CRIMINAL EVIDENCE
EIGHTH EDITION

Norman M. Garland

Second Century Chair in Law
Professor of Law
Southwestern Law School-California

Mc
Graw
Hill
Education

CRIMINAL EVIDENCE, EIGHTH EDITION

Published by McGraw-Hill, Education, 2 Penn Plaza, New York, NY 10121. Copyright © 2020 by The McGraw-Hill Education. All rights reserved. Printed in the United States of America. Previous editions © 2015, 2011, and 2006. No part of this publication may be reproduced or distributed in any form or by any means, or stored in a database or retrieval system, without the prior written consent of The McGraw-Hill Education, Inc., including, but not limited to, in any network or other electronic storage or transmission, or broadcast for distance learning.

Some ancillaries, including electronic and print components, may not be available to customers outside the United States.

This book is printed on acid-free paper.

1 2 3 4 5 6 7 8 9 LWI 21 20 19

ISBN 978-1-259-92060-8 (bound edition)
MHID 1-259-92060-7 (bound edition)
ISBN 978-1-260-68691-3 (loose-leaf edition)
MHID 1-260-68691-4 (loose-leaf edition)

Product Developer: *Francesca King*
Marketing Manager: *Nancy Baudean*
Content Project Managers: *Lisa Bruflodt/Danielle Clement*
Buyer: *Sandy Ludovissy*
Design: *Beth Blech*
Content Licensing Specialists: *Traci Vaske*
Cover Image: *©Couperfield/Shutterstock*
Compositor: *MPS Limited*

All credits appearing on page or at the end of the book are considered to be an extension of the copyright page.

Library of Congress Cataloging-in-Publication Data

Garland, Norman M., author.
    Criminal evidence / Norman M. Garland, Second Century Chair in Law,
    Professor of Law, Southwestern Law School–California.
    Eighth edition. | New York, NY : McGraw-Hill Education, [2020]
    LCCN 2019003461| ISBN 9781259920608 (alk. paper) | ISBN
    1259920607 (bound edition) | ISBN 9781260686913 (loose-leaf edition) |
    ISBN 1260686914 (loose-leaf edition)
    LCSH: Evidence, Criminal–United States.
    LCC KF9660 .G37 2020 | DDC 345.73/06–dc23
    LC record available at https://lccn.loc.gov/2019003461

The Internet addresses listed in the text were accurate at the time of publication. The inclusion of a Web site does not indicate an endorsement by the authors or McGraw-Hill, and McGraw-Hill does not guarantee the accuracy of the information presented at these sites.

This book is dedicated to Melissa Grossan.

ABOUT THE AUTHOR

Norman M. Garland is second century chair in law and professor of law at Southwestern Law School in California, where he teaches Evidence, Criminal Procedure, Advanced Criminal Procedure, and Trial Advocacy. He received his B.S.B.A. and J.D. from Northwestern University; his L.L.M. from Georgetown Law Center, where he was an E. Barrett Prettyman Fellow in Trial Advocacy; and an Honorary LL. D. from Southwestern Law School in 2016. Professor Garland is a member of the Illinois, District of Columbia, and California Bars. He has 10 years of trial experience as a criminal defense attorney, mainly in federal felony cases. In 1968, he joined the law faculty at Northwestern University, where he helped establish the Northwestern Legal Clinic. He joined the faculty of Southwestern Law School in 1975 to help establish the Southwestern Approach to Conceptual Legal Education (S.C.A.L.E.). In the mid-1980s, he spent two summers as Deputy District Attorney in Ventura County, California, where he gained experience as a prosecutor. He is coauthor of *Exculpatory Evidence,* 4th ed. (Lexis-Nexis, 2015), coauthor of *Advanced Criminal Procedure* (West Nutshell, 2d ed., 2006), and author of *Criminal Law for the Law Enforcement Professional*, 4th ed. (McGraw-Hill, 2018). Professor Garland has published a number of CALI Lessons in criminal law and evidence (www.cali.org) and has published numerous articles in legal journals.

BRIEF CONTENTS

CONTENTS

PREFACE

The eighth edition of *Criminal Evidence* presents the basic concepts of criminal evidence applied in the criminal justice environment. *Criminal Evidence,* eighth edition, includes a description of the trial process, types of evidence, the rules relating to relevance, hearsay (including the Confrontation Clause), documentary evidence, qualification of witnesses, privileges, presumptions, judicial notice, photographs, and character. The text also presents the principles relating to the impact of the Constitution of the United States on the admissibility of evidence (i.e., search and seizure, opposing party's statements (admissions) and confessions, the right to counsel, and identification procedures). Finally, the text presents those principles relating to the law enforcement professional as a witness.

This text is written in a clear, lively, and personal style to appeal to criminal justice professionals and students on the way to becoming professionals. Special attention is given to helping students understand the legal aspects of the principles relating to the admissibility of evidence at a criminal court hearing or trial. Students often perceive the law as a complex of incomprehensible rules with uncertain application in the workplace. In *Criminal Evidence,* eighth edition, when an evidence principle is presented, an example or application to the real world of law enforcement immediately follows. Relevant court decisions that affect the admissibility of evidence are discussed in the text, but only to the extent necessary to illustrate the rules. All program components fit into an integrated learning system that helps students learn and apply important course concepts.

ACKNOWLEDGMENTS

I had a lot of help in producing this eighth edition of *Criminal Evidence.* I would like to thank the dean, faculty, and board of trustees of Southwestern Law School for their generous support. I have been fortunate to have two research assistants at Southwestern who worked on this project: Caylin W. Jones and Shahla Jalil-Valles, Southwestern, class of 2019.

For their insightful reviews, criticisms, and suggestions, I would like to thank these colleagues: Pamela Baldwin, Sinclair Community College; John Oare, Solano Community College; Harvey Wolf Kushner, Long Island University.

Finally, and most important, I thank my wife, Melissa Grossan, who was truly my partner in the production of this edition as well as being my loving companion in life.

Changes Made for the Eighth Edition

Chapter 2

▶ Noting the Supreme Court's decision in *Warger v. Shauers,* 135 S.Ct. 521 (2014), holding that FRE 606(b), which makes inadmissible certain juror testimony regarding what occurred in a jury room, precludes a party seeking a new trial from using one juror's affidavit of what another juror said in deliberations to demonstrate the other juror's dishonesty during *voir dire*, because the dishonesty alleged in Warger's new trial motion relates to the juror's personal experience and not to specific knowledge of the case, the Rule's exception for evidence of "extraneous prejudicial information," 606(b)(2)(A), does not apply.

▶ Noting the Supreme Court's decision in *Pena-Rodriguez v. Colorado,* 137 S.Ct. 855 (2017), holding the Sixth Amendment requires that the no-impeachment rule—which recognizes that a verdict, once entered, cannot be challenged based on comments the jurors made during deliberations—must give way in order for the trial court to assess the possible denial of the jury trial guarantee where compelling evidence indicates that a juror relied on racial stereotypes or animus to convict a criminal defendant.

Chapter 7

▶ Noting the Supreme Court's decision in *Ohio v. Clark,* 132 S.Ct. 2173 (2015), holding that the Sixth Amendment's Confrontation Clause did not prohibit prosecutors from introducing statements made by a child abuse victim to his teachers, where neither the child, who was unavailable for cross-examination, nor his teachers had the primary purpose of creating an out-of-court substitute for trial testimony.

Chapter 9

▶ Noting the Supreme Court's decision in *Bailey v. United States,* 568 U.S. 186 (2013), holding that Bailey's detention at a point beyond the immediate vicinity of his apartment while it was being searched by police was not permissible under *Michigan v. Summers*, 452 U.S. 692, as a detention incident to the execution of a search warrant.

▶ Noting the Supreme Court's decision in *Missouri v. McNeely,* 569 U.S. 141 (2013), holding that, in drunk-driving investigations, the natural dissipation of alcohol in the bloodstream does not constitute an exigency in every case sufficient to justify conducting a blood test without securing a search warrant.

▶ Noting the Supreme Court's decision in *Heien v. North Carolina,* 135 S.Ct. 530 (2014), holding that, because it was objectively reasonable for an officer in Sergeant Darisse's position to think that NC law required vehicles to have two functioning brake lights instead of one, Darisse's stop of Heien's vehicle was lawful under the Fourth Amendment.

▶ *Grady v. North Carolina,* 135 S.Ct. 1368 (2015), holding that the NC Court of Appeals erred in concluding that the state's satellite-based monitoring of petitioner for repeated sex offenses was not a 4th A search, but the state courts should determine in the first instance the reasonableness of such a search.

- ▶ Noting the Supreme Court's decision in *Utah v. Strieff,* 136 S.Ct. 2056 (2016), holding that the discovery of a valid pre-existing and untainted arrest warrant attenuated the connection between the unconstitutional investigatory stop of Strieff and the evidence seized.
- ▶ Noting the Supreme Court's decision in *Birchfield v. North Dakota*, 136 S.Ct. 2160 (2016), holding that the Fourth Amendment permits warrantless breath tests incident to arrests for drunk driving but not warrantless blood tests.
- ▶ Noting the Supreme Court's decision in *Collins v. Virginia*, 138 S.Ct. 1663 (2018), holding that partially enclosed top portion of driveway of home, in which defendant's motorcycle was parked, was "curtilage," for purposes of Fourth Amendment analysis of police officer's warrantless search of motorcycle; driveway ran alongside front lawn and up a few yards past front perimeter of house, top portion of driveway sitting behind front perimeter of house was enclosed on two sides by a brick wall about the height of a car and was enclosed on third side by the house, side door provided direct access between this partially enclosed section of driveway and house, and a visitor endeavoring to reach front door of house would walk partway up driveway but would turn off before entering enclosure and instead would proceed up a set of steps leading to front porch. Automobile exception to Fourth Amendment's warrant requirement for searches did not justify police officer's invasion of curtilage of home, for warrantless search of motorcycle covered by tarp and parked in partially enclosed top portion of driveway of home, though officer had probable cause to believe that the motorcycle was the one that had eluded officer's attempted traffic stop; officer invaded not only defendant's interest in the item searched, i.e., the motorcycle, but also invaded defendant's Fourth Amendment interest in the curtilage of the home.

Chapter 12

- ▶ Noting the Supreme Court's decision in *Wearry v. Cain,* 136 S.Cr. 1002, holding that the prosecution's failure to disclose material evidence at petitioner's capital murder trial violated his due process rights under *Brady v. Maryland*.

eTextbooks for *Criminal Evidence*

This text is available as an eTextbook at www.coursesmart.com. At CourseSmart you can save up to 50 percent off the cost of a print textbook, reduce your impact on the environment, and gain access to powerful web tools for learning. CourseSmart has the largest selection of eTextbooks available anywhere, offering thousands of the most commonly adopted textbooks from a wide variety of higher education publishers. CourseSmart eTextbooks are available in one standard online reader with full text search, notes and highlighting, and e-mail tools for sharing notes between classmates. For further details, contact your sales representative or go to www.coursesmart.com.

Connect

Instructors can access additional resources on Connect. An updated Instructor's Manual and lecture PowerPoints are available as well as a complete testbank.

Students—study more efficiently, retain more and achieve better outcomes. Instructors—focus on what you love—teaching.

SUCCESSFUL SEMESTERS INCLUDE CONNECT

FOR INSTRUCTORS

You're in the driver's seat.

Want to build your own course? No problem. Prefer to use our turnkey, prebuilt course? Easy. Want to make changes throughout the semester? Sure. And you'll save time with Connect's auto-grading too.

65%
Less Time Grading

They'll thank you for it.

Adaptive study resources like SmartBook® help your students be better prepared in less time. You can transform your class time from dull definitions to dynamic debates. Hear from your peers about the benefits of Connect at **www.mheducation.com/highered/connect.**

Make it simple, make it affordable.

Connect makes it easy with seamless integration using any of the major Learning Management Systems—Blackboard®, Canvas, and D2L, among others—to let you organize your course in one convenient location. Give your students access to digital materials at a discount with our inclusive access program. Ask your McGraw-Hill representative for more information.

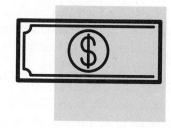

©Hill Street Studios/Tobin Rogers/Blend Images LLC

Solutions for your challenges.

A product isn't a solution. Real solutions are affordable, reliable, and come with training and ongoing support when you need it and how you want it. Our Customer Experience Group can also help you troubleshoot tech problems—although Connect's 99% uptime means you might not need to call them. See for yourself at **status.mheducation.com.**

FOR STUDENTS

Effective, efficient studying.

Connect helps you be more productive with your study time and get better grades using tools like SmartBook, which highlights key concepts and creates a personalized study plan. Connect sets you up for success, so you walk into class with confidence and walk out with better grades.

> " I really liked this app—it made it easy to study when you don't have your textbook in front of you. "
>
> - Jordan Cunningham,
> Eastern Washington University

Study anytime, anywhere.

Download the free ReadAnywhere app and access your online eBook when it's convenient, even if you're offline. And since the app automatically syncs with your eBook in Connect, all of your notes are available every time you open it. Find out more at **www.mheducation.com/readanywhere.**

No surprises.

The Connect Calendar and Reports tools keep you on track with the work you need to get done and your assignment scores. Life gets busy; Connect tools help you keep learning through it all.

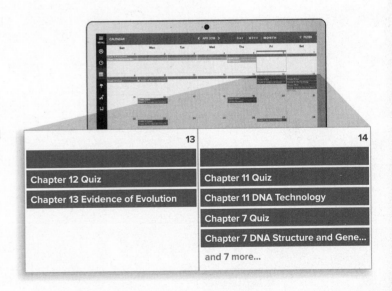

Learning for everyone.

McGraw-Hill works directly with Accessibility Services Departments and faculty to meet the learning needs of all students. Please contact your Accessibility Services office and ask them to email accessibility@mheducation.com, or visit **www.mheducation.com/about/accessibility.html** for more information.

1 INTRODUCTION TO THE LAW OF EVIDENCE AND THE PRETRIAL PROCESS

CHAPTER OUTLINE

CHAPTER OBJECTIVES

This chapter is an introduction to the law of evidence, the court process, personnel, and pretrial process from the law enforcement professional's viewpoint. After reading this chapter you will be able to:

▶ Explain what constitutes evidence.

▶ State the objectives of the rules of evidence.

▶ Name the most common version of evidence law in the United States.

▶ Describe the three basic police functions.

▶ Contrast the jobs of the prosecuting attorney and the defense attorney.

▶ Describe the dual court system in the United States.

▶ Define probable cause to arrest.

▶ State the two alternative ways that a defendant can be formally charged with a serious crime in the United States.

INTRODUCTION TO THE RULES OF EVIDENCE: DEFINITION OF EVIDENCE

Most Americans are aware that there are rules that govern what a jury can hear and see during the trial of a case in an American courtroom. These rules are defined in what is called the **law of evidence.** In this text, we will explore why there is a law that restricts what a jury may hear, the details of the law, and its importance to the effective performance of the law enforcement professional. Before exploring those questions, the reader should know what constitutes evidence.

Most simply stated, **evidence** is information that people base decisions on. In a legal sense, evidence is the information presented in court during a trial that enables the judge and jury to decide a particular case. Technically, evidence consists of testimony or physical items presented to the judge and jury that they use to decide the truth of an assertion, the existence of a fact, and ultimately the guilt or innocence of the accused in a criminal case.

In the American judicial system, a criminal defendant is entitled to have a jury decide his or her guilt or innocence. The jury in all trials makes its final decision based on what it believes the facts are that are involved in the case. Evidence is the means by which those facts are proved or disproved. If this definition were taken literally, then anything that sheds some light on the truth of a fact in question should be revealed during the trial. Perhaps, if the creators of the law trusted juries completely, that would be the way the law of evidence worked. However, the creators of the law believed that juries need some guidance and protection from undue manipulation by competing attorneys during a trial. Therefore, the law limits what constitutes admissible evidence.

Most law enforcement professionals use the term "evidence" with special meaning, since so much of their efforts are concerned with ensuring that physical evidence is usable at trial. So, although law enforcement professionals know that testimony is important, they often refer to evidence as the articles collected at a crime scene, on a suspect, or in the suspect's car or home that are connected to the crime, such as weapons, fruits of a crime, or **contraband** (an object or material that is illegal to possess). Additionally, evidence may mean those things discovered during investigation, such as bloodstains, latent fingerprints, or plaster casts of shoe impressions in the earth.

These items of evidence, once found, are transported to the station and taken to the evidence room, where items are logged in and tagged. On the evidence tag are the date of the booking, the incident report number, the offense, the number of items (pieces), cash, from whom the evidence was taken, the location, the owner, and the signature of the officer who booked in the evidence. The property room officer signs in the evidence and the date received and then deposits the evidence in a secure location known as the **evidence locker**.

Evidence can be checked out (or released) from the evidence locker to the defense attorney, or the prosecutor, or be sent to a laboratory as long as the chain of custody remains intact and each piece of evidence is logged in and out each time it is examined. The last entry in the log is usually the release for the purpose of taking it to court. Some items, such as drugs, blood, or other substances, must be carefully weighed or counted on the initial booking date, weighed or counted again before being checked out, and finally again when returned. Laboratory technicians must also weigh the amount of any substance or material they use for testing purposes.

Unless released for the purposes just described, items remain in the evidence locker, free from illegal tampering, until they can be utilized as exhibits and admitted into evidence during trial proceedings. Legally, these articles found and retained do not become "evidence" until they are introduced in court proceedings and become exhibits. However, if the law enforcement officer does not take the proper precautions with these articles, they cannot be introduced into evidence. This is so because, generally, no item of physical evidence can be introduced at trial unless the law enforcement officer has maintained the proper "chain of custody" of the item. **Chain of custody** refers to how evidence is handled, and by whom, accounting for its whereabouts and condition from the moment it is found until the moment it is offered in evidence. It is the maintenance of custody and control over an object to such a degree that the custodian can prove the object is in the same condition as it originally was when custody was obtained.

The testimony of anyone with personal knowledge pertaining to the case is simply another form of evidence. A good definition of what constitutes evidence is as follows: Evidence is any information about the facts of a case, including tangible items, testimony, documents, photographs, or recordings, which, when presented to the jury at trial, tends to prove or disprove these facts.

Evidence may be classified in many different ways. There is a classification of evidence as real or demonstrative. There are direct evidence and circumstantial evidence. Evidence may be physical or intangible. Testimony of experts often relates to scientific evidence. The differences between these classifications of evidence is fully discussed in Chapter 3.

CHAIN OF CUSTODY The maintenance of custody and control over an object to such a degree that the custodian can prove the object is in the same condition as it originally was when custody was obtained.

THE RULES OF EVIDENCE

"Rules of evidence," or the "law of evidence," as they are also known, are a set of regulations that act as guidelines for judges, attorneys, and law enforcement professionals who are involved in the trials of cases. These guidelines determine how the trial is to be conducted, what persons may be witnesses, the matters about which they can testify, the method by which articles at a crime scene (physical evidence) are collected and preserved, what is admissible, and what is inadmissible. These rules make for the orderly conduct of the trial, promote efficiency, enhance the quality of evidence, and ensure a fair trial. They are the product of many years of judicial evolution and, more recently, legislative study. They were developed by trial and error, through logic and sound judgment, following the basic needs of

FYI

There was a rather famous white Bronco involved in the 1994 O.J. Simpson trial. One of the big problems for the prosecution was the chain of custody of the Bronco. It was towed to a privately maintained storage lot and was not properly secured. During the time the Bronco was there, an employee broke into the vehicle and took some papers. Judge Ito, presiding at the trial of O.J. Simpson, ruled that the bloodstains later discovered on the Bronco's front console were admissible, but the defense, in its attack on the bloodstain evidence, made much of the fact that the Bronco was not properly stored. A proper chain of custody would have reduced or eliminated the impact of the defense's argument.

society. They make for the orderly conduct of the trial and ensure that evidence is properly presented at the trial. For example, the rules prevent one spouse from testifying against another, except in certain instances. The rules also generally forbid the use of hearsay as evidence and prohibit the admission of illegally obtained evidence. Law enforcement professionals should not look upon these rules as roadblocks in their efforts to secure convictions. Instead, they must realize that the objective of these rules is to ensure the integrity of all evidence, protect a defendant's rights, and ensure a fair trial.

History of Trial by Jury

In the days before jury trials, proof of guilt or innocence was decided by ordeal, battle, or compurgation. For the most part, trial by ordeal was an appeal to the supernatural. An example of an ordeal used to determine guilt or innocence consisted of forcing an accused person to remove a rock from the bottom of a boiling pot of water. Any accused whose hands became blistered was found guilty. If the hands did not blister, the accused was acquitted. Acquittals under this system were, not surprisingly, rare.

Another kind of trial was introduced in England as a result of the Norman Conquest in 1066. This was trial by battle or combat, also known as "wager of battle." In this system the victim of a crime and the accused were forced into hands-on combat. Even litigants in civil matters were often required to ascertain who was right and who was wrong by this method of proof, with the one who was right being the winner. It was assumed that God would give victory to the one who was right. In criminal matters, if the accused won, the accused was acquitted. Judicial combat became a prevalent way to establish justice and continued to hold sway for a period of time, but eventually it died out as a means of establishing right and wrong.

A more humane method of ascertaining guilt or innocence utilized from time to time was trial by compurgation, also known as "wager of law." In this system the accused would testify in his or her own behalf, pleading innocence. The accused would be supported by helpers known as "compurgators," or oath helpers, often twelve in number. These supporters or helpers would testify to the good character of the accused and particularly his or her reputation for veracity. These persons would not necessarily know anything about the facts of the case, but merely came forth to tell how good the accused was. This system provided fertile grounds for perjury and proved to be as ineffective at determining the truth as the ordeal and combat methods. But it is considered to be the forerunner of our use of character witnesses.

Later, a trial by jury system began to make its appearance. It was in no way like the trial by jury as we know it. The first juries functioned by charging the accused with a crime, acting in much the same capacity as a grand jury of today. They served to substantiate an accusation, leaving the test of innocence or guilt to be decided by some other means, such as trial by ordeal, battle, or wager of law. As time passed and these methods lost favor, the accusatory jury was given a dual function. Jury members would gather information from the countryside, mostly hearsay (unsworn, out-of-court statements), concerning the alleged crime and, later, would decide whether the accused should be held for trial. If a trial were ultimately held, the same jury would try the accused and render a verdict.

INTRODUCTION TO THE LAW OF EVIDENCE AND THE PRETRIAL PROCESS

Later it was decided that the accusatory jury, known by then as the grand jury, should not also try the accused. Therefore, a separate jury, known as the petit jury, was selected for that function. This jury, like the accusatory jury, relied upon evidence from the countryside. Later this petit jury was composed of individuals with personal knowledge about the case. As time passed, witnesses who had information about the case were called to testify before the jury. However, much of the testimony of the witnesses was based upon hearsay information. Finally, around 1700 the trial by jury as we know it today was becoming a reality, characterized by the swearing in of witnesses and the right to cross-examine those witnesses. Additionally, hearsay evidence began to disappear from jury trials. It was then that our rules of evidence began to develop into what they are today.

Development of the Rules of Evidence

Rules of evidence in jury trials are designed to keep some information from the jury even though it may be relevant. This is because sometimes relevant information cannot be received by the jury without violating some principle or policy that the law seeks to promote. For example, hearsay evidence (a statement made by a person out of court) may be very relevant but is often unreliable and untrustworthy. Hence, the hearsay rule bans the admission of hearsay at a trial, except in specific, defined situations. Likewise, evidence that has been obtained by a law enforcement officer in violation of a suspect's constitutional rights may be declared by the law to be inadmissible in order to deter future misconduct by officers. (The rules governing illegally seized evidence are discussed in detail in Chapter 9.)

Today, the rules of evidence in most jurisdictions are in the form of a statute or code, meaning that they are laws enacted by a legislative body. These evidence laws have supplanted the rules made by judges that evolved over the centuries during the development of the jury system, though many may be traced back to the judge-made rules. By far, the most common codification of evidence law is the **Federal Rules of Evidence** (**FRE**). The FRE apply in all federal courts throughout the United States and in the 43 states that have relied upon them as a model in adopting their own evidence codes.

The evolution of the FRE began in 1942 when the American Law Institute adopted the Model Code of Evidence. The drafting and advisory committees for the Model Code included all the great figures in the field of evidence. The Model Code was considered to be reformist and controversial. So, although the Model Code stimulated debate and development of the law, it was not adopted by any jurisdiction. In 1954, the Uniform Rules of Evidence, authorized by the Commissioners on Uniform State Laws, were produced. While these rules were less radical, they were adopted by only two states. Finally, in 1961, the United States Supreme Court Chief Justice Earl Warren appointed a special committee to determine the feasibility and desirability of a federal evidence code. The committee

FEDERAL RULES OF EVIDENCE (FRE)
The most common codification of evidence law—the rules that apply in all federal courts throughout the United States and in the 43 states that have relied upon them as a model in adopting their own evidence codes.

came back with an affirmative response. An Advisory Committee on Rules of Evidence was appointed to draft proposed rules and, in 1972, a revised draft of proposed rules was promulgated by the Supreme Court as the Federal Rules of Evidence, to be effective July 1, 1973. The rules were referred to Congress, which enacted the rules into law, effective July 1, 1975. The rules have been subsequently amended by Congress but have remained, for the most part, the same since enactment. Effective December 1, 2011, the entire FRE were "restyled," meaning that the language of the rules was simplified to render them more understandable. No substantive changes were made by this amendment to the FRE.

Forty-three state legislatures have adopted evidence codes patterned after the FRE as of January 2013. Those states that have not adopted the rules, however, are some with heavy population centers that account for a substantial number of the state criminal cases generated in the United States. States that have not yet adopted the rules include California, Connecticut (commentators differ about the extent to which the Connecticut Code of Evidence differs from the FRE)[1], Kansas, Massachusetts, Missouri, New York, and Virginia. Although these states follow rules of evidence based on the same general principles that exist in all of Anglo-American evidence law, their rules differ substantially in many respects from the FRE. Therefore, the rules of evidence of each state must be consulted to learn these differences. Moreover, even those states that have patterned their evidence codes on the FRE may have some substantial variances from the FRE.

The FRE, and their state counterparts, cover the entire field of judicial procedure. These rules apply equally in civil and criminal matters. Because the rules are complex, the line between what is admissible and what is inadmissible is very fine. Therefore, these rules may create much confusion for all who deal with them, including the law enforcement professional. Further, it is sometimes difficult to abide by some of the rules, primarily because an appellate court may invalidate or modify what was once perfectly legal and proper. The rules themselves, much like judges' interpretations of the rules, are constantly changing, many times becoming more restrictive on the officer and his or her work.

Despite such problems, the rules of evidence enable officers to know during the investigation what evidence will be admissible at a trial. It is the purpose of this book to concentrate on those rules of evidence most applicable to the work of the law enforcement professional and to help in understanding them.

OVERVIEW OF THE COURT PROCESS: THE PRETRIAL PROCESS

Figure 1-1 is a flow chart of the criminal justice system. It covers the entire process from the observation or report of a crime through investigation, arrest, prosecution, trial, sentencing, appeal, service of sentence, and release. The court process from pretrial to appeal will be briefly described in this section. Later in this chapter, the pretrial process will be described in greater detail. The trial process will be described in greater detail in Chapter 2.

The process begins with an arrest based upon detection, investigation, and/or the filing of a criminal complaint against a person. After arrest, the suspect is booked. **Booking** is a formal processing of the arrested person by the police that involves recording the arrest, fingerprinting, photographing, and inventorying all

BOOKING
A formal processing of the arrested person by the police that involves recording the arrest, fingerprinting, photographing, and inventorying all the personal items taken from the suspect.

the personal items taken from the suspect. The prosecutor will decide whether to proceed with the charges against the defendant. If so, the accused will then make an initial appearance in court, at which time the judge will review the charges to determine the following:

1. that the crime is properly charged (i.e., that all required elements are alleged);
2. that the right person has been named as the defendant;
3. that there is a reasonable basis for the charges;
4. whether the accused has or needs counsel; and
5. what bail or other conditions for release pending trial will be set.

The next step is a preliminary hearing, at which the judge considers the prosecution's case to decide whether there is probable cause to believe the defendant committed the crimes charged. If so, the defendant is held to answer to formal charges in the form of a grand jury indictment or an information.

After the grand jury indicts or the prosecutor files an information formally charging the defendant, the accused appears in the trial court for arraignment and plea. At the arraignment, the defendant can enter a plea of guilty, not guilty, or *nolo contendere* (no contest), or he or she can stand mute. If the defendant pleads guilty (or *nolo contendere*), he or she enters the plea and the judge imposes the judgment of guilt upon the plea. At that time, or shortly after, the judge will impose sentence upon the defendant.

If the defendant pleads not guilty or stands mute at the arraignment, the case will be set for trial. Immediately after this, the lawyers will begin to file papers (pretrial motions) to test legal issues (such as the legality of any searches or seizures or change of venue) before trial, and they will exchange information about the merits of the case. This exchange of information is called **discovery** and is designed to lessen the element of surprise at trial. In most jurisdictions, there are time limits within which such pretrial motions must be filed, often within ten days to two weeks of arraignment. During this post-arraignment, pretrial period, the law enforcement officer will continue to investigate the case, maintain the evidence gathered, prepare further evidence when necessary, and assist the prosecution in any other way appropriate to ensure that the trial proceeds in a timely and effective manner.

DISCOVERY
The right afforded to the adversary in a trial to examine, inspect, and copy the evidence in the hands of the other side.

At the trial, the chief law enforcement officer assigned to the case may be called upon to assist the prosecutor by sitting at the counsel table in the courtroom.

At the very least, all officers who have personal knowledge of significant facts may be called upon to testify on behalf of the prosecution. At the conclusion of the trial, the jury or the judge will render a decision. If the judge or jury convicts the defendant, the judge will set a date for sentencing.

Usually, the probation department will prepare a pre-sentence investigation report (PSI), which recommends a sentence to the judge. The PSI is prepared by a probation officer who investigates all aspects of the defendant's life, seeking to verify all information by public and private records. The recommendation for sentencing contained in the PSI reflects the results of the PSI writer's evaluation of the defendant based upon the information gathered and reference to the sentencing guidelines, if any, that apply in the jurisdiction. If the defendant objects to the PSI, he or she can file an objection to the report, but there is no right of appeal.

The Criminal Justice System

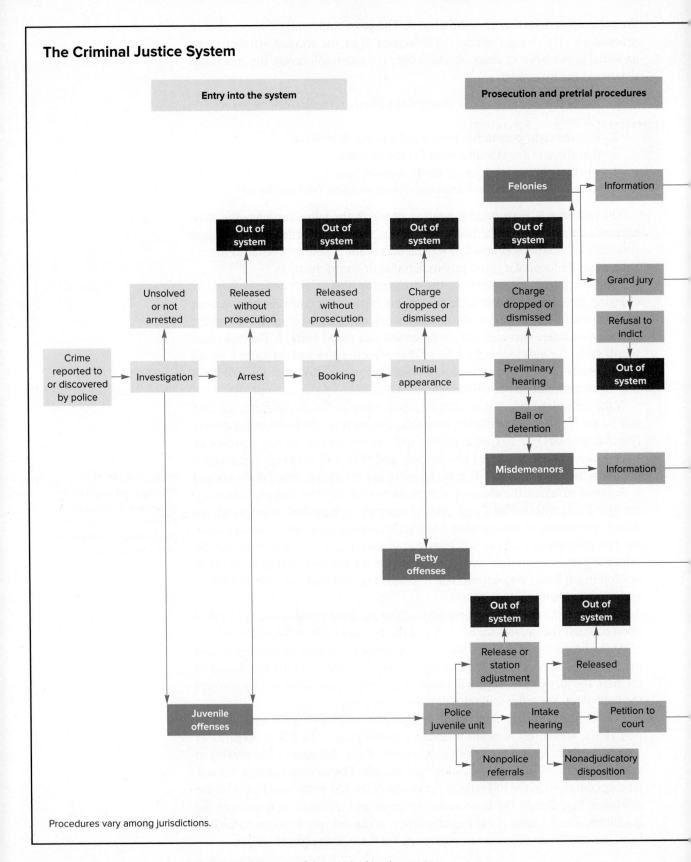

FIGURE 1–1 Overview of the criminal justice system.

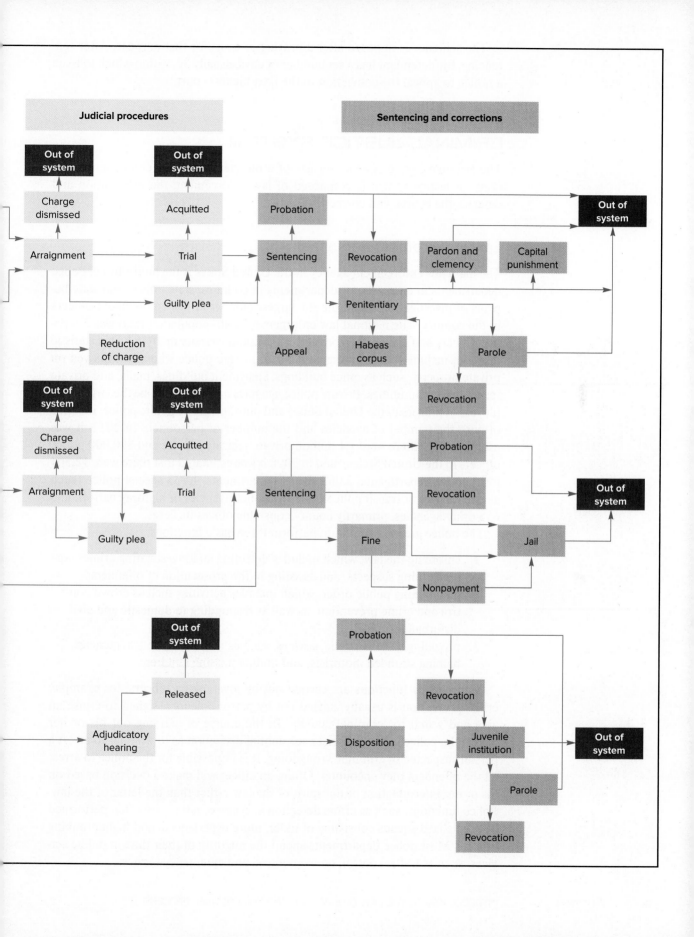

The sentence is imposed after a hearing in court for that purpose. After sentencing, the defendant has a set number of days, usually 30, within which to issue a notice to appeal the conviction to the next highest court.

PARTICIPANTS IN THE CRIMINAL JUSTICE SYSTEM

The criminal justice system consists of a number of distinct components. The criminal justice system is composed of law enforcement, the prosecution and defense, the courts, and corrections.

Law Enforcement Personnel

The main law enforcement agency in the United States is the police force. Police departments in cities, sheriff departments in counties, state police, and state bureaus of investigation constitute the largest number of law enforcement officers in the country. The national law enforcement staff–population ratio was 2.8 police officers and civilian personnel per thousand citizens in 2016.[2] This statistic does not include the enormous number of private police who are employed on private property, such as office buildings, apartment buildings, malls, and private residential communities. Private police agencies are believed to be the largest employers of officers in the United States and outnumber the public police, in terms of both the number of agencies and the number of personnel.[3] In 2017, it was estimated that there were 1.1 million private security officers and 800,000 police officers in the United States,[4] and in 2008 it was estimated that there were 12,501 local police departments, 3,063 sheriff departments, 1,733 special police (such as park service or transit police), 50 state police agencies or highway patrols, and 638 other agencies, primarily county constable offices in Texas.[5]

The police are called upon to perform three basic functions:

1. enforcing the law, which includes detecting and investigating crimes, apprehending suspects, and assisting in the prosecution of offenders;
2. maintaining public order, which includes activities such as crowd control and crime prevention, as well as responding to domestic and civil disturbances; and
3. providing various public services, such as responding to emergencies, helping stranded motorists, and finding missing children.

Many police functions are carried out by low-ranking officers; for example, crime prevention is usually carried out by patrol officers assigned to cruise an area and watch for criminal activity. In the course of carrying out his or her duties, the police officer exercises substantial discretion as to whether to arrest a person suspected of criminal wrongdoing. It is impossible for the police to arrest all the offenders they encounter. Often, an officer will make a decision based on his or her interpretation of the spirit of the law rather than the letter of the law. Police functions, such as crime detection and investigation, are often performed by specialized squads consisting of older, more experienced, and higher-ranking officers. Most police departments spend the majority of their time in public services, such as traffic control, crowd control, and emergency services.

Nationally, the Federal Bureau of Investigation (FBI) is charged with the responsibility of investigating federal law violations. There are a number of other federal law enforcement agencies—notably the Drug Enforcement Administration; the Bureau of Alcohol, Tobacco, and Firearms; ICE (formerly the Customs Service and the Immigration and Naturalization Service, now combined under Homeland Security); the United States Marshals Service; the Border Patrol; the United States Park Service; the Bureau of Postal Inspection; and the Secret Service.

As a component of the law enforcement function, all law enforcement agencies provide assistance to the prosecuting attorneys in presenting evidence in court to prosecute those arrested for criminal activities. Therefore, the gathering of evidence, maintenance of evidence collected, and preparation of evidence for presentation in a court of law are major activities of the law enforcement agencies. In complicated cases, most law enforcement agencies employ specially trained and educated personnel who are familiar with such specialized fields as ballistics, fingerprint analysis, bloodstain analysis, DNA analysis, and other areas utilizing scientific methodology. Such specialists, often called criminalists or forensic investigators, have gained prominence through high-profile trials and popular television programs depicting crime scene investigations. In smaller departments, the officers will do as much of the scientific work as their expertise allows, and then seek help from other law enforcement agencies where necessary.

Depending on the type of case tried, other law enforcement personnel will be involved in the criminal court process. They might include investigators other than those employed by the police department, courtroom personnel (bailiffs, marshals, or other guards), jail personnel, probation officers, and prison personnel.

The staff of the courts, in addition to judges, includes courtroom clerks, judges' clerks, and bailiffs. Bailiffs are law enforcement personnel assigned to keep order in the courtroom, attend to juries, oversee prisoners who are in custody during their court appearances, and otherwise provide security in the courtroom. In many jurisdictions, the bailiff is a deputy sheriff; in the federal courts, the bailiffs are deputy United States Marshals.

Prosecution and Defense

The American criminal justice system is an adversarial one. In it, the accused is presumed innocent until proven guilty and has a right to counsel even before he or she is brought to court. The adversary process by which guilt is determined is competitive, pitting the defense attorney and the prosecuting attorney against each other. The battle lines between these lawyers are often drawn based upon the conduct of the law enforcement officers working on the case. For example, if the investigating officers do a complete, solid job, the defense will find it difficult to argue the quality of the evidence.

The chief prosecuting attorney in most state jurisdictions is a full-time, public, county official, usually elected to office, with a staff of assistant prosecuting attorneys below. Depending on the state, the chief prosecuting attorney may be called the District Attorney, County Attorney, State's Attorney, or Prosecuting Attorney. In some states and in the federal system, the prosecutor is an appointed official. In some rural areas, the office of the prosecutor may be occupied by only one person, who may work only part-time at the job. In many urban areas, the prosecutor's office is very large. For example, the Office of the District Attorney of Los Angeles County, which employs about 1,000 attorneys, may be the largest law office in the country, and certainly the largest prosecutorial office in the United States.[6]

The chief prosecutor in the federal system is the Attorney General of the United States. In each of the 94 federal districts, the chief prosecuting officer is the United States Attorney for that geographic district. The Attorney General and the United States Attorneys are all appointed by the President of the United States. The assistant United States Attorneys are all federal employees.

It is the job of the prosecutor to pursue a case developed by the police until the case terminates by trial, guilty plea, or dismissal. The prosecutor must decide whether to pursue a formal charge and, if so, what crime to charge. The prosecutor is also responsible for conducting any plea negotiations, deciding whether to dismiss charges, and trying the case.

Since the 1970s, the Constitution of the United States has required that a defendant who is sentenced to any time in jail or prison is entitled to an attorney, whether or not he or she can afford one. Also, any suspect who is in custody and interrogated by the police while in custody is entitled to warnings (*Miranda* warnings) about the right to remain silent and to have an attorney present during interrogation, whether or not he or she can afford one. Therefore, state and federal governments provide defense counsel to many criminal suspects and defendants who cannot afford to hire a lawyer on their own. This is accomplished through either the private bar (the local attorneys' association) or a public defender system. Defense counsel must zealously represent the criminal defendant from the point of interrogation through the trial process, demanding that the prosecution respect the defendant's rights, treat the defendant fairly, and meet the burden of proof beyond a reasonable doubt in the event the case goes to trial.

Courts

There is a dual judicial system in the United States: The federal and state courts coexist. The federal court system applies nation-wide, and federal courts are located in each state. These courts coexist with individual state court systems. Whether a defendant is tried in a federal or state court depends on which court has jurisdiction over the case.

JURISDICTION
The power or authority of the court to act with respect to any case before it.

The **jurisdiction** of a court is the power or authority of the court to act with respect to any case before it. The acts involved in the case must have taken place within or have had an effect within the geographical territory of the court, or there must be some statutory authority for the court's power. There are currently federal trial courts in each state and thirteen United States Courts of Appeal, arranged by circuit (eleven numbered circuits, a District of Columbia circuit, and one federal circuit—see Figure 1-2). The lowest level of the federal court system consists of 94 District Courts located in the 50 states (except for the District of Wyoming, which includes the Montana and Idaho portions of Yellowstone National Park); Puerto Rico; the District of Columbia; and the United States Territories of Guam, the Virgin Islands, and the Northern Mariana Islands. Each

FIGURE 1–2 United States Courts of Appeal.
Source: Administrative Office of the United States Courts.

Court of Appeals	Districts Included in Circuit
Federal Circuit	United States
District of Columbia Circuit	District of Columbia
First Circuit	Maine, Massachusetts, New Hampshire, Rhode Island, and Puerto Rico
Second Circuit	Connecticut, New York, and Vermont
Third Circuit	Delaware, New Jersey, Pennsylvania, and the Virgin Islands
Fourth Circuit	Maryland, North Carolina, South Carolina, Virginia, and West Virginia
Fifth Circuit	Louisiana, Mississippi, and Texas
Sixth Circuit	Kentucky, Michigan, Ohio, and Tennessee
Seventh Circuit	Illinois, Indiana, and Wisconsin
Eighth Circuit	Arkansas, Iowa, Minnesota, Missouri, Nebraska, North Dakota, and South Dakota
Ninth Circuit	Alaska, Arizona, California, Hawaii, Idaho, Montana, Nevada, Oregon, Washington, Guam, and the Northern Mariana Islands
Tenth Circuit	Colorado, Kansas, New Mexico, Oklahoma, Utah, and Wyoming
Eleventh Circuit	Alabama, Florida, and Georgia

state has at least one United States District Court, and some, such as New York and California, have as many as four. District Courts are the trial courts of the federal system and have original jurisdiction over cases charging defendants with violation of federal criminal laws. For example, crimes involving such matters as possession and sale of certain dangerous drugs, transportation of stolen property across state lines, and robbery of federally insured banks will be tried in the federal courts even though the crime was committed within a state or local geographical area. In addition, crimes committed on federal lands or property are subject to federal trial court jurisdiction.

Law enforcement officers will hear the term "venue" in connection with the power of a court to hear a case. **Venue** refers to the neighborhood, place, or county in which an act is declared to have been done or, in fact, happened, thus defining the particular county or geographical area in which a court with jurisdiction may hear and determine a case. Venue deals with locality of suit, that is, with the question of which court, or courts, of those that possess adequate personal and subject matter jurisdiction may hear a case. "Venue" does not refer to jurisdiction at all. "Jurisdiction" of the court means the inherent power to decide

VENUE
The neighborhood, place, or county in which an act is declared to have been done or, in fact, happened, thus defining the particular county or geographical area in which a court with jurisdiction may hear and determine a case.

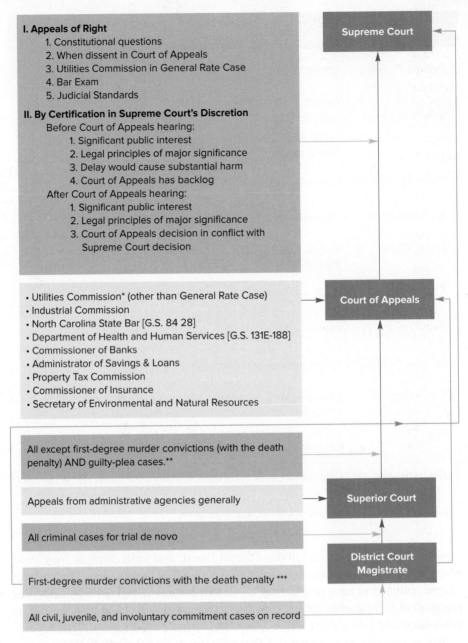

I. Appeals of Right
1. Constitutional questions
2. When dissent in Court of Appeals
3. Utilities Commission in General Rate Case
4. Bar Exam
5. Judicial Standards

II. By Certification in Supreme Court's Discretion
Before Court of Appeals hearing:
1. Significant public interest
2. Legal principles of major significance
3. Delay would cause substantial harm
4. Court of Appeals has backlog
After Court of Appeals hearing:
1. Significant public interest
2. Legal principles of major significance
3. Court of Appeals decision in conflict with Supreme Court decision

- Utilities Commission* (other than General Rate Case)
- Industrial Commission
- North Carolina State Bar [G.S. 84 28]
- Department of Health and Human Services [G.S. 131E-188]
- Commissioner of Banks
- Administrator of Savings & Loans
- Property Tax Commission
- Commissioner of Insurance
- Secretary of Environmental and Natural Resources

All except first-degree murder convictions (with the death penalty) AND guilty-plea cases.**

Appeals from administrative agencies generally

All criminal cases for trial de novo

First-degree murder convictions with the death penalty ***

All civil, juvenile, and involuntary commitment cases on record

Supreme Court

Court of Appeals

Superior Court

District Court Magistrate

* Appeals from agencies must be heard by Court of Appeals before Supreme Court.

** Post-conviction-hearing appeals and reviews of valuation of exempt property under G.S. Ch. 1C are final with Court of Appeals.

*** The only first-degree murder cases with direct appeal to the Supreme Court (tried after December 1, 1995) are those where defendant receives a sentence of death.

a case, whereas "venue" designates the particular county or city in which a court with jurisdiction may hear and determine the case. As such, while a defect in venue may be waived by the parties, lack of jurisdiction may not.

Each state also has its own court system. Most states' structures are similar to that of the federal courts—a trial court, an intermediate appellate court, and a supreme court. (See Figure 1-3, showing the flow of cases in the North Carolina State Court system.) In most states, the trial courts are organized by county.

Furthermore, in most states, the trial courts are divided into two levels, an inferior and a superior court. The inferior court, often called the municipal court or justice of the peace court, conducts preliminary hearings in felony cases and trials in cases involving misdemeanors or petty offenses. The superior court, sometimes called the circuit or district court, is a court of general jurisdiction and has jurisdiction over felony trials.

Federal offenses are prosecuted in federal court and all state offenses are prosecuted in state courts. Since about 1930, the United States Supreme Court has been interpreting the Due Process Clause of the Fourteenth Amendment to have incorporated all but two provisions of the Bill of Rights into constitutional criminal procedural requirements that apply to the states[7]:

▶ the right to trial by jury in cases involving serious offenses (Sixth Amendment);

▶ the right to assistance of counsel in any case in which a sentence of more than six months in jail or prison is imposed (Sixth Amendment);

▶ the privilege against self-incrimination, including a ban against comment by the prosecution on the defendant's failure to testify (Fifth Amendment);

▶ the presumption of innocence and requirement of proof beyond a reasonable doubt (Fifth and Fourteenth Amendments' Due Process Clauses);

▶ the freedom from unreasonable searches and seizures (Fourth Amendment);

▶ the right to silence and counsel during police interrogations (in aid of the Fifth Amendment's privilege against self-incrimination);

▶ the right to compel witnesses' attendance at trial, to confront them, and to cross-examine them (Sixth Amendment);

▶ the right to a speedy and public trial (Sixth Amendment);

▶ the freedom from double jeopardy (Fifth Amendment);

▶ the freedom from cruel and unusual punishment (Eighth Amendment); and

▶ the freedom from racial and sexual discrimination in substantive and procedural criminal law (Fourteenth Amendment).

Violation of any of these constitutional requirements can be the subject of both state appeals and separate federal suits by prisoners, known as *habeas corpus* claims (a form of legal action that seeks to free a prisoner from unlawful confinement).

There is also a juvenile court system in each state. Criminal offenders under a certain age, usually 18 or 16, are dealt with in juvenile courts by way of civil, rather than criminal, proceedings. In cases that are serious, the juvenile may be certified for prosecution as an adult, and the case will then be heard in adult criminal court. Many youthful offenders who commit offenses that would be crimes if committed by an adult are tried in the juvenile courts, the purpose of which is to have specialized judges determine the youth's involvement in the offense and whether the child should receive rehabilitation rather than punishment. Juvenile court procedure was intended to be more informal than criminal courts, but the United States Supreme Court decisions since the 1960s have imposed due process restrictions on the juvenile courts that have caused juvenile proceedings to become more formal.

HABEAS CORPUS
A form of legal action that seeks to free a prisoner from unlawful confinement.

The case of *In re Gault*[8] was the vehicle for the United States Supreme Court to declare that a juvenile is a citizen and is entitled to the protections of the Bill of Rights when juvenile court proceedings result in the child's deprivation of liberty. In the case, the 15-year-old child was committed as a juvenile delinquent to a state industrial school for his involvement in making lewd telephone calls. His commitment followed a hearing in the juvenile court of Arizona, in which he and his parents claimed denial of notice of charges, right to counsel, confrontation and cross-examination of witnesses, and privilege against self-incrimination. The United States Supreme Court agreed that the state had denied these basic constitutional rights and that even state juvenile court proceedings must accord these rights to children in order for due process to be met when a child's liberty is at stake.

JAILS
The facilities used to maintain custody of persons arrested pending prosecution and to maintain custody of those sentenced to short periods of confinement, usually less than one year. Most jails are operated by cities, counties, or both.

PRISONS
Penal institutions maintained by the state or federal government consisting of state penitentiaries, reformatories, and juvenile training facilities.

PROBATION DEPARTMENT
An agency that investigates defendants prior to sentencing, provides a pre-sentence probation report to the court, and supervises persons placed on probation after conviction.

PROBATION
The most frequent sentence imposed on first-time offenders, whereby the offender is released back into the community and required to obey the rules and conditions set out in writing by the probation officer after approval by the judge.

Correctional Institutions and Agencies

Jails are used to maintain custody of persons arrested pending prosecution and to maintain custody of those sentenced to short periods of confinement. On any given day, over 700,000 adults are being held in jail.[9] The majority of inmates are serving sentences for misdemeanor convictions of less than one year. Most jails are operated by cities, counties, or both. Jails provide few services, since most inmates are there temporarily. Usually, there are separate jail facilities for women and juveniles.

All states maintain state penal institutions (**prisons**), consisting of state penitentiaries, reformatories, and training facilities for juveniles. Often, the institutions are graded according to level of security, ranging from high, or maximum, to low, or minimum, security. As of March 2018, there were 1,719 state prison facilities in the United States,[10] with a total population of 2.3 million and of 225,000 federal prisoners.[11] Prison facilities are administered by a separate correctional agency of the state or federal government.

Most court systems have a probation department attached to them. The **probation department** investigates defendants prior to sentencing and provides a pre-sentence investigation probation report to the court. Just over 4.5 million adults were on probation at year-end 2016 in the United States.[12] In addition, the probation department provides supervision over those persons placed on probation after conviction.

Probation is the most frequent sentence imposed on first-time offenders. Probationers are released back into the community and are required to obey the rules and conditions set out in writing by their probation officers after approval by the judge. Conditions include not being in possession of a firearm, not frequenting places where drugs or alcohol are used, obeying all city and state laws and ordinances, not associating with known criminal offenders, attempting to find a job, avoiding the use of alcohol and drugs, submitting to urinalysis, and reporting to a probation officer periodically. The probation service is designed to provide counseling, but because of the overwhelming case-load, probation officers usually are only able to engage in nominal supervision. The sentencing judge gives probation and the judge can take it away if the probationer continually disregards the rules and regulations or is involved in another crime.

If a person is sentenced to a term in prison but is released on parole prior to the expiration of the full sentence, the person is said to be **paroled** under supervision into the community. Supervision on parole is similar to probation supervision, except that the **parole service** is an agency of the state correctional system, rather than the court system. Violations of probation and terms of parole lead to hearings that, in turn, may lead to warning, incarceration, or re-incarceration.

THE PRETRIAL COURT PROCESS

Arrest

The criminal process most often begins with an arrest. An officer can arrest an individual only if probable cause exists. Probable cause deserves a thorough discussion, which it receives in Chapter 9. At this point, it is enough to say that **probable cause to arrest** exists when a police officer has enough evidence to lead a reasonable person to believe that a crime has been committed and that the suspect was the one who committed the crime. An officer possessing probable cause may arrest the suspect without a warrant, unless the suspect is in his or her home.[13] Alternatively, the officer can obtain a warrant from a judicial officer authorizing arrest of the suspect at home if the officer can show sufficient probable cause. Arrests made by police on patrol are made without a warrant because of the need for a speedy response. Warrants are usually obtained during an investigation of a crime.

The law enforcement officer has the responsibility for filing the **criminal complaint**, whether in advance of an arrest in order to obtain an arrest warrant or after an arrest is made without a warrant. The complaint charges the defendant

PAROLED
When a person who has been convicted of a felony and sentenced to a term in prison is released, under supervision, into the community, prior to the expiration of the full sentence.

PAROLE SERVICE
An agency of the state correctional system that is similar to the probation department but supervises those released on parole from the penitentiary.

PROBABLE CAUSE TO ARREST
The level of information required for a police officer to arrest a suspect—enough evidence to lead a reasonable person to believe that a crime has been committed and that the suspect was the one who committed the crime.

CRIMINAL COMPLAINT
A document that charges the defendant with a specific crime, usually signed by a law enforcement officer or prosecutor.

An officer's report may become the focus of intense pretrial scrutiny.

©redhumv/Getty Images

with a particular crime and is supported by an **affidavit**, a written statement, sworn under oath, in which the officer states the facts within his or her personal knowledge that support the complaint.

Not all arrests result in prosecution. The question of whether to prosecute is not made by the police officer. That decision is made by the prosecuting attorney and the courts.

Bail

Most suspects are entitled to release after arrest and booking, either on the accused's own recognizance or on bail. In less serious cases, this release can be approved at the station house. In more serious cases, the judge decides conditions for release at the initial appearance. Often you will hear that a person is released on his or her own recognizance. **Recognizance** is a promise to appear in court. **Bail** is a deposit of cash, other property, or a bond guaranteeing that the accused will appear in court. A **bond** is a written promise to pay the bail sum, posted by a financially responsible person, usually a professional bondsman. Bail is usually not very high, except in cases where it is shown that there is a risk that the accused will fail to appear for trial or poses a threat to the community, as well as in capital cases.

Plea Bargaining

Following arrest, either before or after charges have been made, counsel for the accused and the prosecutor may meet and discuss the charges to be filed against the accused and whether the accused will enter a plea of guilty or not guilty. These discussions are called plea negotiations or plea bargaining. Plea negotiations resolve over 90 percent of all prosecutions filed, both state and federal (94 percent state and 97 percent federal).[14] Plea negotiations may result in a reduction of the original charge, which reduces the level of penalty that the judge may impose upon the accused. Another result of plea negotiations is for the prosecution to recommend a specific sentence to the court, usually involving a lesser punishment than otherwise would be the case. In return, the defense enters a plea of guilty, and the prosecution does not have to go through the time and expense of taking the case to trial.

Charging the Crime

After arrest, the prosecutor will file a charge against the defendant if the prosecutor is satisfied that the evidence is sufficient to support the charge and that the case is worthy of prosecution. After the prosecutor files the charge, a judge holds a **preliminary hearing** to determine whether probable cause exists. In some jurisdictions, the preliminary hearing is minimal, providing only a summary review of the sufficiency of the evidence. In other jurisdictions, the preliminary hearing is very extensive, amounting to a mini-trial.

At the preliminary hearing, the prosecutor is likely to call one or more law enforcement officers to the witness stand. The officer's duty is to testify to those facts known to the officer that prove that there is probable cause to believe that the defendant committed a particular crime. At the preliminary hearing in most jurisdictions, the question of probable cause is one that can be proven by evidence

The law enforcement officer should be careful to give only that information necessary to show probable cause at the preliminary hearing. Testimony by the officer at the preliminary hearing makes a record that defense counsel can use later at trial to try to trip up the officer. Moreover, further investigation from the time of the preliminary hearing, sometimes called the prelim, to the time of the trial may change the way the case is tried. Therefore, the officer should testify only to the bare minimum to show probable cause. On the other hand, the officer cannot be so tight-lipped as to fail to provide the necessary information to supply probable cause.

in the form of hearsay. The issue is whether the information possessed by the prosecution makes it probable that the defendant is the person who committed the crime. Proof beyond a reasonable doubt is not required at the preliminary hearing. On the other hand, the officer will be subjected to cross-examination by the defense in an attempt to attack the prosecution's case. At the very least, defense counsel will try to get as much information as possible about the prosecution's case during the preliminary hearing.

If the prosecution makes its showing of probable cause, the defendant is required to answer to the charge in the trial court. If the crime is a misdemeanor or petty offense, the defendant will respond to the complaint filed by the prosecutor and enter a plea of guilty or not guilty. If the plea is not guilty, the case will be assigned to a court for trial. When the crime is a felony, the procedure is more complex. The common law rule required that a person could be charged with a felony only by a grand jury indictment.

A **grand jury** is a panel of persons chosen through strict court procedures to review criminal investigation and, in some instances, to conduct criminal investigations. Grand juries decide whether to charge crimes in the cases presented to them or investigated by them. The United States Supreme Court has ruled that states can charge using an information rather than an indictment if they so choose. When a grand jury charges a person with a crime, it does so by issuing an **indictment**.

GRAND JURY
A panel of persons chosen through strict court procedures to review criminal investigations and, in some instances, to conduct criminal investigations. Grand juries decide whether to charge crimes, in the form of an indictment, in the cases presented to them or investigated by them.

INDICTMENT
A formal written accusation issued by a grand jury charging a specified person with the commission of a specified crime, usually a felony.

APPLICATION CASE

Early in the development of the criminal justice system in the United States, there was some question whether a state proceeding to prosecute an accused by filing an information following a preliminary hearing, rather than using a grand jury indictment procedure, gave accused persons their required rights under the Fifth Amendment. This question was answered in the 1883 case of *Hurtado v. California*,[15] in which the preliminary hearing, in lieu of a grand jury hearing, was permitted. The Supreme Court of the United States held that the requirement of a grand jury set forth in the Fifth Amendment applies to the federal government, not the states. Furthermore, the Court held that the states did not need to proceed by means of a grand jury indictment in order to satisfy constitutional fairness requirements with respect to felony prosecutions. The *Hurtado* case stands as good case law even today.

In the federal system and in many states, felonies can still be prosecuted only by indictment of a grand jury. In those jurisdictions, after the police investigate a crime, the prosecutor presents the case to the grand jury. The grand jury hears only the prosecutor's case and decides whether to indict the accused. If the grand jury votes to indict, then a bill of indictment, or true bill, is issued. If the grand jury votes not to indict, a no bill is issued. Grand jury proceedings are secret. Only the jurors, the prosecutor, and witnesses are present. The defendant, the defense counsel, and the public cannot be present during grand jury proceedings. When the defendant has been arrested on the street, the case can be presented to the grand jury after arrest. In those jurisdictions that do not follow the grand jury procedure, felony cases are prosecuted by the filing of a formal charge, an **information**, by the prosecutor. The information is merely a piece of paper on which the formal charge appears, and that is signed by the prosecutor.

Every state, except two and the District of Columbia, uses a grand jury to indict. Both the District of Columbia and twenty-three states, i.e., Alabama, Alaska, Delaware, Florida, Kentucky, Louisiana, Maine, Massachusetts, Minnesota, Mississippi, Missouri, New Hampshire, New Jersey, New York, North Carolina, North Dakota, Ohio, Rhode Island, South Carolina, Tennessee, Texas, Virginia, and West Virginia, require the use of indictments to charge certain criminal offenses. These states generally follow federal practice by requiring indictments for serious crimes, while allowing other charging instruments to be used for minor felonies and misdemeanors.

In twenty-five states, i.e., Arizona, Arkansas, California, Colorado, Georgia, Hawaii, Idaho, Illinois, Indiana, Iowa, Kansas, Maryland, Michigan, Montana, Nebraska, Nevada, New Mexico, Oklahoma, Oregon, South Dakota, Utah, Vermont, Washington, Wisconsin, and Wyoming, the use of indictments is optional. Prosecutors can choose an indictment or an information to charge any offense.

Arraignment and Plea

After the formal charges have been filed against a defendant, either by indictment or information, the defendant appears in court at a proceeding called an arraignment or **arraignment and plea**. This is the defendant's appearance to respond formally to the charges. The defendant will enter a plea of guilty, not guilty, or, in some special cases, *nolo contendere* (no contest). If the defendant pleads guilty, then the case will be set for sentencing. If the defendant pleads not guilty, the case will be set for trial. There is usually nothing that the law enforcement officer needs to do at the arraignment and plea. In fact, it is unlikely that the prosecutor will even need the officer present.

Pretrial Motions

After arraignment and plea and before trial, the defense attorney will file certain pretrial motions. The types of motions that will be filed include a motion to suppress evidence based on claimed violations of the defendant's constitutional rights, a motion for severance of defendants or charges, a motion for discovery

---

INFORMATION
A formal written accusation submitted to the court by the prosecutor, alleging that a specified person has committed a specified crime. It is used in many jurisdictions instead of an indictment.

ARRAIGNMENT AND PLEA
The defendant's appearance in court after the filing of a formal charge (either by indictment or information), at which the defendant enters a formal plea to the charges, and at which issues about right to counsel and bail are decided by the judge.

of evidence or information, a motion for change of venue, a motion for a bill of particulars, a motion to determine the defendant's competency to stand trial, a motion for appointment of experts, a motion to continue the trial, or a motion to dismiss the charges.

Often these motions will require that the trial court hold a hearing to decide them. The officers involved in the case may be called upon to testify at those hearings.

Pretrial Issues for the Law Enforcement Professional

The prosecuting attorney will be concerned with some technical legal matters during the time after arraignment and before trial. For example, the defendant has a right to challenge the validity of the indictment or information by moving to dismiss the charges. Any claims that the defendant's constitutional rights have been violated may be raised. Both the defense and the prosecution may ask the trial judge to decide other legal questions, including what evidence will be admissible at trial.

The law enforcement officer will be involved in numerous ways during the pretrial period. First, the officer may continue investigating the case. In many instances, the criminal investigation will continue up to the time of trial and sometimes even during the trial itself.

All the officer's reports will be of potential significance at trial. As a result, the officer will want to organize, review, and summarize his or her own reports and even become familiar with the reports of other officers.

The evidence that has been gathered must be maintained and prepared for trial by either the police or criminalists involved in the investigation. Any new evidence that has been identified should similarly be gathered and properly maintained. Where an officer or a criminalist has been responsible for particular items of evidence, he or she will be called upon at trial to lay the foundation for that evidence's admission and should be aware of the questions the prosecutor will ask and the answers that must be given to lay that foundation. Officers, criminalists, or forensic investigators will also testify as to tests that may have been done to the evidence. This textbook will provide you with the knowledge you will need to gather, prepare, and present evidence in a case in a proper and effective manner.

REVIEW AND APPLICATION

SUMMARY

(1) Evidence is any information about the facts of a case—including tangible items, testimony, documents, photographs, and tapes—that, when presented to the jury at trial, tends to prove or disprove these facts.

(2) The objectives of the rules of evidence are to know what is admissible at a trial, ensure the integrity of all evidence, protect a defendant's rights, and ensure a fair trial.

(3) The most common version of evidence law in the United States is the Federal Rules of Evidence (FRE).

(4) The police are called upon to perform three basic functions:

    (a) enforcing the law, which includes detecting and investigating crimes, apprehending suspects, and assisting in the prosecution of offenders;

    (b) maintaining public order, which includes activities such as crowd control and crime prevention, as well as responding to domestic and civil disturbances; and

    (c) providing various public services, such as responding to emergencies, helping stranded motorists, and finding missing children.

(5) It is the job of the prosecutor to take a case from the police and pursue it until the case terminates by trial, guilty plea, or dismissal. The prosecutor must decide whether to pursue a formal charge and, if so, what crime to charge. Defense counsel must zealously represent the criminal defendant from the point of interrogation through the trial process, demanding that the prosecution respect the defendant's rights, treat the defendant fairly, and meet the burden of proof beyond a reasonable doubt in the event the case goes to trial.

(6) The federal court system applies nation-wide, and federal courts are located in each state. Each state also has its own court system. The federal courts coexist with individual state court systems. Whether a defendant is tried in a federal or state court depends on which court has jurisdiction over that case. Most states' structures are similar to that of the federal courts—a trial court, an intermediate appellate court, and a supreme court.

(7) Probable cause to arrest is when an officer possesses enough evidence to lead a reasonable person to believe that a crime has been committed and that the suspect was the one who committed the crime.

(8) A defendant can be formally charged with a serious crime in the United States either by indictment of a grand jury or by the filing of an information by the prosecution after a preliminary hearing.

KEY TERMS

QUESTIONS FOR REVIEW

1. What is evidence?
2. Describe the purpose of the rules of evidence.
3. What law of evidence exists in a majority of American jurisdictions?
4. List some common activities of police officers.
5. Describe what a prosecuting attorney does. How is this different from the defense attorney's job?
6. What courts are in the federal judicial system? How does this compare with a typical state court system? What are the courts in your state?
7. When may a police officer arrest a person?
8. What is a grand jury indictment? When must it be used?

WORKPLACE APPLICATIONS

1. When an officer secures an item of physical evidence, he or she must ensure a proper chain of custody of it, so that the item can be introduced into evidence in court. Assume that an officer has obtained a knife from the scene of a murder. What steps should the officer take to maintain a chain of custody of the knife up to the time the officer appears in court with the knife for the preliminary hearing?
2. Before a preliminary hearing is held in a criminal case, the law enforcement officer may be approached in person or by telephone by an attorney hired or appointed to represent the defendant. The attorney will want to know what the officer's testimony at the preliminary hearing will be. What do you think an officer should do when contacted by defense counsel before the preliminary hearing?

ENDNOTES

1. *See* 2018 Connecticut Court Order 0411 (C.O. 0411).
2. *2016 Crime in the United States, Overview Table 23,* FBI (2017), https://ucr.fbi.gov/crime-in-the-u.s/2016/crime-in-the-u.s.-2016/tables/table-23/table-23-overview.pdf (last visited 04/22/18).
3. *See* Niall McCarthy, Private Security Outnumbers the Police in Most Countries [Infographic], Forbes https://www.forbes.com/sites/niallmccarthy/2017/08/31/private-security-outnumbers-the-police-in-most-countries-worldwide-infographic/#3f74b015210f (last visited 4/28/18).
4. *Id.*
5. bjs.ojp.usdoj.gov/content/pub/pdf/csllea08.pdf (last visited 01/21/13).
6. The Los Angeles County District Attorney reported in April 2018 that it employed nearly 1,000 Deputy District Attorneys; http://da.lacounty.gov/about/office-overview (last visited 4/28/2018).
7. James J. Tomkovicz & Welsh S. White, *Criminal Procedure: Constitutional Constraints upon Investigation and Proof* xxvi n.2 (8th ed. 2017). Only the Fifth Amendment's requirement of a grand jury indictment for "capital or otherwise infamous crimes" and the Eighth Amendment's prohibition of "excessive bail" have not specifically been incorporated.
8. In re Gault, 387 U.S. 1 (1967).
9. The most recent statistic, mid-year 2016, was that 740,700 inmates were incarcerated in "the nation's local jails." https://www.bjs.gov/index.cfm?ty=pbdetail&iid=6186 (last visited 4/28/18).
10. Peter Wagner & Wendy Sawyer, Prison Policy Initiative, Mass Incarceration: The Whole Pie, https://www.prisonpolicy.org/reports/pie2018.html (last visited 4/28/18).
11. http://www.bjs.gov/content/pub/pdf/p12ac.pdf (last visited 11/8/13).
12. *Id.*
13. Steagald v. United States, 451 U.S. 204 (1981).
14. Erica Goode, *Stronger Hand for Judges in the "Bazaar" of Plea Deals,* N.Y. Times (March 22, 2012), https://www.nytimes.com/2012/03/23/us/stronger-hand-for-judges-after-rulings-on-plea-deals.html (last visited 4/28/18).
15. Hurtado v. California, 110 U.S. 516 (1883).

Design Element: ©Ingram Publishing

2 THE TRIAL PROCESS

CHAPTER OUTLINE

CHAPTER OBJECTIVES

In the prior chapter, we discussed the criminal process from arrest through pretrial. In this chapter, an overview of a criminal trial is presented. After reading this chapter you will be able to:

▶ Describe the sequence of events in a typical criminal trial.

▶ Contrast the level of proof required in a criminal case with the level of proof required in a civil case.

▶ Name the two types of challenges of a juror used during *voir dire.*

▶ Describe the various duties of a judge in a criminal trial.

▶ Cite a working definition of reasonable doubt.

▶ Contrast the roles of the prosecuting attorney and defense attorney.

▶ Describe the burden upon the prosecution in its case-in-chief.

▶ List the five requirements for being a witness.

▶ State the difference between the types of questions allowed on direct and on cross-examination.

▶ Identify the order of presentation of the closing argument.

INTRODUCTION

Each arrest of a person formally accused of a crime must be followed by some kind of prosecutorial action, including dismissal. If the accused enters a plea of guilty to the charge for which he or she was arrested, the prosecutorial procedure is comparatively simple, and the law enforcement officer usually does not become involved. On the other hand, if the accused enters a plea of not guilty, the trial that follows can become a very time-consuming, complicated ordeal. The officer will play an important role in the entire process. For this reason, before beginning a detailed discussion of the law of evidence, a brief review of the structure and procedure of a trial is helpful to gain a better understanding of the rules of evidence and their application. Although the sequence of events in a criminal trial may vary slightly from jurisdiction to jurisdiction, the sequence depicted in Figure 2–1 is typical.

Some people think that a trial is a search for the truth and that juries determine what actually happened in a case by looking at the evidence presented in court. Other people believe that, since it is impossible to determine what truly happened in a case when humans attempt to re-create history through evidence, the true aim of a trial is to bring the competing sides to a peaceful conclusion and to do justice. In either case, a trial is society's last-ditch effort to prevent the chaos that would result if individuals tried to settle disputes themselves. Regardless of which definition of purpose is used, the American justice system is set up as an adversarial system. This means both sides are fighting to win. Winning a trial means convincing the jury or a judge to believe one side's evidence rather than the other side's.

FYI

The problem of re-creating historical fact in a trial is the subject of the classic 1950 Japanese film *Rashomon*. The film depicts a rape-murder and the criminal's subsequent trial in ninth-century Japan. The double crime is depicted four times—from the viewpoints of the three participants (the criminal, the woman he raped, and her husband) as well as from the viewpoint of a woodcutter who witnessed the episode. Each "witness" gives an account of the crime that increases the prestige of his or her conduct. Continuously reconstructing the crime through the "witnesses," the film asks, "How can we ever know the truth?" Anyone who has ever participated in a trial is probably aware of what has come to be known as the "Rashomon syndrome," in which witnesses to the same event present very different accounts of it. The vagaries of human perception, memory, and narrative ability are probably to blame for this fact of life.

Although an American trial is an adversarial proceeding, it provides a forum and a process for telling the story of the case in a logical sequence, so that the judge and jury may more clearly understand the case. Each witness reveals his or her part in the story while testifying to personal knowledge of the pertinent facts. However, since the law does not allow every possible piece of evidence to be heard or seen by the jury, the trial is controlled by a set of rules we refer to as the rules of evidence.

Although there are vast differences between criminal and civil trials, there is very little difference between the rules of evidence applicable in a criminal case and those applicable in a civil matter. Perhaps the most marked difference is the amount of proof necessary. In a criminal case, the prosecution must present enough evidence to convince the jury of the defendant's guilt beyond a reasonable doubt. In a civil trial, only a preponderance of the evidence must be presented on the part of one side or the other to receive a favorable judgment.

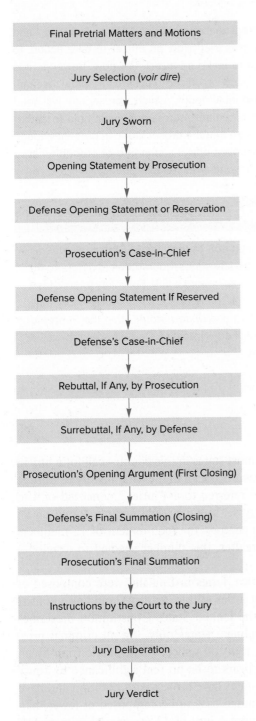

Final Pretrial Matters and Motions

↓

Jury Selection (*voir dire*)

↓

Jury Sworn

↓

Opening Statement by Prosecution

↓

Defense Opening Statement or Reservation

↓

Prosecution's Case-in-Chief

↓

Defense Opening Statement If Reserved

↓

Defense's Case-in-Chief

↓

Rebuttal, If Any, by Prosecution

↓

Surrebuttal, If Any, by Defense

↓

Prosecution's Opening Argument (First Closing)

↓

Defense's Final Summation (Closing)

↓

Prosecution's Final Summation

↓

Instructions by the Court to the Jury

↓

Jury Deliberation

↓

Jury Verdict

FIGURE 2–1 Sequence of events in a typical criminal trial.

Proof beyond a reasonable doubt is not proof beyond all doubt, but it is the highest level, or quantity, of proof that American law demands in any case. Proof beyond a reasonable doubt is far more than 50 percent. On the other hand, proof by a preponderance of the evidence—the quantity required to win in a civil trial—is 50 percent plus a feather. An example of this difference in quantity of proof is the difference in outcomes in the criminal and civil trials of O.J. Simpson in connection with the murders of Nicole Brown Simpson and Ronald Goldman. The jury in the criminal trial was not convinced beyond a reasonable doubt of Mr. Simpson's guilt in the murders and, in October 1995, entered a verdict of acquittal. However, the jury in the civil trial, in February 1997, believed, by a preponderance of the evidence, that Mr. Simpson killed the two victims.

JURY OR COURT TRIAL

Instructions by the Court to the Jury

A criminal trial may be conducted in one of two ways. It may be what is known as a "jury trial" or it may be a "court trial," which is a trial by a judge without a jury (also known as a "bench trial"). Most states permit a defendant to waive a jury, but the right may not be absolute. In some states, the prosecuting attorney may also be required to agree to this waiver in order for the judge to try the case without a jury. In any event, a trial before a judge alone is conducted in much the same manner as a trial before a jury. The structure of the trial is the same, and the same rules of evidence apply.

Chapter 9 will introduce the terms "reasonable suspicion," "Terry Doctrine," and "probable cause." These are the principles that allow an officer to take action, to begin or continue an investigation, and to make an arrest. For now, however, it is enough to know that the standards that allow an officer to act are far below the standards required for "proof beyond a reasonable doubt," which a prosecutor will need for a successful conviction. The law enforcement professional must help to gather and prepare the evidence for trial to ensure that the prosecutor can present enough evidence to fill in the gap between the police officer's standard of probable cause and the prosecutor's standard of proof beyond a reasonable doubt.

APPLICATION CASE

The Sixth Amendment to the Constitution of the United States, as well as provisions in the constitutions of the fifty states, guarantees to a defendant in a criminal trial the right to be tried by an impartial jury. For many years those provisions were interpreted to mean that the defendant must have a jury trial. It was not until 1930, in the case of *Patton v. United States*,[1] that the Supreme Court of the United States gave a qualified approval for a defendant to waive the jury and be tried by a judge alone.

THE JURY

The common law rule and the rule in most states in this country call for a jury in a criminal case consisting of 12 persons. Although in the early history of Europe many of the inquisitory councils, also referred to as "juries," consisted of 4 to 66 members, by the thirteenth century 12 was the usual number found on an inquisitory council. By the fourteenth century, the requirement of 12 members had become more or less fixed. Thereafter, this number seemed to develop a somewhat superstitious reverence.

When the colonists came to America, juries in England were composed of 12 persons, so it was only natural that juries in this country should also consist of 12, yet the Sixth Amendment to the United States Constitution prescribes no set number for a jury. The Amendment states only, "In all criminal prosecutions, the accused shall enjoy the right of a speedy and public trial, by an impartial jury." Inasmuch as there appears to be no real significance to a jury being composed of 12 persons, some states have broken with tradition and have passed laws permitting a jury in a criminal case to be composed of fewer than 12 members. All states, however, require a jury of 12 for capital crimes. The United States Supreme Court has held that a defendant is entitled to a trial by jury when charged with a serious crime,[2] distinguishing trials for "petty" offenses for which an accused is not entitled to a jury trial. An offense is petty, for purposes of the right to trial by jury, when the penalty is incarceration for a period of less than six months.[3] In *Williams v. Florida*,[4] the Supreme Court upheld a conviction for a nonpetty offense on a verdict by a six-member jury. However, a few years thereafter, the Court struck down a state statute providing for five-member

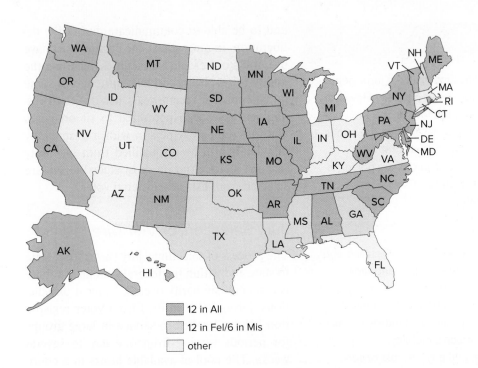

FIGURE 2–2 Number of jurors in criminal cases by state.

Legend:
- 12 in All
- 12 in Fel/6 in Mis
- other

juries in misdemeanor cases in *Ballew v. Georgia.*[5] Taken together, the two cases set the bottom limit for jurors at 6, permitting the states to designate juries of any number between 6 and 12 for trials in which the punishment could exceed six months in jail or prison (see Figure 2-2).

Another important factor involved in trial by jury is the requirement as to how the jury votes. Historically, not only was the jury in a criminal case required to consist of 12 persons, but the verdict reached by the panel was required to be unanimous. In the aftermath of the Supreme Court decisions relating to jury size just discussed, there also arose questions regarding the unanimity requirement. In *Johnson v. Louisiana*[6] and *Apodaca v. Oregon,*[7] two cases decided together, the Supreme Court upheld nonunanimous jury verdicts in criminal trials. All of the juries involved in those cases were panels of 12 persons. A few years after these two decisions, in *Burch v. Louisiana,*[8] the Court clarified the issues by striking down a statute allowing for nonunanimous verdicts of six-person juries for non-petty offenses. The result of all of these cases is that six-member juries are permitted in serious crimes cases, but only if they reach unanimous verdicts. Otherwise, juries of any size greater than six may reach nonunanimous verdicts.

Qualifications of Jurors

Although the qualifications of a trial juror may vary somewhat from state to state, the general qualifications are quite similar. The person must be an adult, meaning 18 years of age or over. He or she must be a citizen of the United States and a resident within the jurisdiction of the court involved. The prospective juror must have a sufficient knowledge of the English language to understand the testimony

As stated in the text, qualifications to be a juror generally include the ability to see, hear, and talk. However, a number of states have adopted laws that permit persons with disabilities to serve as jurors with the necessary assistance. Alaska's statute[10] is illustrative:

(a) A person is qualified to act as a juror if the person is
  (1) a citizen of the United States;
  (2) a resident of the state;
  (3) at least 18 years of age;
  (4) of sound mind;
  (5) in possession of the person's natural faculties; and
  (6) able to read or speak the English language.
(b) A person is not disqualified from serving as a juror solely because of the loss of hearing or sight in any degree or a disability that substantially impairs or interferes with the person's mobility.
(c) The court shall provide, and pay the cost of services of, an interpreter or reader when necessary to enable a person with impaired hearing or sight to act as a juror.

and to be able to communicate during the deliberation. In most states, the person must have use of his or her natural faculties, meaning the ability to see, hear, and talk, although in some jurisdictions in recent years persons with disabilities have been permitted to sit on juries with assistance.[9] A person with a past felony conviction will be disqualified from jury duty in most states. And, in most states, jurors are selected from lists of registered voters.

Jury Selection, or *Voir Dire*

The process of selecting a jury varies from state to state and within the federal system, but there is a general similarity overall. In most jurisdictions, jurors are identified from voter registration lists and called to service in large groups for periods varying from one day to several weeks. The pool of available jurors in a courthouse on any given day provides the pool sent to any one courtroom. The pool of jurors sent to a courtroom is called the **venire**. After that pool enters the courtroom, the judge engages in a general introduction and the initial questioning of the prospective jurors. Usually some jurors are excused from service as a result of this general questioning (e.g., because of the financial hardship from sitting as a juror). However, thereafter begins the more extensive process of questioning prospective jurors to select the final panel, a process known as *voir dire*, which roughly means "to speak the truth."

Voir dire is conducted exclusively by the judge in the federal system and in many states. That means that the attorneys for both sides may only suggest questions for the judge to ask, although attorneys may address the court to challenge jurors for any reason. In those jurisdictions that allow lawyers to conduct *voir dire*, either partially or entirely, the lawyers pose the questions on *voir dire* directly to the prospective jurors.

The purpose of *voir dire* is to eliminate from the jury any person who is incapable of acting impartially. Any prospective juror found by the judge to be biased or prejudiced against the parties because of the type of case, pretrial publicity, or any other factor that may reasonably affect the prospective juror's ability to be fair may be excluded for cause on a motion, made by the prosecution, the defense, or the judge. Such motions are known as **challenges for cause**. There is no limit to the number of challenges for cause that may be made. *Voir dire* usually will also produce information from which the attorneys will decide to exercise peremptory challenges. A juror may be excluded based on a **peremptory challenge** for any reason or no reason whatsoever. The only exception is that neither the prosecution[11] nor the defense[12] may exercise a peremptory challenge in a discriminatory manner that violates the Equal Protection Clause of the Fourteenth Amendment to the Constitution of the United

VENIRE
The pool of prospective jurors from which the jury panel is selected.

JURY *VOIR DIRE*
The process of questioning a panel of prospective jurors to select the final panel; roughly it means "to speak the truth."

CHALLENGES FOR CAUSE
The motion that a prospective juror should be excluded because he or she is incapable of being impartial.

PEREMPTORY CHALLENGE
The motion that excludes a prospective juror from the jury panel without specific reason or justification.

States, particularly with respect to the race of the prospective juror. For example, in *Batson v. Kentucky,* the Supreme Court held that the Equal Protection Clause forbids a prosecutor from challenging potential jurors solely on account of their race, or on the assumption that black jurors as a group will be unable to impartially consider the state's case against a black defendant.[13] The attorney exercising a challenge merely asks the court to exclude the prospective juror. The number of such challenges is severely limited, usually 6 to 10 per side in most states in noncapital cases, 20 in capital cases.

In addition to the jurors selected for the panel, most states require the selection of additional jurors, known as "alternates," who hear all the evidence but do not participate in deliberation unless one or more primary jurors are excused from jury duty during the trial. The process for the selection of alternates follows the same pattern as the process for the selection of regular jurors.

Function of the Jury

In a jury trial, the function of the jury is to determine the facts of the case and render a verdict based on the law explained to them by the judge during jury instructions. In other words, the jury interprets the evidence as it is presented and tries to determine what happened. The jury's ultimate goal in a criminal trial is to ascertain whether the defendant is guilty beyond a reasonable doubt of the crime as charged. This decision is made after the evidence has been submitted to the jury by the prosecution and defense. A defendant in a criminal trial does not have to testify or present any evidence, particularly if the defendant believes the prosecution's case is so weak that there is already a reasonable doubt about his or her guilt. On the other hand, the defendant's evidence may be offered in an effort to overcome that presented by the prosecution. This is done in the hope that it will create a doubt in the minds of the jurors, if that doubt is not already present. The ultimate function of the jury in a criminal case is rendering a verdict of guilty or not guilty.

A jury can participate in determining a defendant's sentence directly or indirectly. In certain instances, in order for a defendant's sentence to be enhanced above a certain minimum, the prosecutor must allege the aggravating factors as part of the charge against the defendant. The jury, will decide whether these factors have been proved at the same time they decide the guilt or innocence of the defendant. In other instances, such as the circumstances described in *Ring v. Arizona,* after the defendant is found guilty of a crime, the prosecution, in a separate phase, presents additional evidence to the jury, so that it can determine whether aggravating circumstances are present. Finally, in six states, the jury, not the court, will pronounce the actual sentence to be received by the defendant in all or some specific types of cases. Those states are Arkansas, Kentuckys, Missouri,

Oklahoma, Texas, and Virginia. In those six states, juries mete out sentences in criminal cases generally or only in some types of cases specified by statute. Under the pertinent United States Supreme Court decisions, juries must make decisions on sentencing in death penalty cases, or cases in which enhancement factors are part of the crime charged.

APPLICATION CASE

In three successive cases, the United States Supreme Court has adopted and applied the principle that the Sixth Amendment right to trial by jury requires that certain facts, in addition to the finding of guilt, must be found by the jury, not the judge. In *Apprendi v. New Jersey*,[14] the Court held that, other than the fact of prior conviction, any fact that increases the penalty for a crime beyond the statutory maximum must be submitted to a jury and proved beyond a reasonable doubt. The case of *Ring v. Arizona*[15] was the vehicle for the United States Supreme Court to decide that, if a jury finds a defendant guilty of a crime subject to the death penalty, the Sixth Amendment principle stated in *Apprendi* requires that a jury determine the presence or absence of the aggravating factors required in order to impose the death penalty. Finally, in *Blakely v. Washington*,[16] the Court declared that a state's sentencing guidelines allowing a trial judge to find the fact necessary to trigger a sentence above the statutory maximum also violated the Sixth Amendment principle stated in *Apprendi*.

Jury Nullification

The jury in a criminal trial in the United States renders an unappealable, unassailable verdict of acquittal of an accused person. Although each juror takes an oath to decide the case by applying the facts, as he or she finds them to be, to the law as the judge states it, there is no redress if the jury violates this oath in favor of a defendant in a criminal case. Should a jury acquit an accused for the wrong reason, or for no reason at all, the law is powerless to correct the error. Also, this means that if the jury does not wish to follow the law, for whatever reason, there is no redress. This power is known as **jury nullification** because it is a fact that the jury may thereby nullify the law. This power is little known and rarely discussed. It is not lawful for a judge or lawyer to tell a jury of its power to nullify.[17] For example, if a person is on trial for drug possession involving possession of marijuana for personal use, a jury might acquit because its members do not believe such drug possession should be illegal even if the prosecution has presented evidence to support all of the elements of the crime.

The federal Constitution, in the Fifth Amendment, contains a provision banning twice putting a criminal accused in "jeopardy." Under this provision, if a trial results in a jury verdict of acquittal, the defendant cannot be retried. Thus, the jury's nullification power stems from this Double Jeopardy Clause of the Fifth Amendment to the Constitution of the United States.

Historically, the jury's nullification power was used to vindicate injustices, where the jury reacted to an unpopular law, or where strict application of the law might have seemed unfair. Examples are the libel prosecutions in the

JURY NULLIFICATION
The power of a jury in a criminal case to acquit a defendant for any reason or no reason at all. When a jury in a criminal case exercises this power, its decision cannot be appealed.

American Colonies by the British government for political protest and the imposition of severe penalties for possession of small quantities of marijuana, as mentioned earlier. In recent years, there has been a growing movement to inform jurors of their power to nullify. However, most states still do not permit this notification.

Law enforcement professionals should be aware that it is possible for a jury to render a verdict in favor of a defendant, using the power to nullify, even though law enforcement did all they could to prepare and present a strong case. As jurors become more aware of their power, such cases may be even more common.

THE JUDGE

The judge's principal responsibility is to see that the defendant in a criminal case gets a fair trial. To accomplish this, the judge has many duties, including deciding what law applies to the case; interpreting the law of the case for the jury; deciding what evidence is and is not admissible; ruling on objections made by the attorneys; determining the qualifications of witnesses; protecting witnesses from overzealous cross-examinations; ensuring that the trial proceeds efficiently and effectively; and, in most states, in most instances, imposing sentence upon the defendant in a criminal case. In some jurisdictions, the judge may comment on the credibility of the witnesses and the weight of the evidence.

In a jury trial, the function of the judge is much like that of a referee. The judge keeps order in the court and sees that the trial progresses properly and smoothly. It is the judge's duty to maintain control over the conduct of those involved in a trial proceeding. To assist in this regard, the judge may exercise the power of contempt. **Contempt** is the power of the court to punish persons for failure to obey court orders or to coerce them into obeying court orders. When a judge holds a person in contempt, the judge fines or jails the person for criminal failures to obey the court. In cases of civil contempt, the judge orders the person to jail until the person complies with the judge's order. A person held in civil contempt is said to "hold the keys to the jail cell in his or her pocket"; if the person complies with the court order, he or she will be released from custody.

When the trial is conducted without a jury, the judge acts in a dual capacity. The judge does the same things he or she would do when presiding over a jury trial, as well as performing the function of the jury in determining the facts of the case. The judge therefore renders the verdict of guilt or innocence.

CONTEMPT
The power of a court to punish persons for failure to obey court orders or to coerce them into obeying court orders.

PROSECUTING ATTORNEY'S RESPONSIBILITY AND THE BURDEN OF PROOF BEYOND A REASONABLE DOUBT

Once a trial begins, the duties of the law enforcement officer are, for the most part, completed, except for testifying. By this time, the officers will have collected physical evidence, interviewed the witnesses, and discussed the case in detail with the prosecuting attorney. All that remains for the officers to do is to testify in a forthright, unbiased, and intelligent manner. The progress of the trial is largely the responsibility of the prosecuting attorney, who assumes the leading role in the judicial process.

Prosecutors, however, have many responsibilities long before the trial begins. Their duty is to prosecute the guilty and to see that the innocent are protected. In the landmark case of *Gideon v. Wainwright,*[18] where the Supreme Court of the United States applied the Sixth Amendment right to counsel in felony cases to the states through the Fourteenth Amendment's Due Process Clause, the Court noted that prosecutors "are everywhere deemed essential to protect the public's interest in an orderly society." In this capacity, prosecutors must decide which criminal charges should be prosecuted and which should be dismissed in the interests of justice. The prosecutor has broad power to decide whether or not to pursue any given case. The public has the right to demand that the prosecutor use that power wisely and impartially.

When the decision to prosecute is reached, the prosecutor must decide which witnesses will be used and what evidence will be presented. It is not necessary that every witness who has some knowledge of the case be called upon to testify. Neither is it required that every bit of physical evidence be presented. The only requirement is that a sufficient number of witnesses be called and sufficient evidence be presented to convince the jury that the accused committed the crime. In deciding what evidence to use, the prosecutor will consider past experience with the particular charge involved, knowledge of the personality of the judge who will be hearing the case, and the potential dramatics of the situation as the trial progresses. In addition, the prosecutor has an obligation to disclose to the defense attorney any evidence that could be used to aid the defense. Any evidence that tends to prove the innocence of an accused is called **exculpatory evidence**. The prosecution has a duty to disclose exculpatory evidence to the defense when requested. Failure to do so, regardless of the good or bad faith of the prosecution, violates the defendant's due process rights. The United States Supreme Court announced this doctrine in the 1963 case of *Brady v. Maryland.*[19] In many states, reciprocal pretrial exchange of information is required and is called **pretrial discovery**.

The United States Supreme Court has held that the Constitution makes it the responsibility of the prosecutor to prove every element of a charged offense beyond a "reasonable doubt." The Court has also held that the "Constitution does not require any particular form of words be used" in instructing the jury on the definition of reasonable doubt.[20] The trial judge may choose not to define reasonable doubt, but, if he or she does choose to define the term, then "taken as a whole the instructions [must] correctly conve[y] the concept of reasonable

EXCULPATORY EVIDENCE
Any evidence that tends to prove the innocence of an accused.

PRETRIAL DISCOVERY
A reciprocal exchange of information between the prosecuting and defending attorneys, before trial, either as ordered by the court in a particular case or required by statute or rule.

ON THE JOB

Law enforcement professionals do not exist in a vacuum. They work long hours in different shifts. This tends to limit their social contacts to people involved in the criminal justice system. It is not uncommon for friendships to develop among law enforcement professionals, including police, criminalists, court bailiffs, court clerks, prosecutors, defense attorneys, and even judges. The trick is to manage such relationships responsibly. When called to testify in court, law enforcement professionals must remember that, when they are in court, the court official, who may be a weekend fishing buddy or shopping companion, is now involved in running a trial that will greatly affect the defendant's life. Therefore, the law enforcement professional must treat the judge, and other court professionals, with the formal respect they deserve whenever they are in the courthouse or in other professional settings. It will enhance both personal and professional respect from other participants.

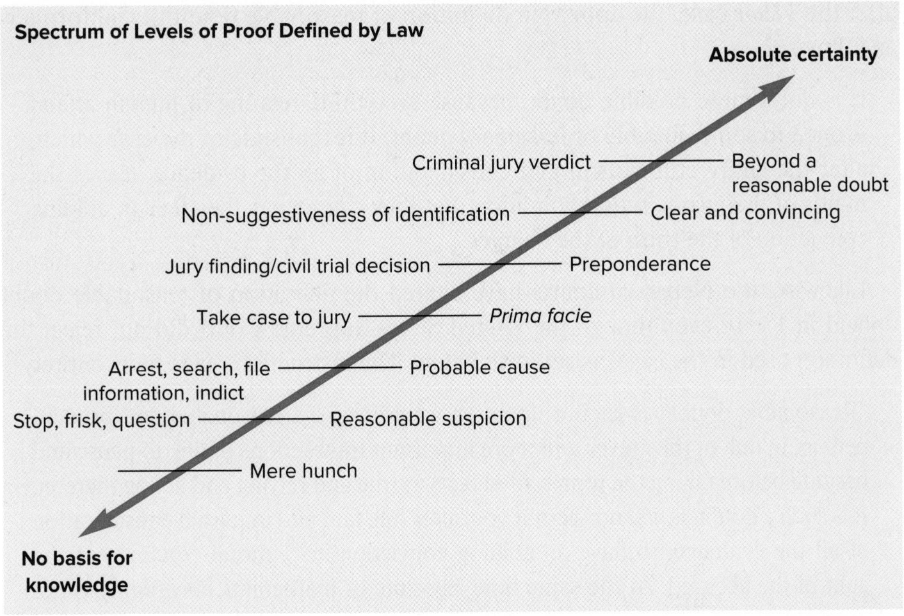

Spectrum of Levels of Proof Defined by Law

Absolute certainty

Criminal jury verdict —————— Beyond a reasonable doubt

Non-suggestiveness of identification —————— Clear and convincing

Jury finding/civil trial decision —————— Preponderance

Take case to jury —————— *Prima facie*

Arrest, search, file information, indict —————— Probable cause

Stop, frisk, question —————— Reasonable suspicion

—————— Mere hunch

No basis for knowledge

FIGURE 2–3 Spectrum of levels of proof.

doubt to the jury."[21] The concept is that proof beyond a reasonable doubt is a high standard of proof, but not one that leaves no doubt at all. In practical terms, the Court has approved a definition that indicates that **reasonable doubt** is a doubt based upon reason: that which would make a reasonable person hesitate to act in connection with important affairs of life.

A number of standards of proof are used in legal definitions. This is a good time to refer to the spectrum of those standards of proof. The first chapter presented the concept of probable cause—that level of proof a police officer needs to arrest a suspect and a prosecutor needs to show in court to formally charge an accused. The standard of proof in a civil case, preponderance of the evidence, was discussed earlier in this chapter. There are a few other levels of proof that the law enforcement officer should be familiar with: mere hunch, reasonable suspicion, *prima facie*, and clear and convincing. A graphical spectrum of these levels of proof is presented in Figure 2–3. Each of these terms will be more fully described at an appropriate point in the text. For now, the focus is on the fact that the requirement of proof beyond a reasonable doubt is the highest level of proof that the law demands.

In recent years, the Supreme Court has addressed the problem of defining reasonable doubt for the jury in a criminal case. The Court disapproved of one definition and approved two others. In the 1990 case of *Cage v. Louisiana*,[22] the Court said that using the words "substantial" and "grave," when coupled with the term "moral certainty," could be understood by a reasonable juror to allow the juror to find an accused guilty "on a degree of proof below that required by the Due Process Clause."[23]

In 1994, in *Victor v. Nebraska*,[24] the Court considered definitions of reasonable doubt from two states, California and Nebraska. The Court held that both definitions were constitutional. Both definitions contained the language relating to "moral certainty." The Court sufficiently questioned use of the term "moral certainty" in modern times to cause the California Supreme Court to consent to the elimination of the phrase from its approved definition thereafter.[25] Thus,

REASONABLE DOUBT The standard of proof in a criminal case. A doubt based upon reason: that which would make a reasonable person hesitate to act in connection with important affairs of life.

after the *Victor* case, the approved definition of reasonable doubt in California is as follows:[26]

> It is not a mere possible doubt; because everything relating to human affairs is open to some possible or imaginary doubt. It is that state of the case which, after the entire comparison and consideration of all the evidence, leaves the minds of the jurors in that condition that they cannot say they feel an abiding conviction of the truth of the charge.

Likewise, the Nebraska courts have altered the definition of reasonable doubt upheld in *Victor*, even though the United States Supreme Court did not reject the definition used in the case, as set forth below. The instruction reads in its entirety[27]

> "Reasonable doubt" is such a doubt as would cause a reasonable and prudent person, in one of the graver and more important transactions of life, to pause and hesitate before taking the represented facts as true and relying and acting thereon. It is such a doubt as will not permit you, after full, fair, and impartial consideration of all the evidence, to have an abiding conviction, to a moral certainty, of the guilt of the accused. At the same time, absolute or mathematical certainty is not required. You may be convinced of the truth of a fact beyond a reasonable doubt and yet be fully aware that possibly you may be mistaken. You may find an accused guilty upon the strong probabilities of the case, provided such probabilities are strong enough to exclude any doubt of his guilt that is reasonable. A reasonable doubt is an actual and substantial doubt arising from the evidence, from the facts or circumstances shown by the evidence, or from the lack of evidence on the part of the state, as distinguished from a doubt arising from mere possibility, from bare imagination, or from fanciful conjecture.

ROLE OF THE DEFENSE ATTORNEY

Among other guarantees, the Sixth Amendment to the Constitution of the United States provides that, "in all criminal prosecutions, the accused shall . . . have the assistance of counsel for his defense." An accused is entitled to assistance of counsel for his or her defense in all instances, except where incarceration is not possible; if the accused cannot afford an attorney, one must be provided. An accused is entitled to the assistance of counsel even before trial—as early as at the time of a suspect's arrest.

Because an accused is entitled to counsel at every stage of a criminal proceeding—from focused investigation or arrest through trial—the defense attorney is an important figure in the administration of criminal justice. Defense counsel's primary function is to make certain that all the rights of the accused are properly protected. Counsel will make certain that the charge against the defendant is a valid one and that there was sufficient probable cause to arrest the defendant or conduct any search or seizure. Defense counsel will conduct pretrial investigation and discovery and otherwise prepare for trial. The defense attorney will advise the accused concerning statements that he or she may or may not make. At the time of the trial, the defense attorney will cross-examine the prosecution witnesses and present any defense necessary under the circumstances. Along with the judge, defense counsel has the responsibility of seeing that the defendant receives a fair trial.

Most important, the defense attorney has an ethical obligation to zealously represent the accused. In our system, every accused person is entitled to full representation and a fair trial. And, though an accused has been brought to trial on the belief by a law enforcement officer, prosecutor, and grand jury or judge that there is probable cause to believe the accused is guilty, the accused enters the courtroom presumed to be innocent; and this presumption continues until the accused is proven guilty beyond a reasonable doubt at trial. It is the job of the defense attorney to demand that the state prove its case under the law with *legally* obtained evidence.

As previously stated, an accused is entitled to counsel in all serious cases; this right may not be denied. However, an accused may waive the right to the assistance of counsel and be entitled to represent himself or herself. However, the judge must be satisfied that the decision is an intelligent and informed one.

OPENING STATEMENT

If the trial is heard by a jury, the judge will read, or have read, to the jury the indictment or information for which the defendant has been brought to trial. When the jury is sworn, that is the point at which jeopardy attaches, i.e., if the accused is later found to be not guilty, he or she cannot be tried again for the same crime.

©New York Post Archives/Getty Images

Colin Ferguson unsuccessfully defended himself in his 1995 trial for the shooting deaths of 6 people and the wounding of 19 others on a Long Island Railroad commuter train.

OPENING STATEMENT
A summary of how the prosecution expects its evidence to show the defendant guilty beyond a reasonable doubt or how the defense attorney expects to raise a reasonable doubt. It is not an argument but rather a road map of the prosecution's case-in-chief.

CASE-IN-CHIEF
That portion of the trial that comprises the main evidence for either the prosecution or the defense.

Whether the trial is heard by a jury or by the judge alone, the prosecution will present its case first. After the charge has been read to the jury, the trial proper begins with the prosecution's opening statement. The **opening statement** is a summary of how the prosecution expects its evidence to prove the defendant guilty beyond a reasonable doubt. The prosecution's opening statement is usually followed by the defense's opening statement, though this right can be reserved and exercised later in the trial. Defense's opening statement is a summary of how there is a reasonable doubt.

An opening statement is not an argument but rather a road map of each side's case-in-chief. The **case-in-chief** is that portion of the case consisting of the main evidence of either the prosecution or the defense. An opening statement is often given in the form of a story, but it is a story in which the attorney promises to support the narrative with positive proof. The attorney often discusses what the evidence will show. The beginning, ending, and sequencing of the story will be constructed in accordance with the lawyer's theory and theme of the case. So, as long as it is clear that the attorney will support the "story" with evidence, this form of opening statement is perfectly acceptable and usually is most effective.

Although the defendant's attorney usually makes an opening statement immediately after the prosecution's opening statement, he or she can reserve the right to do so after the conclusion of the prosecution's case-in-chief. There are benefits and drawbacks to either choice, and, although most defense attorneys will give an opening statement immediately rather than reserving it, the decision is purely tactical.

After opening statements, the prosecution has the burden of going forward with its case-in-chief, presenting witnesses and exhibits. The prosecution proceeds by direct examination with its witnesses. The witnesses are then subject to cross-examination by the defense. After the prosecution has concluded its case, the defense will present its case-in-chief, with the prosecution cross-examining defense witnesses. After both the prosecution and defense have rested their cases, the trial will conclude with closing arguments by both sides, the judge's jury instructions, and, finally, jury deliberation.

FYI

The importance of a lawyer's need to fulfill the promises made in the opening statement was illustrated in the trial of Scott Peterson for the murder of his wife, Laci, and their unborn child. The prosecutor asserted in his opening statement that Peterson had lied to investigators about the day he (Peterson) said he last saw his wife alive because he claimed they watched a Martha Stewart show about meringue. Investigators decided the meringue show had run the day before. To counter this claim, in his opening statement, defense attorney Mark Geragos played a clip of the show in question in which Martha and her guest talked about making meringue cookies. Mr. Geragos played the tape a second time, saying, "I played it twice, just in case the Modesto D.A. couldn't hear it." This was an effective way to cast doubt on the prosecutor's claim that Peterson had lied in this instance. It made no difference, however; he was convicted anyway.

FYI

Some people attribute the acquittal of O.J. Simpson to his attorney, Johnny Cochran's, brilliant theme and theory of the case: "If it doesn't fit, you must acquit." This referred both to the physical evidence of the glove, which the prosecutor was unable to prove fit O.J., and to the message that, if all the pieces of evidence put forth by the prosecution don't add up, the jury must acquit the accused.

MAKING THE RECORD

All felony trials and most other criminal trials today are trials of record. This means that the proceedings are recorded verbatim to preserve a record for appeal in order to preserve

©VINCE BUCCI/Getty Images

O.J. Simpson holds up his hands before the jury after putting on a new pair of gloves similar to the infamous "bloody gloves."

the rights of the accused in the event of a conviction. Historically, the usual method of recording was through a court reporter, a person specially trained and equipped to take down verbatim the official record of the proceedings in a court.

Today, of course, recording may be done mechanically, utilizing sophisticated audio and video equipment. Regardless of the way in which the proceedings are preserved, the fact that a record is made affects the manner in which people act in the courtroom.

Bearing in mind the need to make the record, all communication in court must be audible. Gestures, ambiguous sounds, and inaudible responses cannot be recorded effectively by a stenographer and may be misleading even if mechanically recorded. Only one person may speak at a time, and an individual cannot speak so rapidly as to make it difficult to be understood. In short, the participants in a trial must remain consciously aware that what they are saying and doing must satisfy the requirements for making the record.

In giving testimony, the law enforcement professional must speak clearly and audibly, so that the court reporter (whether human or electronic) can accurately record what is said. A witness must not start to answer a question until it has been completed. If the witness refers to charts, graphs, or certain documents, he or she should discuss with the prosecutor beforehand the procedure for marking the exhibits and referring to them. The witness should not use hand gestures. When the witness is being cross-examined, he or she should wait until the cross-examining attorney completes the question and the prosecuting attorney has had the opportunity to object before answering.

THE PROSECUTION'S CASE-IN-CHIEF

As previously mentioned, a party to a trial presents the thrust of its case in what is known as the case-in-chief. This is particularly significant in a criminal case with respect to the prosecution. Because of the principles of the presumption of

MYTH ▶	◀ FACT
One who is convicted of murder cannot be retried for the crime if he or she kills the same person again. In 1999 the story line of the movie *Double Jeopardy* was based on the assumption that the double jeopardy rule offers a wife the rare opportunity to kill her contemptible husband free from fear of criminal consequences. The wife (Ashley Judd) is in prison, having been convicted of murdering her husband (Bruce Greenwood). He is not dead but has framed her for the murder. After she learns this, she is told by a fellow prisoner that because of double jeopardy she can kill him now and cannot be punished for it.	For two criminal charges to qualify as the "same offense" and come within the double jeopardy ban, some very technical legal conditions must be satisfied. Resolution of the legal issues posed by the movie boils down to a question of whether the relevant conduct for purposes of applying the double jeopardy rule is the death of the husband, in which case she has already been prosecuted and punished for the crime, or the wife's act of killing him, in which case she hasn't. The argument that the staged and actual murders are the same offense is based on the seemingly flawless logic that no one can be killed more than once, no matter how despicable he or she might be and therefore, at most, one crime of murder can be committed on any single individual. But there is an equally compelling argument on the other side of the question that focuses on the criminal act as the relevant fact for double jeopardy purposes. For now at least, the legal issue that is the premise for the movie is unresolved.

But there is one point on which legal scholars agree. Under the dual sovereignty doctrine, the second actual killing is not the same offense as the first staged murder if the two crimes are committed in different jurisdictions. Thus, if the wife makes the mistake of killing the husband in a state other than the one where she was convicted, the Double Jeopardy Clause will not protect her against prosecution for his murder in the second state. |

CORPUS DELICTI
The requirement that the prosecution present sufficient evidence to establish that a crime was committed by someone.

PRIMA FACIE CASE
The amount of proof the prosecution must present in its case-in-chief— evidence sufficient to establish that a crime was committed and that the defendant probably did it.

innocence, the burden of proof, and *corpus delicti* (all of which are discussed at length in the next chapter), the prosecution is required to fulfill certain requirements during the case-in-chief, or the court will enter a judgment against the prosecution.

In short, the prosecution has a burden during its case-in-chief to introduce sufficient evidence to establish that a crime was committed by someone (the *corpus delicti*) and that the accused probably did it. This amount of proof is referred to as a ***prima facie* case**. At this point, the prosecution must have established the jurisdiction of the court, the *corpus delicti* of the specific offense charged, and facts that could lead a reasonable juror to believe that the accused is the responsible person.

After the conclusion of the prosecution's case-in-chief, the prosecution announces that it rests its case. At this time, the defense attorney will ask the trial judge for a judgment of acquittal—a judicial decision on whether the prosecution has satisfied its burden during the presentation of its case-in-chief. That burden is the presentation of evidence on each and every element of the crime(s) charged sufficient for a jury to conclude beyond a reasonable doubt that the accused is guilty. If the motion for **judgment of acquittal** is granted, the case is over. Furthermore, because of the constitutional ban against double jeopardy, there can be no appeal from a judge's entry of a judgment of acquittal in a jury trial.

WITNESS REQUIREMENTS

Immediately after the defense attorney makes an opening statement or reserves the right to do so later, the prosecution calls its first witness. Before the witness takes the seat to testify (frequently referred to as the **witness stand**), an oath is administered to the witness by the judge, the bailiff, or some other officer of the court (in Georgia, the attorney calling the witness administers the oath). The oath consists of words to this effect: "I do solemnly swear (or affirm) to tell the truth and nothing but the truth, so help me God." The reference to God is deleted in the case of a person wishing to affirm rather than swear. In order to qualify as a witness, a person must be able to understand what it means to tell the truth, so that he or she can take the oath (or affirm) that the truth will be told. In most states, serving as a witness also requires that the individual possess personal knowledge of some perceived relevant facts about the case, be able to remember those facts, and be able to communicate them. All other matters relating to being a witness, under modern law, go to the weight of the witness's testimony, not the witness's qualifications. This matter is more fully discussed in Chapter 4.

EXAMINATION OF WITNESSES

Sequence of Witnesses

The sequence in which witnesses are called to testify will depend largely upon the kind of case involved and how the evidence may best be presented in a logical order. It is not necessary that the witnesses be called in the sequence in which the events of a case took place. For example, if a defendant were being tried on a charge of having burglarized a place of business, the order of calling the witnesses could vary greatly. The first witness could be the owner of the burglarized business. Through the testimony of this witness, the first elements of the charge would be established, i.e., that there was an illegal entry and articles were taken without permission. Or the prosecuting attorney could find it more convenient to place the arresting officer on the stand first. Through the testimony of the officer, it could be shown that the defendant was arrested near the scene of the burglary and had in his possession articles taken from the place of business that had been burglarized. Such testimony alone would be a strong indication of the guilt of the accused.

Earlier, in the discussion of the opening statement, the use of story telling was described. Just as the story structure in the opening statement depends upon the theory and theme of the case, so may the attorney's selection of the order of witness presentation. Not all stories are best told in chronological order. Moreover, the story may begin at a different point, depending on one point of view as compared with another. Therefore, a lawyer may decide to call witnesses in some order other than chronological to better present the lawyer's theory and theme of the case.

Following is an example of how witness sequencing can vary, depending on the theory and theme of the case. In this example case, the defendant is charged with first-degree murder in the killing of an acquaintance at a neighborhood tavern. The victim was a well-known bully in the neighborhood, and the accused is a mild-mannered person. Two weeks before the homicide, the victim and the defendant were involved in a verbal dispute in the tavern. The victim accused the defendant of "stealing" some change from the bar counter while the victim was in the restroom. During the dispute, the victim threatened the accused. On the night of the alleged murder, the victim followed the defendant out of the bar onto the street and accosted him. The defendant pulled out a gun and shot the victim as he came toward the defendant. The defendant claims self-defense. The prosecution might well decide to begin the story of this crime with the episode at the bar two weeks before the killing. To that end, the opening statement would begin with the fight two weeks earlier. The first witnesses called by the prosecution would be those who were present at the tavern two weeks before the shooting.

ON THE JOB

Typically, an officer works a forty-hour week, either five eight-hour shifts or four ten-hour shifts, plus whatever overtime or part-time security work is available. The officer may also go to college or have training classes, and family life and personal activities place additional constraints on an officer's time. So, when the inevitable subpoenas start arriving for the arrests and citations the officer has made and issued, it is important that the officer plan ahead.

As soon as the officer is served with a subpoena, he or she should fill out a request to "Records" to generate a copy of any relevant report, since this could take several days, depending on the department's backlog. A trip to the evidence locker is also good insurance; it reassures the officer that the evidence is easily located and lets the evidence custodian know that the officer will soon be needing that piece of evidence. The officer should always keep in mind the need to maintain the proper chain of custody. The officer should make sure that all lab work is complete and that the reports are in order, since forensics is always backlogged. It is vitally important that the officer not wait until the day of trial to discover that a pivotal piece of evidence is missing or that a report appears unprofessional and negligent. The officer does not want to impress the judge and prosecution unfavorably by being ill-prepared. This is also true for other law enforcement professionals. Once served with a subpoena, the criminalist, the crime scene investigator, the laboratory technician, and all other professionals should order all pertinent reports and verify the whereabouts of any evidence needed for court. Just as in the case of the enforcement officer, maintaining the chain of custody of evidence is crucial for it to be admissible in court.

Other factors may also influence the sequencing of witnesses. The work schedules of witnesses coupled with the normal delays of a trial may require an attorney to call a working person who is also a witness out of the sequence the attorney originally planned for the best strategic effect. This may be the case particularly with law enforcement officers, experts, and other professionals whose schedules are less flexible than those of other witnesses.

Direct Examination

The questioning of a witness by the side who calls the witness is known as **direct examination**. Direct examination usually begins by asking the witness his or her name, address, and occupation. Even though this information may be well known to all in the courtroom, it is necessary for the court record of the case. After these preliminary background questions are completed, the general questioning of the witness concerning the specific facts of the case begins.

During the direct examination, whether by the prosecution or the defense, the attorney must form the question in such a manner that the desired answer is not indicated. If the desired answer is stated or suggested in the question, the question is known as a **leading question**. An example of a leading question is "The defendant had a gun in his hand, didn't he?" It is obvious from the wording of this question that the attorney wants the witness to answer in the affirmative. On direct examination, this question would be objected to by the opposing side, and the judge would sustain the objection because of the leading nature of the question. A question about the gun in the defendant's hand that would not be considered leading might be "Did the defendant have anything in his hand?" Leading questions are generally not allowed during direct examination and are discussed at greater length in Chapter 5.

Tradition, custom, and the rules of evidence limit the use of leading questions. They are reserved principally for use on cross-examination. The generally required method of questioning on direct examination is the use of nonleading questions, which elicit information from a witness in the witness's own words. On the other hand, the law prohibits a witness from telling all he or she knows in narrative form. Such a testimony could lead to information coming before the jury that it should not hear and might lead to a prolonged trial, as talkative witnesses tend to ramble. Instead, as a compromise between leading a witness and asking for a narrative, lawyers are expected to ask questions calling for short responses that move the story along.

The forms of questions on direct and cross-examination are significant for all witnesses, including the law enforcement professional. The law enforcement professional, as a principal witness for the prosecution, should be prepared to testify on direct examination in a clear, straightforward manner. He or she should give full answers but not ramble in a narrative fashion. On cross-examination, the law enforcement professional should be direct and forthcoming but should only answer the question asked. A full discussion relating to the conduct of witnesses appears in the final chapter of this book.

Objections

During the questioning of any witness, including the direct examination of the prosecution's witnesses, the opposing attorney will interject **evidentiary objections**. These objections may be based on any one of a number of grounds,

DIRECT EXAMINATION
The questioning of a witness by the side who calls that witness.

LEADING QUESTION
A question that suggests to the witness the answer sought by the questioner.

EVIDENTIARY OBJECTIONS
Legal arguments raised by opposing counsel during trial to prevent a witness from testifying or other evidence from being admitted.

according to the law. Some common grounds are leading, irrelevant, hearsay, calls for opinion, and speculation. Objections may be well founded or may be made principally for effect. For example, an attorney may make an objection to break the concentration of the examining attorney or jury, or merely to interrupt if the opposing counsel is "on a roll." Groundless objections are frowned upon by the court and the jury alike, so, although some objections for psychological effect will be tolerated, most lawyers are careful not to use this tactic excessively.

ON THE JOB

When testifying and there is an objection, a law enforcement professional (any witness, for that matter) should not answer unless the judge overrules the objection. If the judge sustains the objection, the witness should not answer the question at all.

RULINGS ON OBJECTIONS
The judge's decisions on evidentiary objections: overruled, the witness may testify; sustained, the witness must not answer the question.

In any event, when either side makes an objection, the witness must remain silent until the judge has made a ruling, or decision, on the objection. **Rulings on objections** are stated by the judge. The judge either sustains the objection or overrules it. If the objection is sustained, or upheld, the witness must not answer the question. If the judge overrules, or denies, the objection, the witness may answer.

If the witness inadvertently answers the question before the judge can make the ruling and the objection is sustained, or if the sustained objection is made after the witness has already answered, the judge will order the answer stricken from the record and admonish the jury to disregard the answer. The law expects the jury to do so. However, it is practically impossible to erase a thought completely once it has been planted in the minds of jurors. Thus, if the information that the jury heard is too damaging or too prejudicial to the defendant, the judge may declare a mistrial. In that case, the trial is stopped and must be started again with a different jury. Of course, such a situation is very time-consuming and costly. If the information inadvertently comes before the jury because a witness persisted in answering a question before the judge ruled on an objection, and that witness is a law enforcement professional, there may be serious repercussions, for such a professional is expected to abide by court procedure.

Note that the phrase "stricken from the record" does not mean that the offending question or answer is actually removed from the court reporter's record. It is a term of art used to indicate only that the question or answer was not acceptable to the court. Figure 2–4 sets forth the most common grounds of objection and explains each type.

Cross-Examination

CROSS-EXAMINATION
The rigorous examination of a witness by opposing counsel in which the questioner seeks to detract from the witness's credibility.

After the direct examination is completed, the opposing side has the right to cross-examine the witness. The right of cross-examination is considered essential for the discovery of truth during a trial. As one highly regarded evidence scholar has stated, **cross-examination** "is the greatest legal engine ever invented for the discovery of the truth."[28] So, after direct examination is completed, the opposing attorney may, as desired, cross-examine the witness. In most instances, the attorney will cross-examine for several reasons. First, the cross-examiner may hope to shake the witness's story and thereby cause the

Objection	Description of Objection	Federal Rule of Evidence	Chapter of the Book
Irrelevant	The question calls for an answer that does not make a fact of consequence to the case more or less likely.	401–402	2
Incompetent	Witness lacks competence under state law.	601	3
Hearsay	The evidence is an inadmissible out-of-court statement, offered for the truth of what is asserted in the statement.	801–806	6
Insufficient foundation	The preliminary facts or conditions necessary to admit the evidence have not been shown.	901, 803, 804 especially	10, 11, 12
Improper impeachment	Either the content or manner of impeachment is improper.	607–613	3, 5
Cumulative	Resubmission of evidence to prove what has already been shown by other evidence before.	403	2
Not the best evidence	An attempt to prove the content of a writing by secondary evidence.	1001–1007	10, 12
Cross-examination exceeds the scope of direct examination	The subject matter of cross-examination is limited to the scope of the subject matter of direct.	611	1, 5
Redirect examination beyond the scope of the cross-examination	The subject matter of the redirect examination is limited to the scope of the subject matter of cross.	611	1, 5
Privileged material	The question calls for information that is protected by privilege.	501	3
Ambiguous and/or unintelligible question	The question cannot be understood.		
Compound question	The question contains more than one part, so that the witness either cannot tell which part to answer or may inadvertently answer one part without meaning to do so.		

FIGURE 2–4 Common objections to evidence.

jury to give the testimony less weight. Second, the cross-examiner may try to show that the witness is prejudiced and consequently may have testified incorrectly or untruthfully. Third, the cross-examiner may try to show that the witness has made prior inconsistent statements and thus should not be believed by the jury. In any event, cross-examination is frequently a trying experience for the witness involved.

During direct examination, the attorney usually does not try to belittle or embarrass the witness, but upon cross-examination, just the opposite is true. Frequently, the law enforcement officer will be the most damaging witness against an accused. Consequently, in many instances, the officer should expect rigorous cross-examination. Chapter 15 of this book discusses the subject of how to testify effectively.

Daily logs and reports are routinely admitted as evidence at a trial. They are read by judges, prosecutors, defense attorneys, and the jury and are sometimes made public. Officers often consider writing a report a burden, but good report writing should be thought of as insurance. A well-written report will make an officer's time on the witness stand go much more smoothly. Well-written reports will also help keep criminals behind bars, whereas sloppy report writing might let a criminal walk free. Officers should be attentive to grammar and spelling in their report writing, since the reports will be seen and read by judges, lawyers, and jurors who may form an opinion about the officer based on the reports.

If an officer throws away his or her notes after writing a report, defense counsel may try to discredit the officer and the prosecution's case by suggesting that the officer is trying to hide something. A proper response to such a charge is that "everything pertinent from the notes is contained in the report."

Although leading questions are prohibited during direct examination, they are the norm during cross-examination. Remember that a leading question is one in which the examiner tries to put words in the mouth of the witness. Therefore, on cross-examination, the witness must listen carefully to ensure that the facts are not distorted by the examining lawyer's leading questions.

On the witness stand, a law enforcement professional should be very careful to be courteous, especially on cross-examination. No matter how aggressive or hostile the defense attorney may be, the witness should remain cool, answer "yes" or "no" if possible, and say, "I don't know" or "I do not recall," if that is the case. The professional should never guess or assume. If he or she does not understand the question or finds it confusing, the witness should ask defense counsel to clarify the question. The law enforcement professional should avoid humor, and under no circumstances should the witness lose his or her temper or become emotional.

Redirect Examination

REDIRECT EXAMINATION Further questioning, after cross-examination, for the limited purpose of rebutting or clarifying information brought out during cross-examination.

Upon conclusion of cross-examination by the opposing attorney, the direct examiner may further question the witness. This further questioning is known as **redirect examination** and is only for the limited purpose of rebuttal or clarification of information brought out during cross-examination. New matters are not allowed to be brought out for the first time on redirect examination.

Re-Cross- and Subsequent Examinations

RE-CROSS-EXAMINATION Further questioning, after redirect examination, for clarification purposes. This, and subsequent questioning, is purely within the discretion of the trial judge.

After a redirect examination has been conducted, the judge may give permission to the opposing attorney to ask questions limited to further clarification of statements made by the witness during the redirect examination. This questioning is referred to as **re-cross-examination**. Likewise, after re-cross-examination, and thereafter, in rotation, the opposing attorneys may, at the court's discretion, be permitted further questioning. None of these further steps is required, and any questioning past redirect examination is purely within the discretion of the trial judge.

Close of Prosecution's Case-in-Chief

After all witnesses have been called by the prosecution and all other evidence has been tendered to support the charge against the accused in a criminal case, the prosecutor announces that the "prosecution rests its case." As explained earlier, this is an important point because, in most states, lack of adequate proof by the prosecution cannot be corrected after this announcement.

DEFENSE PRESENTATION

After the prosecution rests, the defense will give its opening statement, if the attorney did not do so after the prosecution's opening statement. Then the defense will present its side of the case in an effort to raise a reasonable doubt of the accused's guilt. Because of the presumption of innocence, the defendant does not have to present any evidence at all, for the burden of proving the defendant guilty rests entirely on the shoulders of the prosecution, without any help from the accused. Frequently, the defendant will have no evidence to present and will rest at this point. But, in many cases, the defendant will present some evidence, either alibi, character, justification, or excuse evidence. Or the defendant may testify and deny guilt or support some affirmative defense, such as alibi, self-defense, or insanity. An **affirmative defense** is a reason under the law that allows a defendant to claim to be exonerated, one that the defendant must affirmatively claim and prove.

AFFIRMATIVE
DEFENSE
A reason under the law that allows a defendant to claim to be exonerated, one that the defendant must affirmatively claim and prove.

The same steps that were used in presenting the prosecution's case-in-chief are followed in the defendant's case-in-chief, should the defendant choose to present a case. At the conclusion of the defendant's case, the defense again may make a motion for judgment of acquittal, asking the judge one more time to acquit due to insufficient evidence presented by the prosecution. At this point, in ruling on the motion, the judge may consider the effect of any evidence introduced by the defendant as well as the prosecution.

PROSECUTION'S REBUTTAL

Upon completion of the presentation of all the evidence on behalf of the defendant, the prosecution has the right to call additional witnesses or to present new evidence only to overcome new matters brought out during the defendant's case. Some matters may only be addressed by the prosecution after first being raised by the defense. For example, if a defendant introduces evidence to show that he or she acted in self-defense because of fear resulting from the victim's reputation for violence, the prosecution may rebut that claim by showing that the defendant had previously assaulted the victim. Unless and until the defense introduces the claim of self-defense at trial, the rules of evidence usually prohibit the prosecution from presenting evidence that the defendant committed a prior crime of assault upon the victim. Therefore, the prosecution may introduce the evidence of the defendant's prior assault upon the victim only after the defendant asserts the self-defense claim.

Also, the defense may introduce evidence, such as newly discovered evidence, that is not anticipated by the prosecution but that opens the door for rebuttal evidence. For example, the defendant may have discovered an alibi witness too late in the trial process to notify the prosecution during the prosecution's case-in-chief. In such an event, the prosecution will be permitted to introduce in rebuttal such evidence as it may have uncovered in the interim.

In the absence of one of these reasons for the prosecution to introduce rebuttal evidence, the presentation of evidence will end with the defendant's case. Because of the heavy burden placed upon the prosecution to prove its case beyond a reasonable doubt, as well as the burden of the presumption of innocence, it is traditional for the prosecution to speak first and last. The prosecution's right to put on a rebuttal case, however, cannot be used as an excuse to have the last word by restating its case-in-chief. Thus, although not a rare occurrence, a rebuttal case by the prosecution is not to be expected in every case. In the event the prosecution offers rebuttal evidence, the defense may be permitted to introduce evidence in response, called surrebuttal or rejoinder.

DEFENSE'S SURREBUTTAL

If the prosecution properly introduces new evidence as part of its rebuttal of the defense, the court may allow the defense to introduce surrebuttal evidence. This is the same as rebuttal evidence, except that it is offered by the defense and is limited to the subject matter raised by the prosecution's rebuttal evidence.

CLOSING ARGUMENTS

After both sides have presented their cases, the prosecutor and the defense attorney may make closing, or final, arguments to the jury. These arguments, unlike opening statements (in which the attorneys present a road map of the case), are an opportunity for the lawyers to summarize the case in an overt attempt to persuade the jury to take their view of the evidence. Attorneys are allowed to appeal to the jury based on any inferences that may rationally be drawn from the evidence.

The prosecution opens this segment of the trial with its beginning final argument, followed by the defense's final summation. The prosecution then goes last with its ending closing argument, sometimes referred to as rebuttal. In some states, the prosecution's final argument is severely restricted. However, in most states, the final summation of the prosecution is extensive. In any event, in light of the heavy burden upon the prosecution, the prosecuting attorney is awarded the last word in argument.

INSTRUCTIONS, OR CHARGE, TO THE JURY

When the attorneys for both sides have finished their closing arguments, the judge reads the instructions to the jury. Sometimes the judge instructs the jury before closing arguments; in rarer instances, the judge may even instruct the jury at the beginning of the trial. Judge Ito did this in the O.J. Simpson criminal trial, but he also instructed the jury again at the end of the case. Moreover, during the course of the trial, the judge may find it necessary to relate some rule of law to the jury as evidence is presented.

Jury instructions consist of an interpretation of the substantive and procedural law that applies to the case. The purpose of these instructions is to assist and guide the jury in its review of the evidence in order that they may arrive at a verdict.

Many states and the federal government have published instructions for general purposes and for every kind of civil and criminal case. These instructions are pre-approved by legislatures and courts and are known as "pattern" instructions. Both prosecution and defense attorneys have the opportunity to designate which pattern instructions they wish to be given to the jury. In addition, either side may propose special instructions that arguably apply to the special circumstances of the case. The judge considers both sides' requested instructions at a conference before giving the instructions to the jury.

DELIBERATION AND VERDICT

After the judge has instructed the jury, the jury will retire to the jury room. There, the jury will weigh the evidence presented during trial in light of the judge's instructions and attempt to arrive at a verdict. This review of the evidence is referred to as **jury deliberation**. To prevent the possibility of any outside influence affecting the jury's verdict, the jury's deliberative process is kept secret. Some states require a **sequestered jury** (a jury kept securely removed from any outside influence) during deliberations. In some extremely sensitive cases, the trial court may decide to sequester a jury for the entire trial. One of the most famous such instances was the trial of O.J. Simpson. But that case was unusual; juries are rarely sequestered for an entire trial.

JURY DELIBERATION
The review of evidence by the jury in an attempt to reach a verdict.

SEQUESTERED JURY
A jury removed from any outside influence.

The period of time that a jury may take to deliberate varies considerably. It may be only a matter of minutes, or it may be several days. The seriousness of the charge and the length of the trial often will determine the time the jury takes to deliberate. In most states, the jury must reach a unanimous verdict in a criminal trial. In such cases, deliberation time may grow lengthy because of differences of opinion among the jurors. If the jurors are having difficulty reaching a unanimous verdict, most judges will do everything possible to encourage them to reach a decision. If the jurisdiction requires a unanimous verdict and the jury cannot reach one, the result is known as a **hung jury**. When a jury is hung, the judge must declare a mistrial and discharge the jury. If there is to be a retrial, it must be before an entirely new jury.

HUNG JURY
A jury that cannot reach a verdict.

If, on the other hand, the jury arrives at a verdict, the jury returns to the courtroom and the verdict is announced. In most states, after the verdict has been announced in open court, the jury's function is over and the judge will dismiss the jurors. If the verdict is one of acquittal, the defendant is immediately released from custody and may not be tried again on the same charge in accordance with the Double Jeopardy Clause of the Fifth Amendment to the Constitution of the United States.

SENTENCING THE DEFENDANT

If the jury's verdict is guilty, the defendant must be sentenced. Sentencing procedure varies widely among the states and between the states and the federal government. In most states and the federal system, the judge imposes sentence. The judge's sentencing options are dictated by sentencing guidelines for particular crimes. Two decisions by the United States Supreme Court in 2004 and 2005 seriously question the validity of sentencing guidelines in both the state and federal systems. In *Blakely v. Washington*,[29] the sentencing judge found a fact to exist that the judge then used to impose an aggravated sentence in Blakely's trial.

The Supreme Court held that this violated the defendant's Sixth Amendment right to trial by jury. Then, in *United States v. Booker,*[30] a majority of the Court held that *Blakely* applies to the federal sentencing guidelines, but a different majority held that the guidelines are still viable as advisory. In short, the mandatory sentencing systems contemplated by state and federal sentencing guidelines are now seriously impaired. It remains to be seen how much discretion in sentencing will be restored to trial judges.

If prescribed sentencing guidelines do not exist in a particular jurisdiction, the judge will impose the sentence within statutory limits and alternatives. In a few states, the jury imposes the sentence.

In any case involving the possibility of the death penalty, the sentencing phase is usually separated from the verdict of guilt or innocence phase. In many jurisdictions, the decision whether to impose the death penalty is made by a jury. Either it is made by a completely new jury or, if the same jury decides the penalty, it is decided in a separate trial or phase of the trial. Also, in some states, the jury recommends to the judge whether or not to impose the death penalty, but the judge makes the final decision.

REVIEW AND APPLICATION

SUMMARY

(1) Following is the sequence of events in a criminal trial: (1) final pretrial matters and motions; (2) jury selection (*voir dire*); (3) jury sworn; (4) opening statement by prosecution; (5) defense opening statement or reservation; (6) prosecution's case-in-chief; (7) defense opening statement, if reserved; (8) defense's case-in-chief; (9) rebuttal, if any, by prosecution; (10) surrebuttal, if any, by defense; (11) prosecution's opening argument (first closing); (12) defense's final summation (closing); (13) prosecution's final summation; (14) instructions by the court to the jury; (15) jury deliberation; and (16) jury verdict.

(2) The level of proof required in a criminal case is beyond a reasonable doubt. In contrast, the level of proof required in a civil case is a preponderance of the evidence.

(3) Challenges for cause and peremptory challenges may be used during *voir dire.*

(4) The duties of a judge in a criminal trial include deciding what law applies to the case; interpreting the law of the case for the jury; deciding what evidence is and is not admissible; ruling on objections made by the attorneys; determining the qualifications of witnesses; protecting witnesses from overzealous cross-examinations; ensuring that the trial proceeds efficiently and effectively; and, in most states, in most instances, imposing sentence upon the defendant.

(5) A working definition of reasonable doubt is a doubt based upon reason: that which would make a reasonable person hesitate to act in connection with important affairs of life.

(6) The principal role of the prosecuting attorney is deciding which criminal charges should be prosecuted and which should be dismissed in the interests of justice. The principal function of the defense attorney is to make certain that all of the rights of the accused are properly protected.

(7) In its case-in-chief, the prosecution must introduce evidence sufficient to establish that a crime was committed by someone (the *corpus delicti*) and that the defendant was probably the person responsible (a *prima facie* case). If the prosecution has done this, the court will deny the defendant's motion for judgment of acquittal made at the close of the prosecution's case-in-chief.

(8) The five requirements for being a witness are to (1) understand the duty to tell the truth; (2) take an oath (or affirm) that the truth will be told; (3) possess personal knowledge of perceived facts relevant to the case; (4) remember those facts; and (5) communicate those facts.

(9) On direct examination, only non-leading questions are allowed. On cross-examination, leading questions are permitted.

(10) In closing argument, the prosecutor gives a beginning closing argument, followed by the defense's final summation, followed by the prosecutor's final summation.

KEY TERMS

venire   32
voir dire   32
challenges for cause   32
peremptory
   challenge   32
jury nullification   34
contempt   35
exculpatory
   evidence   36
pretrial discovery   36
reasonable doubt   37

opening statement   40
case-in-chief   40
corpus delicti   42
prima facie case   42
judgment of
   acquittal   43
witness stand   43
direct examination   45
leading question   45
evidentiary
   objections   45

rulings on
   objections   46
cross-examination   46
redirect
   examination   48
re-cross-examination   48
affirmative defense   49
jury deliberation   51
sequestered jury   51
hung jury   51

QUESTIONS FOR REVIEW

1. List the sequence of events in a typical criminal trial.
2. How much proof is necessary for a criminal trial? How is this different from the amount of proof necessary in a civil trial?
3. What is the difference between a jury trial and a bench trial?
4. How many people are required for a jury in a criminal case?
5. List six common qualifications for jurors.
6. What is meant by *voir dire*?
7. What are the two main functions of a jury?
8. What is jury nullification, and why is this power little known?
9. What are the main duties of the judge in a criminal trial?
10. Who has the main responsibility for the progress of a trial? Explain.

THINKING CRITICALLY ABOUT EVIDENCE

1. Why do you think a defendant might prefer to have a jury trial? A bench trial? What are the pros and cons of each?
2. The jury has the power to ignore the law, as well as the facts and evidence presented to it during trial, when reaching its verdict. Write a paragraph stating why you think that the jury has this power, especially when our legal system demands that officers, attorneys, and judges follow the law.

WORKPLACE APPLICATIONS

1. It is a freezing Saturday night in December. You spot a car driving the speed limit with its windows rolled all the way down. You know that drunk drivers frequently use the cold air to help keep themselves awake while driving. The driver's eyes are fixed on the road, and he has what appears to be a death grip on the steering wheel. You follow the car for 10 miles because you have a gut feeling the driver is drunk. Finally, the car weaves in its lane and you pull the driver over for erratic driving. You confirm your suspicion of drunk driving when you smell the odor of alcohol on the driver's breath. The driver fails the field sobriety test and is arrested for drunk driving. Did you have probable cause to stop this motorist? Write a paragraph explaining your answer.
2. You are assisting the prosecutor in preparing for trial in a case you investigated involving a convenience store robbery. The witnesses include the victim, two other eyewitnesses who observed the perpetrator as he entered and left the convenience store at the time of the robbery, the criminalist who identified the perpetrator's fingerprints on the cash register, and the officer who supervised the lineup in which the witnesses identified the perpetrator. The prosecutor asks your advice on the order of the state's witnesses. In what order would you call the various witnesses? Why?

ETHICAL DILEMMAS

1. Assume you are the officer who arrested a defendant for shoplifting at a local electronics store. Assume further that you are on the witness stand at trial and the prosecutor asks the following question: "You observed the defendant take the radio off the shelf and put it in his backpack, didn't you?" In fact, you did not see the defendant do such a thing, but you want to help attain a conviction. What do you say?
2. In order to prosecute a case, the prosecutor must believe there is probable cause that the suspect committed the crime. However, it is also the duty of the prosecutor to reveal all information or evidence that may mitigate, or reduce, the guilt of the suspect. You have some information that may or may not mitigate the guilt of a man charged with rape and murder. You know that if you turn the information over to the prosecutor, he or she will give it to the defense attorney. Do you turn the evidence over to the prosecutor? Does it affect your answer that the evidence will have a substantial impact on the trial or verdict?

ENDNOTES

1. Patton v. United States, 281 U.S. 276 (1930).

2. Duncan v. Louisiana, 391 U.S. 145 (1968).

3. *See* Baldwin v. New York, 399 U.S. 66 (1970).

4. 399 U.S. 78 (1970).

5. 435 U.S. 223 (1978).

6. 406 U.S. 356 (1972).

7. 406 U.S. 404 (1972).

8. 441 U.S. 130 (1979).

9. *See, e.g.,* Cal. Code Civ. Pro. §224 (West 2018). *See also* Nancy L. Dickhuter, *Jury Duty for the Blind in the Time of Reasonable Accommodation,* 32 Creighton L. Rev. 849, 873–74 n. 244 (1999).

10. Alaska Code of Civ. Pro. §09.20.010 (2018).

11. Batson v. Kentucky, 476 U.S. 79 (1986).

12. Georgia v. McCollum, 505 U.S. 42 (1992).

13. Batson v. Kentucky, 476 U.S. 79, 89 (1986).

14. 530 U.S. 466 (2000).

15. 536 U.S. 584 (2002).

16. 524 U.S. 296 (2004).

17. *See* Sparf and Hansen v. United States, 156 U.S. 51 (1895). *See also* Aaron McKnight, *Jury Nullification As a Tool to Balance the Demands of Law and Justice,* 2013 B.Y.U.L. Rev. 1103 (2013).

18. 372 U.S. 335, 344 (1963).

19. Brady v. Maryland, 373 U.S. 83, 87 (1963).

20. Victor v. Nebraska, 511 U.S. 1, 5 (1994).

21. Holland v. United States, 348 U.S. 121, 140 (1954), as cited and quoted in Victor, *supra.*

22. 498 U.S. 39 (1990).

23. *Id.* at 41.

24. 511 U.S. 1 (1994).

25. *See* People v. Freeman, 882 P.2d 249 (Cal. 1994).

26. CALJIC 2.90 (2018). In 2005 the Judicial Council of California Jury Instructions published a plain English set of criminal jury instructions, CALCRIM. The definition of reasonable doubt in CALCRIM is "proof beyond a reasonable doubt is proof that leaves you with an abiding conviction that the charge is true. The evidence need not eliminate all possible doubt because everything in life is open to some possible or imaginary doubt." Judicial Council of California Criminal Jury Instruction 103 (West 2018).

27. Victor v. Nebraska, 511 U.S. at 18. The current approved Nebraska reasonable doubt instruction reads "A reasonable doubt is one based upon reason and common sense after careful and impartial consideration of all the evidence. Proof beyond a reasonable doubt is proof so convincing that you would rely and act upon it without hesitation in the more serious and important transactions of life. However, proof beyond a reasonable doubt does not mean proof beyond all possible doubt." 1 Neb. Prac., NJI2d Crim. 2.0 (2016-2017 ed.) (West 2018).

28. 5 J. Wigmore, Evidence §1367 (3d ed. 1940), as cited in California v. Green, 399 U.S. 149, 1758 (1970).

29. 524 U.S. 296 (2004).

30. 543 U.S. 220 (2005).

Design Element: ©Ingram Publishing

©Pool/Getty Images

3 EVIDENCE—BASIC CONCEPTS

CHAPTER OUTLINE

CHAPTER OBJECTIVES

This chapter introduces the basic concepts of evidence used in the American legal system. After reading this chapter, you will be able to:

▶ List the four general categories of evidence.

▶ Define relevant evidence.

▶ Discuss some of the reasons relevant evidence may be excluded.

▶ Explain the difference between contradictory and corroborative evidence.

▶ Define judicial notice.

▶ Describe four examples of facts that a court may judicially notice.

▶ List the two factual components of a true presumption.

▶ Describe the relationship of a presumed fact to a basic fact.

▶ Describe two examples of rebuttable presumptions.

▶ Explain what a stipulation is.

DESCRIBING EVIDENCE

For clarity, evidence may be categorized within the following four general headings: (1) testimony of witnesses; (2) real, or physical, evidence; (3) documents, or writings; and (4) demonstrative evidence, i.e., visual or audiovisual aids for the jury. These classifications cover all forms of evidence. Other ways of categorizing evidence are sometimes used. For example, there is direct evidence—witnesses' testimony that the jury need not draw an inference from in order to find the facts to exist. There is also circumstantial evidence—evidence from which an inference must be drawn for the jury to find the facts to exist. (Circumstantial evidence is thoroughly described in Chapter 11.) Sometimes evidence is classified on the basis of the distinction between competent and incompetent evidence. Some jurisdictions classify judicial notice and presumptions as kinds of evidence, although they are actually substitutions for evidence. Each of the four categories of evidence listed at the beginning of this paragraph has its own important and unique function in the presentation of facts during a trial proceeding and will be discussed in detail later in this book. First, there are certain terms used to describe or qualify evidence that should be clearly understood. These terms relate to the admissibility of evidence in court. To be admissible in court, evidence must be

- ▶ Relevant
- ▶ On balance, more relevant than unfairly prejudicial
- ▶ Otherwise competent or admissible

Relevant Evidence

All evidence, in the first instance, must relate to the issues of the case. If the evidence is not connected to those issues, it should not be admitted. If the evidence is related, it is said to be relevant. **Relevant evidence** is defined by FRE 401 as evidence that "has any tendency to make a fact more or less probable than it would be without the evidence; . . . and the fact is of consequence in determining the action." Whether the existence of a fact of consequence is more or less probable is a question of common sense and logic rather than an intricate rule of evidence. To be admissible in court, the evidence need only have *any tendency* to make the existence of a fact of consequence more probable or less probable than it would be without the evidence.

The testimony of a witness who saw a man break into a building during the night clearly would be relevant evidence to prove a burglary. Another witness's testimony that the same man was missing from work at the time of the burglary would also be relevant, since it would make the fact that the man could have been committing the burglary "somewhat" more probable. Burglary tools found in the man's possession would also be relevant to prove the man committed the burglary. On the other hand, the fact that the moon was full on the night of the burglary would not be admissible as relevant to assist the jury in determining whether the accused was "unusually likely to have behaved irrationally on that night."[1]

Balancing the Potential for Unfair Prejudice, Remoteness, and the Like

As stated earlier, evidence that is not relevant is not admissible. However, even relevant evidence can be inadmissible. Evidence may be excluded from trial for

RELEVANT EVIDENCE
Evidence that has any tendency to make a fact more or less probable than it would be without the evidence; and the fact is of consequence in determining the action.

reasons that have nothing to do with logical relevance. One such reason for exclusion is when the evidence has a tendency to unduly prejudice or inflame the minds of the jury. For example, gruesome photographs of a bloody victim in a homicide case, or evidence of an accused's prior convictions, may be very relevant to establish guilt, but, because of the prejudicial effect of such evidence, it may be excluded. Relevant evidence may also be excluded if it would tend to cause confusion or create so many side issues that trial time would be wasted if it were admitted. Relevant evidence that is so remote or speculative in time or place that only a weak logical inference can be drawn from it may be excluded. An example of such an exclusion is described in the following case.

A defendant was on trial on a charge of sexual assault (rape). He was observed by an officer near the scene of the crime shortly afterward and fit the description of the assailant. Later, the victim identified the defendant as the man who attacked her. At the time of his arrest, the defendant had, in his wallet, photographs of nude women. The prosecution offered these photographs at trial to show that the defendant had the intent to commit the assault and was therefore the perpetrator. The defendant's possession of the photographs supports an inference that, because of his interest in naked women, he was likely to have committed sexual assault. However, the judge at trial decided to exclude the evidence because the suggested inference was weak but substantially increased the possibility of jury prejudice, confusion, or distraction. The judge concluded that, although the evidence was relevant in showing the defendant's motive, its value was substantially outweighed by its potential for unfairly prejudicing the minds of the jury toward the accused.

It is the responsibility of the trial judge to determine whether evidence meets the test of relevancy. It is also up to the trial judge to decide whether relevant evidence might be excluded because it is too prejudicial, remote, confusing, time consuming, or otherwise unfair. As FRE 403 puts it, the trial judge may exclude relevant evidence if "its probative value is substantially outweighed by a danger of one or more of the following: unfair prejudice, confusing the issues, misleading the jury, undue delay, wasting time, or needlessly presenting cumulative evidence." This **balancing test** is sometimes also referred to as legal relevancy. In the case of the photographs of nude women just discussed, for example, the trial judge balanced the potential prejudice to the defendant against the weight of the evidence on the issue offered. The judge decided the evidence was substantially more prejudicial than probative. The trial judge could have decided to admit the evidence, and that decision probably would not have been criticized by an appellate court, since the balancing decision is within the discretion of the trial judge.

This balancing test has been incorporated into other rules of evidence, both under the common law rules and under the FRE. For example, the accused in a sexual assault case cannot introduce evidence that a victim has had consensual sexual relations with someone else to show that she likely consented to sex with the accused. Even though that evidence may have some arguable relevance on the issue of consent, the policy of promoting the report of sex offenses and protecting victims has been declared by lawmakers to far outweigh the minimum relevant value of such evidence to the accused.

BALANCING TEST
The requirement that relevant evidence be excluded if its "probative value" is substantially outweighed by the danger of unfair prejudice, confusion of the issues, misleading the jury, undue delay, waste of time, or needless presentation of cumulative evidence.

FYI

In a highly publicized prosecution of basketball superstar Kobe Bryant for sexual assault, the case was dismissed by the prosecution when certain critical evidence favorable to the defense became public. Even though Colorado has a rape shield law, the trial judge in the case ruled that evidence about the victim's sexual activities after the alleged rape by Bryant and before the victim had a hospital examination would be admissible at the trial. A defense expert, based on the physical evidence taken from the woman, concluded that she had sex with at least one other person during that time period. The judge stated that the reason for allowing such evidence into the trial under the rape shield law was to show that the victim's physical injuries, particularly vaginal tearing, could have come from that other sexual encounter. This would support Kobe's claim that he had consensual sex with the victim and refute the prosecution's claim that the physical injury proved the sexual encounter with Kobe was nonconsensual. Such use of the evidence is permitted under rape shield law generally, as it was under Colorado's rape shield law.

Relevant evidence may also be excluded because it is inadmissible based on other rules of evidence or other laws. For example, hearsay evidence may be very relevant and not unfairly prejudicial or remote. It still will be excluded if, within the hearsay rule, it does not qualify as admissible evidence. A piece of physical evidence may be highly relevant, yet it may be excluded because it was improperly obtained in violation of the accused's rights under the Fourth Amendment to the Constitution of the United States.

Material Evidence

Many people erroneously use the terms "relevant evidence" and "**material evidence**" interchangeably. "Materiality" refers to whether or not a fact is one of consequence to the case. The issues of balancing and competency are not included in the definition of materiality. Thus, it is appropriate to speak of material or immaterial facts as part of the formula for relevance.

In any case, the judge decides what facts are of consequence, and thus material, based on the definitions of law and the pleadings. The criminal law defines the elements of crimes and defenses that, in part, determine materiality in any given case. The complaint, information, or indictment in a criminal case will also set the limits of what is a material fact in any given case. For example, a defendant is on trial for murder by intentional killing. Evidence of the cost of the shoes the victim was wearing has nothing to do with the case, either under the law of homicide or as the accused was charged. Therefore, that fact is immaterial.

MATERIAL EVIDENCE
Evidence that pertains to a fact of consequence to the case on trial.

The question of the admissibility of evidence of parental sexual abuse in the 1994–1996 trials of Erik and Lyle Menendez for the murders of their mother and father illustrates the concept of materiality. Under California law, self-defense may be shown only if the defendants had an honest belief that their parents were about to kill them and that their belief was reasonable, that is, that a reasonable person would be justified in such a belief. The trial judge, in both trials of the brothers, concluded that, at the time of the killing, the parents posed no threat to the brothers, so they were not entitled to a self-defense theory. Further, in the first trial, the judge ruled that if, under California law, the jury believed the brothers had an honest *but unreasonable* belief in the threat, then the jury could find them guilty of the lesser crime of voluntary manslaughter rather than murder. This is called imperfect self-defense because the defendant tries to prove self-defense and fails to do so under the law's definition.

During their 1994–1996 trials for the murders of their mother and father, Erik and Lyle Menendez were denied use of the self-defense theory.

Since the trial judge said California law defined the crime of voluntary manslaughter in that way, the defendants were permitted to introduce evidence of their parents' abuse during the first trial. The abuse evidence was admissible on the material fact of the honest but unreasonable belief of the brothers on the issues related to imperfect self-defense, even though that evidence was immaterial on the issues related to complete self-defense. However, in the second trial, the trial judge ruled that, under a more recent decision by the California Supreme Court, even imperfect self-defense could not be used by the brothers, since there was no immediate threat to their well-being posed by the parents. That ruling made the sexual abuse evidence immaterial and therefore inadmissible. Both brothers were convicted of first-degree murder in March 1996.

Competent (or Incompetent) Evidence

Ordinarily, the term "competency" is used when a judge decides whether a person is competent or qualified to testify in a trial proceeding. However, it is also used to describe whether certain evidence is admissible or not. Competent evidence has been described as evidence that is admissible. Incompetent evidence is evidence that the law does not allow to be used in evidence at all. For example, a confession may shed light upon the facts of a case, yet, because of some irregularity in obtaining it, the judge may rule that it is not admissible. Evidence of such a confession may be termed "incompetent." Because the terms "competent" and "incompetent" evidence are somewhat confusing, it is better to substitute the terms "admissible" and "inadmissible" evidence, avoiding the term "competency." The use of "competency" as it relates to witnesses will be discussed in detail in Chapter 4.

Prima Facie Evidence

***Prima facie* evidence** is that evidence which, standing alone, unexplained or uncontradicted, is sufficient to establish a given fact or a group of facts constituting a party's claim or defense. In other words, it is the bare minimum of evidence necessary to sustain a position by the side offering the evidence. The term *"prima facie"* means "at first sight" or "on the face of it." Further, the phrase *"prima facie* case," in the context of a criminal trial, is the measure of evidence the government must present if the case is to go to the jury. If there is no *prima facie* case made in the government's case-in-chief, the defendant is entitled to a judgment of acquittal. A ***prima facie* criminal case** is made when the prosecution has established that a crime has been committed and that the accused probably committed it. In some jurisdictions, the evidence necessary in a criminal proceeding to support a charge at a preliminary hearing is called a *prima facie* showing or case.

Prima facie evidence is often associated with the violation of a statute. For example, if the operator of a vehicle exceeds the posted speed limit, the excess speed is *prima facie* evidence of a traffic violation and is sufficient to prove the violation unless some evidence is presented by the operator to justify the excess speed. To cite another example, if one individual sees another shoot a third person, this is *prima facie* evidence that a homicide has been committed. The offender, though, may attempt to overcome the *prima facie* evidence by presenting evidence that the shooting was done in self-defense.

Contradictory and Corroborative Evidence

Contradictory evidence and corroborative evidence are two opposite forms of evidence. **Contradictory evidence** is evidence used to prove a fact contrary to what has been asserted by a party or witness. **Corroborative evidence** is evidence that is supportive of other evidence already given, tending to strengthen or confirm the prior evidence. Corroborative evidence may be seen as evidence necessary to the party's claim or defense. Corroborative evidence must also be distinguished from cumulative evidence, mentioned previously in connection with the judge's discretion to balance probative value against the needless presentation of such evidence. **Cumulative evidence** is evidence that repeats earlier testimonial or tangible evidence, whereas corroborative evidence is additional evidence of a different character supporting the same point.

To illustrate the difference between contradictory evidence and corroborative evidence, consider the facts of the following hypothetical case. The defendant is on trial for selling narcotics on the night of April 13 at 8 P.M. Testifying in his own behalf, the defendant introduces an alibi defense. He alleges that he could not have committed the crime, as he was at a place other than where the crime was committed and had been mistakenly identified as the seller. The defendant claims that on the night in question he was attending a movie with his wife, sister, and mother. He testifies that they saw the movie *Black Panther* at the Odeon Cinema and that it was raining that night. The wife, sister, and mother all testify to the same facts, which is considered cumulative evidence, since the three women repeat the testimony of the defendant. After the wife testifies, the judge is justified in excluding the cumulative testimony of the sister and mother as a waste of court time.

The manager of the Odeon Cinema is called as a witness and testifies that on the night of April 13 the movie *Black Panther* was showing. The manager's testimony *corroborates* the defendant's testimony. The prosecution then calls as a witness in rebuttal an official of the weather bureau, who testifies that it was partly cloudy with no chance of rain on the night in question. The weather bureau official's testimony *contradicts* the testimony of the defendant and his wife, sister, and mother.

JUDICIAL NOTICE

The law of evidence is designed to ensure the accuracy of evidence presented at trial. Each point must be properly and legally presented and proved. This proof must be presented, with few exceptions, by witnesses who have personal knowledge of the facts about which they are testifying. However, the verification of every fact by a witness with firsthand knowledge results in a very costly procedure from the standpoint of time, energy, and money. Under some circumstances, a substitute for evidence may be allowed.

One category of an allowed substitute for evidence is when there are certain facts that may be accepted by the court without formal proof, in the form of testimony or tangible evidence, being presented. These facts, of which a judge may take **judicial notice**, must first be "not subject to reasonable dispute:" Generally, such undisputed facts fall within two categories; they either (1) are "generally known within the trial court's territorial jurisdiction or (2) can be accurately and readily determined from sources whose accuracy cannot reasonably be questioned."[2] In the first category are facts that have been established through common knowledge, for example, the fact that it is light during the day and dark at night or that a stone sinks when thrown into a pond. The second category includes facts that are readily verifiable by referring to an indisputable, accurate source. An example is that the location of an intersection may be verified by a street atlas, or that the stopping distances of automobiles at various speeds may be determined by referring to the appropriate table. Certain facts may already be known by the judge, and reference to an outside source may be unnecessary. However, not having personal knowledge of a fact need not prevent a judge from taking judicial notice of its existence. There are some facts judges may accept immediately and others that they may accept after referring to some record or other source.

For example, FRE 201(c)(2) requires a court to take judicial notice of a fact if one of the parties makes a request for notice and supplies the court with the necessary information to verify the fact. Once a request for judicial notice is made, the opposing party is entitled to oppose the request. Therefore, a party cannot unilaterally ask for a fact to be judicially noticed without giving the other party an opportunity to discuss the matter with the court. Additionally, a court may *sua sponte* (on its own) take judicial notice of a fact even if neither of the parties has requested it to do so.

Judicially noticed facts are treated differently in civil and criminal trials. According to FRE 201(f), "In a civil case, the court must instruct the jury to accept

JUDICIAL NOTICE
The acceptance of a fact by a judge without formal proof, in the form of testimony or tangible evidence, being presented. A substitute for evidence.

the noticed fact as conclusive. In a criminal case, the court must instruct the jury that it may or may not accept the noticed fact as conclusive." A criminal jury must be given discretion to accept or reject a judicially noticed fact, or the defendant's Sixth Amendment right to trial by jury will be violated. In other words, for a trial judge in a criminal case to *require* the jury to accept the judicially noticed fact as true would usurp the jury's function as trier of fact and violate the Sixth Amendment.

If a judge refuses an attorney's request to take judicial notice of a pertinent fact, then that attorney will have to present adequate proof to establish the existence of the fact.

Judicial notice may be taken at any time or at any stage of any proceeding. Thus, any court may take judicial notice at any point in a trial, even after the side seeking judicial notice has rested its case. Additionally, a court may take judicial notice of a fact on appeal.

The following are some of the more common facts of which a judge might take judicial notice in a criminal trial.

Notice of Public Statutes

Most jurisdictions permit judges to take judicial notice of all public statutes, or laws, of the United States, as well as those of their own state. Under the FRE, most state and federal court judges take judicial notice of statutes of "sister states." This is because the laws of most states and the federal government are readily ascertainable by anyone who knows how to look them up. Some forms of laws, such as municipal codes, are not codified or published regularly, or at all, and thus must be the subject of proof, not judicial notice.

Lawyers cannot assume that judges know every law or city ordinance. Therefore, lawyers must often present the judge with sufficient references and information to convince the judge that the law was enacted and is still in force. This must be done even for the laws of the state in which the judge is sitting. The material submitted to the judge citing the relevant law is not considered evidence; it is only the basis for the judge to take judicial notice of public law.

ON THE JOB   A court may take judicial notice of the location of streets and highways within a county or city. However, the law enforcement officer should be prepared to testify that the events under investigation took place in the town, city, or county in which the case is on trial in order to supply the proof that the trial is taking place in the proper court. This is important because a court usually has the power, or jurisdiction, over a criminal case only when the crime was committed in the county in which the court is located.

Notice of Geographical Facts

Many well-established geographical facts fall within the category of judicial notice or knowledge of the court. These include state boundaries, international borders, city limits, and the location of streets and highways. The navigability of certain waters is also recognized, as are the differences in temperature between the North and the South. In some cases, a judge may not have personal knowledge of the geographical fact in question and may wish to consult an official map or other source of information that is not subject to reasonable dispute.

Notice of Words, Phrases, and Abbreviations

The court will take judicial notice of commonly known words, phrases, or abbreviations. For example, the words "whiskey" and "wine" will be recognized as intoxicating beverages. The abbreviations "A.M." and "P.M." are well known and will be accepted in court. Slang will be judicially noticed. For example, "piece" will be recognized as "gun," and "waste him" will be acknowledged to mean "kill him." A judge may even take notice of jargon or terms used in the vernacular when the meaning of the term is in widespread use. For example, the term "coke" is so well known in certain contexts to mean "cocaine" that a judge may take judicial notice of that fact.

Notice of Time, Days, and Dates

Many facts about time are judicially recognized, such as 24 hours make a day or 7 days make a week. January 1 is recognized as the beginning of the new calendar year, and July 4 is accepted as a national holiday in the United States. However, because of differences in religious beliefs, Sunday is not accepted as being the Sabbath.

Scientific and Medical Facts

For a scientific or medical fact to fall within the realm of judicial notice, it must be an established fact. Scientific and medical theories progress from the unknown, to the debatable, to the generally accepted, and then eventually to established facts.

Perhaps no area of judicial notice is more subject to change than that of science and medicine. With the research and progress made in these fields, what was once an accepted fact is now nothing more than an ancient myth. At one point, it was accepted fact that the earth was flat, flying to the moon was impossible, tuberculosis meant certain death, and tomatoes were poisonous. Likewise, many scientific/medical principles that were at one time unknown are now commonly accepted, such as the sterilization of milk; immunization against disease; and visualization of the structure of human cells, tissues, and organs using magnetic resonance imaging.

The question of whether a scientific or other principle can be judicially noticed by a judge is different from the question of whether an expert may rely

ON THE JOB

Whenever possible, a law enforcement officer should be specific in his or her use of language in court. Although "coke" is widely accepted as "cocaine," other terms may not be as clear. For example, while "speed" is a term generally used for amphetamines and methamphetamines, in some cases it is used to refer to cocaine.

upon the principle in rendering an opinion in expert testimony. The prevailing FRE approach to qualification of a subject for expert testimony, including the United States Supreme Court's standard stated in its 1993 and 1999 decisions in the *Daubert* and *Kumho Tire*[3] cases, is discussed in Chapter 5. In summary, a scientific or other fact may be sufficiently recognized to be used by an expert in giving opinion testimony but insufficiently accepted to be judicially noticed by a judge.

The acceptance of many scientific and medical facts has worked to the advantage of law enforcement professionals. For example, courts take judicial notice of radar as a means of determining speed, although the accuracy and efficiency of the apparatus will depend upon the officer who uses it. It is up to the officer to convince the jury of his or her ability. The courts routinely accept the analysis of fingerprints, DNA, bodily fluid secretions, blood types, and hair structure to connect a suspect to a crime scene. However, the issue of whether the questioned fingerprints, secretions, blood, or other materials match the criminal defendant is a fact the jury will decide.

There are several scientific and medical principles that have not gained acceptance and thus are not judicially recognized. Controversy over the acceptance of these principles has raged for years. Two of the most significant are the validity of the results of the polygraph, or lie detector, and the effects of hypnosis on stimulating a person's memory. The universal rule in the United States is that polygraph results are inadmissible in court, even though many law enforcement agencies and other organizations continue to use them for investigative purposes. Witnesses whose memories have been hypnotically refreshed are not banned from testifying, but there are severe restrictions upon the use of the portion of the testimony that may have resulted from hypnosis. Most courts refuse to recognize the validity of such memory recall techniques.

APPLICATION CASE

A number of states have ruled that hypnotically enhanced testimony should be excluded at trial on the grounds that it tends to be unreliable. There is substantial evidence that hypnosis may induce false memories. In *Rock v. Arkansas*,[4] the United States Supreme Court held that Arkansas' exclusionary rule could not apply to a defendant who wanted to testify after hypnosis to explain how the gun that killed her husband went off accidentally. The Court held that an automatic rule of total exclusion of a hypnotized person's testimony, established by the state courts or legislature, could not be applied to a *defendant* even if the rule could apply to *witnesses*. It should be noted that the Court's decision was founded on a defendant's right in a criminal case to "present relevant testimony," which is found in the Compulsory Process Clause of the Sixth Amendment to the United States Constitution. This decision, however, has led to continued debate over the validity of hypnotically refreshed testimony.

In the 1987 case of *Rock v. Arkansas,*[5] the United States Supreme Court approved the rule adopted by many states that a witness who is not a defendant and whose memory has been hypnotically refreshed cannot testify about the matters recalled under hypnosis. But a witness who recalled certain matters *before* being hypnotized may testify about those matters even after being hypnotized. To preserve the record of what testimony has and has not been affected by hypnosis, the law enforcement officer *must* record, preferably on video, the witness's recall at all stages. The officer must take great care in preparation, as it is impossible to "undo" mistakes in documentation or interviewing. The officer would be wise to role play the interview beforehand with a colleague. Another recommended tactic is to have other persons present during interviews, even if recorded. These additional witnesses are then available to corroborate the recorded events.

PRESUMPTIONS

Like judicial notice, a presumption is a device that substitutes for evidence. When allowed to operate, a **presumption** permits (or requires) the fact-finder (often the jury) to conclude that, because a party has introduced evidence that one fact exists (called the "basic fact"), another fact (called the "presumed fact") exists, even though the party has not introduced any other evidence of the existence of the presumed fact. The following two examples will help explain this concept. In the first example, the law states that a letter properly addressed, stamped, and placed in the mail is presumed to have been delivered. In the second example, a person who has been missing and unheard of for seven years is presumed to be dead. In these two examples, the basic facts are, respectively, the proper mailing of a letter and the disappearance of a person who has not been heard of in seven years. The presumed facts are delivery of the letter and death of the missing person. The subject of presumptions involves a number of concepts that must be understood. In the law of evidence, a presumption is a term of art that has limited and specific effects in operation. Presumptions may be "mandatory" or "rebuttable." In recent years, the United States Supreme Court has severely restricted the use of true presumptions in criminal cases because, otherwise, criminal defendants would be deprived of the right to have the jury decide the facts in a criminal case beyond a reasonable doubt. When a true presumption operates, the jury is told that they "must" find a presumed fact to exist, even when there is no evidence of the presumed fact other than the evidence of the basic fact.

PRESUMPTION
A substitute for evidence whereby the fact-finder is allowed to conclude that a certain fact exists because some other fact is found to exist.

Inferences and "Conclusive" Presumptions Distinguished

The term "presumption" is often misused. Even in everyday communications, we often say we are "presuming" something, when what we really mean is that we are making an **inference**, or drawing a conclusion from an observation or a series of observations. A presumption as used in the law of evidence is when the jury is told that, if they believe that fact A exists, they must find that fact B exists. For example, a defendant is charged with possession of a pound of cocaine with intent to sell it. In this case there is a presumption of "intent to sell"

INFERENCE
A conclusion drawn from an observation or a series of observations.

that the law infers based upon the quantity of illicit drugs a person possesses. The presumption would operate in this example if the jury were told "If you believe that the defendant had possession of one pound of cocaine, you must conclude that he had the intent to sell it." Note that this example of a presumption is not proper because concluding that the defendant had intent to sell would be merely an inference.

CONCLUSIVE PRESUMPTION
A presumption that the law demands or directs be made from a set of facts and that cannot be refuted by evidence. Usually a misnomer for a substantive law rule.

Another misapplication of the term "presumption" is what the law sometimes refers to as a "conclusive" presumption. A **conclusive presumption** is one that the law demands or directs be made from a set of facts and that cannot be refuted by other evidence. Conclusive presumptions are also referred to as "irrebuttable" presumptions. In truth, conclusive presumptions are rules of law and therefore the term is not widely used. The following example of a conclusive presumption may help clarify the concept. In California, until the mid-1990s, when a child was born to a married couple who were having relations at the time of conception and the husband was not impotent or sterile, a conclusive presumption arose that the husband was the father of the child. No evidence that some other man could have been the child's father would have been admissible to rebut this presumption. The basis for this presumption was the law's desire to avoid children's illegitimacy.[6]

Conclusive presumptions cannot be used to prove an element of the crime charged in criminal cases because, as in the case of a court taking judicial notice, imposing such conclusive presumptions would relieve the prosecution of the burden of proving the defendant guilty beyond a reasonable doubt. Such an action would violate the Sixth Amendment of the United States Constitution. For example, consider the case of *Leary v. United States.*[7] In this case, Timothy Leary was convicted of "possession of marijuana knowing it was imported into the United States." The statute under which he was convicted established a presumption of knowledge of illegal importation from mere possession of the marijuana. The Supreme Court of the United States held that the law was unconstitutional because it established a presumption that had a conclusive effect and was therefore improper in this criminal case.

In some states, however, conclusive presumptions are still recognized and have been held constitutional as a substantive rule of law that must be followed in noncriminal cases. For instance, in California, a tenant is not permitted to deny the title of his or her landlord at the time a lease begins. The title is conclusively presumed to be valid.

TRUE PRESUMPTION
A presumption that requires that, when the jury finds the basic fact to exist, it must find the presumed fact to exist in the absence of evidence to the contrary being introduced.

In contrast to an inference or a conclusive presumption, a **true presumption** applies in the following manner: If the basic fact is found to exist, then the jury must find the presumed fact to exist in the absence of evidence to the contrary being introduced. Using the example of the proper mailing of a letter, if the proponent of the presumption introduced evidence of proper mailing, then the jury would be instructed that it must find the letter to have been delivered, unless the opposing party offered evidence that the letter was not received. Using the example of the missing person, if the party seeking the benefit of the presumption offered evidence that the person was missing and unheard of for seven years, the jury would be instructed that it must find that the missing person was dead, unless the opponent of the presumption offered evidence to the contrary.

The Policy Behind Presumptions

Presumptions are conclusions that the law requires to be drawn from certain sets of facts. They are recognized because they follow in the normal course of human experience. Experience has proven that, each time a given set of facts arises, the end results of the set are very likely to be the same. Under these circumstances, it is logical to presume that the same results will continue to take place. The examples of delivery of a properly mailed letter and death of a missing and unheard-of person fit this pattern. These are logical presumptions, since they are what normally take place in these situations. They are the most probable results. Thus, one reason presumptions are recognized is that they are based on the law of probability.

The acceptance of presumptions is also based on the social habits of human beings. Consider again the example of presuming dead a person who has been missing and unheard of for seven years. Most people are gregarious creatures with family ties, and they do not normally vanish without making contact with either friends or family unless a tragedy has taken place. If there has been no information about a person for seven years, the logical deduction or presumption is that the person is dead. There is nothing particularly significant or magical about the seven-year period, which probably comes from old English statutes that declared that a person who went to sea or was otherwise absent from the kingdom for seven years was presumed to be dead. Some people assert that this period is now too long, arguing that it no longer reflects the reality of high-speed transportation and communication, and that a period of three years is more appropriate.

Because the basis of a presumption is either probability or human experience, the question arises whether a presumption that is not probable or is not within common experience is valid. The Supreme Court of the United States has also addressed this issue. The Court has declared that, at a minimum, the presumed fact must flow from the basic fact measured by a standard of a preponderance of evidence. A preponderance of the evidence is said to be "fifty percent plus a feather." In other words, in judging the validity of a presumption, one must conclude that the presumptive fact follows from the basic fact more likely than not.

The preponderance of the evidence standard is the formulation for what is known as a permissive presumption, as distinguished from a mandatory presumption. In contrast, the standard of proof of a mandatory presumption is "beyond a reasonable doubt," according to the Supreme Court. This distinction will be examined again after the difference between mandatory and permissive presumptions is discussed.

The Effects of Presumptions: Jury Instructions and Burden of Proof

A presumption has very limited, but significant, effects. The first effect relates to what the jury is told about the presumption. For example, when delivery of a mailed letter is defined as a rebuttable, mandatory presumption in the state in which the trial is taking place and the opponent of the presumption offers no evidence to rebut the conclusion, the judge would tell the jury that if they find that the letter was properly mailed, they *must* find that it was delivered.

The second effect of a presumption is the effect on the burden of proof. The **burden of proof** is a party's obligation to introduce evidence in a lawsuit and to persuade the fact-finder that the evidence is believable. The burden of proof, therefore, has two elements: (1) the burden of producing evidence **(production burden)** and (2) the burden of persuading the trier of fact **(persuasion burden)**. If the party having the burden of production fails to produce any evidence, then that party loses for that reason alone, and the judge can direct a verdict without the case ever going to the jury. If the party having the production burden introduces evidence, that evidence must be strong enough to convince the jury of the facts the evidence supports.

A presumption usually just affects the burden of production by shifting it to the party against whom the presumption operates. In other words, the presumption affects the burden of producing evidence by putting the burden on the party that needs to prove the claim. For example, consider the presumption of delivery from proper mailing to illustrate this concept. Assume the party seeking to use the presumption introduces evidence of proper mailing. The presumption will operate and the jury will be instructed that they must find delivery if they believe the evidence of proper mailing, unless the opponent of the presumption comes forward and introduces evidence to rebut the presumption. In most states (and under the FRE), the only effect of a presumption is that it shifts the production burden. In those states, once the opponent of the presumption has introduced any evidence rebutting the presumed fact—in this case, testimony of nondelivery—the presumption disappears, and the jury hears the conflicting evidence on both sides (proper mailing versus nondelivery). The jury decides the fact as it wishes and is told nothing about presumptions in such a case.

Distinguishing Mandatory from Permissive Presumptions: Presumptions in Criminal Cases

Presumptions may be incorrect. For some unknown reason, a letter may not have been delivered. Or, due to unexpected events, the person who has been missing and unheard of for seven years may not be dead but instead may be quite well and living peacefully in some distant community. For this reason, the law usually provides for a **rebuttable presumption**, which means the opponent of the presumption may introduce evidence to rebut the presumption's conclusion. Thus, for example, in the face of an attempt to use the presumption of receipt of a letter based upon evidence of the fact that a letter was properly mailed, the addressee could take the stand and testify that the letter was not received. Therefore, the presumption would cease to operate in the case in most states. Then the jury could decide the matter considering the logical inferences from proper mailing, on the one hand, and the testimony of nonreceipt on the other.

However, if the presumption continues to operate in the case, even if the presumption is rebuttable, we must consider whether the effect of the presumption on the jury is to require it to find the presumed fact to exist. That is, we must consider whether the presumed fact should be *required* to be found to exist when the basic fact has been proven, or whether the jury should merely be *allowed* to find the presumed fact *if the jury chooses to do so.* A true presumption *requires* the jury to find the presumed fact from the existence of the basic fact and may be called a **mandatory presumption**. In other words, the permissive form operates only as an inference. Therefore, for a presumption to operate at all requires it to be mandatory in effect.

The reason it is necessary to distinguish between permissive and mandatory presumptions is that the United States Constitution has a number of provisions affecting the rights of persons accused of crimes. Such rights include due process of law, under the Fifth and Fourteenth Amendments, and the Sixth Amendment's provisions of the right to trial by jury. The United States Supreme Court has held that the right to a fair trial by jury in criminal cases carries with it the requirement that the prosecution prove the case against the accused by evidence beyond a reasonable doubt as to every element of the crime charged. Thus, the burden of proof is upon the prosecution, and the defendant is entitled to a presumption of innocence unless and until the prosecution satisfies its burden. If a presumption in favor of the prosecution were to operate in a criminal case to relieve the prosecution of its burden of producing evidence or persuasion, the right of the accused to a fair trial by jury would be violated.

Some Common Rebuttable Presumptions and Their Status Under the Law

There are many rebuttable presumptions that are valid because they do not conflict with constitutional principles or some state statute. Law enforcement professionals need to be familiar with the following presumptions commonly encountered in criminal cases.

Presumption of Innocence

Perhaps there is no better known rebuttable presumption than that "a person is presumed innocent until proved guilty" or, as it is sometimes stated, "a person is presumed innocent of a crime or a wrong." This presumption of innocence is based upon the needs of a free society; it is a part of our national heritage and has been described as a person's guarantee against injustice and oppression. It is this presumption that the prosecution must overcome if the prosecuting attorney is to prove the defendant guilty beyond a reasonable doubt.

Presumption of Sanity

There is a general presumption that all persons are sane. This presumption of sanity stems from the fact that sanity is the normal human condition. It permits the prosecution to proceed with a criminal trial without having to first prove the defendant to have been sane at the time that the crime was committed. However, once insanity is raised or put in issue in the case, the situation changes. In all federal prosecutions, if the defendant raises an affirmative defense of insanity, the Insanity Defense Reform Act of 1984 places the burden of proof upon the defendant to establish insanity by clear and convincing evidence.[8] In the absence of such a statute, the presumption of sanity would disappear, and the prosecution would have to prove sanity beyond a reasonable doubt or by a preponderance of the evidence standard. The degree of evidence that the defendant claiming insanity is required to produce may vary in those states that have followed the lead of the Insanity Reform Act; some jurisdictions require "some" evidence, others require "slight" evidence, and others permit "any" evidence to raise the issue.

Children Under a Certain Age Are Not Capable of Committing a Crime

Under this common law rule, it was "conclusively presumed" that a child under the age of seven was not capable of committing a crime—a presumption of incapacity. Not all states in this country recognize this presumption as conclusive; some term it a rebuttable presumption. In addition, the common law rule was that a child between the ages of seven and fourteen was presumed to be incapable of committing a crime. This presumption could be rebutted by evidence that the child knew that the act done was wrongful. Some states still retain this rebuttable presumption, although the ages to which it applies may differ from state to state.

Miscellaneous Rebuttable Presumptions

The following are some additional better-known rebuttable presumptions. If any state laws still contain mandatory language (i.e., "must"), that language cannot be used in a criminal case. In the 1979 case of *Sandstrom v. Montana*,[10] the United States Supreme Court ruled that a presumption cannot be applied mandatorily in a criminal case. In other words, the jury may be told that they *may infer* that the defendant acted with intent, but it is not mandatory they find it from a presumption. Thus, many of the following presumptions under the common law rule are now applicable in a criminal case only as allowable inferences:

- ▶ People intend the ordinary consequences of their voluntary acts.
- ▶ An unlawful intent is presumed from doing an unlawful act.
- ▶ Evidence willfully suppressed would be adverse if produced.
- ▶ Official duty has been regularly performed.
- ▶ The ordinary course of business, or routine practice, has been followed.
- ▶ A date on a writing is correct.
- ▶ A man and a woman reporting themselves as husband and wife are legally married.
- ▶ The law has been obeyed.
- ▶ A ceremonial marriage is valid.
- ▶ The identity of a person can be determined by the person's name.

Knowledge of the Law

There is no established legal presumption that a "person is presumed to know the law." However, there is a maxim or rule of law providing that everyone is assumed to know the law and that ignorance of the law is no defense for a criminal act. Additionally, the claim that one did not know that an act was punishable is not a defense. This maxim is based on the demands of society. Otherwise, successful prosecutions could be defeated if offenders were able to claim ignorance of the law as their defense.

Presumptions, Not Evidence

Today, in an overwhelming majority of jurisdictions, a presumption is not evidence. This is an important point, for if a presumption is classified as evidence, it may confuse the jury into giving the presumption as much weight as witness testimony and tangible evidence. By declaring that presumptions are not evidence, the law materially lessens the burden upon the jury, as the jurors may, with a clear conscience, give greater weight to the evidence presented than to the deduction that must be drawn from a presumption. Thus, in the majority of states where a presumption is not evidence, the jury will likely see it as the mere procedural device it is and not give it undue weight.

BURDEN OF PROOF

As mentioned earlier, the burden of proof is the responsibility to present evidence in a case that persuades the fact-finder of the truth of the claims the evidence is offered to support. In a criminal trial, the prosecution has the burden of going forward with the evidence initially and proving the defendant guilty beyond a reasonable doubt. This is a necessity arising from the fact that a person is presumed innocent until proven guilty, a presumption that is the bedrock of our criminal justice system.

However, a state legislature may pass a law defining a crime in such a way as to eliminate certain facts from the elements of the crime. The same law can then make certain facts pertinent to defenses, rather than to the elements of the crime. If the law treats the facts as relating to defenses, rather than elements of the crime's definition, then the defendant has the burden to raise those facts as a defense. In addition to the burden of asserting the defense, the defendant has the burden of introducing evidence in support of the defense, as well as proving the defense by at least a preponderance of the evidence. For example, in one case, the state of Maine required an accused to prove that he acted "in the heat of passion on sudden provocation" in order to reduce the homicide he was charged with from murder to manslaughter.[11] The United States Supreme Court held that, since the law of Maine distinguished between murder and manslaughter as a matter of definition of the elements of the crime, it was an unconstitutional shift of the burden of proof to the defendant to require him to prove heat of passion rather than requiring the prosecution to disprove it.

On the other hand, in another case, New York law designated an affirmative defense to murder where the "defendant acted under the influence of extreme emotional disturbance for which there was a reasonable explanation or excuse."[12] The affirmative defense had to be proved by the defendant. Under New York law, such an accused could be convicted of the offense of manslaughter. The United States Supreme Court held that this method of placing the burden on the accused to plead and prove an affirmative defense did not violate due process.

STIPULATIONS

Other facts may be presented during a trial without formal proof being required. These are facts upon which the parties and their attorneys agree. This agreement may take place either before or during the trial. Once agreement has been reached, it will not be necessary to call witnesses to present the facts. Rather, the facts to which they have all stipulated will be told to the jury at the proper time, either by one of the attorneys or the judge. The jury will be instructed that these facts included in a **stipulation** are to be taken into consideration in arriving at a verdict.

Stipulations are usually made concerning facts that are relatively unimportant to the trial, or to facts about which there is little or no dispute. The primary reason for a stipulation is to save trial time and expense. In addition, stipulations are generally seen with chain of custody issues.

Occasionally, though, an attorney may offer to stipulate to a fact in order to avoid the emotional impact a witness's testimony may have on the jury. In that situation, the opposing side may not agree to the stipulation. For example, in the case in which the defendant alleged that he attended the Odeon Cinema on the night of April 13, the prosecution could have stipulated to those facts to avoid the necessity of the theater manager appearing as a witness. His testimony did not actually prove any significant fact involved in the case. There was no allegation that the movie *Black Panther* had not been showing on the night of April 13. However, the defense attorney might refuse to accept the prosecutor's offer to stipulate in order that the defendant's alibi be supported, even circumstantially, by someone other than his relatives.

STIPULATION
Facts upon which the trial parties and their attorneys agree that may be presented during the trial without formal proof being required.

REVIEW AND APPLICATION

SUMMARY

(1) The four general categories of evidence are (1) testimony of witnesses; (2) real, or physical, evidence; (3) documents, or writings; and (4) demonstrative evidence, i.e., visual or audiovisual aids for the jury.

(2) Relevant evidence is evidence with any tendency to make the existence of any fact that is of consequence to the determination of the action more probable or less probable than it would be without the evidence.

(3) Relevant evidence may be excluded if it has a tendency to unduly prejudice or inflame the minds of the jury, will cause confusion or create too many side issues, is so remote or speculative that only a weak logical inference can be drawn from it, or is inadmissible based on other rules of evidence or other laws.

(4) Contradictory evidence is evidence used to prove a fact contrary to what has been asserted by a party or witness, whereas corroborative evidence is evidence that is supportive of other evidence already given, tending to strengthen or confirm the prior evidence.

(5) Judicial notice is the process or act by which a judge accepts a fact as true, without requiring formal proof, where that fact either (1) is generally known within the territorial jurisdiction of the trial court or (2) can be accurately and readily determined from sources whose accuracy cannot reasonably be questioned.

(6) A court may judicially notice (1) the existence and content of public laws; (2) geographical facts, such as boundaries and location of streets and highways; (3) the existence and meaning of common words, phrases, and abbreviations; and (4) many facts about time, days, and dates.

(7) A true presumption consists of a basic fact and a presumed fact.

(8) The existence of a basic fact is the basis for presuming the existence of a presumed fact.

(9) Two examples of rebuttable presumptions are (1) people intend the ordinary consequences of their voluntary acts and (2) the date on a writing is accurate.

(10) A stipulation is a particular fact or group of facts upon which the parties and their attorneys agree. A stipulated fact need not be proven by evidence and is simply told to the jury by one of the attorneys or the judge.

KEY TERMS

relevant evidence 58	cumulative evidence 62	production burden 70
balancing test 59	judicial notice 63	persuasion burden 70
material evidence 60	presumption 67	rebuttable
prima facie evidence 62	inference 67	presumption 70
prima facie criminal	conclusive	mandatory
case 62	presumption 68	presumption 71
contradictory evidence 62	true presumption 68	stipulation 74
corroborative evidence 62	burden of proof 70	

QUESTIONS FOR REVIEW

1. What are four general categories of evidence?
2. Describe what makes evidence relevant.
3. What are some reasons for excluding relevant evidence from trial?

4. How is contradictory evidence different from corroborative evidence?
5. What is judicial notice?
6. Name some types of facts that can be the subject of judicial notice.
7. What are the two factual components of a true presumption?
8. How is a presumed fact related to a basic fact?
9. What is the main characteristic of a rebuttable presumption?
10. How does a stipulation work?

THINKING CRITICALLY ABOUT EVIDENCE

1. Relevant evidence often is excluded because it is unfairly prejudicial. Photographs of the scene of a homicide are most likely to generate a defense objection as to prejudice. Can you think of ways to reduce the potential for unfair prejudice that might be produced when photographs of a homicide scene are exhibited?

2. A defendant is suspected of armed robbery of a bank. The robbery was very dramatic and received major media coverage. One of the facts reported is that a clear set of fingerprints was discovered at the scene. After the robbery and before his arrest, the defendant went to a plastic surgeon and had his fingers surgically altered. Is this evidence relevant to the pending robbery charge? Explain.

WORKPLACE APPLICATIONS

1. John Jones is under suspicion for having murdered his wife to collect her life insurance. An officer assigned to the investigation observes Mr. Jones at a jewelry store buying an expensive diamond ring. The officer follows him and sees him visit a woman known to be his close friend. Mr. Jones enters her home and spends the night there. Based on these facts and observations, the officer decides to seek a search warrant for the woman's home in order to get the ring as evidence in the murder investigation. Draft a statement of the rationale spelling out the inferences necessary to support the request for the warrant. Note ways that the inferences may be confirmed by the search.

2. Three people were involved in the robbery of a local computer store—the defendant, an unknown masked accomplice who entered the store with him, and the driver of an automobile that the trio used to get away. A passerby noticed the plates of that vehicle as the robbery was in progress and reported it to the police. The vehicle was later traced and discovered to have been stolen two days before the robbery. The day after the robbery, the car was recovered and the defendant's fingerprints were found on the passenger door panel. Is this evidence admissible at the defendant's trial for the robbery charge? Explain why or why not.

ENDNOTES

1. Daubert v. Merrell Dow Pharmaceuticals, Inc., 509 U.S. 579, 591 (1993). The full moon example stated in the text was used by the Court in *Daubert's* majority opinion.

2. Fed. R. Evid. 201(b).

3. Daubert v. Merrell Dow Pharmaceuticals, Inc., 509 U.S. 579 (1993); Kumho Tire Company, Ltd. v. Carmichael, 526 U.S. 137 (1999).

4. Rock v. Arkansas, 483 U.S. 44 (1987).

5. *Id.*

6. The California presumption of paternity referred to in the text still exists, Cal. Fam. Code §7540; however, the presumption can now be rebutted by blood test evidence [Cal. Fam. Code §7541 (West 2018)] or by other factors [Cal. Fam. Code §7611 (West 2018) (certain provisions of the Uniform Parentage Act)]. In fact, it is possible for there to be competing presumed fathers, in which case the courts must determine which of them shall be declared the father ultimately. In other words, a presumption of paternity, even one declared to be conclusive, is rebuttable now under California law. *See* In re Jesusa V., 10 Cal. Reptr. 3d 205 (Cal. 2004).

7. Leary v. United States, 395 U.S. 6 (1969).

8. 18 U.S.C. §17 (West 2018).

9. Cooper v. Oklahoma, 517 U.S. 348 (1996).

10. Sandstrom v. Montana, 442 U.S. 510 (1979).

11. Mullaney v. Wilbur, 421 U.S. 684 (1975).

12. Patterson v. New York, 432 U.S. 197 (1977).

Design Element: ©Ingram Publishing

4 WITNESSES—COMPETENCY AND PRIVILEGED COMMUNICATIONS

CHAPTER OUTLINE

CHAPTER OBJECTIVES

This chapter introduces the basic concepts of evidence used in the American legal system. After reading this chapter, you will be able to:

▶ Explain the qualifications required to be considered competent to be a witness.

▶ List the three characteristics that constitute witness capacity.

▶ State the rationale for privileged communications.

▶ Explain the difference between the spousal incapacity and marital communications privileges.

▶ State when the attorney-client privilege is created.

▶ Describe two exceptions to the physician-patient privilege that often make the rule irrelevant.

▶ Explain why there is no compelling need for a physician-patient privilege, according to the United States Supreme Court.

▶ State the strong policy justifications for the psychotherapist-patient privilege.

▶ State when the government may refuse to reveal the identity of an informer.

▶ Explain when the news reporter–news source privilege yields.

INTRODUCTION

Most of the evidence in any trial is presented through the oral testimony of witnesses. Therefore, the rules of evidence pertaining to witnesses deserve thorough study. A witness is a person who has some knowledge about the facts of a case. The testimony of a witness is taken under oath (or affirmation) in a trial. An oath is a solemn, formal declaration or promise to testify truthfully, calling on God as witness. An affirmation is a solemn declaration given in place of an oath by a person who conscientiously objects to taking an oath.

The common law rule required that a witness be competent. The trial judge determined the competency of a witness, and there were many grounds for **incompetency**, including tender (young) age, old age, infirmity of mind, lack of religious beliefs, prior criminal conviction, and an interest in the outcome of the case. These historical standards no longer hold true.

FRE 601 states: "Every person is competent to be a witness unless these rules provide otherwise." Under the FRE, only judges and jurors sitting in the case on trial are declared incompetent to testify. Generally, the only requirements for a person to be able to testify are that the individual have personal knowledge of facts pertinent to the case, have the ability to understand the obligation to tell the truth, and willingly take an oath (or affirm) that he or she will tell the truth. No mental or moral qualifications for testifying as a witness are specified in the federal rules.

In a criminal trial, the witnesses must appear personally to face the defendant. This requirement stems from the Confrontation Clause of the Sixth Amendment of the United States Constitution, which states: "In all criminal prosecutions, the accused shall . . . be confronted with the witnesses against him." Because of the Confrontation Clause, it is not usually possible to use a witness's written statement in a criminal case. In certain circumstances, a witness's written statement—an affidavit (a sworn written statement), a declaration (another name for an affidavit), or a deposition (sworn testimony under questioning before trial and usually in a private office, not in a courtroom)—may be introduced in a criminal trial under the hearsay rule or one of its exceptions. The circumstances in which out-of-court "testimonial" statements, whether written or oral, may be admitted into evidence depend upon satisfaction of the Confrontation Clause, as well as the hearsay rule. This, as well as the hearsay rule in general, is discussed in Chapter 7. However, because a witness must face the accused in a criminal trial, the following discussion of the rules of evidence for witnesses will be confined, for the most part, to oral testimony.

INCOMPETENCY
The inability to act as a witness. Today, there are few grounds for incompetency, and in federal courts and all states except Arkansas (where atheists are not competent), all persons are competent to be a witness.

MYTH ▶	◀ FACT
A person must demonstrate a certain mental fitness in order to testify.	Other than being able to demonstrate personal knowledge of facts pertinent to the case on trial and to understand the obligation to tell the truth, no mental fitness is required of a person in order to be a witness.

WHO IS A COMPETENT WITNESS?

The primary purpose of a trial is to arrive at the truth in a particular case. In a trial, it is mandatory to have persons who will tell the truth when they testify. The common law rule viewed certain categories of persons as being unable to testify truthfully. These common law restrictions have been abolished in most states. Today, in federal courts and all states except for Arkansas, where the state constitution provides that atheists are not competent, all persons are competent to be a witness. The absence of a religious belief, a lack of mental capacity, being a party to a suit, or having been convicted of a crime does not make a person incompetent as a witness. The presence of any of these conditions may affect the weight of the testimony in the eyes of the jury, but it will not prevent the person from becoming a witness.

Although everyone is competent to testify, a person must possess three basic characteristics in order to be a witness. They are the ability to perceive, remember, and narrate in an understandable manner. These three characteristics make up **witness capacity**. A fourth element of capacity, sincerity, is sometimes added, but the advisory committee to the FRE noted that "it seems merely to be an aspect of the three already mentioned."[1]

In addition to the basic capacity mentioned previously, in most states, an individual must meet three requirements in order to be a witness: (1) A person must have personal knowledge of facts relevant to the case; (2) a person must understand the obligation to tell the truth; and (3) a person must take an oath (or affirm) that he or she will testify truthfully. A person who possesses witness capacity and meets the other three requirements is qualified to testify. Therefore, it is more accurate to talk about **qualifying to be a witness** rather than to speak in terms of competency to be a witness. Nonetheless, many lawyers and judges still speak of witness competency when discussing the qualifications of witnesses.

There are some problems that recur in qualifying a person to testify as a lay, or ordinary, witness. Is a child too young to understand or communicate? Is a person too mentally feeble to understand or communicate? What about drug addicts or alcoholics? When these problems arise, the trial judge will usually hold a hearing out of the presence of the jury to decide the questions relating to the witness's qualification. This hearing or process is often referred to as a **witness *voir dire*** of the witness. However, if the question presented is whether the witness has personal knowledge of the facts related to the case, the members of the jury will usually listen to the witness's testimony and decide for themselves whether they believe the witness has personal knowledge.

Children as Witnesses

Since all persons are competent to testify under the law of most American jurisdictions, even a young child can be a witness. The common law rule was that a child under the age of seven was too young to be competent. That is not the law in most jurisdictions today. However, when a child is very young, even the basic questions of capacity and ability to understand the obligation to tell the truth can arise. The judge will have to determine if the child is able to understand what is going on around him or her, to remember events, to relate

WITNESS CAPACITY
The elements of witness capacity are the ability to perceive, remember, and narrate in an understandable manner, as well as sincerity.

QUALIFYING TO BE A WITNESS
To qualify to be a witness, a person must possess witness capacity: have personal knowledge of facts relevant to the case, be able to understand the obligation to tell the truth, and take the oath or affirm that he or she will testify truthfully.

WITNESS *VOIR DIRE*
The process or hearing, usually conducted out of the presence of the jury, by which a judge decides the qualification of a witness to testify.

the knowledge intelligently to others, and to appreciate what it means to tell the truth. If a child meets this test, the child can testify. For example, one court approved the trial court's acceptance of a six-year-old as a witness in a child sexual assault case. The prosecutor asked the child if she knew what it meant to tell the truth and the child answered "yes." The prosecutor then asked whether she knew what happened if one did not tell the truth and the child answered "you get punished."[2]

ON THE JOB

When interviewing small children as witnesses, taking their statements, and writing reports based on this information, the law enforcement officer should approach them in much the same manner as the judge does. The officer should ask the child questions to determine if he or she understands the need to tell the police the truth and the consequences of lying to the police, as well as determine if anyone has told the child to lie to the police.

For example, the officer can ask these questions: Do you know what it means to tell the truth? Do you know what it means to lie? What happens to you if you lie? Usually, the child will indicate some sort of punishment as a consequence of lying. From this interchange, the officer should be able to assess whether the child can be trusted. This is very similar to the questioning the judge will use at the hearing or trial.

The burden of proving to the satisfaction of the judge that a child is qualified to testify rests upon the side producing the child as a witness. It is not necessary that the child understand the oath as such, but the child must know that he or she must tell the truth when testifying. In the *voir dire* hearing, the usual procedure is for the judge to ask the child whether it is wrong to "tell a lie," or a similar inquiry. If a child has learned that telling a falsehood brings punishment, this is sufficient to prove that the child knows the necessity for telling the truth.

Age, therefore, is no longer a barrier to becoming a witness. If this were not the case, most child-molesting cases would go unprosecuted because of the unavailability of the principal witness, the child victim. In cases involving young victims, the Confrontation Clause of the Sixth Amendment and the hearsay rule may prevent out-of-court statements of absent child victims from being admitted into evidence against a criminal defendant. If a youthful victim is found incapable of testifying, the victim's statements can only be introduced against a defendant if deemed to be "non-testimonial" and fall within certain hearsay exceptions. The Confrontation Clause, the hearsay rule, and its exceptions are explained in Chapter 7.

Finally, the argument is often made, usually by the accused, that caution should be exercised in permitting a very young child to become a witness because of possible injustice to the defendant as a result of some imaginary act of misconduct the child may have invented or had planted in his or her mind. These issues must be addressed when evaluating the credibility of the child. Investigators must exercise great care when initially talking to young children to avoid planting ideas in their minds. It is up to the judge and jury in the final analysis, however, to evaluate the defense claim that the child is not credible. As it is argued by lawyers, these questions go to the weight of the evidence, not admissibility.

In the summer of 1984, John Stoll was accused of being the ringleader of a band of child molesters and pornographers in Bakersfield, California. Stoll and his friends constituted one of eight alleged child molestation rings in town, allegedly committing a litany of sex acts against children, authorities said. The "witch hunts," as critics called them, were the first in a wave of multiple-victim child molestation cases to sweep the nation in the mid-1980s.

Stoll had long maintained his innocence, claiming there was no evidence for any of the charges. No indecent photographs were ever found, and the child victims, including his own son, were never examined by a physician. As in many of the cases, Stoll's conviction was based almost solely on the testimony of child witnesses, who defense attorneys maintained had been badgered and brainwashed by overzealous investigators. In early 2004, four of the alleged victims trooped to the witness stand to describe horrifying treatment, not at the hands of Stoll but of law enforcement and prosecutors. Investigators cajoled, badgered, and even threatened them to convince them to testify to sex acts they now said never happened. On May 1, 2004, Stoll's conviction on 17 counts of child molestation was overturned due to improper questioning of the child witnesses.[3]

To address the very sensitive problems related to questioning child victims and witnesses, training is available to help child abuse investigators learn the proper protocol for interviewing young children. This training helps ensure that the information the child gives is both admissible and believable. In cases in which the child is the victim of a crime, it may be advisable to have the child's testimony taken some place other than in the presence of the defendant in the courtroom. Taking into account how stressful such a situation is for a child, the Supreme Court of the United States approved the use of closed-circuit televised testimony in *Maryland v. Craig*.[4] The defendant in such a case still has the right to confront the child witness, but the Court held that as long as the defendant, trial court, and jury could observe the witness while testifying, the defendant's right to confrontation is satisfied. Most states permit the use of closed-circuit television testimony or video recorded deposition testimony of child victims, enabling such witnesses to avoid facing their accused abusers. See Figure 4–1, a map showing which states permit closed-circuit and video recorded testimony of child witnesses. As Figure 4-1 shows, as of 2018, 4 states permit video recorded testimony only, 15 states permit closed-circuit *or* video recorded testimony, 3 states allow alternative methods that amount to closed-circuit testimony, and 1 state has no legal provision. All the remaining 27 states allow closed-circuit testimony only.

Persons of Questionable Mental Stability

In addition to children, persons who are mentally challenged, are senile, have been declared mentally unbalanced, or are drug addicts or alcoholics may also become witnesses because they may still have lucid moments. In most jurisdictions, the only requirement is that they meet the same test as any other person, that is, demonstrate basic capacity (the ability to perceive, remember, and narrate) and qualify to

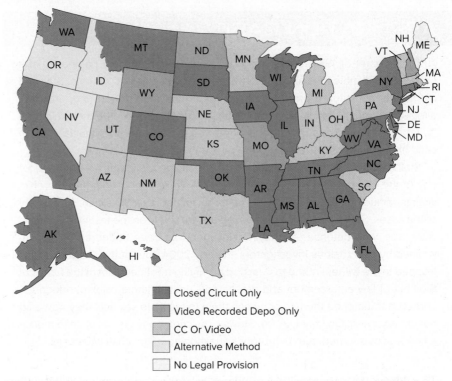

FIGURE 4–1 States that allow child victims to testify via closed-circuit TV or video recorded deposition.

Closed Circuit Only
Video Recorded Depo Only
CC Or Video
Alternative Method
No Legal Provision

testify (possess personal knowledge of relevant facts, understand the obligation to tell the truth, and take an oath [or affirm] that they will testify truthfully).

Judges and Jurors as Witnesses

Under the common law rule, there were certain circumstances under which a judge could be called as a witness. However, FRE 605 declares that a judge presiding at trial may not testify as a witness. A judge not presiding at trial is held to the same competency standards as everyone else.

FRE 606 provides that, like the presiding judge, a member of the jury is incompetent to testify in the trial in which the juror is sitting. Also, once a verdict has been reached, neither side can delve into the juror's mind or emotions during deliberations to cloud the validity of the verdict. A juror may only testify on the question of whether "extraneous prejudicial information" or "outside influence" was brought to the juror's attention or had some bearing upon any juror.

APPLICATION CASES

The rule prohibiting evidence of jurors' deliberative process is the subject of two major United States Supreme Court decisions. The first is *Tanner v. United States*.[5] In that case, the Court held that FRE 606(b) barred jury testimony on drug an alcohol use by jurors during trial. Then, in *Warger v. Shauers*,[6] the Court held that Rule 606(b)(2)(A)'s exception for evidence of "extraneous prejudicial information" did not apply to allow one juror's affidavit of what another juror said in deliberations to demonstrate that juror's dishonesty during *voir dire*. The dishonesty revealed in the affidavit was that the juror did not truthfully disclose her bias. During *voir dire*, she said she could impartially decide the case and award damages; however, during deliberations she revealed that her daughter had been at fault in an accident similar to the one at trial and that a lawsuit would have ruined her life. In short, the Supreme Court found that the juror's deliberation statements could not be admitted into evidence in both cases.

Finally, more recently, the Supreme Court rendered another decision involving this no-impeachment rule, this time allowing evidence of a comment made by a juror during deliberations. In *Pena-Rodriguez v. Colorado*,[7] the Court held that the no-impeachment rule must give way where compelling evidence indicates that a juror relied on racial stereotypes or animosity to convict a criminal defendant. The trial court needed such evidence in order to assess the possible denial of the Sixth Amendment's jury trial guarantee.

PRIVILEGED COMMUNICATIONS

Introduction

Special circumstances may arise under which a person may refrain, or be prohibited, from testifying concerning certain matters or information. This condition occurs when a person is in possession of information gained as a result of certain confidential relationships. Public policy in the United States seeks to encourage and protect select relationships. These relationships are of such importance that society is willing to protect them by maintaining the secrecy of confidences exchanged during such a relationship. By removing the fear that the confidences might be revealed in court, the law promotes the relationship. Legally, such exchanges of confidential information are known as **privileged communications**. If a privilege exists, evidence of any communication made within the privilege is barred from any legal proceeding, unless the privilege is waived or an exception to the privilege exists.

Recognition of a privilege may result in important relevant information being excluded in the trial of a particular case. However, the policy of the law is that maintaining privileged communications as secrets between those involved outweighs the benefit that society would derive from their disclosure. Privileged relationships are strictly limited because any privilege claimed can act as a block to uncovering the truth during a trial. Since privileges prevent the full disclosure of the facts in a trial, they are not favored in the law.

Some privileges were recognized by the common law in accordance with principles that can be simply stated:[8]

> [T]he public . . . has a right to every man's evidence. When we come to examine the various claims of exemption, we start with the primary assumption that

PRIVILEGED COMMUNICATIONS Exchanges of confidential information between persons who are in a privileged relationship.

FYI

Sometimes jurors submit to media interviews after rendering a verdict, especially in high-profile cases. The evidence rule that declares jurors incompetent as witnesses is consistent with this phenomenon. Any statements made by jurors in the media are not evidence. Even if a juror revealed something to the media about the deliberation process, such information could not be used as evidence unless the juror revealed that there was an outside influence brought to bear upon the jury.

there is a general duty to give what testimony one is capable of giving, and that any exemptions which may exist are distinctly exceptional. . . .

The justification for an exception from the general rule against privileges could be found only for "public good transcending the normally predominant principle of utilizing all rational means for ascertaining the truth."[9] In other words, there must be strong public interest in fostering a relationship in order for a privilege to be recognized in the law of evidence.

In addition to the fostering of relationships, privileges are sometimes based upon reason. For example, in the clergy-communicant relationship, a priest would not disclose the confidence, whether or not there existed a privilege, because the rules of the church prohibit disclosure. If there were no attorney-client privilege, a lawyer, who has a duty to zealously represent his or her client, might feel compelled to lie in order to fulfill that duty of zealous representation.

The relationships and circumstances giving rise to a privilege are, therefore, limited and unique. An eminent legal scholar has helpfully stated four fundamental conditions that must be established before a person is exempted from testifying in a judicial proceeding based on a claim of privilege:[11]

1. The parties to a communication must believe that their communication is *confidential* and will not be disclosed to others;
2. this element of *confidentiality must be essential* to the full and satisfactory maintenance of the relationship between the parties;
3. the *relationship* must be one which, in the opinion of the community, ought to be promoted and protected; and
4. the injury that would be caused to the relationship by the disclosure of the communications must be *greater than the value* of the conversation to the proper resolution of the court case.

The third condition requires that the relationship be one that the community, and therefore the law, wishes to foster. A limited number of such relationships are recognized as giving rise to privilege, though not all are recognized in all states. Included in these relationships are

1. husband and wife;
2. parent and child;
3. attorney and client;
4. physician and patient;
5. psychotherapist and patient;
6. clergy and communicant;

7. law enforcement officer and informant;
8. accountant and client; and
9. news reporter and news source.

Because of the importance of these relationships, each will be discussed in detail.

There are also many worthy relationships that the law does not recognize as privileged. Most jurisdictions do not recognize a parent-child privilege. This relationship, like that of attorney-client and husband-wife, is one in which the persons may feel compelled to lie rather than to reveal confidences. Thus, in a way, the failure of the law to recognize the relationship as a privileged one may be encouraging perjury. Other relationships that are not universally recognized as privileged include accountant-client, newsperson–news source, and other counseling relationships, such as social worker–patient, sex abuse counselor–client, and domestic violence advocate–victim.

In 1972, the Chief Justice of the United States transmitted to Congress the Proposed Rules of Evidence for United States Courts and Magistrates. The rules had been formulated by a committee that reported to the Supreme Court and had been approved by a conference of the federal judiciary and by the Supreme Court. The Proposed Rules defined nine testimonial privileges:

1. required reports;
2. lawyer-client;
3. psychotherapist-patient;
4. husband-wife;
5. communications to clergy;
6. political vote;
7. trade secrets;
8. secrets of state; and
9. identity of informer.

Congress rejected this recommendation and instead adopted FRE 501, which states:

> The common law—as interpreted by United States courts in the light of reason and experience—governs a claim of privilege unless any of the following provides otherwise:
>
> ▶ the United States Constitution;
> ▶ a federal statute; or
> ▶ rules prescribed by the Supreme Court.
>
> But in a civil case, state law governs privilege regarding a claim or defense for which state law supplies the rule of decision.

Thus, the only federal privileges would be those recognized in the federal common law that existed at the time, plus any privileges recognized in subsequent judicial decisions. The common law privileges then existing probably included attorney-client and husband-wife and, perhaps, some others. However, it was the intent of Congress to "reflect the view that the recognition of a privilege based on a confidential relationship . . . should be determined on a case-by-case basis."[12] Since the adoption of the FRE, at least through 2018, the Supreme Court has altered one major existing common law privilege (the husband-wife privilege in *Trammel v. United States*[13]) and adopted a new common law privilege (the psychotherapist-patient privilege in *Jaffee v. Redmond*[14]) pursuant to this language. In this latest move, the Court stated: "The Rule [501] thus did not freeze the law governing the privileges of witnesses in federal trials at a particular point in our history, but rather directed federal courts to 'continue the evolutionary development of testimonial privileges.'"[15]

The effect of the Supreme Court's actions with respect to FRE 501 and the federal common law of privileges are discussed in the sections of this chapter dealing with spousal privileges and the psychotherapist-patient privilege. Equally as significant, however, is the effect of the **Proposed Privilege Rules** (those privilege rules drafted but not adopted as the FRE) upon the states. Many of the provisions of those draft rules were adopted by various states. Thus, there is now greater uniformity among the states with respect to the various privileges than there was before the FRE were proposed, though some relationships, including social worker–patient, various types of victim counselors, accountant-client, and news reporter–source, are not recognized as privileged in many states.

PROPOSED
PRIVILEGE RULES
Those privilege rules drafted but not adopted as the Federal Rules of Evidence.

General Principles

Some general principles apply to all privileges. A few of these principles will also be discussed in the following sections dealing with specific privileges. However, introducing the principles now will lead to a better general understanding of the nature of privileges.

The matter of when and where a privilege may be recognized is important. Usually, a rule of evidence applies only in court proceedings. However, privileges are recognized in all proceedings, even those in which the rules of evidence do not apply. For example, the rules of evidence do not apply in preliminary determinations made by the judge, but privilege rules always apply in all proceedings.

A privilege is held by one or more of the persons involved in the privileged relationship. Most privileges cover only two persons, but there can be more, for example, when two or more people consult with an attorney together. Usually, all of the persons in the relationship hold the privilege, meaning they are capable of asserting the privilege and therefore need not answer questions before a judge and jury. However, if no one is present to assert the privilege, in some circumstances, the court is obligated to assert it on behalf of the holder. A holder of a privilege has the power to waive it.

HOLDER OF A
PRIVILEGE
That person who benefits from the privilege and who has the power to waive it.

The **holder of a privilege** can waive the privilege by either disclosing a significant part of the communication or consenting to disclosure of the communication by someone else. The waiver must be made without coercion. Failure to claim a privilege when a holder is able to do so may waive the privilege. If a holder of a privilege waives it for any purpose, it is waived for every other purpose. If two or more persons hold a privilege, such as when several people consult with an attorney, waiver by one holder does not usually affect the right of the other to claim the privilege.

If a privilege is claimed by a holder of it but there are questions as to whether the privilege should be recognized, the trial judge determines if the privilege exists and to whom it belongs. This issue will be argued by attorneys for each side in a **hearing *in camera***, which the judge conducts for this purpose in chambers, with only the privilege holder and the attorneys present.

Finally, many jurisdictions prohibit any attorney or the court from commenting upon a person's invocation of a privilege at trial. Where this rule is in effect, the jury will be instructed that it may not draw any inference from the invocation of the privilege. This instruction applies to the credibility of the witness as well as any matter at issue in the proceeding.

HEARING *IN CAMERA*
A judge's consideration, privately, in chambers, of the validity of a claim; here, specifically, a claim that a privilege does or does not exist.

Competency Versus Privileged Relationships

Privileged relationships do not necessarily bar the persons involved from becoming witnesses. The existence of a privileged relationship merely restricts what testimony may be given from the witness stand. In other words, if information is gained as a result of the confidential relationship, the persons involved may wish to refrain or be prohibited from revealing this information. So, a witness who has knowledge of a privileged communication may still testify as to any matter *except* the content of the privileged communication. But still the witness may testify to the privileged communication only if the privilege holder waives the privilege. The privilege may be waived by the privilege holder by explicitly waiving the privilege, consenting to the testimony, or failing to claim the privilege in a timely manner.

HUSBAND AND WIFE RELATIONSHIP

The relationship of husband and wife is fundamental in American society. Therefore, it is not surprising that the law has long sought to encourage harmony within the marital relationship by recognizing that the privacy between husband and wife should be granted the status of a privilege. There are actually two distinct privileges applicable to the husband and wife relationship. One is a rule of disqualification as a witness, which is actually a rule of incompetence or disqualification. The other is the communications privilege. Each will be treated separately.

Spousal Incapacity or Disqualification

The rule that disqualifies one spouse from testifying against another has a long history. It actually results from two medieval canons of jurisprudence. The first was the rule that an accused was incompetent as a witness because of interest in the outcome of the case. In other words, a criminal defendant, like any party to a case was incompetent to be a witness. The second was the principle that husband and wife were one. In 1980, the United States Supreme Court considered the spousal incapacity privilege under federal law in the case of *Trammel v. United States*.[16] At the time of the decision, 33 states recognized the privilege but treated it in three different ways under state evidence law. The Court pointed out that, in some states, one spouse was incompetent to testify against the other in a criminal proceeding. In other states, there existed a privilege against adverse spousal testimony that could be asserted by either spouse or by the defendant-spouse alone. In yet other states, only the spouse called as a witness was allowed to assert

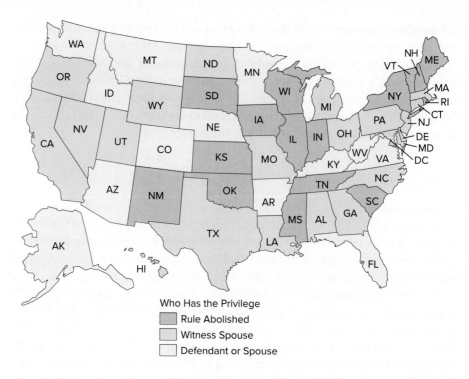

FIGURE 4–2 Spousal incapacity rule.

Who Has the Privilege
- Rule Abolished
- Witness Spouse
- Defendant or Spouse

SPOUSAL INCAPACITY
PRIVILEGE
The marital privilege that
gives a spouse called to
testify against his or her
spouse the privilege to
refuse to testify.

the privilege and refuse to testify against the defendant-spouse. In the remaining states, the privilege had been abolished in criminal cases.

The Court in *Trammel* concluded that the **spousal incapacity privilege** is held only by the spouse acting as a witness. The Court reasoned that "[w]hen one spouse is willing to testify against the other in a criminal proceeding—whatever the motivation—their relationship is almost certainly in disrepair."[17] In that circumstance, the justification for the privilege—marital harmony—no longer exists.

So, *Trammel* set the rule for federal criminal trials, not as a constitutional requirement but as an evidence rule within the Supreme Court's supervisory power over the federal judiciary. Thus, the states may still design their own evidence rules on this subject. As reflected in Figure 4-2, as of 2018, 16 states have abolished the spousal incapacity rule; 21 follow *Trammel*, holding that only the witness spouse can assert the privilege (if called as a witness); and 13 states allow either the defendant *or* the witness/spouse to assert the privilege. Remember, this is the law with respect to the spousal incapacity privilege. The law regarding the marital communications privilege is described next.

Marital Communications Privilege

Up to this point, the discussion has been primarily concerned with whether one spouse could testify for or against the other because of the marriage relationship. Another issue is what protection should be given to information that is gained strictly through communication during the marriage. This problem may arise in two different situations: first, in those cases in which a spouse is willing to testify against the other and, second, when there has been a dissolution of the marriage and one spouse is called upon to testify about communication between spouses during the time that the marriage was intact. It is an accepted fact that, for a successful and wholesome marriage relationship to exist, there must be a free exchange of communication between spouses. The law recognizes this relationship as one in which the mutual exchange of confidential information not only is encouraged but must take place. Consequently, the privileged communications doctrine is made applicable to the husband-wife relationship.

To promote the institution of marriage, any communication between spouses during the marriage is privileged. This privilege is known as the **marital communications privilege**. If the communication was intended to be a confidential one, was communicated between spouses, did not involve a crime upon one of the spouses by the other, and was not overheard by a third person, the communication is privileged and cannot be the subject of testimony by a spouse, even after the marriage has been dissolved by divorce, an annulment, or death. In other words, situations may arise in which a spouse may not be able to testify concerning confidential matters communicated during the marriage, even though the couple are no longer married.

It is well known that many private conversations take place between a husband and wife. These conversations pertain to many things, even to crimes committed or acts of misconduct. Such communications are considered confidential. Under the privilege, a spouse cannot reveal this information in court when the privilege is claimed by either spouse, even after the marriage has been dissolved. A few jurisdictions do not recognize the privileged communications doctrine when the communication pertains to criminal acts; however, others extend the privilege doctrine to all confidential exchanges of information, even though the marriage has been dissolved and the information pertains to crimes. This is based upon the theory that one spouse should not be made hesitant about revealing to the other some secret for fear that it might someday be revealed in court should a divorce take place. It is believed that by this freedom of exchange of confidential information, the dissolution of marriages may be avoided.

The privilege for confidential communications between spouses is not to be confused with information gained by one spouse concerning the other that was not exchanged in confidence between the two. For example, assume a wife observes her husband rob a service station. In most jurisdictions, the wife cannot be compelled to testify against her husband as long as the marriage is intact. But, once the marriage is dissolved, she can be compelled to testify against her former husband because she did not gain her information as a result of any confidential exchange of communications. On the other hand, if the wife did not see her husband rob the service station, but the husband came home and in private told his wife that he had committed the robbery, in most jurisdictions the wife could not testify about this confidential information, even though the marriage had been dissolved.

Information Gained Before Marriage

In those jurisdictions in which the husband-wife relationship prohibits one from testifying against the other, the prohibition relates to all matters, regardless of when the information was gained. It includes knowledge of facts learned prior to the marriage, as well as during the marriage. If it can be proved that the marriage was carried out under false pretenses, i.e., that it took place merely to prevent the testimony, the privilege will not apply, since the reason for the rule, to protect the sanctity of marriage, does not, in fact, exist. Nor does the privilege apply in cases in which the marriage was void from the outset, for example, an incestuous marriage.

Once the marriage has been dissolved by divorce or annulment, the rule prohibiting one spouse from testifying against the other changes. Testimony concerning information gained before marriage may then be compelled. However, even in such cases, the spouse serving as a witness is prohibited from testifying to the contents of communications that occurred during the marriage.

Crime or Fraud Exception

An exception to the spousal incapacity and marital communications privilege exists when one spouse commits a crime or fraud against the other. The basis for the privilege lies in society's desire to foster the relationship between marital partners. When one of the partners threatens or commits a crime or fraud upon the other, this so threatens the fabric of the relationship as to destroy it. In short, there is no longer any harmony in the home to protect.

For this reason, most states have enacted laws allowing a spouse to testify about crimes or frauds threatened or committed. In most jurisdictions, the victimized spouse can be compelled to testify, irrespective of his or her wishes.

Communication Between Husband and Wife Heard by Third Persons

The first requirement for any confidential communication to be within a privilege is that the communication be made in confidence. If the communication is made *directly in the presence of others*, who themselves are not in a confidential relationship with the spouses, then the first requirement is not met. Nothing prevents the third person who overhears a communication between spouses from revealing that communication. Therefore, communications between spouses in the presence of others are not privileged.

Slightly different considerations are involved when spousal communications are *overhead by a third person indirectly*. Two sets of circumstances may apply in such a situation. In the first, the spouses could anticipate a third party overhearing the communication. In the second, the couple could not anticipate being heard. This includes a situation in which the third party is an intentional eavesdropper. In cases in which the husband and wife speak in public, or when they should know other people can hear them, the privilege is not recognized. For example, if a married couple is at home with guests in the next room and they speak to one another loud enough for the guests to hear, their communication is not in confidence.

On the other hand, if the couple exchanges confidences under circumstances where they would not expect anyone to overhear, the privilege still applies. For example, assume the party is over and the couple believes all the guests have departed, but one person remains, unobserved by the couple. If the husband and wife were to exchange confidences not knowing of the presence of the guest, and they could not be expected to have anticipated that anyone would overhear them, many states would recognize the privilege. Similarly, if the husband and wife were to exchange confidences in the privacy of their bedroom, but, unbeknownst to them, an eavesdropper were lurking outside their bedroom, then that exchange would be entitled to the cloak of the privilege in most jurisdictions. This is so whether the eavesdropper gains access to the conversation by electronic means or by simply drawing near and listening.

If the interception of the communication is due to the betrayal or connivance of one spouse, most jurisdictions hold that the privilege applies. The rationale is that the spouse would not be able to disclose confidential spousal communications, and therefore should not be able to circumvent the privilege through betrayal or connivance.

PARENT-CHILD PRIVILEGE

The recognition of a parent-child privilege is a recent development in the law of the United States. Support for it has grown largely from the realities of life. Even judges and respected members of society confess that they would perjure themselves rather than testify against their children, which "reflects traditions regarding the sanctity of family ties."[18] As one commentator puts it in arguing for such a privilege,[19]

> Imagine that your teenage child calls and asks you to pick him or her up from a corner near the party he or she was attending. When you arrive, you see your child's clothing smeared with blood. Without thinking, you ask, "What happened?" Though this instinctive human response of a parent to a child in trouble is developmentally correct, it is risky as a matter of law [absent a parent-child privilege], because the same knowledge that helps the parent understand how best to help the child exposes the parent to the risk of being served with a government subpoena to testify against that child.

The public sentiment in favor of a parent-child privilege peaked in outraged reaction to special prosecutor Kenneth Starr's subpoenaing Monica Lewinsky's mother to learn the intimate details of Monica's relationship with President Clinton. The sentiment grew so strong that two bills came before Congress to enact a federal parent-child privilege, though no laws have been enacted to date.

Many commentators and jurists support the enactment of this privilege. In the mid-1990s, the Criminal Justice Section of the Defense Function Committee of the American Bar Association proposed the ABA Model Parent-Child Privileges Statute. Under the scheme envisioned by the ABA, there are two privileges: First, section 102 of the proposed act establishes an adverse testimonial privilege that protects parents and children from testifying when either is a defendant in any type of criminal proceeding, including those before a grand jury. The privilege is inapplicable when "the proceeding concerns an offense against the person or property of the witness or a family member that is purported to have been committed by the witness's parent or child" and when there is joint criminal activity. Second, section 103 establishes a jointly held confidential communications privilege that may be asserted by a parent or child when either is a party to any proceeding, including those before a grand jury. Exceptions to the privilege exist where the parent and child are opposing parties jointly involved in criminal activity or where the parent or child is a party in any criminal or juvenile proceeding, if the basis of the proceeding is alleged acts committed against the person or property of a family member.[20]

Currently, only five jurisdictions recognize a parent-child privilege: New York's privilege is established in a judicial decision,[21] and the privileges in Connecticut, Idaho, Massachusetts, and Minnesota are established by statute.

ATTORNEY-CLIENT PRIVILEGE

The attorney-client relationship is another one in which the law recognizes a privilege. It is mentioned in the old Roman laws and was adopted early in English judicial procedure. There are a number of justifications for the attorney-client privilege. One is that maintaining a confidential exchange between an attorney and his or her client makes for a more orderly court procedure. At one time, people brought their own cases into court and adversaries defended themselves. As time went on, court procedures grew steadily more complex. As a result, providing officers of the court to assist the litigants became necessary. These officers are known as barristers, attorneys, or lawyers, and they are still considered to be officers of the court. It is through their efforts that the rules of evidence are followed and that trials run more smoothly.

Another reason for the attorney-client privilege is to reduce undue or excessive litigation. A client being free to communicate all the facts, even unfavorable ones, to an attorney allows the attorney to assess more accurately the merits of taking the matter to trial or whether to accept the client's employment at all.

Public policy in the United States demands that the exchange of information between an attorney and a client be kept confidential. In criminal matters, the "right to counsel" is a constitutional guarantee. If this guarantee is to be given its full force and effect, there must be a free exchange of communications without fear that information will work to the detriment of the client.

The point in time at which such an attorney-client relationship is created, and whether there is such a relationship, can be problematic. Therefore, defining who is an attorney and who is a client becomes necessary. An **attorney** is one who is authorized to practice law in a given state or nation. A **client** is one who goes to an attorney seeking professional services or advice. To be licensed, the attorney must have complied with certain rules of the legal profession set forth in the various states' statutes.

There is no problem in the attorney-client relationship when a client consults an attorney who is properly licensed to practice law in the state in which the consultation takes place. Such a person definitely falls within the definition of an attorney. However, the status of the purported attorney is not

FYI

An event occurred in connection with the first criminal trial of O.J. Simpson that bears upon the issue of what constitutes an attorney-client relationship. Mr. Simpson delivered one of his travel bags to Robert Kardashian upon his return from Chicago, the day after the murders of Nicole Brown Simpson and Ron Goldman. At that time, Mr. Kardashian was not actively licensed to practice law in California because he was on inactive status. He had not paid dues and did not need an active attorney's license for the work he was doing at the time. Such inactive status for lawyers is not unusual. Since Mr. Kardashian was not then technically a lawyer in California, he could not claim any attorney-client privilege on behalf of Mr. Simpson with respect to the bag or its contents, unless Mr. Simpson could claim that he believed Mr. Kardashian was still acting as a lawyer. The issue was never litigated, however, because the prosecution never sought to recover the bag or its contents.

ATTORNEY
One who is authorized to practice law in a given state or nation.

CLIENT
One who goes to an attorney seeking professional services or advice.

always so clear in some situations, such as when the attorney has failed to renew his or her license to practice, is licensed in another state, or has completed law school but has not taken or passed the bar examination. Another ambiguous situation occurs when the client consults with a person whom the client believes to be an attorney but that person is, in fact, not an attorney. There is also ambiguity when the client communicates with an attorney's secretary, paralegal, investigator, or law clerk.

In the past, these situations plagued the courts. Now, however, a majority of jurisdictions have dealt with these problems by recognizing the privilege whenever a client reasonably believes the person he or she is consulting is an attorney licensed in any state or nation. Also, the attorney-client privilege has been extended to any communication between the client and any person present to further the interest of the client, including employees or agents of the attorney, such as secretaries, paralegals, investigators, and clerks.

When Is the Privilege Created?

The rules concerning the time when the relationship of an attorney and a client is created are clear and universally recognized. The moment a client consults an attorney on legal matters, the attorney-client relationship, and hence the privilege, is created. This is true even if the attorney rejects the case or the client decides to seek other counsel. The right of a client and an attorney to confer and exchange information to enable both to make a choice is a necessary part of the privileged-communications rule. If the privileged-communications rule were otherwise, a client would have to accept the first attorney who would handle a case for a fee without knowing any facts of the case. There need be no agreement concerning payment or fee for the attorney-client relationship to be created.

MYTH ▶	◀ FACT
For the attorney-client privilege to exist, the client must "hire" the attorney or pay a retainer.	The attorney-client relationship comes into being the moment that a person consults with an attorney for legal advice, regardless of whether any payment for services is made or the attorney takes the case.

MYTH ▶	◀ FACT
While a client is speaking with an attorney, the presence of another person violates the attorney-client privilege.	There are a number of people who may be present during an attorney-client consultation without destroying the privilege. Anyone who is an employee or agent of the attorney, whose presence is necessary to carry out the attorney's mission, including secretaries, paralegals, law clerks, investigators, and experts, will not destroy the privilege.

Communications Made in the Presence of a Third Person

As stated in the introduction to the subject of privileges, the first requirement for a privilege is that the communication in question must be made in confidence. Thus, if a client and an attorney communicate in the presence of others, on the face of the situation, it cannot be said that the communication was intended to be confidential. In addition, the communication must pertain to the attorney-client relationship. The "third person" confidentiality requirement does not apply to the presence of agents or employees of the attorney whose presence is necessary, such as a secretary. This also includes an agent of the client who, while acting for the client, furnishes information to the attorney.

However, if a communication is made in the presence of someone who accompanied the client, the privilege rule is not applicable to either the third person or the attorney. The client, under these circumstances, will be found not to have intended the communication to be a confidential one. On the other hand, if the person who accompanied the client was also seeking the services of the attorney in the same case, the privilege would be binding on all present.

The Communication Between Attorney and Client

As in the case of the husband–wife relationship, it must be determined what is included in a privileged communication between an attorney and a client. In other words, does a privileged communication comprise oral and written statements only, or does it include acts? The general view is that any information a client furnishes to an attorney as a result of the professional status is considered to be a privileged communication. This includes oral and written statements and acts on the part of the client. If, during the consultation with the attorney, the client displays a gun, a sack of money, or scars or marks, these, too, fall within the privilege rule. These acts must have some connection with the case about which the attorney was being consulted in order to be covered under this privilege.

The attorney cannot be a depository for criminal evidence. The fact that the client turned the evidence over to the attorney may be privileged, but the attorney cannot withhold evidence from the court. Therefore, within a reasonable time, the attorney who has come into possession of such evidence must take steps to turn it over to the proper authorities while maintaining the attorney-client privilege with respect to the source of the evidence. An example of this is an infamous manila envelope delivered by the defense to a magistrate in the O.J. Simpson criminal trial. The public never found out what was in that envelope because it was turned over to the magistrate (a judicial officer not involved in the trial) for her eyes only. Trial watchers speculated that the defense found a knife that Mr. Simpson had bought and that the prosecution was claiming was the murder weapon. The prosecution had searched for the knife but was unable to locate it. At the preliminary hearing, the state introduced evidence about Mr. Simpson's purchase of the knife, but no other evidence about the knife was ever introduced. The world will probably never know for sure what was actually in the manila envelope.

A client may make a complete confession to an attorney about a crime. If this confession is made during the consultation on the case, the attorney cannot reveal the information. Even if the client confesses, the attorney may still have the client enter a plea of "not guilty" and endeavor to get an acquittal for the client. This may seem to be a parody of justice. However, under the American system of criminal justice, and based on the Constitution, the defense attorney is required to do this. The Constitution places the burden of proof in a criminal case upon the prosecution, and the defendant is presumed innocent until proven guilty beyond a reasonable doubt by a fair trial.

Many lawyers cannot go this far with a clear conscience. Those lawyers may find it impossible to defend a person who has confessed to a crime or one who they think is guilty. For that reason, those attorneys will not accept the case, which is their prerogative. In this instance, any information exchanged between the defendant and an attorney who subsequently does not accept the case is still considered privileged. It is important to remember that under the American criminal justice system, even the guilty are entitled to assistance of counsel and a fair trial.

Crimes Exception to Attorney-Client Privilege

The attorney-client privilege does not apply when a person consults an attorney concerning the commission of a future crime or for the purpose of concealing the defendant after a crime has been committed. The policy of the privilege is to promote the administration of justice. It would then be a perversion of the privilege to allow a client to seek advice from an attorney to aid in carrying out an illegal scheme or assist in the furtherance of a crime or fraud. If an attorney should become involved in a crime or conspire to commit a crime, the attorney and the client become associated in the crime and the privilege does not exist.

Waiver of the Privilege

Rarely will the accused in a criminal case be called upon by the circumstances to waive the attorney-client privilege. However, it does happen. It is possible for a witness to be asked to waive the privilege. The client, as the holder of the attorney-client privilege, has the power to waive it.

PHYSICIAN-PATIENT AND PSYCHOTHERAPIST-PATIENT PRIVILEGES

Many people are surprised to learn that historically there was no physician-patient privilege. The common law did not recognize it, it was not included in the FRE, and even the Supreme Court of the United States did not recognize it. In recent times, however, the need for privacy between doctor and patient has been deemed important enough to warrant a privilege. And the person who seeks psychological support has been protected even before recognition of the privilege between patient and doctor. This is so because a patient with a mental difficulty will frequently seek help only if assured that his or her communications will remain totally confidential.

Physician-Patient Privilege

The common law did not recognize a privilege for communications between patients and their doctors. Although doctors may have been under a professional obligation to be discreet, they could be forced to testify when called as a witness. New York was the first state to adopt a statutory physician-patient privilege in 1828.[22] Most states today have a physician-patient privilege, but a few still do not (Alabama, Florida, Georgia, Kentucky, Maryland, Massachusetts, South Carolina, Tennessee, and West Virginia). Also, there is no federal physician-patient privilege.

The Health Insurance Portability and Accountability Act of 1996 (HIPAA), however, authorized the United States Department of Health and Human Services (HHS) to adopt regulations governing standards for the security and privacy of health information. Generally, these standards provide for disclosure of medical information only under certain conditions. In addition, the standards provide a right of privacy for medical information to patients—i.e., they must be notified of the circumstances under which the information will be disclosed. However, this is not a privilege, in that, if the requester and health plan comply with HIPAA, the information will be disclosed. Because it is a federal law, HIPAA preempts any state laws relating to the disclosure of medical records, unless the particular state's law is more stringent.

Most significantly, the Proposed Rules, which have dramatically affected the state privilege laws since the early 1970s, had no provision for a physician-patient privilege, although they did have provision for a psychotherapist-patient privilege. FRE 501 provides that, in cases in which the law of a particular state applies (principally, civil cases involving diversity of citizenship suits), the privilege law of that state also applies. However, even in such a case, if the law of the state does provide for a physician-patient privilege, federal courts may refuse to recognize the privilege, since there is none under federal common law.[23] Even in those states that have recognized the privilege, there are numerous exceptions

In addition to reporting gunshot wounds to the police, the attending physician must reveal in court anything the victim tells him or her regarding the circumstances of the shooting.

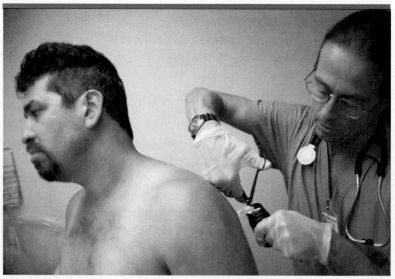

©Mark Richards/PhotoEdit

MYTH ▶	◀ FACT
The physician-patient privilege is universally recognized.	The physician-patient privilege is not universal; it does not exist in common law, in federal common law, and in a number of states. If, while investigating a case in Alabama, Kentucky, Maryland, Massachusetts, South Carolina, Tennessee, or West Virginia, a law enforcement officer encounters a doctor who is withholding pertinent information, the officer could remind the physician of this fact.

among them excluding this privilege in criminal cases. In most states, if a party makes his or her mental or physical condition an issue in a case, the privilege is waived. These two exceptions to the privilege make it irrelevant even in those states where it exists. In addition, in most states doctors are required to report gunshot wounds.

There is a twofold rationale for the physician-patient privilege. First, the privilege exists in the interest of maintaining the patient's privacy in matters pertinent to medical diagnosis and treatment. Second, similar to the attorney-client privilege, the law's policy promotes full and free communication between patient and physician. In the absence of the privilege, patients may be deterred from giving the doctor complete information. However, this justification is not universally accepted. In the 1996 case of *Jaffee v. Redmond,*[24] a case that actually dealt with a person seeking psychotherapy, the United States Supreme Court also addressed the issue of physician-patient privilege. The Court pointed out that there is no compelling need for confidences in the physician-patient setting. The Court stated that "[t]reatment by a physician for physical ailments can often proceed successfully on the basis of a physical examination, objective information supplied by the patient, and the results of diagnostic tests."[25]

Psychotherapist-Patient Privilege

The psychotherapist-patient privilege is even newer than the physician-patient privilege, but it is recognized in all 50 states, the District of Columbia, and, since June 1996, all federal courts.[26] Most states place the physician-patient and psychotherapist-patient privilege in the same statute or code provision. However, in many states, the two privileges are separate, and the reach of the psychotherapist privilege is much greater than that of the physician privilege because the class of professionals qualifying as psychotherapists is quite broad.

The breadth of the privilege is necessary to extend coverage to patients who seek psychotherapy from a nonphysician therapist. The psychotherapist-patient privilege is supported by stronger policy justifications than the doctor-patient privilege; as a result, some states have adopted only the therapist-patient privilege. A psychotherapist is more likely to be the recipient of damaging, embarrassing, and personal information than an ordinary doctor. Moreover, deterrence is a more significant consideration. Patients would be less likely to go to a psychotherapist if there were a threat that information exchanged would be made public.

A **patient** within this privilege is any person who consults a psychotherapist or physician for the purpose of the diagnosis or the treatment of a mental or emotional condition. A **psychotherapist** is a person who has been authorized to practice medicine and devotes a substantial portion of his or her time to the practice of psychiatry or a person who is recognized by the laws of the particular jurisdiction as a certified psychologist. Thus, the privilege applies to licensed psychiatrists and psychologists. However, a number of jurisdictions extend the privilege to other licensed professionals who engage in psychotherapy, for example, licensed social workers and various types of victim counselors, such as sexual abuse and domestic violence counselors.

PATIENT
Any person who consults a psychotherapist or physician for the purpose of the diagnosis or the treatment of a mental or emotional condition.

PSYCHOTHERAPIST
A person who has been authorized to practice medicine and devotes a substantial portion of his or her time to the practice of psychiatry or a person who is recognized by the laws of the particular jurisdiction as a certified psychologist. Some jurisdictions extend the definition to include social workers.

APPLICATION CASE

In *Jaffee v. Redmond*,[27] the United States Supreme Court recognized a psychotherapist-patient privilege under federal law. In doing so, the Court relied upon FRE 501's authority to create common law privileges when reason and experience require it. Moreover, the Court declared that the privilege extends not only to licensed psychiatrists and psychologists but also to licensed social workers engaged in psychotherapy.

In *Jaffee,* the survivors of a man shot and killed by a police officer sued the officer and the village by which the officer was employed. The officer was responding to the scene of a "fight in progress" when the shooting occurred. The officer later participated in over 50 counseling sessions with a licensed clinical social worker. The plaintiffs wanted access to the social worker's notes to use at the trial. The Supreme Court held that the notes contained privileged communications and, therefore, could not be obtained or used by the plaintiffs.

Confidences expressed by the patient that may assist in the diagnosis or treatment by a psychotherapist are privileged, even though they may pertain to criminal matters. Generally, there is little in the way of physician-patient communication that would pertain to criminal matters and would assist the physician in the treatment of the patient. In the case of a psychotherapist, however, it may be necessary for the patient to make a full disclosure of crime-related facts that may be causing some mental or emotional disturbance in order for proper treatment to take place. This disclosure could even entail confession. In these circumstances, the communications are privileged.

Exceptions to Privilege

There are a few situations in which the psychotherapist-patient privilege is not recognized. One instance is when an accused is charged with a criminal act and raises the defense of insanity or mental distress, thus making the accused's mental state an issue. The need to have access to the accused's mental processes by both the prosecution and defense has led to an exception to the privilege in most jurisdictions.

APPLICATION CASE

The California Supreme Court, in *Tarasoff v. Regents of University of California*,[28] held that, when a therapist determines, or pursuant to the standards of his or her profession should determine, that his or her patient presents a serious danger of violence to another, the therapist incurs an obligation to use reasonable care to protect the intended victim against such danger. In *Tarasoff,* a college student at a University of California campus consulted a university therapist for depression, making statements that he intended to harm a woman friend whom he viewed as having jilted him. The therapist, after consulting with colleagues, decided not to break the confidentiality of the therapy sessions and did not take any steps to identify, locate, and warn the woman mentioned by the patient. The patient went to the woman's home and murdered her. The case involved the right of the woman's family to sue the university.

Another exception to the privilege exists in most states if the psychotherapist has reasonable cause to believe that the patient is in such mental or emotional condition as to be dangerous to himself or herself, or to another person or another's property, and that disclosure of the communications is necessary to prevent the threatened danger. This is called the **dangerous patient exception** to the privilege. There is yet another exception to the privilege that exists in most states: if the psychotherapist has reasonable cause to believe that the patient is involved in child or elder abuse, as either the perpetrator or the victim.

DANGEROUS PATIENT EXCEPTION
An exception to psychotherapist-patient privilege, existing in most states, which provides that, if the psychotherapist has reasonable cause to believe that the patient is in such mental or emotional condition as to be dangerous to himself or herself, or to another person or another's property, the disclosure of the communications is necessary to prevent the threatened danger.

APPLICATION CASE

In *Menendez v. Superior Court*,[29] the California Supreme Court considered a claim of the psychotherapist-patient privilege. The Menendez brothers were charged with murdering their mother and father. In the case, the prosecution sought to obtain from the brothers' psychotherapist audiotapes containing recordings of four therapy sessions in which information was transmitted in the course of the relationship. The prosecution wished to use the tapes at the brothers' trial. The therapist-patient privilege was asserted. The court found that the tapes of all four therapy sessions were privileged communications, but it also found that the tapes of two of the sessions were admissible in evidence as being within the dangerous patient exception to the psychotherapist-patient privilege.

The court held that the two tapes were not privileged because they involved threats by the brothers against the doctor, the doctor's spouse, and the doctor's lover, and disclosure was necessary to prevent any harm. Under the dangerous patient exception, the court held that the doctor was authorized to disclose the danger to the people threatened because the doctor had a duty to avert danger to others. In addition, however, the court held that the dangerous patient exception also acts to destroy the privilege generally. The protective privilege ends when public peril begins. Therefore, the portions of the audiotapes that contained threats to the doctor or others were not privileged and were admissible in evidence.

CLERGY-COMMUNICANT PRIVILEGE

The common law did not recognize a privilege for the exchange of information between a member of the clergy and a parishioner. Nonetheless, as a practical matter, the law had to adjust to accept the privilege because Catholic priests were forbidden to break the secrecy of the confessional and would rather go to prison than reveal communicants' confessions. A privilege protecting confidential communications between clergy and communicants has now been adopted in all of the 50 states and is recognized as part of the federal common law.[30]

The practicality of this privilege was recognized early in Anglo-American history. Even one of the great eighteenth-century criminal justice thinkers, Jeremy Bentham, an arch-critic of privileges in general (and the attorney-client privilege in particular), acknowledged the futility of trying to force the clergy to breach the seal of the confessional.[31] Clergy who are bound by secrecy of the confessional will not violate that trust, regardless of the command of the civil law. Therefore, it is understandable that the civil law developed a privilege recognizing this reality. Moreover, because of our society's religious heritage, public policy demands that a person be permitted to confess sins and seek spiritual guidance without the fear that those confessions will be revealed.

A member of the **clergy** is a priest, minister, religious practitioner, or similar functionary who has been ordained by a religious denomination or organization. Today, the term "religious advisor" is commonly used in the criminal justice system as a generic description. A **communicant** is one who seeks out the clergy in a religious capacity for the purpose of securing spiritual advice. In most jurisdictions, the privilege has developed to cover any person who desires to speak in confidence to someone in the professional role of a spiritual advisor.

In the past, in order to fall within the privilege, the communication must have been a confession. Most jurisdictions today, however, define any communication for purposes of spiritual guidance as a privileged communication. A penitential communication is any communication between the penitent and the clergy that was made in confidence to assist the penitent in receiving spiritual aid. Just how far this definition can be extended is difficult to determine. For example, a penitent asking a minister to hide a gun used in a crime, or a sack of money stolen

CLERGY
Priests, ministers, religious practitioners, or similar functionaries who have been ordained by a religious denomination or organization.

COMMUNICANT
One who seeks out the clergy in a religious capacity for the purpose of securing spiritual advice.

in a crime, would not be considered a penitential communication. However, the privilege might apply if the request is made in connection with the penitent's desire to repent and then to take some action toward absolution.

A majority of jurisdictions consider the clergy-communicant relationship primarily for the benefit of the communicant and therefore hold that only the communicant may claim or waive the privilege. However, there are instances in which the law has granted the clergy the right to refuse to disclose a communicant's communication, even though the communicant has waived the privilege. This right has been granted to the clergy in some jurisdictions because certain religious denominations hold that it is a violation of church principles for the clergy to reveal penitential communications under any circumstances.

Legislators and courts have generally held that for a penitential communication to come within the privilege, the member of the clergy and the communicant do not have to belong to the same faith. All that is necessary is that the communicant seek the member of the clergy for the sincere purpose of spiritual guidance.

IDENTITY OF INFORMER PRIVILEGE

The identity of informer privilege is an offshoot of the well-established governmental privilege protecting military and state secrets established by the common law. The common law governmental privilege protects the government against compulsory disclosure of military, diplomatic, or other state secrets when it is in the best interest of the people to do so. This common law privilege has been embodied in the statutes of the various states and has been enlarged upon to permit government officials to keep certain information confidential. The statutes creating this privilege usually state words to the following effect: "The government has a privilege to refuse to give evidence and to prevent any person from giving evidence upon a showing of reasonable likelihood of danger that the evidence will disclose a secret of state or official information."[32] The identity of informer privilege that has been adopted in most jurisdictions is often patterned upon the language contained in the Proposed Federal Rules of Evidence:[33]

> The government or a state or subdivision thereof has a privilege to refuse to disclose the identity of a person who has furnished information relating to or assisting in an investigation of a possible violation of law to a law enforcement officer or member of a legislative committee or its staff conducting an investigation.

Such a statute, or rule of evidence, permits a law enforcement officer to withhold the identity of an informer *unless disclosure is necessary to the defendant's fair trial* on the merits. The purpose of this right was stated by the United States Supreme Court in the case of *Roviaro v. United States,* in which the Court said:[34]

> The purpose of the privilege is the furtherance and protection of the public interest in effective law enforcement. The privilege recognizes the obligation of citizens to communicate their knowledge of the commission of crimes to law enforcement officials and, by preserving their anonymity, encourages them to perform that obligation.

Although the Court spoke of the obligation of a person to report crimes to officials, generally there is no legal obligation as such to report knowledge of a crime. The common law provides that it is a crime to have knowledge of a serious crime and not report it. This crime is known as "misprision of a felony." Today, "misprision of a felony" is not a crime in most states; however, it is still a crime under federal law. In the *Roviaro* case, the courts realized that there is a need to encourage those who have such knowledge to come forward and report it. Common sense suggests that under certain circumstances a person may be reluctant to report information about criminal activities unless it can be done in complete secrecy.

Although the identity of informer privilege has been recognized, it is not absolute. The *Roviaro* case recognized the limitations upon the privilege:[35]

> The scope of the [officer-informant] privilege is limited by its underlying purpose. Thus, where the disclosure of the contents of a communication will not tend to reveal the identity of an informer, the contents are not privileged. Likewise, once the identity of the informer has been disclosed to those who would have cause to resent the communication the privilege is no longer applicable.
>
> A further limitation on the applicability of the privilege arises from the fundamental requirements of fairness. *Where the disclosure of an informer's identity, or of the contents of his communication, is relevant and helpful to the defense of the accused, or is essential to a fair determination of a cause, the privilege must give way.* In these situations the trial court may require disclosure and, if the government withholds the information, dismiss the action.

Thus, the identity of the informer may be required to be disclosed when there is a full trial on guilt or innocence and the accused needs the information in order to have a fair trial. As the *Roviaro* Court also stated, however, there is no fixed rule, and "[t]he problem is one that calls for balancing the public interest in protecting the flow of information against the individual's right to prepare his defense."[36] On the other hand, it is not necessary for the prosecution to reveal the identity of an informant who has provided information for a determination of probable cause under most circumstances. The United States Supreme Court, in *McCray v. Illinois,*[37] held that, where the officer testifies to the underlying information provided by an informer supporting a probable cause determination, the officer need not identify the informer. The Court pointed out that the *Roviaro* case did not involve a preliminary hearing, but the trial on the issue of guilt or innocence. *McCray* held that nothing in the Constitution required the privilege to be waived under the circumstances.

As a result of the right of discovery in many states, which is discussed in detail in Chapter 12, the number of instances in which an officer has had to reveal the identity of the informant has deprived the identity of informer privilege of some of its significance. Furthermore, if knowledge of the existence, identity, or communications from an informer would provide evidence tending to exonerate the accused, the prosecution has an obligation to reveal such evidence to the defense under the Supreme Court's rule announced in *Brady v. Maryland.*[38] The *Brady* rule is also discussed in detail in Chapter 12. Finally, the Freedom of Information Act (FOIA), passed by Congress in 1966, and similar statutes passed by some state legislatures require the government to turn over information to the public upon request, with certain exceptions. Under the FOIA, the government is exempted from releasing information pertaining to confidential informants, but only if the government shows that the information was given with the express or implied promise that the identity of the informant would remain confidential. However, the determination of the status of information as confidential under the FOIA does not mean that if the defendant needs the information to achieve a fair trial the government may withhold the information when discovery in a criminal trial requires disclosure of the information.

APPLICATION CASE

In *United States Department of Justice v. Landano*,[39] an inmate convicted of murder of a police officer sought to obtain FBI files under the FOIA. The government claimed that it was entitled to a presumption that all sources supplying information to the FBI in the course of a criminal investigation are confidential sources entitled to protection against release of information under a certain provision of the FOIA. The Court held that no such presumption exists. The Court also noted that either discovery rules or the Constitution might require divulgence of the identity of an informer, including the circumstance where the informer was required to testify at trial. Even so, the Court held that the FOIA does not require release of an informer's identity and the information provided, if the informer's statement was initially given in confidence. Thus, even though the government is not entitled to a blanket exception from the FOIA for all informers' information, neither does the FOIA permit blanket release of informers' confidences merely because they might be discovered in a criminal trial under the discovery rules or the principles of *Roviaro* and *McCray*.

ACCOUNTANT-CLIENT PRIVILEGE

The common law holds no provisions for testimonial privilege for communications between a person and his or her accountant. Communications to accountants are privileged in 29 states (see Figure 4–3). No such privilege exists in federal law in criminal cases; however, since July 1998 there has been a federal confidentiality privilege relating to taxpayer communications. A communication between a taxpayer and a federally authorized practitioner is a privileged communication if it would be a common law privileged communication between a taxpayer and an attorney. This privilege only applies to any noncriminal tax matter before the Internal Revenue Service and any noncriminal tax proceeding in federal court brought by or against the United States.

Federal courts dealing with issues in state cases have even refused to apply the state accountant-client privilege statute but have adhered to the common law rule.[40] The state privileges are narrow, applying mostly to communications between clients and certified public accountants. Most have a crime-fraud provision like the attorney-client privilege and do not allow the privilege to interfere with bankruptcy proceedings.

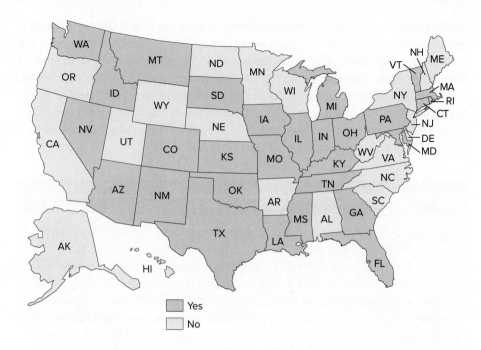

FIGURE 4–3 States that have adopted the accountant-client privilege.

Yes
No

NEWS REPORTER–NEWS SOURCE PRIVILEGE

The protection of news reporters against the compulsory disclosure of sources of information was not recognized as common law, but a qualified privilege has been recognized by the federal government and a number of states. Prior to 1972, news reporters sought to have news sources recognized as privileged. They did not want to have to reveal sources of information or even to be compelled to appear before grand jury hearings or other judicial proceedings. Reporters claimed this privilege under the "freedom of the press" guarantee of the First Amendment to the United States Constitution.

This First Amendment-based privilege was rejected by the United States Supreme Court in *Branzburg v. Hayes*,[41] in which the Court ruled that the First Amendment guarantee of freedom of the press does not afford any privilege to a newspaper reporter from appearing before a grand jury or other judicial proceeding, nor from revealing the identity of news and information sources. The Court in that case stated:[42]

> The public through its elected and appointed law enforcement officers regularly utilizes informers, and in proper circumstances they may assert a privilege against disclosing the identity of these informers. But the purpose of the privilege is the furtherance and protection of the public interest in effective law enforcement. . . . [But] such informers enjoy no constitutional protection. Their testimony is available to the public when desired by the grand juries or at criminal trials; their identity cannot be concealed from the defendant when it is critical to his case. . . .

As noted previously, the common law recognized no such [news reporter] privilege, and the constitutional argument was not even asserted until 1958. From the beginning of our country, the press has operated without constitutional protection for press informants, and the press has flourished. The existing constitutional rules have not been a serious obstacle to either the development or retention of confidential news sources by the press. . . .

We see no reason to hold that [news] reporters, any more than other citizens, should be excused from furnishing information that may help a grand jury in arriving at its initial determinations.

The *Branzburg* decision merely held that the First Amendment guarantee of freedom of the press did not *automatically* grant a news reporter-source privilege. That decision did not bar Congress or state legislatures from passing statutes that would grant some protection to news reporters relating to their news sources. As a result, many courts and state legislatures have, by judicial decision (12 state courts have adopted the qualified privilege) and by statute (34 states and the District of Columbia have enacted the privilege), granted the newspaper reporter the qualified privilege of not being held in contempt of court for refusing to reveal a source of information (see Figure 4-4). Most federal courts that have considered the issue have held that a qualified news reporter's privilege exists under federal law.[43] The privilege is qualified in the sense that the reporter's claim of privilege in any given case will be weighed by the trial judge to determine whether the information sought is vital to the prosecution or defense of a criminal case. If the trial judge determines that the information is vital, then the news reporter's privilege will yield. If the reporter refuses to reveal the information, he or she will be held in contempt until the information is forthcoming.

Two other issues relating to the news reporter-news source privilege are who is covered by the privilege and what information is within the privilege. The statutes that have been enacted granting a **news reporter** protection against revealing a news source have specified that those covered by the privilege include

NEWS REPORTER
A publisher, an editor, a reporter, or other person connected with or employed by a newspaper, magazine, or other periodical publication or by a radio or television station.

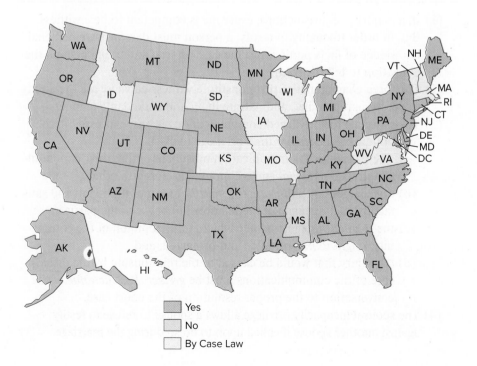

FIGURE 4–4 States that have adopted the news reporter–source privilege.

Yes
No
By Case Law

publishers, editors, reporters, and other persons connected with or employed by a newspaper, magazine, or other periodical publication or by a radio or television station. The privilege usually covers the information discovered by the reporter, including the sources and background data. Also included are the reporter's notes, photographs, tapes, and edited materials. Usually, it is the source of the information that is protected and not the information itself, as was stated in the case of *Lightman v. State*:[44]

> The Maryland [news reporter's privilege] does not protect against the disclosure of communications; it privileges only the source of the information and the privilege is not that of the informant but of the newsman. . . . Where a newsman, by dint of his own investigative efforts, personally observes conduct constituting the commission of criminal activities by persons at a particular location, the newsman, and not the persons observed, is the "source" of the news or information [and the privilege does not apply].

Thus, a news reporter may not refuse to appear in a judicial proceeding and furnish the requested information when commanded to do so without being held in contempt of court, but the news reporter may refuse to reveal the source of that information without being held in contempt in those jurisdictions in which the privilege is recognized.

REVIEW AND APPLICATION

SUMMARY

(1) In a majority of jurisdictions, everyone is competent to be a witness. But, in order to qualify to testify, a person must demonstrate personal knowledge of facts pertinent to the case on trial and to understand the obligation to tell the truth.

(2) The three characteristics that constitute witness capacity are the ability to perceive, remember, and narrate in an understandable manner.

(3) The rationale for privileged communications is best expressed in the four conditions necessary for a privilege to exist:

  (a) The parties to a communication must believe that their communication is *confidential* and will not be disclosed to others;

  (b) this element of *confidentiality must be essential* to the full and satisfactory maintenance of the relationship between the parties;

  (c) the *relationship* must be one which, in the opinion of the community, ought to be promoted and protected; and

  (d) the injury that would be caused to the relationship by the disclosure of the communications must be *greater than the value* of the conversation to the proper resolution of the court case.

(4) The spousal incapacity privilege allows a spouse to refuse to testify against another spouse if called upon to do so during the marriage.

The marital communications privilege operates to keep confidential all communications made during the marriage. The incapacity privilege is held by the witness-spouse and ends when the marriage ends. The communications privilege is held by both spouses and continues even after the marriage ends.

(5) The moment a client consults an attorney on legal matters, the attorney-client relationship, and hence the privilege, is created.

(6) The two exceptions to the physician-patient privilege that often make the rule irrelevant are the exception in criminal cases and the waiver of the privilege in civil cases if a party makes his or her mental or physical condition an issue in a case.

(7) Treatment by a physician for physical ailments can often proceed successfully on the basis of a physical examination, objective information supplied by the patient, and the results of diagnostic tests.

(8) The strong policy justification for the psychotherapist-patient privilege is that a psychotherapist is more likely to be the recipient of damaging, embarrassing, and personal information than an ordinary doctor. Moreover, deterrence is a more significant consideration. Patients would be less likely to go to a psychotherapist if there were a threat that information exchanged would be made public.

(9) The government may refuse to reveal the identity of an informer except at trial or such other time when it is found by the trial judge to be necessary to preserve the defendant's right to a fair trial.

(10) The news reporter's qualified privilege to refuse to reveal a news source yields when the trial judge finds that the information is vital for the prosecution or defense of a criminal case.

KEY TERMS

QUESTIONS FOR REVIEW

1. What are the general requirements for a person to be a witness?
2. What are the characteristics of witness capacity?
3. What is the rationale for privileged communications?
4. What is the spousal incapacity privilege? How does the marital communications privilege differ?
5. At what point in time is the attorney-client privilege created?

6. What aspect of the physician-patient privilege makes that privilege irrelevant in criminal cases?
7. Why, according to the United States Supreme Court, is there no compelling need for a physician-patient privilege?
8. What is the policy behind the psychotherapist-patient privilege?
9. When can the government refuse to reveal the identity of an informer?
10. When must a news reporter reveal his or her source?

THINKING CRITICALLY ABOUT EVIDENCE

1. You are having some remodeling done on the roof of your house and want to have a valid contract drawn up with the roofer. A good friend introduces you to her cousin and tells you that he practices "all kinds of law." You talk to the cousin and never ask any questions, but the cousin gives you the advice "on the house," telling you that the contract is fine. Six months later, when the snow is packed six inches high on your leaking roof, you discover that not only was the cousin's advice wrong but he had never been to law school and had received all his legal knowledge as a jail-house attorney during his latest prison sentence. Do you have any recourse?

2. According to the attorney-client privilege, attorneys must "seal their lips" if their client confesses to a crime and enter a "not guilty" plea if the client requests it. However, if the same client brings evidence of the same crime to the attorney, the attorney is required to turn it over to the prosecution. Why must attorneys keep a client's confession confidential but turn over any evidence revealed by their client?

3. Your neighbor is a used car salesman, yet he frequently buys new boats and furniture and takes exotic vacations. Recently, he claimed another one of his wealthy relatives had died, leaving him with yet another small fortune. You read in the local newspaper that your neighbor is suing his attorney for malpractice and embezzlement of client funds. You have been friends with the attorney since elementary school and believe her when she says that the car salesman has really been embezzling money from the car dealership. Is there any way that the attorney can prove her innocence without violating the attorney-client privilege?

WORKPLACE APPLICATIONS

1. You have been working in the Narcotics Unit for several years and have primarily focused on cocaine trafficking from South America. You have a confidential informant from Mexico who ranks high in an extremely violent cocaine ring that you have been targeting for about a year. The informant fed you confirmed, invaluable information for about six months prior to the biggest cocaine bust in the history of your state. The informant agreed to give you information only after you agreed to her complete anonymity and confidentiality. You are now called to testify at the preliminary hearing of several members of the drug ring who have been indicted. The defense attorneys are demanding to know the informant's identity, so that they can call

the informant. Write down the reasons that the informant's identity should not be revealed. Will the informant be required to testify? Why or why not?

2. Assume you are a police officer and are at the department's Policeman's Ball. You strike up a conversation with a man whom you previously did not know and discover that he is an attorney. Because you have been having landlord problems lately, you casually ask what your legal rights are in case the situation gets worse. You buy the man a drink but do not pay him for his advice, get his name, or even get his business card. Has an attorney-client privilege relationship begun?

3. Assume you are a police officer assigned as a canine handler and have just been named in a lawsuit. You, the rest of the officers on the scene, and the city council are being represented by the city attorney's office. The attorney in charge of your case sets a meeting to discuss the facts of the case; when you arrive, she tells you she is on her way to an unexpected meeting with a judge. She tells you that her capable law clerk is knowledgeable about the case and will be able to conduct the meeting. You discover that the law clerk is in her first year at law school. You discuss the case with the clerk without the attorney present. Has an attorney-client privilege been established?

ETHICAL DILEMMA

1. A citizen tells you that he will give you information only if you keep it confidential. The information is very valuable, but you know that you cannot keep it a secret if asked about it in court. The citizen is insistent. Do you give your word as an officer and agree to keep the information confidential, knowing that legally you can't?

ENDNOTES

1. Advisory Committee's note preceding Article VIII of Federal Rules of Evidence.

2. Reckard v. State, 234 A.2d 630, 633 (Md. Ct. Spec. App. 1967).

3. John Johnson, *Conviction Tossed After 19 Years,* L.A. Times, May 1, 2004, at B.

4. 497 U.S. 836 (1990).

5. 483 U.S. 107 (1987).

6. ___ U.S. ___, 135 S.Ct. 521 (2014).

7. ___ U.S. ___, 137 S.Ct. 855 (2017).

8. Jaffee v. Redmond (518) U.S. 1, 9 (1996), citing United States v. Bryan, 339 U.S. 323, 331 (1950) (quoting 8 John H. Wigmore, Evidence § 2192, p. 64 (3d ed. 1940)).

9. *Id.,* citing Trammel v. United States, 445 U.S. 40, 45 (1980), quoting Elkins v. United States, 364 U.S. 206, 234 (1960) (Frankfurter, J., dissenting).

10. Kentucky Rules of Evidence, Rule 501.

11. David Louisell, *Confidentiality, Conformity and Confusion: Privileges in Federal Court Today,* 31 Tul. L. Rev. 101, 109–15 (1956), quoting Dean Wigmore.

12. S. Rep. No. 93-1277, p. 13 (1974), as cited in Jaffee v. Redmond, 518 U.S. 1, 8, 116 S. Ct. 1923, 1927 (1996).

13. 445 U.S. 40 (1980).

14. 518 U.S. 1, 116 S. Ct. 1923 (1996).

15. *Id.,* at 8–9, quoting Trammel v. United States, 445 U.S. 40, 47 (1980).

16. 445 U.S. 40 (1980).

17. *Id.* at 52.

18. Catherine J. Ross, *America–Implementing Constitutional Rights for Juveniles: The Parent-Child Privilege in Context,* 14 Stan L. & Pol'y Rev. 85, 86 (2003).

19. *Id.*

20. The proposed ABA Model parent-child Privilege Statute was described in the case of In re Grand Jury Proceedings, Unemancipated Minor Child, 949 F. Supp. 1487 (E.D. Wash. 1996).

21. In re A & M (People v. Doe), 403 N.Y.S.2d 375 (N.Y. App. Div. 1978) (common law recognition of a parent-child privilege through the constitutional right to family privacy); People

v. Fitzgerald, 422 N.Y.S.2d 309, 312 (N.Y. App. Div. 1979) (extending the parent-child privilege to an older child; holding that the privilege is not limited to minors); In re Ryan, 474 N.Y.S.2d 931, 931 (N.Y. Fam. Ct. 1984) (recognizing a grandmother as a parent for parent-child privilege purposes). But *see* People v. Hilligas, 670 N.Y.S.2d 744, 747 (N.Y. Sup. Ct. 1998) (rejecting Fitzgerald for independently living adults).

22. 8 John H. Wigmore, Evidence § 2280, p. 819 (McNaughten rev. 1961).

23. United States v. MHC Surgical Centers Associates, Inc., 911 F. Supp. 358 (N.D. Ind. 1995).

24. 518 U.S. 1, 116 S. Ct. 1923 (1996).

25. *Id.* at 10, 116 S. Ct. at 1929.

26. *Id.* at 13.

27. 518 U.S. 1, 116 S. Ct. 1923 (1996).

28. 551 P. 2d 334 (Cal. 1996).

29. 834 P. 2d 786 (1992).

30. In re Grand Jury Investigation, 918 F.2d 374 (3d Cir. 1990) reviews the development of the clergy-communicant privilege in the federal courts. *See also* Russell G. Donaldson, Annotation, *Communications to Clergyman as Privileged in Federal Proceedings*, 118 A.L.R. Fed. 449 (1994) (Updated Weekly West 2018).

31. J. Bentham, 4 Rationale of Judicial Evidence 588-91 (1st ed. 1827), as quoted in John H. Wigmore, 8 Evidence § 2396 (McNaughten rev. 1961).

32. The quoted language is that of Proposed Fed. R. Evid. 509.

33. Proposed Fed. R. Evid. 510.

34. *Id.* at 59.

35. *Id.* at 60-61 (footnotes omitted) (emphasis added).

36. *Id.* at 62 (emphasis added).

37. 386 U.S. 300 (1967).

38. 373 U.S. 83 (1963).

39. 508 U.S. 165 (1993).

40. Couch v. United States, 409 U.S. 322, 335 (1973). There is no "justification for such privilege where records relevant to income tax returns are involved in criminal investigation or prosecution."

41. 408 U.S. 665 (1972).

42. *Id.* at 667-99, 702 (footnotes omitted).

43. Schoen v. Schoen, 5 F.3d 1289, 1292 & n.5 (9th Cir. 1993) (reviews the cases, by federal circuit, which have held that the privilege exists).

44. 294 A.2d 149, 156-57 (Md. App.), *aff'd per curiam*, 295 A.2d 212, *cert. denied*, 411 U.S. 951 (1972).

5 WITNESSES—LAY AND EXPERT

CHAPTER OUTLINE

CHAPTER OBJECTIVES

This chapter explores the basic elements related to serving as a witness, both lay and expert. After reading this chapter, you will be able to:

▶ State the one essential characteristic required before a person may become a witness.

▶ Name the two rights the Constitution guarantees to an accused person that assure the accused may call witnesses on his or her behalf.

▶ Define a leading question.

▶ List five exceptions to the rule prohibiting leading questions on direct examination.

▶ Define impeachment.

▶ Name the five methods of impeachment.

▶ List the subjects typically within the purview of lay opinion.

▶ State the circumstances under which testimony may be introduced.

▶ Explain how a witness may be qualified as an expert.

▶ List the three foundational requirements for an expert's testimony.

▶ State the three bases for expert opinion.

▶ Explain when and how a witness's recollection may be refreshed.

▶ List the steps that must be taken before a witness's recorded recollection may be admitted into evidence.

BECOMING A WITNESS

A person becomes a potential witness by having personal knowledge about the facts of a case that is going to trial. Personal knowledge may have been acquired through something seen, heard, smelled, or touched. A law enforcement professional who is called as a witness usually has gained knowledge through individual investigation of a case or a certain portion of the case. Witnesses are called upon during the course of a trial to relate their knowledge. Witnesses are seldom surprised when they are called to testify, especially in criminal cases. Before most criminal trials, law enforcement professionals conduct extensive investigations and usually advise the persons being interviewed that they may be called upon as a witness.

Although many people willingly serve as witnesses, others, for a variety of reasons, serve reluctantly. Some wish not to become involved; some fear reprisal; others fear cross-examination. Still others may wish to cooperate but are reluctant to lose time at work. Trials are unpredictable. Often the flow of the trial is such that witnesses appear on the date and time planned, only to find they are not needed until some other day. This necessitates taking another day from work to return each time a case is set for trial—a procedure that can become expensive for a wage earner.

However, an individual does not always have a choice whether or not to appear as a witness. Anyone with information that may be of value in arriving at the truth in a trial may be compelled to be a witness. This power to compel a witness to attend a trial is based on two clauses appearing in the Sixth Amendment to the Constitution of the United States: the Confrontation Clause and the Compulsory Process Clause. The Confrontation Clause provides that "the accused shall enjoy the right . . . to be confronted with the witnesses against him." The Compulsory Process Clause states that "the accused shall enjoy the right . . . to have compulsory process for obtaining witnesses in his favor." Both of these rights are available to the accused in federal and state trials.

APPLICATION CASE

The Supreme Court of the United States held that the Confrontation Clause applies to the states through the Fourteenth Amendment's Due Process Clause in the case of *Pointer v. Texas.*[1] In that case, the Court stated:

> The Sixth Amendment is a part of what is called our Bill of Rights. In *Gideon v. Wainwright* [372 U.S. 335 (1963)] in which this Court held that the Sixth Amendment's right to the assistance of counsel is obligatory upon the States, we did so on the ground that "a provision of the Bill of Rights which is fundamental and essential to a fair trial is made obligatory upon the States by the Fourteenth Amendment." . . . We hold today that the Sixth Amendment's right of an accused to confront the witnesses against him is likewise a fundamental right and is made obligatory on the States by the Fourteenth Amendment.
>
> It cannot seriously be doubted at this late date that the right of cross-examination is included in the right of an accused in a criminal case to confront

the witnesses against him. . . . The fact that this right appears in the Sixth Amendment of our Bill of Rights reflects the belief of the Framers of those liberties and Safeguards that confrontation was a fundamental right essential to a fair trial in a criminal prosecution.

Likewise, the Compulsory Process Clause has been applied to the states via the Fourteenth Amendment by the United States Supreme Court.[2] This right is not absolute. Favorable testimony can be excluded if it is incompetent, irrelevant, privileged, or inadmissible under the rules of evidence.[3] Further, a violation of a rule of procedure, such as discovery rules, can cause a court to constitutionally exclude such favorable testimony.[4] Although the Compulsory Process Clause of the Sixth Amendment does not create an absolute right, it is important to note that a criminal defendant is entitled to government assistance in obtaining witnesses favorable to him or her.[5]

Attendance of Witnesses

To ensure that a witness appears to testify, most lawyers will compel the witness's attendance by issuing a subpoena. A **subpoena** is an official document issued by a judge, the clerk of a court, or an attorney and delivered to, or "served upon," the witness. See Figure 5-1 for an example of a subpoena in a criminal case. In criminal cases, the subpoena sets forth the name of the defendant to be tried and the name of the person called as a witness, and it orders that person to appear at a specific time and place and to remain in attendance until released. If the person has papers, records, or other physical evidence needed for the trial, the person will be served with a **subpoena** *duces tecum.* This subpoena also directs the person to bring specific material to court.

Naturally, a person does not have to be served with a subpoena to become a witness; he or she may appear voluntarily or at the oral request of an attorney representing either side. However, if a witness does not appear in accordance with an oral request, it is not a violation of a court order and no penalty can be imposed. A witness's failure to appear in response to a subpoena, however, is a violation of a court order and subjects the violator to the full range of judicial sanctions. For this reason, the usual procedure is to serve a subpoena on each person desired as a witness, even those who are "friendly" and who voluntarily agree to appear.

SUBPOENA
An official document issued by a judge, the clerk of a court, or an attorney and delivered to, or "served upon," a witness compelling his or her attendance in court.

SUBPOENA *DUCES TECUM*
A subpoena ordering a witness to appear in court and to bring specified documents or other physical evidence in his or her possession or control.

MYTH ▶ ◀ FACT

MYTH	FACT
Trials are smoothly running operations, beginning on schedule and remaining on schedule until completion. The watchwords are "smooth sailing."	Trials are unpredictable, slow moving at best, and most often proceeding in fits and starts. The watchwords are "hurry up and wait!"

<table>
<tr><td>

CASE NUMBER

The People of the State of California, Plaintiff

vs.

Defendant(s)

Disobedience to this subpoena may be punishable as contempt of court. (Penal Code Section 1331)

> *Unless special instructions indicate differently*
> **YOU ARE COMMANDED TO APPEAR AT:**
> **DATE:**   **TIME:**   **COURTROOM:**
> **ADDRESS:** 800 S. Victoria Ave., Ventura, CA 93009
> **CALL IMMEDIATELY (805) 654-3006**
> Para Asistencia en Español llame al (805) 654-3708

If you have agreed with a member of the District Attorney's Office to appear at a time other than specified in the subpoena, your failure to appear at the time agreed upon may be punishable as contempt of court. (Penal Code Sec. 1331.5) **Read witness information on reverse.**

</td><td>

WITNESS SUBPOENA – CRIMINAL CASE

Gregory D. Totten, District Attorney
County of Ventura, State of California

The People of the State of California, to:

Phone No. (Bus.)   (Res.)

    Special Instructions to Witness:

           SHERIFF'S RETURN COPY

</td></tr>
</table>

FIGURE 5–1 Sample witness subpoena form–criminal.

There can be severe consequences for failing to honor a subpoena or subpoena *duces tecum*. The court can hold a recalcitrant person in criminal contempt. Sanctions for criminal contempt of court can be a monetary fine, imprisonment, or both. If the court chooses to imprison the person, the imprisonment will be for a fixed period of time and may continue even if the person later submits to the court's authority. Should a person answer a subpoena but intentionally refuse to give testimony or produce the physical evidence ordered, the court may find the witness in civil contempt. The court may order the uncooperative witness placed in jail until the witness complies with the orders of the court.

Method of Subpoenaing Witnesses

In most jurisdictions, the attorneys (either the defense attorney or prosecutor) issue their own subpoenas to compel the appearance of a witness. In a few jurisdictions, the clerk or judge must issue the subpoena, and the attorneys' duty is to furnish to the clerk a list of persons who are needed as witnesses. Although in most states anyone may serve a subpoena, in criminal cases, the subpoenas are usually given to an officer of the court—a deputy sheriff, a constable, or a marshal—to be served on the person named in the subpoena. The service of the subpoena consists of personally handing the subpoena to the person. In some jurisdictions, sending the subpoena by certified mail or leaving the subpoena at a witness's home or place of work is acceptable as proper service.

It is the duty of all citizens to testify when needed. Organized society is based on the civic contribution of its members. It is also considered to be an inherent right of our courts to compel a person to appear as a witness. Few circumstances will excuse a person from attendance as a witness—the needs of the criminal justice system take precedence over the convenience of the witness. Being a witness

Imagine that you are a homicide detective, sitting at your desk, when suddenly the shift lieutenant walks through and drops 20 subpoenas into your basket. "Prelim in three weeks," he growls. "The D.A. wants to interview these people as soon as possible; find them." The case is a seven-year-old homicide. Experience tells you that you'll probably find a few people locally, but the long period of time since the crime occurred means many of the potential witnesses have moved away.

There are several places to start, but most commonly you read through the police and district attorney's files first and note any phone numbers of parents or other relatives and friends. Phone calls to these old numbers, with patient explanations and subtle inquiries, will lead to your next level of contacts. Contacting old business numbers may provide more information. Don't ignore the obvious. A quick check of area phone books often yields surprising results. Also check jail records and the department of corrections. If the person being sought has a criminal record, he or she may have been arrested or incarcerated.

The next level involves technology—use of an Internet search on the name, a 50-state driver's license check, a criminal history report from the FBI, and a credit profile utilizing a credit reporting company, such as TRW. In extreme cases, assistance by the Internal Revenue Service assures that most, if not all, of the subpoenas will be served. One final tip: Technology is fine, but develop good people skills and learn to listen when people talk to you.

is deemed to be a civic duty owed by a person to society; therefore, a witness at a criminal trial may or may not be compensated, depending on local law.

There may be a limit placed upon how far a witness may be required to travel in order to testify without being compensated. Legally, a subpoena is valid anywhere within the state in which it is issued. But if a witness is required to travel from one county to another, or within a prescribed distance, the witness is usually paid a mileage fee and some small compensation for the expenses involved. Generally, when a witness resides in a county other than the one in which the subpoena is issued, the court issuing the subpoena will designate on the subpoena that the witness is material to the trial and will be compensated for appearing at the trial.

Out-of-State Witnesses

As pointed out, a subpoena is valid only within the state in which it is issued. Consequently, in the past, when a material witness in a criminal trial resided in another state, compelling an appearance could be a problem. But, today, all 50 states, the District of Columbia, Puerto Rico, and the Virgin Islands have addressed this issue by adopting the Uniform Act to Secure the Attendance of Witnesses from Without the State in Criminal Cases. This act permits a court to issue a subpoena to an out-of-state witness and to have the subpoena sent to a court in that state. The witness will be commanded to appear in that court, where a hearing will be held to determine whether he or she is a material witness. If it is determined that the witness is material, he or she will be ordered to appear in the court where the original subpoena was issued. A witness who fails to appear as ordered may suffer the same contempt sanctions as a witness within the state. Again, the witness is entitled to compensation for appearing.

Segregation of Witnesses, or the Rule on Witnesses

RULE ON WITNESSES
The rule of evidence requiring that witnesses be excluded from the courtroom during the testimony of other witnesses.

Although the defendant in a criminal trial is entitled to a public trial, it is not unusual to exclude the witnesses from the courtroom during the trial. This is known as the **rule on witnesses**. The reason for segregating or excluding the witnesses is to prevent witnesses from hearing each other's testimony and being affected by it, either intentionally or unintentionally. From a practical standpoint, a complete separation of the witnesses is almost impossible. They may still meet in the halls of the courthouse during recesses or at other times when the trial is not in session. However, the rule on witnesses is designed to prevent the most overt form of witnesses' collaboration. Judges will also direct witnesses not to discuss their testimony among themselves while waiting to appear in the courtroom. Witnesses are often placed in a hallway or a separate room and monitored by an officer of the court. This, of course, does not prevent witnesses from talking with one another away from the courthouse.

FYI

It is common for the law enforcement professional in charge of a criminal investigation to sit at counsel table with the prosecutor to assist in the presentation of the case, even though the officer is a witness at the trial and the judge invokes the rule on witnesses. The same is true for any person who is a party to the case or an expert who assists either lawyer.

ON THE JOB

Most people in the community consider the courthouse a place where the serious business of the law takes place. However, on more and more occasions, this solemnity has given way to gunshots as the legal process has inadvertently brought together warring factions. Gang violence is probably the most common, but feuds between individuals and groups of all sorts also occur. For example, in a scheduled preliminary hearing on a homicide case, a courtroom in Las Vegas took on an international flavor as witnesses and victims from Honduras came face to face with witnesses and defendants from San Salvador, two groups who had been locked in combat for many years. Although no violence ensued, the situation was extremely tense.

It is the law enforcement officer's responsibility to inform the prosecutor of any conflicts between the parties in a case that might erupt into violence in the courtroom. If the prosecutor is not concerned by the threat of violence, the officer should at least speak with the bailiff of the court. The bailiff has special training in courtroom security and is handpicked by the presiding judge.

The law enforcement officer must remain vigilant in the courtroom. This was made clear once again in July 2016, when Larry Darnell Gordon, who was a county jail inmate awaiting court appearance on several charges, in an apparent escape attempt, tried to take hostages inside the Berrien County Courthouse in St. Joseph, Michigan. He shot and killed two bailiffs and wounded a deputy, when he himself was shot dead.

LAY, OR ORDINARY, WITNESSES

Witnesses have been classified into two categories: (1) lay, or ordinary, witnesses and (2) expert witnesses.

A **lay witness** is a person who has some personal knowledge about the facts of the case and who has been called upon to relate this information in court. The law enforcement officer will usually fall within the lay witness category, but other law enforcement professionals more frequently testify as experts, too. The lay witness is permitted to testify about facts only and, with few exceptions, may not state personal opinions. This restriction on opinions or conclusions may be most frustrating to the witness. Much of our daily conversation is made up of conclusions and opinions. When a witness is prohibited from making such statements on the stand, he or she may become virtually tongue-tied. As a result, the method in which a witness relates information becomes very important to the court proceeding.

LAY WITNESS
A person who has some personal knowledge about the facts of the case and who has been called upon to relate this information in court.

Methods of Interrogating Witnesses

The Federal Rules of Evidence have traditionally viewed it as improper for an attorney to ask leading questions of the witness during direct examination. A **leading question** is one that suggests to the witness the answer sought by the questioner. The law prefers open-ended, or non-leading, questions on **direct examination** because leading questions are, by definition, suggestive. Leading questions could induce a witness to inadvertently adopt the questioner's suggestion. This is especially likely when the attorney posing the leading question prepared the witness to testify and the witness has some relationship with the party represented by that attorney.

LEADING QUESTION
A question that suggests to the witness the answer sought by the questioner.

DIRECT EXAMINATION
Presentation of the proponent witness's testimony by means of open-ended, non-leading questions.

One of the major functions of the trial attorneys is to aid witnesses in properly relating their story while on the stand. Thus, although leading questions are generally improper during direct examination, tradition and the FRE[6] allow some exceptions to this rule. These exceptions occur (1) with respect to undisputed preliminary or inconsequential matters; (2) when a witness is hostile, unwilling, frightened, or biased; (3) with respect to a child or adult witness who has difficulty communicating; (4) when a witness's recollection is exhausted; and (5) when laying a necessary foundation under certain circumstances. All five of these exceptions relate to the need to develop the witness's testimony under specific circumstances. In addition, a lawyer sometimes finds it necessary during direct examination to attack the credibility of a witness (impeach the testimony). When that occurs, the examination becomes a cross-examination, and leading questions are permitted.

Unless one of the previously mentioned exceptions applies, direct examination must be by non-leading questions. Nonetheless, the questions may be highly directive, requiring only a short answer, and may even be answered simply "yes" or "no" without being condemned as leading. As long as the answer is not suggested in the question, the question is not, technically, leading.

There is a spectrum of suggestiveness, ranging from completely closed-ended leading questions to questions that direct the witness to the subject matter but are technically not leading. An example of a closed-ended leading question is "You saw the defendant hit the victim over the head with a beer bottle, didn't you?" An example of a question that directs the witness to the subject matter but is less leading is "As you were standing in the bar, did you see the defendant strike the victim?" A lawyer who uses the latter form frequently, or with respect to critical facts, would surely be called for leading. On the other hand, a lawyer who uses such a form of question sparingly, and only in regard to noncritical facts, would probably not be interrupted by an objection.

Another method by which the witness may be interrogated is the **narrative** form. In this method, the witness is requested to state in his or her own words what happened in a particular instance. This permits the witness to tell the story in a logical sequence, normally making it easier for the jury to follow the evidence. Narrative questioning has its drawbacks and is usually not permitted by the courts. The witness, not being fully informed on the rules of evidence, may testify concerning many things that are incompetent, irrelevant, or inadmissible, bringing objections by the opposing side and requests to strike the testimony from the record. The judge must then admonish the jury to disregard the testimony. This procedure can be very time-consuming. It is also difficult for the jury to disregard something a witness has said, even though it is stricken from the record and the judge instructs the jury not to consider it.

There is another disadvantage to the use of narrative presentation during the direct examination. While telling his or her story, the witness may go into matters the attorney did not intend to include at that time. Or the witness may include irrelevant material, which would result in extensive cross-examination and could be detrimental to the case.

Even though both the narrative form of interrogation and leading questions have their weaknesses, it is sometimes necessary to use one of them or a combination in order to get the facts to the judge and jury. Both are time-consuming and may help account for the lengthy ordeals that many trials are.

CROSS-EXAMINATION
The rigorous examination of a witness by opposing counsel in which the questioner seeks to detract from the witness's credibility, often by using leading questions.

On **cross-examination**, the right to use leading questions is almost universally recognized. As FRE 611(c)(1) puts it, "Ordinarily, the court should allow leading questions . . . on cross-examination." The official note to this rule points out that it "conforms to tradition in making the use of leading questions on cross-examination a matter of right." Thus, questions asked by the cross-examiner usually demand a "yes" or "no" answer. This is done for a purpose—the cross-examiner is better able to control the information related by the witness.

No question may be asked on cross-examination unless its subject was brought up during direct examination. This does not mean that the exact matter must have been raised during direct examination, but the subject matter must have at least been implicated during that phase. For example, a witness who testifies that he saw the accused on a particular occasion could be asked on cross-examination whether he, the witness, wears glasses, even though no such question was posed on direct examination. The scope of the testimony, seeing and recognizing the accused on the occasion in question, implicates the subject matter of the witness wearing glasses.

ADVERSE WITNESS
A witness aligned with the opposing side.

Usually, the witness under cross-examination is an **adverse witness** (one aligned with the opposing side), who may, because of conscious or unconscious hostility engendered by the cross-examination, take advantage of the situation and try to volunteer additional information to the advantage of the opposing side. This is an ever-present hazard of cross-examination for both the witness and the cross-examiner. The attorney, in fact, has more to lose than the witness. Cross-examination is, at best, a dangerous procedure. Although lawyers are taught only to ask questions to which they know the answers on cross-examination, the cross-examiner can be surprised by unfavorable or unanticipated answers. In most instances, the damaging effects of such answers are impossible to reverse. For these reasons, effective cross-examination is a skill developed by only the most capable attorneys. Many attorneys hold cross-examination to a minimum, or waive it entirely, because of this potential for disaster.

When done correctly, cross-examination is an indispensable method of either eliciting testimony favorable to the examiner's case or impeaching the witness's testimony. In eliciting favorable testimony, an attorney on cross-examination might simply seek to have the witness testify to disputed facts favorable to the examiner's case. Or the attorney could have the witness repeat favorable testimony already stated on direct examination. The cross-examiner might also try to get the witness to qualify or explain damaging testimony given during direct examination. At the very least, the cross-examiner could try to put the witness's testimony in the light most favorable to the examiner's case and iterate or reiterate the examiner's theory of the case to the jury.

Perhaps the most important purpose of cross-examination is to persuade the jury to disbelieve the testimony of a witness, or impeach the witness. **Impeachment** is a process or a result that diminishes or destroys the believability of a witness's testimony. There are five basic methods of impeachment: (1) by contradiction; (2) by proof of bad character for truthfulness; (3) by proof of prior inconsistent statement; (4) by proof of bias or motive to falsify; and (5) by proof of lack of or diminished witness capacity.

Impeachment by **contradiction by cross-examination** consists of asking the witness about facts that are directly in opposition to those testified to on direct examination. For example, assume a defendant is charged with the unlawful sale of cocaine and that he takes the stand and testifies, denying the transaction and stating that he has never had any contact with any drugs. If the defendant had been tested for drugs as a condition for his release pending trial a year before and the test was positive, on cross-examination, the prosecution would be permitted to contradict the accused's testimony by inquiring about the fact that the accused had tested positive for cocaine.[7]

Impeachment by proof of bad character for truthfulness can be done in only two ways. First, the witness can be impeached by proof that he or she was convicted of certain crimes. Second, the witness can be impeached by questioning on cross-examination about specific acts that involve dishonesty but did not result in a conviction. The crimes that can be shown to impeach for bad character for truthfulness are (1) a crime involving dishonesty and (2) any crime punishable by imprisonment in excess of one year. Crimes involving dishonesty include perjury, fraud, and embezzlement. Crimes punishable by imprisonment in excess of one year include most felonies. Questions about bad conduct not amounting to a conviction can uncover activities that show that the witness has been dishonest, and therefore untruthful, even though the witness was not convicted or even arrested. For example, the lawyer could ask the witness on cross-examination, "Isn't it true that you regularly took money from the cash register at the store you work at?"

To complete the impeachment, the cross-examiner is allowed to prove the fact of the conviction, should the witness deny it. However, an answer to a question about an act that did not lead to a conviction must be accepted and cannot be the subject of further proof by the cross-examiner.

A law enforcement professional should testify truthfully, rather than with a focus on obtaining a conviction. If a police officer is testifying to get a conviction, then there is an obvious prejudice that might be exploited by the defense on cross-examination and in closing argument. Some defense attorneys, however, would like young law enforcement professionals to believe they are neutral parties in the courtroom. The truth is that law enforcers have collected a paycheck for their effort to solve the crime and undoubtedly believe in their own work product. While they must tell the truth and divulge exculpatory information right along with all the information that damages the defendant, they are prosecution witnesses and not part of the defense team. The law enforcement professional needs to present testimony completely and thoroughly, without sympathetic regard for the potential that the defendant will be convicted.

PRIOR INCONSISTENT STATEMENT
A witness's previously made statement that contradicts the witness's current in-court testimony.

Impeachment by **prior inconsistent statement** consists of the cross-examiner asking the witness about the fact that the witness previously made statements contradicting his or her testimony given on direct examination. Obviously, if a witness has made contradictory statements, the jury might think that the witness is either mistaken or lying, or has changed his or her mind for some other reason. The only requirement in the FRE and in most states for the cross-examiner to prove the content of a prior inconsistent statement is that the witness be given an opportunity to explain or deny the statement and the opposing party be afforded an opportunity to interrogate the witness about the statement.[8]

BIAS
A witness's interest in the case or its outcome.

Impeachment for **bias** may take many forms. Any interest the witness may have in the case or its outcome may be investigated on cross-examination to show bias or motive to falsify. A relationship between the witness and a party involved in the case; a financial connection, such as employment; and hatred or dislike for a party are all examples of provable bias. In general, the law finds bias almost always provable in any case. Particularly, ethnic or racial bias has been held to be provable.[9]

Finally, the cross-examiner may seek to impeach a witness by showing a lack of capacity or impaired capacity. Witness capacity consists of perception, memory, narration, and sincerity. Poor eyesight, hearing, memory, or ability to speak effectively are all matters that a cross-examiner may attempt to emphasize. Clearly, if a witness has problems in any of these areas, the jury will weigh his or her testimony carefully and might well disregard or give less weight to it. The final category, sincerity, is an evaluation of all aspects of the witness's demeanor and testimony.

If there is any chance of impeaching a witness's testimony by the cross-examination, the cross-examiner will attempt to do so. For a law enforcement professional acting as a witness, the cross-examination can become very unpleasant. This is probably because officers and other law enforcement witnesses are the most damaging witnesses insofar as the defendant's case is concerned. Unfortunately for such witnesses, some defense attorneys will go to any length to confuse, belittle, or embarrass them on the stand in an effort to diminish their testimony. Although such tactics may be difficult for the witness to endure, they often work to the advantage of the prosecution. If a law enforcement professional is able to maintain composure and control, the jury may feel more sympathetic toward the witness than toward the defense attorney. The witness should bear this in mind while testifying. (This matter will be discussed in further detail in Chapter 15.) Even though the witness may dislike the experience of cross-examination, in most instances, the defense attorney would also avoid it if it were not considered necessary for proper representation of the defendant.

APPLICATION CASE

Perhaps the most famous instance of impeachment by proof of bias is that involving Detective Mark Fuhrman, a prosecution witness in the O.J. Simpson trial. The defense was very successful in impeaching Fuhrman's testimony. Fuhrman, in response to defense questions, denied being racist or otherwise carrying out his police duties with a racist attitude. The defense was able to present to the jury a number of instances in which Fuhrman exhibited a racist attitude in his police work. Furthermore, the defense called a witness who had interviewed Fuhrman for a movie script she was writing. This witness testified to particular statements made by Fuhrman that were blatantly racist. Needless to say, all of Fuhrman's testimony was placed in doubt, and Fuhrman, along with the entire police department, was thoroughly embarrassed by the episode.

Witness Must Answer Questions

A witness must answer all questions the judge permits, whether the questions are on direct examination or cross-examination. Sometimes the witness is reluctant to answer a question that may be adverse to the side for which the witness has been called, particularly during cross-examination. To make matters worse, a witness subject to cross-examination may not be given a chance to explain his or her answer. However, the witness may be given the opportunity to explain the answer on re-direct examination.

Detective Mark Fuhrman's testimony in the O.J. Simpson trial was impeached under cross-examination.

©Ted Soqui/Getty Images

The one exception to the requirement that a witness must answer all questions is with respect to a self-incriminating question. The guarantee of the Fifth Amendment to the Constitution of the United States and the provisions of the constitutions of the various states give a witness, as well as the defendant, the right against self-incrimination.

Refusal to Answer a Question

Occasionally, a witness will refuse to answer a question asked by an attorney. This is more likely to occur during cross-examination. As pointed out previously, a witness is usually favorable to one side and will answer its questions. The entire testimony of a witness who refuses to answer a question may be stricken from the record. This is based on the premise that the witness must reveal the entire truth, not just the portion believed beneficial to one side.

When an answer given to a question is not responsive, the unresponsive answer may be stricken from the record. An **unresponsive answer** is one that does not address the subject matter of the question that was asked or goes beyond the scope of the question and relates to some other matter. The mere fact that an answer does not fulfill the expectations of the cross-examiner is not sufficient grounds to have it removed from the record. Receiving an unexpected answer, or one less favorable than expected, is also insufficient grounds for having the answer stricken from the record. When an answer is stricken from the record, the jury will be instructed to disregard the answer and not to consider it as evidence in the case.

If a witness absolutely refuses to answer a question, and if the question is not incriminating, the witness can be held in contempt of court in addition to having his or her entire testimony stricken from the record. Moreover, if a witness knowingly makes a false statement about a matter material to the case, or swears or affirms the truth of a statement made previously that he or she knows to be untrue, the witness may be guilty of **perjury**. Perjury may be a misdemeanor or a felony carrying corresponding criminal penalties of fines or imprisonment.

Opinion Testimony of Lay Witnesses

Most of the time, lay witnesses may relate only facts, not opinions. However, under the common law rule and the FRE, lay witnesses may testify in the form of opinion or make an inference under certain circumstances. Such testimony, called **lay opinion testimony**, is restricted to those opinions or inferences that are "rationally based on the witness's perception; and . . . helpful to clearly understanding the witness's testimony or to determining a fact in issue."[10] Often, the line between fact and opinion is very finely drawn. An opinion has been defined as an inference or a conclusion drawn from a fact known or something observed. Even though the term "conclusion" is often used as a synonym for "opinion," a **conclusion** is the ultimate inference drawn from a fact observed. As it relates to the testimony of a lay witness, it would be an inference drawn from something the witness observed. There are situations that can only be intelligently described or expressed in the form of inference or opinion.

UNRESPONSIVE ANSWER
A witness's answer that does not address the subject matter of the question or goes beyond the scope of the question asked and relates to some other matter.

PERJURY
Knowingly making a false statement about a matter material to a case or swearing or affirming to the truth of a previously made statement that one knows to be untrue. It may be a misdemeanor or a felony.

LAY OPINION TESTIMONY
Testimony by nonexpert witnesses in the form of opinion; it must be based on rational inference from the facts observed and necessary for a clear understanding of the witnesses' testimony.

CONCLUSION
The ultimate inference drawn from a fact observed; a synonym for "opinion."

For example, a witness may state that the defendant was angry when he came home. Is this a conclusion made by the witness or is it a fact? Such a statement may appear to be a conclusion, yet it is generally recognized that even a small child quickly senses anger or a parent's displeasure. This emotion is felt so keenly that it may be a fact. Then, too, how would one describe what makes the witness conclude the defendant was angry? Therefore, the law allows opinion testimony in such circumstances. If the court, to avoid any misperception, then demands that the witness relate what was actually seen and heard, the witness might state that when the defendant came home his face was red; his mouth was drawn; his eyes were wild; and he spoke in a loud, abrasive manner. Not much would be gained by such a detailed description. Besides, such statements as the defendant's eyes were wild, his face was red, or his mouth was drawn are themselves opinions. Thus, it is not always easy to determine whether a matter is a fact or an opinion of the witness.

Consequently, the law has set guidelines by which a lay witness may relate information in the form of an opinion. As previously stated, the opinion testimony must be rationally based on the witness's perception. In other words, the opinion must be one that a person could normally form from observed facts. Second, the opinion testimony must be "helpful to clearly understanding the witness's testimony or determining a fact in issue." The jury should clearly understand the witness who says, "The defendant was angry when he came home." On the other hand, a description similar to that given in the earlier example could be entirely misconstrued by the jury as fear instead of anger. Such a misinterpretation by the jury could be the determining factor between a first-degree murder verdict (if the defendant was angry) and one of not guilty based on the belief that the killing was done in self-defense (if the defendant was fearful). Accordingly, the lay witness's opinion testimony could be crucial.

In addition to those concerning human emotion, there are many occasions within common experience when an ordinary person may render an opinion. In one case, a California court stated: [11]

[T]he exception [to the rule prohibiting opinion testimony by a lay witness] . . . applies to questions of identity, handwriting, quantity, value, weight, measure, time, distance, velocity, form, size, age, strength, heat, cold, sickness, and health; questions also concerning various mental and moral aspects of humanity, such as disposition and temper, anger, fear, excitement, intoxication, veracity, general character, etc. . . . We identify men. We cannot tell how, because expressions of the face, gestures, motions, and even form, are beyond the power of accurate description. Love, hatred, sorrow, joy, and various other mental and moral operations, find outward expression, as clear to the observer as any fact coming to his observation, but he can only give expression to the fact by giving what to him is the ultimate fact, and which, for want of a more accurate expression, we call opinion.

Before a lay witness may express an opinion, a proper foundation must be laid to prove that the witness had personal knowledge of the facts upon which the opinion is formed. Personal knowledge may be shown by evidence in the form of the witness's own testimony. Therefore, a witness may not testify that something smelled like marijuana unless it is established that the witness, from prior experience, knows what marijuana smells like. Moreover, it is important to note that the opinion of the lay witness may be only about something that the witness observed, heard, or smelled and not in answer to some hypothetical question pertaining to the witness's opinion of the matter.

A great deal of discretion has been given to the trial judge in determining when a witness may relate an opinion. The appellate courts have stated that the trial judge is in a better position to make this decision in accordance with what is taking place at the time, and the appellate courts are therefore reluctant to reverse decisions of this kind unless there is a material error in judgment.

Some of the more commonly encountered opinions that may be expressed by a lay witness in criminal matters are discussed in further detail in the following sections.

State of Emotion

In criminal trials, a lay witness is frequently called upon to express an opinion as to the state of emotion of the accused or of the victim of a crime. It may be most important to know whether the accused was angry or excited at a particular time or whether the victim was afraid, happy, or in love. If the lay witness had an opportunity to observe the accused or the victim at the pertinent time, the witness may express an opinion of the state of emotion of either.

Speed of Vehicles

A lay witness who has observed a moving vehicle is permitted to state an opinion as to the speed of the vehicle. The witness need not be able to drive in order to state an opinion as to the speed, but some experience verifying that the witness is familiar with various speeds may need to be shown. Witnesses have been permitted to state that a vehicle was going very fast or that it was going faster than other vehicles in the area. A lay witness may even be permitted to state that a vehicle was going fast or very fast merely from hearing the sound of the vehicle pass an area. A lay witness may not give an opinion about speed merely from observing skid marks, as this falls within the purview of an expert witness. Neither may a lay witness state that a person was driving negligently or dangerously, as this may be the very issue in question and must be decided by the jury.

Distances

Opinion testimony of a lay witness is permitted with respect to distances between two objects, so long as the testimony is rationally based on the personal knowledge of the witness. For example, a witness may give an opinion as to the approximate distance between an intersection light that turned red and a car that ran the red light as probative of the time the driver had to stop before hitting a pedestrian. If a proper foundation is laid showing that the witness was at the intersection or nearby, and personally observed the facts testified to, then such testimony will be admitted. Moreover, in evaluating an opinion expressed by a witness concerning distances, the witness is often tested by being asked to estimate distances between objects within the courtroom.

Sobriety or Intoxication

Often, a person's sobriety or intoxication at a particular time is in issue, either in establishing guilt or mitigating to a lesser offense. A lay witness may testify to an opinion that an individual was intoxicated or sober if it is sufficiently established that the witness, from prior experience, knows how an intoxicated or sober person appears. For instance, a bouncer employed by a bar may testify that the defendant appeared intoxicated, therefore lacking the requisite intent for first-degree murder, when the defendant killed the victim by breaking a bottle over the victim's head. In establishing the proper foundation for the witness's testimony, the witness may testify to the fact that, by being a bouncer at a bar, he observed intoxicated individuals on a daily basis and is therefore able to determine if someone is sober or intoxicated. Accordingly, on this the bouncer may testify that the defendant appeared intoxicated in light of the bouncer's prior experience.

Age, Identity, and Physical Condition of a Person

A lay witness may give an opinion of the estimated or approximate age of a person whom the witness has observed. If a lay witness is acquainted with another person or has observed that person, the witness may express an opinion about whether a photograph is a good likeness of the individual. The witness may also state an opinion as to whether a voice heard over a telephone or through a closed door was that of someone whose voice the witness is able to recognize. Likewise, a lay witness may give an opinion about the general physical characteristics of a person. This includes such opinions as whether a person appeared to be strong, weak, feeble, or ill. Generally, a lay witness may not give an opinion about a type of illness or any internal physical condition. Lay opinions should be confined to things that are observable.

Opinions on Miscellaneous Matters, Such as Weight, Color, and Value

Because of the familiarity of the average person with a great number of nontechnical matters, the lay witness may express an opinion on such matters. These include opinions about the approximate weight, size, or color of an object. The witness may state an opinion on matters of taste, smell, and touch. The witness may also, on a limited basis, give an opinion of the value of certain objects or property. If value is an important issue in the case, the services of an expert may be called upon.

Character of a Person

A witness may testify, in the form of opinion, as to another witness's character for truthfulness or untruthfulness. This is an express exception to the general rule prohibiting the use of character evidence for purposes of showing a propensity to act in a certain way. Character evidence will be discussed in more detail in Chapter 6, but for the present it is important to note that proving a witness's character for veracity is permissible. As in all forms of opinion testimony, any such testimony offered to prove the character of a witness must be rationally based on the perception of the witness and must be helpful to a clear understanding of the witness's testimony or the determination of a fact in issue. The witness must have sufficient personal knowledge or experience from which an inference may be drawn showing another witness's character for telling the truth. For instance, a witness may testify that he or she perceived the other witness telling lies and that, in her opinion, the other witness is not a truthful person. However, the witness giving such an opinion may not testify about those specific instances of conduct. Only the opinion testimony is permitted.

Character witnesses can often be embarrassed or easily discredited by the opposing side. According to the rules of evidence, during cross-examination, a character witness may be asked questions such as "Did you know that the defendant has been arrested for shoplifting, loitering, and public nuisance five times in the past?" The question must have some basis in fact; however, since people rarely know everything about friends' and coworkers' pasts, the opposing side can generally find some damaging "secret" to reveal. Because character witnesses can be so easily embarrassed or discredited, their use is not common.

Sanity

There are occasions when a lay witness may even express an opinion on the sanity of a person with whom he or she is intimately acquainted. However, as a general rule, a lay witness may not express an opinion of whether the acquaintance knew the difference between right and wrong, as that is a fact that the jury is called upon to decide during a trial. In some jurisdictions, the lay witness may not express an opinion as to the sanity of a person but may merely express an opinion as to whether the person in question acted in a rational or irrational manner. The courts have stated that it is not necessary that the witness have any prior acquaintance with the person in order to give this sort of opinion. This decision is based on the supposition that a rational person reacts in a certain "normal" manner and that an irrational person deviates from this normal manner. An observer can generally draw a conclusion as to whether a person appeared rational after viewing the person for a short time. In order that a jury may better evaluate an opinion, it is considered proper procedure for the lay witness to relate as accurately as possible the actions and words from which he or she drew the conclusion as to the person's sanity or rationality. All but four states allow such testimony: New York and Massachusetts do not, and Delaware and Hawaii are undecided on the issue.[12]

Opinions About Handwriting

In many instances, a lay witness may state an opinion about the genuineness or identification of the handwriting of another. The use of the lay witness in this regard stems from our country's legal history. The common law rule, both in England and in this country, often required the authentication of a document or of a person's handwriting. In earlier days, handwriting experts were unknown, so the services of the lay witness were used through necessity. It was held that, if a witness had seen another person write or had received correspondence or documents from the person, the lay witness could express an opinion about the genuineness of the writing. This kind of opinion must not be confused with the

A police officer's demeanor in the courtroom is crucial in establishing his or her credibility. A police officer is most often a lay witness as described in the text. Thus, the officer is subject to the limitations imposed on nonexpert witnesses. However, the standard rules do not account for society's expectations and the manner in which a jury views a police officer's testimony. Police officers hold a special place of responsibility in the community, and, despite recent fallout from recent events and highly publicized criminal and civil trials, jurors will look to the officer's demeanor in court as the all-important initial indicator of the officer's credibility. Four specific guidelines for police officers' testimony follow:

1. In terms of proper clothing in court, as a general rule, the officer should testify dressed as he or she was at the time of his or her involvement in the case, unless the officer was undercover. If the officer was in uniform at the time of the arrest, then he or she should testify in uniform. If the officer was wearing civilian clothing, then civilian clothing should be worn to court. If there is any question about the officer's credibility, a freshly pressed uniform with shined leather gear and shoes is sure to make the proper impression on the jury.

2. The officer is "on display" the moment he or she enters the courthouse. Any loud or embarrassing behavior with other officers should be limited to the locker room.

3. The officer should conduct himself or herself as a professional. He or she is a witness for the state, but jurors do not expect blind loyalty to the prosecution. An officer's testimony should, at all times, be factual, accurate, and limited to the officer's firsthand knowledge of the incident in question. It is important that the officer not appear overtly biased in favor of the prosecution. Jurors tend to expect police officers to be fair and impartial.

4. A career in law enforcement requires dedication and integrity from the moment the individual decides to pursue such a vocation. Honor and integrity are keystones to success, both on the street and in the courtroom. No defendant is worth an officer's career. An officer should never commit perjury. Once an officer has committed, or is believed to have committed, perjury, his or her effectiveness as a witness is ruined. Some agencies will dismiss an officer who is guilty or suspected of perjury.

opinions that are expressed by an expert witness in the field of handwriting comparisons. The lay witness merely observes a questioned handwriting and, being familiar with the handwriting of the person, expresses an opinion as to whether it is genuine.

Terminology of Lay Witnesses

Terminology alone does not convert a witness's admissible factual testimony into inadmissible opinion testimony. In general conversation, people frequently start a statement with such phrases as "in my opinion," "it is my belief," or "I believe." This would seem to imply that the person using such phrases is expressing a conclusion. In reality, the witness may be stating a fact. When a witness uses such a phrase, the attorney conducting the examination may have to question the witness further to clarify that a fact, not a conclusion, is being stated. Even if a witness is testifying to a conclusion or an opinion, such testimony may be admissible, provided the conditions already explained are met.

EXPERT WITNESSES

No matter how sophisticated a jury panel may be, it inevitably will be called upon to make judgments about many matters, some of which may be beyond the understanding of its members. Matters involving specialized knowledge are often presented to the jury in even the most mundane case. To assist the jury in its search for the truth, and in the best interests of justice, the services of expert witnesses come into play. As many everyday matters continue to become more technical and specialized, expert witnesses will play an even more important role in trial proceedings in the future. Expert witnesses may come to be viewed as assistants to the jury. An expert witness gives the jury the benefit of knowledge of a particular science or skill. By such knowledge, the jurors are assisted in arriving at the truth. Although the jury need not accept the opinion, an expert is permitted to express an opinion or draw conclusions concerning a particular set of facts or about the examination of some evidence.

Generally speaking, under the FRE an expert may testify if the scientific, technical, or other specialized knowledge he or she provides will assist the jury in understanding the evidence or in determining a material fact. Before an expert may testify, the judge must first determine whether the witness is qualified as an expert in the particular field by knowledge, skill, experience, training, or education and that the testimony will help the jury arrive at the truth.

Definition of an Expert Witness

An **expert witness** is a person skilled in some art, trade, science, or profession. An expert must have knowledge, skill, experience, training, or education that is beyond that of the average person. In this respect, therefore, an expert is in a position to assist the jurors because they do not have such a background.

Contrary to popular belief, the expert witness does not have to be a person of great educational background or training. All that is necessary to qualify as an expert witness is scientific, technical, or "specialized" knowledge that the ordinary person does not have. The witness may have gained this knowledge through longtime work experience in that field. For example, a cement mason may have very little educational background but, because of experience in the cement and concrete trade, may qualify as an expert in that field. A mason may be in a position to express an opinion about how long it takes concrete to harden before it can be driven upon without doing damage. On the other hand, there are certain areas in which the expert witness may have to show extensive study and training. This would be true in matters pertaining to medical or scientific examinations, for example, identification by fingerprints or matching DNA samples.

It is possible to become an expert witness through self-instruction and experience. Many crime laboratory experts, better known as criminalists, fall within this category.

The Foundation for Expert Testimony

To utilize the testimony of an expert witness, three requirements must be established to the satisfaction of the trial judge. First, the subject matter of the expert's proposed testimony must be relevant in the sense that it will assist the jury "to understand the evidence or to determine a fact in issue."[13] Second, the expert's field must be one requiring scientific, technical, or specialized knowledge. Third, the witness must be shown to have the background necessary to qualify as an expert in the field.

The first and third foundational requirements pose no unusual burdens upon the trial judge. Relevance determinations and qualifications of witnesses are routine matters and easily understood by all judges. Although some unusual cases may present complex issues, and the ingenuity of trial lawyers may tax the trial court's resources at times, these foundational requirements are usually not problematical. However, the second foundational requirement, qualifying the subject as a valid one, has generated substantial controversy.

The United States Supreme Court's decisions in *Daubert v. Merrell Dow Pharmaceuticals, Inc.*[14] and *Kumho Tire Co. Ltd. v. Carmichael*[15] set the standard for the trial court's determination of the foundation for expert testimony with respect to scientific principle under the FRE. Prior to the Supreme Court's decision in *Daubert,* the *Frye*[16] standard for admissibility of this aspect of expert testimony was the general rule. Under the *Frye* **test**, only such expert testimony as was based on a scientific methodology "generally accepted as reliable in the relevant scientific community" was admissible. In contrast, the *Daubert-Kumho* **test** requires the trial judge to determine that the subject of an expert's testimony has achieved the stature of "scientific knowledge" based on five factors: (1) testing of the theory or technique; (2) peer review and publication of the theory or technique; (3) the scientific technique's known or potential rate of error; (4) the existence and maintenance of standards controlling the technique's operation; and (5) the theory or technique's "general acceptance." Even if not generally accepted by the scientific community, it is possible for a scientific theory to be used in a trial if consideration of the other four factors favors the use of the evidence. In *Kumho,* the Court extended *Daubert*'s holding to apply not only to scientific principles but to technical and specialized knowledge as well. The Court has referred to the function of the trial court in making the *Daubert-Kumho* determination as the gatekeeper for deciding the admissibility of an expert's opinion testimony.

FRYE TEST
The former test for admissibility of expert testimony. It required that the testimony be based on scientific methodology "generally accepted as reliable in the relevant scientific community."

DAUBERT-KUMHO TEST
The new test for admissibility of expert testimony, requiring the trial judge to determine that the subject of an expert's testimony has achieved the stature of "scientific knowledge" based on five factors: (1) testing of the theory or technique; (2) peer review and publication of the theory or technique; (3) the particular scientific technique's known or potential rate of error; (4) the existence and mantainence of standards controlling the technique's operation; and (5) the theory or technique's "general acceptance."

FYI

On February 18, 2009, the National Research Council issued its much anticipated report on the fractured state of forensic science in the United States.[17] This report criticizes the very foundation of much scientific expert evidence presented in criminal trials in the United States, calling for a massive reform of the forensic institutions responsible. Here is a critical excerpt from the summary section of the report: "With the exception of nuclear DNA analysis, however, no forensic method has been rigorously shown to have the capacity to consistently, and with a high degree of certainty, demonstrate a connection between evidence and a specific individual or source."[18] It is not known whether, and to what extent, courts may react to the report and exclude forensic evidence under the *Daubert-Kumho* standards for the admission of evidence reliant upon scientific, technical, or specialized knowledge principles.[19]

CRIMINALIST
A specialist in the
application of science to
crime and the law.

A **criminalist** is a specialist in the application of science to crime and the law. Because criminalists are the most familiar type of expert witness, such a professional will serve as an example in examining when an expert witness may be used. When the criminalist makes a bullet comparison or compares a latent fingerprint with that of a suspect, the expert's opinion is necessary in the trial, since the average person is unable to analyze such findings without assistance. Therefore, by enabling the jury to understand better the evidence before it, the criminalist's testimony concerning the bullet or fingerprint comparison satisfies the first criterion of admissibility. The second criterion requires that the scientific principles involved in ballistics and fingerprint comparisons must qualify as reliable under the *Daubert-Kumho* test. Since these principles have been accepted in courts for many decades, they easily satisfy this criterion.

The third requirement is that the witness must be qualified as an expert in these fields. No set foundation is required, since an expert may be qualified by knowledge, skill, experience, training, or education. Therefore, if the criminalist has had formal education in ballistics and fingerprint analysis, this information would be elicited first by the prosecutor on direct examination. However, even if the witness has had no formal education, the prosecutor can qualify the criminalist as an expert by eliciting information about the witness's special training and experience. Even if our hypothetical criminalist had no formal education, he or she could have studied related subjects. For example, in the case of the ballistics examiner, it would be to his advantage to have a knowledge of metals, physics, chemistry, and criminalistics, although there is no requirement that he must have studied these courses in order to qualify. Although not a requirement, if an expert can show formal study in addition to experience and training, the testimony will probably be given greater weight by the jury.

Qualifying the Expert: *Voir Dire*

VOIR DIRE OF A
PROPOSED EXPERT
WITNESS
The questioning process
by which an expert witness
is qualified.

The process of qualifying a witness as an expert is called *voir dire.* This term means "the questioning or examination into the character and possible biases."[20] Just as when it is applied to the selection of a jury, a ***voir dire* of a proposed expert witness** requires that the witness answer questions about his or her qualifications. However, unlike the *voir dire* of a jury, the qualification of an expert witness places a burden upon the side producing the expert witness to prove qualification. So, in a typical criminal case, the qualification process involves preliminary questions asked of the witness about education, experience, training, and work in order to establish the witness's basic qualifications. In addition, the attorney will want to qualify the witness as persuasively as possible by going beyond the essential qualifications in order to give the witness as much stature as possible in the eyes of the jury. Often, opposing counsel, knowing the witness will be admitted as an expert, will offer to accept the witness without going through the usual qualification questions and answers. The side offering the witness as an expert will, of course, want the jury to hear as much of the witness's credentials as possible. Persuasive qualification is particularly important in cases in which the opposing parties each intend to use expert testimony with respect to a specific issue.

For example, consider a crime laboratory technician who specializes in bloodstain examinations. The prosecuting attorney would call the technician to the stand and, after asking the witness's name and occupation, would probably ask about educational background, as college training in science (especially chemistry and biology) would improve the witness's image. In addition to any educational qualifications, the witness's work experience, including training under the supervision of other experts in the field, would be introduced. Also, the length of time that the technician has been engaged in this kind of examination would be revealed, particularly if a considerable period. With respect to any expert witness, it would be persuasive for an attorney to examine areas beyond the basic qualifications of education and experience, for example, specialized training, continuing education courses, teaching and lecturing positions, licenses and certifications, publications, consulting experience, professional memberships, awards, and other professional honors. The more qualifications the prosecuting attorney can introduce, the more likely the expert is to impress the jury, and the more inclined the jury is to accept the expert's conclusions as accurate.

It is necessary in some jurisdictions, once qualifications have been completed, to *formally tender* the witness to the court as an expert in a particular field, after which the opposing counsel may attack the expert's qualifications.[21] The procedure described in the text has come to be disfavored. The reason to disfavor such tendering of a witness as an expert to avoid the trial court putting a stamp of authority on a witness's opinion. Though the ABA proposal was made in the context of civil trials, the report also said that the policy should be extended to criminal cases. The purpose of tendering the witness as an expert is to inform the court that qualification has been concluded. The opposing attorney then has an opportunity to conduct a *voir dire* examination of the witness and to force that opposing *voir dire* to take place before the witness's opinions have been elicited. Thus, the *voir dire* allows the opposing counsel to attempt to show that the technician is not qualified through a cross-examination limited to the witness's qualifications before the witness gives an opinion. Opposing counsel might attempt to show that the technician has had little education in a related scientific field, or that the witness has had limited experience. Or counsel may attempt to discredit, if not disqualify, the expert by exposing other factors, such as out-of-date credentials or irrelevance of specialties. Even if the opposing attorney is not able to bar the witness from testifying as an expert, the attorney may seriously damage the effect of the witness's testimony. Consequently, a person endeavoring to qualify as an expert witness should be prepared to show as extensive an amount of personal skill in and knowledge of the relevant subject matter as is possible.

If during the qualification procedure it has been shown that the witness is a highly qualified individual, the opposing attorney may waive *voir dire* entirely. Although such a waiver precludes defense counsel from attacking the witness's qualifications as an expert, it does not preclude the defense attorney from cross-examining the expert with respect to the expert's opinions given on direct examination. In many cases, an opposing attorney has lessened the effect of the expert testimony through cross-examination, although cross-examination of an expert witness can be a difficult task for an attorney, since he or she usually has very little knowledge of the field. For this reason, it is often necessary for the attorney or paralegal to conduct extensive research to become acquainted with that field.

The final determination of whether a person qualifies as an expert witness is made by the trial judge, and, unless the decision is beyond all reason, it will not be overruled on appeal. Once the judge accepts the witness as an expert witness, the weight given to that person's testimony is determined by the jury. If the trial judge decides that a person tendered as an expert does not qualify, it is unlikely that the person can then testify as a lay witness, especially since the 2000 amendment to FRE 701 prohibiting a lay witness to give evidence based on scientific, technical, or otherwise specialized knowledge. As the advisory committee's note accompanying the amendment put it, the rule was changed to prevent evading the requirements for expert testimony by tendering an "expert in lay witness clothing."

Testimony of the Expert Witness

The opinions and conclusions of an expert witness may be based upon information gained in one of three ways. First, specific information possessed by the expert, gained through examination of a particular piece of evidence, may be the basis of his or her opinion or conclusion. Such opinion testimony may be elicited simply by asking the expert what conclusions were reached after examining the evidence.

Second, the expert may rely upon data supplied from another source in any form, as long as it is within the usual practice in the field to rely on such data. Moreover, under FRE 703, the facts or data upon which the expert bases an opinion need not be admissible at trial, provided that such data or facts are of a type reasonably relied upon by experts in that field.

ON THE JOB

From May 2003 to January 2004, a Los Angeles police chemist botched evidence in 47 narcotics cases by failing to properly weigh drugs before testing.[22] The errors raised questions about the credibility of the chemist, who had analyzed drugs for the LAPD since May 2003. Following are some of the possible consequences of this chemist's sloppy work:

▶ In cases that have already gone to trial, defense attorneys can file a motion for a new trial based on the claim that the chemist's testing was incorrect. As one defense attorney put it, "Any time you have law enforcement not doing their job accurately, it undermines the potential legitimacy of the evidence they want to present."

▶ In future cases, if a prosecutor believes the errors undermine the chemist's expertise, the facts of the prior errors must be disclosed to the defense. As one defense attorney pointed out, "An argument could be made that this evidence indicates that [the] chemist is a 'careless' and/or 'incompetent' scientist." Prosecutors are obligated to turn over the information if they know the chemist made even one mistake.

▶ Thus, as a result of sloppy work, in each future case in which this chemist takes the stand as an expert witness, each defense attorney will be able to cross-examine him by asking if his results in drug testing have ever been found to be inaccurate. The defense attorney will be able to bring out the fact that convictions were reversed and evidence thrown out due to his sloppy work. In closing argument, the defense attorney can point out that the prosecution's own expert testimony was discounted by the prosecution.

▶ As a result, this expert's testimony will not be helpful in any future cases, and he will probably not be used as an expert witness again.

Third, the expert may be presented with a set of hypothetical facts from which the expert is asked to draw conclusions. This type of presentation is not used frequently in criminal cases. Most often, expert testimony in criminal cases results from an actual examination of a piece of physical evidence. This is particularly true of testimony given by criminalists. A criminalist's appearance as an expert witness generally originates from an earlier examination of an article found at a crime scene. This does not preclude the defense attorney, or the prosecuting attorney, from also presenting certain hypothetical questions to the expert.

As an example, a criminalist may conduct DNA tests on a blood sample. From those tests, he or she can express the opinion that the DNA found at the crime scene matches that of the accused or the victim. DNA tests are not exclusive to blood evidence but may also be conducted on saliva, hair, or semen left at the crime scene. In conducting the DNA test, the criminalist is able to extract a genetic "fingerprint," which can then be compared with the genetic fingerprint of a DNA sample taken from the accused. Both DNA evidence and blood grouping evidence are forms of statistical proof—DNA evidence being the most useful in determining identity. For example, blood grouping evidence may narrow the range of other potential suspects with the same blood type to one out of two hundred, whereas DNA evidence may, as a practical matter, eliminate any possibility that there exists another potential perpetrator by identifying the specific genetic "makeup" of the accused.

One may assume that blood and DNA typing are scientifically proven facts and not mere opinions of the witness. Science definitely accepts that blood will react to certain chemicals, that human blood will react in a different manner than animal blood, and that blood can be grouped. Moreover, DNA testing is a scientifically accepted procedure and is readily admitted at trial. However, since the results of DNA testing are statistical projections, it is merely an opinion of the expert that, for example, the stains found on a shirt were the blood of the accused and that the bloodstains were genetically identical to some found at the crime scene. Because of the expert's skill and knowledge in such matters, the witness may give opinions resulting from the examination of the evidence for the benefit of the jury. The jury may or may not believe the opinions to be true, depending upon how well qualified it considers the witness to be and how convincing it finds the testimony.

MYTH	◀ FACT
The testimony of a criminalist pertaining to the blood typing or genetic identification of a blood sample is a matter of fact that must be accepted by the jury.	Such testimony is a matter of mere opinion and may be completely disregarded by the jury if it thinks the criminalist is not a convincing witness or if it has doubts about any other aspect of the bases for the opinions.

The O.J. Simpson trial did much to bring DNA evidence into the public eye. The prosecution in the Simpson case relied heavily upon DNA evidence. Blood samples of both the victims and Simpson were taken from the murder scene. DNA evidence extracted from these samples was then matched to DNA extracted from blood samples found in Simpson's home and car. Although the DNA evidence linked Simpson to the crime scene and all but eliminated the possibility that anyone else with the same genetic "code" as Simpson could have been present at the crime scene, the sloppy manner in which the police and the criminalists collected, handled, and tested the blood caused the jury to discount the expert DNA testimony. Poor police and crime lab procedures led the jury to doubt the validity of the otherwise strong expert testimony.

HYPOTHETICAL QUESTIONS
Questions based on facts, data, or opinions that have some relation to the matter at issue and upon which the expert witness is asked to render an opinion.

The second way that experts may get data upon which to base an opinion is from a source generally relied upon by experts in the field. Rarely will an expert testify based upon information transmitted only by word of mouth, but an expert may often be presented with written reports gathered by others, which the expert will read and analyze, and upon which he or she will render an opinion. For example, a doctor specializing in orthopedics may rely upon the report of a radiologist, who interprets an X-ray, in rendering an opinion with respect to a bone fracture.

The third basis for an expert opinion involves the use of **hypothetical questions**. Although hypothetical questions have historically been criticized "as encouraging partisan bias . . . and as complex and time consuming,"[23] the FRE continue to allow the use of such questions. It is within the discretion of the trial judge whether to allow hypothetical questions. Thus, an expert may be a witness even though he or she has not examined any evidence and has no knowledge, either directly or indirectly, about the case. Instead, a set of hypothetical facts, data, or opinions that has some relation to the matter at issue will be given to the expert, who will then be asked for an opinion, based on his or her experience and knowledge of what would happen, given a certain set of circumstances. Only if the jury were to find each of the hypothetical facts to be proven could it even consider the expert's opinion based on the proposed hypothetical scenario.

©POOL/Getty Images

In the O.J. Simpson trial, the jury doubted the validity of the DNA evidence presented by criminalist Dennis Fung.

For example, a medical doctor may be placed on the witness stand and asked, "Assuming that a man had been in the habit of drinking four cans of beer each night before supper for more than two years, would this in your opinion retard his reaction time?" As long as the facts contained in the hypothetical scenario are ultimately supported by evidence, the jury will be permitted to consider the expert's opinion.

When facts and data not admitted into evidence are used in forming a hypothetical question, the trial judge will usually give an instruction to the jury not to consider those facts and data in its deliberations.

Whatever the source of information upon which an expert bases an opinion, that information must be of a type reasonably relied upon by experts in that field. Even if the evidence relating to that underlying information is inadmissible, as long as the facts, data, or opinions are of a type reasonably relied upon by experts in that field in forming opinions, then the attorney questioning the expert may pose questions disclosing such information. For example, a medical examiner may rely upon all of the reports contained in a police file, as well as the autopsy, in determining the cause of death of a homicide victim. Even though the written reports might be inadmissible hearsay, the fact that medical examiners rely upon such reports allows the information contained in those reports to be the subject of questions posed by the lawyer during examination of the expert witness, as long as the trial judge determines that the probative value of the evidence in assisting the jury to evaluate the expert's opinion substantially outweighs the evidence's prejudicial effect. Even then, the trial judge will instruct the jury only to consider such evidence insofar as it assists the jurors in evaluating the expert's testimony. This was affirmed in *Williams v. Illinois*,[24] when the United States Supreme Curt ruled an expert witness may state an opinion based on facts the expert assumes, but does not know to be true. Certain requirements must be met. See further discussion of the *Williams* case at the end of Chapter 7. Under FRE 703, the jury cannot consider the inadmissible evidence in any other way.

The prosecution or the defense may call expert witnesses, or the judge, on his or her own initiative, may request that an expert be called in for some purpose. Court appointment of expert witnesses frequently occurs if a question of insanity is involved or some physical ailment is alleged. With respect to court appointment of experts, FRE 706 (a) provides: "On a party's motion or on its own, the court may order the parties to show cause why expert witnesses should not be appointed and may ask the parties to submit nominations. The court may appoint any expert that the parties agree on and any of its own choosing. But the court may only appoint someone who consents to act."

Kinds of Expert Witnesses

It would be next to impossible to list all of the kinds of expert witnesses that may be encountered. However, a few of the better-known areas in which experts appear in criminal cases are reviewed here.

Medical Examiner or Coroner

In homicide cases, the cause of death must be established. This is invariably done by the **medical examiner** or **coroner**. The prosecution will call the examiner as an expert witness to give an opinion of the cause of death as a result of his or her examination of the body. It is only after the coroner or medical examiner has made a complete examination of the body that he or she can conclude that the death was due to stabbing and not to a heart attack or that a death was due to strangulation and not to accidental drowning.

MEDICAL EXAMINER OR CORONER
The government medical expert called to give opinion testimony as to the cause of death in a homicide.

Document Examiner

DOCUMENT
EXAMINER
An expert in the analysis of
documents who identifies
documents, paper,
handwriting, and the like.

A **document examiner** is usually skilled in making comparisons of both handwritten documents and documents produced by other means. Such a person would be able to qualify as a handwriting expert and as an expert in the field of document examination generally. A handwriting expert is seldom acquainted with the person whose writing he or she examines. Instead, the expert's examination is purely a comparison of two or more writing samples. The expert may compare two checks in an effort to determine whether they were written by the same individual. Or the expert may compare a known sample of a person's handwriting against a questioned check or document to determine if the same person wrote the second document.

An expert in the field of document examination may examine a document and express an opinion about the method used to create the document. In the case of a document produced on a typewriter, computer, facsimile, copier, or printer, the expert might examine the document and a known sample from a particular piece of equipment and express an opinion as to whether the document was produced by that device. In many cases, a document examiner will be able to express an opinion identifying the manufacturer of the paper used and the approximate date of its manufacture.

Although many people consider themselves to be authorities on handwriting and questioned document comparisons, it requires a great deal of study and experience to be accepted as an expert in this field. There is much that must be taken into consideration when comparing handwriting and documents, yet to date there is little in the way of formal schooling on this subject. Thus, this is one area in which an extensive educational background in the skill may be difficult to show. Still, juries are usually impressed by college degrees, even when it comes to this kind of examination and testimony. A general study in the field of criminalistics would add weight to the testimony of an expert witness who was commenting on handwriting and questioned documents.

Fingerprint Expert

The officer who examines a crime scene or piece of evidence for latent fingerprints usually testifies at trial as a lay witness. Although it takes a certain amount of skill and knowledge to lift and develop latent prints properly, it is not a field in which one must qualify as an expert witness to state that latent prints were located and developed. If an officer has had considerable experience in developing latent prints, the prosecuting attorney may introduce this information. If so, it is done merely to give more weight to the testimony and not for the purpose of qualifying the officer as an expert witness. In many large law enforcement agencies, the person who searches for and develops latent prints is frequently the **fingerprint expert**. However, most small departments must rely on the officer in the field to develop and lift the prints, which are in turn given to the expert for a comparison with a suspect's prints.

FINGERPRINT EXPERT
An expert in the
identification of fingerprints
by comparing unknown
and known samples of
fingerprints.

The services of the fingerprint expert become important when it is necessary to make a comparison of a latent fingerprint at a crime scene and the prints of a known suspect to determine whether the prints match. If an identification is made, the examiner will, in most instances, be called as a witness to prove the basis upon which the identification was made. In these circumstances, the examiner will have to qualify as an expert in the field of fingerprint examinations. Here again, little in the way of formal education is available to an expert, but such a witness will have to show some study, training, and experience to qualify as an expert.

Skid-Mark Expert, Speed Expert, and Accident Reconstructionist

Serious motor vehicle accidents are a fact of life in many countries. In many instances, there are few, if any, eyewitnesses to automobile accidents, so the determination of the speed of the vehicles involved in accidents is not easily made. However, speed is often an important factor in such a case. Therefore, an **accident investigator** is often called upon to give an opinion as to the speeds of the vehicles involved. Such an opinion is based on the skid mark or marks left at the accident scene or other observable data. Through the use of calculus, computers, and scientific knowledge, the speed of a vehicle involved in an accident can be determined with a fair degree of accuracy. Also, accident investigators are frequently called upon to state opinions concerning what may be safe speeds in accordance with certain road conditions. These opinions are usually based upon hypothetical questions. Such questions may be phrased in the following manner: "Based on your training and experience, assuming ideal road conditions—for instance, in the middle of the summer, no snow, no wetness—what would be the reasonable or safe speed in and about the area of the accident?" The expert would then give the jury the benefit of an opinion to assist them in deciding whether a driver involved in a serious or fatal accident may be held criminally responsible.

ACCIDENT INVESTIGATOR The person who investigates the causes and results of vehicle accidents. An accident investigator can also be a skid-mark expert, a speed expert, and an accident reconstructionist.

Experts on Bookmaking, Narcotics, and Other Specific Types of Crimes

Officers who have had extensive experience in working on particular types of crimes may become qualified as **crimes experts** with respect to those crimes. For example, officers who work on bookmaking cases may become qualified as experts on the material and paraphernalia used by bookmakers.

Likewise, officers experienced in drug investigations may qualify as experts on drug users' methods of taking drugs. They may also express their opinion about scars that they believe to have been made by injections, or whether certain paraphernalia found at a crime scene were used by those engaged in the use or sale of narcotics. The narcotic content of a pill or powder, however, would have to be determined by a person skilled in the field of chemistry.

CRIMES EXPERTS Persons, often law enforcement officers, who are experts in the methodology and paraphernalia involved in the commission of specific crimes, for example, bookmaking or narcotics.

Criminalist or Forensic Scientist

It is next to impossible to list all the areas in which individual experts in a crime laboratory, usually called criminalists, may be involved. But a few of the more commonly encountered areas are ballistics, spectroscopic examinations, hairs and fibers, soils, toxicology, glass and glass fractures, blood and other body fluids, paints, and chemicals.

DNA Experts

The use of DNA evidence requires the assistance of highly educated and trained experts. It would be impossible for an officer or another person, by way of training or experience only, to give an opinion with respect to such evidence. Consequently, it is necessary to have experts educated in the fields of genetics, biology, chemistry, and other sciences to testify as **DNA experts** concerning such evidence. Often, scientists with advanced degrees in the sciences will be required to testify, as this lends more credibility to their testimony in the eyes of the jury.

Footprint Experts

Footprints are admitted in evidence when their similarity to the shoes worn by a defendant justifies an inference that the prints were made by the defendant's shoes. Often, there is not much that science can add to a comparison of a cast or photograph made of a footprint found at a crime scene with the shoe of a suspect. Thus, recognizing similarities in any peculiar markings between the cast or photograph and the shoe, as well as comparing their sizes, can often be done by the jury with as much proficiency as an expert witness. In many cases, therefore, expert testimony is not needed or permitted. Of course, if the identification involves the use of scientific methods requiring technical expertise, then an expert witness will be required.

Even though expert testimony is not necessary when comparing footprints with a suspect's shoes, there are times when a footprint may have other significance to a case, and an analysis of the print may require the services of a **footprint expert**. Also, there are persons who are expert trackers or who have made a study of walking patterns; as experts, these persons can determine certain facts with considerable accuracy by examining tracks at a crime scene. For example, an expert may determine whether the suspect walked or ran from the scene, walked with a limp, was carrying something heavy, or was having difficulty with equilibrium. Additionally, there are experts in the examination of footwear. These experts are trained in determining the size and type of shoe that made an imprint at a crime scene. For example, the prosecution in the first criminal trial of O.J. Simpson called an expert to testify with respect to the bloody shoe prints leaving the scene of the double murder. The expert was highly qualified; he had a master's degree in forensic science, had extensive training in analyzing shoe prints as an FBI analyst, taught classes, and authored articles and a book concerning shoe print evidence. The expert testified, based on his examination of the bloody shoe prints, to the size, brand, and style of the shoe worn by the person tracking the blood while leaving the scene.

Psychologists and Psychiatrists

It is recognized that doctors specializing in psychiatry or psychology may state their opinion on the sanity of a person, but a perplexing problem arises as to whether a psychologist or psychiatrist may state an opinion on the sanity issue. It is known that sanity is a matter of mental illness; thus, a psychologist or psychiatrist who is trained and experienced in mental illnesses may qualify as an **expert on mental illness** and express an opinion on the sanity of a person. The problem arises in criminal cases in which the expert may testify that the accused suffered from a mental illness, but the expert may not state that the accused did or did not have the mental state or condition constituting an element of a crime or defense thereto; that issue is for the jury to determine.[25]

Polygraph Examiners

Concerted efforts have been made by those interested in polygraph examinations to have the results of these examinations admitted in evidence by the courts. **Polygraph experts** claim that the polygraph is now beyond the experimental stage and is a recognized scientific instrument capable of detecting when a person is being truthful or not. Although the courts have agreed that there has been substantial progress in improving the equipment and the operator techniques used in administering polygraph tests, very few courts will allow polygraph evidence to be admitted for any purpose.[26] The judicial aversion to polygraph evidence is attributable to the view that such evidence lacks reliability. It is alleged that too many factors can affect the reliability of the polygraph test. These factors include the emotional condition of the person being examined and his or her physical condition. Such physical factors as high or low blood pressure, drunkenness, fatigue, or use of drugs can lead to unreliable results. The experts in the field readily admit that these factors can and often do affect the tests, but they argue that, when these conditions exist, they will be taken into consideration and the results, if not reliable, will not be used. They also contend that, when conditions are normal, as is true in most instances, the results should be introduced in evidence for whatever assistance they may have in aiding the jury in arriving at a verdict. However, the courts fear that the weight given to the polygraph test by the jury would, in effect, permit the test to usurp the function of the jury.[27] It is believed that juries often find it difficult to accept the polygraph results as only an expert's opinion as to whether the person taking the polygraph test was truthful or not, and not a proven fact. Some courts take this view even though the judge may instruct the jury that the test result presented by the polygraph

POLYGRAPH EXPERTS
Persons expert in the workings, use, and results of tests using polygraphs.

APPLICATION CASE

In *United States v. Scheffer*,[28] the Supreme Court followed the nation-wide trend of rejecting polygraph evidence, even though a strong constitutional argument was offered in support of it. Scheffer, a member of the Air Force, applied for a job as an undercover drug investigator. As part of the routine qualification for the job, Scheffer submitted urine samples for drug testing. After submitting the urine sample but before its results were known, he also submitted to a polygraph test, the results of which indicated "no deception" when Scheffer denied using drugs. The urinalysis indicated the presence of methamphetamine. Scheffer was charged with, among other things, use of methamphetamine at a court-martial. Under Military Rule of Evidence 707, Scheffer's attempt to introduce the polygraph test results was rejected. He appealed, claiming that the exclusion of the evidence that would prove he did not know he took any drugs—"innocent use"—denied him a fair trial in violation of the Due Process Clause. In rejecting this constitutional claim, the Court held that the government has a greater interest in ensuring that only reliable evidence is admitted at trial. The Court reaffirmed the view that polygraph evidence is insufficiently reliable to be admitted in a trial to prove that the subject of a test was either lying or telling the truth.

examiner is only an opinion and the jury members may accept the opinion or reject it as they see fit. A significant number of courts will allow polygraph test results to be admitted, provided there is a stipulation by the parties. In other words, the results can be admitted if there is an agreement among the prosecutor, the defense attorney, and the defendant to admit such evidence.[29]

In those jurisdictions in which the courts have not accepted polygraph results, some prosecuting attorneys have endeavored to have the courts accept in evidence the refusal of a defendant to take a polygraph test on the grounds that the refusal proved guilty knowledge or consciousness of guilt. However, the courts have not generally accepted this refusal in evidence on the grounds that an accused may refuse to take a polygraph test, not because he or she fears that it will reveal a consciousness of guilt, but because the test may be unreliable. The courts likewise have refused to accept in evidence a defendant's expressed willingness to take a polygraph test. The courts state that a guilty suspect may be willing to risk taking the test in the hope that it will erroneously record innocence, knowing that, even if the test does not reflect innocence, the results cannot be used as evidence.[30]

Voiceprint Expert

ACOUSTICAL SPECTROGRAPHY The branch of science that consists of composing the voice or sound into harmonic components and obtaining a visual pattern of the sound—a spectrogram.

VOICEPRINT EXPERT An expert in voice identification, using the science of acoustical spectrography.

Individuals have been accepted by the courts as experts in the method of voice identification known as voiceprints. This method of voice identification consists of identifying or eliminating an unknown voice among several that are known by both listening to the voices and visually inspecting a spectrogram. **Acoustical spectrography** is the branch of science that consists of composing the voice or sound into harmonic components and obtaining a visual pattern of the sound. This pattern is called a spectrogram.

Generally, a **voiceprint expert** is utilized when a victim receives threatening calls about bombs, kidnapping, extortion, or other similar dangers and there is an opportunity to record the assailant's voice in some manner. Thereafter, if a suspect is located, his or her voice is also recorded, and the voiceprint expert will listen to the recordings and endeavor to determine similarities between the two recorded voices. The expert will also compare the voiceprint patterns displayed on the spectrograms and form an opinion as to whether the threatening voice of an unknown individual is identical to that of the known suspect. The expert, if properly qualified and if called upon to do so, may thereafter express an opinion concerning the identity of the threatening caller during the trial of the suspect.

Some courts have permitted the voiceprint expert to state an opinion on identity because it has been held that the voiceprint method of identification has reached a stage of acceptable reliability whereby the results are accepted as evidence. Some courts state that the test of admissibility of scientific evidence is whether or not it has received general acceptance by recognized experts in the field. The experts in the field of voiceprint

FYI

In the California case against Scott Peterson for the murder of his wife, Laci, and unborn child, an investigator for the California Department of Justice, who was the department's polygraph examiner, testified about his interview with Scott Peterson the day after Laci Peterson vanished. It was not disclosed to news sources whether the investigator administered a polygraph to Peterson during the interview. Even if he had administered a polygraph to Peterson, it would not have been admissible in court. Jurors were not even told that the investigator was a polygraph examiner.[31]

identification attest to its reliability. It is interesting to note that scientific voiceprint identification has entered the investigative field recently, compared with polygraph testing, yet voiceprint identification has received general acceptance by the courts, whereas polygraph results are accepted on a very limited basis, if at all.

Photographers

Except for certain scientific photographs, such as the spectrograph, micrograph, or X-ray, a photographer does not have to be an expert in the field of photography to have photographs admitted in evidence. (For further details, see Chapter 14, on photographic evidence.)

REFRESHING RECOLLECTION

If a witness, whether lay or expert, is incapable of testifying for the simple reason that his or her memory has failed, an attorney may refresh the witness's memory. Anyone who is going to testify about matters contained in detailed records, including law enforcement officers, should review the case file and become thoroughly familiar with it before a hearing or trial. All witnesses should also meet with the attorney, who will question them and discuss the testimony before trial. This is not so the witnesses can be told what to say, but to prepare them for their appearance in court. Despite thorough preparation, a witness may forget a fact while on the stand. Witnesses are, after all, just human. Fortunately, the law of evidence provides for assistance in such a situation—the process of **refreshing recollection**.

For example, FRE 612 allows for a witness to refer to a "writing" before or during testimony in an effort to revive his or her memory. The witness whose memory is to be refreshed must first testify that his or her memory has temporarily failed and that he or she cannot remember the facts. In some states, the attorney may refresh the recollection of a witness even if that witness has not appeared to have a faulty memory. The reason for this more lenient position is simply that witnesses may believe that they have remembered everything; examining the writing helps them remember additional facts.

There is a seemingly infinite number of items that may constitute a writing for purposes of refreshing a witness's memory. Moreover, the writing itself does not have to be admissible in evidence. In fact, a writing does not need to be used to refresh recollection. All that is required is that the witness testify that his or her personal recollection is revived after reading or seeing whatever was used to refresh recollection.

The witness need not even have prepared the writing, if one is used. In fact, the witness need not have any connection with the writing. Nor is it necessary that the writing be made at or near the time of the occurrences remembered. Finally, the Best Evidence Rule, which will be discussed in later chapters, is not applicable to

REFRESHING RECOLLECTION The process or fact of reviving a witness's memory by a variety of means.

An attorney may refresh the memory of a witness by the use of leading questions during examination. While FRE 612 deals only with the use of a writing to refresh memory, FRE 611(c) allows for the use of leading questions. As discussed earlier, leading questions are permitted on direct examination when necessary to develop the witness's testimony and are ordinarily permitted on cross-examination. Accordingly, refreshing recollection of a witness may occur upon either direct examination or cross-examination.

writings used to refresh a witness's memory. In sum, anything may be used to revive a witness's memory, as long as it is genuinely calculated to accomplish such a purpose. Examples include a note, a memorandum, a report, a photograph, a newspaper article, an object, a recording of a song, or an aroma.

Some technical aspects of FRE 612 deserve consideration. If the witness refers to a writing while testifying, opposing counsel has an absolute right to inspect the writing referred to, to cross-examine on it, and to introduce pertinent portions of it into evidence for any relevant purpose. On the other hand, if the witness refers to a writing prior to testifying, opposing counsel may inspect the writing "if the court decides that justice requires the party to have those options."[32] In either event, if a party claims that the writing used to refresh memory contains matters not related to the subject matter of the testimony, the judge will examine the writing *in camera* (privately, in the judge's chambers) and excise any unrelated portions of the writing. The judge will then return the remainder to the party seeking to refresh memory. Additionally, if, in a criminal case, a writing is not produced or delivered by the prosecution pursuant to a court order, the court may strike the testimony from the record or even declare a mistrial.

Past Recollection Recorded

A common situation at trial, especially for witnesses who testify about matters recorded in extensive reports or who testify often, is that the witness's memory cannot be refreshed as described in the previous section. When this occurs, an honest witness should admit to the problem, as quite often the forgotten fact has been recorded in a writing that will qualify as evidence as **past recollection recorded**. If the witness whose memory has failed and cannot be revived is able to testify that the writing used to attempt to refresh recollection contains an accurate account of the forgotten fact, then the contents of the writing itself are admissible in evidence in lieu of the witness's testimony.

There are a few technical aspects to the matter of past recollection recorded. First, before the writing may be used as past recollection recorded, the witness must be shown to have exhausted present recollection by failing to have recollection refreshed. Second, the writing must have been prepared by the witness, prepared at the witness's direction, or adopted by the witness. Third, the witness must be in a position to swear that at one time he or she had knowledge of the contents and that the contents were true and correct. Fourth, the evidence in the form of the writing is hearsay. (Hearsay will be discussed in greater detail in Chapter 7.) Fifth, the evidence is admissible hearsay because, as Chapter 7 will explain, there is an exception to the hearsay rule for past recollection recorded. Finally, the evidence, though admissible, may only be read to the jury; the writing is not admissible unless offered by the opponent.

FRE 803(5) contains the rule relating to past recollection recorded as an exception to the hearsay rule and states:

> **Recorded recollection.** A record that (a) is on a matter the witness once knew about but now cannot recall well enough to testify fully and accurately; (b) was made or adopted by the witness when the matter was fresh in the witness's memory; and (c) accurately reflects the witness's knowledge.

PAST RECOLLECTION RECORDED
A record of a fact, known by a witness at one time but not presently remembered, that will qualify as evidence.

If admitted, the record may be read into evidence, but may be received as an exhibit only if offered by an adverse party.

Thus, if a law enforcement professional conducts an investigation and while doing so writes down findings in a notebook, or records an interview in a notebook while questioning a person, the notebook may be used to refresh recollection. If, after reviewing the notes, the witness still does not recall the facts, the contents of the notebook may be offered as evidence.

Because the notepad is a potentially integral piece of evidence, great emphasis has been placed on it and on its continuing retention and preservation. The emphasis has been so great that many an officer's locker is so cluttered with old notepads that it resembles the back room of a secondhand bookstore. In certain instances, the defendant may be granted a right of discovery, allowing the defendant to review the officer's notes. Both state and federal courts, though, are reluctant to permit a defendant to inspect notes, memoranda, or reports prepared by law enforcement personnel in connection with a particular case. Such notes and memoranda constitute privileged information, as the work product of the officers, and only in compelling and exceptional circumstances may the accused inspect such notes.

An accused may overcome the privilege and obtain discovery if the officer is testifying as a witness. Several conditions may apply. First, the right to inspect the officer's notes may arise if the officer is using such notes to refresh his or her memory while on the stand. Second, if the officer was an eyewitness to the crime or is a witness to place the defendant at the scene of the crime, the accused may have the right to inspect the officer's notes or report in connection with the crime. Finally, and most important, the accused is absolutely entitled

In the law enforcement academy, students are taught to carry a small notepad in their shirt pocket. This notepad will be used to write down witness information, dates and times of incidents, arrival and departure times, special notes about crimes and criminals, informant information, and other work-related information that a patrol officer needs on a day-to-day basis. The section on past recollection recorded noted that, if an officer still cannot recall the pertinent information, his or her notes may be offered as evidence. If an officer's notepad is offered into evidence and is accepted by the court, *that notepad* may be open for inspection and analysis in court. This means that even the non-work-related information will be viewed by the judge and attorneys, including defense counsel. Additionally, and perhaps even more potentially damaging to an officer's professional reputation, defense counsel will have the opportunity to *cross-examine* the officer, in open court, based on that information. Many officers have been red-faced in front of the court and the jury when personal information meant for their eyes only was suddenly the topic of a blistering cross-examination in open court.

Officers should not tear out any pages of their notepads. If they do, the missing pages will be used against them on cross-examination. Some agencies require officers to save all notes. However, most allow the officer to write a report from the notes and then destroy them. In an instance in which notes have been destroyed, should the officer be questioned about their destruction, he or she should reply that all pertinent information is contained in the official report.

to have the prosecution provide all exculpatory evidence (evidence that exonerates the accused) within the prosecution's possession. Moreover, if the accused requests such information, then the prosecution must carefully scrutinize all evidence in searching for any exculpatory information. If the prosecution, either intentionally or unintentionally, fails to provide requested exculpatory evidence, the accused's right to due process of law or a fair trial may be violated. The right of discovery is discussed in more detail in Chapter 12.

Investigative Report as a Means of Refreshing Recollection and Past Recollection Recorded

An officer's investigative report, much like the officer's notepad, may be used to refresh the officer's memory while he or she is testifying as a witness. The report, as previously mentioned, need not have been prepared by the officer or at the officer's direction for purposes of refreshing his or her memory. Accordingly, the report may be one prepared by a police stenographer as dictated by the officer, or the report may be one prepared by another officer. Additionally, the report need not have been made at or near the time of the events that are reported.

Laying the Foundation for Past Recollection Recorded

The rules regarding refreshing memory are simple when compared with the steps that must be taken before an officer's investigative report may be admitted into evidence as a recorded recollection. If a proper foundation is laid for the recorded recollection exception to the hearsay rule, the investigative report or notepad may then be read into evidence in lieu of the officer's testimony.

The prosecuting attorney must carefully follow correct procedure before a police record or memorandum can be introduced into evidence. First, the attorney must show that the officer-witness once had personal knowledge of the matters contained in the record or memorandum; this issue is determined by the jury, whereas the remaining conditions are determined by the judge. Second, it must be shown that the officer made or adopted the record or memorandum when the matters were fresh in the officer's memory. This second step does not mean that the officer must have adopted or made the investigative report or notes at the same time or immediately following the events reported, only that the events were still fresh in the officer's memory when the report was made. The time lapse between the events and the recording of those events, though, is probative in determining whether the matters were still fresh in the officer's memory. Third, the record or memorandum must accurately reflect the knowledge the officer once had. Finally, the prosecuting attorney must show that the testifying officer currently has insufficient recollection to enable him or her to testify fully and accurately. This final requirement is satisfied if it is shown that the record or memorandum fails to refresh the officer's recollection. Of course, the defense attorney is still entitled to cross-examine the officer, but such questioning will be limited because there is no testimony. The attorney may cross-examine the officer regarding who made the report if the officer-witness adopted the report, or the officer may be questioned about how soon the report was made after the occurrence of the event. Otherwise, there is little that may be asked on cross-examination.

Some examples of laying the foundation for recorded recollections may be helpful at this point. The witness may testify that he or she remembers making an accurate recording of the event in question, which he or she now no longer sufficiently remembers. Alternatively, the officer may testify that he or she routinely makes accurate and complete records of this kind. If the officer has totally forgotten the situation within which the recording was prepared, then the officer may testify that he or she is confident from the circumstances that he or she would not have made or adopted such a description of the facts unless that description accurately reflected the observations at the time.

In the event that the record or memorandum is admitted into evidence, it may only be read into evidence by the witness or the attorney. This means that the investigative report or officer's notepad may not be received as an exhibit for the jury to take into the deliberation room. The only occasion in which the report or notepad may be received as an exhibit is when the defense offers it as evidence.

REVIEW AND APPLICATION

SUMMARY

(1) The one essential characteristic required before a person may become a witness is that he or she has personal knowledge of the matter to which he or she testifies.

(2) The Constitution, in the Sixth Amendment, gives the accused the right to compulsory process and to confrontation of his or her accusers. These rights guarantee the accused the right to call witnesses.

(3) A leading question is one that suggests the answer in the question.

(4) Five exceptions to the rule prohibiting leading questions on direct examination are questioning (1) with respect to undisputed preliminary or inconsequential matters; (2) when a witness is hostile, unwilling, frightened, or biased; (3) with respect to a child or adult witness who has difficulty communicating; (4) a witness whose recollection is exhausted; and (5) when laying a necessary foundation under certain circumstances.

(5) Impeachment is a process or a result that diminishes or destroys the believability of a witness's testimony.

(6) The five basic methods of impeachment are (1) by contradiction; (2) by proof of bad character for truthfulness; (3) by proof of prior inconsistent statement; (4) by proof of bias or motive to falsify; and (5) by proof of lack of or diminished witness capacity.

(7) The subjects on which lay people may give opinions include state of emotion; speed of vehicles; distances; sobriety or intoxication; age, identity, and physical condition of a person; weight, color, and value; character of a person; sanity; and handwriting.

(8) Generally speaking, under the FRE an expert may testify if the scientific, technical, or other specialized knowledge he or she provides will assist the jury in understanding the evidence or in determining a material fact.

(9) All that is necessary to qualify as an expert witness is scientific, technical, or "specialized" knowledge that the ordinary person does not have.

(10) The three requirements for expert testimony are (1) the subject matter of the expert's proposed testimony must be relevant; (2) the expert's field must be one requiring scientific, technical, or specialized knowledge; and (3) the witness must be shown to have the background necessary to qualify as an expert in the field.

(11) The three bases for expert opinion are (1) personal knowledge of the expert by actual examination of the evidence; (2) information from any source usually relied upon by experts in the field; and (3) hypothetical facts from which the witness is asked to draw conclusions.

(12) A witness's recollection may be refreshed when the witness experiences a temporary failure of memory or, in some states, when the answer given clearly indicates to the questioning attorney that there has been a failure of memory. Anything may be used to refresh recollection, for example, notes, memoranda, reports, photographs, newspaper articles, objects, song recordings, or aromas.

(13) The steps required before a witness's recorded recollection may be admitted into evidence are (1) the witness's present memory must be shown to have failed; (2) any attempt to refresh recollection must also fail; (3) the witness's recollection has been shown to be exhausted; (4) the witness must identify some recording of the recollection that the witness can swear was complete and accurate at the time it was made, and that the witness at one time had personal knowledge of the information recorded; and (5) the recorded recollection may only be read to the jury, not shown to them.

KEY TERMS

QUESTIONS FOR REVIEW

1. What must a person possess in order to be a witness?
2. What two rights in the Constitution guarantee that an accused person may call witnesses on his or her behalf?
3. What is a leading question?
4. What are the five exceptions to the rule prohibiting leading questions on direct examination?
5. What is impeachment?
6. What are the five methods of impeachment?
7. What are some subjects on which lay persons may give opinion testimony?
8. Under what circumstances can expert testimony be introduced?
9. How may a witness be qualified as an expert?
10. What are the three foundational requirements for an expert's testimony?
11. What are the three bases for expert opinion?
12. When and how may a witness's recollection be refreshed?
13. What are the steps that must be taken before a witness's recorded recollection may be admitted into evidence?

WORKPLACE APPLICATIONS

1. You know that many of the daily reports you write could end up being used in court to prove a defendant's guilt. Keeping in mind that you will be called as a lay witness to explain your report, write a narrative report describing a domestic dispute call. Describe the emotions of the quarreling parties in a way that is free from misinterpretation by the jury and is difficult for the defense attorney to misconstrue during your cross-examination.
2. After 15 years in the narcotics division and hundreds of drug arrests and court appearances, the head of the division thinks you are ready to qualify as a drug detection expert. List the factors that would qualify you as an expert.
3. You are called upon to testify in a drug trafficking case. You have written several reports over the course of your first year on the job, have had your deposition taken, and have testified before a grand jury. You read all these statements before trial and discover that, over the period involved, there have been some innocent inconsistencies in your story. As a result of these inconsistencies, you may appear to the jury to be mistaken, confused, or even lying. The opposing lawyer may be able to discredit you totally during cross-examination. What can you do to lessen the impact of the inconsistencies without damaging the case? What do you tell the prosecutor, if anything?
4. While serving as a training officer several years ago, you had a new trainee take and write up a burglary report. You have now been called to testify

about the burglary. The trainee is no longer with the department and is unavailable to testify. You have no recollection of the incident, and reading the not-so-well-written report does not help. The prosecutor wants to admit the report as a past recollection recorded. You are uncertain about the accuracy of the report because you remember that the trainee was not a very good report writer. Can the report be admitted?

ETHICAL DILEMMA

1. The prosecutor asks you to locate a witness, so that he can be subpoenaed to appear in a murder trial. You know that the witness is hostile and could damage the case. You use the normal procedures to find the witness, but without success. You know that the court will be satisfied with your efforts and deem the witness unavailable. Then you hear a reliable rumor that places the witness in a specific town in another state. Should you pursue the rumor further, tell the prosecutor about it, or just let the matter drop?

ENDNOTES

1. 380 U.S. 400 (1965).

2. The United States Supreme Court has interpreted the Compulsory Process Clause as giving criminal defendants the right "to the government's assistance in compelling the attendance of favorable witnesses at trial and the right to put before a jury evidence that might influence the determination of guilt." Miriam Riskind, *Can a Client Be Held Liable for Attorney's Misconduct? Let the Client Beware!* 15 T. Marshall L. Rev. 103, 114 (1989–1990) (citing the Court's opinion in Pennsylvania v. Ritchie, 480 U.S. 39 (1987)).

3. *Id.* at 115.

4. *Id.* at 103, citing Taylor v. Illinois, 484 U.S. 400 (1988).

5. *Id.* at 114, citing Pennsylvania v. Ritchie, 480 U.S. 39 (1987).

6. Fed. R. Evid. 611(c) addresses the subject of leading questions.

7. This hypothetical example is based on United States v. Copelin, 996 F.2d 379 (D.C. Cir. 1993).

8. *See* Fed. R. Evid. 613(b), for the federal requirement.

9. United States v. Abel, 469 U.S. 45 (1984).

10. Fed. R. Evid. 701.

11. Holland v. Zollner, 102 Cal. 633, 638–39 (1894).

12. Massachusetts and New York still have the bar against lay testimony concerning the sanity of the accused. Gorham v. Moor, 84 N.E. 436 (1908); Matter of Estate of Vickery, 561 N.Y.S.2d 937 (N.Y. App. Div. 1990). Neither Delaware nor Hawaii has specifically decided the question yet.

13. Fed. R. Evid. 702.

14. 509 U.S. 579 (1993).

15. 526 U.S. 137 (1999).

16. The *Frye* standard was derived from the case of Frye v. United States, 293 F. 1013 (D.C. Cir. 1923).

17. This report is available to read online at no charge: *see* http://www.nap.edu /catalog.php?record_id=12589#toc (last visited 3/28/09).

18. The summary is also accessible online: http://books.nap.edu /openbook.php? record_id =12589&page=5 (and the page following, last visited 3/28/09).

19. *See* op ed piece of Professor Jennifer Mnookin, appearing in the *Los Angeles Times* on February 19, 2009: http://www.latimes.com/news /opinion/commentary/la-oe -mnookin19-2009feb19,0,709564 .story (last visited 12/1/13).

20. Marshall v. State, 51 A.3d 641, 652 (Md. 2012).

21. *See* AMERICAN BAR ASSOCIATION, Criminal Justice Forensic Science Task Force, Report, ADOPTED BY THE HOUSE OF DELEGATES, FEBRUARY 6, 2012.

22. Anna Gorman, *LAPD Narcotics Analyst Erred; Botched Evidence Raises Questions on Credibility. Public Defender's Office Demands an Accounting,* Los Angeles Times, September 4, 2004, at B1.

23. Fed. R. Evid. 705, advisory committee's note.

24. 567 U.S. 50 (2012).

25. *See,* for example, Fed. R. Evid. 704(b): In a criminal case, an expert witness must not state an opinion about whether the defendant did or did not have a mental state or condition that constitutes an element of the crime charged or of a defense. Those matters are for the trier of fact alone.

26. State v. Thompkins, 891 So.2d 1151 (Fla. Ct. App. 2005).

27. State v. McNaught, 713 P.2d 457, 469 (Kan. 1986).

28. Cassamassima v. Florida, 657 So.2d 906 (Florida Ct. App. 1995).

29. 523 U.S. 303 (1998).

30. *See* West Virginia v. Chambers, 459 S.E.2d 112, 114 (1995) ("reference to an offer or refusal by a defendant to take a polygraph test is inadmissible in criminal trials to the same extent that polygraph results are inadmissible").

31. Diana Walsh & Stacy Finz, *The Peterson Trial,* S.F. Chronicle, July 7, 2004, at B1.

32. Fed. R. Evid. 612 (a) (2).

Design Element: ©Ingram Publishing

6 CREDIBILITY AND IMPEACHMENT

CHAPTER OUTLINE

CHAPTER OBJECTIVES

The previous chapter discussed witnesses and touched briefly upon the subjects of this chapter, credibility and impeachment. After reading this chapter, you will be able to:

▶ Name the four components of witness capacity.

▶ List the five basic methods of impeaching a witness.

▶ Name the two types of criminal convictions that may be admitted to impeach a witness.

▶ Explain the difference between the balancing test applied to the admission of evidence of a conviction of a criminal defendant who testifies and the balancing test of FRE 403.

▶ Describe the types of crimes that are automatically admissible to impeach a witness.

▶ Explain the principal restriction upon impeachment by the use of evidence of misconduct not resulting in a conviction of a witness.

▶ Name the one requirement for the introduction of extrinsic evidence of a prior inconsistent statement.

▶ State the rule governing the impeachment of a witness on the grounds of bias.

▶ State the rule governing the impeachment of one's own witness.

▶ Describe when a witness may invoke the privilege against self-incrimination.

▶ Name the prevailing form of witness immunity in the United States.

CREDIBILITY

CREDIBILITY
The quality in a witness
that renders the witness's
evidence worthy of belief.

Credibility is the quality in a witness that renders the witness's evidence worthy of belief. If a witness is able to impress the jury with the ability to observe correctly, to retain observations, and to relate them convincingly on the witness stand, the witness will be perceived by the jury as being very credible. In other words, the credibility of a witness is entirely dependent upon how much the jury believes the testimony—how much credit the jury gives it. A jury may believe the entire testimony, or it may believe part of it and not believe other parts. It is not unusual for a jury to disbelieve all the testimony given by a witness.

ON THE JOB

One way for a law enforcement professional to appear credible to a jury is to be prepared. As with any witness, he or she should review any prior testimony or statements that he or she made or wrote. He or she should also try to meet with the prosecutor before trial to run through the important trial issues and to discuss the types of questions that will be asked on direct examination, as well as potential cross-examination questions. The goal is not to rehearse the witness's answers but, rather, to make the witness more comfortable, relaxed, and ultimately more credible to the jury. Maintaining good eye contact with the jury, prosecutor, and judge also helps build credibility.

Not all false testimony is the result of lying. A witness may give testimony that is truthful, accurate, and clear, or a witness may give testimony that is untruthful, inaccurate, or distorted. Moreover, a witness's testimony may be false because the witness is lying or merely mistaken. Figure 6–1 shows the general credibility instruction given to jurors in criminal cases in federal trials in the United States.

Before testifying, a witness is required to take an oath or affirm to tell the truth. However, a witness might not tell the truth for a number of different reasons. Recall that witness capacity, discussed in Chapter 5, consists of perception, memory, narrative ability, and sincerity. A deficiency in perception, for instance, if the witness was unable to observe correctly, can result in the witness honestly believing that he or she saw something that was not, in fact, the reality. Poor memory may lead to original observations becoming so confused that a witness gives an unintentionally inaccurate account of what was seen. A person who cannot speak effectively, because of a speech impediment, for example, cannot be understood. In terms of sincerity, a witness may have some interest in the case, sympathy for one side or a prejudice against the other, or a financial interest in the outcome. Any of these factors may cause a witness to consciously or unconsciously color testimony toward a particular side. In addition, some persons, for any number of reasons, intentionally falsify their testimony.

All of these possibilities affect the credibility of the witness. If the jury is unaware of these factors, jurors may still believe the story as related by a witness, irrespective of how false or inaccurate the testimony may have been.

You . . . are the sole and exclusive judges of the credibility of each of the witnesses called to testify . . . and only you determine . . . weight that their testimony deserves. . . .

[In deciding the weight] you should carefully scrutinize all of the testimony given by that witness, the circumstances under which each witness has testified, and all of the other evidence which tends to show whether a witness, in your opinion, is worthy of belief. Consider each witness's intelligence, motive to falsify, state of mind, and appearance and manner while on the witness stand. Consider the witness's ability to observe the matters as to which he or she has testified and consider whether he or she impresses you as having an accurate memory or recollection of these matters. Consider also any relation a witness may bear to either side of the case, the manner in which each witness might be affected by your verdict, and the extent to which, if at all, each witness is either supported or contradicted by other evidence in the case.

Inconsistencies or discrepancies in the testimony of a witness or between the testimony of different witnesses may or may not cause you to disbelieve or discredit such testimony. Two or more persons witnessing an incident or a transaction may simply see or hear it differently. Innocent misrecollection, like failure of recollection is not an uncommon human experience. In weighing the effect of a discrepancy, however, always consider whether it pertains to a matter of importance or an insignificant detail and consider whether the discrepancy results from innocent error or from intentional falsehood. . . .

(The testimony of a defendant should be judged in the same manner as the testimony of any other witness.)

FIGURE 6–1 The federal general credibility instruction. **Source:** Kevin F. O'Malley, Jay E. Grenig, and Hon. William C. Lee, 1A Fed. Jury Prac. & Instr. § 15:01 (6th ed.) (West 2018).

ON THE JOB

Out in the field, law enforcement professionals make a lot of credibility assessments. They decide which witnesses to believe or which ones to give little credence to. Many times, a person's credibility will have to be judged based upon that person's behavior. Factors that the professional will evaluate include a person's body language, such as his or her refusal to look the investigator in the eye or excessive fidgeting; a witness's emotions, such as a father not being upset about his missing infant; and possible motivations, such as a grandmother trying to protect her gang-member grandson. Sometimes the law enforcement professional bases the assessment of the witness on a gut feeling that someone is lying or that his or her story does not ring true.

Thus, in effect, when the law enforcement professional writes reports, he or she is the first person to record credibility factors that will help the prosecutor decide whether to charge a person with a crime or determine which witnesses to call, and ultimately will aid the jury in reaching a verdict. With this in mind, the law enforcement professional should be sure to record his or her perceptions in this regard.

BASIC METHODS OF IMPEACHMENT

IMPEACHMENT
The process by which the credibility of a witness is attacked.

Impeachment is the process by which the credibility of a witness is attacked. There are five basic methods of impeaching a witness:

1. by showing that the witness has a bad character with respect to the trait of truthfulness;
2. by contradiction;
3. by showing that the witness has made statements inconsistent with his or her present testimony;
4. by showing that the witness is biased; and
5. by showing that the witness has a failure or deficiency in the ability to perceive, remember, or narrate.

The need for impeachment of a witness is, of course, very much a function of the significance of the witness's testimony to the outcome of the case. In many instances, counsel will not even attempt to impeach a witness's testimony because the testimony is not significant enough to warrant the time and effort. However, the testimony of the law enforcement professional is usually very significant in a criminal trial. Therefore, there is normally a strong incentive for the defense to attack the witness's credibility in such cases. For this reason, the various methods of impeachment, discussed in detail in this chapter, should be carefully studied.

Before discussing the methods of impeachment in detail, it will be useful to consider the general procedure followed in making attacks upon the credibility of witnesses. As pointed out in Chapter 2, detracting from the witness's credibility, if possible, is a major goal of cross-examination. In almost all instances, impeachment begins with cross-examination of the witness. But another goal of cross-examination is to present the witness's testimony in the light most favorable to the cross-examiner's case, if possible. And yet another goal of cross-examination is to safeguard the accuracy and completeness of the testimony. Certain points mentioned during direct examination may be clarified. Or such points may be brought forth in greater detail and their accuracy measured. During this measurement of accuracy, it may be determined that the witness did not actually recall the details and is now confused concerning them. Thus, the process of impeachment begins.

Attempts to impeach a witness may be well founded. If a witness has inaccurately related facts on the witness stand, the inaccuracies should be brought out during the cross-examination, and an attack upon the witness's credibility is in order. Not all witnesses are impeachable, however. If a witness's testimony seriously damages the cross-examiner's case, there will be every incentive to attack the witness's credibility. However, an attack upon the witness that fails to shake the witness's credibility may very well backfire and hurt the cross-examiner's case even further.

If the cross-examination is aimed at impeachment, a witness may be questioned on a number of matters that seem to have no relationship to the issues of the case. Remember that the scope of cross-examination is limited to the subject matter that was introduced during direct examination. However, a witness's credibility is almost always relevant for cross-examination. Even if a judge is strict in ensuring that the scope of the subject matter is carefully limited, he or she will usually permit considerable liberty in allowing questions that address credibility. If questions seem misdirected, the cross-examiner may have to prove to the satisfaction of the trial judge that the questions are designed for impeachment purposes. However, the lengths to which the cross-examiner may go in questioning the witness are entirely up to the discretion of the trial judge.

In some instances, the effort to impeach a witness may not take place through the cross-examination but, rather, through the use of testimony of an impeaching witness or the introduction of an impeaching document or object. The impeaching witness may merely contradict the testimony of the first witness. The impeaching witness may, however, testify that a witness has a bad reputation for truthfulness or testify in an effort to prove bias or prejudice on the part of the first witness. A document may be introduced to prove that, contrary to what a witness testified, he or she did make a statement inconsistent with that prior testimony. In many instances, efforts to impeach a witness may be made by a combination of cross-examination and impeaching witnesses or other evidence.

BAD CHARACTER FOR TRUTHFULNESS

Proof of a trait of character relating to untruthfulness may take the form of the following:

1. evidence of conviction of certain crimes;
2. questioning about bad conduct that did not result in a conviction;
3. evidence of a reputation for untruthfulness; or
4. opinion testimony regarding untruthfulness.

This evidence is restricted in both form and content. Proof of character is severely restricted under the law of evidence and will be discussed in detail in Chapter 11. In short, according to the **character evidence rule**, evidence of a trait of character to prove a person's conduct in conformity with that trait is inadmissible, with a few exceptions. For example, introducing proof that a defendant in an auto theft case previously stole a car, to help prove guilt in the current case, is prohibited by the rule. One of those few exceptions is proof of a trait of bad character of a witness for truthfulness.

CHARACTER EVIDENCE RULE
The rule that states evidence of a trait of character to prove a person's conduct in conformity with that trait is inadmissible, with a few exceptions.

Evidence of Conviction of Certain Crimes

A common law rule relating to witness competency was that a convicted felon was incompetent to testify. As described in Chapter 4, the modern law of evidence declares that all persons are competent to testify, thus eliminating the common law grounds for incompetency, including conviction of a felony. However, the modern rules of evidence relating to character and impeachment still retain vestiges of the old incompetency notions. One of these vestiges is the rule that a person convicted of a crime punishable by imprisonment for a term of more than a year or by death (essentially, a felony) may be impeached by proof of that conviction. This is so even if the conviction is for a crime that has nothing to do with truthfulness or honesty. For example, a crime of violence, such as assault or rape, does not involve dishonesty as does a crime such as perjury or deceptive practices. The theory underlying the admission of evidence of conviction of such crimes is that a person who would commit such a serious offense is of questionable credibility as a witness. At the very least, the jury is entitled to consider the fact of the conviction as it relates to the witness's credibility.

Two types of criminal convictions may be admitted to impeach a witness. First, as already stated, is a conviction for a crime that is punishable by more than one year's imprisonment or by death, essentially a felony. Second, a conviction for a crime involving dishonesty or false statement, regardless of the potential or actual punishment, may be admitted. These rules are according to the FRE (see Rule 609) but are consistent with those found in most states prior to the adoption of the FRE. In those states where the FRE have not been adopted, there may be some deviation from the rules as stated.

If the witness is *not* the accused in a criminal case and the conviction is one punishable by imprisonment in excess of a year or by death, under the FRE,[1] the evidence of the conviction must also be found by the trial judge to be logically relevant without being substantially outweighed by the danger of unfair prejudice, and the like, under FRE 403. When the witness is also the accused in a criminal case, a different balancing test applies to convictions under this rule. In such a case, the evidence is inadmissible if the unfair prejudicial effect of the evidence merely *outweighs* the probative value. This special balancing test differs from the Rule 403 test in that the word "substantial" has been removed and, therefore, the prejudicial value has only to be slightly greater than the probative value for the evidence to be prohibited. If the conviction is one for a crime involving dishonesty or false statement, under the FRE,[2] the evidence is automatically admissible and is not subject to either balancing test.

Felony convictions that qualify for admissibility for impeachment are those for offenses that are *punishable* by imprisonment for more than a year or by death. It does not matter what the actual sentence was. Even if a person was not imprisoned, the conviction would still qualify for impeachment purposes under the rule. For example, assume that a person is convicted of grand larceny for stealing a diamond ring from a department store. Assume further that, since it was his first offense, or for other reasons, the judge imposed a sentence of five years but suspended the sentence and placed the defendant on probation. This conviction could be used to impeach the convicted person, should he appear as a witness at a subsequent trial.

The crimes that qualify for impeachment regardless of the penalty imposed, and without balancing for the potential prejudicial nature of the evidence, are

MYTH ▶   ◀ FACT

MYTH ▶	◀ FACT
A person convicted of a serious crime, a felony, is not competent to be a witness.	A person convicted of a felony is competent to be a witness, but the felony conviction may be introduced to impeach the witness's credibility.

much more narrowly defined. Crimes involving dishonesty or false statement include "perjury or subornation of perjury [inducing another to commit perjury], false statement, criminal fraud, embezzlement, or false pretense or any other offense . . . the commission of which involves some element of deceit, untruthfulness, or falsification bearing on the accused's propensity to testify truthfully."[3] Beyond this description contained in the legislative history of the FRE, there is substantial difference of opinion as to what crimes are within the rule.

There are some other restrictions on the admissibility of evidence of convictions of crimes for impeachment purposes under the FRE. Generally, only convictions ten years old or less are admissible (the ten years is measured from the date of release from confinement). Evidence of a conviction is not admissible if the conviction was the subject of a pardon, an annulment, or a certificate of rehabilitation under certain circumstances. Evidence of juvenile adjudications is generally not admissible. With respect to both the time limit and juvenile adjudications, the trial court may, under certain circumstances, allow the evidence to be used.

Misconduct Not Resulting in a Conviction

Evidence relating to conduct that might show the witness is not to be trusted is not admissible if it did not result in a conviction. For example, evidence that the witness lied on his or her income tax returns for the last ten years would be inadmissible in court, even though it could shed some light on the witness's credibility, unless the witness was actually convicted of tax evasion. However, under FRE 608(b), inquiry may be made into specific acts of misconduct that relate to truthfulness. Thus, the cross-examiner of the witness who lied on his or her tax returns but was not convicted of a crime could ask, "Isn't it true that you lied on your tax returns for the past ten years?" There are two requirements or restrictions that must be met before the cross-examiner can even ask this question. First, the cross-examiner must have a basis-in-fact for asking the question. In other words, no unfounded fishing expeditions are permitted for this form of cross-examination. Second, the cross-examiner must accept the witness's answer. No evidence may be presented to prove the acts of misconduct. There may be further cross-examination of the witness in an effort to bring the misconduct to light, but, if this questioning is still unproductive, the inquiry ends despite the cross-examiner's wishes.

MYTH ▶	◀ FACT
Only misconduct resulting in a criminal conviction may be introduced in evidence to impeach a witness.	Any misconduct that relates to a witness's character for truthfulness may be raised on cross-examination to impeach a witness. However, if the witness was not convicted of a crime, the interrogator must accept the witness's answer and cannot introduce evidence of the misconduct if the witness denies it.

Opinion and Reputation Evidence Relating to Truthfulness

Two other forms of evidence permitted to prove character are opinion and reputation evidence. A person who has sufficient personal knowledge of another individual may well be in a position to render an opinion or testify to the reputation of the character of the person in question. This witness is often referred to as a **character witness**. A character witness's testimony is limited to opinion or reputation evidence that the first witness's character for truthfulness, honesty, or integrity is bad. An opinion is expressed in terms of what the character witness believes the first witness's character for truthfulness is. Reputation evidence is expressed in terms of what the character witness has heard about the character of the first witness for truthfulness. Reputation evidence, although hearsay, is admissible within an exception to the hearsay rule.[4]

To qualify as a character witness when the testimony is in opinion form, the character witness must be shown to have close contact with the witness whose character is being attacked. The contact must be close enough to enable the character witness to have a sufficient knowledge of the person upon which to base an opinion as to character. However, the character witness is forbidden to testify to specific instances of conduct. The testimony is limited to the character witness's general opinion.

Similarly, the character witness who testifies to the subject witness's reputation for truthfulness must be in a position to know what others say and think about that person. For this purpose, it is usually necessary to prove that the character witness has some community with the subject witness, that is, resides or works in the same area as the subject witness or travels in the same social circle. Here, too, the character witness is not permitted to testify about specifics, with respect to the subject witness's conduct or specific conversations.

As a response to an attack on a witness's character for untruthfulness, dishonesty, or lack of integrity, the side that called the impeached witness may itself call witnesses in rebuttal. These character witnesses may also testify in the form of opinion or reputation that the original witness has a good character for truthfulness, honesty, and integrity. However, evidence of such good character cannot be presented until the character of the witness has been attacked.

CONTRADICTION

Impeachment by **contradiction** is the act of saying the opposite of a statement or specifically denying a statement. In its simplest form, impeachment by contradiction is the cross-examiner's act of merely asking the witness to deny the fact or facts previously stated on direct examination. Of course, this form of contradiction is rarely, if ever, successful. Moreover, asking a witness to deny his or her previous testimony borders on being argumentative, which is not permitted.

Contradiction through cross-examination may also be achieved by artful questioning that demonstrates the witness could not be correct. The goal of artful questioning is to contradict a witness on a small point, and then to use this small point to impeach the witness's entire testimony. Taking certain details and reorganizing them might show that the witness could not have been correct about the time, location, distance, or some other detail of the direct examination testimony. For example, assume that the witness was the victim of a robbery at gunpoint. The witness then testifies to the identity of the accused from a photographic lineup on April 15, 2019. If cross-examination demonstrated that the witness was, at that date and time, at the IRS offices miles away, delivering a request for extension of filing of personal income taxes, the date of the identification would be contradicted and the credibility of the witness's entire testimony would come under question.

Contradiction may be achieved by calling a witness to testify to a fact that directly contradicts a fact testified to by a prior witness. In the case just described, the cross-examiner might elicit a reaffirmation of the date, time, and circumstances surrounding the photographic identification on cross-examination. Then, the cross-examiner, during his or her next opportunity to present evidence, could call a witness to testify to seeing the previous witness at the IRS offices at the day and time that the photographic identification was supposedly taking place. As long as the testimony or other evidence offered in contradiction is relevant and a proper foundation is laid, the testimony or evidence is admissible.

PRIOR INCONSISTENT STATEMENTS

One of the most frequently used means of impeachment is to show that the witness has made prior statements inconsistent with those being made in the present testimony. These inconsistent statements may have been made at any time before the trial, or they may be made during the trial. A witness's statement during cross-examination that is inconsistent with the witness's testimony on direct examination may impeach the witness. In fact, one of the reasons for extensive cross-examination is to determine whether the witness will give inconsistent answers.

Inconsistent statements are logically relevant to impeach a witness because a person who speaks inconsistently is less likely to be accurate or truthful. Therefore, any inconsistent statement demonstrates a weakness of credibility, regardless of the circumstances under which the statement is made. When an inconsistent statement is used for impeachment purposes, its relevance does not depend upon the content of the statement being true. Inconsistent statements offered only for impeachment purposes need not be made under oath.

In a majority of states, particularly those that have adopted the FRE, there is no special foundation required for the introduction of a prior inconsistent statement. Therefore, if a witness makes a statement during direct or cross-examination that is inconsistent with a statement made at any other time, that statement may be introduced by the opposing party during the time that the party introduces its

INCONSISTENT STATEMENTS
Statements inconsistent with the present testimony. Such statements are logically relevant to impeach a witness because one who speaks inconsistently is less likely to be accurate or truthful.

MYTH ▶ ◀ FACT

MYTH ▶	◀ FACT
For a prior inconsistent statement to be used in a trial to impeach a witness, the statement must have been made under oath and/or at a trial, hearing, or other proceeding.	A prior statement is admissible to impeach a witness, regardless of when or how made, as long as it is inconsistent with the trial testimony of a witness, is relevant, and meets certain other minimal requirements.

©Bettmann/Getty Images

Several powerful politicians, including former U.S. Attorney General John Mitchell, shown here, were convicted of perjury during the Watergate scandal of the early 1970s.

own evidence. The only requirement is that the witness who is being impeached must be afforded an opportunity to explain or deny the statement, and the opposing party must be afforded an opportunity to interrogate the witness with respect to the statement.[5] As an example, assume that a witness testifies for the defense in a criminal case, stating that the witness was with the accused in another city on the day and at the time the crime was committed. Before the trial, the witness told one of her friends, during a casual conversation, that she was home alone on the day and at the time the crime took place. On cross-examination, the prosecutor could ask the witness to reaffirm her testimony that she was with the accused at the pertinent time. Then, during the rebuttal case, the prosecution could call the witness's friend to present contradictory testimony. If the jury believes the friend's testimony, the original witness's statement is impeached by a prior inconsistent statement.

The previous example is but one way to use a prior inconsistent statement to impeach a witness. Perhaps a more common approach is for the cross-examiner to confront the witness with the inconsistent statement. This approach would have the questioner direct the witness's attention to the circumstances surrounding the making of the inconsistent statement and asking the witness if the statement was, in fact, made. If the witness admits making the statement, then the cross-examiner has succeeded in showing a prior inconsistent statement. If the witness denies making the statement, then the opposing party will have satisfied the requirements of FRE 613(b) and may introduce evidence of the prior inconsistent statement when the next opportunity presents itself.

A pretrial statement by a defendant may also be admitted for impeachment purposes as a prior inconsistent statement. There are special considerations for such statements, however. First, the defendant's statements are independently admissible as opposing parties' statements (see the next chapter, "The Hearsay Rule"). Whether in the form of a confession, either formal or informal, or just a passing remark, anything an accused says that is relevant and usable against him or her is admissible insofar as the hearsay rule is concerned. An example of a usable passing remark is the following: A police officer arrests Joe and says, "Joe, you are under arrest for robbery." Joe says, "What robbery?" The officer says, "Maria's robbery." Joe blurts out, "I was out of town yesterday afternoon."

Second, any statement sought to be used against the accused must meet constitutional and procedural requirements. At the very least, if the statement was made while the accused was in custody, the familiar warnings required by *Miranda v. Arizona*[6] must have been given. The warnings must be given and the accused must waive the *Miranda* rights before the statement is made, in order for the statement to be admissible.[7] There are also other constitutional requirements that could make an accused's statements inadmissible. These include the Fourth Amendment's prohibition against unreasonable search and seizure; the Fifth

ON THE JOB

A law enforcement officer should be very careful about what he or she says and how it is said when speaking with defense counsel. This is especially so when an officer is engaged in casual conversation about the case, particularly in halls and the courtroom before and during the proceedings. *Anything* an officer says can be used against the officer as a prior inconsistent statement. People are particularly prone to quote others out of context and claim that the quotation is inconsistent with prior testimony. Officers cannot avoid speaking with counsel, but caution should be the watchword. A good rule is for the law enforcement officer to avoid allowing defense counsel to draw him or her into conversations.

Amendment's Due Process Clause, which prohibits coerced confessions; and the Sixth Amendment's Right to Counsel, prohibiting interrogation of an accused in the absence of counsel after indictment. If any of these requirements have been violated, any statement made by an accused person is rendered inadmissible by the **exclusionary rule**. Chapter 9 discusses search and seizure law in detail.

If the statement of an accused is offered by the prosecution in a criminal case to impeach the testimony of the accused, then the exclusionary rules may not apply and the evidence may be admissible. In other words, if the defendant testifies at trial and makes statements inconsistent with statements made at the time of arrest, the prior inconsistent statement may be used to impeach the defendant, even if it was made under circumstances that violated *Miranda*.[8] In fact, the accused's statements may be used for impeachment purposes even if the inconsistency is asserted by the accused for the first time during cross-examination by the prosecution.[9] If the inconsistency is contained in the testimony of a witness other than the accused, then a statement taken from the accused in violation of *Miranda* cannot be used to impeach.[10]

EXCLUSIONARY RULE
The rule that provides that illegally obtained evidence will be excluded from use in a criminal trial.

BIAS OR MOTIVE TO FALSIFY

One effective way to discredit the testimony of a witness is to show that the witness entertains a feeling for or against one side in the trial. For example, a defense witness may be a close relative of the defendant, and a favorable bias would be natural. However, aside from pointing out the close relationship by

MYTH ▶	◀ FACT
A person who is very biased, such as the mother of the accused, is so interested in the outcome of the case that he or she is incompetent to be a witness.	Although bias is always provable in any case, the witness's bias, prejudice, or interest in the outcome of the case does not make the witness incompetent. The jury is merely entitled to take the matter into account in evaluating the witness's testimony.

questioning the witness, it may be difficult to prove bias. On the other hand, a witness who entertains a feeling of hostility or prejudice toward one side may have expressed such hostility to someone through words or acts. These hostile words or acts may be the subject of testimony, either by the witness or by other witnesses who have heard the words or seen the acts. For example, a defense witness may have made hostile remarks to an officer during the arrest of the defendant or may have attempted to strike the officer. Although this hostility on the part of a defense witness would not necessarily result in untruthful testimony, there could well be a prejudice against the prosecution that would color the testimony. If a witness has made statements showing hostility toward the police, the victim, or society in general, the prosecuting attorney may be permitted to ask the witness about those statements. If the witness admits making them, the witness will be given an opportunity to explain the statements. If the witness denies making the statements, the prosecution may present other witnesses in an effort to prove that the statements were made by the witness or that a hostile act was committed.

APPLICATION CASE

Perhaps the most famous instance of bias or prejudice of a witness took place in the O.J. Simpson trial when Detective Mark Fuhrman was cross-examined with respect to his prejudice against African Americans and his use of the expletive "nigger." The prosecution fought hard to prevent F. Lee Bailey from pursuing the cross-examination into these matters, but Judge Ito ruled that Bailey could do so. The result was Fuhrman's denial and the defense's introduction into evidence of excerpts of tape-recorded statements and other testimony proving that Fuhrman's statements and conduct did demonstrate his prejudice. As Bailey argued, the Supreme Court of the United States has held that bias is always relevant and the denial of an accused's right to prove it with respect to important witnesses is a constitutional issue.[11]

Bias can take many forms. Any relationship to the parties or subject matter of a case could give rise to an inference that a witness is biased. In addition to the more obvious motives to color testimony, a common ground for impeachment for bias occurs when one coparticipant in a criminal endeavor agrees to testify against another. If the witness has agreed to testify in exchange for more favorable treatment by law enforcement, the prosecution, or the courts, these facts may be brought out on cross-examination to show that self-interest is involved.

No matter how biased a witness may appear, however, bias is not a ground for excluding the witness's testimony. Moreover, juries regularly believe the testimony of witnesses who are shown to have interests that could support the conclusion that they are biased. Everyone is biased or prejudiced to some extent; jurors decide what weight to give a witness's testimony by taking into account all the relevant factors.

WITNESS INCAPACITY

As discussed in Chapter 4, the elements of **witness capacity** are the ability to perceive, remember, and narrate in an understandable manner, as well as sincerity. If there is any physical or mental weakness related to any aspect of these elements, the witness is subject to attack and impeachment. Such an attack is usually made through cross-examination of the witness rather than through the introduction of other evidence.

Thus, a witness's eyesight, hearing, or sense of smell could be questioned on cross-examination. If the witness usually wears corrective lenses or a hearing aid and on the occasion of the events testified to he or she did not, then the witness could be impeached as to his or her ability to perceive. The witness's intoxication or drug use at the pertinent time might be introduced to raise doubts about the witness's perceptive capacity. Similarly, if the witness was suffering from some mental infirmity that affected perception, this fact would be the subject of cross-examination inquiry. Tender years or old age could influence a witness's ability to understand what was taking place at the time of the incident. The ability to see in daylight or at night and the distance from the event in question are additional factors to consider.

Any such weakness could also affect the witness's ability to remember or narrate the events accurately. An attack upon a witness on any of these grounds could cause the jury to give the witness's testimony less weight. Of course, if the witness denied the infirmity or weakness on cross-examination, the examiner could introduce affirmative evidence of the fact at the next opportunity.

FYI

After the trial of Martha Stewart for obstruction and securities fraud concluded in 2004, Larry Stewart (no relation), the government's self-described "national expert for ink," was arrested and charged with perjury for false testimony. Larry testified that he conducted tests on an ink notation of "@60" that Peter Bacanovic, Martha's former broker, scribbled next to a list of Martha's ImClone holdings and determined that Bacanovic had added the "@60" at a later time. The indictment for perjury arises out of the fact that Larry took credit for tests another employee performed and that he never conducted or participated in the exams.

Larry was indicted for perjury after Martha was found guilty. Martha's lawyers made motions for a new trial based on the indictment of the government witness. This motion was denied because there was no evidence that the prosecution in Martha's case was aware of the false testimony. The judge presiding at Martha's trial concluded, "Because there is no reasonable likelihood that this perjury could have affected the jury's verdict, and because overwhelming independent evidence supports the verdict, the motions are denied." Nonetheless, this information surely could have been used to impeach the government witness, had it been known by the defense during Martha's trial.

Ultimately, Larry was acquitted of the perjury charges. When interviewed afterwards, jurors at his trial said Larry's ego may have caused him to overstate his role in testing key pieces of evidence at Martha's trial. Larry said he would not return to the agency that suspended him.

WITNESS CAPACITY
The elements of witness capacity are the ability to perceive, remember, and narrate in an understandable manner, as well as sincerity.

IMPEACHMENT: OTHER ISSUES

Self-Impeachment

All too frequently, a witness discredits his or her own testimony without any attack having been made on the witness. This may be the result of conduct on the stand, such as the witness's attitude or manner of speaking. It may be because of an inability to testify convincingly. It is entirely possible for a witness who is testifying truthfully to hesitate, repeat, or become confused to such an extent that the jury believes the witness is actually fabricating a story. To help prevent such an occurrence, the law enforcement professional who is a witness should be thoroughly familiar with the subject of his or her testimony before taking the witness stand.

Lack of Religious Belief

Impeachment by questioning a witness about religious beliefs or opinions is prohibited by FRE 610. As Rule 610 puts it, "Evidence of a witness's religious beliefs or opinions of a witness is not admissible to attack or support the witness's credibility."

Rehabilitation of Impeached Witness

When the credibility of a witness has been attacked by an opposing attorney, the side that produced the witness need not stand idly by and do nothing to restore the witness's credibility in the eyes of the jury. The rules of evidence permit some effort to be made to rehabilitate the attacked witness.

When a witness has been attacked on the basis of a prior conviction, rehabilitating witnesses may be produced to testify in the form of an opinion that the impeached witness is truthful or that the impeached witness has a good reputation for truthfulness. It must be remembered that the mere fact that a person has been convicted of a crime does not mean the person cannot testify truthfully. On the other hand, the jury may remain suspicious of the testimony of a person convicted of a crime, especially one involving fraud or deceit.

Similarly, an attack upon a witness by cross-examination as to misconduct not amounting to a crime is grounds for rehabilitation by character witnesses. Such witnesses may attest to the impeached witness's good character for truthfulness, either in the form of opinion or reputation testimony. However, evidence of a witness's bias does not constitute an attack on the witness's character for veracity and would not justify rehabilitation through the presentation of character witnesses.[12]

Prior consistent statements are not automatically admissible to rehabilitate a witness who has been impeached by the introduction of evidence of a prior inconsistent statement. Prior consistent statements are not generally admissible, based on the reasoning that, if a witness is inclined to make false statements, the mere repetition of previous statements does not make the present testimony any more truthful or credible. On the other hand, if the impeached witness has been attacked with a claim, express or implicit, that he or she fabricated a story for some recently developed reason, the fact that the witness made similar statements in the past may be admissible to overcome this alleged recent influence or motive. If the prior consistent statements were made before the impeached witness allegedly developed the improper influence or motive to falsify, then the prior consistent statements would be admissible to rehabilitate.[13] In fact, prior consistent statements offered to rebut a charge of recent fabrication or improper influence are not limited to use for rehabilitation but may be considered as proof of the matters stated under FRE 801(d)(1)(B). This matter is discussed further in Chapter 7, which deals with hearsay.

Reasons for Impeaching One's Own Witness

The common law rule was that a party who called a witness vouched for that witness. Therefore, a party could not impeach its own witness. This is an archaic rule and has been universally abandoned. The reason for the rule is obscure, but it may have had its roots in the custom long ago of trying cases by the number of witnesses who could be procured to swear to the facts. In any event, the rule today states: "Any party, including the party that called the witness, may attack the witness's credibility."[14]

Each side in a trial prepares a list of witnesses to be called to testify. Through the testimony of the prosecution's witnesses, the elements of the crime are established and efforts are made to prove beyond a reasonable doubt the guilt of the defendant. In most instances, these witnesses have been interviewed by the investigating officer and their stories have been incorporated into the investigative report. It is logical to assume that, when interviewed, these persons related facts that they will repeat in their testimony on the witness stand. They become witnesses for the prosecution. The defendant's attorney will also have witnesses for the defense, through whom an effort will be made to establish the innocence of the accused or to cast doubt on his or her guilt. These are the defendant's witnesses.

Generally, a witness belongs to the side calling him or her. This is because that side needs that witness's testimony. Neither the prosecution nor the defense has the power to decide who shall be a witness in the sense of choosing people because of their superior ability to perceive, testify, or appear sincere. Moreover, sometimes one side must call a witness who is necessary to its case but who is not sympathetic to, or cooperative with, the side calling the witness. In a sense, then, such witnesses do not really belong to the side who has called them. Additionally, witnesses do not always come forth with the information expected or present the information in the form anticipated. When this occurs, it may become necessary for the examining attorney to impeach the witness.

There are a variety of reasons an attorney may decide to impeach his or her own witness. An attorney who calls a witness to testify usually presumes that the witness will testify favorably toward that side. However, attorneys frequently find that a witness cannot be depended upon to give the testimony anticipated. This may be especially true for the prosecution, particularly, for example, in domestic violence cases. Prosecutors do not like to proceed with cases involving reluctant principal witnesses, but sometimes, in the public interest, it is necessary to do so. In such a case, the reluctant witness may completely reverse his or her story on the witness stand. If the testimony is left uncontested, the prosecution is placed in an unfavorable position. Such a case is the most common example of when an attorney should impeach his or her own witness.

On occasion, a law enforcement officer may be called as a witness for the "other side." This is especially true in civil cases, in which an officer may be sued in his or her official or individual capacity. In these cases, the officer becomes the defendant and the person filing the suit is the plaintiff. The plaintiff's side may call the officer as its witness, attack the officer's credibility, and attempt to impeach the officer. Plaintiff's counsel may limit questions posed to the officer to those that attack the officer's credibility. In this manner, the plaintiff's counsel hopes to cast doubt on the officer's credibility before the jury ever gets to hear the officer's side of the story.

There are many other situations in which an attorney might wish to impeach a witness called for his or her side. Even the most cooperative and well-intentioned witnesses have memory lapses or change their story on the witness stand. Most of the time, the attorney may jog the witness's memory by reminding him or her of some prior statement. However, if that fails, and the fact is important to the case, the attorney has to resort to some form of impeachment in order to preserve the fabric of the case. In such an instance, the attorney will not hesitate to impeach the witness, even though the person was called as the attorney's own witness.

SELF-INCRIMINATION

As described in an earlier chapter, when a person receives a subpoena to be a witness, he or she must obey the order to appear, willing or not. A witness is also required to answer truthfully the questions asked, irrespective of whom the answers may help or hurt. There is one exception to this rule—the witness has the right to refuse to answer any question that will be self-incriminating. The privilege against self-incrimination is probably the most frequently invoked constitutional guarantee in the courtroom. Certainly, the privilege has been both idealized and vilified in the media.

PRIVILEGE AGAINST SELF-INCRIMINATION The constitutionally based right that permits a witness to refuse to answer any question if the answer would tend to show that the witness is guilty of a crime and would subject the witness to the danger of prosecution and conviction.

The **privilege against self-incrimination** permits a witness to refuse to answer any question if the answer would tend to show that the witness is guilty of a crime and would subject the witness to the danger of prosecution and conviction. The witness can refuse to answer even though the answer may not be a complete admission of guilt. The witness may refuse if the answer merely connects the witness with a crime or would identify evidence that could link the witness with a crime.

The privilege extends not only to witnesses in criminal trials but also to witnesses in any kind of trial and most official hearings. It is applicable to the defendant in a criminal trial as well as to other witnesses. This is why the courts so carefully scrutinize the admissibility of confessions. The subject of confessions will be discussed in greater detail in Chapter 8.

Claiming the Privilege Against Self-Incrimination

How far a witness may go in claiming the privilege against self-incrimination may create problems at trial. Whether a witness may claim the privilege is not solely the decision of that witness. The decision is within the discretion of the trial judge. If the question asked is obviously incriminating, the witness may refuse to answer and that refusal will be upheld by the judge. If the question asked does not appear to be one that would incriminate the witness, the witness may still claim the privilege. The judge may then decide to question the witness in order to determine whether the witness should be permitted to invoke the privilege. The witness may be compelled to answer a question when it is clear the answer is not incriminating, even though the witness may regard it as so. If the witness absolutely refuses to answer the question after being ordered to do so, he or she may be held in contempt.

In making a determination whether a question is such that the answer may incriminate the witness, the judge will take into account the immediate setting of the testimony, other testimony, and the likelihood of possible prosecution of the witness. To meet the test of possible incrimination, the judge must attempt to determine whether there is any possibility that the witness has committed a crime and that the answer might, in some way, link the witness to that crime. The witness may not refuse to answer a question because he or she anticipates that the next question might be incriminating. Also, the fact that the answer will incriminate someone else is not grounds for refusal to answer the question. The mere fact that the answer to a question will embarrass or degrade the witness is not sufficient grounds for refusing to answer.

If a witness is not aware of his or her privilege against self-incrimination, it is incumbent upon the trial judge to inform the witness. Under some circumstances, it may be necessary for the witness to seek advice of counsel before going forward with the testimony and, in appropriate circumstances, the trial court might even have to appoint counsel to provide the necessary advice.

Waiver of Privilege Against Self-Incrimination

A witness may waive the privilege against self-incrimination. In other words, the witness may testify concerning matters that may incriminate the witness if he or she so chooses. This is the right of the witness, alone. No one else may claim the privilege for a witness (a lawyer, for example). Furthermore, if the privilege is waived, it is waived for the entire matter. The witness may not testify about some of the facts favorable to the side calling the witness and then claim the privilege for other unfavorable facts during cross-examination.

The defendant may decide to take the stand and testify, but not waive his or her privilege against self-incrimination. Although this is unusual, it is possible.

MYTH ▶	◀ FACT
If the defendant in a criminal case takes the witness stand in his or her own behalf, he or she may testify only to favorable matters and refuse to answer questions about matters that are unfavorable to his or her case.	The accused in a criminal case may take the stand and testify in his or her own behalf. However, doing so usually constitutes a waiver of the privilege, in which case the privilege is waived with regard to the entire matter. The accused cannot testify about matters favorable to him or her and then refuse to answer questions on cross-examination relating to unfavorable matters.

Unless the defendant, during direct examination, testifies in such a way as to deny the crime generally or testifies to facts and circumstances relating to the crime, there is no waiver of the privilege and the defendant cannot be compelled to testify about those facts and circumstances. For example, assume the defendant is on trial for armed robbery of the patrons of a beauty salon. One of the victims also testifies at trial against the accused and, after identifying him as the perpetrator, states that she recognized him because she saw him "around the high school" she attended some eight years earlier. If the defendant took the stand during the defense's case-in-chief and testified only that he did not attend the high school in question, the defendant's privilege against self-incrimination would not be waived. In such a case, the prosecution would be limited in its cross-examination of the defendant to the subject matter of his presence at the high school during the time in question.

Witness's Immunity Against Prosecution: Procedure in Granting Immunity

Frequently in the course of criminal investigations, persons are discovered or apprehended who, for one reason or another, would make better witnesses than defendants. For example, in a criminal conspiracy there are normally instigators, leaders, and followers. Under the law, all may be equally culpable, but the prosecutor may have difficulty proving the case against the leaders without the testimony of one or more followers. To secure the testimony necessary to convict the "big fish," the prosecution might prefer to have the testimony of the "small fry" rather than placing him or her on trial also. However, if such a witness were to relate the necessary facts, the witness could subject himself or herself to prosecution. To overcome this difficulty, rules termed **witness immunity** have been developed under which a witness may be spared prosecution if the witness furnishes facts that might otherwise incriminate himself or herself. When afforded this immunity, the witness can be compelled to answer all relevant questions. If the witness refuses to answer, he or she may be held in contempt.

WITNESS IMMUNITY Rules that allow a witness to be spared from prosecution if the witness furnishes facts that might otherwise incriminate himself or herself.

There are two types of immunity: (1) use and derivative use immunity and (2) transactional immunity. Use and derivative use immunity prohibits the use of any testimony that is specifically immunized, and any evidence derived from it, in the prosecution of the immunized witness. Transactional immunity protects the immunized person from prosecution for all activity the witness mentions in his or her immunized testimony. Transactional immunity is sometimes referred to as "blanket immunity." Most jurisdictions utilize use and derivative use immunity rather than transactional immunity to limit the effects of immunization.

Prior to 1972, when the United States Supreme Court held that use and derivative use immunity is consistent with the scope of the privilege against self-incrimination,[15] case law was believed to require only transactional immunity. Since the Supreme Court ruling, a state may prosecute a witness granted use immunity as long as the evidence used has been obtained from sources other than the witness's testimony.

Not only is use and derivative use immunity widely utilized today in the United States but, when such immunity is granted, both state and federal courts must recognize each other's grant of immunity. In the case of *Murphy v. Waterfront Commission,*[16] the United States Supreme Court held that, whenever a state compels testimony by immunizing a witness, testimony and any derivative evidence must be excluded from federal prosecutions. On the other hand, the Court held that, to be effective, federal grants of immunity must include use and derivative use immunity sufficient to bar state prosecutions.

There are times when a witness who has been granted immunity will refuse to testify even after being jailed for contempt. This incarceration is not a punishment, but an attempt to coerce the recalcitrant witness into testifying. The witness "holds the keys" to the jail in the sense that his or her agreement to testify will open the jail-house doors.

Defendant's Privilege Against Self-Incrimination

Although a person can be compelled to be a witness, this compulsion does not apply to the defendant in a criminal trial. The defendant cannot be compelled to take the witness stand. There was a time, under the common law rule, when any party, including the defendant, could be prohibited from taking the stand, even if he or she chose to do so. Today, the defendant has a right to testify in his or her own defense, but there is no requirement that the defendant do so, even though he or she may be in the best position to furnish the information needed to arrive at the truth in the case. The defendant has the right to remain completely silent. If the defendant chooses to remain silent, the prosecution and judge may not comment upon the defendant's failure to testify. Such comments have been held by the Supreme Court of the United States to compel the defendant effectively to be a witness against himself or herself in violation of the privilege against self-incrimination.[17]

What Is Not Self-Incrimination

The privilege against self-incrimination relates to "testimonial compulsion." The courts have generally held that requiring the defendant to perform certain physical acts or provide specific physical evidence is not considered testimony on the part of the defendant. Providing blood, fingerprints, and hair samples and even speaking words before a witness for voice identification purposes are matters that are not within the privilege. Even compelling the accused to exhibit himself or herself before a jury is not testimonial compulsion within the privilege. The courts have been divided on the question of whether a suspect can be compelled to give a DNA sample. The Maryland Court of Appeals, in 2012, decided that requiring such a sample from an arrestee violated his Fourth Amendment rights. The United States Supreme Court overturned that decision, holding that, when officers arrest a suspect for a serious offense, taking and analyzing a cheek swab of the arrestee's DNA is, like fingerprinting and photographing, a legitimate police booking procedure that is reasonable under the Fourth Amendment.[18]

SUMMARY

(1) The four components of witness capacity are (1) perception, (2) memory, (3) narrative ability, and (4) sincerity.

(2) The five basic methods of impeaching a witness are (1) by contradiction; (2) by showing that the witness has a bad character with respect to the trait of truthfulness; (3) by showing that the witness has made statements inconsistent with his or her present testimony; (4) by showing that the witness is biased; and (5) by showing that the witness has a failure or deficiency in the ability to perceive, remember, or narrate.

(3) The two types of criminal convictions that may be admitted to impeach a witness are (1) conviction of a crime that is punishable by more than one year imprisonment or by death, essentially a felony, and (2) conviction of a crime involving dishonesty or false statement, regardless of the potential or actual punishment.

(4) The balancing test applied to the evidence of a criminal defendant's conviction prohibits the evidence if the unfair prejudicial effect simply outweighs the probative value. This balancing test operates against the admissibility of even slightly unfair prejudicial evidence. In contrast, the balancing test of Rule 403 allows evidence unless the probative value is *substantially* outweighed by the prejudicial effect. This balancing test operates in favor of admissibility of unfairly prejudicial evidence unless it is substantially more prejudicial than probative.

(5) Crimes automatically admissible to impeach a witness are those involving dishonesty or false statement, including perjury or subornation of perjury, false statement, criminal fraud, embezzlement, or false pretense or any other offense, the commission of which involves some element of deceit, untruthfulness, or falsification bearing on the accused's propensity to testify truthfully.

(6) A cross-examiner seeking to impeach a witness for engaging in misconduct not resulting in a conviction must have a basis-in-fact for asking a question about misconduct relating to untruthfulness. The cross-examiner must accept the witness's answer and cannot introduce extrinsic evidence to prove the misconduct.

(7) The only requirement for the introduction of extrinsic evidence of a prior inconsistent statement is that the witness who is being impeached must be afforded an opportunity to explain or deny the statement, and the opposing party must be afforded an opportunity to interrogate the witness with respect to the statement.

(8) The rule governing the impeachment of a witness on the grounds of bias is that a witness's bias is always, or almost always, provable in a case.

(9) The rule relating to the impeachment of one's own witness is that the credibility of a witness may be attacked by any party, including the party calling the witness.

(10) A witness may invoke the privilege against self-incrimination if the answer would tend to show that the witness is guilty of a crime and would subject the witness to the danger of prosecution and conviction.

(11) The prevailing form of witness immunity in the United States is use and derivative use immunity.

KEY TERMS

credibility   156

impeachment   158

character evidence
   rule   159

character witness   162

contradiction   162

inconsistent
   statements   163

exclusionary rule   165

witness capacity   167

privilege against self-
   incrimination   170

witness immunity   172

QUESTIONS FOR REVIEW

1. What are the four components of witness capacity?
2. What are the five basic methods of impeaching a witness?
3. What two types of criminal convictions may be admitted to impeach a witness?
4. What is the difference between the balancing test applied to the admission of evidence of a conviction of a criminal defendant who testifies and the balancing test of FRE 403?
5. What types of crimes are automatically admissible to impeach a witness?
6. When may evidence of misconduct that has not resulted in a criminal conviction be used for impeachment of a witness?
7. When may evidence of a prior inconsistent statement be used in a trial?
8. When may evidence of bias be used to impeach a witness?
9. When may a party impeach a witness called to testify for that party?
10. When may a witness invoke the privilege against self-incrimination?
11. What is the prevailing form of witness immunity in the United States?

THINKING CRITICALLY ABOUT EVIDENCE

1. The court generally makes it more difficult to admit evidence of actual convictions than it does to admit evidence based on reputation, including rumors. For example, a murder conviction cannot be admitted into evidence if more than ten years has elapsed since the murder conviction or release of the defendant from prison, whichever is later, except under unusual circumstances. However, a witness's statement that a person had a reputation of being a murderer could be admitted, even if it were not true. Why would the court allow such a statement? What are the circumstances under which the court would allow it? As you determine your answer, consider a defendant's claim of self-defense based upon fear of the victim.

2. David is charged with the murder of Victor. David claims that he and Victor were having an argument when Victor took a swing at him. David said he responded in self-defense by knocking Victor to the ground and "head butting"

him until Victor passed out. Victor subsequently died of a brain hemorrhage. The prosecutor wants to introduce the testimony of William, who, in an earlier argument with David, was "head butted" by the defendant until he passed out. The prosecutor states that the testimony is relevant character evidence, as it demonstrates that David's *modus operandi* in a fight is to "head butt" his opponent. Should William's testimony be admitted? What is the reasoning for your answer?

WORKPLACE APPLICATIONS

1. A police officer responds to a domestic dispute call for the second time in one day at the same address. The house is located in an affluent neighborhood, and the officer recognizes the husband as the CEO of a major local corporation and a pillar of the community. The wife is a homemaker with three small children. On the first call, the wife told the officer that she tore her blouse and got the bruises on her arms and legs "by falling down the stairs." The officer suspected that she had some "help" down the stairs, but not enough to justify an arrest. When the officer arrives the second time, several hours later, she notices the wife has new bruises, a puffy lip, and a black eye. However, the wife still denies that her husband has beaten her. Pursuant to a statute in the state allowing the officer to arrest a person suspected of spousal abuse without the abused's permission, the officer arrests the husband. What point could the officer note in her report that would help the prosecutor attack the credibility of the husband? Since the wife will likely make a statement supporting her husband, what further action could the officer take that would help the prosecutor overcome the wife's statement?

2. A law enforcement professional's behavior, on and off duty, can become the subject of scrutiny in a court case as the defense counsel attempts to attack the person's testimony. Seemingly unrelated personal revelations can become very damaging and embarrassing when raised in the courtroom, for example, if a person is caught cheating on income taxes. This information could be used by the defense to attack the witness's truthfulness. Think of and list five "off-duty" activities that could be used to attack a law enforcement professional's credibility.

ETHICAL DILEMMAS

1. An escaping murder suspect is shot and killed by a police officer after the officer saw a gun in the suspect's hand. The murder suspect's accomplice did not witness the shooting. The suspect had a gun in hand, pointed at the ground, and was turning toward the officer in response to the officer's warning to freeze. It was at this point that the officer shot the suspect. By testifying to this scenario, the officer could be subject to murder charges. The officer does not believe there were any witnesses, the victim was a wanted felon with a gun, and, if the officer had waited a split-second longer, there would not have been any question about the officer's actions. At the

accomplice's trial, the defense counsel asks the officer if the victim threatened the officer's life. How should the officer answer the defense counsel's question?

2. A police officer responds to a loud party call about midnight. While arguing with the officer about the officer's decision to shut down the party, the homeowner uses a long list of obscenities, in both English and German. While waiting for a back-up unit, and listening to this tongue-lashing, the officer mutters under his breath, "Shut up, you stupid Kraut," referring to the owner's obvious German accent. The homeowner hears the officer and files a lawsuit against him. Did the officer say anything legally wrong? Ethically wrong? Can the officer's statement be used against him in court? How?

ENDNOTES

1. Fed. R. Evid. 609(a)(1).

2. Fed. R. Evid. 609(a)(2).

3. Fed. R. Evid. 609, Conference Report, H.R. Fed. Rules of Evidence, Conf. Rep. No. 1597, 93d Cong., 2d Sess., p. 9 (1974).

4. Fed. R. Evid. 803(21).

5. Fed. R. Evid. 613(b).

6. Miranda v. Arizona, 384 U.S. 436 (1966).

7. Missouri v. Seibert, 542 U.S. 600 (2004).

8. *See* Harris v. New York, 401 U.S. 222 (1971).

9. *See* United States v. Havens, 446 U.S. 620 (1980).

10. *See* James v. Illinois, 493 U.S. 307 (1990).

11. *See, e.g.,* United States v. Abel, 469 U.S. 45 (1984).

12. Fed. R. Evid. 608(a), advisory committee's note.

13. In United States v. Tome, 513 U.S. 150, 156–57 (1995), the Supreme Court held that, in order for a prior consistent statement to qualify for use to rebut a charge of recent fabrication or improper influence of a witness under Fed. R. Evid.

801(d)(1)(B), there is a premotive temporal requirement.

14. Fed. R. Evid. 607.

15. Kastigar v. United States, 406 U.S. 441 (1972).

16. Murphy v. Waterfront Commission, 378 U.S. 52 (1964).

17. Griffin v. California, 380 U.S. 609 (1965).

18. Maryland v. King, 569 U.S. 435 (2013).

Design Element: ©Ingram Publishing

7 THE HEARSAY RULE

CHAPTER OUTLINE

CHAPTER OBJECTIVES

This chapter examines the rule against hearsay and its many exceptions. After reading this chapter you will be able to:

▶ Define hearsay.

▶ Explain the rationale for the hearsay rule.

▶ Explain the FRE's assertion-based definition of a statement.

▶ List the five subcategories of statements that are not offered for the truth of the matter asserted (NOTMA).

▶ Name the two general categories of exemptions from the hearsay rule under the FRE.

▶ List the three types of prior statements by witnesses that are exempt from the hearsay rule.

▶ Identify the five types of admissions by a party opponent that are exempt from the hearsay rule.

▶ List the four foundational requirements for the dying declaration exception to the hearsay rule.

▶ Name the two species of spontaneous declarations exceptions to the hearsay rule and state the difference between them.

▶ Identify a major limitation upon the state of mind exception to the hearsay rule.

▶ List the foundational requirements for the statements for purposes of medical diagnosis exception to the hearsay rule.

▶ Name the foundational requirements for the former testimony exception to the hearsay rule.

▶ State the foundational requirements for the business records exception to the hearsay rule.

INTRODUCTION

HEARSAY
A statement that the declarant does not make while testifying at the current trial or hearing and a party offers in evidence to prove the truth of the matter asserted in the statement.

There are numerous ways to define hearsay. In simplest terms, hearsay evidence is based on something a witness has heard someone else say, rather than on what the witness has personally seen or otherwise perceived. In the words of the courts, the definition most commonly used in the United States is that of the Federal Rules of Evidence (FRE), which defines **hearsay** as "a statement that (1) the declarant does not make while testifying at the current trial or hearing; and (2) a party offers in evidence to prove the truth of the matter asserted in the statement."[1] A major portion of this chapter is devoted to explaining the application of that definition, since analysis and understanding of the hearsay rule are much more than the definition.

The hearsay rule grew out of the fear of convicting an accused person based upon the untested, out-of-court statements of those not present in front of the jury and subject to observation, oath, and cross-examination. Perhaps the worst form of hearsay is rumor. Prior to the development of the hearsay rule, trial by rumor was more the norm than a mere possibility. The hearsay rule was developed by the common law to prevent the miscarriage of justice that would result from the acceptance of extreme forms of untested, unsworn statements by persons not present in court.

From the outset of the development of the hearsay rule in England in the eighteenth century, it was evident that not all hearsay evidence should be condemned and considered inadmissible. For this reason, the hearsay rule generally prohibits hearsay evidence, but with numerous exceptions, resulting in the admission into evidence of many out-of-court statements.

APPLICATION CASE

The trial of Sir Walter Raleigh in 1603[2] exemplifies the freedom, historically, with which hearsay evidence was admitted in courts. Raleigh was on trial for conspiring to overthrow the king of England. The prosecution relied almost exclusively on witnesses testifying to statements made by one individual, Lord Cobham. Raleigh objected to this evidence, demanding the production of the witness against him. Raleigh was unsuccessful in his own defense and was found guilty of high treason. Although he was released to conduct a second exploratory expedition to Guiana, ultimately he was executed after the expedition failed. As this chapter will demonstrate, the rule against hearsay has evolved into a considerable body of law since the days of Sir Walter Raleigh.

MYTH ▶   ◀ FACT

MYTH ▶	◀ FACT
All hearsay evidence is inadmissible.	Much hearsay evidence is, in fact, admissible. There are numerous exemptions from and exceptions to the hearsay rule that permit evidence that is hearsay by definition to be used in court.

In fact, learning the hearsay rule requires at least as much understanding of the exceptions as of the rule itself. In short, hearsay evidence by definition is suspect, but not all hearsay evidence is inadmissible.

Through the media, even a person with the most limited knowledge of the judicial process is aware that some forms of hearsay evidence are not admissible in a trial proceeding. This was not always the case, however. The rule against hearsay was not developed until the early 1700s, when courts began to take a dim view of such evidence.

The significance of the hearsay rule to the law enforcement professional cannot be overstated. Many statements taken from witnesses, victims, suspects, and fellow law enforcement professionals are hearsay.

The reports written by law enforcement professionals are also hearsay, or contain much hearsay. A law enforcement professional's understanding of the hearsay rule will help the professional to take statements and write reports in

©Bettmann/Getty Images

Accused of plotting to overthrow the king, Sir Walter Raleigh—soldier, explorer, writer, and businessman—was convicted in 1603 on the written evidence of Henry Brooke, Lord Cobham.

DECLARANT
A person who makes a statement.

CONFRONTATION CLAUSE
The provision of the Sixth Amendment to the Constitution of the United States that guarantees the defendant in a criminal case the right "to be confronted with the witnesses against him."

such a way as to enhance the possibility that the professional's observations will yield investigative results that can be used effectively at trial. A law enforcement professional who understands the hearsay rule will be more focused when questioning people, be able to phrase questions more precisely with respect to the requirements of the hearsay rule, and know how to figure out if the witness's statements fit within a hearsay exemption or exception, or the ban of the Confrontation Clause. Given the most recent decisions by the United States Supreme Court dealing with the Confrontation Clause and its interrelationship with the hearsay rule, it is even more imperative that the law enforcement professional know and understand the parameters of this subject.

RATIONALE FOR THE RULE AND CONSTITUTIONAL CONSIDERATIONS

Because hearsay is a statement made by a person out-of-court, questions of truthfulness are always present. A key principle underpinning the hearsay rule is the preference that the **declarant** (the person who makes a statement[3]) be present in court, under oath, and subject to cross-examination. If the declarant cannot be present in court but certain requirements are met, the hearsay rule may allow admission of the out-of-court statement into evidence.

The rule's preference for the presence of the declarant seeks to ensure that the fact-finder (the trial judge or jury) is in a position to evaluate the declarant's ability to perceive initially, remember accurately, and narrate correctly. In short, the fact-finder is then able to evaluate personally the declarant's sincerity. When the declarant is a witness in court and subject to cross-examination, the judge and jury are able to observe demeanor and are therefore in a better position to decide what weight to give to the testimony. All of these safeguards are lost when the declarant is not present in court and hearsay evidence is admitted. In addition to the problems of truthfulness inherent in hearsay, constitutional problems arise as well.

The **Confrontation Clause** of the Sixth Amendment to the Constitution of the United States guarantees the defendant in a criminal case the right "to be confronted with the witnesses against him." This guarantee requires that any evidence in the form of a statement by a person be made by that person under oath, subject to cross-examination by the defendant. If the Confrontation Clause were applied literally, no hearsay evidence could ever be admitted at trial in a criminal case.

The Supreme Court of the United States has had occasion to consider the constitutionality of hearsay exceptions in connection with a defendant's right of confrontation and, until March 2004, found most of the exceptions to be constitutional. Up to that time, the Court found that, if hearsay evidence was within a "firmly rooted" exception to the hearsay rule, then the evidence was likely reliable enough to be admitted in criminal cases without violating the Confrontation Clause. In March 2004, the Court decided the case of *Crawford v. Washington,*[4] in which the Court redefined the Confrontation Clause, rejecting the "firmly rooted" analysis adopted in prior cases. Instead, the Court held that the Confrontation Clause bans use at trial of uncross-examined statements of absent declarants when the statements are "testimonial." Although the Court left "for another day"[5] a comprehensive definition of "testimonial," the Court stated that the Confrontation Clause clearly bans statements made

▶ in the form of testimony given at a formal proceeding (including trial, preliminary hearing, grand jury, and plea allocution) and
▶ to police or other government personnel during interrogation.

The Court also used language, however, to indicate that the ban of the Clause might apply to any statement "made under circumstances which would lead an objective witness reasonably to believe that the statement would be available for use at a later trial,"[6] which could include the following:

▶ all manner of statements such as police reports, forensic reports, and witness interview notes;
▶ public records created under such circumstances; and
▶ excited utterances made to law enforcement or other officers.

Two years after *Crawford,* the Court again addressed the definition of "testimonial" for Confrontation Clause purposes, this time focused on statements made in 911 calls and to police officers at the scene of a crime. In *Davis v. Washington,*[7] the Court addressed the issues in the context of domestic abuse cases (*Davis* was consolidated with the case of *Hammon v. Indiana*). In resolving the issues, the Court concluded, "Statements are nontestimonial when made in the course of police interrogation under circumstances objectively indicating that the primary purpose of the interrogation is to enable police assistance to meet an ongoing emergency. They are testimonial when the circumstances objectively indicate that there is no such ongoing emergency, and that the primary purpose of the interrogation is to establish or prove past events potentially relevant to later criminal prosecution."[8]

Davis left open the question of how broadly the Court would treat the "ongoing emergency" doctrine and how it would go about trying to determine what the primary purpose of an interrogation was. The Court began to give answers in *Michigan v. Bryant.*[9] The case centered on statements made by a shooting victim, while lying badly wounded on the pavement outside a gas station. The victim told several police officers who arrived on the scene that he had been shot by the defendant a half hour earlier and six blocks away. Several hours later, the victim died of his wounds. There was no proof, however, that at the time of his statements he anticipated imminent death, so his statement could not qualify as a dying declaration. During trial, the testimony of the officers regarding the victim's statements were challenged. The Supreme Court held that the statements were not testimonial and that they were properly admitted at trial. Rather, the statements were made for the purpose of addressing the emergency created by the shooting. The Court used the "Primary Purpose" test adopting "[a] combined inquiry that accounts for both the declarant and the interrogator" in determining from whose perspective a court should make the assessment of purpose. The majority concentrated its discussion mainly on the police officers, for as they arrived at the scene they knew little or nothing of what was going on.[10]

The Court again addressed the Primary Purpose test in 2015 in *Ohio v. Clark*.[11] There, the Court held that the Confrontation Clause did not prohibit prosecutors from introducing statements made by a child abuse victim to his teachers, where neither the child, who was unavailable for cross-examination, nor his teachers had the primary purpose of creating an out-of-court substitute for trial testimony. The child was three years old at the time he made the statements.

In both *Crawford* and *Davis,* the Court noted two exceptions to the testimonial rule: dying declarations and "forfeiture by wrongdoing." The Court did not expand on those exceptions in either case. Then, two years after *Davis,* in *Giles v. California,*[12] the Court clarified the forfeiture by wrongdoing exception to the Confrontation Clause, holding that an accused can only be found to have forfeited his or her right to confront if the accused is found to have purposely caused the absence of the declarant at trial.

A more comprehensive analysis of the impact of the *Crawford, Davis,* and *Giles* decisions on the law enforcement professional's approach to investigation and gathering of witnesses' statements appears later in this chapter. For now, let it be said that statements taken from victims and witnesses may not be expected to be used at trial if the victim or witness is unavailable for cross-examination and has not previously been cross-examined by the defendant, unless the statements were made to assist police to meet an ongoing emergency, the statements qualify as dying declarations, or the defendant intentionally caused the victim or witness to be absent from trial to prevent him or her from testifying against the accused.

COMPONENTS OF THE HEARSAY RULE

The Definition of a Statement

Only evidence that is in the form of a statement not presently made in court can be hearsay. If the evidence is in any other form, such as a witness's present testimony in court or a tangible object, such as a gun, then there is no application of the hearsay rule to the evidence. Also, since words uttered or written and conduct exhibited by a person may or may not involve issues of truthfulness, not all utterances, writings, and conduct are within the concern of the hearsay rule. The definition of a statement, in the first instance, is one way that the law distinguishes between hearsay and nonhearsay.

FRE's Assertion-Based Test

The FRE definition focuses on what is known as an "assertion-based" test. Under this test, evidence is a statement, and therefore may be hearsay, only if the declarant intended the utterance, writing, or conduct to assert something.[13] For example, assume a defendant in a criminal murder trial claimed another man committed the murder and offered evidence that the other man was so distraught over his crime that he committed suicide. The act of suicide, on its face, was not intended by him as an assertion of anything—he was just trying to

MYTH ▶	◀ FACT
Anything uttered by a person out-of-court is a hearsay statement.	In order for an utterance to be a statement for purposes of the hearsay rule, it must be intended by the person speaking to be an assertion. Ordinarily, questions and directions are not assertions, although some questions and directions may be shown, in context, to be intended as assertions. An example is a statement in question form, such as "You don't think I know that?" Likewise, conduct that implies a belief, but was not intended by the actor to assert the belief, is not a statement for purposes of the hearsay rule in most jurisdictions.

end his misery. However, his act implicitly revealed his belief that he was guilty of murder (among other possibilities). Therefore, the evidence would be relevant to his guilt and would not be hearsay because the conduct was not a statement. On the other hand, if the person who committed suicide was heard to cry out, "I just cannot live with the shame of murdering a person," just before he killed himself, that statement would be an assertion by the person related to the crime and would be hearsay.

The Common Law's Declarant-Based Test

Some states do not follow the FRE's assertion-based approach to the definition of a statement and use a "declarant-based" test instead. Under this test, in the previous example, committing suicide would be considered under the hearsay rule even in the absence of a specific statement by the person. This is because the evidence involves evaluation of the person's belief in order to be relevant to the issue of guilt. Under this approach, since the jury would have to rely upon the credibility of the actor, the conduct qualifies for consideration under the hearsay rule. Under a declarant-based definition of hearsay, an out-of-court statement (or conduct) is hearsay when it depends upon the credibility of the declarant (his or her truthfulness) for its value, regardless of the assertive intent of the declarant or actor.[14]

The operative language of the FRE definition is that the declarant intends to assert something by words or conduct. Usually, when words are uttered, there is no doubt that an assertion was intended. However, if the declarant gives a direction or asks a question, both of which are nondeclarative forms of utterances, there is no assertion and, technically under the FRE, the evidence of such utterances would not involve the hearsay rule.

In contrast to the suicide example, it is an assertion when a victim points at a suspect in a lineup as a substitute for saying the words "That's him!" The sole purpose of the victim's conduct is to assert a belief as to the identity of the perpetrator. Once it is determined that a statement was made out-of-court, further inquiry into the statement's relevance is required before it is possible to decide if the statement is, in fact, hearsay.

Offered for the Truth of the Matter Asserted or Not?

The next phase of analysis under the definition of hearsay is whether a statement is offered by the proponent of the evidence to prove the truth of the matter asserted. If the statement can help to prove a fact in the case only if it is true, then the statement is hearsay. Conversely, a statement may not have to be true but may have some value in determining what happened in a case. It is important to remember that the definition of a statement is not limited to spoken words or conduct—a statement may also be information written or typed by the declarant, such as information in letters, notes, or other documents.

To illustrate the problems involved in determining whether evidence of a statement needs to be true to be probative and is therefore hearsay, consider the following scenario. Assume that a defendant has been charged with bank robbery, and a witness takes the stand and testifies that a neighbor told the witness that the defendant robbed a bank. In this case, the witness has no personal knowledge about the acts of the defendant; he or she knows only what the neighbor said. Because the witness has knowledge only of what the neighbor said, the neighbor, as the declarant, must have personal knowledge of the defendant's acts. The out-of-court declarant's statement that the defendant robbed the bank is, by itself, insufficient to show any personal knowledge on his or her part. In other words, the testimony by the witness on the stand that the defendant robbed a bank is inadmissible hearsay.

Even though the witness is telling the truth about what the neighbor said, the accuracy of the facts is dependent upon the neighbor, who is not in court. It is possible that the information given by the neighbor is true, but it may not be. It is conceivable that the neighbor may have obtained the information from another person and just repeated it, so that the truthfulness of the statement is now dependent upon a third individual. Up to this point, the identity of the neighbor has not even been considered, and, in reality, it doesn't matter. The neighbor, if called to testify, may not even be a qualified witness. He or she may be a child of tender years or a senile person without the ability to perceive the situation correctly, or the person may have a reputation for not telling the truth (which would not disqualify the person as a witness but would surely detract from the witness's credibility). Another danger in admitting hearsay evidence is that the witness may not accurately relate what was heard. Since the original declarant is not present to correct any inaccuracies, the hearsay, if admitted, might be given more credit than it deserves. Thus, it can readily be seen that hearsay can be dangerous and may give little assistance to the jury in its search for the truth. The rule excluding hearsay was developed because the usual safeguards for trustworthiness are lacking in hearsay evidence.

Exceptions to and Exemptions from the Hearsay Rule

Numerous exceptions and exemptions that have been established over the years recognize some recurring situations. These exceptions and exemptions are the result of custom, tradition, or necessity. Many hearsay exceptions and exemptions apply in situations in which the statements have a reasonably high level of trustworthiness. For example, excited utterances, those statements that are blurted out in the heat of excitement, are particularly trustworthy. The declarant, having no time to think about anything, is likely to have been truthful in the assertion. Custom dictates that a dying person's statement about the cause of his or her death is acceptable evidence. The dying declaration is also an example of necessity, since the declarant, having died, is not available to testify in court.

Statements that are within an exception to the hearsay rule are hearsay but are admissible nonetheless. Statements that are within an exemption from the hearsay rule are not even considered to be hearsay at all. Examples of statements exempted from the hearsay rule are certain prior consistent and inconsistent statements by witnesses, and opposing parties' statements (admissions).

Although the FRE and common law include a large number of exceptions to and exemptions from the hearsay rule, only those frequently encountered in criminal matters will be considered in this book for more detailed discussion. FRE 803, 804, and 807 contain the exceptions to the hearsay rule, and 801(d) contains the exemptions from the rule. For purposes of the law enforcement professional, the exceptions and exemptions to be discussed are

1. dying declarations,
2. spontaneous declarations,
3. state of mind,
4. statements for purposes of medical diagnosis or treatment,
5. former testimony,
6. business records,
7. pedigree,
8. past memory recorded,
9. prior statements of witnesses,
10. opposing parties' statements (admissions) and confessions, and
11. declarations against interest.

There is no particular significance in the order in which these exceptions or exemptions will be discussed. With respect to opposing parties' statements (admissions) and confessions, however, this chapter will deal only with the hearsay rule, while Chapter 8 will explain opposing parties' statements (admissions) and confessions from the standpoint of constitutional issues. Figure 7–1 depicts the decisions to be made when determining if an item of evidence is hearsay or not.

FIGURE 7–1 How to determine what is hearsay.

The Hearsay Rule

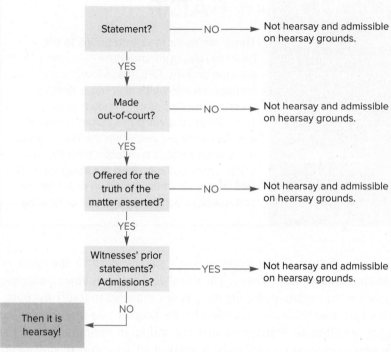

STATEMENTS THAT ARE NOT HEARSAY BECAUSE THEY ARE NOT OFFERED FOR THE TRUTH OF THE MATTER ASSERTED

As noted earlier, when dealing with the hearsay rule, the first question to consider is whether the evidence in dispute is a statement. If the evidence is a statement, and if the statement was made out-of-court, then the next matter for consideration is whether the statement is being offered in evidence by the proponent of the evidence to prove the truth of the matter the declarant intended to assert in the statement. This inquiry focuses on the statement and examines whether the statement needs to be true in order to prove the fact for which the statement is offered in evidence. There are two ways a statement may tend to prove something:

1. just the fact that the statement was made or was heard by a particular person, regardless of its truth or falsity, may tend to establish a fact in the case; or
2. the content of the statement may have to be true in order to prove a fact.

If the content of a statement must be true to prove a fact, then the statement is hearsay and needs to fall within an exemption from or exception to the hearsay rule in order to be admissible. However, if the statement proves a fact just because the statement was made, regardless of whether it is true or not, the statement is not hearsay and is therefore admissible insofar as the hearsay rule is concerned. For example, a robber's statement "If you don't give me your money, I'll shoot you" is evidence of the threat of violence just because the statement was uttered.

The following categories of statements do not fall within the definition of hearsay because they are not offered for the truth of the matter asserted (NOTMA).

1. Operative legal fact
2. State of mind of the hearer
3. State of mind of the declarant
4. State of mind (knowledge) of the declarant on the "traces of the mind" theory
5. Statements that are otherwise not offered for the truth of the matter asserted (NOTMA) but to prove something else

Following is a more comprehensive explanation of each category.

Operative Legal Fact

The utterance of an **operative legal fact** creates or destroys a legal relationship, right, power, or duty. The following is an example of an operative legal fact. Person A says to Person B, "I will pay you $5,000 if you will kill V." Person A's statement is significant merely because it was uttered. The statement is the solicitation of Person B to do an illegal act and is itself an element of the crime of solicitation. The statement need not be true to qualify as a solicitation. Other examples of statements that are operative legal facts in a criminal law context include the threat as an element of robbery (mentioned before) or extortion, solicitation of a bribe, solicitation for prostitution, and solicitation to buy narcotics or stolen goods.

OPERATIVE LEGAL FACT
A statement that creates or destroys a legal relationship, right, power, or duty.

State of Mind of the Hearer

In many instances, what a person thinks at a particular moment in time is extremely relevant and important to a case. We cannot see inside a person's head to determine what he or she is thinking. One way to tell what a person is thinking is by what he or she says. Another way is by what he or she does. Yet another way to determine what is in a person's mind is to know what he or she has seen and heard. Thus, if we know that someone told a person about something, then

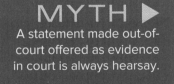

MYTH ▶   ◀ FACT

A statement made out-of-court offered as evidence in court is always hearsay.

Not all such statements are hearsay. Only those statements that must be true in order to prove the fact for which the statement is offered in evidence are hearsay. If the statement tends to prove a fact in the case without the content of the statement having to be true, then, by definition, it is not hearsay and is admissible insofar as the hearsay rule is concerned.

STATE OF MIND OF
THE HEARER
A statement that creates
or affects the state of mind
of another who hears the
statement.

we can say that the hearer, or auditor, "knows" about that fact. The **state of mind of the hearer** principle includes statements made by a person that create or affect the state of mind of another who hears those statements. For example, in a murder case, the defendant, prior to the killing, heard another man say that the victim was a violent man who always carried a knife. If the defendant is claiming self-defense, these statements are relevant to show that, at the time of the killing, the defendant was in a state of mind of fear of the victim. Moreover, under the definition of self-defense, the defendant must have only a reasonable belief in the truth of the threat or justifying circumstance in order for self-defense to be validly claimed. Therefore, the statements heard by the defendant in such a case as hypothesized do not have to be true. It is necessary only that the defendant thought they were true. Thus, if such statements are made in the presence of the accused and are heard and believed, those statements are relevant and admissible and are not hearsay. It would be up to the jury to decide whether the defendant heard and believed such statements.

ON THE JOB

Many crimes require a "guilty mind," or *mens rea,* to be complete. For example, burglary requires an intent to commit a crime in a dwelling or structure before or at the time the perpetrator enters. One way to prove *mens rea* is by evidence of statements made by the suspect showing his or her state of mind at the time he or she committed the crime. A suspect's statement to a friend an hour before the burglary that "I plan to steal all the silver in the house" will make the offense burglary because the requisite *mens rea* is shown. However, the statement to the same friend that "I'm going to enter the house only to get out of the rain and cold" shows a lack of *mens rea* for burglary because the suspect's state of mind or decision to steal the silver did not occur until after the entry was made. If the suspect entered the house to get warm and then decided to steal the silver, the suspect would be guilty only of theft and not of burglary. When interviewing a suspect or witness, the officer should pay close attention to the exact words used by the person and record any pertinent statements as they are made. Many cases are decided upon the exact wording of a statement.

State of Mind of the Declarant

STATE OF MIND OF
THE DECLARANT
A statement offered to
show the state of mind of
the person who uttered
the statement, not of the
person who heard the
statement.

In **state of mind of the declarant**, a statement is offered to show the state of mind of the person who uttered the statement, not of the person who heard the statement. The statement cannot be offered as truth but may be offered so that the fact-finder can infer the declarant's state of mind at the time the statement was made. For example, if a young man claims, "I am Henry the Eighth," such a statement may be offered to prove that the young man is suffering from a delusion. Obviously, the statement is not true (the declarant cannot be Henry the Eighth), but the inference from the statement lends insight into the declarant's state of mind. As another example, assume the defendant in a murder case said something negative about the victim's character, such as "Harry [the victim] is the most horrible person in the world." Such a statement would be relevant not to prove that Harry was the most horrible person in the world but to prove that the defendant, who is also the declarant, had ill will toward Harry and, for that reason, had a motive to kill him.

State of Mind (Knowledge) of the Declarant on the "Traces of the Mind" Theory

The **"traces of the mind" theory** allows into evidence statements that prove the person making the statement has knowledge that he or she could have gained only by actually having perceived some unusual event, circumstances, or surroundings. A statement may be relevant to prove that a person has been to a particular place because he or she has a distinct knowledge of what the place looks like. For example, assume a young girl has been kidnapped and locked up in a room. The child is then released and describes the contents of the room to an investigating officer. The description of the room can be offered to prove that she had indeed been in that room because she could not have such knowledge of the room's contents unless she had actually seen them. It is important to note that the details of the place must be proven by evidence other than that contained in the child's statement. Photographs of the room and its contents would satisfy this requirement in this case.

"TRACES OF THE MIND" THEORY
The theory that allows into evidence statements that prove the declarant has knowledge that he or she could have gained only by actually having perceived some unusual event, circumstances, or surroundings.

APPLICATION CASE

An example of a statement by a person admissible under the "traces of the mind" theory occurred in a much publicized case involving the late pop superstar Michael Jackson. A young boy claimed to have been molested by Jackson and described a unique mark on Jackson's genitalia. The criminal case never developed into a prosecution, and the potential civil case was settled on undisclosed terms. During the investigation, however, Jackson was searched, and his body was inspected and photographed. In the event of a criminal trial, the boy's statement describing the unique mark could have been admitted under the "traces" theory, and the photograph could have been admitted to display the mark for comparative purposes.

Statements That Are Otherwise Not Offered for the Truth of the Matter Asserted but to Prove Something Else

Anytime a statement is offered for a reason other than to prove the truth of the matter asserted in the statement, it is, by definition, nonhearsay and admissible if relevant. For example, sometimes the mere fact that a person spoke is relevant, even though the content of the statement is not. Suppose there is a dispute over whether a murder victim survived for a few minutes before dying. If someone overheard the victim utter a statement, that statement is relevant to prove that the person was alive. This stems from the fact that dead people cannot talk. The content of the statement is not important. The victim might have said, "I'm alive."[15] Even so, the mere fact any statement was uttered shows that the person was still alive, and what the person actually said is unimportant.

It must be remembered that all of the subcategories discussed in this section are particular instances of statements not offered for the truth of the matter asserted (NOTMA). These are not rigid categories, but they have been grouped together because of the frequency of their occurrence. When determining if a statement qualifies as hearsay, consider if the statement needs to be true to be relevant. If the answer is no, then the statement is nonhearsay and is therefore admissible.

HEARSAY EXEMPTIONS

If a statement is logically relevant only if the content of it is true, then it is offered for the truth of the matter asserted, is hearsay, and is only admissible if it falls within an exemption or exception. In a sense, any utterance that is not a statement and any statement that is NOTMA are exempt from the hearsay rule by definition. However, there is another set of hearsay exemptions under FRE 801(d). They fall into two categories:

1. certain kinds of prior statements of a witness and
2. opposing parties' statements (admissions).

Figure 7–2 depicts the two categories of exemptions from the hearsay rule. After determining that the evidence is in the form of a statement, and that it is offered to prove the truth of the content of the statement, it must then be determined whether the statement is within one of the exemptions.

Prior Statements by Witnesses

In order for a prior statement by a witness to be admissible, the person must be available to testify in court and be subject to cross-examination. It may seem that, since the witness is available to testify, his or her statements offered for the truth of the matter asserted are not hearsay. But it is important to remember that any out-of-court statement offered for the truth of the matter asserted is hearsay even if the person who made the statement is available to testify. There are three types of prior statements by witnesses:

1. prior inconsistent statements,
2. prior consistent statements, and
3. statements of prior identification.

FIGURE 7–2 Two categories of exemptions from the hearsay rule.

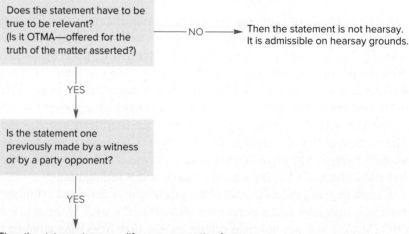

Exemptions from the Hearsay Rule

Does the statement have to be true to be relevant? (Is it OTMA—offered for the truth of the matter asserted?) —— NO ——▸ Then the statement is not hearsay. It is admissible on hearsay grounds.

YES

Is the statement one previously made by a witness or by a party opponent?

YES

Then the statement may qualify as an exemption from the hearsay rule and be admissible on hearsay grounds.

A **prior inconsistent statement** is a statement by the witness that contradicts the witness's current in-court testimony. For example, a witness to a robbery testifies in court that the getaway car was a green, two-door Chevrolet Camaro. The same witness had previously testified at the preliminary hearing that the getaway car was a red, four-door Ford Taurus. The preliminary hearing statement is a prior inconsistent statement that is now admissible during the cross-examination of the witness. However, according to the FRE and in most jurisdictions, in order for the prior statement to qualify as an exemption under this heading, the prior statement must have been made under oath and must have been subject to the penalty of perjury at a trial, at a hearing, at another proceeding, or in a deposition. Inconsistent statements not under oath are not admissible under this exemption.

Prior consistent statements do not have to be under oath and thus may be out-of-court statements. A **prior consistent statement** is a statement made previously that is consistent with the present testimony of the witness. Under the FRE, it is admissible only "to rebut an express or implied charge that the declarant recently fabricated it or acted from a recent improper influence or motive in so testifying." For example, suppose a child claimed that she had been abused by one of her parents. Subsequently, the parents decide to get divorced, and both parents want custody of the child. At the child abuse hearing, the child is called to testify about the alleged abuse. In defense, each parent claims that the child is fabricating the story of abuse to remain with the other parent after the divorce. On re-direct examination of the child, the prosecution will seek to offer a prior consistent statement that the child gave to a police detective at the time of the alleged abuse. This statement was given before the parents decided to get divorced and therefore could not be tainted by any motive to stay with a particular parent.

Statements of prior identification are simply out-of-court statements identifying a person made after the declarant has seen that person. In criminal cases, there are several types of out-of-court identifications, including in-person lineups, photo lineups, and show-ups (the accused is presented to the witness alone because the circumstances require swift action). All statements made in connection

PRIOR INCONSISTENT STATEMENT
A statement by the witness that contradicts the witness's current in-court testimony.

PRIOR CONSISTENT STATEMENT
A statement made previously that is consistent with the present testimony of the witness. It is admissible only to rebut an express or implied charge that the declarant recently fabricated it or acted from a recent improper influence or motive in so testifying.

STATEMENTS OF PRIOR IDENTIFICATION
Out-of-court statements identifying a person made after the declarant has seen that person.

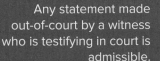

MYTH ▶   ◀ FACT

Any statement made out-of-court by a witness who is testifying in court is admissible.

An out-of-court statement made by a witness and offered to prove the truth of the matter asserted in the witness's statement is, by definition, hearsay. Only those prior witnesses' statements that are within the specified exemptions are admissible. These statements include prior consistent statements (but only when offered to rebut a charge of recent fabrication), prior inconsistent statements (but only if made under oath at a prior proceeding), and statements of prior identification of a person.

with such identifications are admissible within this exemption. This allows the fact-finder to have all the information needed to assess any eyewitness identifications presented at a criminal trial.

Opposing Parties' Statements (Admissions)

OPPOSING PARTY'S STATEMENT (ADMISSION)
A statement that is attributed to a named party in a civil lawsuit or a statement attributed to a criminal defendant, and offered *against* the declarant pary.

An **opposing party's statement (admission)** is a statement that is attributed to a named party in a civil lawsuit or a statement attributed to a criminal defendant. There are five types of opposing parties' statements, the last three of which are vicarious statements (statements made on behalf of another person):

1. the party's own statement,
2. the party's statement by adoption,
3. a statement by a person authorized by a party to speak,
4. a statement by an agent or employee of a party, and
5. a statement by a co-conspirator of a party.

Any statement by a party qualifies as an opposing party's statement if it was made by the party, whether the statement was against the interest of the person when made or not. All that is required is that the statement was made and that it is offered in evidence against the party. Opposing parties' statements are not required to have been made under oath or under any particular circumstances. Under certain circumstances, a statement of admission of guilt by an accused in a criminal case is also called a confession. A more comprehensive discussion of confessions and admissions of criminal defendants follows in Chapter 8.

ADOPTIVE OPPOSING PARTY'S STATEMENT (ADMISSION)
A "statement" that occurs when a party, though not making the statement himself or herself, adopts a statement made by another, usually by silence in the face of an accusation.

An **adoptive opposing party's statement (admission)** occurs when the party, though not making the statement himself or herself, adopts a statement made by another, usually by silence in the face of an accusation. For example, as two men are walking toward each other on the street, one points to the other and says, "That's the man who killed my brother." If the other man hears the statement but does not respond with a denial, then such a lack of response will constitute an adoption of the statement as truth. An adoptive opposing party's statement will be found when, under the circumstances, a reasonable person would be expected to respond and deny the accusation.

MYTH ▶	◀ FACT
In order for an admission to qualify as evidence, it must be against the best interests of the party who made it at the time it was made.	Any statement made by a party to a lawsuit is admissible as an admission if it is offered by the opposing party, whether the statement was against the interest of the declarant at the time it was made or not. Thus, a statement made by an accused at the time of arrest that is later offered at trial against him or her is admissible as an admission, whether or not the statement was incriminating at the time it was made.

A **vicarious opposing party's statement (admission)** is a statement not actually made by the party but by an individual acting on behalf of the party. Such an individual may be acting as a person expressly authorized to speak on behalf of the party, an agent or an employee, or a co-conspirator. If the statement was made by someone authorized to speak for the party opponent, then the statement must concern the subject matter about which the person was authorized to speak. If the statement was made by an employee, the statement must concern a matter within the scope of employment and must be made during the time of employment.

A co-conspirator's statement is one made by a co-conspirator during the course of the conspiracy and in furtherance of the conspiracy. Not all co-conspirators' statements are admissible. If a co-conspirator makes a statement after the conspiracy has ended, usually after the arrest, such statements are not admissible within the co-conspirator's statements exemption.

SPECIFIC HEARSAY EXCEPTIONS

In addition to the exemptions from the hearsay rule discussed earlier, there are other specific *exceptions* to the hearsay rule. Many of the exemptions were treated as exceptions under the common law rule. They have been treated separately in this discussion because they are treated separately in the FRE. However, in those states that have not adopted the FRE, the exemptions will be called exceptions.

STATEMENTS MADE UNDER SENSE OF IMPENDING DEATH (DYING DECLARATIONS)

The dying declaration exception to the hearsay rule is the most restricted of all in terms of foundation for admissibility. For a **dying declaration** to be admissible, there must be an initial showing of unavailability of the declarant. Then, according to the exception under the FRE, Rule 804(b)(2), "[i]n a prosecution for homicide or in a civil case, a statement that the declarant, while believing the declarant's death to be imminent, made about its cause or circumstances" constitutes a dying declaration. The usual justifications underlie the dying declaration exception, namely, necessity and reliability. Originally, the declarant of a dying declaration had to die for the statement to be admissible. Although no longer a requirement, in most situations today, the declarant of a dying declaration is deceased, thus allowing the admission of a statement of an absent declarant. Reliability under the old common law tradition was predicated on the assumption that no one would be willing to lie when about to meet his or her Maker. Today, this assumption is more questionable. The necessity of presenting all the facts to the jury, however, is still a forceful justification for this exception.

Under the common law rule, a dying declaration could only be used in prosecutions for homicide. In most cases, the killer and the victim were the only ones present at the time that the assault took place and were therefore the only ones who knew what happened. It was thought that if, after the assault, the victim should live long enough to make some declaration concerning the cause of his or her injuries, the declaration should be introduced in evidence at the trial against the accused killer. Otherwise, the killer might go free to prey upon others, and justice would not be done.

Foundation for the Modern Exception

There are four foundational requirements for a dying declaration:

1. the declarant must be unavailable,
2. the trial must be either a prosecution for homicide or any civil action,
3. the statement must be made while the declarant believes that death is imminent, and
4. the statement must concern the cause or circumstances of what the declarant believed to be impending death.

Unavailability of the Declarant

FRE 804(a) specifies five ways in which a declarant may be found unavailable for all the exceptions to the hearsay rule that require a finding of unavailability. A declarant is unavailable as a witness if he or she

1. is exempted by privilege;
2. persists in refusing to testify even when ordered by a court to do so;
3. testifies to a lack of memory;
4. is unable to be present because of death, illness, or infirmity; or
5. is absent because the person offering the evidence has been unable to secure the declarant's attendance by process or other reasonable means.

Declarant's Belief in Impending Death

The judge must decide the admissibility of any statement claimed to be a dying declaration. The major issue presented to a judge in determining admissibility pursuant to FRE 104(a) is the third foundational requirement: the state of mind of the declarant at the time the statements were made. Only if the judge is satisfied by a preponderance of the evidence that the declarant was under a belief of impending death will the statements be admitted. In other words, the judge considers whether there were sufficient circumstances, known to the declarant, that caused the declarant to be under the belief that death was imminent. The declarant is not required to say, "I know that I am going to die." Indeed, the declarant's belief in impending death may be created by another person's utterance. For example, a friend's statement to the declarant, "Oh, man, a truck can drive through that hole in your chest," can create a belief in the imminence of death. Other examples showing the declarant's belief that death is inevitable might be his or her request for the final

MYTH ▶

Any statement made by a dying person is admissible in evidence as a dying declaration.

◀ FACT

Only the statements of victims of homicides or attempted homicides are admissible as dying declarations. The statements must be made while the victim believes he or she is dying and must concern the person or persons responsible for the victim's death.

rites of the church, an expression of concern that the family be properly cared for, and an expression of a desire to see some family member one last time.

The declarant's belief in impending death is essential to the admissibility of these statements. It may be perfectly obvious to all present that the declarant has no chance of survival. The declarant may have even been told by a doctor that death is near, but, unless the declarant is convinced that he or she is about to die, the test of trustworthiness is not met. It is the solemnity of impending death that leads the declarant to speak the truth.

It is not necessary that the declarant die immediately after making the declarations for them to be introduced in evidence. In fact, the declarant need not even die, although many cases involve the homicide or death of the declarant. As long as the statement was made under the belief of imminent death and concerns the cause or circumstance of what the declarant believed to be imminent death, it will be admissible. Moreover, there is no prescribed time period following the assault in which the declaration must be made. Admissibility hinges on the frame of mind of the declarant at the time the declarations were made. Admissibility is, therefore, not defeated if, after making a declaration under a belief in impending death, the condition of the declarant improves. As long as the declarations were made at a time the declarant believed that death was imminent, the test of trustworthiness is met.

Dying Declarations Must Relate to the Cause of Death

For a dying declaration to be admissible, the subject matter of the declaration must be confined to facts about the injuries that created the belief of impending death. More specifically, the declaration must relate to the cause or circumstances of what the declarant believes is his or her imminent death. The statements may include things that took place just prior to the injurious event, as well as those that happened closely enough thereafter to be considered an integral part of the event. Dying declarations may include not only the facts of how the injuries were received or inflicted but also information that identifies the assailant, as this may pertain to the cause of death. The declarant does not have to identify the assailant by name, but any descriptive data that assist in the assailant's identification may be admitted.

For example, a victim of a fatal stabbing made a final statement to police at the scene of the crime that, while walking in the park, she was grabbed by a man with a beard and long hair who was wearing a red shirt and, when she screamed, he stabbed her. This statement pertains to the cause or circumstances of the woman's death and is therefore admissible, provided it was made under the belief of imminent death. Where she was at the time that injury was inflicted, the act of grabbing, and the scream followed by the stabbing are all facts pertaining to the injury from which she likely believed she would die. The description of the assailant is a part of the event and pertains to identification.

Form of the Dying Declaration

There is no prescribed form that a dying declaration must follow to be admissible. An oral or written statement, a sign, a nod of the head—all are acceptable. A dying declaration can be in the form of a very simple statement, such as "John shot me." The declaration may be the spoken answer to a question asked of the victim, or it may be merely a nod of the head when the victim is asked whether he or she knows who caused the injury. In this example, if the next question were one that identified the assailant—such as "Was it John?"—a simple nod by the victim would again be sufficient. Also, the victim might be asked to point to the person who assaulted him or her. Such an action by the victim is also considered a valid form of dying declaration. When a declaration is an act and not an actual statement made by the victim, it may become necessary to prove that the victim's mental condition was not perceptibly affected or impaired by his or her injuries. Most important, once it has been established that the declarant has a sense of impending death, utterances made concerning injuries are admissible whether the statements are volunteered by the victim or in response to questions.

A witness who testifies at trial that the victim believed that death was imminent is often the witness who repeats the content of the victim's dying declaration. However, this need not be the case. One witness might present facts to prove that the declarant was under the sense of impending death, while another witness presents the dying declaration itself.

Who May Use Dying Declarations

From a practical standpoint, dying declarations are almost always introduced by the prosecution to aid in the proof of guilt. However, there is no restriction that prohibits the defendant in a homicide case from introducing dying declarations in his or her defense. Likewise, in civil cases, dying declarations may be introduced by either the plaintiff or the defendant. In those states that continue to restrict the admissibility of dying declarations to homicide prosecutions, it is difficult to envision a situation in which the defendant would be able to utilize a dying declaration. In such a state, the only realistic scenario would be if the defendant could produce a witness who had heard the deceased declarant state that the fatal injury had been inflicted by someone other than the defendant.

Weight to Be Given to Dying Declarations

It is primarily the responsibility of the trial judge to determine whether the utterances of a declarant meet the test of trustworthiness—whether the declarant was truly under the impression that death was near. Under FRE 104(a), the judge must determine, as a preliminary question of fact, whether the declarant had the requisite state of mind. The judge may consider inadmissible evidence in resolving this issue and, until the judge determines by a preponderance of the evidence that the declarant was under the belief of impending death, the dying declaration is inadmissible.

Once the dying declaration has been admitted in evidence, the jury decides the weight to be given to it. A jury may give great weight to a declaration because of the solemn circumstances under which it was given. Or the jury may become emotionally involved in the pathos of the situation, believing that in these circumstances no one would utter anything but the truth. On the other hand, the jury may believe that, when the utterances were made, the declarant was in a state of shock. The victim may have been in extreme pain, and his or her thoughts and memories were confused. It is also possible that the jury will find that the declarant was seeking revenge, taking advantage of his or her last moments on earth to accuse an enemy. In sum, it is up to the jury to decide whether the declarant was sincere and speaking of things within his or her personal knowledge.

Thus, even though the judge permits the declarations to be introduced as dying declarations, the jury may also measure the statements' trustworthiness and weigh the statements accordingly. If the jury were to conclude that the declarations were made when the declarant was not under a belief that death was impending, the jury could give the dying declaration little or no weight.

DECLARATIONS AGAINST INTEREST

Sometimes confused with an opposing party's statement (admission) is a declaration against interest. Unlike an opposing party's statement, a **declaration against interest** is a statement made by a person who is not a party to the case and who is unavailable as a witness. Furthermore, the person's statement, to qualify as a declaration against interest, must have been contrary to the person's interests at the time it was made. If the statement were one made by a party to the case, for instance, an accused in a criminal case, then the statement would be admissible as an opposing party's statement and would never even be considered as a declaration against interest.

There are two basic requirements for this exception:

1. the declarant must be unavailable as a witness and
2. the statement must have been against the financial or penal interest of the declarant at the time it was made.

DECLARATION AGAINST INTEREST An exception to the hearsay rule for a statement made by a person who is not a party to the case and who is unavailable as a witness. To qualify as a declaration against interest, the person's statement must have been contrary to the person's interests at the time it was made.

The Rationale for the Exception

The declaration against interest exception exists in recognition of the principle that a person would not say something that would expose him or her to loss of property or liberty unless the statement was likely true. Thus, such potentially damaging statements are viewed as reliable. But the law does not view declarations against interest as being so reliable that they are admissible in all situations.

However, because of the increased likelihood of reliability of such a statement, if the speaker is not available as a witness, the law does allow the statement to be admissible as evidence in many instances.

Unavailability of the Declarant

Just as with the dying declarations exception, unavailability for declarations against interest is defined in FRE 804(a). The same five reasons for unavailability may be shown for a declaration against interest as for a dying declaration. If the declarant is not shown to be unavailable for one of those reasons, the statement will not be admissible.

Requirements for Admissibility: What Is Against Interest?

Any statement that exposes a potential financial loss is a declaration against interest that is admissible under this exception. For example, a statement by a person that he or she owes money to another person is a declaration against interest. Likewise, a statement that could lead to a person's prosecution for a crime would be a statement against penal interest and would be admissible under this exception. For example, a statement in which a person said that he or she committed a robbery would qualify as a declaration against interest. Note that such an admission by a person who is the defendant in a robbery trial would be an opposing party's statement or a confession and would be admissible as such. Such a declaration against interest might be used in a situation in which a defendant seeks to use another person's statement to prove that the other person, not the defendant, committed the crime. It should be noted that, under FRE 804(b)(3)(B), if the statement "is offered in a criminal case as one that tends to expose the declarant to criminal liability," the statement must be "supported by corroborating circumstances that clearly indicate its trustworthiness."

When a suspect in a criminal case makes an incriminating statement that also might be used to incriminate a third person, the prosecutor usually cannot use such statements as declarations against penal interest. This is so due to decisions rendered by the United States Supreme Court. First, in *Williamson v. United States,*[16] in 1994, a plurality of the Court held that FRE 804(b)(3)'s declarations against penal interest exception to the hearsay rule do not allow admission of non-self-inculpatory statements that shift the blame to another, even if they are made in a broader narrative that is generally self-inculpatory. In the case, a man named Harris had admitted his part in a drug transportation scheme but also said that Williamson was the person in charge of the scheme. Some of the justices believed that no part of Harris' statement qualified as a declaration against penal interest, so a majority of the Court agreed that Harris' statement should not have been admitted against Williamson.

In short, according to this case, a declarant's statement such as "I did it, but Joe made me do it" should not be admitted against Joe.

Then, in 1999, in *Lilly v. Virginia,*[17] the Court reviewed a case involving the admission of a blame-shifting declaration against interest admitted in evidence in a state prosecution under Virginia's evidence law. According to Virginia law, such a blame-shifting statement was admissible within the state-defined exception. A majority of the Supreme Court held that admission of the evidence violated the Sixth Amendment's Confrontation Clause rights of the defendant, even if it was admissible under Virginia law.

Finally, in 2004, in *Crawford v. Washington,*[18] the Court redefined the Confrontation Clause and proclaimed that testimonial statements made by an absent declarant not available for cross-examination cannot be admitted against an accused in a criminal case. Blame-shifting declarations against penal interest made to law enforcement professionals would clearly be within *Crawford*'s ban.

SPONTANEOUS UTTERANCES: PRESENT SENSE IMPRESSIONS AND EXCITED UTTERANCES (A.K.A. *RES GESTAE*)

Many times people spontaneously react or say something in response to an unusual event or condition that they have perceived. This spontaneity provides the justification for two exceptions to the hearsay rule: present sense impressions and excited utterances. The rationale is that, when spontaneous reactions or utterances result from a provocative event, time to reflect on the event, and therefore a person's ability to fabricate a lie, are both limited. Thus, anything the person says or does is viewed as inherently more trustworthy. This justification, however, has been undermined somewhat by social science research, which indicates that people may be less accurate in their perceptions when they are excited or surprised. Nonetheless, the justification has continued to be accepted by the law.

The present sense impression and excited utterance exceptions have their origins in what was known as the *res gestae* exception to the hearsay rule. Perhaps in no other area of the rules of evidence is there a term more ambiguous and confusing than that of *res gestae*. Literally, the term **res gestae** means "the things done." The term is more generic than specific, and many distinct exceptions fall within its definition in addition to spontaneous utterances, although the spontaneous utterance exceptions are most commonly associated with the term. Many commentators on evidence have criticized the term as so encompassing that it creates an incentive for judges and lawyers to avoid precision by simply referring to *res gestae*. The use of the term is frowned upon by the courts; when seeking the admission of evidence under the doctrine, a specific exception, rather than the doctrine itself, should be referred to.

RES GESTAE
Literally, "the things done." The term is used most commonly to refer to the spontaneous utterance exceptions to the hearsay rule but could be meant to encompass any number of other exceptions. Therefore, it is ambiguous and its use should be avoided.

Spontaneous Utterances Defined: Present Sense Impressions and Excited Utterances

A **present sense impression** is defined by FRE 803(1) as "[a] statement describing or explaining an event or condition, made while or immediately after the declarant perceived it." This exception to the hearsay rule has two limiting principles. First, the subject matter of the statement must *describe* or explain some event or condition. The statement cannot simply *relate* to an event or a condition. Second, the statement must be made while the declarant was perceiving an event or *immediately* after perceiving that event. Therefore, a slight lapse in time will not defeat admissibility, but, if the time lapse can be measured in minutes rather than seconds, it will likely be considered too long.

PRESENT SENSE IMPRESSION
A statement describing or explaining an event or a condition, made while or immediately after the declarant perceived it.

Unlike the restrictions on subject matter and time, the event or condition that is perceived and explained can be any event or condition, and the declarant's participation in the event is not required. The event need not be startling, provocative, or unusual. In fact, a present sense impression may describe an event as innocuous as noticing the colors of a bird that landed on a tree in the witness's backyard.

The following are examples of present sense impressions that would likely be admissible. A girl observing a man in a department store says to her friend, "That leather outfit with spikes that man is wearing is funny looking"; a husband says to his wife while observing their neighbor, "John's running quite fast; looks like he's late for work"; a woman sees a car drive through an intersection against the red light and says immediately thereafter, "That man drove right through that red light." Anyone who overheard these statements may testify to them, provided there is sufficient evidence to show that the declarant actually perceived these events.

The second form of spontaneous declarations is the excited utterance exception to the hearsay rule. FRE 803(2) defines an **excited utterance** as "[a] statement relating to a startling event or condition, made while the declarant was under the stress of excitement that it caused." The event or condition that the declarant perceives must be startling, as distinguished from the present sense impression exception, in which any event or condition is sufficient. The content of the statement,

EXCITED UTTERANCE
A statement relating to a startling event or condition, made while the declarant was under the stress of excitement that it caused.

on the other hand, is much more expansive than the present sense exception. Excited utterances need only relate to the startling event or condition. Moreover, the excited utterance exception may have a much broader time frame, depending on the circumstances, than a present sense impression. The statement satisfies this qualification if it was made under the stress of excitement prompted by a startling event. For example, consider the case of an assault victim, hospitalized for seven weeks with brain damage, who upon coming home from the hospital was shown a newspaper article containing a photograph of the defendant accused of the assault. Upon seeing the photograph, the victim, in great distress, pointed to the picture and said, "He killed me, he killed me." The court considering the testimony describing these events and the retelling of the statement held that the statement was admissible within the excited utterance exception to the hearsay rule.[19]

Examples of statements that fall within the excited utterance exception may be helpful for a working understanding of the exception. A wife observing her husband being shot by a member of the family may run from the home, screaming, "John just killed my husband"; or the husband may stagger from the house in a dazed condition and state, "John shot me"; or a pedestrian who was almost run over by a car may exclaim, "I can't believe that idiot in the Camaro." Anyone who overhears these statements may testify to the content of the statement. Although it must be shown that the declarant perceived the startling event, the statement itself is usually proof enough.

ON THE JOB

Most officers carry a digital recorder in their pocket or a smartphone to record encounters with victims, witnesses, and suspects. Although most officers record these conversations to protect themselves from false accusations, there is another valuable use for such recordings. The officer is able to obtain the exact wording of dying declarations, excited utterances, and other statements. This makes the police report more accurate and assists the judge in ruling on the admissibility of the hearsay statements.

Foundation and Rationale for the Exceptions

The requirements that must be met in order for a present sense impression to be admissible as an exception to the hearsay rule are:

1. the declarant must explain or describe an event or condition; and
2. the description must be made while the declarant is perceiving the event or condition or immediately thereafter.

For a statement to be admissible under the excited utterance exception to the hearsay rule, the utterance:

1. must relate to a startling event; and
2. must have been made while the declarant was under the stress of excitement caused by the event.

With both exceptions, there are a number of potential problems regarding other foundational matters. These potential problems include proving the existence of the event using the statement itself, proving personal knowledge of the declarant, and determining what to do when the statement is in the form of an opinion.

The rationale for the present sense impression exception is that substantial contemporaneousness makes the chance of deliberate or conscious fabrication or misstatement unlikely. The best example of a present sense impression would be a sports announcer's play-by-play description of a basketball game, where the ability to reflect upon a particular play is all but eliminated. Truthfulness is thus ensured because of the involuntary spontaneity of the announcer's declarations.

The same principle underlies the exception for excited utterances. The ability of the declarant to reflect upon and alter the perception of a startling event is temporarily suspended by the condition of excitement prompted by a startling event.

It is important to note that a person's answer to a question is likely to be viewed by a court as not being within the present sense impression exception because the court will not view the statement as spontaneous. If there is no startling event, and if the speaker is not saying anything about his or her own state of mind, the court is more likely to find that there was an opportunity for the speaker to reflect and be untruthful when answering a question.

The Time Element

A major problem involved in the admissibility of spontaneous declarations is the determination of the time element involved. How soon after the event took place must the excited utterance or present sense impression be made to be admissible? As already explained, the time frame is different for each exception. Present sense impressions must be made while the event is occurring or immediately subsequent to the event. The lapse of time from event to statement must be very brief, consistent with the theory of spontaneity underlying the exception.

APPLICATION CASE

In the case of *Booth v. State*,[20] the defendant was charged with the premeditated murder and robbery of James Edward ("Pie") Ross. In the prosecution's case, it was necessary to place Booth at the home of Ross on the evening of the killing. Among the evidence presented for that purpose was the testimony of Regina Harrison, who testified that she telephoned Ross on the evening of his murder. She further testified that she heard on the telephone the door to Ross' home open and that she asked Ross who was there. According to Harrison, Ross said that it was "some guy . . . behind the door." Other evidence linked the defendant to the scene that night. Ross' statement was admitted as a present sense impression statement, and the Maryland Court of Appeals upheld the conviction of the defendant on the evidence, including this statement.

On the other hand, excited utterances require that the statement be made under the stress of excitement. This requirement has at least two component parts, a time element and a mental element. As to the time element, the requirement poses the question whether there was sufficient lapse of time between the event and the inquiry for the declarant to reflect upon what happened and thereby be able to misrepresent the facts. The mental element poses the question whether the declarant was still in such a state of mind that he or she was not likely to have told a falsehood. Thus, for excited utterances, the primary test of trustworthiness is not so much the time factor as it is the state of mind of the declarant. Was the utterance made while the mind was still so overwhelmed by the nervous excitement of the event that the power to reflect was nonexistent? If so, the utterance is admissible. It is not possible to form any firm criteria for measuring either time lapse or state of mind, as conditions could well vary from one person to another, as well as from one situation to another.

APPLICATION CASE

In one case illustrative of an excited utterance, the declarations made by a victim of a robbery were held admissible even though the declarations were in response to inquiries. The victim-declarant was knocked unconscious after being robbed. The victim was taken to the hospital still in the state of unconsciousness some 45 minutes later. An officer requested that the emergency room nurse ask the victim what had happened to him. About 20 minutes after arriving at the hospital, the victim regained consciousness for about 4 or 5 minutes. During this time, the nurse asked the victim what had occurred. He replied either, "I was beaten," or "I was robbed." He was next asked if he knew who attacked him and he replied, "No." Then the nurse asked, "Was there more than one attacker?" He replied that there was more than one. Finally, she asked if there were more than two, and the victim said, "Maybe two or three." The appellate court upheld the admission of all the statements made to the nurse as excited utterances. The Supreme Court of California stated: "Neither lapse of time between the event and the declarations nor the fact that the declarations were elicited by questioning deprives the statements of spontaneity if it nevertheless appears that they were made under the stress of excitement and while the reflective powers were still in abeyance."[21] The victim had been unconscious for most of the time between the beating and the nurse's questioning and, therefore, was unable to reflect on his answers.

Utterance Must Relate to the Event Just Preceding It

The second requirement for a spontaneous declaration (meaning a present sense impression *or* excited utterance) to be admissible is that it must relate to the event that just preceded the utterance. In the case of an excited utterance, the declaration need only relate to the startling event. The exception for present sense impressions, however, requires that the declaration describe or explain the event. Whichever of these two exceptions is applied, the declaration may not pertain to things that happened the day before or at some other time, such as threats previously made.

In the case of *Houston Oxygen Co. v. Davis,*[22] Mrs. Cooper was riding in an automobile when she saw a Plymouth car go by, at which time she stated, "They must be drunk; we will find them somewhere on the road wrecked if they keep that rate of speed up." Fifteen minutes later, the car in which Mrs. Cooper was riding came upon the scene of an accident involving the Plymouth and a truck belonging to the Houston Oxygen Company. Mr. Sanders, a passenger in the car along with Mrs. Cooper, overheard her statement and was called upon to repeat it in court at a trial brought by the passengers of the Plymouth against the Houston Oxygen Company. The trial court held that the statement was inadmissible. Mrs. Cooper was also called to testify at the trial and, although she was permitted to state her opinion of the speed of the passing Plymouth, she, too, was prevented from repeating her own statement predicting the fate of the vehicle. The appellate court overruled the trial court, holding that the statement should have been admitted as a present sense impression. According to the court, the form of her statement "was one in which the witness was alluding to an occurrence within her own knowledge in language calculated to make her 'meaning clearer to the jury' than would a mere expression of opinion as to the speed at which the passing car was moving."[23]

Availability of the Declarant as a Witness

Under FRE 803, which includes present sense impressions and excited utterances, the availability of the declarant is immaterial, and therefore no showing of unavailability of the declarant is required. In fact, some students of evidence and a majority of the Supreme Court of the United States[24] think that spontaneous utterances may have more reliability than the testimony of the declarant given while on the witness stand. This point of view is based upon the fact that the declarant may not even recall having made the utterance or may have been in such a state of shock as to not be able to recall accurately what took place. If the original declarant is not called upon to testify, generally it is not necessary to explain or give any reason for not calling the declarant. Even if the original declarant is called upon to testify, his or her spontaneous utterance may be related by another witness who heard the utterance. This is most likely to take place if the opposing side makes an allegation that the declarant had falsely testified.

There are times when an utterance of a victim of a homicide may be introduced as a spontaneous declaration, particularly when the utterance does not meet the foundational requirements as a dying declaration. The utterance, however, must meet the foundational requirements of either an excited utterance or a present sense impression.

STATE OF MIND

The state of mind exception to the hearsay rule, being an exception that once fell under the *res gestae* doctrine along with excited utterances and present sense impressions, has its roots in the old common law. This exception allows a declarant's assertion of his or her then-existing **state of mind** to be admitted into evidence to prove that the person actually had that state of mind. As the exception now exists under the modern rules of evidence, there are three requirements:

1. the statement must relate to the declarant's condition of mind or emotion existing at the time he or she made the statement,
2. the statement cannot be one of memory or belief used to prove a fact remembered or believed, and
3. the statement must have been made under circumstances indicating apparent sincerity.

The seminal case that brought the state of mind exception to the forefront in the United States was *Mutual Life Insurance Co. v. Hillmon,*[25] decided by the Supreme Court in 1892. The *Hillmon* case was an action on a life insurance policy, and the question was whether Hillmon had actually died. A body had been found at Crooked Creek, Colorado, which was Hillmon's destination, on March 5. The plaintiff contended that Hillmon and a man named Brown were at Crooked Creek when Hillmon was accidentally shot. The insurance company, on the other hand, maintained that a man named Walters had accompanied Hillmon to Crooked Creek and that it was Walters' body, not Hillmon's, that was found. A letter from Walters to his sister containing the statement "I expect to leave for Crooked Creek on or about March 5th, with a certain Mr. Hillmon" was offered to show Walters' state of mind. The Court held the statement admissible to prove the future conduct of the declarant, Walters, and Hillmon.[26]

State of Mind Declarations Defined

FRE 803(3) defines the state of mind exception to the hearsay rule as "[a] statement of the declarant's then-existing state of mind . . . or emotional, sensory, or physical condition." The rule further provides specific examples, such as statements of intent, plan, motive, design, mental feeling, pain, and bodily health. Memory of events is specifically excluded. If the exception allowed the memory of events to be encompassed within the state of mind definition, the virtual destruction of the hearsay rule would result. To prevent this result, the drafters of the FRE excluded a "statement of memory or belief to prove the fact remembered or believed" from the scope of the rule.

Accordingly, the then-existing state of mind of the declarant will not include statements such as "I was hungry on the flight over from New York," or "I wanted to punch him at the party last Friday," or "I remember that the red car was driving too fast when it hit the bus this morning." The exception includes statements that are backward-looking, except if the statement relates to the execution, revocation, identification, or terms of the declarant's will. For purposes of the law enforcement professional, a statement of memory or belief used to prove a fact remembered or believed will always be inadmissible.

The following are examples of statements that would generally be admissible as within state of mind exceptions to the hearsay rule: "I don't trust Jim"; "I hate people who don't signal"; "I love Nancy—I would never do anything to hurt her"; "I'm leaving for London tonight." These statements describe the declarant's state of mind at the time the statement was made. The first statement may be indicative of the declarant's motive for refusing to entrust Jim with money. The second statement could show the declarant's motive for getting out of his car and attacking another driver. The third statement may show the declarant's lack of motive for the murder of Nancy. Finally, the last declaration indicates that the declarant was planning to take a trip to London.

Anyone who overhears declarations of a declarant's state of mind may testify to them in court, as these statements assist in arriving at the truth in each situation. These statements may be used to prove an element of a crime or defense, or they may tend to show that the declarant acted in conformity with a then-existing intent or plan. For instance, an element of first-degree murder is intent. If one can show the existence or lack of intent from the declarant-defendant's statement, then either the prosecution or the defense may be able to sustain its case.

Foundation and Rationale for the Exception

The principles of reliability and necessity justify the state of mind exception, as well as all other exceptions to the hearsay rule. Statements falling within the exception are generally considered reliable because the declarant is deemed to be the best commentator on his or her own state of mind. Reliability is furthered because, since the statement is limited to the then-existing state of mind of the declarant, there is a reduced possibility for untruthfulness, at least with respect to memory. Of course, a person can always lie about what is on his or her mind, but, unless the circumstances show some basis for suspicion along those lines, the statement will be admitted. Necessity also justifies this exception, in that evidence of a person's state of mind is limited to what the person says and does. Obviously, we cannot look inside a person's head to see what he or she is thinking, so the declarant's state of mind commentary is the most accurate reflection of these thoughts. Moreover, later repetition of this statement in court is the sole means of bringing the statement before the fact-finder. The exception basically rests on a single principle—the declarant is the best witness to what is in his or her own mind.

The major foundational question upon which admissibility turns is whether the statement, when made, related the declarant's "then-existing" state of mind. Does the statement reveal what the declarant was feeling, mentally, emotionally, or physically, at the time the statement was made? Also, is the statement forward-looking? In other words, is the statement by the declarant as to then-existing intent a basis from which one can infer the declarant's subsequent conduct?

Inferring Declarant's and Second Party's Subsequent Conduct

On its face, the state of mind exception to the hearsay rule seems to impose no limitation upon the use of a statement to prove the subsequent conduct of a person, be it the declarant or another. In fact, under the Supreme Court's decision in the *Hillmon* case, a statement of the declarant's intent to do something that involves another person was allowed to be used to prove the future conduct of that person. In that case, the declarant was Walters, who stated that he intended to go to Crooked Creek with Hillmon. The Supreme Court approved the use of

Walters' statement to prove not only that Walters went to Crooked Creek but also that Hillmon went with him. This use of a declarant's statement to prove the conduct of another has been controversial.

The state of mind exception under the FRE, however, was intended by the drafters to limit statements of intent by a declarant by making statements admissible only to prove the declarant's future conduct, not the future conduct of another person.[27] Pursuant to this limitation, statements speculating about the future acts of any other person, either directly or by inference, are to be excluded from evidence. Therefore, in many of those states that have adopted the FRE, the use of a declarant's state of mind statement is not admissible to prove the conduct of a person other than the declarant. That is the position of the courts in Arizona, for example.[28] This view is not uniformly held, however. Both federal and state court decisions have taken the view that a declarant's statement of intent to act in the future with a third person may be used to prove both the declarant's act and the third person's act if there are foundational safeguards. This was the view adopted by the New York Court of Appeals (the highest New York court) in *People v. James.*[29] The foundational safeguards that court established were a showing that

1. the declarant is unavailable;
2. the statement of the declarant's intent unambiguously contemplates some *future* action by the declarant, either jointly with the nondeclarant defendant or that requires the defendant's cooperation for its accomplishment;
3. to the extent that the declaration expressly or implicitly refers to a prior understanding or arrangement with the nondeclarant defendant, it must be inferable under the circumstances that the understanding or arrangement occurred in the recent past and that the declarant was a party to it or had competent knowledge of it; and
4. there is independent evidence of reliability, i.e., a showing of circumstances that all but rule out a motive to falsify and evidence that the intended future acts were at least likely to have actually taken place.[30]

In a footnote, the New York Court of Appeals collected the decisions it claimed followed a similar approach to the *Hillmon* doctrine.[31] The reader is cautioned that he or she may have to ascertain the approach currently taken in any particular federal circuit or state court.

APPLICATION CASE

In *United States v. Pheaster,*[32] the court was confronted with a kidnap-ransom conspiracy in which the victim was still missing. The court allowed, over objection, a friend of the victim to testify that on the night of the abduction the victim had told him and others that he was going to the parking lot to meet the defendant to pick up a pound of marijuana and would be right back. The court held that it was permissible for the fact-finder (judge or jury) to draw the inference that the declarant actually carried out his intention and met with the defendant on that night, since the case was tried under the state of mind exception as defined before the FRE went into effect. If the trial had been held after the FRE went into effect, the victim's statement of intent to meet the defendant could not have been admitted to prove that he had been with the defendant.

People v. Alcalde,[33] a California case from 1944, was decided under the old common law view of the state of mind exception. In *Alcalde,* the supreme court of California upheld a conviction of a man for the murder of a woman on evidence that the victim said that she was going out with the defendant that night. The court held that, under the *Hillmon* doctrine, the victim's statement of her intent to do an act in the future was admissible to prove she did it, even if it included the inference that another person was involved.

Availability of the Declarant as a Witness

The state of mind exception does not require a showing that the declarant is unavailable as a witness. The declarant is in the best position to know what is going through his or her own mind and, because state of mind commentary is most accurate when made, the statement possesses sufficient circumstantial guarantees of trustworthiness so that the declarant's availability as a witness is immaterial.

When considering hearsay, it is necessary to discuss "regular" hearsay as well as "totem pole" hearsay. Say that you record an out-of-court statement, such as "He's the killer." Another layer of hearsay is added by your police report that includes the statement—your report is also an out-of-court statement. Therefore, the prosecutor will need to find an exception or exemption for each layer of the hearsay in order to get the statement admitted into court. For example, your report may be within the business records exception, while the witness's statement might be within the excited utterance exception.

Foundation and Rationale for the Statements for Purposes of Medical Diagnosis or Treatment Exception

There is another hearsay exception that encompasses a declarant's state of mind. It is the exception for the **statements for purposes of medical diagnosis or treatment**. According to FRE 803(4), such a statement "is made for—and is reasonably pertinent to—medical diagnosis or treatment; and describes medical history; past or present symptoms or sensations; their inception; or their general cause." For example, if a person goes to a doctor and says, "I fell down the stairs this morning and my back is killing me," that statement would be within this exception and admissible.

The admissibility of such statements is premised on the assumption that the declarant has a strong motivation to be truthful and accurate; the desire for proper diagnosis or treatment outweighs any motive to falsify. In addition, because the declarant is usually describing his or her own condition, the risks of inaccuracy are diminished. The risks of misperception or faulty memory are also decreased, as the declarant is the best commentator on his or her own condition.

STATEMENTS FOR PURPOSES OF MEDICAL DIAGNOSIS OR TREATMENT
The exception to the hearsay rule that allows into evidence statements that are made for—and are reasonably pertinent to—medical diagnosis or treatment; and describe medical history; past or present symptoms or sensations; their inception; or their general cause.

Thus, statements for purposes of medical diagnosis are admissible under FRE 803(4) if the statements

1. are made for purposes of medical diagnosis or treatment;
2. are made by the patient or someone speaking on his or her behalf;
3. are made to a doctor or other medical person;
4. describe medical history, pain, symptoms, or causes (but not attributing fault) thereof; and
5. are reasonably pertinent to the diagnosis or treatment.

Who Can Make the Statement

Statements made for purposes of diagnosis or treatment may be made by either the patient or someone with an interest in the patient's well-being. For example, a mother of a child suffering from an illness may describe to a doctor the symptoms her child was experiencing that led her to believe the child was sick, and the mother's statement would be admissible within this exception. In determining whether the declarant is someone with an interest in the well-being of a patient, the relationship between the declarant and patient is most important. If the statement as to the condition or symptoms of the patient is made by a disinterested bystander, then such a statement will likely be held inadmissible.

To Whom the Statement Can Be Made

Statements under this exception are not limited to those made to a medical doctor. Qualifying statements may be made to anyone associated with providing medical services, including paramedics, nurses, or even family members. In every case, however, the statements must be made for purposes of medical diagnosis or treatment and must be reasonably pertinent to the diagnosis or treatment.

Additionally, statements made for purposes of diagnosis or treatment are admissible even if they are made after filing a lawsuit. Such statements can be made to either an examining or a treating physician. The exception covers statements made to examining physicians who conduct the examination solely to enable them to testify at trial. Therefore, statements made to a doctor who will be testifying at trial, or even in anticipation of litigation, are admissible. This position is consistent with the liberal approach taken by the FRE in admitting expert testimony; Rule 703 allows experts to base their testimony on inadmissible evidence if the evidence is of a kind ordinarily relied upon by experts in the field and the evidence is more probative than prejudicial.

Even if the statement is found by the trial judge not to have been made for purposes of medical diagnosis or treatment, admissibility may still be granted. In cases in which Rule 803(4) is not satisfied, the statement may still be admissible under the present sense, excited utterance, or state of mind exception.

Statements of Cause of Condition or Pain

The exception extends to statements of causation that are reasonably pertinent to the diagnosis or treatment of the patient's condition. A limit exists as to when statements of causation will fall within the exception. Under Rule 803(4), statements of fault will not ordinarily qualify under this exception to the hearsay rule. For example, a patient's statement that he was "struck by an automobile" would qualify, but his statement that the "car was driven through a red light" would not.[34] In any given case, the question of whether or not a statement made to medical personnel and describing fault is within the exception is one for the trial judge to make based on the facts and circumstances.

FORMER TESTIMONY

The testimony given by a witness at a prior proceeding is admissible in a subsequent trial in certain circumstances as an exception to the hearsay rule. As with the other exceptions, specific requirements must be met before the **former testimony** may be introduced in evidence. The essential requirement for the admissibility of the former testimony is the present unavailability of the witness who gave the former testimony. Under the common law rule, the exception applied only if both the party offering the former testimony and the party against whom it is being offered are the same parties as in the prior proceeding. Further, the common law allowed former testimony only if the issues in both proceedings were identical. Federal Rule of Evidence 804(b)(1) now allows the exception to apply even if the parties and the issues in the two proceedings are not the same. However, with respect to former testimony used in a criminal trial, the defendant must have been a party to the former proceeding and have had the full opportunity to examine the witness whose testimony is being offered under the exception. This exception is most often utilized in criminal cases when a witness who testified at a preliminary hearing or a prior trial is unavailable in the first or subsequent trial of an accused.

Sometimes a deposition given in the presence of the opposing side and with the opposing side given the opportunity to examine the witness qualifies as former testimony. A **deposition** is a written declaration, under oath, made upon notice to the adverse party for the purpose of enabling the adversary to attend and cross-examine. This declaration is usually in question-and-answer form and is much the same as if it were actually related on the witness stand. In a criminal case, the use of a deposition under the former testimony exception usually occurs because there is some sufficient reason the witness cannot appear. The most common acceptable reasons for witness unavailability are death, illness, and hardship, as well as when the witness is planning to leave the state and cannot return to testify at the trial.

FORMER TESTIMONY
The exception to the hearsay rule that allows into evidence testimony given by a now unavailable witness at a prior proceeding.

DEPOSITION
A written declaration, under oath, made upon notice to the adverse party, during which the adversary is present and cross-examines.

Foundation and Rationale for the Exception

By definition, the evidence within this exception consists of testimony given by a witness in person, under oath, and subject to examination (direct, cross-, re-direct, and re-cross) at some other trial or proceeding. The only difference when compared with regular testimony is that the "witness" is now absent and the fact-finder has no opportunity to observe the witness.

Since the exception applies only when the declarant is unavailable, the true rationale for the exception is necessity. The rule states a preference for live testimony, if possible, allowing the use of the recorded prior testimony only when absolutely necessary. The Constitution demands, through the Confrontation Clause of the Sixth Amendment, that the accused in a criminal case be given the right to face his or her accusers. When the accuser has previously testified and satisfied the requirements of the former testimony exception, the courts have held the Confrontation Clause to be satisfied. The courts have so held since 1895.[35]

The foundational requirements for former testimony are

1. the witness must be shown to be unavailable in accordance with one of the situations set forth in FRE 804(a);
2. the testimony sought to be introduced must have been under oath and subject to cross-examination; and
3. either the opponent of the testimony or a party with a similar motive must have had an opportunity to question the declarant in the earlier proceeding by way of direct examination, cross-examination, or re-direct examination. Former testimony may *not* be used against a criminal defendant who was *not* a party to the earlier proceeding.

Opportunity to Have Effective Cross-Examination

Rule 804(b)(1)(B) allows the admissibility of former testimony if the testimony is "offered against a party who had—or, in a civil case, whose predecessor in interest had—an opportunity and similar motive to develop it by direct, cross-, or re-direct examination." The clear meaning of the rule prohibits the use of former testimony against a criminal defendant if the defendant was not a party in the prior proceeding.

As the rule states, the party against whom the former testimony is now being offered must have had an "opportunity" and "similar motive" to develop the testimony of the declarant as the party in the former proceeding. If the party chose not to examine the declarant-witness for tactical or other reasons, the requirement will still be satisfied. The party need only have had the opportunity to examine the witness, and the fact that the party chose not to take advantage of that opportunity does not destroy the opponent's ability to use the evidence.

BUSINESS OR PUBLIC RECORDS
The hearsay exceptions that permit certain written reports or records that record acts, events, conditions, opinions, or diagnoses to be admitted into evidence without requiring the person with knowledge of the facts contained in the records to be called as a witness.

BUSINESS AND PUBLIC RECORDS

Certain reports or records that record acts, events, conditions, opinions, or diagnoses may be admissible as either **business or public records** if certain requirements are met by the proponent of the evidence. These exceptions were developed in the early 1900s as a result of the law's recognition that, if businesses and governments were relying on records of regularly conducted activities, then such records should be sufficiently reliable to be admissible in court.

The exceptions are quite remarkable in that they permit the proof of underlying facts by paper records without requiring the person who has knowledge of the underlying facts to be called as a witness. For example, if the prosecution wanted to prove that the defendant in a criminal case had telephoned the homicide victim just an hour before the murder, the custodian of records of the telephone company could be called to submit the pertinent records. With proper foundation, the record would be admitted to show that the telephone call was, in fact, made from the telephone number assigned to the defendant. In this example, the custodian has no knowledge of the fact that the defendant made any particular telephone call; perhaps no one other than the defendant (and the dead victim) would have that knowledge. Nonetheless, the telephone company's records would be admissible as business records to prove that the call was made.

The matters that are subject to proof under this exception are almost limitless. In recent years and in many states, however, there has developed a limitation upon the use of the exception in criminal cases to prohibit proof of matters observed by law enforcement officers. The effect of this limitation is to prevent the introduction of the contents of police reports on behalf of the prosecution in a criminal case.

Business Records—Description and Foundation

For the business records exception, both the common law rule and FRE 803(6) require that the record must be identified as one

1. made at or near the time of the event;
2. by, or from information transmitted by, a person with knowledge;
3. made in the regular course of business; and
4. kept in the course of regularly conducted business activity.

A record made by someone who does not have knowledge of the transaction or event recorded is still admissible if the underlying information was transmitted by a person in the business who did. Consider a record typed by a clerk who was not a witness to the transaction in question. If the information came through regular business channels from the person who conducted the transaction, the record would qualify. The clerk might not even know who the source of the information was, only that it came through regular channels.

Also, the record must be written at or near the time of the event or transaction; the passage of time may make the record inadmissible. For example, a receipt written six months after the sale of goods would not qualify for the exception.

The traditional method for laying the foundation for a business record is for the custodian of records for the business, or some other qualified person, to testify to the regular practice of keeping the business records and how the record in question was kept. By an amendment to FRE 803(6) effective in 2000, this foundation can be laid by a written declaration of the custodian or other qualified person stating the necessary foundational facts. Such written declaration must be "certified" and comply with another rule of evidence, FRE 902(11) or 902(12). Both of those rules relate to certification, and the authentication through certification, of documents or facts. This amendment makes it much easier for proof of business records by the admission into evidence of the documents without the necessity of sponsoring live witnesses.

If the person testifying (or making a written declaration) is not the custodian of records, the witness must merely be able to describe the business practices sufficiently to satisfy the trial judge that the record was, in fact, made and kept in the regular course of the business and contains information by or from a person with knowledge within the business.

Public Records—Description and Foundation

A record kept by a public agency—a branch of the federal, state, or local government— like a business record, may be introduced into evidence within the public records exception to the hearsay rule. The exception, under FRE 803(8), encompasses "[a] record or statement of public office." There are three types of public records. First are those that set forth "the office's activities."[36] This form of public record is admissible in any type of case. One example is a report by a city police department of the number of arrests made in a certain police district during a particular time period.

The second type of public record is one setting forth "a matter observed while under a legal duty to report."[37] On its face, this category of public record would include police reports containing records of observations by police officers and reports containing analyses of suspected drugs by government chemists. However, this exception under the FRE specifically excludes "in a criminal case a matter observed by law enforcement personnel."[38] By this language, Congress specifically prohibited the use of police reports, as contrasted with the testimony of the officer, to be admitted into evidence against an accused in a criminal case. Since the FRE have been adopted in 43 states, this is the law throughout most of the United States—California, Kansas, Massachusetts, Missouri, New York, and Virginia are the six states that have not adopted the framework of the FRE.

The third type of public record is one setting forth "factual findings from a legally authorized investigation."[39] An example of this type of public record is an investigative report of an officer of the Judge Advocate General of the Navy containing an opinion as to the cause of the crash of a Navy training aircraft.[40] However, public records within this category are permitted only in civil proceedings and when offered into evidence against the government in criminal cases. In other words, such evaluative reports cannot be used by the prosecution in a criminal case.

The foundation required for public records is a showing

1. that the record is an official document of the agency,
2. that it was recorded by an employee of the agency, and
3. that the employee had a duty by law to report such information accurately.

SELF-AUTHENTICATION
The principle that authenticity of a document may be determined on its face, without resort to outside evidence.

Unlike the foundation for authentication required for most objects and documents, public records are self-authenticating. Chapters 11 and 13 cover the general foundations for authentication. **Self-authentication** means that the authenticity of the document may be determined on its face, without resort to outside evidence. In the case of public records, self-authentication is usually provided by a certification of correctness by the custodian of records or other person authorized by the agency to make certifications.[41]

Law Enforcement Reports May Not Be Admissible in Criminal Cases

In criminal cases, police and other law enforcement reports may not be admissible in the prosecution's case-in-chief for policy reasons, even though they are both business and public records. This is because of the Confrontation Clause, as previously discussed. This issue is not completely settled or clear, however. The business records exception, under the FRE, contains no specific prohibition against the use of police and other law enforcement reports in criminal cases, as does the public records exception. Therefore, it may be argued that such law enforcement reports may be offered pursuant to the business records exception. If a law enforcement report is offered to prove only simple matters, is based on the firsthand knowledge of the maker of the report, does not involve conclusions, and is indicated to be trustworthy by the circumstances of its preparation, most state and federal courts will admit the report when offered by the prosecution.[42] Although one court has specifically held that even these conditions for admissibility are not proper, the matter is far from settled.[43]

The Supreme Court's 2004 decision in the *Crawford*[44] case also limits the use of police reports as evidence under the Confrontation Clause, to the extent that such reports contain records of witnesses' statements made to law enforcement personnel. The case banned the introduction of such statements if they are found to be "testimonial," and one of the specific types of statements said to be "testimonial" was witnesses' statements to police officers that a reasonable person would expect to be used later at trial.

The Court further defined what constitutes testimonial statements by witnesses to law enforcement personnel in the 2006 decision in *Davis v. Washington*.[45] The decision was rendered in a consolidation of two cases, one involving a 911 call reporting a domestic violence attack by the victim (*Davis*) and the other involving statements by a victim of domestic violence made to investigating police officers responding to a call (*Hammon*). The Court found that the 911 caller's statement, speaking about events as they were actually happening and facing an ongoing emergency, even though questioned by the 911 operator (who was an agent of the police), was not testimonial under the *Crawford* test. In contrast, the victim's statements to the police officers who came to the scene in response to the call were made when no emergency was in progress and when the police were seeking to determine what had happened in a past suspected criminal event. These statements were testimonial under the *Crawford* standard.

Another possibility involving witnesses' and victims' statements, often arising in domestic abuse cases, is the situation in which the victim- or witness-declarant is absent from the defendant's trial because the defendant has committed some act to keep the declarant from appearing. The most extreme such situation is where the defendant is charged with killing the declarant and the prosecution wishes to introduce statements made by the declarant reporting the defendant's threats against the declarant. That was the case in *Giles v. California*.[46] The defendant was charged with killing the declarant, his ex-girlfriend. At trial, the prosecution introduced statements made to police responding to a domestic violence call a week before the homicide. The victim reported that Giles had threatened to kill her. The California courts held that the statements were admissible because the defendant had forfeited his confrontation rights by killing the victim—his intentional criminal act was what made the victim unavailable to testify.

The Supreme Court reversed the state courts and held that, in order for the forfeiture by wrongdoing exception to the Confrontation Clause to apply, the act causing the declarant's unavailability at trial must have been intended to prevent the victim from testifying. In the *Giles* case, the lower courts had not found that to be so; hence, the exception from the Confrontation Clause could not apply. The Court did note that it would be possible in domestic abuse cases for the evidence of past abuse to support a trial court's finding that the defendant did act to prevent the declarant-victim from testifying by killing the victim.[47] However, if the defense wishes to introduce part of a police report, then it may do so. Once part of the police report is admitted, pursuant to the doctrine of completeness, the prosecution may ask for the whole report to be admitted. The **doctrine of completeness** provides that if a party seeks to admit part of a document, the opposing party may "require the introduction at that time of any other part or any other writing or recorded statement which ought in fairness to be considered contemporaneously with it."[48]

The United States Supreme Court further defined what is testimonial under *Crawford* in connection with state laboratory analysts' certificates of analysis of a substance as cocaine. In the case, *Melendez-Diaz v. Massachusetts,*[49] the defendant had been convicted of drug offenses. In a 6-3 opinion (with a concurrence by Justice Thomas), Justice Scalia concluded that the introduction of the lab analysts' affidavits were testimonial and introduction of such evidence violated the defendant's confrontation rights.

In 2011, in a five-Justice majority, the Supreme Court reaffirmed its *Melendez-Diaz* decision in *Bullcoming v. New Mexico.*[50] In *Bullcoming*, the results of a blood test were necessary to prove an aggravated form of a DUI offense. Unlike *Melendez-Diaz*, the prosecution presented a live witness from the lab, rather than simply the report. The analyst who actually performed the test, however, was on unpaid administrative leave, and the state did not bring him to court. Instead, the state presented the testimony of a supervisor who could speak from personal knowledge about the lab's procedures, but who had not participated in or observed performance of any part of the test on the defendant's blood. The majority opinion, authored by Justice Ginsburg, concluded on the basis of *Melendez-Diaz* that the analyst's report was testimonial. The New Mexico Supreme Court had not denied the report was governed by *Melendez-Diaz* but held that the analyst's report was not governed by the Confrontation Clause. The court reasoned that, because the analyst had transcribed the results of a gas chromatograph machine without offering any additional interpretation, he was a "mere scrivener," with the true accuser being the machine itself. Justice Ginsburg's opinion rejected this theory, however, stating that the analyst's report did more than repeat numbers yielded by the machine. Rather, it amounted to a certification of the entire manner in which the test was conducted. Therefore, the Supreme Court held that the Confrontation Clause does, in fact, apply to such testimony, and lab analysts are no different in this regard from other witnesses.

The New Mexico Supreme Court in *Bullcoming* had also held that the lab supervisor could substitute for the analyst because he was qualified to testify about the machine and the laboratory's procedures. Justice Ginsburg shot down this argument, stating that the supervisor could not testify to what the analyst knew—not only about the test but about why the analyst had been put on unpaid leave. More fundamentally, the "Clause does not tolerate dispensing with confrontation

DOCTRINE OF COMPLETENESS
The rule that provides that, if a party seeks to admit part of a document, the opposing party may "require the introduction at that time of any other part or any other writing or recorded statement which ought in fairness to be considered contemporaneously with it."

simply because the court believes that questioning one witness about another's testimonial statements provides a fair enough opportunity for cross-examination."[51]

Five days after deciding *Bullcoming*, the Supreme Court granted review of *Williams v. Illinois*.[52] In *Williams*, an in-court expert testified that two DNA profiles matched; one of them was reported by an out-of-state lab, from which no witness came to testify at trial. That lab's report was not introduced, but the essence of it—the deduction of a DNA profile that, according to both a computer program and the in-court expert, matched that of the accused—was made clearly known to the judge, sitting as trier of fact. In a plurality opinion written by Justice Alito, along with the four dissenters from *Melendez-Diaz* and *Bullcoming*, they agreed that the DNA profile was not testimonial. The opinion emphasized that the report at issue not only appeared to be reliable but also did not accuse a targeted individual of a crime. When considering forensic evidence, therefore, formal forensic reports are testimonial. This means that any type of testing including, but not limited to, drug, blood alcohol, and fingerprint reports that involve forensic testing by an analyst and that are clearly incriminating will be inadmissible without the testimony of the original analysts.

Proof of Absence of Business or Public Records Entry

Sometimes it is necessary to prove, through the absence of an entry in business or public records, that an event did not occur. Such a fact could be just as important as proof of the affirmative. Of course, the relevance of the absence of an entry to prove an event did not take place is that if the records of a business or public entity do not contain a record of an event, and the records are regularly complete, then it is not likely the event occurred. Thus, it is not surprising that there are hearsay rule exceptions for the absence of both business [FRE 803(7)] and public [803(10)] records.

PEDIGREE OR FAMILY HISTORY

Frequently, a person's vital statistics, such as birth, baptism, marriage, divorce, or death, must be proven in court. Such information is easily proven by a person who has personal knowledge of the event, such as a witness to the event. However, many times there is no such witness available or it would be difficult or a waste of time to track down that witness and call him or her to the stand. Both under the common law rule and the FRE, there are provisions for proof of such personal information. Under the FRE, two forms of hearsay are admissible to prove personal statistics or history: (1) by written record of certificate and (2) by reputation concerning personal or family history.

Written Records

Written records of births, marriages, legitimacy, death, and so on are liberally admissible to prove their existence. Under FRE 803(9), all records of births, deaths, or marriages are admissible if the reports were made to a public agency pursuant to requirements of law. This exception is different from the public records exception, because the person filling out the report does not necessarily have to witness the event recorded. Under FRE 803(11), the records of religious organizations, if kept regularly by the organization, are admissible to prove birth, marriage, divorce, legitimacy, ancestry, and relationship by blood or marriage. Certificates of the person who administered the ceremony are also admissible under FRE 803(12). Also, family records such as entries in a Bible, genealogies, charts, engravings on rings, and engravings on portraits or tombstones are admissible under FRE 803(13).

Reputation to Prove Family History

Finally, reputation among a person's family or community members concerning a person's birth, adoption, marriage, divorce, death, legitimacy, relationship by blood, or other personal or family history is admissible under FRE 803(19). Such reputation evidence is presumed to be reliable.

PAST RECOLLECTION RECORDED: ONLY READ INTO THE RECORD

A witness, even a law enforcement professional, may have trouble remembering specific facts while testifying on the stand. As discussed in Chapter 5, the lawyer may, at this point, show a witness a memorandum or record concerning a matter that the witness once had personal knowledge of and that was written when the matter was fresh in the witness's memory. However, if this writing still does not refresh the witness's memory, the writing then may be introduced as past recollection recorded under FRE 803(5). The key to past recollection recorded is that the writing was written at or near the time of the event when the witness's memory was fresh. Too much passage of time may disqualify the writing from admissibility. The writing must be one that was either written or "adopted" by the witness whose memory has failed. In other words, the witness must be able to testify that the writing contained the correct information at the time that the writing was made, even though the witness cannot now remember the details.

If admitted, the writing may only be read into the record by the proponent of the evidence and may not be received as an exhibit unless the opposing party offers the writing as an exhibit. More simply, the writing is read by the attorney or witness into the record and in front of the jury. However, the jury will not have the document to look at during its deliberation unless the opposing party offers the writing into evidence.

Figure 7–3, in the Review and Application section, summarizes the hearsay rule and the exclusions, exemptions, and exceptions thereto.

REVIEW AND APPLICATION

SUMMARY

(1) Hearsay is an out-of-court statement offered in evidence to prove the truth of the matter asserted in the statement.

(2) Although there are numerous reasons for the hearsay rule, the principal rationale is that the law prefers the declarant of a statement to be

present in court, under oath, and subject to cross-examination rather than to have someone repeat in court what the person said out-of-court.

(3) A statement, for purposes of the hearsay rule under the FRE, is an oral or written assertion or nonverbal conduct intended by the declarant as an assertion.

(4) The five subcategories of NOTMA are (1) operative legal fact, (2) state of mind of the hearer, (3) state of mind of the declarant, (4) state of mind (knowledge) of the declarant on the "traces of the mind" theory, and (5) statements that are otherwise not offered for the truth of the matter asserted (NOTMA) but to prove something else.

(5) The two general categories of exemptions from the hearsay rule under the FRE are prior statements of witnesses and admissions by a party opponent.

(6) The three types of statements by witnesses that are exempt from the hearsay rule are prior inconsistent statements, prior consistent statements, and statements of prior identification of a person.

(7) The five types of admissions by a party opponent that are exempt from the hearsay rule are
   (a) the party's own statement,
   (b) the party's admission by adoption,
   (c) an admission by a person authorized by a party to speak,
   (d) an admission by an agent or employee of a party, and
   (e) an admission by a co-conspirator of a party.

(8) The four foundational requirements for the dying declaration exception to the hearsay rule are
   (a) the declarant must be unavailable,
   (b) the trial must be either a prosecution for homicide or a civil action,
   (c) the statement must be made while the declarant believes that death is imminent, and
   (d) the statement must concern the cause or circumstances of what the declarant believed to be impending death.

(9) The two species of spontaneous declarations exceptions to the hearsay rule are present sense impressions and excited utterances. The difference between them is that a present sense impression must be made while the declarant is perceiving the event described or immediately thereafter, while an excited utterance need only relate to an exciting or startling event and may be made at any time that the declarant is still under the influence of the excitement of the event.

(10) A major limitation upon the state of mind exception to the hearsay rule is that the statement must reflect the then-existing thoughts of the declarant. The statement may be forward-looking, as in stating an intent to do something in the future. However, the statement cannot contain an assertion of a fact remembered or believed.

(11) The foundational requirements for the statements for purposes of medical diagnosis or treatment exception to the hearsay rule are that the statement must
   (a) be made for purposes of medical diagnosis or treatment;
   (b) be made by the patient or someone speaking on the patient's behalf;

(c) be made to a doctor or other medical person;

(d) describe medical history, pain, symptoms, or causes (but not attributing fault) thereof; and

(e) be reasonably pertinent to the diagnosis or treatment.

(12) The foundational requirements for former testimony are

(a) the witness must be shown to be unavailable in accordance with one of the situations set forth in FRE 804(a);

(b) the testimony sought to be introduced must have been under oath and subject to cross-examination; and

(c) either the opponent of the testimony or a party with a similar motive must have had an opportunity to question the declarant in the earlier proceeding by way of direct examination, cross-examination, or re-direct examination.

(13) The foundational requirements for the business records exception to the hearsay rule are that the record must be identified as one

(a) made at or near the time of the event;

(b) by, or from information transmitted by, a person with knowledge;

(c) made in the regular course of business; and

(d) kept in the course of regularly conducted business activity.

KEY TERMS

hearsay 180
declarant 182
Confrontation
    Clause 182
operative legal
    fact 189
state of mind of the
    hearer 190
state of mind of the
    declarant 187
"traces of the mind"
    theory 188
prior inconsistent
    statement 190
prior consistent
    statement 190

statements of prior
    identification 190
opposing party's
    statement
    (admission) 191
adoptive opposing
    party's statement
    (admission) 191
vicarious opposing
    party's statement
    (admission) 192
dying declaration 192
declaration against
    interest 196
res gestae 198

present sense
    impression 198
excited utterance 198
state of mind 203
statements for purposes
    of medical diagnosis
    or treatment 206
former testimony 208
deposition 208
business or public
    records 209
self-authentication 211
doctrine of
    completeness 216

QUESTIONS FOR REVIEW

1. What is a simple definition of hearsay? How is hearsay defined by the courts?

2. What is the rationale for the hearsay rule?

3. How is a statement defined in the FRE?

4. What are the five subcategories of statements that are not offered for the truth of the matter asserted (NOTMA)?

5. What are the two general categories of exemptions from the hearsay rule under the FRE?

6. What are the three types of prior statements by witnesses that are exempt from the hearsay rule under the FRE?

7. What are the five types of admissions by a party opponent that are exempt from the hearsay rule under the FRE?

8. What are the four foundational requirements for the dying declaration exception to the hearsay rule?

9. What are the two species of spontaneous declarations exceptions to the hearsay rule and what is the difference between them?

10. What is a major limitation upon the state of mind exception to the hearsay rule?

11. What are the foundational requirements for the statements for purposes of medical diagnosis or treatment exception to the hearsay rule?

12. What are the foundational requirements for the former testimony exception to the hearsay rule?

13. What are the foundational requirements for the business records exception to the hearsay rule?

THINKING CRITICALLY ABOUT EVIDENCE

1. In the prosecution of a defendant, John, for the murder of Bill, the state calls a witness to testify that he heard Debbie (a friend of the defendant) say to the defendant, "Bill is a gang member who has knifed several people." Is this statement hearsay? Is it admissible?

2. A defendant is on trial for assault with a deadly weapon. In order to prove that the defendant was carrying a knife at the time of the attack, the prosecution calls a witness to testify that, as the defendant was walking past him on the day and time in question, the witness's wife said, "Look, that guy has a knife." Is this statement hearsay? Is it admissible?

3. In a criminal homicide prosecution, the defense, in order to prove its defense of insanity, calls a witness to testify that the defendant repeatedly told people, "I am the President of the United States." Is this evidence hearsay? Is it admissible?

4. In the prosecution of a defendant for burglary, the prosecution calls the arresting officer to testify that, on the way to the police station after he was arrested, the defendant confessed that he had committed the crime. Is this evidence hearsay? Is it admissible?

WORKPLACE APPLICATIONS

1. A police officer arrived at the scene of a gang initiation party to find one of the inductees stabbed several times as part of his test for membership. The inductee had lost a lot of blood and was near unconsciousness. When the officer asked the wounded man who stabbed him, the man replied, "Baby Killer," a rival gang member. The victim recovered but could not be found and called as a witness at Baby Killer's criminal trial. At the trial, the prosecutor calls the police officer to testify to the victim's statement as a dying declaration. Can the statement be admitted? Explain why or why not.

2. A police officer responds to a domestic dispute call. The wife has some bruises on her arms. When the officer asks her what happened, she points

to her husband and says, "He did it to me. He threw me around the room like a rag doll." The husband does not say anything but stands with his head hanging down, shaking it back and forth. Should the husband's reaction or lack thereof be admitted as an adoptive admission?

ETHICAL DILEMMA

1. Assume that you are a police officer and a witness in a trial of a brutal homicide that you investigated. You are on the witness stand and cannot remember the date that you collected critical bloodstain evidence from the scene of the crime. The prosecutor asks you if your memory could be refreshed if you examined your report. You respond affirmatively, the prosecutor hands you a copy of your report, and you read it. You still don't remember the date but now, having read the report, you see the date on it. The prosecutor next asks, "Now, is your memory refreshed?" How should you answer? Explain.

ENDNOTES

1. Fed. R. Evid. 801(c).

2. J.G. Phillmore, History and Principles of the Law of Evidence, 357 (1850), as cited and presented in Roger C. Park & Richard D. Friedman, Evidence, *Cases and Materials* 197 (12th ed. 2012).

3. Fed. R. Evid. 801(b) defines a declarant as a person who makes a statement.

4. 541 U.S. 36, 124 S.Ct. 1354 (2004).

5. *Id.* at 1374.

6. *Id.* at 1364.

7. Davis v. Washington, 547 U.S. 813 (2006).

8. Davis v. Washington, 547 U.S. 813, 822 (2006).

9. 562 U.S. 344 (2011).

10. *Id.* at 367-70.

11. ___ U.S. ___, 135 S.Ct. 2173 (2015).

12. Giles v. California, 554 U.S. 353 (2008).

13. Fed. R. Evid. 801(a): "Statement" means a person's oral assertion, written assertion, or nonverbal conduct, if the person intended it as an assertion.

14. *See* Roger C. Park, *I Didn't Tell Them Anything About You: Implied Assertions as Hearsay Under the Federal Rules of Evidence,* 74 Minn. L. Rev. 783 (1990).

15. This example was created by the late John Kaplan to illustrate the very point made in the text in the form of a made-up case. This was included in his casebook on evidence. The current version of the casebook is Park & Friedman, *supra,* note 2, at p. 203.

16. 512 U.S. 594 (1994).

17. 527 U.S. 116 (1999).

18. 541 U.S. 36, 124 S.Ct. 1354 (2004).

19. United States v. Napier, 518 F.2d 316 (9th Cir. 1975).

20. 508 A.2d 976 (Md. Ct. App. 1986).

21. People v. Washington, 459 P.2d 259, 263 (Cal. 1969).

22. 161 S.W.2d 474, 476 (Tex. Comm. App. 1942).

23. *Id.* at p. 477.

24. *See* White v. Illinois, 502 U.S. 346, 355-56 (1992).

25. 145 U.S. 285 (1892).

26. The Hillmon case was extremely controversial, and the controversy persisted for many decades in the courts. A few years ago, Professor Mimi Wesson led a project to exhume the body interred at Oak Hill Cemetery in Lawrence, Kansas, to see if modern science could end the controversy. In February 2007, a professor of anthropology from the University of Colorado issued a report asserting the body was, in fact, that of John Hillmon. *See* http://www.thehillmoncase.com/results.html [http://perma.cc/TAH8-R6HU].

27. Fed. R. Evid. 803(3), advisory committee's note.

28. State v. Krone, 797 P.2d 621, 625-26 (Ariz. 1995) (concurring opinion).

29. People v. James, 717 N.E.2d 1052, 1057-60 (N.Y. 1999).

30. *Id.* at 1060.

31. *Id.* at 1058 n. 4.

32. 544 F.2d 223 (9th Cir. 1976).

33. 148 P.2d 627 (Cal. 1944).

34. Fed. R. Evid. 803(4), advisory committee's note.

35. Mattox v. United States, 156 U.S. 237 (1895).

36. Fed. R. Evid. 803(8)(A)(i).

37. Fed. R. Evid. 803(8)(A)(ii).

38. *Id.*

39. Fed. R. Evid. 803(8)(A)(iii).

40. *See* Beech Aircraft Corp. v. Rainey, 488 U.S. 153 (1988).

41. *See* Fed. R. Evid. 902(4).

42. *See* State v. Bertul, 664 P.2d 1181 (Utah 1983), a seminal case cited by many state courts. The court in Bertul cited and quoted from United States v. Smith, 521 F.2d 957 (D.C. Cir. 1975), another oft-cited

decision. With respect to federal courts' treatment, see Robert A. Brazener, Annotation, *Admissibility of Police Reports Under Federal Business Records Act (Federal Rules of Evidence, Rule 803, and predecessor amendments,* 31 A.L.R. Fed. 457, § 3 (West. 2018). With respect to state courts' treatment, see George L. Blum, Annotation, Admissibility in State Court Proceedings of Police Reports as Business Records, 111 A.L.R.5th 1 (West 2018).

43. Compare United States v. Oates, 560 F.2d 45 (2d Cir. 1977) (held: Custom's Service chemist's report that substance was cocaine not admissible in criminal case under Fed. R. Evid. 803(8) or 803(6)), with United States v. Rosa, 11 F.3d 315 (2d Cir. 1993) (held: autopsy report of medical examiner not a law enforcement report within the Oates decision and, therefore, it is admissible in criminal case).

44. Crawford v. Washington, 541 U.S. 36, 124 S.Ct. 1354 (2004).

45. Davis v. Washington and Hammon v. Indiana, 547 U.S. 813 (2006).

46. Giles v. California, 554 U.S. 353 (2008).

47. *Id.* at 377.

48. Fed. R. Evid. 106.

49. Melendez-Diaz v. Massachusetts, 557 U.S. 305 (2009).

50. Bullcoming v. New Mexico, 564 U.S. 647 (2011).

51. *Id.* at 2708.

52. 132 S.Ct. 2221 (2012).

Hearsay Exclusion,[1] Exemption,[2] Exception[3]	Rationale or Reasoning	Example
Statement—exclusion	Only an intended assertion raises credibility issues	The act of suicide, offered to prove guilty conscience
Offered for the truth of the matter asserted—exclusion	No credibility issue involved	"Your money or your life" threat in robbery
Prior inconsistent statement of a witness—exemption	Declarant available and prior statement made under oath, subject to penalty of perjury	Contradictory description of getaway car made at preliminary hearing in contrast to testimony at trial
Prior consistent statement of a witness—exemption	Declarant available and usable only for limited purpose of rebutting attack on credibility	Consistent statement made by declarant at a time before motive to fabricate existed
Prior identification statement of a witness—exemption	Declarant available and fact of identification is highly probative of identity	"That's the man who attacked me" while victim picks out defendant at a lineup
Opposing party's statement (admission)—exemption	The adversary system: anything a party does or says can be used against him or her; "You said it; you explain it"	Defendant attempted to cover up his movements on the day the victim was killed
Adoptive opposing party's statement (admission)—exemption	People ordinarily deny accusations against them if they are untrue	Defendant stands silent as victim's wife says to him, "You killed my husband"
Authorized opposing party's statement (admission) by agents, employees, and co-conspirators of a party opponent—exemption	Statements made by agents of parties are usable against the parties just as though they had made the statements themselves	"I am selling this heroin for me and the defendant" (there must be evidence that the seller and the defendant were partners in the heroin business)
Dying declaration—exception	People who know they are dying do not lie when they make statements about what they believe to be the cause of their impending death, and the law needs such evidence in homicide cases	"I know I am about to die and the defendant is the one who shot me"

FIGURE 7–3 Hearsay principles and examples. *(continued)*

Hearsay Exclusion,[1] Exemption,[2] Exception[3]	Rationale or Reasoning	Example
Declaration against interest—exception	People ordinarily do not make statements exposing themselves to civil or criminal liability unless the statements are true	"I am the one who took the money"
Present sense impression—exception	People who make statements describing events while they are happening do not have time to reflect and lie about them	"The defendant sure looks mad enough to kill someone"
Excited utterance—exception	People who make statements relating to exciting events while they are under the stress of the excitement do not reflect about them and lie	"Oh, my goodness, that red car hit the woman in the cross walk like the driver was aiming at her"
State of mind—exception	People do not likely lie about what is then and there on their minds and, besides, how else could we know?	Defendant's statement "I hate John," made the day John was murdered
Statements for medical diagnosis or treatment—exception	People are not likely to lie to their doctors when they seek medical treatment	"Doctor, I have never suffered from insomnia before the murder I witnessed; now I can't sleep at all"
Former testimony—exception	Testimony by a witness under oath, fully examined at a prior legal proceeding, is almost as good as live testimony	"The defendant is the man who attacked me," testified to at a preliminary hearing by a witness who is now dead but was fully examined by both sides' lawyers at the preliminary hearing
Business records—exception	If it is reliable enough for the business to use it, it is good enough for the courts	The telephone company's record that shows the telephone call threatening the victim came from the phone assigned to the defendant
Public records—exception	Public employees under a legal duty to report facts are going to do so accurately	The Department of Motor Vehicles report shows the getaway car was registered to the defendant
Pedigree, or family history—exception	Information about births, deaths, and other family history, whether written in a Bible or in a church record, or part of family reputation, is relied upon and therefore is likely accurate	The church record of the marriage between defendant and his wife proves that they are married and therefore she has a marital privilege not to testify against him if she wishes
Past recollection recorded—exception	People who swear that they wrote down details accurately at the time should be believed even if they cannot now remember the details	"I know that I wrote down the license number of the getaway car accurately on this slip of paper, even though I cannot remember the number"

[1] "Hearsay exclusion" means excluded from the hearsay rule by definition.
[2] "Hearsay exemption" means exempted from the hearsay rule by FRE 801(d)(1) or (2).
[3] "Hearsay exception" means that although the evidence is hearsay, it is admissible within a specific exception to the hearsay rule.

Design Element: ©Ingram Publishing

OPPOSING PARTY'S STATEMENTS (ADMISSIONS) AND CONFESSIONS

CHAPTER OUTLINE

CHAPTER OBJECTIVES

This chapter examines specifically the law of evidence as it relates to statements made by the accused in a criminal case, commonly known as opposing party's statements (admissions) and confessions. After reading this chapter you will be able to:

▶ Define an opposing party's statement (admission).

▶ Distinguish between confessions and opposing party's statements (admissions).

▶ State the fundamental requirement for a confession to be usable as evidence.

- ▶ Describe the test for voluntariness of a confession.

- ▶ State the requirements of *Miranda*.

- ▶ Define custody for purposes of *Miranda*.

- ▶ Define interrogation for purposes of *Miranda*.

- ▶ State the burden of proof required to prove a waiver of *Miranda* rights by a suspect.

- ▶ Describe when interrogation of a suspect who has invoked the right to counsel may resume.

- ▶ List the three exceptions to the requirement of *Miranda* warnings.

- ▶ Explain when the Sixth Amendment right to counsel attaches.

- ▶ State the rule governing interrogation of a suspect when right to counsel has attached.

- ▶ Define what constitutes deliberate elicitation.

- ▶ Explain the procedures to determine the admissibility of a confession at trial.

INTRODUCTION—OPPOSING PARTY'S STATEMENTS (ADMISSIONS) AND CONFESSIONS GENERALLY

OPPOSING PARTY'S STATEMENT (ADMISSION)
Any statement, verbal or otherwise, made by a party that can be used in evidence against him or her.

Under the FRE, any statement made by a party is an **opposing party's statement (admission)** and can be used in evidence against him or her as long as the statement is relevant to the case. Opposing party's statements cover a broad category of evidence. Also, an opposing party's statement presents no hearsay problems, as pointed out in Chapter 7, because opposing party's statements are exempt from the hearsay rule.

Opposing party's statements are not limited to verbal statements made by a party–they can be inferred from a person's demeanor, conduct, and acts, or even silence. Statements made before trial by criminal defendants are also opposing party's statements and can be used as evidence at trial. However, a defendant's statement made while in police custody may be inadmissible unless the prosecution proves that the statement was made voluntarily and that specific rights (*Miranda* and the Sixth Amendment right to counsel) were waived before the statement was made.

CONFESSION
A conscious acknowledgment of guilt by an accused.

Certain opposing party's statements by criminal defendants are also known as confessions. A defendant's statement is a **confession** when the statement is a conscious acknowledgment of guilt by an accused. Both opposing party's statements generally and confessions must be voluntarily given to be admissible against an accused in a criminal case.

Confessions and opposing party's statements frequently overlap, and it is sometimes difficult to decide which type of statement was given. A dictionary definition of a confession is "a full and direct acknowledgment of all the elements of the crime."[1] The distinction between a confession and an opposing party's statement (admission) has been stated this way by one court: "A confession is an admission of the crime itself. An opposing party's statement (admission) concerns only some specific fact which, in turn, tends to establish guilt or some element of the offense."[2] For purposes of the law enforcement professional's understanding, the most important fact is that both opposing party's statements (admissions) and confessions must be voluntarily made in order to be used in court against a person accused of a crime. Moreover, the FRE does not have a rule specifically covering confessions, and therefore the distinction between opposing party's statements (admissions) and confessions is of little importance in terms of determining admissibility in most jurisdictions.

<table>
<tr><td>

MYTH ▶

In order for a statement to qualify as an opposing party's statement (admission), it must be a conscious acknowledgment of guilt or complicity at the time it was stated.

</td><td>

◀ FACT

An opposing party's statement (admission) is any statement by a party (that is, a defendant in a criminal case or either plaintiff or defendant in a civil case) that is offered in evidence by an opponent (the prosecution in a criminal case) at trial. The statement need not have been against the interest of the party making the statement at the time it was made. The only requirement is that the statement be relevant to some issue at trial.

</td></tr>
</table>

The law of evidence is not nearly as important in deciding the admissibility of opposing party's statements (admissions) and confessions as is the Constitution of the United States. The United States Supreme Court has imposed requirements on law enforcement professionals in connection with opposing party's statements and confessions stemming from the Fourth, Fifth, Sixth, and Fourteenth Amendments. After briefly describing how the law of evidence affects opposing party's statements by a criminal defendant, this chapter will explore the impact of these constitutional provisions on the admissibility of defendants' confessions in a criminal trial.

OPPOSING PARTY'S STATEMENTS (ADMISSIONS)

Statements or acts by an accused before trial that are not an acknowledgment of guilt but do link the accused with a crime or are in some ways incriminating are opposing party's statements (admissions). The accused need not intend to incriminate himself or herself for the statement or act to be an opposing party's statement (admission). An opposing party's statement (admission) may be a simple acknowledgment of being at the crime scene or of being acquainted with the victim of a crime; it may also be a denial of being at the scene. Any statement or act could become incriminating once coupled with other evidence. For example, assume an officer arrests the accused and states, "You are under arrest for robbery." The accused then responds, "I was out of town yesterday afternoon." Since the officer said nothing about the place and date of the robbery, the accused's response discloses peculiar knowledge that only the perpetrator of the crime would know. The response constitutes a "false denial" and is admissible against the accused on a theory of consciousness of guilt.

Acts as Opposing Party's Statements (Admissions)

Acts are also classified as a form of opposing party's statement if they are inconsistent with an accused's innocence. Thus, acts such as trying to escape detection and arrest and attempting to hide a crime are an opposing party's statements and may be introduced against the accused at a trial. For example, an act that constitutes an opposing party's statement would be a defendant nodding his head when the officer asks him if he committed the crime. However, these opposing party's statements by conduct fall more logically under the subject matter of consciousness of guilt, which will be discussed in detail in Chapter 11.

Opposing Party's Statement (Admission) by Silence in Response to Accusatory Statements

The defendant's silence in circumstances in which a person would normally speak out may constitute an opposing party's statement (admission). Whether or not this silence may be introduced as an opposing party's admission of guilt depends upon the conditions under which the silence occurred. If a person makes a statement in front of another, accusing him or her of committing a crime and no reply or denial is made, this is considered to be an **implied, or adoptive, opposing party's admission** of guilt as long as it is clear that the accused person was in a position to hear and understand the accusation. A person does not ordinarily remain silent in the face of an accusation of having committed a crime unless the accusation is true. For example, assume the defendant said nothing in response to her mother's statement "You robbed our neighbor, didn't you? I know you did!" Faced with this accusation, it is presumed that an innocent person would deny the validity of the statement. Silence is an indication that the statement or accusation is true, that the accused has "adopted" or made the statement his or her own, and carries an implication of guilt.

Additionally, if an accused denies an accusation, the accusatory statement and the denial are both inadmissible because the denial is a "self-serving statement" and is inadmissible as hearsay. However, if the accused makes a statement not amounting to a denial, it may be introduced if the effect is the same as an opposing party's admission by silence. For example, when the mother asked her daughter what she did with the jewelry she stole from the neighbors, the daughter replied, "Who, me?" This is not a denial, and the inference of guilt may be drawn just as if she had remained silent.

Statements by an Accused While in Police Custody

A statement made by a person while in police custody is usually not an adoptive opposing party's admission because a person in custody is not required to say anything. Even if a suspect is not in custody, just being in the presence of officers and under suspicion is enough to cause a reasonable person to remain silent in the face of an accusation. For example, assume an officer asks the defendant, "You ran over that kid with your car, didn't you?" The defendant's silence probably would not be an opposing party's statement (admission) because many people accused of a crime wish to consult with an attorney before they speak with the police, even if they are innocent.

CONFESSIONS—GENERAL PRINCIPLES AND CONSIDERATIONS

Throughout human history, statements have been coerced from people by a variety of means that are unacceptable today. For this reason, opposing party's statements (admissions) and confessions are often subject to close scrutiny.

IMPLIED, OR ADOPTIVE, OPPOSING PARTY'S ADMISSION Silence in the face of an accusation when a reasonable person would respond.

For some time, courts have taken a rather dim view of confessions as evidence. In the twentieth century, the United States Supreme Court developed the exclusionary rule, and the Court continues to develop complex and strict rules pertaining to the admissibility of confessions in evidence. It is important for the law enforcement professional to be aware of how these rules were developed through a succession of Supreme Court decisions. Studying this progression of cases will lead to a better understanding of how to obtain confessions that will be admissible in court.

Development of the Free and Voluntary Rule

The use of confessions as a tool to convict persons of crimes dates far back into human history. History also reveals that, in the past, many confessions used to obtain convictions were coerced through various forms of torture, such as the rack and screw or the application of red-hot irons to bare flesh. Many of these confessions were false, since a person suffering excruciating pain will say anything just to get immediate relief. As the use of coerced confessions as evidence fell into disfavor, the law developed the fundamental requirement that a confession, to be usable as evidence, must be made freely and voluntarily.

ON THE JOB

Often, the exact wording of the defendant's admission or confession is of extreme importance to a successful prosecution. Out in the field, the officer should use a personal recorder. At the police station, interviews should be recorded. Such recordings may also document the circumstances and conditions under which the statements were made. Recording using a device that captures both visual and audio is preferable to simply recording audio alone because it records more information. Along with the recording, a signed and witnessed statement from the defendant should also be obtained. The statement should include the content of the defendant's admissions or confessions along with any waiver of constitutional rights that might be applicable.

For a confession to have been made freely and voluntarily, the person making the confession must have been in a position to exercise complete mental freedom at the time the confession was made. The courts have been strict in their interpretation of what will affect this "complete mental freedom" and have ruled that any pressure applied to induce a confession will be considered interference, causing the confession to be excluded from evidence at trial.

At first, courts were primarily concerned with whether the confessor had been subjected to any physical abuse to induce the confession. Later, the courts came to recognize that other factors might affect freedom of the mind, such as psychological pressures upon the accused before or during interrogation. Psychological pressure has been interpreted as any act or statement that may place the accused under a mental strain, such as a threat of violence, a threat against members of the accused's family, extreme deception, a promise of reward, or duress.

The requirement that the confession must be given freely and voluntarily satisfies two concerns of modern jurisprudence. First, unless the confession is so given, there may be a doubt about the fundamental fairness of its use at trial against the accused; second, unless it is given freely and voluntarily, the accused's right against self-incrimination may be violated.

Development of Additional Requirements

Until about the middle of the twentieth century, the admissibility of confessions was entirely dependent upon meeting the requirement that the confession be freely and voluntarily given. If it was, the confession was admitted in evidence against the accused. This approach required the courts to decide each case individually with respect to the admissibility of a confession, rather than deciding on the case according to a categorical rule. Then, beginning in the 1940s, the Supreme Court of the United States began taking an entirely new approach to judging the admissibility of confessions.

First, the high Court developed a *per se* rule applicable only in the federal courts. This rule excluded potentially coerced confessions by addressing the practice of detaining arrested persons in isolation for an extended period of time. Admissibility did not depend on whether the confession was voluntary, but rather was based on whether an arrested suspect was brought before a committing magistrate for arraignment "without unnecessary delay" following the suspect's arrest. This requirement became known as the *McNabb-Mallory*[3] rule, named after two Supreme Court decisions establishing the rule. Under the *McNabb-Mallory* rule, unnecessary police delay in arraigning a suspect who was in police custody led to the exclusion of any statement obtained during the period of unnecessary delay, regardless of whether it was given freely and voluntarily.

PROMPT
ARRAIGNMENT RULE
The rule requiring an arrested person to be brought before a committing magistrate without unnecessary delay. Such a delay can cause statements made by the arrested person to be found inadmissible. Also known as the *McNabb-Mallory* rule.

The **prompt arraignment rule**, or requirement, is still contained in Federal Rule of Criminal Procedure 5(a). However, the *McNabb-Mallory* rule, which was not constitutionally based, never applied to the states and has been overshadowed by the Supreme Court's decision in *Miranda v. Arizona*,[4] which is discussed later.

The Supreme Court also extended the basis for a finding of a coerced confession from threatened and actual physical coercion to psychological coercion as well. In 1944, in *Ashcraft v. Tennessee*,[5] the Court held that 36 hours of continuous interrogation alone was enough to render the accused's confession coerced. Also, in the 1959 case of *Spano v. New York*,[6] the Court held that psychological pressures rendered a confession inadmissible because of coercion. Three justices agreed with the outcome of the *Spano* case but stated that they would have found Spano's confession inadmissible for another reason also. The justices pointed out that Spano, who had already been indicted for the murder he was later convicted of, was not provided counsel when he was interrogated. At the time of the *Spano* decision, the Sixth Amendment right to counsel had not yet been held to apply to the states. The requirement of the right to counsel was applied to the states in 1963 with respect to felony trials[7] and with respect to nonfelony criminal trials in 1972.[8]

In 1964, in *Escobedo v. Illinois*,[9] the Supreme Court found that a police interrogation of a suspect violated the Sixth Amendment right to counsel. Escobedo had not been formally charged and, during a lengthy questioning, his attorney had tried repeatedly to see his client. The Court said that, since Escobedo's attorney was trying to see him, in the absence of any warning, Escobedo's statement should be excluded from trial as a violation of the right to counsel. Also in 1964, the Court held in *Massiah v. United States*[10] that police interrogation (defined as deliberate elicitation) of an indicted person in the absence of an attorney (or waiver by the accused) is a violation of the Sixth Amendment's right to counsel.

Up to the time of the *Escobedo* and *Massiah* decisions, the Supreme Court had been seeking ways to curtail what it perceived to be police abuses in the context of private (incommunicado) interrogations of suspects. Although the use of actual violence and even psychological coercion had been condemned, the Court was still dissatisfied with what it believed to be more sophisticated forms of abuse. The Court's decisions from *McNabb* to *Escobedo* also reflected a dissatisfaction with the free and voluntary rule as an effective means of dealing with perceived police excesses in obtaining confessions. Under the free and voluntary rule, each case required a factual assessment of the accused's claim that his or her confession was coerced.

Thus, the stage was set for the Court's revolutionary 1966 ruling, *Miranda v. Arizona.*[11] *Miranda* requires the police to inform a suspect in custody

1. of his or her right to remain silent,
2. that anything the suspect says might be used in court against the suspect,
3. that the suspect has the right to have counsel present during questioning, and
4. that counsel will be appointed for the suspect if the suspect cannot afford counsel.

In the absence of these **Miranda warnings** and a waiver of the rights to remain silent and to counsel during police interrogation, any statement obtained by the police cannot be used against the accused at trial, even if the statement is not coerced.

Beginning almost immediately after the Court's *Miranda* decision, judges and legal scholars began asserting that *Miranda*'s warnings were not constitutionally mandated. Some decisions of the Supreme Court even endorsed this notion. In 2000, in *Dickerson v. United States,*[12] however, the Court settled the matter, reconfirming that the United States Constitution requires that *Miranda* procedures be followed. The effect of the *Dickerson* decision will be discussed more fully later in this chapter in connection with the coverage of the topic of the exclusionary rule and *Miranda*. Since *Dickerson,* it is clear that *Miranda*'s requirements must still be followed by state and federal law enforcement professionals.

MIRANDA WARNINGS The warnings required by the case of *Miranda v. Arizona* to be given to a suspect in custody before interrogation by a police officer can be valid.

CONFESSIONS EXCLUDED DUE TO VIOLATION OF DUE PROCESS OF LAW: COERCED CONFESSIONS

There are a variety of reasons for condemning the use of coerced confessions.[13] A coerced confession could be unreliable. Even if the confession is reliable, it should be excluded from evidence because the police should "obey the law while enforcing the law."[14] Moreover, the American criminal justice system is accusatorial, not inquisitorial—our founders abhorred coercive techniques of inquisition. Thus, the use of coerced confessions is inherently offensive to the American conception of justice. In addition, the principle of personal autonomy dictates that a confession that is not freely and voluntarily given should not be used. Finally, the exclusion from evidence of a coerced confession will, arguably, deter police misconduct.

Underlying all of the reasons for excluding a coerced confession is the fundamental requirement that a confession must be freely and voluntarily given. The test for voluntariness, according to the Supreme Court of the United States, is

TOTALITY OF THE
CIRCUMSTANCES
The test for voluntariness
of a confession.

the **totality of the circumstances.**[15] The question is whether, under the totality of the circumstances, the defendant's will was overborne when the defendant confessed. Any conduct by law enforcement officers that, under the totality of the circumstances, could cause a reasonable person in the position of the accused to feel coerced would violate these principles.

In order for a defendant to claim that a confession was involuntarily given, there must be some action by a federal or state agent. Action by a private citizen, or self-induced compulsion, will not lead to the exclusion of the statement from trial unless there is some state statutory provision to the contrary.

APPLICATION CASE

In *Colorado v. Connelly,*[16] a man who was suffering from a severe mental disturbance (he heard the voice of God order him to confess to a murder or commit suicide) approached a police officer on the street and confessed to a murder. Connelly told the officer that he had been in several mental institutions. The officer recited *Miranda* warnings to Connelly and then questioned him about the crime. Connelly's confession and statements were admitted at his trial, and he was convicted of the murder. The Supreme Court of the United States held that the confession was admissible because Connelly's confession was compelled by the voice in his head, not by any agent of the government.

Confessions Coerced by Physical Force

It is unfortunate that at times law enforcement officers, eager to solve crimes and attain convictions, resort to physical force to acquire confessions. The term "third degree" has been used to describe such conduct. When courts began to address this conduct, they took a dim view of the use of such confessions as evidence against an accused. Therefore, the courts have long excluded confessions obtained through the use of violence or inhumane treatment of the accused. The exclusion of such confessions goes beyond the fact that the confession might be untrue; fundamental fairness requires that the court not be a party to the use of evidence obtained through such coercion.

APPLICATION CASE

In one of the first state court decisions involving confessions to be reviewed by the United States Supreme Court, in 1936, the confessions were obtained through the use of physical force. In *Brown v. Mississippi,*[17] the Court reversed a murder conviction of three African American defendants who had been convicted in a local court primarily on the basis of their confessions. The three defendants had been whipped by local law enforcement authorities until they confessed. During the trial, the confessions were admitted before the manner in which they were obtained was proven. The defense argued that, by the introduction of these confessions, the defendants had been denied due process of law.

The Supreme Court held that inasmuch as the confessions had been induced by brutal treatment, the defendants had been denied due process of law, and the conviction was reversed. The appeal was made strictly upon the contention that due process of law had been denied; the guarantee against self-incrimination contained in the Fifth Amendment was not argued.

Although the type of inhumane treatment found in many early cases involving physical abuse is rare today, courts are still skeptical about the procedures used by officers in interrogating suspects, and a number of extremely restrictive rules have been enacted. Not only will actual physical mistreatment of the accused cause a confession to be excluded, but extreme discomfort suffered by the accused during the interrogation might also lead to statements being ruled inadmissible. Even lengthy, uninterrupted questioning, without providing food, rest, or bathroom use, could be sufficient grounds for a court to exclude a statement from trial as involuntary.

APPLICATION CASE

In *Ashcraft v. Tennessee,*[18] the defendant was suspected of involvement in the murder of his wife. State law enforcement officers took him to an office in the county jail 12 days after his wife's death, where for 36 hours he was held incommunicado, without sleep or rest, and relays of officers, experienced investigators, and highly trained lawyers questioned him without respite. The state then claimed that Ashcraft confessed to hiring a man to kill his wife. The defendant and the state disagreed on many of the facts of the case, but, based on those facts not disputed, the Supreme Court concluded that the situation was inherently coercive. The Court ruled that mental freedom could not have existed in a situation in which the police clearly brought substantial coercive force to bear on a lone suspect. Therefore, the Court concluded that the confession was not voluntary and that the 36-hour interrogation itself violated due process. The Court ordered the conviction to be reversed.

Confessions Coerced by Psychological Pressure

Overcoming the will of a suspect can be achieved just as effectively by application of psychological pressure as it can by application of physical force. Psychological pressure, or "mental stress," takes many forms. It may result from a mere suggestion that, if the accused will confess, "things will go easier" for him or her. It may be some other promise or reward, such as an assurance that no action will be taken against the accused's spouse, or that every effort will be made to assist the family of the accused in procuring welfare aid if the confession is made. The mental stress may be created by a threat of action to be taken against the family of the accused, such as taking his or her children and placing them with domestic services, unless a confession is forthcoming.

Other forms of psychological pressure may be brought to bear upon an accused that could lead a court to conclude that the suspect's confession was not freely and voluntarily given. Interrogation techniques are often aimed at manipulation of individual weaknesses. Such ploys as showing false sympathy, criticizing the victim, making deceptive claims about the strength of the case against the accused, or playing "good cop, bad cop" could cause a court to find that a statement was coerced. The operative word in such a situation is "coerced." Some deception, or even an outright lie, may be permissible, as long as the action by the government agent is not so outrageous as to overcome the free will of the suspect. In recent years, the Supreme Court has been more tolerant of deception than the decisions of earlier Courts might suggest.[19]

APPLICATION CASE

In *Spano v. New York*,[20] the Supreme Court of the United States held that a confession that was gained by the application of psychological pressure was involuntary and therefore inadmissible in a criminal trial. Spano, a young man with only a junior high school education, shot and killed a man who bullied, humiliated, and beat him. After disappearing for a week, during which time he was indicted for murder, Spano telephoned a close friend, Bruno, who was a rookie police officer. Spano told Bruno about the killing and said he was going to get a lawyer and give himself up. Bruno relayed this information to his superiors. The following evening Spano, accompanied by an attorney, surrendered to the police.

Spano was questioned, out of his attorney's presence, for about five hours but, heeding his attorney's instructions, he refused to talk. Spano requested to see his attorney, but the request was denied. At that point, those in charge of the investigation thought that Bruno could be of assistance. They called Bruno and told him to inform Spano that Spano's telephone call to him had caused him a "lot of trouble." Further, the investigators instructed Bruno to try to win sympathy from Spano for Bruno's wife and children. Bruno played his part, but Spano still refused to answer any questions. It was not until Bruno's fourth effort to gain Spano's sympathy that the suspect finally agreed to tell the authorities about the shooting and offered a confession. The confession was introduced in evidence at trial, and the jury convicted Spano. The Supreme Court reversed the conviction, finding that the confession was obtained in violation of the Due Process Clause of the Fourteenth Amendment based on a totality of the circumstances. The Court's decision relied particularly on four factors:

1. the official pressure from a barrage of questioning by several different people,
2. the effect of denying Spano's requests to speak with his attorney,
3. the fatigue resulting from the interrogation's length and the time of night, and
4. the sympathy falsely created by Bruno.

EXCLUSION OF CONFESSIONS DUE TO VIOLATION OF RIGHTS SECURED UNDER *MIRANDA v. ARIZONA*

Perhaps no legal decision is more widely known by the general public than *Miranda v. Arizona*[21]–the case that imposed the requirement that police inform criminal suspects of their rights to remain silent and to have an attorney present during questioning. Also, perhaps no legal decision has generated more criticism and debate. Not only has the law enforcement community criticized *Miranda,* but even Supreme Court justices have voiced concern. As a result, *Miranda,* decided by a bare five-Justice majority, has been narrowly applied.

A recent controversy over *Miranda* has been generated. The surviving Boston Marathon Bomber suspect, Dzhokhar Tsarnaev, was charged with federal crimes while in serious condition in a Boston hospital. Prior to the charges being brought, the Attorney General of the United States announced that Tsarnaev would not be given his *Miranda* warnings. This touched off a heated debate among legal observers and commentators. A magistrate judge and a representative from the U.S. Attorney's office went to Tsarnev's hospital room after 16 hours of interrogation of him and did read him his *Miranda* warnings, after which Tsarnev immediately stopped talking. In any event, the initial failure to give warnings might be justified by the public safety exception, discussed later in this chapter. Also, if the warnings were not given, there is no constitutional violation unless any improperly obtained statements are admitted in court against the suspect.

The *Miranda* rule requires that a law enforcement officer read *Miranda* warnings to a suspect *before* custodial interrogation. The officer must advise the suspect that the suspect has the right to remain silent; that anything the suspect says can and will be used against the suspect at trial; that the suspect has a right to an attorney being present during questioning; and that, if the suspect cannot afford an attorney, one can be provided at no cost to the suspect. After issuing these warnings, the law enforcement officer must verify that the suspect understands those rights and, before questioning the suspect, the officer must secure an affirmative waiver by the suspect of these rights.

In the establishment of the famous *Miranda* warnings, the Supreme Court brought together elements of an accused's right to remain silent, right to an attorney, and right to be protected against coercion by agents of the government. Originally, the Court imposed the procedures at the earliest stage of contact between government and a criminal accused (when the person first became the focus of the investigation)–long before formal charges were brought. Later decisions of the Court have revised that to impose the procedures whenever there is "custodial interrogation."

Miranda was actually one of four cases decided by the Supreme Court at the same time, each of which presented the issue of the admissibility of statements made by a suspect in custody. In the *Miranda* case, the defendant was arrested at his home and taken in custody to a Phoenix police station. There, the complaining witness identified him as the person who had kidnapped and raped her. After a two-hour interrogation, the police emerged from the interrogation room with a written confession by Miranda. The confession and the officer's testimony describing Miranda's prior oral confession were admitted against him. The jury convicted Miranda of kidnapping and rape.

The Supreme Court reversed Miranda's conviction, holding that the officer's failure to advise Miranda of his right not to be compelled to incriminate himself and his right to have an attorney present during the interrogation rendered the defendant's confessions inadmissible at trial. The Court announced the requirements of the now-famous *Miranda* warnings:[22]

> Prior to any questioning, the person must be warned that he has a right to remain silent, that any statement he does make may be used as evidence against him, and that he has a right to the presence of an attorney, either retained or appointed. The defendant may waive effectuation of these rights, provided the waiver is made voluntarily, knowingly and intelligently. If, however, he indicates in any manner and at any stage of the process that he wishes to consult with an attorney before speaking there can be no questioning. Likewise, if the individual is alone and indicates in any manner that he does not wish to be interrogated, the police may not question him. The mere fact that he may have answered some questions or volunteered some statements on his own does not deprive him of the right to refrain from answering any further inquiries until he has consulted with an attorney and thereafter consents to be questioned.

ON THE JOB

Most police departments issue credit card-sized *Miranda* cards that list the rights that must be read to and waived by the suspect before questioning may begin. The officer should not recite these rights from memory but rather read them from the issued card, for several reasons. First, an officer might omit a right. Second, an officer might recite the rights using slightly different language. Finally, when the officer testifies in court about the reading of the rights, the officer can produce the actual card used and confidently state that he or she read the warning, word for word, from the card.

In those situations in which the officer is faced with a suspect who does not speak English or for whom English is a second language, a different problem is presented. For such instances, many police departments have issued *Miranda* rights cards in other languages, such as Spanish, Chinese, Korean, or Vietnamese. However, only officers who qualify as translators should administer warnings in a language other than English.

In *Miranda,* the Supreme Court of the United States ended its search for a way of dealing with the "problem" of claims by criminal suspects that they were being subjected to improper police tactics during the interrogation process. The Court imposed upon law enforcement a set of procedures to be followed in questioning suspects, which, if followed, would lead to admission in evidence at trial of any statements made during custodial interrogation. On the other hand, failure to follow these guidelines results in any such statements being inadmissible. In other words, these rules have an "automatic" result. The Court made the rules automatic to avoid the necessity of relitigating the question of the voluntariness of a confession in every case. Instead, the trial courts can look to see whether the police followed the *Miranda* rules and decide each case on that basis.

Even though the rules are "automatic," a defendant may still claim that he or she was actually coerced or actually denied the right to counsel. However, a statement made after law enforcement compliance with *Miranda* would most likely be ruled valid. In addition, as will be seen in the next chapter, if a confession is the poisoned fruit of an illegal search or seizure, then it may be held inadmissible on that ground alone.

Today, the *Miranda* requirements apply to **custodial interrogations** of suspects by law enforcement officers. When an officer has a suspect *in custody* and engages in interrogation, the officer must inform the suspect of *Miranda* rights, and the officer cannot interrogate the suspect unless the suspect affirmatively waives those rights. If the suspect invokes his or her rights at any time, the officer must cease interrogation and scrupulously honor the rights the suspect asserts. Only if the suspect reinitiates communication with the officer and again affirmatively waives his or her *Miranda* rights may the officer further interrogate the suspect. In the event that the police do obtain a statement from a suspect in violation of the *Miranda* rules, the statement itself will be excluded, but any evidence derived as a result of the statement may not be subject to the exclusionary rule. Finally, there are court-created exceptions to the *Miranda* rule.

Thus, the relevant topics for discussion relating to the *Miranda* rules are (1) what is custody for purposes of *Miranda,* (2) what is interrogation for purposes of *Miranda,* (3) what constitutes a valid waiver of *Miranda* rights, (4) what constitutes a valid waiver after a suspect has asserted his or her rights, (5) what are exceptions to the *Miranda* rule, and (6) what is the effect of the exclusionary rule on statements taken in violation of *Miranda.*

What Constitutes Custody for Purposes of *Miranda*

In the *Miranda* decision, the Supreme Court stated that the *Miranda* rules apply when a person is "taken into custody or otherwise deprived of his freedom of action in any significant way."[23] The Court has viewed this language as referring to an actual arrest, rather than the act of merely stopping and questioning a suspect. **Custody** results when a police officer restrains a person in a manner consistent with a formal arrest, regardless of the situation or intent of the officer. Anytime a person is taken into custody, the officer is required to give *Miranda* warnings before asking any substantive questions about the offense.

Just prior to the *Miranda* decision, the Court decided the case of *Illinois v. Escobedo.*[24] The Court held in the *Escobedo* case that the defendant was entitled to his Sixth Amendment right to counsel, even though the police interrogation occurred before the accused was formally charged. The Court said that, as the focus of the investigation, the defendant was entitled to his right to counsel. However, the Court's decision was limited to the specific circumstances of the case—the defendant was interrogated in custody, his lawyer had instructed him not to talk, the police did not inform him of his right to have his lawyer present, and the lawyer was trying to contact the defendant. Therefore, the *Miranda* definition of "custody" as the trigger for the required warnings has supplanted the *Escobedo* test of whether or not the defendant is the "focus" of the investigation. Though the *Escobedo* decision has never been overruled, it is now of little more than historical interest.

CUSTODIAL INTERROGATIONS
Interrogations conducted with the suspect *in custody.* Such interrogations can occur only after the suspect has been read, and waived, his or her *Miranda* rights.

CUSTODY
Custody results when a police officer restrains a person in a manner consistent with a formal arrest, regardless of the situation or intent of the officer.

Whether the suspect is in custody under the *Miranda* test is, as stated earlier, a matter of whether, under a totality of the circumstances, a reasonable person would think his or her freedom was restrained in any significant way. The custody test is an objective one, but in 2011, in *J.D.B. v. North Carolina*,[25] the Supreme Court, in a 5-4 opinion held that a child's age is a factor in assessing that determination so long as the age was known to the officer at the time of police questioning, or would have been objectively apparent to a reasonable officer. In *Miranda* itself, the Court talked about its concern with the coercive atmosphere of the police station. However, a coercive atmosphere could exist anywhere, and the fact that a suspect is questioned in a police station does not necessarily mean that he or she is in custody for purposes of *Miranda*. Two contrasting cases illustrate the point. First, in *Orozco v. Texas*,[26] the Court held that the accused was in custody when four officers questioned him in his own bedroom at 4 o'clock in the morning. One of the officers testified that the accused was under arrest at the time of the questioning, even though the officer did not tell Orozco that he was under arrest.

On the other hand, in *Oregon v. Mathiason*,[27] the Court held that a suspect who met a policeman in an office in the police station was not in custody for purposes of *Miranda*. The defendant was a parolee whom the officer suspected of committing a burglary. The officer contacted Mathiason and asked him to meet the officer at the police station. The officer told Mathiason that he was not under arrest, and Mathiason was released after confessing that he had committed the crime.

What Constitutes Interrogation for Purposes of *Miranda*

When an officer has a suspect in custody and specifically asks him or her direct questions about the incident under investigation, the officer is engaged in interrogation within the meaning of the *Miranda* rule. But many circumstances arise where there are serious questions about whether or not the conduct of an officer amounts to such interrogation. For example, if officers discuss matters pertaining to the case while transporting a suspect to the station, it could cause the suspect to make a statement, especially if the officers' conversation plays upon some weakness of the accused. That was the case in *Rhode Island v. Innis*,[28] in which the Supreme Court of the United States adopted a test for deciding whether an officer has engaged in interrogation of a suspect in custody. The Court stated that **interrogation** as used in *Miranda* refers to "either express questioning or its functional equivalent."[29] Furthermore, the Court defined "functional equivalent" as "any words or actions on the part of the police (other than those normally attendant to arrest and custody) that the police should know are reasonably likely to elicit an incriminating response from the suspect."[30]

INTERROGATION
Express questioning or its functional equivalent, that is, any words or actions on the part of the police (other than those normally attendant to arrest and custody) that the police should know are reasonably likely to elicit an incriminating response from the suspect.

ON THE JOB

A general rule of thumb will help the officer in the field clarify when *Miranda* should be given:

Custody + Questioning = *Miranda* + Waiver

Anytime an officer effectively places a suspect in custody and wishes to question the suspect, the officer must read the *Miranda* warnings and request a waiver in order to proceed with the questioning. A few exceptions to the rule exist and will be discussed later in this chapter, but an officer would be wise to apply this rule in almost all cases.

In *Rhode Island v. Innis,*[31] officers arrested the accused in connection with the shotgun murder of a taxi driver. The weapon had not been recovered at the time of the defendant's arrest. Officers advised him of his *Miranda* rights on more than one occasion, and the accused said he wanted to speak to a lawyer. Officers then placed the defendant in a caged wagon in order to transport him to the central police station. En route to the station, one of the officers initiated a conversation with another officer concerning the missing shotgun. He mentioned that a school for handicapped children was located nearby and stated, "God forbid one of them might find a weapon with shells and hurt themselves."[32] The other officer said nothing, but then the first officer also said it would be too bad if a little girl "would pick up the gun, maybe kill herself."[33] At that point, Innis interrupted the conversation and led the officers to the weapon.

The *Innis* Court developed the test for interrogation in the context of *Miranda.* If police engage in express questioning of a suspect, they have engaged in interrogation. In addition, if the police engage in the functional equivalent of express questioning, then interrogation has also occurred. The Court defined the functional equivalent of express questioning as any words or actions on the part of the police (other than those normally relating to arrest and custody) that the police should know are reasonably likely to elicit an incriminating response from the suspect. Applying that test to the case before it, a majority of the Justices concluded that the officers' statements did not amount to the functional equivalent of interrogation, therefore affirming the defendant's conviction.

According to the *Innis* Court, the *Innis* test focuses primarily upon the perceptions of the suspect, rather than the intent of the police. This is consistent with the basis of the *Miranda* rule—seeking to protect a suspect in police custody from coercion. Thus, the Court emphasized the *should have known* language of the rule, saying that officers are accountable only for words or actions that they *should have known* were reasonably likely to elicit an incriminating response from the suspect. However, in a footnote, the Court cautioned that any knowledge that an officer may have concerning the "unusual susceptibility of a defendant to a particular form of persuasion"[34] might be taken into account in determining what the officer should have known would likely induce the suspect to speak.

An example of what the Court was likely referring to in *Innis* was involved in the case of *Brewer v. Williams.*[35] In that case, the police were transporting a defendant who was in custody for the murder of a young girl. The girl's body had not been found and, during the trip, one of the officers made a "Christian burial" speech. The officer made the speech, addressing the accused as "Reverend," knowing that the accused was a highly religious person and had recently escaped from a mental hospital. The officer testified at trial that, in giving the speech, he intended to provoke the accused into revealing the location of the girl's body.

Williams had appeared before a magistrate before being transported; thus, the officer's intentional attempt to elicit information from him was in violation of Williams' Sixth Amendment right to counsel. Therefore, in *Williams,* the Supreme Court did not decide the case on *Miranda* grounds. Rather, the Court held that the deliberate elicitation by the officer violated Williams' right to counsel under the Sixth Amendment. The point is that, although the *Innis* test for interrogation is an objective one that focuses on the perceptions of the suspect, the officer's subjective intent may play a role, as it did in *Williams.*

What Constitutes a Valid Waiver of *Miranda* Rights

In the *Miranda* decision, the Supreme Court stated that the prosecution has a "heavy burden" of proof that any claimed waiver of rights by an accused was made voluntarily, knowingly, and intelligently.[36] Moreover, the Court warned that "a valid waiver will not be presumed simply from the silence of the accused after warnings are given or simply from the fact that a confession was in fact obtained."[37] In cases after *Miranda,* the Court has clarified these statements.

With respect to the "heavy burden," the Court subsequently held that it is met by the prosecution's proof of the validity of a waiver by a preponderance of the evidence.[38] In making its evaluation of the conditions under which the *Miranda* rights were waived, the Court has repeatedly stated that it will consider all circumstances concerning the procurement of the waiver, and that an oral or written statement of waiver is not conclusive proof. The watchwords for officers and prosecutors are "Follow procedures and be careful."

APPLICATION CASE

In *North Carolina v. Butler,*[39] the defendant was convicted of kidnapping, armed robbery, and felonious assault. At his trial, evidence of statements Butler made to an FBI agent was introduced against him. Prior to making the statements, Butler refused to sign an "Advice of Rights" form containing, and waiving, the *Miranda* warnings. When told his rights and asked if he understood them, he replied that he did. Although he refused to sign the form, he did agree to speak with the agents.

On appeal, the North Carolina Supreme Court reversed Butler's conviction, holding that he had refused to sign a waiver and had not made a *specific* oral waiver. The case then went to the United States Supreme Court, which disagreed with the North Carolina Supreme Court's decision. The United States Supreme Court held that, even in the absence of an express waiver and under the "heavy burden" test of *Miranda,* a waiver could be inferred in some cases based on the conduct of the accused, thereby reversing the decision of the North Carolina Supreme Court.

In other cases, the Court has rendered decisions that illuminate its interpretation of what constitutes a waiver. In one case,[40] the Court held that the fact that the accused thinks he is being questioned about one crime but then is asked about another does not affect his waiver of the rights of silence and counsel. In another case,[41] the accused was in custody on a murder charge when a lawyer called the police and said that she would act as his attorney if the police were going to question him that night. The attorney was told there would be no interrogation. Later that night, however, the police gave the suspect his warnings, failing to mention anything about the lawyer's call. The accused waived his rights and made incriminating statements. The Court held that the defendant's waiver of his *Miranda* rights was valid, even though he was not informed of the attorney's telephone call.

Berghuis v. Thompkins[42] involved a contention that the defendant's words and acts were not sufficient to waive his *Miranda* right to remain silent. A five-Justice majority rejected this contention, noting that waivers "can be established even absent formal or express statements of waiver." Defendant was arrested as a suspect in a shooting murder. While in custody awaiting transfer, two officers interrogated defendant for about three hours. At the outset, the officers gave warnings and a form waiver, but defendant refused to sign. During the interrogation, defendant remained largely silent but never said he wanted to remain silent, giving a few limited verbal responses. Two hours and 45 minutes into the interrogation, an officer asked if defendant believed in God, whether he prayed, and if he prayed to God to forgive him for the shooting. Defendant answered "yes" and this statement was admitted at his murder trial.

In a different setting, in *Salinas v. Texas*,[43] the Court considered introduction into evidence of a suspect's silence. Salinas came in voluntarily for questioning about a murder. He was not in custody and he answered questions until he was asked about whether he thought the shell casings from the murder scene would match his shotgun. He did not answer the question. The questioning then continued and he continued answering other questions. At his subsequent trial for the murder, the fact of his silence in response to the shotgun shell question was admitted against him and he was convicted. A plurality of the Supreme Court (Justice Alito, joined by Roberts and Kennedy) held that the admission of the fact of his silence did not violate his rights. He was not entitled to *Miranda* warnings, since he was not in custody. He did not invoke his Fifth Amendment right to remain silent, and his remaining silent thus could be used against him. Two other Justices (Thomas, joined by Scalia) agreed with the result on the grounds that commenting on Salina's silence caused him no penalty, unlike the situation in *Griffin v. California*,[44] which should not be extended to a precustodial interview.

What Constitutes a Valid Waiver After a Suspect Asserts His or Her Rights

In *Miranda,* the Court stated that, if a suspect, prior to or during interrogation, indicates in any manner that "he wishes to remain silent, the interrogation must cease."[45] Likewise, the Court said that, if an individual says that "he wants an attorney, the interrogation must cease until an attorney is present."[46] However, in subsequent cases, the Court established two separate rules governing resumption of questioning—one dealing with a defendant who had invoked the right to remain silent, the other dealing with a defendant who had invoked the right to counsel.

In the first case, *Michigan v. Mosley*,[47] the Court held that the "interrogation must cease" language in *Miranda* does not mean that the police may never resume questioning a suspect after he or she invokes the right to remain silent. Rather, the Court concluded that statements made in response to subsequent questioning will be admissible if the police "scrupulously honored" the suspect's right to cut off questioning. In this case, the defendant was arrested in connection with recent robberies. The arresting officer advised him of his *Miranda* rights, after which Mosley read and signed the police department's constitutional rights notification certificate. The officer began questioning him. Mosley said he did not want to answer any questions, and the officer promptly ceased the interrogation. More than two hours later, a homicide detective took Mosley from the cell block to the Homicide Bureau for questioning about a shooting, a crime distinct from the robberies for which Mosley had invoked his right to silence. The detective advised Mosley of his *Miranda* rights, and Mosley signed the departmental form. At first, Mosley denied any participation in the killing, but, when the detective falsely stated that another man had confessed to participation in the crime and had named Mosley as the shooter, Mosley made statements implicating himself in the homicide. The statements were admitted against him at trial, and he was convicted of first-degree murder.

The Supreme Court of the United States held that the admission in evidence of Mosley's incriminating statement did not violate the principles of *Miranda*. In reaching this conclusion, the Court rejected the proposition that police may never resume questioning after a suspect asserts the right to remain silent; rather, the test of the admissibility of a statement made under such circumstances is whether the police scrupulously honored the suspect's assertion of the right to remain silent.

On the other hand, in *Edwards v. Arizona*,[48] the Supreme Court dealt with a case in which a suspect in custody invoked his *right to counsel*, but the police reinitiated contact with him the next morning and questioned him without his attorney being present. The Court held that, even though the police advised Edwards of his *Miranda* rights, and although he was willing to talk, the police-initiated custodial interrogation without counsel present violated *Miranda*. The Court thus created a stricter rule dealing with the resumption of questioning by police after a suspect has invoked the *right to counsel* than when a suspect invokes the right to remain silent. In very clear language, the Court stated that law enforcement officials cannot further interrogate a suspect who, being *Mirandized*, invokes the right to counsel, "unless the accused himself initiates further communication, exchanges, or conversations with the police."[49] In a subsequent case, the Court held that, when a suspect, having invoked the right to counsel,[50] has met with counsel, police may not subsequently interrogate the suspect outside the presence of counsel.

In *Maryland v. Shatzer*[51] in 2010 a nearly unanimous Supreme Court severely restricted the *Edwards* rule. Shatzer was in prison on a sex abuse conviction when an officer came to question him about abuse of his own 3½-year-old son. Shatzer refused to speak without an attorney. Two years and six months later, a different officer came to the defendant, who was still in custody but in a different prison, to question him about the same abuse of his son. The officer gave Shatzer warnings and, when he agreed to talk, he made incriminating statements. Those statements were admitted against him at his subsequent trial.

The Court held that *Edwards* did not require exclusion of the statements in these circumstances. The Court reasoned that, when "a suspect has been released from his pretrial custody" after a request for counsel and "has returned to his normal life" for some time before a subsequent attempted interrogation, there is little reason to think that his change of heart regarding interrogation has been coerced. In Shatzer's case, return to the general prison population was a return to his normal life. The Court also adopted a 14-day limitation as a measure of the appropriate break in custody, thus putting a time limit on the *Edwards* rule in general.

In *Minnick v. Mississippi*,[52] a suspect in custody, after being warned that he did not have to answer questions without a lawyer present, said, "Come back Monday when I have a lawyer." The FBI agents who were interviewing him ended the interview. The suspect did consult with appointed counsel and then, two days later, state law enforcement officers came to see him. The suspect's jailers told him he had "to talk" to the officers and, even though the suspect refused to sign a waiver of rights form, the officers questioned him. Statements he made at that time were admitted against him at a state trial, and he was convicted of capital murder and sentenced to death.

The United States Supreme Court reversed Minnick's conviction. The Court held that, merely because Minnick had consulted with an attorney, *Miranda*'s right to counsel rule had not been satisfied under the *Edwards* rule requiring that counsel be present during interrogation once the suspect invokes the right to counsel.

Exceptions to the *Miranda* Rule

The Supreme Court of the United States has created three exceptions to the requirement that a police officer give a suspect in custody *Miranda* warnings before interrogating him or her: (1) the public safety exception, (2) the routine booking question exception, and (3) the undercover police questioner exception. By establishing these exceptions, the Court has limited the fruit of the poisonous tree doctrine as applied to *Miranda* violations and has created an impeachment exception to the exclusionary rule as applied to such violations. Although the Court, in the *Dickerson*[53] case, affirmed *Miranda*'s constitutional base, the Court has also reaffirmed the vitality of the Court-created exceptions to the exclusionary rule and fruit of the poisonous tree doctrine as applied to *Miranda*.[54] The application of the exclusionary rule and fruit of the poisonous tree doctrine to *Miranda* is discussed more fully in the next section of this chapter.

The **public safety exception** holds that *Miranda* should not apply to a situation in which police officers ask questions reasonably prompted by a concern for the public safety. In the case establishing the exception, *New York v. Quarles*,[55] a police officer entered a supermarket in pursuit of a rape suspect who was believed to be carrying a gun. When the officer spotted and approached the accused, who matched the description of the assailant, the officer ordered him to stop and put his hands over his head. With three other officers present, the first officer frisked the defendant, finding an empty shoulder holster. The officer then handcuffed the defendant and asked him where the gun was. The defendant nodded in the direction of some cartons and responded, "The gun is over there." At trial, the trial court excluded both the defendant's statement and the gun because of the officer's failure to give the defendant *Miranda* warnings before questioning him about the gun. The Supreme Court reversed this ruling, holding that, on the facts of the case, there was a "public safety" exception to the requirements of the *Miranda* rule. The Court further stated that the public safety exception applies regardless

PUBLIC SAFETY EXCEPTION
An exception to the requirement of *Miranda* warnings when police officers ask questions reasonably prompted by a concern for the public safety.

of the officer's motivation, as long as the situation is one in which police officers ask questions reasonably prompted by a concern for the public safety.

ROUTINE BOOKING QUESTION EXCEPTION
An exception to the requirement of *Miranda* warnings that allows questions to be asked to secure the biographical data necessary to complete booking or pretrial services.

The **routine booking question exception** was adopted by four Justices of the Supreme Court of the United States in the case of *Pennsylvania v. Muniz*.[56] The Justices concluded that questions posed to an arrestee during booking, such as those relating to name, address, weight, eye color, date of birth, and age, are within a "routine booking question" exception, "which exempts from *Miranda*'s coverage questions to secure the 'biographical data necessary to complete booking or pretrial services.'"[57] Thus, even though the accused is in custody and the answers are given in response to direct questioning under *Innis,* the routine booking question exception applies.

In *Muniz,* the United States Supreme Court addressed the question of whether *Miranda* warnings must be given by a police officer to a person who is in custody and suspected of driving under the influence of alcohol. A police officer, who had reason to believe Muniz was operating his vehicle while under the influence of alcohol, pursued the suspect, pulled him over, and asked him to perform three field sobriety tests. Muniz performed these tests poorly and stated that he did so because he had been drinking. The officer placed Muniz under arrest and transported him to the county's central booking facility.

The booking facility, following standard practice, videotaped the ensuing proceedings. Muniz was not at this time, or previously, advised of his *Miranda* rights. The booking officer asked Muniz his name, address, height, weight, eye color, date of birth, and current age. Muniz gave slurred answers to these questions and could not give the date of his sixth birthday. Muniz's inability to make the calculation from his birth date to his sixth birthday was incriminating, since it showed his mental faculties were impaired. The officer then had Muniz perform the same sobriety tests that he had performed on the roadside. He again performed them poorly. Muniz next refused to take a breathalyzer test. At this point the officer gave Muniz his *Miranda* warnings for the first time. Muniz waived his rights in writing and admitted he had been driving while intoxicated. At trial, the videotape was admitted in evidence against Muniz, as were the first officer's testimony describing Muniz's performance on the sobriety tests and the incriminating statements made by the defendant.

Muniz appealed his conviction, claiming the officers' failure to give him his *Miranda* warnings rendered the evidence of his subsequent acts and statements unlawfully obtained and used against him. The Supreme Court of the United States held that the slurred nature of his speech in response to the questions and his physical responses to the sobriety tests at the booking center were not testimonial and, therefore, did come within the *Miranda* rule. Four Justices also agreed that the first seven questions asked by the officer at the booking station regarding Muniz's name, address, height, weight, eye color, date of birth, and current age were not covered by *Miranda* because they fell within a "routine booking question" exception to the *Miranda* rule. The Court, however, viewed the question concerning the defendant's sixth birthday as involving "testimony." As a result, the Court held *Miranda* was violated and the evidence about the question and answer should not have been admitted in the trial.

Miranda, by its terms, applies only to situations in which a suspect perceives that he or she is in police custody and, from that perspective, is subject to a police-dominated atmosphere that is coercive. When an undercover police officer questions an accused, therefore, there is no violation of *Miranda*. If the defendant does not believe that the person to whom he or she is talking is a police officer, then there is no need for the protection of the *Miranda* warnings. This is particularly the case when an accused is incarcerated and the questions are asked by a cellmate. The fact that the cellmate is an undercover law enforcement officer does not matter for purposes of requiring *Miranda* warnings. It is important to note, however, that, if the accused has made a court appearance or has been indicted and the *right to counsel* has attached, *any questioning* by law enforcement in the absence of counsel will violate the Sixth Amendment right. This is so because the *right to counsel* under the Sixth Amendment protects an accused more completely once formal charges have been brought.

APPLICATION CASE

In *Illinois v. Perkins*,[58] a prison inmate told the police he had learned about a homicide from a fellow inmate. The police recognized the description of the homicide as possibly being one under investigation. Consequently, the police placed an undercover agent in the cellblock with the informant and the defendant. The defendant was being held at that time for another crime unrelated to the homicide. The undercover officer engaged the defendant in a conversation about killing and asked the defendant if he had ever "done" anybody. The officer did not give the defendant *Miranda* warnings before the conversation. The Supreme Court of the United States held that the statements were admissible against the defendant and did not violate the requirements of *Miranda*. Although the accused was in custody, the Court held that "an undercover law enforcement officer posing as a fellow inmate need not give *Miranda* warnings to an incarcerated suspect before asking questions that may elicit an incriminating response."[59]

Some amount of deception in the form of a ploy to get a suspect to make incriminating statements has been held by the United States Supreme Court not to amount to sufficient coercion to violate either due process or *Miranda*. For example, in *Illinois v. Perkins*,[60] the Court approved a law enforcement officer pretending to be a prison inmate to secure a statement from a "fellow inmate." The Court said that "[p]loys to mislead a suspect or lull him into a false sense of security that do not rise to the level of compulsion or coercion to speak are not within *Miranda*'s concerns."[61] In *Michigan v. Mosley*,[62] Mosley made incriminating statements to a homicide detective after the detective stated falsely that an accomplice of Mosley's had confessed and implicated Mosley in the killing as the "shooter." In affirming Mosley's conviction, the Court noted the false statement by the detective but said nothing about it being improper. In contrast, the use of deception in the *Spano* case[63] was condemned by the Supreme Court as being violative of due process. In that case, Spano's friend, a police officer, falsely stated that he would be in trouble if Spano did not confess.

Miranda, the Exclusionary Rule, and the Fruit of the Poisonous Tree Doctrine

EXCLUSIONARY RULE
The rule that provides that illegally obtained evidence will be excluded from use in a criminal trial.

When there is a violation of any constitutional provision relating to criminal procedure, the evidence gained as a result of such violation may be inadmissible at trial because of the **exclusionary rule**. This is the case with respect to any confession that is obtained by coercion in violation of due process. On the face of it, one would expect that the violation of the *Miranda* rule would also lead to application of the exclusionary rule. This is true, insofar as any statement taken in violation of *Miranda* is usually inadmissible per the exclusionary rule applied to *Miranda.* Nonetheless, the matter is a bit more complex than might otherwise appear. Although the exclusionary rule will be discussed even more fully in the next chapter with respect to violations of Fourth Amendment rights, some aspects of the exclusionary rule as applied to violations relating to *Miranda* and related rights must be discussed here.

The *Miranda* opinion, by its terms, seemed to be derived from the Fifth Amendment privilege against self-incrimination. A few years after *Miranda,* however, in the 1974 Supreme Court decision in the case of *Michigan v. Tucker,*[64] the Court developed the theory that a *Miranda* violation is not actually a violation of a constitutional right. In *Tucker,* the Court, in an opinion authored by then Justice Rehnquist, stated that *Miranda* was a non-constitutional, prophylactic rule developed to prevent violations of suspects' rights against compelled incrimination. Under this view, any statements obtained in violation of the *Miranda* rule were inadmissible, but not because of an actual constitutional violation. The Supreme Court's decision in *Dickerson v. United States,*[65] however, is inconsistent with this view expressed in *Tucker.* The Court held in *Dickerson* that *Miranda* was a constitutional decision.

But the view that *Miranda* is not constitutionally based, as expressed in *Tucker,* gave rise to another effect—the impact on the fruit of the poisonous tree doctrine when dealing with a *Miranda* violation. When there is a violation of a defendant's constitutional rights, in addition to the direct fruit of the violation being inadmissible, any evidence derived from the violation is also inadmissible under the **fruit of the poisonous tree doctrine**. For example, consider a case where the police have *actually coerced* a confession from a suspect and, in that confession, the suspect disclosed the location of a gun used in the crime. The confession is inadmissible as the direct "fruit" of the illegal government conduct, and the gun is inadmissible as the derivative "fruit" of the illegality. The theory of the fruit of the poisonous tree doctrine is that, if the root of the tree is poisoned, the fruit of the tree is also poisoned. It is important to note that in some instances the case may have to be dropped if, without the inadmissible evidence, the case against the accused is insufficient to support a conviction.

FRUIT OF THE POISONOUS TREE DOCTRINE
The principle that any evidence derived from a violation of a defendant's constitutional rights is inadmissible.

APPLICATION CASE

In *Michigan v. Tucker,*[66] the police failed to give the accused adequate warnings, and his statements obtained in violation of *Miranda* were held inadmissible at his trial. However, through the inadmissible statement, the police found a witness, who was called to testify at Tucker's trial. The Court held that the statement itself was inadmissible because it violated the *Miranda* rule but, since the *Miranda* rule is not constitutionally based and is only a protective rule, the evidence derived from information in the illegally obtained statement was admissible. The decision was based, in part, on the fact that the derivative "evidence" was a live human being who, himself, could decide whether or not to be a witness.

In 1985, in *Oregon v. Elstad,*[67] the Supreme Court reaffirmed the non-constitutionality of the *Miranda* rule and the inapplicability of the fruit of the poisonous tree doctrine to violations of *Miranda* where the statement taken from an accused was not actually coerced and the statement of the accused was his own voluntary "testimony." In *Elstad,* two police officers went to the home of the 18-year-old defendant with an arrest warrant for a burglary charge. While one officer was in another room talking to the defendant's mother, the other officer spoke to the defendant in the living room. The officer questioned the accused without advising him of his *Miranda* rights. Elstad made an incriminating statement. The officers then took Elstad to the sheriff's headquarters, where, for the first time, they advised him of his rights. Elstad waived his rights and signed a written confession. The written confession was admitted against Elstad at trial, and he was convicted of burglary.

The Supreme Court of the United States held that the first incriminating statement's inadmissibility because of the *Miranda* violation did not affect the admissibility of the second statement. The Court specifically held that "a suspect who has once responded to unwarned yet uncoercive questioning is not thereby disabled from waiving his rights and confessing after he has been given the requisite *Miranda* warnings."[68]

The *Dickerson* decision, proclaiming the *Miranda* case as being a constitutional decision, might well be considered as undermining the *Tucker* and *Elstad* exceptions to the exclusionary rule and fruit of the poisonous tree doctrine applicable to *Miranda.*[69] The Court, however, in *Dickerson* itself, noted that these cases (including the public safety exception case of *Quarles*) "simply"

illustrate the principle . . . that no constitutional rule is immutable. No court laying down a general rule can possibly foresee the various circumstances in which counsel will seek to apply it, and the sort of modifications represented by these cases are as much a normal part of constitutional law as the original decision.[70]

As a result, it can be said at this time that, if there is a violation of *Miranda,* any statement obtained in violation of *Miranda* will be excluded, but if that statement leads to the discovery of other evidence, that derivative fruit of the poisonous tree is not barred by the exclusionary rule applied to *Miranda.* The Court made this point very clear in its decision in *United States v. Patane,*[71] decided in 2004. In *Patane,* a detective was provided with information that a convicted felon illegally possessed a pistol. While arresting the suspect, the officers attempted to advise him of his *Miranda* rights, but the suspect interrupted, asserting that he knew his rights. The suspect then revealed the location of a pistol in response to the officer's questioning. The Court allowed the pistol to be admitted into evidence, despite the lack of *Miranda* warnings. The Court found that the introduction of non-testimonial evidence obtained as a result of voluntary statements does not violate a suspect's constitutional rights, or *Miranda,* by negligent or non-deliberate failures to provide full *Miranda* warnings. If the violation of *Miranda* is deliberate, however, the subsequent statement, taken after the giving of warnings, is inadmissible unless the police take "curative measures" before the later statement is made, according to the Court's decision in *Missouri v. Seibert.*[72]

APPLICATION CASE

In the case of *Missouri v. Seibert,*[73] the United States Supreme Court considered the constitutional validity of a police procedure that some have called the Missouri two-step. The police, following this procedure, would interrogate a suspect without first giving *Miranda* warnings. If the suspect confessed, then the officer or officers would give the suspect the required warnings, secure a waiver, and then obtain a repeated incriminating statement. The second statement would then be presented at the subsequent trial of the accused.

With a 5-4 vote, the Court affirmed the opinion of the Missouri Supreme Court that this procedure violated the defendant's rights. Only four of the five Justices voting in the majority, however, agreed on the test that determined this outcome. Mr. Justice Kennedy, agreeing with the result in the case, would have applied a narrower test than the other four Justices: banning only those two-step interrogations that are deliberately calculated to circumvent *Miranda,* not just those that had such a result regardless of deliberation. Further, Justice Kennedy was of the view that, even where the result is calculated, a warning between the two steps that explains the likely inadmissibility of the pre-warned statement could be curative.

IMPEACHMENT
EXCEPTION
An exception to the exclusionary rule that applies to *Miranda* or the Fourth Amendment, which allows statements taken in violation of *Miranda* or the Fourth Amendment to be used at trial to impeach the testimony of the accused.

Finally, the Supreme Court created an **impeachment exception** to the rule that excludes statements taken by the police in violation of *Miranda*. If a defendant (1) takes the witness stand and (2) testifies untruthfully, the prosecutor can use a statement obtained in violation of *Miranda* to impeach the defendant's testimony.[74]

EXCLUSION OF CONFESSIONS DUE TO VIOLATION OF THE SIXTH AMENDMENT RIGHT TO COUNSEL

The right to counsel is one of the guarantees of the Sixth Amendment to the United States Constitution. This fundamental right applies to the states through the Due Process Clause of the Fourteenth Amendment. By its terms, a criminal accused has a right to counsel for "his defense." The Supreme Court of the United States has held that the right attaches only at a **critical stage** of a prosecution,[75] which means when adversarial judicial proceedings have been initiated, "whether by way of formal charge, preliminary hearing, indictment, information, or arraignment."[76] (Although in *Escobedo,* the Court relied on the right to counsel when the accused had not yet been formally charged with a crime, that case has been restricted narrowly to the facts of the case by the Court.)

Miranda protects a suspect's right to counsel to aid the accused in preserving the right to remain silent in a custodial arrest situation. The Sixth Amendment right to counsel, after adversary criminal charges (formal charges) have been instituted, is an entirely different matter.

In *Massiah v. United States,*[77] the Supreme Court addressed the Sixth Amendment right to counsel. The Court used the exclusionary rule as a means of discouraging police misconduct in obtaining incriminating statements from suspects. The thrust of the Supreme Court's rulings in this area is that, if judicial proceedings have been initiated against an accused, law enforcement officers cannot deliberately elicit incriminating information from the accused without defense counsel being present. To understand this rule more fully, the law enforcement professional must explore when the rule applies, what constitutes deliberate elicitation as opposed to interrogation, when and how an officer can communicate with an accused after the right to counsel has attached, and how an accused can waive the right to counsel. Figure 8–1 summarizes the constitutional rights of an accused at different stages of the criminal justice process.

> **CRITICAL STAGE**
> That stage of a criminal prosecution at which time the Sixth Amendment right to counsel attaches. It is that point at which adversarial judicial proceedings have been initiated against the accused, whether by way of formal charge, preliminary hearing, indictment, information, or arraignment.

APPLICATION CASE

In *Massiah v. United States,*[78] the defendant had been indicted for violating federal narcotics laws by transporting cocaine on a ship from South America to the United States. The defendant had pleaded not guilty, had retained a lawyer, and was released. Another man, Colson, was also charged in the indictment. Colson agreed to cooperate with government agents in their continuing investigation of the case. To that end, Colson allowed a radio transmitter to be installed in his car. Colson and Massiah then had a lengthy conversation in the car while it was parked on a New York street. A government agent in another car monitored by radio the conversation between Colson and Massiah. Massiah made several incriminating statements, which the agent repeated in his testimony at Massiah's trial. The defendant was convicted.

The Supreme Court of the United States overturned Massiah's conviction, holding that he was denied the basic protections of the Sixth Amendment's right to counsel when "there was used against him at his trial evidence of his own incriminating words, which federal agents had deliberately elicited from him after he had been indicted and in the absence of counsel."[79]

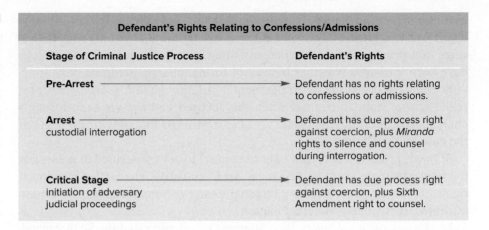

FIGURE 8–1 Constitutional rights of an accused.

Defendant's Rights Relating to Confessions/Admissions	
Stage of Criminal Justice Process	**Defendant's Rights**
Pre-Arrest ————————————————————➤	Defendant has no rights relating to confessions or admissions.
Arrest ————————————————————➤ custodial interrogation	Defendant has due process right against coercion, plus *Miranda* rights to silence and counsel during interrogation.
Critical Stage ————————————————➤ initiation of adversary judicial proceedings	Defendant has due process right against coercion, plus Sixth Amendment right to counsel.

When the Right to Counsel Rule Applies

The Sixth Amendment right to counsel attaches when adversarial judicial proceedings have commenced in a criminal case. Once the accused has obtained and actually met with counsel, police conduct amounting to deliberate elicitation of incriminating statements from the accused violates the accused's right to counsel. If the defendant, after commencement of adversarial proceedings but before counsel has been retained or appointed, initiates conversation with the police and waives *Miranda* rights, then the accused's statements are not given in violation of the right to counsel and are admissible at trial.[80] Moreover, an accused who has a right to counsel may waive that right, as is explained at the end of this section.

What Constitutes Deliberate Elicitation Versus Interrogation

Conducting a custodial interrogation without providing the suspect with the warnings of the right to remain silent and the right to counsel is prohibited by *Miranda.* The ruling in the *Massiah* case condemned deliberately eliciting incriminating statements after counsel has been obtained and in the absence of counsel. The test for interrogation for purposes of *Miranda* is set forth in the *Innis*[81] case. The *Innis* test to determine if an "interrogation" has taken place focuses on the effect on the accused—whether, objectively, what the officer did would likely result in the suspect providing incriminating information. The "deliberate elicitation" test applicable to the Sixth Amendment right to counsel, on the other hand, focuses on the subjective purpose of the officer. In other words, **deliberate elicitation** occurs when the law enforcement officer acts with the purpose of eliciting an incriminating response from a suspect after counsel has been obtained or the adversarial proceeding has begun and counsel is not then and there present.

There is a range of law enforcement activities that can come within the deliberate elicitation language of *Massiah.* One such activity involves a government agent directly seeking to elicit incriminating information, such as in the *Massiah* case. Another example is an officer purposefully attempting to provoke an incriminating statement, such as the Christian burial speech given by the officer in the *Williams* case. Finally, there is the use of undercover agents, or plants, to set up situations in which incriminating information is likely to be obtained. In all of these

DELIBERATE ELICITATION
When the law enforcement officer acts with the purpose of eliciting an incriminating response from a suspect after counsel has been obtained or the adversarial proceeding has begun.

situations, it is the fact that the government agents know their conduct is likely to lead the accused to make an incriminating statement that causes the statement to come within the definition of deliberate elicitation and thus be inadmissible.

APPLICATION CASE

In *United States v. Henry*,[82] the government planted a paid FBI informant in a jail cell with the accused after the accused had been indicted. The informant was paid on a contingent fee basis but was told not to initiate conversations with the accused. The Supreme Court held that the statements reported by the informant were inadmissible as violative of the Sixth Amendment right to counsel because the government must have known that the informant's presence would likely lead to the incriminating statements. This case contrasts with the *Perkins* case discussed in the *Miranda* section, in that the right to counsel under the Sixth Amendment is more absolute than it is under the *Miranda* decision. After formal charges have been initiated against a criminal defendant, no officer or agent of the government may question the defendant without counsel being present.

When and How an Officer Can Communicate with an Accused After the Right Attaches

After adversarial judicial proceedings have been initiated, any attempt by a law enforcement professional to elicit incriminating information deliberately will violate the right to counsel. In some cases, however, adversarial judicial proceedings may have commenced against an accused but no attorney has been hired or appointed. In such a situation, an officer can inform the accused of his or her rights under *Miranda* and secure a valid waiver. If the accused does not ask to exercise the right to counsel, then any incriminating statements obtained will not be a violation of the Sixth Amendment right to counsel.[83] Should the accused request counsel but no counsel has been appointed, an officer may inform the accused of his or her *Miranda* rights and secure a valid waiver.[84] If an attorney has been hired or appointed but the accused has not yet consulted with the attorney, caution dictates that no communication with the accused be initiated by law enforcement without counsel being present.

How an Accused Can Waive the Right to Counsel

A waiver of the right to counsel is possible in all situations where the accused is informed of the right and makes a voluntary, knowing, and intelligent waiver of that right. These principles were established in the 1938 Supreme Court decision of *Johnson v. Zerbst*.[85] By definition, there can be no waiver of the right to counsel when the method of eliciting information is by an undercover or secret agent—the accused would have no knowledge of the right to counsel and thus could not waive it. In all other circumstances, an accused against whom adversarial criminal proceedings have commenced is adequately informed of his or her Sixth Amendment right to counsel when read the *Miranda* warnings. That the *Miranda* warnings are sufficient to secure a valid Sixth Amendment waiver of the right to counsel was specifically held to be so by the Supreme Court in *Patterson v. Illinois.*[86]

CONFESSION GIVEN AFTER AN UNLAWFUL SEARCH AND SEIZURE MAY BE EXCLUDED

The exclusionary rule and the fruit of the poisonous tree doctrine both apply to the products of an unlawful search or seizure. Therefore, if a person subjected to an unlawful search and seizure makes incriminating statements, those statements are inadmissible under the exclusionary rule of the Fourth Amendment. Such inadmissibility is unrelated to the Due Process Clause, *Miranda,* or the Sixth Amendment right to counsel. The fact that an officer gives *Miranda* warnings to such an accused (one who has been subjected to an unlawful search and seizure), who then waives those rights, does not automatically lead to the incriminating statements being admissible.[87] When a defendant confesses after an unlawful arrest, it is possible for the statement and the fruit of the statement to be admissible under the attenuation doctrine. This doctrine holds that, if evidence resulting from illegal police conduct is sufficiently removed from the primary illegality, the fruit of the poisonous tree doctrine need not apply. Intervention of the free will of a person has been held to be sufficient to attenuate the taint of the unlawful arrest. The attenuation doctrine is discussed more fully in the next chapter.

APPLICATION CASE

In *Brown v. Illinois,*[88] the Supreme Court of the United States held that incriminating statements made by Brown after an unlawful arrest were inadmissible, even though Brown had been advised of his *Miranda* rights. The Court held that the statements were the fruits of a poisonous tree, that is, the unlawful arrest. The Court, however, stated that its decision in the *Brown* case was a limited one. The United States Supreme Court did not rule that all statements made after an unlawful arrest would be inadmissible, but that if there were sufficient intervening circumstances to purge the taint of the unlawful arrest, the statements could be admissible. The Supreme Court disagreed with the Illinois Supreme Court. That court had held that advising the accused of his *Miranda* rights always purged the taint of the unlawful arrest, thereby making any incriminating statement by the accused admissible.

THE CONTINUED IMPORTANCE OF CONFESSIONS AS EVIDENCE

There are many technical rules that limit the admissibility in evidence of incriminating statements. Nonetheless, such statements remain a critical weapon in law enforcement's arsenal in the war on crime. In fact, the *Miranda* Court specifically pointed out that "confessions remain a proper element in law enforcement,"[89] and confessions continue to play a major role in law enforcement.

©Paul Conklin/PhotoEdit

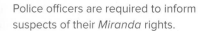
Police officers are required to inform suspects of their *Miranda* rights.

Many crimes are committed in which, even after the most clever, intelligent, and scientific investigation has been conducted, practically no evidence has been discovered to aid in determining the perpetrator's identity. Even when police investigation develops sufficient probable cause to arrest, it is frequently difficult to develop evidence sufficient to attain a conviction under the beyond a reasonable doubt standard. This is particularly true in murder cases. In most cases, the murderer and the victim are the only ones present at the time of the slaying, and frequently there is little physical evidence at the scene except the dead victim. The killer often disposes of the murder weapon miles from the scene. The identification of the killer and a successful prosecution become very difficult. Frequently, it is only through interrogations of persons connected to the victim, as well as possible witnesses, that evidence sufficient to convict can be developed.

Given the important role of defendants' statements in the prosecution of criminal cases, the law enforcement professional cannot afford to conduct interrogations that produce inadmissible evidence. It is incumbent upon the law enforcement professional, therefore, to know the rules that determine whether a suspect's confession, admission, or incriminating statement will be admissible at trial.

PROCEDURE FOR INTRODUCTION OF CONFESSIONS

A confession is usually introduced through the testimony of the officer to whom it was made. If the defense attorney objects to a confession, a preliminary inquiry will be held by the trial judge to determine admissibility. Two equally valid procedures are used in the United States. All questions relating to the admissibility of incriminating statements under the *Miranda* decision, the Sixth Amendment right to counsel, and Fourth Amendment search and seizure are questions of law and fact for the trial judge to rule on. Questions relating to whether a confession was freely and voluntarily made for purposes of due process may require different treatment.

The states follow one of two procedures to determine whether a confession was freely and voluntarily made—the orthodox procedure or the Massachusetts procedure. Under the **orthodox procedure**, the trial judge decides if, given the circumstances, the confession is voluntary. If it is, the confession is introduced into evidence and the judge instructs the jury to consider the confession along with all the other evidence presented. Under the **Massachusetts procedure**, if the judge decides that the confession is voluntary, the judge instructs the jury on the definition of voluntariness and tells them to consider the confession as evidence only if they find that the confession was voluntary.

APPLICATION CASE

At one time, in many jurisdictions in the United States, the inquiry into the voluntariness of a confession was heard by both the judge and the jury. If the judge decided that the confession was involuntarily given, it would be excluded. If there were some doubt about the voluntariness, the judge would admit the confession and instruct the jury that it should decide the issue. If the jury believed that the confession was involuntarily given, the jury was instructed to disregard the confession. If the jury believed the confession was voluntary, it was instructed to consider the confession as evidence. This was known as the New York procedure.

In *Jackson v. Denno*,[90] the United States Supreme Court held that the New York procedure violated due process. The Court concluded that it is unrealistic to expect a jury that hears a confession to disregard it, even if the jury believes it to have been involuntary. Therefore, the Court concluded that the jury that decides the guilt or innocence of an accused cannot decide, in the first instance, the question of the voluntariness of a confession. The Court thus proclaimed the procedure used in *Jackson* to be unconstitutional. The Court did approve the continued use of the orthodox and Massachusetts procedures, in which a clear-cut decision on the voluntariness question is made preliminarily by a trial judge.

Under both procedures, all that is necessary to challenge a confession is for the defendant to object to its introduction at trial. During such an inquiry or hearing, the burden is on the prosecution to prove that the confession was properly obtained. The prosecuting attorney must present evidence, through the testimony of witnesses, that the confession was voluntarily given and that all the other rights and procedures were properly followed in obtaining the confession. The judge must be convinced by a preponderance of the evidence that the confession was lawfully obtained.[91]

At this inquiry, the defendant is permitted to offer evidence in an effort to contradict the evidence presented by the prosecution. If the judge decides that the confession was not properly obtained, the confession will be excluded, and the trial will have to be conducted without the benefit of the confession. If the judge concludes that the confession was properly obtained, he or she will permit the confession to be introduced during the trial.

If the defendant is convicted, the defendant may appeal, and the appellate court will make an independent review concerning the manner in which the confession was obtained. If the appellate court concludes from the record of the case that the confession was improperly obtained, the conviction will be reversed unless the prosecution can prove beyond a reasonable doubt that evidence of the confession did not prejudice the outcome of the trial.[92]

WORDING OF CONFESSIONS

There is no prescribed wording for a statement or a confession. According to its definition, a confession is an acknowledgment of guilt by one accused of a crime. This acknowledgment may be merely an affirmative answer to a question. In other words, an accused may be asked, "Did you kill Richard Roe?" An answer of "Yes" would serve as a complete acknowledgment of guilt and would be classified as a confession. Or the confession may be a simple statement, such as "I killed Molly Brown with a hatchet."

On the other hand, the confession may be a lengthy acknowledgment in which the accused relates in detail every phase of the crime. This may include the facts leading up to the commission of the act, the details of the act itself, and the actions on the part of the accused after the commission of the crime, such as the method of getaway, the disposal of the fruits of the crime, or other related matters.

Although there is no requirement that a confession be in written form, from an evidentiary standpoint, it is preferable that the confession be written and signed by the accused. It is also advisable to record the process leading up to the confession, as well as the confession itself.

The following warnings are standard under the *Miranda* decision:

> You have the right to remain silent. If you talk about this case, anything you say can and will be used against you. You have the right to consult an attorney and to have your attorney present while you are being questioned. If you cannot afford an attorney, one will be provided for you without cost to you. Do you understand these rights? Do you wish to speak to me?

If the interrogation of the accused is recorded by an electronic device, each question and each answer should be included at the outset of the interrogation.

If the interrogation is to be recorded by a stenographer and in question-and-answer form, these questions and the answers should be included at the beginning of the statements. If the interrogation is to be written in a summary narrative form of statement, a preamble should be included as the first paragraph of the statement of the accused. The preamble should read in substance as follows:

> I, (the name of the accused), make this voluntary statement to officer (name of officer or officers conducting the interrogation). I make this statement without threats or promises being made to me. I have been advised of my right to remain silent. I have also been advised of my right to consult an attorney and to have that attorney present during the time that I am being questioned by the officer. I was also advised that, if I could not afford an attorney, one would be provided for me free of charge. I was advised that, if I did say anything, it could be used against me in court. I wish to state that I understand my right to remain silent and my right to an attorney, but I waive these rights and wish to make the following statements to (officer's name).

In addition to setting forth this preamble to the confession, it is suggested that, as a concluding paragraph, the accused in his or her own handwriting include a statement to this effect: "I have read the foregoing statement consisting of (number) pages, and it is true and correct to the best of my knowledge and belief." The accused should then sign the confession in the presence of witnesses other than the person to whom it was given. If the accused cannot read, the written record of the confession should include a notation that the confession was read to the accused and should set forth the names of those present during the reading. Those persons present should sign the statement acknowledging that the confession was read to the accused in their presence and that the accused affirmed the statement.

If corrections are made in the confession, they should be made by the accused in his or her own handwriting and initialed. The accused should also initial each page of the statement if it consists of more than one page. This will overcome any allegation on the part of the accused that other pages that he or she had not seen were added to the confession.

The written confession may be in question-and-answer form, or it may be a narrative of the accused's statement. The question-and-answer form is better, as it more truly reflects the exact statements of the accused. Producing such a statement in written form is time-consuming and, without stenographic assistance, it can become an arduous task. For that reason, some officers prefer a narrative form of statement, which is a summary of the facts as related by the accused. The difficulty with a narrative statement is that it is too frequently in the officer's words, not those of the accused. In reading the statement, the jury may believe that the officer put words in the mouth of the accused and that the statement was not, in fact, that of the accused. With a recorder, there is little need to worry about stenographic assistance at the time a confession is given, as the recording can be transcribed and signed at a later time.

In reducing any confession to writing, the officer is faced with the problem of including only those facts relevant to the crime for which the accused is to be tried. If the written statement includes too many irrelevant details or other incriminating evidence, the written confession may be objectionable at the time of the trial and thereby be excluded.

If a suspect is willing to talk freely about the case, as well as other matters, and the interrogation is being recorded, the entire conversation should be recorded. A second statement can then be obtained, including only those matters relevant to the case at hand.

CONFESSION IMPLICATING A CODEFENDANT

Officers frequently encounter a situation in which a crime is committed by two or more defendants and one defendant confesses to the crime, implicating the other. The other defendant, however, refuses to make any statement, much less to confess. In this situation, the principle of limited admissibility, which would ordinarily solve the problem, will not apply.

Limited admissibility allows evidence admissible for one purpose but inadmissible for another purpose to be introduced for the allowable purpose. The jury is then instructed, at the time the evidence is admitted and before deliberation, to disregard the evidence for the improper purpose. Limited admissibility is a concept that is followed in all jurisdictions. FRE 105 states the doctrine of limited admissibility as it exists in a majority of jurisdictions. However, in the case of one defendant incriminating a codefendant, the United States Supreme Court concluded it is likely a jury would not be able to disregard the facts about the other defendant.[93] Introduction of the confession under those circumstances would violate the Confrontation Clause rights of the codefendant who did not confess. The possibility of such a violation increases when the confessing defendant does not testify and cannot be cross-examined.

Various procedures have been suggested to overcome this problem. First, the trial court can permit a joint trial of all the defendants if all parts of the confession implicating any nonconfessing codefendants can be and are effectively deleted (redacted) from the confession. This will work only if the redaction does not still allow the jury to infer that the nonconfessing codefendant is implicated in the confession. Second, the trial court may grant separate trials if the prosecutor insists upon using the confession and it appears that effective deletions cannot be made. If severance of the trials is not judicially feasible and effective deletions cannot be made, the confession must be excluded from evidence.

These rules create a problem for an officer in an interrogation of a suspect if the interrogation is being electronically recorded. As stated before, it is probably advisable to permit the suspect to talk freely of his or her activities, as well as those of any associates, and thereafter either record a second statement or have the statement taken down stenographically, so that any necessary redaction can be accomplished without affecting the statement's worth to the prosecution.

This procedure may be done by merely having the suspect tell of his or her own activities, admit to being one of those who committed the crime, and not mention the names of others who participated in the crime. By deleting the identity of the codefendants, the confession can be introduced during a joint trial without prejudice to the codefendants. Otherwise, either the confession may not be introduced or it will be necessary to have separate trials. These rules are applicable even if the charge is one involving a conspiracy. A conspiracy has ended by the time of the interrogation, and the statements of a co-conspirator are not binding on the other conspirators once the conspiracy has ended.

PROOF OF THE CRIME IN ADDITION TO A CONFESSION— THE REQUIREMENT OF *CORPUS DELICTI*

CORPUS DELICTI
Required proof, other than a confession, that a crime has been committed.

It is generally conceded in this country that a person cannot be convicted of a crime upon an extrajudicial confession alone. There must be some proof of the crime in addition to the acknowledgment of guilt by the accused—some outside proof of the *corpus delicti*, that is, proof that a crime has been committed. The amount of proof required is usually a *prima facie* showing (some evidence on all elements). Moreover, circumstantial evidence coupled with the confession itself may suffice. The proof of the *corpus delicti* does not have to connect the confessor with the crime but merely prove that a crime was committed.

The reason for the rule requiring additional proof of a crime beyond a confession is deeply ingrained in Anglo-American jurisprudence. The best interests of justice demand that we not convict persons who may be innocent of a crime. Not infrequently, people who suffer from mental instability confess to imaginary crimes or to real crimes for which the unstable person is not responsible. For reasons of their own, people sometimes confess to crimes committed by others.

REVIEW AND APPLICATION

SUMMARY

(1) An opposing party's statement (admission) is any statement, verbal or otherwise, made by a party that can be used in evidence against him or her.

(2) A confession is an admission of the crime itself. An opposing party's statement (admission) concerns only some specific fact that, in turn, tends to establish guilt or some element of the offense.

(3) A confession, to be usable as evidence, must be made freely and voluntarily.

(4) The test for voluntariness, according to the Supreme Court of the United States, is the totality of the circumstances. Specifically, the test is whether, under the totality of the circumstances, the defendant's will was overborne when the defendant confessed. Any conduct by law enforcement officers that, under the totality of the circumstances, could cause a reasonable person in the position of the accused to feel coerced would violate these principles.

(5) The requirements of the *Miranda* decision are that, before a criminal suspect is subjected to custodial interrogation by a law enforcement officer, the officer must advise the suspect that he or she has the right

to remain silent; that anything the suspect says can and will be used against the suspect at trial; that the suspect has a right to an attorney being present during questioning; and that, if the suspect cannot afford an attorney, one can be provided at no cost to the suspect. After issuing these warnings, the law enforcement officer must verify that the suspect understands his or her rights and, before questioning the suspect, the officer must secure an affirmative waiver of these rights by the suspect.

(6) Custody results when a police officer restrains a person in a manner consistent with formal arrest, regardless of the situation or intent of the officer.

(7) Interrogation for purposes of *Miranda* consists of either express questioning or its functional equivalent. The functional equivalent of interrogation is any words or actions on the part of the police (other than those normally attendant to arrest and custody) that the police should know are reasonably likely to elicit an incriminating response from the suspect.

(8) The Supreme Court has stated that the prosecution has a heavy burden to prove that a suspect has waived his or her *Miranda* rights, but it has set the burden of proof at a preponderance of the evidence.

(9) Authorities cannot further interrogate a suspect who, being *Mirandized,* invokes his or her right to counsel unless the accused initiates further communication, exchanges, or conversations with the police.

(10) The three exceptions to the requirement of *Miranda* warnings are the public safety exception, the routine booking question exception, and the undercover police questioner exception.

(11) The Sixth Amendment right to counsel attaches only at a critical stage of a prosecution, which means when adversarial judicial proceedings must have been initiated against the accused, whether by way of formal charge, preliminary hearing, indictment, information, or arraignment.

(12) The rule governing police interrogation of a suspect when his or her right to counsel has attached is that law enforcement officers cannot deliberately elicit incriminating information from the accused without defense counsel being present.

(13) Deliberate elicitation occurs when the law enforcement officer acts with the purpose of eliciting an incriminating response from a suspect after counsel has been obtained or the adversarial proceeding has begun.

(14) In *Jackson v. Denno,* the Court approved two procedures for determining the admissibility of a confession at trial—the orthodox and Massachusetts procedures. Under the orthodox procedure, the trial judge decides whether the confession is voluntary, in which case the confession is introduced into evidence and the judge instructs the jury to consider the confession along with all the other evidence presented. Under the Massachusetts procedure, if the judge decides that the confession is voluntary, the judge instructs the jury as to the definition of voluntariness and tells the jury to consider the confession as evidence only if it finds that the confession was voluntary.

KEY TERMS

QUESTIONS FOR REVIEW

1. What is an opposing party's statement (admission)?
2. How do confessions and opposing party's statements (admissions) differ?
3. What is the fundamental requirement for a confession to be usable as evidence?
4. What is the test for voluntariness of a confession, according to the Supreme Court of the United States?
5. What are the requirements of the *Miranda* decision?
6. What is the definition of custody for purposes of *Miranda?*
7. What is the definition of interrogation for purposes of *Miranda?*
8. What is the burden of proof on the prosecution to prove a waiver of *Miranda* rights by a suspect?
9. When may authorities resume interrogation of a suspect who has invoked the right to counsel?
10. What are the three exceptions to the requirement of *Miranda* warnings?
11. When does the Sixth Amendment right to counsel attach?
12. What is the rule governing police interrogation of a suspect when his or her right to counsel has attached?
13. What constitutes deliberate elicitation for purposes of the Sixth Amendment right to counsel?
14. What are the procedures approved by the United States Supreme Court in *Jackson v. Denno* to determine the admissibility of a confession at trial?

WORKPLACE APPLICATIONS

1. Your captain has asked you to write the department *Miranda* waiver form to be used and signed by all persons who have been read their *Miranda* rights, whether they have waived them or not. Prepare a form using all of the required rights and questions. Remember to account for persons who waive some of their rights and invoke others. Signature and/or initial blanks should be made available for the officer, the translators, and the suspect.
2. You have just arrested two suspected gang members for painting graffiti—gang symbols—on the courthouse wall. They are in custody and have invoked

their *Miranda* right to silence. You decide to place them in the same police car with a hidden tape recorder running to see if they make any incriminating statements. The tape recording, made while you were outside the car, reveals that the gang members discussed committing the crime and concocted an alibi to give to the police. Have you interrogated the suspects or violated their rights? Explain your answer fully.

3. You have arrested a suspect in the kidnapping of a six-year-old boy. The suspect has waived his *Miranda* rights and has agreed to talk to you. You know that the suspect's accomplice has been found after apparently killing herself. The kidnapping has received major nation-wide media attention. Locating the child and returning him to safety is your top priority. The suspect is denying any knowledge of the kidnapping. You turn up the temperature of the interrogation room a little and order that the suspect get warm drinking water and that his meals be served cold. You lie to the suspect and tell him his accomplice confessed to the kidnapping and said that she knew where the boy was before the police killed her in a gun battle. However, you truthfully tell the suspect that the boy has diabetes and, if he does not get his insulin shot, he will die within 24 hours, adding charges of murder to the kidnapping charges. Is this interrogation coercive? Why or why not?

4. Late one night, a highway patrol officer observes a car with its right tail light out. She follows the car, which is traveling very slowly, and after a mile or so pulls it over. As the officer approaches the car, she observes a driver and passenger; as she nears the driver's side window, she smells marijuana smoke. The driver's reactions are very slow, and both driver and passenger appear to be in an advanced stage of intoxication. The officer orders them out of the car and, after confirming that both are seriously physically impaired, she orders them into the back of the cruiser. The officer calls for backup to secure the car and, after the suspect's car has been impounded, the officer drives off toward the station. Along the way, the passenger perks up enough to yell at the driver, "Man, why'd you throw that joint out of the window? I paid $20 for that." Upon making the statement, the passenger seems to fade out. Does the officer have to stop and read the two suspects their *Miranda* warnings? Would the statement be admissible in court? Why or why not?

ETHICAL DILEMMAS

1. You respond to a robbery in progress call at a neighborhood park. When you arrive, you find that a child has been shot to death in the park, and some parents chased the fleeing suspect through the park and captured him some distance from the crime scene. The suspect had hidden the gun somewhere in the park before his capture. Concerned about the safety of their children with the missing gun in the vicinity, the parents beat the suspect until he confessed to the crime and revealed the location of the missing gun. You arrive just in time to hear the confession and are the only one who saw a fellow officer standing back behind some bushes, watching the entire exchange between the suspect and parents. Is this confession coerced? What do you do now?

2. You are acting undercover as a fence dealing in stolen property. You have an informant who knows you are a police officer and keeps you supplied with information about criminal activities. You are after a "rival" fence who has just been arraigned on 15 counts of receiving stolen property. You casually mention the name of this defendant to your informant but do not specifically ask for any information on him. Several weeks later, the informant tells you several incriminating statements that the defendant made to the informant. Have you violated the defendant's right to counsel? Explain your answer fully.

ENDNOTES

1. People v. Kelly, 157 Misc. 2d 554, 556, 598 N.Y.S.2d 423, 425 (Sup. Ct. 1993), citing (Richardson on Evidence) § 540.

2. Gladden v. Unsworth, 396 F.2d 373, 376 (9th Cir. 1968), citing Jones v. United States, 296 F.2d 398, 402 (1962).

3. McNabb v. United States, 318 U.S. 332 (1943); Mallory v. United States, 354 U.S. 449 (1957).

4. 384 U.S. 436 (1966).

5. 322 U.S. 143 (1944).

6. 360 U.S. 315 (1959).

7. Gideon v. Wainwright, 372 U.S. 335 (1963).

8. Argersinger v. Hamlin, 407 U.S. 25 (1972).

9. 378 U.S. 478 (1964).

10. 377 U.S. 201 (1964).

11. 384 U.S. 436 (1966).

12. 530 U.S. 428 (2000).

13. The requirement that confessions be voluntary is predicated on a complex of values. *See* Joshua Dressler, Understanding Criminal Procedure § 22.02 (2), at p. 393 (7th ed. 2017) citing Blackburn v. Alabama, 361 U.S. 199, 207 (1960).

14. Spano v. New York, 360 U.S. 315, 320 (1959).

15. *See* Culombe v. Connecticut, 367 U.S. 568, 606 (1961).

16. 479 U.S. 157 (1986).

17. 297 U.S. 278 (1936).

18. 322 U.S. 143 (1944).

19. *See* Joshua Dressler, Understanding Criminal Procedure § 22.02[B][4][d], at pp. 401–02 (7th ed. 2017).

20. 360 U.S. 315 (1959).

21. 384 U.S. 436 (1966).

22. *Id.* at 444.

23. *Id.*

24. 378 U.S. 478 (1964).

25. 564 U.S. 261 (2011).

26. 394 U.S. 324 (1969).

27. 429 U.S. 492 (1977).

28. 446 U.S. 291 (1980).

29. *Id.* at 300–301.

30. *Id.* footnote 6 omitted.

31. *Id.*

32. *Id.* at 294–95.

33. *Id.*

34. *Id.* at 302, n. 8.

35. 430 U.S. 387 (1987).

36. 384 U.S. 436, 444.

37. *Id.* at 475.

38. Colorado v. Connelly, 479 U.S. 157 (1986).

39. 441 U.S. 369 (1979).

40. Colorado v. Spring, 479 U.S. 564 (1987).

41. Moran v. Burbine, 475 U.S. 412 (1986).

42. 560 U.S. 370 (2010).

43. 570 U.S. 178 (2013).

44. 380 U.S. 609 (1965)

45. 384 U.S. 436, at 473–74.

46. *Id.* at 474.

47. 423 U.S. 96 (1975).

48. 451 U.S. 477 (1981).

49. *Id.* at 484–85.

50. Minnick v. Mississippi, 498 U.S. 146 (1990).

51. *Id.*

52. Dickerson v. United States, 530 U.S. 428 (2000).

53. *See* United States v. Patane, 542 U.S. 630 (2004).

54. 467 U.S. 649 (1984).

55. 559 U.S. 98 (2010).

56. 496 U.S. 582 (1990).

57. *Id.* at 601.

58. 496 U.S. 292 (1990).

59. *Id.* at 300.

60. 496 U.S. 292 (1990).

61. *Id.* at 297.

62. 423 U.S. 96 (1975).

63. Spano v. New York, 360 U.S. 315 (1959).

64. 417 U.S. 433 (1974).

65. 530 U.S. 428 (2000).

66. 417 U.S. 433 (1974).

67. 470 U.S. 298 (1985).

68. *Id.* at 318.

69. Joshua Dressler, Understanding Criminal Procedure § 24.06 [C][1], at pp. 445–47 & 474 (7th ed. 2017).

70. Dickerson, 530 U.S. 428, at 441 (2000), as quoted in Dressler, *Id.* at § 24.11[A], p. 468 text accompanying n. 200.

71. 542 U.S. 630 (2004).

72. Missouri v. Seibert, 542 U.S. 600 (2004).

73. *Id.*

74. Harris v. New York, 401 U.S. 222 (1971).

75. United States v. Wade, 388 U.S. 218, 227 (1967).

76. Kirby v. Illinois, 406 U.S. 682, 689 (1972).

77. 377 U.S. 201 (1964).

78. *Id.*

79. *Id.* at 206.

80. *See* Patterson v. Illinois, 487 U.S. 285 (1988).

81. Rhode Island v. Innis, 446 U.S. 291 (1980).

82. 447 U.S. 264 (1980).

83. Patterson v. Illinois, 487 U.S. 285 (1988).

84. Montejo v. Louisiana, 556 U.S. 778 (2009), overruling Michigan v. Jackson, 475 U.S. 625 (1986).

85. 304 U.S. 458 (1938).

86. 487 U.S. 285 (1988).

87. *See* Brown v. Illinois, 422 U.S. 590, 603 (1975).

88. 422 U.S. 590 (1975).

89. 384 U.S. 436, 481 (1966).

90. 378 U.S. 368 (1964).

91. Lego v. Twomey, 404 U.S. 477 (1972).

92. *See* Arizona v. Fulminante, 499 U.S. 279 (1991).

93. Bruton v. United States, 391 U.S. 123 (1968).

Design Element: ©Ingram Publishing

9 THE EXCLUSIONARY RULE— SEARCH AND SEIZURE

CHAPTER OUTLINE

CHAPTER OBJECTIVES

This chapter explores the law of search and seizure, which stems from the Fourth Amendment to the Constitution of the United States. The focus of this chapter is the exclusionary rule. After reading this chapter you will be able to:

▶ State the main purpose of the exclusionary rule.

▶ Explain the two-pronged test for determining whether there is a search.

▶ Identify the procedure and requirements for obtaining a valid search warrant.

▶ Explain the meaning of probable cause and possible ways of establishing probable cause.

▶ Discuss the requirements and limitations of a search incident to lawful custodial arrest.

▶ List the three ways in which a vehicle may be searched without a warrant.

▶ Identify two requirements for a valid consent.

▶ Discuss the additional requirement for a valid consent if a third party is giving consent.

▶ Review those circumstances that have been recognized as exigent, allowing an officer to search without a warrant.

▶ State the elements that must be satisfied before an officer may seize an object pursuant to the plain view doctrine.

▶ Discuss the justification needed to conduct a stop and frisk.

▶ Explain the standing requirement for a defendant's assertion of a constitutional violation by law enforcement officers.

INTRODUCTION: WHAT IS THE EXCLUSIONARY RULE?

EXCLUSIONARY RULE
The rule that provides that illegally obtained evidence will be excluded from use in a criminal trial.

The **exclusionary rule** is one of the simplest rules in the legal system. It provides that illegally obtained evidence will be excluded from use in a criminal trial. Generally speaking, this rule excludes the introduction of evidence whenever police obtain the evidence in a manner that violates a person's constitutional rights. As a practical matter, the rights guaranteed by the Fourth Amendment to the Constitution of the United States, freedom from unreasonable searches and seizures, are most often involved when evidence is excluded due to application of the exclusionary rule. However, the exclusionary rule sometimes involves other constitutional guarantees. The Sixth Amendment right to counsel, the Fifth Amendment privilege against self-incrimination, and the Fifth and Fourteenth Amendments rights to due process of law are all subject to violation, potentially triggering the exclusionary rule. In addition, as discussed in Chapter 8, the protections afforded by the *Miranda* decision,[1] if violated, may also result in the application of the exclusionary rule and the suppression of evidence at trial. Thus, it would perhaps be more accurate to refer to "exclusionary rules," plural. Nonetheless, the reference to the "exclusionary rule," singular, should be taken to refer to the rule that excludes evidence in a criminal case because of violations of any of a citizen's rights.

The exclusionary rule is not truly a rule of evidence. Rules of evidence were developed to regulate the flow of information presented in a courtroom in order to find the historical facts of a legal dispute. At the same time, the rules of evidence developed in part because of a mistrust of the jury—a recognition that the jury has limitations with respect to what it can hear without being improperly swayed. Thus, principles of trustworthiness, reliability, and necessity came to bear in formulating the rules of evidence. The exclusionary rule seeks to promote a different value—to protect certain constitutional rights of individual citizens or, as the Supreme Court has said in recent years, to deter unlawful police misconduct.

The exclusionary rule is court-created and came into being early in the twentieth century. In 1914, in *Weeks v. United States,*[2] the United States Supreme Court adopted the Fourth Amendment exclusionary rule for the first time, but it was not until 1961 that the Court applied the rule in state trials in the case of *Mapp v. Ohio.*[3] In *Mapp,* the Supreme Court stated a number of justifications for the exclusionary rule, including deterrence of unlawful police conduct and the notion that the courts should not participate in such illegality by allowing the fruits of it into evidence. The exclusionary rule has been controversial from the outset, mostly because its result is often that "[t]he criminal is to go free because the constable has blundered."[4] As a result, the Supreme Court has interpreted the exclusionary rule in a limited manner in recent years, stating that the only purpose of the rule is to deter unlawful police conduct. Therefore, if a situation presents itself in which a law enforcement officer has violated a constitutional mandate but excluding the evidence would have no deterrent effect on the police, the Court has found that the exclusionary rule does not apply or has proclaimed an exception to it.

Development of the Exclusionary Rule and Its Exceptions

At common law, the fact that evidence was illegally obtained did not prevent it from being admitted in court against the accused. The rule was that, if evidence was relevant to the case and aided in proving an issue at trial, then the evidence should be admitted. The courts did not concern themselves with how the evidence was obtained. Moreover, the exclusionary rule was at one time unique to the American system of justice. The English legal system has yet to adopt an exclusionary rule, although Canada does have such a rule.

Six years after the *Weeks* case announced the exclusionary rule, the case of *Silverthorne Lumber Co. v. United States*[5] was decided, and an additional restriction was placed upon federal officers and the admissibility of evidence. *Silverthorne* held that not only is illegally obtained evidence inadmissible, but any other information derived from the illegal evidence is also inadmissible. The **fruit of the poisonous tree doctrine** was thus established. This doctrine has been reiterated many times over the decades, and it continues to be asserted in recent decisions. According to the doctrine, if the search itself is illegal, it is like a poisonous tree. Any information gained as a result of such a search is also tainted by the illegal search and is inadmissible against the defendant—it is poisonous fruit of a poisonous tree. The exclusionary rule and the fruit of the poisonous tree doctrine apply to evidence derived from violations of a person's Fifth and Sixth Amendment rights to the same extent that they apply to unlawful searches and seizures that violate a person's Fourth Amendment rights.

The Court in the *Silverthorne* case did not close the door on all information that may be gained through an illegal search. The *Silverthorne* Court established the **independent source doctrine**, which is one of three exceptions to the fruit of the poisonous tree doctrine. If the prosecution can show that the same information or knowledge was also gained through another, independent source unrelated to the illegality, the information can then be admissible through this source but not through the illegal search. Since evidence admitted under this and the other

FRUIT OF THE POISONOUS TREE DOCTRINE
The principle that, under the exclusionary rule, not only is illegally obtained evidence inadmissible, but any other information derived from the illegality is also inadmissible.

INDEPENDENT SOURCE DOCTRINE
One of three exceptions to the fruit of the poisonous tree doctrine. This exception holds that, if the same information or knowledge is also gained through a source independent of the illegality and this fact can be shown by the prosecution, the information can be admissible through this source but not through the illegal search.

two exceptions to the fruit of the poisonous tree doctrine are also admitted into evidence notwithstanding the exclusionary rule, one could say that these are also exceptions to the exclusionary rule.

ON THE JOB

The fruit of the poisonous tree doctrine works as follows. A murder suspect is taken into custody and the arresting officer threatens the suspect with a cocked gun, causing the suspect to confess to the murder, revealing where the gun is hidden and leading the officer to the body. All this evidence would be inadmissible in court because it is tainted by the officer having coerced the suspect into confessing in violation of Fifth Amendment due process. The confession would be direct fruit of the initial illegality, and the gun and body would be derivative fruit of the initial illegality, that is, fruit of the poisonous tree.

ATTENUATION DOCTRINE
The exception to the fruit of the poisonous tree doctrine in which the connection between the unlawful conduct of the police and the discovery of the challenged evidence is so unrelated as to dissipate the taint.

There are two other exceptions to the fruit of the poisonous tree doctrine: the attenuation doctrine and the inevitable discovery doctrine. The **attenuation doctrine** applies when the connection between the unlawful conduct of the police and the discovery of the challenged evidence is so unrelated as to dissipate the taint. The attenuation doctrine was most famously stated and applied in the case of *Wong Sun v. United States.*[6] In this case, the police seized a man who told them that he had purchased narcotics from the defendant. The seized man was not known to the police beforehand and so was not a reliable informant. The police then went to the defendant's home and arrested him illegally, that is, without probable cause. While being interrogated, the defendant refused to make any statements. Two days after the defendant was released on bail, he voluntarily returned to the police station and made incriminating statements to the police. The Supreme Court found that the defendant's statements were admissible because the connection between the illegal arrest and the making of the statements was so attenuated as to purge the statements of the primary illegality. More specifically, the defendant's voluntary act of returning to the police station could not be attributable to any police misconduct. Therefore, the illegal arrest had little or nothing to do with the defendant's subsequent incriminating statements.

In 2016, the United States Supreme Court applied the attenuation doctrine in the case of *Utah v. Strieff.*[7] In *Strieff*, an officer stopped a man without any cause after the man exited a residence that the officer was surveilling based on an anonymous tip that drug transactions were going on in the house. The officer got Strieff's identification and learned from a police dispatcher that there was an outstanding warrant for his arrest on a traffic violation. The officer arrested Strieff and found drugs and paraphernalia on him. Strieff's appeal from his conviction was affirmed by the United States Supreme Court, which held that the discovery of a valid pre-existing and untainted warrant attenuated the connection between the unconstitutional investigatory stop of Strieff and the evidence seized.

APPLICATION CASE

In *Hudson v. Michigan,*[8] the United States Supreme Court decided that a violation of the knock and announce requirement for police executing a search warrant did not, in the circumstances, require exclusion of the evidence seized as a result of the ensuing search. The officers waited only three to five seconds after announcing before entering Hudson's home. The state conceded that this was a violation of the knock and announce rule, but the Court concluded that the purpose of the knock and announce rule is to protect life, limb, and property and this did not relate to the securing of the evidence. In this sense, the seizure of the evidence was attenuated from the violation of the rule, and the exclusion of the evidence was not an appropriate remedy. Instead, the Court said, an appropriate remedy would be a civil suit.

Much like the independent source doctrine, the **inevitable discovery doctrine** is a simple and straightforward legal concept. According to this exception, the challenged evidence is admissible if the prosecution can show that the evidence would have been inevitably discovered, even in the absence of the police illegality. For example, in *Nix v. Williams*,[9] the police violated the defendant's Sixth Amendment right to counsel. As a result of the violation, the defendant made incriminating statements and was induced to lead the police to the body of the murder victim. At the same time, search teams were looking for the body and were within a few miles of its location. The Supreme Court held that the evidence related to the discovery of the body of the murder victim was admissible despite the violation of the defendant's rights. The Court stated:[10]

> If the prosecution can establish by a preponderance of the evidence that the information ultimately or inevitably would have been discovered by lawful means—here the volunteers' search—then the deterrence rationale has so little basis that the evidence should be received. Anything less would reject logic, experience, and common sense.

Similarly, if the police had unlawfully searched the defendant's house and obtained the information regarding the location of the body from the defendant's personal diary, then the result would have been the same. The search teams were already on their way to discovering the body, and the information acquired from the diary pursuant to the unlawful search would have made no difference.

Before 1960, state officers who obtained evidence illegally could hand it over to federal officers for prosecution in federal court. This was known as the **silver platter doctrine**. The silver platter doctrine ended with the 1960 United States Supreme Court case of *Elkins v. United States*.[11] There, the Court held that evidence illegally obtained by a state officer was inadmissible in a federal prosecution. The test now requires that evidence obtained unlawfully by a state officer be treated the same as if it had been obtained in a similar manner by a federal officer.

Keep in mind that the exclusionary rules initially were applicable only to federal officers. The states were still free to establish their own procedures regarding searches, seizures, and admissibility of evidence without interference from the federal courts. Many states did not see fit to adopt the exclusionary rule until the Court rendered its decision in *Mapp* in 1961, making the Fourth Amendment exclusionary rule applicable to the states through the Due Process Clause provisions of the Fourteenth Amendment. The Court in *Mapp* stated, "We hold that all evidence obtained by searches and seizures in violation of the Constitution is, by that same authority, inadmissible in a state court."[12]

INEVITABLE DISCOVERY DOCTRINE
An exception to the fruit of the poisonous tree doctrine that states that the challenged evidence is admissible if the prosecution can show that the evidence would have been inevitably discovered, even in the absence of the police illegality.

SILVER PLATTER DOCTRINE
The doctrine that allowed state officers who obtained evidence illegally to hand it over to federal officers for prosecution in federal court.

In the *Mapp* case, Dollree Mapp was convicted for having obscene materials in her possession, a conviction that was affirmed by the Ohio Supreme Court and appealed to the United States Supreme Court. Acting upon information that a suspect in a bombing case was hiding in the home of Ms. Mapp and that policy paraphernalia (material connected with illegal betting activities) was hidden there, the city police went to Ms. Mapp's home and asked permission to search it. Ms. Mapp called her attorney and then refused to admit the officers unless they had a search warrant. The officers left but returned later and again sought admittance.

When Ms. Mapp failed to come to the door, the officers broke the outer door to the residence and started up the stairs to her residence, where they were met by Ms. Mapp. She asked to see their search warrant. One of the officers displayed a paper purporting to be a search warrant. Ms. Mapp grabbed the paper and tried to stuff it in her brassiere. A scuffle ensued, and the paper was retrieved by one of the officers. The officers then searched Ms. Mapp's apartment and found the obscene material that brought about her conviction. No "search warrant" was ever produced at trial. The United States Supreme Court held that this invasion of Ms. Mapp's residence and the subsequent search were unreasonable and therefore violated the Fourth Amendment to the Constitution. Moreover, the Court declared the exclusionary rule to be an essential part of both the Fourth and Fourteenth Amendments, thereby reversing Ms. Mapp's conviction. With that conclusion, the Supreme Court adopted a new philosophy, which caused the exclusionary rule to become the standard in all states.

Philosophy of the Exclusionary Rule

The *Mapp* Court gave a number of rationales for its decision. The first and most significant rationale, or justification, is the **deterrence rationale**. To deter police officers from disregarding the Constitution, it is necessary to exclude from evidence at trial the evidentiary fruits of illegal police conduct. Additionally, the Court stated that the need to maintain judicial integrity justifies the application of the exclusionary rule to the state—judges cannot be accomplices to illegality by allowing the introduction of illegally obtained evidence. In recent years, as the composition of the Court has changed, and under the leadership of Chief Justices Burger, Rehnquist, and Roberts, only the deterrence rationale has survived. As a result, the Court has been able to fashion a number of exceptions to the exclusionary rule and the fruit of the poisonous tree doctrine. These exceptions have blunted somewhat the exclusionary rule's adverse effect of letting the criminal go free to prey upon society again because the officer blundered. In addition to the independent source, attenuation, and inevitable discovery doctrines already discussed as exceptions to the fruit of the poisonous tree doctrine, the Court has fashioned two exceptions to the exclusionary rule: the good faith and impeachment exceptions.

In *United States v. Leon,*[13] the Court established the "good faith" exception to the Fourth Amendment exclusionary rule. In *Leon,* police officers executed a warrant under a good faith belief that the warrant was supported by probable cause. But, as it later turned out, the warrant was invalid for lack of probable cause. If the Supreme Court were to adhere to its prior decision in *Mapp,* the

DETERRENCE RATIONALE
The rationale for the exclusionary rule that rests upon the view that, to deter police officers from disregarding the Constitution, it is necessary to exclude from evidence at trial the evidentiary fruits of illegal police conduct.

evidence seized by the officers in *Leon* would be held inadmissible. The Supreme Court, contrary to precedent, allowed the evidence to be introduced, by holding that "[i]n the absence of an allegation that the magistrate abandoned his detached and neutral role, [exclusion of evidence] is appropriate only if the officers were dishonest or reckless in preparing their affidavit or could not have harbored an objectively reasonable belief in the existence of probable cause."[14] The good faith exception to the exclusionary rule applies only to cases involving warrants.

As elaborated by the Court, the essential test for the **good faith exception** exists when an officer, in executing a search warrant, has an objectively reasonable belief that the warrant is valid. The evidence may then be admissible at trial even if there is some technical defect in the warrant. However, when a reasonably well-trained officer should realize that a search warrant is invalid, then the good faith exception does not apply.

In short, *Leon*'s good faith exception applies when the illegality is due to the conduct of the magistrate, not the law enforcement officer. Consistent with the overriding deterrent rationale of the Supreme Court, correcting magistrates' mistakes by applying the exclusionary rule will not yield any deterrence of law enforcement misconduct.

Criticism of the good faith exception is at least two-fold. First, by exempting erring magistrates from the exclusionary rule, the Court may be encouraging magistrates to rubber-stamp police warrant applications and to be generally sloppy in the judicial review function. Second, the way the good faith exception works is logically questionable. The test for probable cause assumes a reasonable officer's view that the search or seizure is justified. If a magistrate approves a warrant that lacks such reasonable support, how can it be said that "a reasonably well-trained" officer would have believed in the validity of the warrant? The dissenters in *Leon* pointed out this logical inconsistency, but to no avail.

Notwithstanding some controversy over the good faith exception, including the fact that some states have rejected it,[15] one must bear in mind that the exception only applies to warrant cases and other limited circumstances, such as statutory authorization later found unlawful.[16] Generally, law enforcement action taken without a warrant is not subject to the exception, even though arguments for such application can be made. Hence, the exception applies to a relatively "small class of cases."[17] The United States Supreme Court has extended the good faith exception to three other circumstances: (1) seizures made in reasonable reliance on erroneous computer records indicating the existence of a warrant where the error was attributable to a judicial branch employee (*Arizona v. Evans*);[18] (2) similar reliance on erroneous computer records by a county warrant clerk working in the sheriff's department who checked with his or her counterpart in a neighboring county (*Herring v. United States*);[19] and (3) reliance on "objectively reasonable reliance on binding appellate precedent" that was subsequently overruled (*Davis v. United States*).[20] In the computer records and state statute cases, the Court found that no deterrent effect of police misconduct was involved because the errors were made by judicial personnel in one case and the legislature in another. In the most recent computer records case, *Herring v. United States,* the error was made by an employee of a law enforcement department, the county sheriff. Nonetheless, the Court found that the error was merely one of negligent

GOOD FAITH EXCEPTION
This exception to the exclusionary rule allows the admission of evidence even if there is some technical defect in the warrant, as long as the executing officer has an objectively reasonable belief that the warrant is valid.

conduct by a clerk, not flagrant misconduct by arresting officers, and, applying a cost-benefit analysis, a majority refused to apply the exclusionary rule.[21] In the reliance on binding appellate precedent case, *Davis v. United States*, officers searched a vehicle incident to the arrest of recent occupants. At the time, extant Eleventh Circuit precedent interpreting *New York v. Belton* authorized that vehicle search. Two years later, the Supreme Court decided *Arizona v. Gant*, which interpreted *Belton* narrowly, thereby restricting the scope of vehicle searches incident to arrest. (Both *Belton* and *Gant* are fully discussed later in this chapter.) Relying on prior good-faith exception decisions, the majority decided that, when officers rely upon binding appellate precedent authorizing a search, the deterrent premises of the exclusionary rule and the balance of costs and benefits dictate the admission of any evidence obtained.

APPLICATION CASE

In *Maryland v. Garrison*,[22] the Supreme Court addressed the issue of the good faith of officers who executed a warrant that was later found to be deficient because it was overbroad. Police obtained a warrant to search the third-floor apartment of a person named McWebb. It was unknown at the time that the third floor had more than one apartment. The officers discovered paraphernalia in the Garrison apartment, which was not included in the warrant. The officers, although they didn't know it, were in the wrong apartment, and they seized items they weren't even looking for! Nonetheless, the Supreme Court found the search valid. The Court determined that a reasonable police officer, based on the information available at the time of execution of the warrant, would have believed he or she was executing (conducting) a valid search. Accordingly, the search was reasonable because the officers executed the search warrant under a good faith, though mistaken, belief that they were acting within the scope of the warrant.

APPLICATION CASE

In *Groh v. Ramirez*,[23] a federal agent prepared and signed an application for a warrant to search Ramirez's ranch. The application included an affidavit stating that the agent believed that certain specific weapons, explosives, and records were on the ranch. The agent gave the magistrate a completed warrant form, but it did not list any of the specific property to be seized. The magistrate failed to notice that the warrant was defective and signed it. When the warrant was executed, none of the items sought were found. Ramirez brought suit for violation of his Fourth Amendment rights. The Supreme Court held that the warrant was patently invalid in that it failed altogether to comply with the particularity requirement of the Fourth Amendment. Had any property been located and seized, it would not have been admissible in any trial against Ramirez, and the *Leon* good faith exception would not have applied.

Another exception to the exclusionary rule is the **impeachment exception**. This exception allows the prosecution to use evidence illegally seized from the accused in violation of his or her Fourth Amendment or Fifth Amendment *Miranda* rights for the limited purpose of impeaching the accused during direct examination or cross-examination. This exception is justified on the grounds that the use of illegally seized evidence to impeach a defendant's false testimony aids in the determination of truth. In addition, this exception is consistent with the deterrent rationale underlying the exclusionary rule in that it is unlikely that officers will be encouraged to violate the Fourth or Fifth Amendments in the hopes of gaining evidence for impeachment purposes.

IMPEACHMENT EXCEPTION
An exception to the exclusionary rule that applies to *Miranda* or the Fourth Amendment, which allows statements taken in violation of *Miranda* or the Fourth Amendment to be used at trial to impeach the testimony of the accused.

THE SCOPE OF SEARCHES AND SEIZURES

The Fourth Amendment prohibits unreasonable searches and seizures and provides that no warrants for a search or a seizure shall be issued without probable cause. One generally thinks of searches and seizures in connection with obtaining physical evidence, but they also pertain to the receipt of information through wiretaps, recording devices, inspection of papers, and even conversations. Thus, the search for and seizure of evidence are not confined to physical, tangible objects. The objects of a search or seizure may be the fruits of a crime, the materials used in a crime, the evidence of a crime, weapons, contraband, or a person. Whether or not the information or objects looked for (searched) and taken (seized) may be used as evidence in a judicial proceeding depends entirely upon whether the search for and the seizure of the evidence were reasonable or unreasonable.

Although people have a tendency to use the term "search and seizure" as if it were one act, legally and technically, this is incorrect. A search is one act and a seizure is another; it is possible to conduct a search and not make a seizure, or there may be a seizure without a search. It is quite possible to have authority to search but not to seize, or authority to seize but not to search.

The legality of a seizure of an object is usually dependent upon the legality of the search, but an illegal seizure may stem from a legal search. This is particularly true when things are taken other than those described in a search warrant. An illegal search may follow a lawful seizure, such as when an automobile is stopped (seized) because of a traffic violation but then, without probable cause to search, an officer searches the vehicle and finds contraband.

WHAT IS A SEARCH?

There was a time when a search required a physical intrusion—a trespass. According to this definition, police officers were required to step into a person's home, or other constitutionally protected area, in order to observe something. A person was deemed to have Fourth Amendment protection in his or her home or other areas in which the person had a property interest. If the police physically intruded onto such property, even in the slightest way, then a search occurred. The United States Supreme Court's 1967 decision, in *Katz v. United States*,[24] dramatically changed the meaning of "search" in Fourth Amendment jurisprudence. The *Katz* ruling allowed a search to occur without a physical entry.

Katz was convicted of transmitting wagers in interstate commerce through the use of a pay telephone booth. The telephone booth was completely enclosed, a type that is rarely seen in modern times. FBI agents had attached an electronic listening device to the booth and recorded Katz's conversations. The recordings were used as evidence at trial. On appeal, Katz contended that there had been an unreasonable seizure of his conversations, since his privacy had been invaded. The United States Supreme Court upheld Katz's claim and reversed the conviction. The Court stated: [25]

> *[T]he Fourth Amendment protects people, not places.* What a person knowingly exposes to the public, even in his own home or office, is not a subject of Fourth Amendment protection. . . . But what he seeks to preserve as private, even in an area accessible to the public, may be constitutionally protected. . . .
>
> It is true that the absence of penetration was at one time thought to foreclose further Fourth Amendment inquiry . . . for that Amendment was thought to limit only searches and seizures of tangible property. . . . But "the premise that property interests control the right of the Government to search and seize has been discredited. . . ." We have expressly held that the Fourth Amendment governs not only the seizure of tangible items, but extends as well to the recording of oral statements overheard without any "technical trespass under . . . local property law." . . . Once this much is acknowledged, and once it is recognized that the Fourth Amendment protects people—and not simply "areas"—against unreasonable searches and seizures, it becomes clear that the reach of that Amendment cannot turn upon the presence or absence of a physical intrusion into any given enclosure. (Emphasis added.)

Katz recognized for the first time that Fourth Amendment protections extend to intangibles, including conversations. Equally significant, the language of the decision recognizes it is a person's expectation of privacy that establishes the protection, even in a public environment. On the other hand, what a person exposes to public view, even if the person believes it to be private, is not within the Fourth Amendment's protection.

With respect to the meaning of the language quoted previously, note that, whenever a person exposes activities or objects to public view, there is no search if an officer perceives the activity or object from a lawful vantage point when making the observation. Thus, in *Katz,* the officers' observations of Katz in the glass-enclosed telephone booth were not searches. The Fourth Amendment was not triggered by the officers' conduct in viewing Katz from the public street. The theory upon which this conclusion is based is that anything in open or plain view, that anyone can perceive by one of the five senses, is not subject to Fourth Amendment protection. The officers' conduct in wiretapping Katz's conversations went beyond what Katz had exposed to the public and, therefore, constituted a search.

APPLICATION CASE

Observation of activities from a lawful vantage point is not limited to the sense of sight but extends to all the senses. In *Minnesota v. Dickerson,*[26] an officer conducting a lawful patdown felt a small lump in the front pocket of the suspect's jacket. The officer continued to feel the object further and determined that it was crack cocaine, which he seized. Although the Court held that the seizure of the cocaine was unlawful for reasons that will be discussed later in this chapter, the Court said that, under certain circumstances, the observation of an object through the sense of touch is not a search—thereby recognizing the "plain touch" doctrine.

The Reasonable Expectation of Privacy Test

In a concurring opinion in *Katz,* one consistent with the majority's opinion on the meaning of the Fourth Amendment, Justice John Marshall Harlan stated a two-pronged test for determining whether a search has occurred. In the years following the *Katz* decision, the Supreme Court chose Harlan's test to decide whether, in any given case, a search has occurred. The test examines whether

1. the person alleging that a search occurred has exhibited an actual, subjective expectation of privacy in the place searched; and
2. the person's expectation is one that society is prepared to recognize as reasonable or legitimate.

If both conditions are present, then there is a search.

This test contains both a subjective prong and an objective prong. There is some question as to whether the subjective prong (number 1 in the list) is necessary or appropriate, and, in many cases, the subjective prong is assumed to exist even if it is not clear that the citizen truly expected privacy. In any event, the significant aspect of the test is whether a person claiming a violation of his or her Fourth Amendment rights can be said to have a personal, reasonable expectation of privacy measured by objective standards.

There are a number of recurring scenarios involving search issues that the Supreme Court has addressed in the context of a reasonable expectation of privacy. Those scenarios are the false friend, open fields, technologically enhanced activities, and aerial surveillance.

The False Friend

Prior to *Katz,* the Supreme Court had held that, when a paid government informant insinuated himself or herself into the confidence of a suspect and reported to the government statements made by that suspect, the suspect's Fourth Amendment rights were not violated. In the early 1960s, a government informant was present at a number of meetings between Jimmy Hoffa, who was on trial for perjury, and his attorney. The informant was invited into the meetings during which Hoffa talked freely about his actions. The informant relayed to the FBI what Hoffa had said, and that information helped lead to Hoffa's subsequent indictment and conviction of attempting to bribe a juror. Hoffa then appealed to the United States Supreme Court.

In *Hoffa v. United States,*[27] the Court relied upon an "assumption of the risk" theory to conclude that there was no search in this situation. What a person willingly reveals to another on the assumption that the other is a friend is thereby revealed to the world if the so-called friend turns out to be no friend at all. This is known as the **false friend doctrine**.

After *Katz,* the Supreme Court reaffirmed the false friend principle in *United States v. White.*[28] The "expectation of privacy" terminology from *Katz* was used by the Court to say that a citizen does not have a reasonable expectation that a person with whom he or she is conversing will not then or later reveal the conversation to the police. The difference between *White* and *Hoffa* was that the false friend in *White* was wired and, while the conversations were taking place, they were transmitted to an officer nearby. The *White* Court did not find this difference significant enough to warrant a different result and declared that no search had occurred.

However, in *Carpenter v. United States*[29] the Court held that a phone company handing over transactional records to the government, including the date and time of calls, and the approximate location where calls began and ended, did not fall within the false friend doctrine. Although, when an individual places a phone call he or she voluntarily gives the phone company the approximate GPS location and thus assumes the risk of what the company may do with that information, there is nonetheless a reasonable expectation of privacy in such an intrusive type of information. Thus, a search warrant is needed to gain such information.

Open Fields Doctrine and Curtilage

Prior to *Katz,* the Supreme Court had declared that entry into "open fields" did not constitute a search under the Fourth Amendment in *Hester v. United States.*[30]

This principle was reaffirmed in *Oliver v. United States,*[31] when federal officers had gone past "No Trespassing" signs onto private property where they saw marijuana growing. The marijuana was growing in fields that were not visible unless one entered the private property. The officers walked around a gate and through a private woods in two separate instances. The Court concluded, under the **open fields doctrine**, that people do not have a legitimate expectation of privacy in open fields, even if law enforcement officers trespass upon private property in order to observe the open fields. The main justification for this conclusion is that open fields do not provide the setting for those intimate activities that the Fourth Amendment is intended to shelter from government intrusion or surveillance.

In *Oliver,* the Court distinguished open fields from the **curtilage**, i.e., the land immediately surrounding and associated with a home. A citizen's activities in the open fields, unlike those usually conducted within the curtilage, are not entitled to Fourth Amendment protection. Thus, whereas an individual would expect that there would be no warrantless entry into the curtilage by officers, the same expectation is not justified with respect to open fields.

In *Collins v. Virginia,*[32] the United States Supreme Court, in a near-unanimous decision, found the Fourth Amendment's warrant requirement for searches applied to a police officer's invasion of curtilage of a home for a warrantless search of a motorcycle covered by a tarp and parked in a partially enclosed top portion of a driveway of the home.

FALSE FRIEND DOCTRINE
The doctrine, in defining one's reasonable expectation of privacy, that what a person willingly reveals to another, on the assumption that the other is a friend, is thereby revealed to the world if the so-called friend turns out to be no friend at all.

OPEN FIELDS DOCTRINE
The doctrine, in determining one's reasonable expectation of privacy, which states that people do not have a legitimate expectation of privacy in open fields, even if law enforcement officers trespass upon private property in order to observe the open fields.

CURTILAGE
The land immediately surrounding a home and associated with it, where one has a reasonable expectation of privacy, as contrasted with open fields, where one does not.

©Ira Wyman/Getty Images

The Supreme Court has held that, if the government gains information that a citizen has knowingly exposed to the public, the use of enhanced surveillance techniques does not violate the Fourth Amendment protections. Recent decisions by the Court have narrowed this principle when applied to extended surveillance and digital data contained in cell phones and the like.

Technologically Enhanced Activities

The use of technology to enhance criminal investigations presents a wide variety of issues under the Fourth Amendment. While pointing a flashlight at night to illuminate an area open to public view does not trigger Fourth Amendment issues, there are a variety of devices that could lead to such issues, ranging from parabolic microphones to electronic and wireless tracking devices. The Supreme Court has decided a number cases in this area, holding that, if the government gains information that the citizen has knowingly exposed to the public, then the use of an enhancement device will not violate the Fourth Amendment.

First, in *Smith v. Maryland,*[33] the Court found that the installation and use of a pen register (a device that records the numbers dialed by a telephone) by the telephone company was not a search under the Fourth Amendment. The Court distinguished this case from *Katz* on the ground that, instead of learning of the contents of a telephone conversation, the government in *Smith* learned only the numbers called. But pivotal to the Court's decision was the fact that telephone users were well aware that they were sending the numbers dialed to the telephone company. Thus, like the false friend situation, the Court reasoned that the telephone user has no reasonable expectation of privacy in information turned over to a third person—in this instance, the telephone company.

The "third-party" doctrine had its roots in *United States v Miller,*[34] where federal agents subpoenaed two banks and received all of Miller's bank records. As a result, Miller was indicted for tax fraud. The United States Supreme Court had held, three years before *Smith,* that bank customers do not have a reasonable expectation of privacy in their bank records because they voluntarily give information contained in the records to the bank and such records are observable by the bank's employees. An individual who volunteers information to a

The decisions of the Supreme Court of the United States set the *minimum* standard for what violates the Fourth Amendment (or any constitutional right of a criminal defendant). The states are free to impose a higher standard than that set by the Supreme Court. Therefore, in the area of technologically enhanced government conduct, some states have defined searches as including the use of pen registers, the audiotaping of conversations without the knowledge of all the participants in the conversation, and other means of obtaining information that may or may not be below the standards established by United States Supreme Court cases. The law enforcement professional should determine the status of technologically enhanced searches under the law of the state in which he or she is working.

third party assumes the risk that the third party is not going to hand over the information to the government. And, remember, in *Carpenter v. United States*, the Court declined to extend the third-party doctrine to cell-site location information. The Court reasoned the level of intrusiveness in extensive cell-site data gathered over 120 days, giving an individual's approximate GPS location weighed against the application of the third-party doctrine. Thus, the Court held narrowly that the government will need a warrant to access cell-site location information. The Court distinguished its prior beeper cases, *Knotts* and *Karo*, discussed in the next paragraph. *Carpenter* was a 5-4 decision with strenuous separate dissents by Justices Kennedy, Thomas, Alito, and Gorsuch.

The use of electronic beepers to monitor movements of suspects was involved in two other cases, *United States v. Knotts*[35] and *United States v. Karo*.[36] The result in both cases turned upon the Court's view of whether the information obtained by the government was or was not open to public view. In *Knotts*, officers placed a beeper in a chemical container that they knew would be sold to the suspects. The beeper emitted a radio signal that the officers monitored to track the suspects' movements on the streets and highways. Using visual as well as electronic monitoring, the officers were able to locate the suspects via their possession of the "beeperized" container, even though the officers lost visual contact with the suspects. The Court held that, since the officers gained only as much information as they would have gotten through visual surveillance (even though they lost visual contact), there was no search. Also of importance to the Court was the fact that the beeper was of limited use—the officers did not track the suspects' movements within a private area, such as the dwelling the suspects entered.

In contrast to *Knotts*, the *Karo* scenario was quite different in the Court's eyes. *Karo* also involved a beeper in a chemical container, but the police used it to monitor the suspect's movements within private houses as well as public places. The Court found this monitoring to be a search, since the monitored property had been removed from public view.

In addition, in *Kyllo v. United States*,[37] the Court found the use of a thermal imaging device was an unconstitutional search because the sense-enhancing device obtained information about Kyllo's home that could not otherwise have been obtained without physical intrusion into the home. In *Kyllo*, an agent from the Department of the Interior suspected that Kyllo was growing marijuana in his home, which was part of a triplex. The agent scanned the exterior walls of the triplex with a thermal imaging device to detect the heat that emanates from lamps commonly used for cultivating marijuana plants. The scan showed that the roof over the garage and a side wall of Kyllo's home were relatively hot compared with the rest of the home and substantially warmer than neighboring homes in the triplex. The agent concluded that Kyllo was using halide lights to grow marijuana in his house, which indeed he was. Based on the thermal imaging readout, the agent obtained a search warrant for Kyllo's home, where he found more than 100 marijuana plants. The Supreme Court reversed Kyllo's conviction, holding that, when the government uses devices that are not in general public use to acquire information that would otherwise be unknowable, such surveillance is a search and is presumptively unreasonable without a warrant.

Thus, the *Kyllo* case turned on the fact that thermal imaging devices were not generally in use by the public. With respect to devices that are readily and commonly used by the public, a different result will probably occur, as there is no reasonable expectation of privacy against the use of such devices by the public at large. For example, assume that a person uses a cordless telephone to conduct illegal betting activities. One day a neighbor inadvertently overhears the conversations on her own telephone, contacts the police, and, at the police's instruction, electronically records the next betting conversation intercepted on her telephone. Since it is widely known that cordless telephones may be overheard by neighbors, passersby, or others, a person cannot be said to have a legitimate, objective belief that conversations conducted on such a telephone will be private. Currently, thermal imagers, infrared scanners, parabolic microphones, and other ultrasensitive listening devices that "look" or "hear" through walls have not been approved by the Court. On the other hand, a person may not have an expectation of privacy in what is said in a public place or an open field, even if it is intercepted through the use of an ultrasensitive listening device.

Finally, in *United States v. Jones*,[38] the Court held that the government's installation of a GPS tracking device on a suspect's vehicle, and use of the device to monitor the vehicle's movements for 28 days, constituted a "search" under the Fourth Amendment. In *Jones*, the defendant was arrested for conspiracy relating to drug trafficking after the police attached a tracker to his vehicle, without a warrant, and used it to follow him. At trial, the government introduced the data derived from the GPS tracking system, which connected the defendant to the alleged conspirator's stash house. A jury found the defendant guilty; however, the Court of Appeals reversed the conviction because the admission of evidence obtained by use of the GPS device without a warrant violated the Fourth Amendment. The Supreme Court rejected the government's argument that there is no reasonable expectation of privacy in a person's movement on public streets, and affirmed the lower court's ruling.

In *Jones*, a unanimous Supreme Court concluded that the government's actions qualified as a "search" under the Fourth Amendment. The Justices divided sharply, however, over the reasoning supporting that conclusion. Only five Justices joined Justice Scalia's majority opinion, which endorsed the theory that attaching the GPS on the vehicle constituted a trespass. According to the majority, a "physical intrusion" of that sort "would have been considered a search" at the time the Fourth Amendment was adopted. The majority conceded that, beginning with *Katz*, later decisions of the Court "deviated from th[e] exclusively property-based approach," focusing instead on reasonable expectations of privacy; however, these decisions, "did not repudiate" the historical understanding of the Fourth Amendment—that it "embod[ies] a particular concern for government trespass upon the areas ('persons, houses, papers, and effects') it enumerates."

Four Justices concurred in the judgment but the result could be reached by the reasonable expectation of privacy standard of *Katz* and its progeny. Though Justice Sotomayor joined the majority opinion, she emphasized the need to apply *Katz* to GPS monitoring that does not involve a trespassory installation. It remains to be seen whether the majority approach in *Jones* marks a significant deviation from the expectation of privacy test and a return to the physical intrusion test of the past.[39] The physical intrusion theory of *Jones*, as opposed to the expectation of privacy theory of *Katz*, was applied again in *Florida v. Jardines*.[40] In *Jardines*, a five-Justice majority concluded that a dog sniff on the porch of a home constituted a search. *Jardines* is discussed more fully later in this chapter.

APPLICATION CASE

The physical intrusion theory of *Jones* and *Jardines* was applied again in the case of *Grady v. North Carolina*,[41] where the Supreme Court of the United States considered the validity under the Fourth Amendment of a state statute requiring satellite-based lifetime monitoring of Grady for repeated sex offenses. The state courts found that the Fourth Amendment did not apply, so Grady's opposition to the application of the statute to him was denied. The United States Supreme Court reversed the holding of the state courts, finding that the Fourth Amendment did apply, but remanded the case to the state courts for an initial determination of the reasonableness of the search, which had not been determined by any state court. On remand, the Court of Appeals of North Carolina concluded that such monitoring was unreasonable under the Fourth Amendment.[42]

Aerial Surveillance

Another recurring scenario in cases involving the expectation of privacy is aerial surveillance. The Supreme Court has decided in two cases that, as long as the officer is in airspace navigable by the public and conducts the surveillance in a nonobtrusive and nontechnologically enhanced manner, such aerial surveillance does not constitute a search, even though the observations are of activities taking place within the curtilage of private dwellings. In *California v. Ciraolo*,[43] the Court upheld a fixed-wing airplane flyover at 1,000 feet; in *Florida v. Riley*,[44] the Court upheld surveillance from a helicopter hovering at 400 feet. In both cases, the Court found that the observations took place from positions within publicly navigable airspace under Federal Aviation Administration (FAA) regulations. In both cases, the officers resorted to flyovers because their attempts to observe suspected marijuana cultivation within the curtilage of the dwellings had been frustrated by a fence and a partially enclosed greenhouse, respectively.

Miscellaneous Matters Pertaining to Defining a Search

One common thread running throughout the Supreme Court's analyses of the expectation of privacy issues in the cases previously discussed is the test of how much and what kind of information has been obtained by the law enforcement activities. As we saw in the aerial surveillance cases, if the information obtained was available to the public, then the Court has concluded that there was no search. The nature of the information revealed in certain specific circumstances is a factor in determining whether a search occurred and whether the expectation of privacy was violated. Specific circumstances addressed in court cases have included chemical field testing, inspection by drug-sniffing dogs, inspection of garbage, and abandoned property.

Whether police conduct constitutes a search may depend upon such factors as the quantity or quality of information the conduct reveals. In *United States v. Jacobsen,*[45] a package shipped by Federal Express had broken partially open. FedEx employees opened it all the way to repack it in accordance with company policy and noticed in the package a baggie containing a suspicious white, powdery substance. This conduct by the FedEx employees did not trigger the Fourth Amendment because no government conduct was involved. The FedEx employees then called the Drug Enforcement Administration (DEA). The federal agent, who responded to the FedEx office, subjected the white powder to a color indicator chemical test to establish whether it was likely that the substance was cocaine. The Supreme Court held that, since the only information that the DEA agent's test revealed was whether the substance was contraband, there was no government violation of a legitimate expectation of privacy. This ruling rests on two principles: first, that there can be no legitimate expectation of privacy in contraband and, second, that when the information revealed by the government action is very limited, there is no search.

The Court reached a similar result based upon substantially similar reasoning in a case holding that subjecting luggage to a sniff test by a dog trained to signal upon smelling narcotics does not constitute a search. In the case, *United States v. Place,*[46] the Court based its decision on the facts that there was no serious intrusion, the information revealed was very limited in nature, and the information would only disclose the presence or absence of contraband, which cannot be legally possessed. In *Illinois v. Caballes,*[47] the Court turned the dicta of *Place* into a holding. The Court declared that its holding in *Caballes* was "entirely consistent" with the conclusion that the use of a thermal imager on a home is a search. "Critical" to the decision on the thermal imager in *Kyllo* "was the fact that the device was capable of detecting lawful activity," including intimate details, such as the hour at which the lady of the house might take a daily bath. In contrast, the Court noted, a dog sniff conducted during a lawful traffic stop, as it was in *Caballes,* that reveals "no information other than the location of a substance that no individual has any right to possess does not violate the Fourth Amendment."[48] Moreover, in *Florida v. Harris,*[49] the Court held that a dog certified in drug detection provided probable cause for a search of a vehicle when the dog alerted during a routine traffic stop.

Yet another dog sniff case, *Rodriguez v. United States,*[50] involved a stop for a traffic violation. Unlike the situation in *Caballes*, the officer detained the suspect after completion of the "mission" of the stop—issuing a citation—in order to subject the car to a dog sniff. The Court held that a police stop exceeding the time needed to handle the matter for which the stop was made violates the Constitution's shield against unreasonable seizures."[51]

The case of *Florida v. Jardines*[52] also involved a dog sniff, this time of the front door of a home, accessible by the officer walking on the porch. The trained drug detection dog alerted to the presence of drugs, confirming a report that marijuana was being grown within the home. Based on that alert, the officers obtained a warrant, entered the home, searched, and discovered marijuana plants. A five-Justice majority adopted the approach set forth in the *Jones* case the year before concluding that the warrantless dog sniff constituted a search in violation of the Fourth Amendment. Citing both *Jones* and *Katz*, the majority concluded that "[t]he officers were gathering information in an area belonging to Jardines and immediately surrounding his house—in the curtilage of the house, which we have held enjoys protection as part of the home itself. And they gathered that information by physically entering and occupying the area to engage in conduct not explicitly or implicitly permitted by the homeowner."

Finally, the status of a citizen's expectation of privacy in relation to garbage and abandoned property must be examined. When one places garbage for collection in containers out on the street, there is no legitimate expectation of privacy. In *California v. Greenwood*,[53] the Supreme Court noted that the garbage was outside the curtilage and concluded that the Fourth Amendment does not protect information knowingly exposed to the public (relying on the aerial surveillance cases) or voluntarily turned over to others (relying on the pen register case). Both of these principles also relate to material that has been abandoned.

WHAT IS A SEIZURE?

The Fourth Amendment extends to persons, houses, papers, and effects and requires that searches and seizures thereof not be unreasonable. Seizures of objects implicate different values than seizures of persons. A **seizure of property** occurs "when there is some meaningful interference with an individual's possessory interests in that property."[54] Destroying property, taking property from the person's possession, and preventing persons from entering or leaving their homes constitute meaningful interferences with individuals' possessory interests.

The **seizure of a person** may be by means of a formal arrest or by lesser means of restriction of freedom. Formal arrest, when a person is handcuffed and taken to the station, is clear-cut. More complex issues arise when there is no formal arrest and the defendant argues that he or she was seized within the meaning of the Fourth Amendment. The United States Supreme Court has provided a definition by which to judge whether a person is seized. A person is seized when, (1) by means of physical force or show of authority, the person's freedom of movement is restrained and only if, (2) in view of all of the circumstances surrounding the incident, a reasonable person would not have believed he or she was free to leave.[55]

In *Florida v. Bostick*,[56] two officers, with badges and insignia, boarded a bus bound from Miami to Atlanta during a stopover in Fort Lauderdale. One of the officers held a zipper pouch, which contained a plainly visible pistol. The officers were executing a plan of random checks on buses and, without any ability to state a suspicion, approached the defendant, who was sitting in the back of the bus, identified themselves, and questioned him. During the questioning, the officers requested and received permission to search the defendant's luggage, in which they found narcotics. The Supreme Court held that, under these circumstances, the defendant was not necessarily seized by the officers' approach and questioning. The Court stated that the correct standard for determining whether a person in Bostick's position has been seized is not whether a reasonable person would

SEIZURE OF PROPERTY
A seizure that occurs when there is some meaningful interference with an individual's possessory interests in that property.

SEIZURE OF A PERSON
A seizure of the person occurs when, (1) by means of physical force or show of authority, the person's freedom of movement is restrained and only if, (2) in view of all of the circumstances surrounding the incident, a reasonable person would not have believed he or she was free to leave.

feel free to leave. The correct standard is whether "a reasonable person would feel free to decline the officers' requests or otherwise terminate the encounter."[57] According to the Court, this new standard is logical because the defendant's freedom of movement is already restricted by being a passenger on a bus, a factor not attributable to any action by the police.

If there is a show of authority by the officer and, under the circumstances, a reasonable person would not feel free to leave, there must also be a submission to authority before the encounter can be deemed a "seizure." As the Supreme Court in *California v. Hodari D.* stated, a seizure "requires either physical force or, where that is absent, submission to the assertion of authority."[58] A seizure occurs when there has been an application of physical force to the person, even when the person manages to break free and escape. On the other hand, when an officer asserts his or her authority, be it by flashing lights or a pointed gun, and the suspect flees, no seizure has occurred until that suspect is captured or gives up.

APPLICATION CASE

In *United States v. Drayton,*[59] the Court applied the *Bostick* test to another bus sweep and found that those passengers had not been seized. In *Drayton,* one police officer knelt on the driver's seat, facing the rear of the bus, while another stood at the back of the bus, facing forward. A third officer walked forward from the back of the bus, stopping next to each passenger, to whom he spoke. The police did not tell the passengers that they had the right not to cooperate. In upholding the ensuing consensual searches, the Court found nothing that would suggest to a reasonable person that he or she was barred from leaving the bus.

WAYS OF MAKING A REASONABLE SEARCH AND SEIZURE

Three methods have been developed whereby a search or seizure is generally accepted as reasonable, thus allowing the fruits of the search or seizure to be introduced at trial:

1. searches and seizures made pursuant to a search warrant;
2. warrantless searches and seizures that have been declared reasonable via a "well-delineated exception" to the warrant clause; and
3. less intrusive searches and seizures, which are made on less than probable cause, such as searches and seizures under the *Terry* doctrine, discussed later in this chapter (see p. 322), based on a "reasonable suspicion."

Searches and seizures conducted pursuant to a valid warrant require probable cause. In determining the existence of probable cause, the courts examine the sources of information provided by the officer in support of the warrant. In addition to the requirement of probable cause, a valid warrant must satisfy the requirements that the place to be searched and the person or thing to be seized be specifically set out. The courts review warrants and warrant applications from a practical, common-sense point of view with respect to the issuance and service of the warrant. The six "well-delineated" exceptions to the warrant clause are

1. search incident to a lawful arrest (SILA);
2. consent;
3. vehicle and container searches;
4. inventory searches;
5. exigent circumstances searches; and
6. plain view searches.

Finally, beginning in 1968, the Supreme Court of the United States began to interpret the Fourth Amendment's unreasonable search and seizure prohibition to encompass a balancing of governmental interests against the privacy interests of citizens. This balancing allows that, under certain circumstances, reasonable searches and seizures without warrants and without probable cause can occur. Thus, under the decision in the *Terry* case, discussed later in this chapter (see p. 322), in certain circumstances, searches and seizures may be valid based on reasonable suspicion rather than probable cause.

Even though these methods of search are generally acceptable, they are not without their complications. Involved in each method are a number of legal technicalities that must be observed or the search may still be deemed unreasonable. However, space will not permit a complete discussion of all the ramifications of the laws as they pertain to search and seizure. No other field relating to criminal evidence has been explored in writing more than the subject of search and seizure.

SEARCH PURSUANT TO A SEARCH WARRANT

The Fourth Amendment to the United States Constitution guarantees to the people the right to be secure against unreasonable searches and seizures. The framers of this constitutional provision realized that there would be times when reasonable searches and seizures would be necessary and expedient for the protection of the people—when a crime has been committed and the perpetrator of that crime has attempted to conceal himself or herself or the fruits of the crime. Therefore, the framers included a provision in the Fourth Amendment that searches and seizures may be properly conducted pursuant to a warrant that will not be issued, "but upon probable cause, supported by oath or affirmation, and particularly describing the place to be searched, and the persons or things to be seized." These requirements specifically prohibit general warrants, preventing a "general, exploratory rummaging in a person's belongings."[60] If these requirements are not carefully adhered to, the search may be deemed unreasonable and the seized evidence excluded.

Definition of a Search Warrant

A **search warrant** is a written order, issued in the name of the people, upon probable cause, by a neutral and detached magistrate to a peace officer directing the officer to search a particular person or place and to seize specifically described property and bring it before the magistrate.

SEARCH WARRANT
A written order issued upon probable cause by a neutral and detached magistrate, in the name of the people, to a peace officer directing the officer to search a particular person or place and to seize specifically described property and bring it before the magistrate.

Grounds for Issuing a Search Warrant

Although the grounds for the issuance of a search warrant may vary slightly from one jurisdiction to another, they are generally the same. A search warrant may be issued when it authorizes a search for particular

1. property that is the **fruit of a crime**, such as stolen or embezzled property;
2. property that is an **instrumentality of a crime**, meaning that the property was used as the means of committing a crime, such as a gun used in a robbery;
3. property that is **evidence of a crime**, tending to show that a felony has been committed or that a particular individual has committed a felony, such as a bloody shirt;
4. property that is **contraband**, meaning any property that is unlawful to produce or possess, such as narcotics; or
5. persons for whom there is **probable cause** to believe that they have on their person one of the types of property named in the first four categories, or for whom there is a warrant for their arrest.

Procedure to Obtain a Search Warrant

An officer may not merely go to a magistrate and request that a search warrant be issued for the search of a person or a place. The officer must be able to show that there is sufficient reason, or probable cause, to believe that one of the foregoing grounds for the issuance of a search warrant exists. This belief must be based on facts articulated in a written and sworn application for a warrant. This application is known as an affidavit. The officer must then seek approval of the warrant application from a supervisor or, in some jurisdictions, a prosecutor. Once supervisory approval is obtained, the officer can then go to a judge or magistrate to submit the warrant application and secure the issuance of the warrant. The person issuing the warrant must be a **neutral magistrate** or judge. The officer usually will find the judge in the courthouse, but, if the circumstances demand, the officer may even have to go to the judge's home outside normal working hours. It is also possible for a judge to issue a warrant by telephone. The procedure and circumstances for issuance of a telephonic warrant vary from jurisdiction to jurisdiction.

Before issuing the warrant, the magistrate must be satisfied that the facts set forth in the affidavit give rise to probable cause. If the affidavit contains hearsay information, such as from an informant, the judge will closely scrutinize the affidavit. If the magistrate does not think that the officer has enough facts to establish probable cause, or that the hearsay information is unreliable, the magistrate may, in some jurisdictions, question the officer. The questioning may provide additional facts and circumstances sufficient to support the belief that the items sought are at the place where they are alleged to be. Or the questioning may supply a more complete description of the thing or person to be seized in order to meet the "rule of particularity," i.e., the requirement of specifying the items sought. These questions and answers will be reduced to writing and made a part of the affidavit filed by the officer. If, after this questioning takes place, the magistrate is convinced that sufficient probable cause exists, the magistrate will issue the warrant. Magistrates usually spend only a few minutes reviewing an affidavit, and few applications for warrants are rejected by magistrates. See Figure 9–1 for a sample search warrant and affidavit (the sample is from the 1994 O.J. Simpson criminal case).

FRUIT OF A CRIME
Property that is seizable by a police officer, such as stolen or embezzled property.

INSTRUMENTALITY OF A CRIME
Property that is seizable by a police officer that was used as the means of committing a crime, such as a gun.

EVIDENCE OF A CRIME
Any object that demonstrates that a crime has been committed.

CONTRABAND
Property that is seizable by a law enforcement officer that is unlawful for anyone to possess.

PROBABLE CAUSE
Although the Fourth Amendment provides that no warrant shall be issued except upon probable cause, it does not spell out what probable cause is. The definition of probable cause has been developed primarily through court decisions and interpretation.

NEUTRAL MAGISTRATE
A person who acts as magistrate (or judge) who can issue a warrant upon application of a law enforcement officer. Such person cannot be associated with law enforcement or the prosecution.

SW No. 940093

STATE OF CALIFORNIA–COUNTY OF LOS ANGELES
SEARCH WARRANT AND AFFIDAVIT
(AFFIDAVIT)

Philip L. Vannatter, being sworn, says that on the basis of the information contained within this Search Warrant and Affidavit and the attached and incorporated Statement of Probable Cause, he/she has probable cause to believe and does believe that the property described below is lawfully seizable pursuant to Penal Code Section 1524, as indicated below, and is now located at the locations set forth below. Wherefore, affiant requests that this Search Warrant be issued.

Philip L. Vannatter,

NIGHT SEARCH REQUESTED: YES [ ] NO [X]

(Signature of Affiant)

(SEARCH WARRANT)

THE PEOPLE OF THE STATE OF CALIFORNIA TO ANY SHERIFF, POLICEMAN OR PEACE OFFICER IN THE COUNTY OF LOS ANGELES: proof by affidavit having been before me by Philip L. Vannatter, that there is probable cause to believe that the property described herein may be found at the locations set forth herein and that it is lawfully seizable pursuant to Penal Code Section 1524 as indicated below by "x"(s) in that it

_____ was stolen or embezzled

____X____ was used as the means of committing a felony

_____ is possessed by a person with the intent to use it as means of committing a public offense or is possessed by another to whom he or she may have delivered it for the purpose of concealing it or preventing its discovery.

____X____ tends to show that a felony has been committed or that a particular person has committed a felony.

_____ tends to show that sexual exploitation of a child, in violation of >Penal Code Section 311.3 has or is occurring.

YOU ARE THEREFORE COMMANDED TO SEARCH:

360 Rockingham Avenue, West Los Angeles, California. A single family residence located on the southeast corner of Rockingham Avenue and Ashford Street. The residence is two stories constructed of light brown wood trim and beige stucco. The property is fenced by a solid plant hedge with green wrought iron gates facing Rockingham Avenue and Ashford Street. The number 360 is clearly painted on the curb adjacent to the Rockingham Gate.

FOR THE FOLLOWING PROPERTY:

Presence of traces of human blood, clothing, surfaces, or any material that may contain blood, any object that may have been used to inflict the fatal injuries to the victims, including but no limited to objects capable of inflicting blunt force trauma, firearms or knives. Paperwork indicating the identity of the occupants of the residence to which the occupants have access, and the 1994 Ford Bronco, California license 3CWZ788.

AND TO SEIZE IT IF FOUND and bring it forthwith before me, or this court, at the courthouse of this court. This Search Warrant and incorporated Affidavit was sworn to and subscribed before me this 13th day of June, 1994, at 10:45 A.M. Wherefore, I find probable cause for the issuance of this Search Warrant and do issue it

Linda K. Lefkowitz,

NIGHT SEARCH APPROVED: YES [ ] NO [ ]

Judge of the Superior/Municipal Court, Los Angeles Judicial District

Your affiant Philip L. Vannatter # 14877 is a Police Detective for the Los Angeles Police Department, assigned to Robbery-Homicide Division, Homicide Special Section. Your affiant has been a police officer for the City of Los Angeles for over 25 years. Your affiant has been assigned to Robbery-Homicide Division for the past 15 years working the Officer-Involved Shooting Section and Homicide Special Section.

Your affiant worked homicide at West Los Angeles and Wilshire Division prior to being assigned to Robbery-Homicide Division, and has investigated in excess of 200 homicides. Your affiant has attended numerous training sessions and seminars, and has qualified in Los Angeles County Municipal and Superior Court as a homicide expert.

On Monday June 13, 1994 at 0430 hours your affiant and his partner F.D. Lange #13552 were assigned the investigation of the double murder of Nicole Brown AKA Nicole Simpson and an unidentified male, White at 875 South Bundy Drive, West Los Angeles the residence of Nicole Brown. The facts contained herein are summarized as follows:

During the course of the investigation it was determined that Nicole Brown was the ex-wife of O.J. Simpson and had two children by Simpson. The children were located and were removed from the residence on Bundy Drive.

During the course of the investigation detectives followed up to 360 Rockingham Avenue, West Los Angeles, the residence of O.J. Simpson in an attempt to make a notification. Upon arriving at the location detectives were unable to arouse anyone at the residence. Detectives observed a 1994 White Ford Bronco, California license 3CWZ788 registered to Hertz Corporation parked at the west side of the residence headed north on Rockingham Avenue. Detectives observed what appeared to be human blood, later confirmed by Scientific Investigation personnel to be human blood on the driver's door handle of the vehicle.

Detectives subsequently aroused O.J. Simpson's daughter, Arnell Simpson, at the residence and determined Simpson was not at home. During the interview of Simpson's daughter, she identified the Ford Bronco as belonging to her father, who was the primary driver. Blood droplets were subsequently observed leading from the vehicle on the street to the front door of the residence.

During the securing of the residence a man's leather glove containing human blood was also observed on the south side of the residence. This glove closely resembled a brown leather glove located at the crime scene at the feet of the unidentified male, White victim.

It was determined by interviews of Simpson's daughter and a friend, Brian Kaelin, Simpson had left on an unexpected flight to Chicago during the early morning hours of June 13, 1994, and was last seen at the residence at approximately 2300 hours, June 12, 1994.

It is prayed that a search warrant be issued to search 360 Rockingham Avenue for the presence of traces of human blood, clothing, surfaces, or any material that may contain blood, any object that may have been used to inflict the fatal injuries to the victims, including but not limited to objects capable of inflicting blunt force trauma, firearms or knives. Paperwork indicting the identity of the occupants of the residence to show dominion and control of the residence. Any and all garages or outbuildings associated to the residence to which the occupants have access, and the 1994 Ford Bronco, California license 3CWZ788.

FIGURE 9–1 Sample search warrant and affidavit.

Probable cause to search "exists if the facts and circumstances within [the officers'] knowledge and of which they [have] reasonably trustworthy information [are] sufficient in themselves to warrant a man of reasonable caution in the belief that *an item subject to seizure will be found in the place to be searched*."[61] There must be a "fair probability"[62] that the property subject to being seized by the government (contraband, fruits, instrumentalities, or evidence of a crime) is presently in the specific place to be searched. In other words, if it is alleged that certain stolen property is believed to be at a particular place, there must be enough facts presented to cause a person of reasonable caution to believe, by a fair probability, that the stolen property is at that place. A fair probability has not been defined by the courts affirmatively but has been specifically said to be less than a preponderance of the evidence, meaning somewhat less than a 50 percent likelihood.[63]

PROBABLE CAUSE TO SEARCH
When the facts and circumstances within an officer's knowledge, and of which he or she has reasonably trustworthy information, are sufficient in themselves to warrant a person of reasonable caution in the belief that *an item subject to seizure will be found in the place to be searched*.

APPLICATION CASE

In *Maryland v. Pringle*,[64] an officer stopped a car, with three occupants, for speeding. When the driver, a man named Partlow, opened the glove compartment to retrieve the vehicle registration, the officer observed a large amount of rolled-up money in the glove compartment. When the officer asked for permission to search, Partlow consented. The search of the vehicle yielded $763 from the glove compartment and five plastic glassine baggies containing cocaine from behind the backseat armrest. The officer questioned all three occupants about the ownership of the drugs and money and told them that, if no one admitted to ownership of the drugs, he was going to arrest them all. The men offered no information regarding the ownership of the drugs or money. All three were placed under arrest and transported to the police station. Later, defendant Pringle, who was the front seat passenger, confessed that the cocaine was his. A jury convicted him of possession with intent to distribute cocaine and possession of cocaine.

Appealing the conviction, Pringle argued that his confession should have been suppressed because he was illegally arrested. More specifically, he claimed that the officer had no probable cause to arrest him, because the officer did not know whom the cocaine belonged to, since there were three occupants of the car, the cocaine was in the backseat behind an armrest, and Pringle was in the front seat. The United States Supreme Court rejected Pringle's argument and affirmed the conviction, stating,

> We think it "an entirely reasonable inference from" these facts "that any or all three of the occupants had knowledge of, and exercised dominion and control over, the cocaine. . . . Thus, a reasonable officer could conclude that there was probable cause to believe Pringle committed the crime of possession of cocaine, either solely or jointly.

The Supreme Court's ruling overturned the decision of the Maryland high court, which had reversed Pringle's conviction for lack of probable cause. The Maryland court had "dismissed" the money as a factor for the officer to consider in finding probable cause. The Supreme Court disapproved of the Maryland court's "consideration of the money in isolation," reaffirming that the police officer was justified in taking into account the money and everything else in the "totality of the circumstances" supporting the probable cause conclusion.

Like probable cause to search, probable cause to arrest is defined in terms of the information possessed by the arresting officer. Thus, **probable cause to arrest** exists when the facts and circumstances within the officer's knowledge, and of which he or she has reasonably trustworthy information, are sufficient to warrant a person of reasonable caution to believe, by a fair probability, that a particular individual has committed, or is committing, a particular offense.

PROBABLE CAUSE TO ARREST
When the facts and circumstances within the officer's knowledge, and of which he or she has reasonably trustworthy information, are sufficient to warrant a person of reasonable caution to believe, by a fair probability, that a particular individual has committed, or is committing, a particular offense.

APPLICATION CASE

In *Draper v. United States,*[65] an informant told the police that the defendant had gone to Chicago on a particular day and would return on a certain day with three ounces of heroin in his possession. The informant further described with particularity what the defendant would be wearing, the tan zipper bag he would be carrying, and the defendant's habit of walking fast. However, the informant did not state how he obtained his information. Nonetheless, the Supreme Court held that the hearsay information supplied by the informant was sufficiently reliable to support probable cause. The informant described the criminal activity of the defendant in such detail, which was corroborated by the officers' observations, to support the inference that the informant's information was reliable.

Source of Information

In order to establish probable cause, it is not necessary for the officer seeking a search warrant to have personal knowledge of the facts stated in the application or affidavit. The officer's information may stem from a variety of sources. The officer may receive it from a superior officer, a confidential informant, an anonymous telephone call, a reliable person in the community, another officer who is an expert in a particular field (such as narcotics or bookmaking), or personal observations. The source of information is often hearsay in nature, and the information might not be admissible at trial. But the information must have been supplied by a source that an ordinarily prudent person would accept as reasonably trustworthy. Whether the information provided in the affidavit is reliable will be determined by a magistrate, taking into account the "totality of circumstances" surrounding the application for the warrant.

Confidential Informant or Anonymous Source

Many times, when information is furnished to an officer, it is deemed advisable to keep the identity of the informant confidential. The informant does not have to be identified in the affidavit in order to establish probable cause for issuing a search warrant, but there must be enough facts set forth to enable the magistrate to determine the reliability of the information furnished.

If the information that the officer provides in the affidavit is hearsay, by way of an informant or an anonymous source, then the magistrate must decide whether the information is reliable based on the "totality of circumstances." This means that the magistrate must make a practical, common-sense decision whether, given all the circumstances set forth in the affidavit, including the veracity (or believability) and the basis of knowledge of persons supplying the hearsay, and corroboration through other sources of information, there is a fair probability that the thing to be seized will be found in a particular place. The basis of knowledge of the person supplying the hearsay may be shown if the informant states that he or she personally observed the reported facts. Or it may also be demonstrated by self-verifying detail—when

APPLICATION CASE

In *Illinois v. Gates,*[68] the Bloomingdale, Illinois, Police Department received an anonymous letter informing them that a married couple in town was dealing in large quantities of marijuana, which they transported by automobile from Florida. The letter predicted a drug run, giving specific details and a specific date. Detective Mader, acting on this tip, investigated the couple's activities, corroborating much of the predicted behavior. On the basis of the tip and the investigation, the detective sought and obtained a warrant to search the couple's home and automobile upon their return from Florida. In upholding the issuance of the warrant and the subsequent search and seizure of 350 pounds of marijuana, the Court stated that the *Aguilar v. Texas*[69] and *United States v. Spinelli*[70] two-pronged test for probable cause based upon an informant's tip should not be rigidly applied. Instead, the Court adopted a totality of the circumstances test for probable cause. In the totality of the circumstances, an informant's basis of knowledge and veracity are factors to be taken into account but should not be rigidly applied. Following is the *Gates* Court's statement describing the test it adopted:[71]

> [W]e reaffirm the totality of the circumstances analysis that traditionally has informed probable cause determinations. . . . The task of the issuing magistrate is simply to make a practical, common-sense decision whether, given all the circumstances set forth in the affidavit before him, including the "veracity" and "basis of knowledge" of persons supplying hearsay information, there is a fair probability that contraband, or evidence of a crime will be found in a particular place.

FYI

In both the *Draper* and *Gates* cases, the information provided by the informant "contained a range of details relating not just to easily obtained facts and conditions existing at the time of the tip, but to future actions of third parties not easily predicted."[72] In short, the United States Supreme Court was persuaded that a source seemingly possessed of inside information could be counted as reliable.

the informant describes the criminal activity in such detail as to allow an inference that he or she gathered the information in a reliable way. Accordingly, if information is furnished by an unnamed informant, such information should be set forth in the affidavit in as much detail as possible in order to establish the informant's basis of knowledge.

The veracity of the person supplying hearsay information may be shown by evidence demonstrating either that the informant is a credible person or that his or her information is reliable. For instance, believability may be shown if the officer relates that prior information furnished by the same informant has been found to be true and reliable. The number of times information has been furnished, or the period of time over which reliable information has been given, will assist the magistrate in making a determination that the informant is credible or his or her information is reliable.

If either the basis of knowledge or the veracity factors (or both) are lacking, there may be some other means of corroborating the hearsay. It may be possible to determine the reliability of the information by reference to investigative leads. Probable cause can be established by investigations that verify, or tend to confirm, the information provided by the informant or anonymous source. In these circumstances, the officer would be establishing probable cause from his or her own observations and knowledge and not that of an informant. However, this confirming knowledge must have been gained through proper conduct and not by an illegal entry, trespass, or other violation of the law.

Judicial Review of Probable Cause

Just because a search or seizure was made pursuant to a search warrant does not ensure in all instances that the search or seizure will have been reasonable. The trial court, and later an appellate court, when called upon by the accused, will make a careful review of the issuance of a warrant and make an independent decision. Recent United States Supreme Court decisions require an appellate court to be deferential to a magistrate's finding of probable cause.

As discussed previously, probable cause is determined from the **totality of the circumstances for probable cause**, which is a fluid concept based on nontechnical,

TOTALITY OF THE CIRCUMSTANCES FOR PROBABLE CAUSE The test for probable cause, which is a fluid concept based on nontechnical, common-sense considerations.

common-sense considerations. Probable cause, therefore, is not determined under a neat set of legal rules but is determined in light of how reasonable people act in everyday life. The Supreme Court has defined probable cause this way because it felt that a rigid set of legal rules would unduly hamper law enforcement. As one might logically conclude, an appellate court should defer to a magistrate's finding because the magistrate is in a better position to determine probable cause under the "totality of circumstances" existing at the time of the application. The magistrate's determination of probable cause does not depend upon certainty but upon probability, and, more particularly, upon a **fair probability**.

FAIR PROBABILITY
The test for the amount of belief of suspicion required for a determination of probable cause.

APPLICATION CASE

An officer may be possessed of probable cause and reasonable suspicion if the suspicion is based on a mistake of fact or law. In *Heien v. North* Carolina,[73] an officer was following a suspicious vehicle and noticed that only one of the vehicle's brake lights was working. The officer stopped the vehicle, got consent to search the vehicle, found cocaine, and arrested Heien. The officer believed that state law required two working brake lights. This was a mistake of law because the applicable state law required only a single "stop lamp" on the rear of the vehicle. In upholding the officer's reasonable suspicion of a law violation, the United States Supreme Court noted that mistakes of fact had long been recognized as properly supporting a finding of probable cause, because it only requires probability not certainty. As long as the mistake is reasonable, then there is no violation of the Fourth Amendment. The Court found in this case that the same principle applies to mistakes of law and reasonable suspicion.

The Supreme Court reaffirmed the fluidity of the totality of the circumstances test of *Gates* in the 2013 decision in *Florida v. Harris*.[74] Officer Wheetley pulled over Harris' truck because it had an expired license plate. When Wheetley observed that Harris was extremely nervous, Wheetley brought his trained narcotics detection dog, Aldo, to the truck. Wheetley walked Aldo around the truck for a "free air sniff." When Aldo signaled that he detected drugs at the driver-side door handle, Wheetley searched the truck, finding the ingredients for making methamphetamine, but none of the drugs Aldo was trained to detect. Harris was convicted of possessing one of the ingredients for use in manufacturing methamphetamine.

Harris' motion to suppress the evidence was denied by the trial court on the grounds that Wheetley had probable cause to search based on Aldo's alert. The Florida Supreme Court reversed, holding that, to sustain a probable cause finding based on a trained detection dog's alert, the state had to introduce extensive evidence of the dog's field performance records, which the state had failed to do in this case. The United States Supreme Court unanimously reversed the decision by the Florida court, holding that the Florida court had "flouted" the "fluid" probable cause concept of the totality of the circumstances test of *Gates* and its progeny. Aldo's certification and training programs, according to the Court, themselves provided sufficient reason for Officer Wheetley to trust his alert.

Consequently, given that a magistrate determines probable cause under such amorphous concepts as "fair probability" and "totality of circumstances," an appellate court will not likely reverse a magistrate's determination.

When applying for a warrant, sometimes it is necessary to leave out specific details about an informant for his or her safety. For example, it would be unwise to include detailed information about the date or time of an informant's controlled narcotics buy from a drug dealer. Through the process of elimination, the drug dealer would be able to determine the informant's identity, thus jeopardizing the informant's life.

Particularity of Description of Property to Be Searched or Seized

The Fourth Amendment to the United States Constitution provides that the place to be searched and the things to be seized must be particularly described. Since "particularly described" is not spelled out, court decisions have set forth certain guidelines.

First, the court considers the purpose of the requirement of particular description. The requirement of particularity seeks to prevent an indiscriminate, blanket authority to search a place or an area and to prohibit a wholesale seizure without limits. Consequently, the court will look very carefully at the description of the place to be searched. If it is not specifically designated, the magistrate may refuse to issue the search warrant. The following is an example description in which the premises to be searched are a dwelling house: premises located at 129 Main Street, Walnutville, Maine, consisting of a white, one-story dwelling with blue trim, with an attic, a basement, a detached garage, and a tool shed (if the grounds surrounding the residence and outbuildings are to be included in the search, notation to that effect should be made in the search warrant). If the occupant of the premises is known, the occupant's name should also be included in the description of the premises searched.

Being vague or mistakenly describing the premises to be searched does not necessarily invalidate a warrant. For instance, in *Maryland v. Garrison,*[75] the police had a warrant to search the third-floor apartment of one McWebb. The officers did not know at the time that the third floor had more than one apartment. The police mistakenly searched the apartment of the defendant, Garrison, thinking it was McWebb's. They found contraband in this apartment and charged Garrison with its possession. The Supreme Court upheld the search and seizure as objectively understandable and reasonable. Although in retrospect the warrant was overbroad, the police, in light of the information available to them at the time of the search, executed the warrant under a good faith belief that they were acting within the scope of the warrant.

Discovery of Other Property—the Plain View Doctrine

Under the particularity requirement for warrants, the scope of the search authorized is limited to those items named in the warrant. Thus, the officer, while executing a warrant, may only seize those items that are described in the warrant.

However, if the officer, while conducting a search within the reasonable scope of the warrant, observes material that the officer has probable cause to believe is subject to seizure, he or she may seize it. As long as the material is within plain view and the officer is in a lawful position when the observation is made, anything that the officer recognizes to be fruits, instrumentalities, contraband, or evidence may be seized. Under this doctrine, the officer does not have to be blind to other items that may be observed on the premises, even though those items are not described in the search warrant.

The plain view doctrine is actually an exception to the requirement of a warrant for a seizure and is discussed under the warrant clause exceptions later in this chapter. There is a significant aspect of that doctrine as it applies to the issues related to warrants. Even if an officer is aware that certain objects not listed in the warrant may be present and discovered during the search, the officer may seize those items if they are discovered in plain view during the course of the search authorized by the warrant. In other words, inadvertence is not a requirement for the plain view doctrine to apply.

An example will help demonstrate the relationship between inadvertence and the plain view doctrine. In *Horton v. California*,[76] an officer investigating an armed robbery obtained a warrant to search a suspect's home. Evidence led the officer to suspect the accused, and the officer applied for a warrant. In the affidavit, the officer referred to police reports that described the weapons used in the robbery as well as the proceeds—jewelry and cash—but the warrant issued by the magistrate authorized only a search for the proceeds, including three specifically described rings.

The officer searched the residence pursuant to the warrant, but he did not find the stolen property. During the course of the search, however, he did discover the weapons in plain view and seized them, along with other items of evidence that were not the proceeds. The Court held that, although the officer knew about the weapons before the search and did not list them in the warrant, the seizure of them in plain view was valid. Since the officer did not extend the search beyond that authorized by the warrant, and the search as conducted was supported by probable cause, the seizure of the weapons was legitimate. If the officer had found the proceeds before discovering the weapons, the search authorized by the warrant would have been completed and the weapons could not have been the subject of a valid search and seizure.

Night Service of a Warrant

A common law tradition held that a person's right to privacy in his or her home was especially strong during the nighttime hours. Consequently, there existed a belief that nighttime service of a warrant required a degree of certainty greater than just probable cause. However, in 1974, the Supreme Court held that there is no Fourth Amendment requirement that warrants may be served only at night upon a showing of special circumstances.[77] Similarly, a majority of the states do not have special rules for the service of warrants at night. However, in 28 states, the execution of search warrants is limited to daytime hours, absent some special reason and authorization. Fourteen other states expressly allow the execution of a search warrant at any time. The remaining 13 states have no rules, either court made or statutory, that restrict the execution of search warrants to the day.[78]

See Figure 9-2, listing those states with restrictions upon nighttime execution of search warrants and requiring some special showing by law enforcement that will have to be made before a nighttime search warrant will be issued. A common restriction is that the affidavit supporting the search be "positive" that the property being sought is in the place to be searched.[79] This means that the officer must include information in the affidavit that will justify the assertion of a positive belief that the particular property is in the place to be searched. Another common restriction is that a nighttime search warrant will only be issued for "good cause," which focuses on the need to search the premises in the nighttime, rather than the likelihood that the property being sought is on the premises. Good cause will ordinarily require that the officer show that the nighttime search is justified by some exigency, such as apprehending a fleeing killer or a risk that evidence will be destroyed.

ON THE JOB

When seeking a search warrant, remember to list *everything* and *everyone* that you anticipate finding and *everywhere* you intend to search. This is important for several reasons. First, assume just one or two items are listed on the warrant, such as the gun used in a homicide, yet you expect to find the rest of the instrumentalities, fruits, and evidence during the search. In such a case, if you found the gun quickly, you would no longer be authorized to continue the search because the warrant was limited in scope to the gun. Anything seized after the gun was found would probably be inadmissible.

Second, you can be precluded from searching certain areas or places if you list only some of the items you are seeking. For example, if you believe burglary tools and stolen televisions will be found at a residence but list only the televisions, then you cannot search any area that is too small for a television, such as in drawers, small cabinets, and cupboards or under the furniture.

Finally, you should carefully list all the areas you want to search so that the magistrate can determine the reasonableness of the request. For example, assume you have reliable information that stolen money is buried in the backyard of a residence. If you were to write "search of the backyard" on the warrant, the magistrate might issue a warrant thinking that an above-ground search has been approved. However, your intent was to bring in a backhoe and dig up the yard. A magistrate will expect much more information in order to approve the digging up of a backyard than to conduct an above-ground search.

Also, for the purpose of executing a warrant, there is no uniformity as to what constitutes daytime or nighttime. One view is that nighttime is that period between sunrise and sunset. Other states take the view that search warrants may be executed only during specified hours, such as 8 A.M. to 8 P.M.

Who May Serve a Warrant

A search warrant may be served only by a peace officer, not by a private citizen. A search warrant may be served by any one of the officers, or class of officers, mentioned in the warrant. If a particular officer, and no others, is named in the search warrant, that officer, or someone who is aiding him or her while the named officer is present, must serve the warrant.

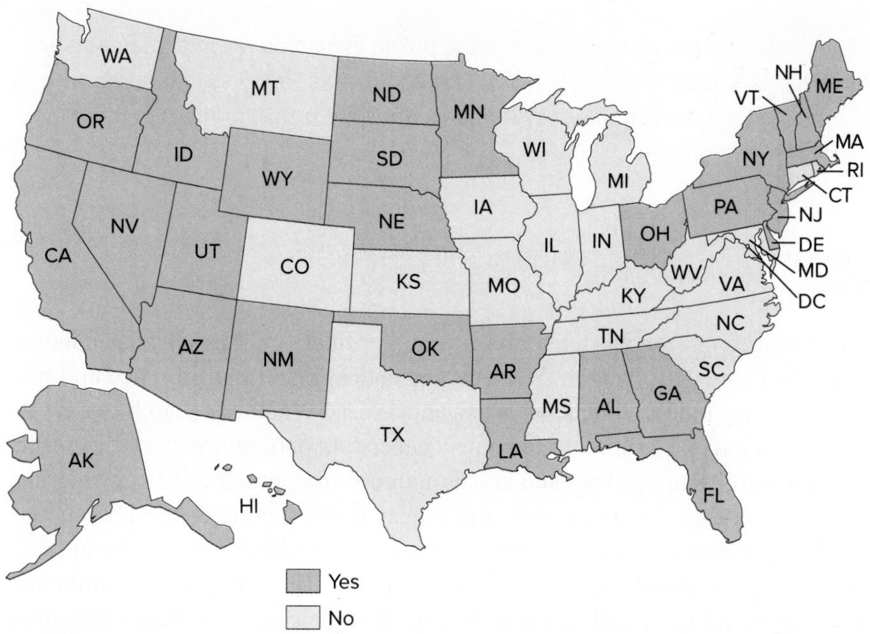

FIGURE 9–2 States with special restrictions upon service of warrants at night.

Yes

No

Usually, the officer has the search warrant in his or her possession at the time the officer is going to execute the search but not all states have statutes requiring this. The usual practice is that, when a search is made pursuant to a search warrant, the officer executing the search shows the original search warrant to the occupant of the premises to be searched. The officer then furnishes the occupant with a copy of the warrant and the affidavit before the search. If there is no one present at the time of the search, a copy of the search warrant and affidavit should be posted in a conspicuous place inside the premises. Taping the warrant on a living room TV screen works well, since people usually notice that their premises have been entered and usually check to see if portable items, such as TV sets, have been stolen.

APPLICATION CASE

In *Wilson v. Layne*,[80] the Wilsons brought a civil suit against the United States Marshals Service and the local Sheriff's Department (Montgomery County, Maryland), claiming that their Fourth Amendment rights were violated when the peace officers brought the media to observe and record the execution of arrest warrants for their son, Dominic Wilson. Dominic was a wanted suspected violent criminal, one of many who were the subject of a major operation of the Department of Justice aimed at apprehending dangerous criminals. The officers were not aware that the residence they entered was the home of Dominic's parents, not Dominic. The Supreme Court agreed with the Wilsons and held that it violates the homeowner's Fourth Amendment rights "for police to bring members of the media or other third parties into a home during the execution of a warrant when the presence of the third parties . . . was not in aid of the execution of the warrant."[81] When the police execute a warrant, their power to intrude is limited to the objectives of the intrusion. Bringing journalists who do not aid in the execution of a warrant exceeds the power granted to them by the Fourth Amendment.

Knock and Announce and the Use of Force in Execution of a Warrant

KNOCK AND ANNOUNCE, OR KNOCK AND NOTICE
The constitutional requirement that, before an officer may execute a search warrant by forcibly entering the premises, the officer must knock and announce his or her presence and purpose for entering.

Before an officer may execute a search warrant, the officer must **knock and announce** (this requirement is also known as **knock and notice**) his or her presence and purpose for entering, unless some kind of exigency exists. Whether a search of a dwelling is ruled reasonable or unreasonable may depend, in part, on whether the officers executing a search warrant knocked and announced their presence before entering. If, after making this announcement, the officer is not admitted, the officer may break into the premises in order to make the search. An officer may use the amount of force reasonably necessary to carry out the search. The officer may restrain persons who try to interfere with the search, and, in some cases, the officer may even arrest the ones who interfere. The officer may break into locked rooms and closets if admittance is not otherwise granted. But the search warrant does not give the officer blanket authority to do damage to the premises not necessary to accomplish the search or to otherwise act unreasonably in conducting the search.

ON THE JOB

Officers' actions in the execution of a search warrant must be reasonable. For example, when searching a bedroom for small items (such as drugs), it is reasonable for officers to remove, search, and place items (such as clothing) in a central location in the room (such as the bed). They may also remove, search, and replace picture frames, perfume bottles, and similar items on shelves or move or turn over furniture. It would be unreasonable for the officers to throw picture frames, other easily breakable items, computers, televisions, or clothes maliciously onto the floor or fail to return furniture to an upright position. Officers should place perishable food back into the refrigerator and place medicines back into medicine cabinets. In other words, reasonable actions are based on common sense. While it is not necessary to reorganize the closets or refold the clothes that have been searched, items should not be recklessly or maliciously destroyed.

APPLICATION CASE

The Fourth Amendment's reasonableness requirement has been interpreted to include, as a factor for determining reasonableness of a police entry into a dwelling based on a warrant, whether the officers knocked and announced their authority. In 1995, the Supreme Court of the United States stated in *Wilson v. Arkansas*[82] that knock and announce was a factor in deciding the constitutionality of a police entry into a dwelling.

In *Wilson,* the officers went to Wilson's house to search for narcotics and to arrest her and a codefendant. The officers entered the home without knocking and announcing their identity and purpose. On appeal of her conviction to the Supreme Court, the state contended that the arresting officers did not need to knock and announce because they reasonably believed that a prior announcement would have placed them in peril, given their knowledge that one of the suspects had threatened a government informant with a semiautomatic weapon and that another suspect had previously been convicted of arson and firebombing. The state also argued that prior announcement would have produced an unreasonable risk that the suspect would destroy easily disposable narcotics evidence.

The state courts did not think that knock and announce was required by the Fourth Amendment. The Supreme Court held that "the common-law knock-and-announce principle forms a part of the Fourth Amendment reasonableness inquiry."[83] The Court specifically recognized that there are exigent circumstances under which officers need not knock and announce, for example, when doing so would endanger the officers or others or would lead to destruction of evidence. However, since the state courts had not decided whether the facts of the case justified the police failure to knock and announce, the Supreme Court reversed the conviction and sent the case back to the state courts to decide. Subsequently, in *Richards v. Wisconsin*,[84] the Supreme Court held that there is no blanket exception to the Fourth Amendment's knock and announce requirement for felony drug investigations.

In yet another subsequent case, *Hudson v. Michigan*,[85] the Court reaffirmed the principles announced in previous knock and announce cases. In *Hudson*, the officers knocked and announced but waited only three to five seconds before entering the home to execute the warrant. The state conceded a knock and announce violation, and the only question before the Court was the remedy. The Court opined that the knock and announce rule has never protected the citizen's interest in preventing the government from seeing or taking evidence described in a warrant. Rather, the interests protected by the rule are life, limb, and property. Thus, the Court held that the exclusionary rule is inapplicable to a knock and announce violation. The remedy for such violation is a civil suit.

APPLICATION CASE

In *United States v. Ramirez*,[86] the police obtained a "no-knock" warrant to enter and search a home for a dangerous escaped prisoner, believed to be armed. When the police went to the house to search, an officer broke a single window in Ramirez's garage. Awakened by the noise and fearful that he was being burglarized, Ramirez grabbed his gun and shot into the ceiling of his garage. Realizing he had shot at the police, he immediately surrendered and was arrested, charged, and convicted of being a felon in possession of a firearm. On appeal, Ramirez argued that the police violated the Fourth Amendment because they broke into his house and smashed his window while executing the warrant, thus making his arrest and seizure of the evidence illegal. The Supreme Court rejected this argument, holding that the police acted reasonably because they are not held to a higher standard than "no-knock" entries when "no-knock" entry results in the destruction of property.

There are times when announcing the officer's purpose prior to entering the premises is not necessary. If the occupants are already alerted to the officer's presence, then a knock and announcement is not required. Also, if the officer has probable cause to believe that his or her life, or that of others, may be in danger, the officer need not announce his or her presence or the purpose of the visit prior to entering the premises. Additionally, the officer may enter the premises without prior announcement and request for admission if there is reason to believe that evidence may be destroyed as a result of the announcement, or if the officer is in close pursuit of a fleeing suspect. If the officer has an honest belief that the premises to be searched are unoccupied, no announcement need be made, and the evidence seized is admissible, even if it turns out that there were occupants in the premises at the time. If the officer applying for the warrant believes that the situation requires an entry without a knock and announcement, the officer would be wise to seek the magistrate's approval in the issuance of the warrant. Some jurisdictions may even require a "no-knock" endorsement on the warrant when officers anticipate an unannounced entry.

Time Limit on Length of Search

There is no time limit placed on how long officers may take to execute a search warrant, but the existence of a search warrant does not permit a search to continue indefinitely. However, any search must be thoroughly made and can be time-consuming. The kind of premises to be searched and the kind of property or evidence sought are determining factors in the length of time that a search may reasonably take. If stolen electronics equipment were being sought in a private residence, the search would probably take no more than an hour or two. On the other hand, a search for stolen automobile parts in an automobile-parts warehouse or a junkyard could easily extend into several days.

There is no limit on the number of officers that may aid in a search. However, to avoid overreaction from the public or the suspect, it is advisable that the number of officers be appropriate for the situation. The search of a private residence should, under ordinary circumstances, require fewer officers than the search of a large warehouse.

One must bear in mind that a search warrant permits an invasion of a person's privacy. Though a valid search warrant makes the invasion a reasonable and legal one, the appellate courts could very well take the view that the search went beyond the limits of reasonableness if the length of time, number of officers, or treatment of persons and property seems unreasonable.

Time Limit on Execution of Warrant: The Staleness Doctrine

STALENESS DOCTRINE
The principle that, once a warrant is issued, it may not be held indefinitely by the officer before the search is made.

According to the **staleness doctrine**, a search warrant, once issued, may not be held indefinitely by the officer before the search is made. Warrants are issued on the basis of probable cause to believe that the objects of the warrant are in a particular place, yet many objects sought via a search warrant are portable and cannot be presumed to remain in one place indefinitely.

Time limitations on the execution of search warrants exist because, as time passes, probable cause may dissipate. If probable cause to search no longer exists and a search takes place anyway, a Fourth Amendment violation will occur. This is logical because probable cause to search is based on the probability that a particular item is presently in a specific place; if too much time elapses, the item to be seized may no longer be on the premises. Probable cause, therefore, becomes stale.

Specific laws usually set the length of time within which a search warrant must be executed, measured from the time the warrant was issued. The usual time is ten days. If the search is not made within that time, the search warrant becomes void. If the officer still wishes to make a search, a new search warrant must be obtained. In most jurisdictions, the time cannot be extended.

In some jurisdictions, there is no prescribed time within which the search warrant must be executed. The law of these jurisdictions merely provides that the execution of the search warrant be "immediate" or within a "reasonable time" after issuance. Many of these provisions have been interpreted liberally. However, seldom will the time for service be extended beyond a two-week period.

An arrest warrant, unlike a search warrant, does not become stale in most instances. Once probable cause to arrest arises, it does not lapse, unless the original basis for belief in the guilt of the suspect was incorrect. Therefore, once an arrest warrant has been issued, there is no specified time limit in which the subject must be arrested.

A related timeliness issue is the so-called **anticipatory warrant**, a warrant issued with a provision that it be executed upon the occurrence of a triggering condition. This type of warrant was upheld in the 2006 Supreme Court decision in *United States v. Grubbs.*[87] In *Grubbs,* a postal inspector applied for a warrant to search and seize a videotape containing child pornography ordered by the defendant. The warrant application specified that the warrant would not be executed unless and until the parcel ordered by the defendant was delivered, but it did not specify that the condition had occurred. Because of this, the defendant contested the validity of the search and seizure, claiming that the anticipatory nature of the application rendered this warrant a violation of the particularity requirement of the Fourth Amendment. The Court held that so-called anticipatory warrants do not violate the Fourth Amendment's particularity requirement. The Court noted that all warrants are anticipatory in the sense that probable cause to search amounts to a prediction that the item sought will still be there when the warrant is executed. Thus, all warrants require the issuing magistrate to determine that it is now probable that contraband, evidence of a crime, or a fugitive will be on the described premises when the warrant is executed. Anticipatory warrants merely contain a triggering condition, which must be met before the warrant is valid.

Return of the Search Warrant

After a search has been made pursuant to a search warrant, a **return of the search warrant** must be made to the magistrate who issued the warrant. In most instances, this return is a separate document. It gives a list of the property seized in connection with the search. The officer maintains custody and control of the property seized until the court orders its proper disposition.

A criminal defendant may allege that an officer who applied for a warrant (the affiant; see Figure 9–1) supplied false information in the application. Under the usual test for probable cause, it does not matter if the information possessed by an officer is wrong or false. However, if the officer knew or should have known the information was false, then the defendant's allegation may lead to a finding that the warrant was issued improperly.

The defendant's claim is governed by the *Franks* test, named after the case of *Franks v. Delaware.*[88] Under this test, the burden is on the defendant to show that false information was supplied by the officer to the magistrate in support of probable cause. The defendant must show that a false statement was included in the affidavit that was made knowingly and intentionally, or with a reckless disregard for the truth. For the defendant's attack to be successful, the defendant must also show that such false statement was necessary to the magistrate's finding of probable cause. If the defendant is successful, the court will determine whether probable cause still exists without the false statement. If the court finds that probable cause is lacking without the false information, then the search warrant must be voided and the fruits of the search excluded.

Attack on the Search Warrant

The mere fact that a search warrant was issued and property seized pursuant to the warrant does not prevent an attack from being made by the defendant on the search warrant. If the attack is successful, the property may be excluded from evidence, or a conviction may be reversed upon appeal. If an attack is made, the burden is on the defendant to prove that the search warrant was invalid or improperly issued, or that some other defect or improper procedure resulted. The attack may be made on any of several grounds. The defendant may allege that there was insufficient probable cause for the issuance of the search warrant, that the place to be searched or the thing to be seized was not "particularly" described, or that it was not properly executed. Examples of improper execution include an unreasonable breaking and entering without prior request for admission into the premises and a failure to execute the warrant within the prescribed, or a reasonable, time.

REASONABLE SEARCHES WITHOUT WARRANT: EXCEPTIONS TO THE WARRANT REQUIREMENT

The second method by which a reasonable search may be made is by an exception to the warrant requirement. As stated earlier, there are six "well-delineated exceptions" to the warrant requirement:

1. search and seizure incident to lawful arrest;
2. vehicle searches;
3. inventory searches;
4. consent searches;
5. exigent circumstances searches; and
6. plain view searches.

Specific conditions must be met before a search may be considered reasonable as an exception to the warrant requirement. Each of these exceptions will be discussed in further detail.

Search and Seizure Incident to a Lawful Arrest

A search incident to a lawful arrest (SILA) is one of the well-delineated exceptions to the warrant requirement. Based upon the necessity to protect the officer and prevent destruction of evidence, the exception no longer requires either necessity to be shown in a given case—it applies automatically upon or after arrest.

SEARCH INCIDENT TO A LAWFUL ARREST (SILA)
One of the well-delineated exceptions to the warrant requirement that permits an officer, without a warrant and further probable cause, to search the person of and certain areas around an arrestee incident to a lawful arrest.

For a search incident to arrest to be reasonable, the arrest must be a lawful one and the search must be limited to the following:

1. the person of the arrestee and the area within his or her immediate control (including any containers on the person or within the area);
2. if the arrest is made in a house or other structure, any area adjoining the room in which the arrest is made in which a person might be present who could immediately launch an attack upon the arresting officers (limited to those spaces large enough to conceal a person); and
3. if the arrest is made while or immediately after the arrestee was a passenger in a vehicle, the passenger compartment of the vehicle and any containers therein, open or closed. If the arrestee was in a vehicle, SILA does not apply if the arrestee is, as usually is the case, secured and does not have access to the vehicle. An exception to this is if the search of the vehicle is for evidence of the crime of arrest.

APPLICATION CASE

In *Chimel v. California*,[89] the Supreme Court, for the first time, set forth some guidelines on the area that may be searched incident to an arrest. Chimel was arrested in his residence on a charge that he had burglarized a coin shop. Incident to the arrest, the entire house was searched, including the attic and garage. The search took between 45 minutes and an hour to conduct. Items found in the bedroom and sewing room were taken and introduced against Chimel at his trial. The Supreme Court affirmed that the arrest was valid but held that the search of the entire residence incident to that arrest went beyond the area that was within the immediate control of the accused, and therefore the search and seizure was illegal. Thus, the items seized were illegally admitted into evidence at trial, and the Court reversed the conviction. The Court stressed the importance of the warrant requirement before a search may be deemed reasonable. Accordingly, in *Chimel,* it would have been unreasonable to allow officers to search the entire premises, as Chimel had already been arrested and could not destroy any evidence or obtain a weapon in the bedroom or sewing room, as these areas were beyond the defendant's reach.

If the arrest is made in compliance with a warrant for arrest, it is generally recognized as lawful with very little difficulty. If the arrest occurs within a felony suspect's dwelling, an arrest warrant will, in most instances, be required. On the other hand, if a suspect is arrested in a public place, no warrant is required as long as the officer has probable cause to believe that the suspect has committed a felony or is then and there committing any crime, no matter how minor, in the officer's presence.

In *United States v. Robinson,*[90] decided four years after *Chimel,* a police officer arrested a motorist for the offense of driving without a permit. Under the
law of the jurisdiction, the District of Columbia, the officer was required to arrest
the offender. The officer conducted a full search of the offender incident to the
arrest and discovered illegal drugs. In upholding the accused's conviction for
possession of the drugs, the United States Supreme Court stated that the facts
that the offense was of a minor nature and that the officer did not have probable cause to believe the arrestee could gain control of a weapon or destructible
evidence were of no consequence. As long as the officer had probable cause
to arrest, had probable cause to believe the arrestee was driving without a permit, and made the arrest lawfully, the search incident to the arrest was justified.

A person who has been arrested is subjected to complete loss of personal
liberty. Loss of privacy is so complete that the intrusion of a search incident
to that arrest is either overshadowed by the arrest or minimal in comparison.
In any event, a lawful arrest alone gives the officer authority to search incident
to the arrest—without any additional justification. Accordingly, the authority to
conduct a search incident to arrest does not depend on what a court may later
determine was the likelihood in a particular arrest situation that weapons or evidence would, in fact, be discovered.

Perhaps the most compelling policy behind the SILA exception is the desire
to create a bright-line rule for law enforcement officers. This is desirable in the
context of searches incident to arrest, so that officer safety and the preservation
of evidence will not be compromised, and so that law enforcement officers will
not have to hesitate under dangerous circumstances to consider their actions.

In *Knowles v. Iowa,*[91] a police officer pulled Knowles over for speeding and
issued a citation. The officer, without Knowles' consent or probable cause,
conducted a search of Knowles' car, which yielded a "pot pipe" and some
marijuana. The officer arrested Knowles. Knowles moved to suppress the "pot
pipe" and the marijuana on the ground that, since he had not been arrested
for speeding, the search was not justified by the SILA exception. On review,
the Supreme Court agreed with Knowles, refusing to recognize a search incident to a citation exception to the warrant requirement. The Court found that
the policy reasons behind the SILA exception, officer safety and the need to
preserve evidence, did not exist in the case of a traffic citation. First, the threat
to officers from issuing a citation is less than that of a custodial arrest. Second,
the need to preserve evidence does not exist at a traffic stop because, once
Knowles had been issued a traffic citation, all evidence needed for prosecution
had been obtained.

Scope of the Search: Person of the Arrestee and Area Within Immediate Control

The general rule is that when a person is arrested, a search may be made of the person and the area that is under his or her "immediate control."[92] The search of the person is clear and generally presents few problems. The extent of the area under the arrestee's immediate control, or "wingspan," however, is not always so easily determinable.

The area within the immediate control of the person arrested was defined in *Chimel* as "the area into which an arrestee might reach in order to grab a weapon or evidentiary items."[93] It has been said that the area within the immediate control of the arrestee is that area within his or her wingspan. Since this formulation is also a bit tricky, it may be helpful to return to the reason behind the rule—to seize weapons by which injury or escape may be accomplished or to seize evidence that may be quickly destroyed—to establish some type of criterion.

If an arrest takes place within a home or other structure, a **protective sweep** may be made of any area adjoining the room in which the arrest is made. Thus, arresting officers, without further justification, may also search "closets and other spaces immediately adjoining the place of arrest from which an attack could be immediately launched."[94]

When a person is arrested, he or she loses all liberty rights. Therefore, whether a complete search of the person is effected at the time and place of the arrest or later at the police station is of no consequence. In *United States v. Edwards*,[95] the arrestee's clothing containing incriminating evidence was taken from him in the jail several hours after a late-night arrest. The Court said, "It is . . . plain that searches and seizures that could be made on the spot at the time of arrest may legally be conducted later when the accused arrives at the place of detention."[96]

PROTECTIVE SWEEP
A quick and limited search of a premises, incident to an arrest and conducted to protect the safety of police officers or others. It is narrowly confined to a cursory visual inspection of those places in which a person might be hiding.

APPLICATION CASE

In *Maryland v. Buie*,[97] six officers, armed with an arrest warrant for the defendant, entered the defendant's house to arrest him for a crime allegedly committed by the defendant and an accomplice. As the police entered the premises, they discovered a basement, and, while standing on the ground floor, an officer ordered everyone to come out of the basement. The defendant came out of the basement and was arrested and handcuffed. Then another officer went into the basement to see if anyone else was down there and, though finding no other person there, discovered evidence related to the crime in plain view. The Supreme Court upheld the search of the basement as a "protective sweep," which was necessary for the safety of the officers on the premises. The Court defined a protective sweep as "a quick and limited search of a premises, incident to an arrest and conducted to protect the safety of police officers or others. It is narrowly confined to a cursory visual inspection of those places in which a person might be hiding."[98] An officer needs no justification, other than a lawful custodial arrest, to "look in closets and other spaces immediately adjoining the place of arrest from which an attack could be immediately launched."[99]

However, an officer may only conduct a cursory visual inspection of those places immediately adjoining the place of arrest, and any search beyond that requires additional justification, namely, a belief that a person posing a danger to the officer is in the area to be searched.

Finally, if a custodial arrest takes place while the arrestee is in a vehicle or has just emerged from a vehicle, an officer may search, as incident to the arrest, the area immediately within the control of the arrestee. According to the Supreme Court, this includes not only the passenger compartment of the vehicle but also any containers, open or closed, in that compartment.[100] If the arrestee who emerged from the vehicle has been secured and is not within reaching distance of the passenger compartment at the time of the search, the search is not within the exception.[101] However, there is some question as to whether a locked container is within the Court's language. The area subject to search does not extend to the trunk.

APPLICATION CASE

In the case of *New York v. Belton,*[102] a state trooper arrested the occupants of a car that had been stopped for a traffic violation. The trooper smelled burnt marijuana coming from the vehicle and observed an envelope on the floor of the vehicle that appeared to contain marijuana. The trooper removed the occupants from the car and arrested them. The trooper then returned to the vehicle and searched the envelope to verify that it contained marijuana. He then searched the passenger compartment of the car. On the backseat he found a leather jacket belonging to one of the accused. The trooper unzipped a pocket and found cocaine. The United States Supreme Court held that the search was reasonable and concluded that the search was incident to the lawful arrest in that it was conducted "immediately upon" arrest, even though the search took place after the accused had been removed from the vehicle.

APPLICATION CASE

In the case of *Thornton v. United States,*[103] the Supreme Court applied and extended the reasoning of *Belton.* In *Thornton,* an officer became suspicious of Thornton, followed him, ran a check on his license plates, and found they had been issued to a different type of car than the one Thornton was driving. Before the officer could pull Thornton over, Thornton drove into a parking lot, parked, and got out of his car. The officer quickly followed, stopped Thornton, questioned him, and discovered cocaine in the course of a consensual pat-down search. The officer then searched the car and found a handgun under the driver's seat. Thornton was charged and convicted of drug and firearms offenses. On appeal, he claimed that the search that turned up the weapon was unlawful. The Court rejected the argument, holding that the vehicle search was proper under *Belton.* The Court reasoned that the rationale for SILA did not require *Belton* to be limited solely to situations in which suspects were still in their vehicles when approached by the police. Since Thornton was in "close proximity, both temporally and spatially," to his vehicle, the Court concluded that his status as a "recent occupant" of a vehicle was the same as that of Belton, justifying the application of SILA to the search of the car he recently exited.

APPLICATION CASE

In the case of *Arizona v. Gant,*[104] the Supreme Court of the United States clarified the reach of the search incident to arrest exception to the warrant requirement applied to recent occupants of vehicles. Gant was arrested for suspected drug-related crimes after he got out of his car. The arresting officers handcuffed and locked Gant in the back of a patrol car and then searched Gant's car, finding evidence used to convict him of the drug-related offenses. A majority of the Court held that the search was unreasonable under *Belton,* finding that the SILA rationale authorizes police to search a car incident to a recent occupant's arrest only when the arrestee is unsecured and within reaching distance of the passenger compartment at the time of the arrest. The Court added that circumstances unique to the vehicle context justify a search incident to arrest when it is reasonable to believe evidence relevant to the crime for which the arrestee was arrested might be found in the car.

APPLICATION CASE

In the case of *Riley v. California,*[105] the Supreme Court of the United States addressed an equally, if not more important, question regarding the scope of search incident to a lawful arrest applied to the search of a "person." The Court held that cell phone digital data searches exceeded the scope of the automatic search of the person that is reasonable following an arrest for any offense. Riley's car was impounded after he was caught driving with expired registration tags. Before the car was impounded, the police performed an inventory search of the vehicle, found two guns, and subsequently arrested Riley. Riley had his cell phone in his pocket when he was arrested. A gang unit detective examined the videos and photographs found in the cell phone. The videos and photographs showed Riley making gang signs and engaging in other gang-related activity, which were used to determine whether Riley was gang-affiliated. The Court held that this violated Riley's Fourth Amendment right to be free from unreasonable searches. The Court held that the warrantless search exception following an arrest exists for protecting officer safety and preserving evidence, neither of which is at issue in the search of digital data. The Court described cell phones as minicomputers full of private information, which distinguished them from the usual items that can be seized from an arrestee's person, such as a wallet. However, the Court held that *some* warrantless searches of cell phones might be permissible in an emergency: when the government's interests are so compelling that a search would be reasonable, which was not the case here. The majority opinion notably commented, "[M]odern cell phones, which are now such a pervasive and insistent part of daily life that the proverbial visitor from Mars might conclude they were an important feature of human anatomy."

Blood Samples and Driving Under the Influence

The extent to which an officer may search an accused incident to an arrest has its limitations. This has been particularly true in cases of arrests for driving under the influence, when blood, breath, or urine samples are sought for purposes of chemical analysis for alcoholic content. Does drawing blood go beyond what is authorized in a search incident to a lawful arrest? The answer to this question was squarely met in *Schmerber v. California*.[106] In this case, Schmerber was convicted of driving under the influence of alcohol. Schmerber was arrested in a hospital, where he was receiving treatment for injuries sustained in a car accident. While in the hospital, a blood sample was drawn from his body by a doctor at the direction of a police officer. The blood sample revealed that Schmerber was intoxicated at the time of the accident and was admitted in evidence. Although the Supreme Court found the extraction of blood from Schmerber was a reasonable warrantless search and upheld the conviction, it did so on grounds other than the SILA exception.

The Supreme Court made clear that searches involving intrusions beyond the body's surface involve greater dignity and privacy interests than do searches of an arrestee's outer body. With this in mind, the Court held that there must be some kind of justification for the search other than the mere fact of a lawful arrest. Specifically, the Court stated that there must be "a clear indication" that evidence will be found in the blood taken from the accused. This has been interpreted to mean three things: (1) that the officer must have probable cause to believe that the blood of the arrestee contains criminal evidence, namely, a criminally high blood-alcohol level; (2) that there must be an exigency that evidence will be destroyed if an officer were required to apply for a search warrant; and (3) that the means and procedures employed by the officer be reasonable. In the *Schmerber* case, the means and procedures employed were reasonable, in that blood was taken by a physician in a hospital environment according to accepted medical practices.

In *Missouri v. McNeely*, [107] the United States Supreme Court, in 2013, further refined the *Schmerber* exigent circumstances rule. In *McNeely*, the Court held that an individual arrested for driving under the influence of alcohol cannot be assumed to present an exigency justifying a warrantless blood testing in all cases. Rather, "exigency in this context must be determined case by case based on the totality of the circumstances."[108] In *Birchfield v. North Dakota*,[109] the Court did distinguish between breath and blood tests, holding that the Fourth Amendment permits warrantless breath tests incident to arrest for drunk driving.

Refusal to Give Samples—Admissible Evidence

Although it has been held in most jurisdictions that giving blood samples, submitting handwriting exemplars, or speaking for identification is not a violation of the privilege against self-incrimination, there is no way to force an accused to furnish this evidence. However, an accused who refuses to give the evidence should be advised that it is not a violation of the privilege against self-incrimination, and that there is no constitutional right to refuse to furnish the requested evidence. Depending upon the jurisdiction, the accused should also be advised that refusal to give the evidence can be used against him or her in court.

Except in the case of post-indictment identification lineups, the accused is not entitled to the assistance of counsel in giving physical evidence. However, if counsel has been appointed, the accused has the right to have the attorney present when exemplars are taken. The counsel should be advised of any contact made with the accused for the purpose of obtaining physical evidence.

The Vehicle Exception

There are three methods by which an officer may search a vehicle without a search warrant. The first method is a search incident to arrest, under the *Belton* case discussed in the previous section. Another is the inventory exception, discussed in the next section. The third is the subject of this section, the vehicle exception to the warrant requirement.

Under the **vehicle exception**, an officer may search the interior of a vehicle if he or she has probable cause to believe that the vehicle contains contraband or fruits, instrumentalities, or evidence of a crime.[110] The rationale behind the vehicle exception is that vehicles are inherently mobile and, therefore, the opportunity to search is only momentary. If the occupants of the vehicle are alerted, and if a search warrant is necessary, then the vehicle might never be found again, let alone the contents of the vehicle. Because of this rationale, searches are limited to vehicles that are being used on public ways and vehicles that are in stationary positions but are readily capable of use on the highway. Another rationale for the vehicle exception is that people have a lesser expectation of privacy in a vehicle. This is because a vehicle is exposed to public view on a daily basis[111] and because a vehicle is subject to much regulation by the government, such as registration, mechanical inspection, ticketing, and in some states smog checks.[112]

VEHICLE EXCEPTION Another of the well-delineated exceptions to the warrant requirement by which an officer may search the interior of a vehicle if he or she has probable cause to believe that the vehicle contains contraband or fruits, instrumentalities, or evidence of a crime.

APPLICATION CASE

In *Collins v. Virginia*,[113] the United States Supreme Court, in a near-unanimous decision, held that the vehicle exception to the Fourth Amendment's warrant requirement for searches did not justify a police officer's invasion of curtilage of a home for a warrantless search of a motorcycle covered by a tarp and parked in a partially enclosed top portion of a driveway of the home, even though the officer had probable cause to believe that the motorcycle was the one that had eluded the officer's attempted traffic stop.

I n *Florida v. White*,[114] two months after the police observed White delivering cocaine in his car, the police arrested him at his work and seized his car from the parking lot. The arresting officers did not obtain a warrant to seize the car because they had probable cause to believe that White used his car as an instrumentality for drug trafficking, making the vehicle itself forfeitable contraband. During a subsequent inventory search, the police found two pieces of rock cocaine in the ashtray. White was convicted of possession of crack cocaine. Upon review, the Supreme Court upheld the seizure of White's car without a warrant, stating that the Fourth Amendment does not require the police to obtain a warrant before seizing an automobile from a public place when they have probable cause to believe the automobile itself is contraband.

The vehicle exception has very expansive applications. First, the search of the vehicle may take place away from the scene, for example, at a police station. The police may seize the car without searching it, move it to another location, and search it there, regardless of the reason for doing so. All of this may be accomplished without a warrant.[115] Once the police seize the vehicle, the probable cause to search that allowed them to seize it originally may continue indefinitely.[116] At some point, the police retention of the vehicle may continue so long that the seizure becomes permanent. In that case, the police may search the vehicle pursuant to the inventory exception (discussed in the following section), if applicable. It may seem that, once the police decide to seize the vehicle and search it elsewhere, the vehicle lacks mobility and the search no longer meets the main rationale for the exception. However, the Supreme Court has stated that the vehicle retains its mobility wherever it may be taken by the police. Also note that the vehicles within this exception include all motorized vehicles, such as trucks, airplanes, motor homes, campers or trailers attached to cars, boats, and houseboats.

I n *California v. Carney*,[117] the defendant was convicted of possession of marijuana for sale. The police had probable cause to believe that the defendant was selling drugs for sex from inside a motor home parked in a public lot. Two officers, without a warrant or the defendant's consent, searched the motor home and found marijuana. The Supreme Court upheld the search, stating that the motor home was inherently mobile and the facts that it might be used as a home and was much larger than an ordinary car were of no consequence.

During a lawful vehicle exception search, an officer may search any containers found inside the vehicle. The officer must have probable cause to believe the vehicle contains some seizable evidence and, in certain instances, may only have probable cause to search a certain area of the vehicle. If a container is discovered during a vehicle exception search, its contents may be examined only if the container is capable of holding the object of the search; this limitation does not apply to SILA searches, as these searches do not require probable cause. For instance, if an officer observes a suspect place a large bag, which the officer has probable cause to believe contains ten pounds of marijuana, in the trunk of a car, the officer may search the trunk and examine the contents of the bag. But the officer may not search other areas of the car, unless the officer has probable cause to believe such areas contain other seizable objects. Furthermore, if, during the search of the trunk, the officer discovers a small pocket pouch, he or she may not examine its contents, since such a pouch is incapable of holding ten pounds of marijuana.

APPLICATION CASE

In *Wyoming v. Houghton*,[118] a police officer stopped a motorist for speeding and driving with a faulty brake light. While questioning the driver, the officer noticed a hypodermic syringe in the driver's shirt pocket. When asked why he had the syringe, the driver said he used it to take drugs. Houghton was one of two female passengers in the vehicle and, when she left the car upon back-up officers' instructions, she left her purse on the backseat. The original officer went back and searched the car for contraband. He picked up Houghton's purse, opened it, and found a syringe and methamphetamine in it. Houghton was charged with possession of methamphetamine. She moved to suppress the syringe and the methamphetamine found in her purse. The Supreme Court upheld the search, stating that where there is probable cause to search a car for drugs, as in this case, the police may open any and all containers, "without a showing of individualized probable cause for each one."

Inventory Searches

The third method by which an officer may search a vehicle without a search warrant is an inventory search. In fact, most jurisdictions require neither a warrant nor probable cause before a lawful inventory search may be conducted. The rationales behind the inventory exception are that such searches protect the owner's property while it is in police custody, protect police against claims of loss or theft, and protect the police and others from dangerous items that might be hidden inside. Inventory searches are not limited to vehicles but extend to persons as well.

Police departments have established standard **inventory search** procedures for vehicles and other property lawfully in police custody (impoundment). These procedures are designed to protect the rights against unreasonable searches and seizures guaranteed in the Fourth Amendment and are an attempt to prevent "a general, exploratory rummaging" in people's belongings. Some leeway is allowed, such as when department procedures provide searching officers with some discretion as to which containers in the car will be searched.

INVENTORY SEARCH
Another of the well-delineated exceptions to the warrant requirement that permits a police officer to inventory the property of a vehicle or person for the protection of the property and the police.

The same rules apply to inventory searches of persons who are lawfully within police custody. The search must be conducted pursuant to routine or standard procedures incident to booking and jailing. The person who is searched must be lawfully in police custody, meaning that he or she has been arrested lawfully and is expected to be jailed for a period of time.

APPLICATION CASE

In *Flippo v. West Virginia*,[119] the police received a 911 call from Flippo that he and his wife had been attacked in their hotel room. The police arrived at the hotel and found Flippo's wife murdered. After Flippo had been taken to the hospital for treatment of his injuries, the police began to process the crime scene by taking photographs, collecting evidence, and searching the contents of the room, including a photograph contained in a closed briefcase belonging to Flippo. At trial, the photograph was used to establish motive that Flippo killed his wife because she was having an affair with the man in the photograph. The Supreme Court, reviewing his conviction, found there is no crime scene exception to the warrant requirement. Hence, the Court found that the evidence found at the scene should not have been admitted against Flippo at his trial.

Consent Searches

A **consent search** is another exception to the warrant requirement of the Fourth Amendment, as well as an exception to the probable cause requirement. Therefore, an officer needs no justification to conduct a search pursuant to valid consent. If a person gives consent to be searched or to have his or her property searched, logically, that person has no basis to question the legality or reasonableness of the search at a later time. However, a number of conditions affect the giving of the consent that, in turn, may affect the legality of the search. The validity of **consent** turns on whether consent was voluntarily given, taking into account all of the surrounding circumstances. Moreover, the person who gives consent must be in control of the premises or property searched, meaning that he or she has authority, or at least apparent authority, over the property. If a valid consent is given for a search, any attack on a seizure of property pertinent to a crime is not effective, unless the search was extended beyond the scope of the consent.

APPLICATION CASE

In *Schneckloth v. Bustamonte*,[120] a police officer stopped a car when he observed that one headlight and its license plate light were burned out. Six men were in the vehicle, one of whom, Joe Alcala, produced a license and explained that the car belonged to his brother. The officer asked to search the car, and Alcala replied, "Sure, go ahead." In the trunk, the officer found three checks that had been stolen from a car wash. Those checks were admitted at trial against another of the passengers, Bustamonte, who was convicted. Bustamonte challenged the search, claiming that the consent was invalid because no one informed Alcala that he had the right to refuse consent.

The Supreme Court held that, to prove consent, the prosecution must prove that the consent was voluntarily given, that voluntariness is a question of fact to be determined from all the circumstances, and that the subject's knowledge of a right to refuse is a factor to be taken into account. However, the Court specifically stated that the prosecution is not required to demonstrate the subject's knowledge of the right to refuse consent as a prerequisite to establishing a voluntary consent and upheld the conviction in this case.

The prosecution has the burden of showing that consent was, in fact, voluntarily given and not the result of coercion or duress. This does not mean that the prosecution must show that the accused had knowledge of his or her right to refuse consent, or that the accused was advised of the right to refuse consent by the police. Whether or not a consent was voluntarily given may depend on many things. Any showing that the consent was induced by a threat, promise, duress, fear, coercion, or deceit will affect the validity of the consent.

APPLICATION CASES

In *Ohio v. Robinette,*[121] a deputy pulled Robinette's car over for a speeding violation. The deputy checked Robinette's license, issued a verbal warning, and gave his license back to him. Before Robinette drove away, the deputy asked Robinette whether he had any contraband in his car and if he could search it. Robinette consented to a search, which revealed a small amount of marijuana and a pill that turned out to be an unlawfully possessed controlled substance. Robinette argued that his consent to search the car was *per se* involuntary because the officer did not inform him that he was free to go when he gave the consent. The Supreme Court rejected this argument, holding that the Fourth Amendment only requires that an officer obtain consent to search in a reasonable manner and that failure to inform a detainee that he or she is free to go before gaining consent does not, by itself, vitiate that consent. Similarly, in *United States v. Drayton,*[122] the Court held that the Fourth Amendment does not require a passenger asked to consent to the search of her luggage and her person during a suspicionless bus sweep to be advised of her right to refuse permission in order for her consent to be voluntary.

TOTALITY OF THE CIRCUMSTANCES FOR CONSENT
The test for consent that takes into account all of the circumstances surrounding the giving of consent to determine whether a person has voluntarily consented.

Whether an officer's conduct falls within the standards of valid consent depends upon all of the facts and circumstances. The test for a valid consent is whether, under the **totality of the circumstances for consent**, the accused voluntarily consented. The totality of the circumstances includes consideration of the characteristics of the person giving consent, such as age, education, emotional state, and mental condition, as well as whether there was a show of force by the officer requesting consent. The officer's conduct and the characteristics of the individual giving consent, considered together, may create the inference that the person's free will was overwhelmed by the officer's conduct. If so, the consent is invalid.

APPLICATION CASE

Florida v. Bostick,[123] discussed previously in this chapter in defining seizure of the person, also dealt with the doctrine of consent. In the case, two officers from the Broward County, Florida, Sheriff's Department, pursuant to a drug interdiction plan, routinely boarded a bus en route from Miami to Atlanta during a stopover in Fort Lauderdale. Their purpose was to try to identify law violators by picking persons at random, or based on vague suspicion, and asking them potentially incriminating questions. The officers wore badges and insignia, and one held a zipper pouch containing a plainly visible pistol. Without articulable suspicion, the officers picked out the defendant and asked to inspect his ticket and identification. Noting nothing unusual, the officers nonetheless persisted in their questioning, ultimately asking for consent to search the defendant's bags. Bostick consented, and the officers found cocaine in his bag. Bostick was arrested and charged with trafficking in cocaine. The Florida Supreme Court held that, because the encounter took place in the close space of a bus, Bostick felt he had no choice but to consent to the officers' request. The United States Supreme Court disagreed. In upholding Bostick's conviction, the Court held that the question of whether a person would feel free to refuse had to be decided as a matter of fact, based on a totality of the circumstances, not merely because the encounter took place on a bus.

It is the responsibility of the trial judge to determine whether the consent was voluntarily given. The judge will make a decision from the facts presented by the prosecution about the manner in which the consent was obtained. Thus, the circumstances surrounding the consent are most important to the prosecution—the admissibility of the physical evidence will be completely dependent upon the validity of the consent. If there is doubt about the voluntariness of the consent, the search will be considered unreasonable, and the exclusionary rule will be triggered.

Form of Consent

No formal wording is necessary for a consent to be considered freely and voluntarily given, but there should be some affirmative response, not merely a failure to object to the search. Silence alone is not deemed to be a consent. It is possible, under the totality of the circumstances, that silence followed by some action or gesture would be tantamount to consent. For example, if an officer should go to a house and ask the occupant for permission to search the premises, and the occupant steps back and motions the officer into the building, such a gesture would be considered a consent to search.

Although consent may be given either orally or in writing, when possible, it is highly desirable that the consent be reduced to writing and signed by the person giving it. This does not preclude the person from later alleging that consent was not given for the search, but it does provide some evidence that the matter was discussed and that an affirmative response was given. It is suggested that the following preamble be made in the first paragraph of a written consent to search: "I, (name of person giving consent), give my free and voluntary consent to have a search made of the premises located at (address of place to be searched). I give this consent without any threat or promise being made to me." (Note: In jurisdictions where a warning of the right to withhold consent must be given, the following should also be included in the written consent: "I have been advised of my constitutional right to refuse to permit a search to be made.") This written consent should be signed and dated by the person giving it and witnessed by someone other than the officer receiving it. Whether any additional information is included in the written consent should be left to the discretion of the officer at the time.

Consent is a right of the person giving it. It may be limited in area, scope, or purpose, and it may be withdrawn at any time. If consent is withdrawn, the officer will have to resort to some other authority to search further, such as obtaining a search warrant or making an arrest. Otherwise, the officer may be completely stymied in the continuation of the search.

The fact that consent to search was freely given does not permit continual and repeated invasion of the premises thereafter. How soon the search has to be made after consent is given depends largely upon the circumstances. As a practical matter, the search should be made as soon as possible, because the consent may be withdrawn at any time. Although the courts have not established any prescribed time within which a search must be made once consent is given, an undue delay between the consent and the search might lead the court to conclude that the police abandoned the search effort and require a new consent for the search to continue.

Who May Give Consent

If the search is to be of a person, the person who is to be searched is the one to give the consent. In the case of a person of unsound mind or a child too young to understand the meaning of the request, consent may be given by the guardian or parent. If a search is to be made of a certain property or premises, consent must be given by one who has, or reasonably appears to have, common authority over the property or premises for most purposes. It is not always easy to determine who has this authority.

The validity of a third party's consent depends on whether the third party and the defendant have common authority over the property or premises searched. **Common authority** has been defined by the Supreme Court as mutual use of the property searched by persons generally having joint access to or control over the property for most purposes.[124]

If the place to be searched is a residence, the occupant of that residence is the proper person to give the consent. If there is more than one occupant of the residence, any one of the occupants present at the time may give consent to a

COMMON AUTHORITY Mutual use of the property searched by persons generally having joint access to or control over the property for most purposes.

search. However, if more than one occupant has common authority and one of the occupants refuses consent, then the police cannot enter. This was the holding in the 2006 Supreme Court decision in *Georgia v. Randolph*.[125] The occupant giving consent, however, must have common authority, for most purposes, over the area to be searched. For instance, the spouse of the accused would most likely have common authority over the couple's dwelling, but roommates with separate rooms may have common authority over portions of their common dwelling but not over their separate sleeping quarters.

The rule for testing third-party consent was first established by the Supreme Court of the United States in the case of *United States v. Matlock*.[126] Matlock was arrested in the front yard of a house in which he was living with his girlfriend. The girlfriend allowed the officers to search a bedroom of the house that she and the defendant shared. The Court held that the consent given by the defendant's girlfriend was valid. The girlfriend and the defendant had joint access to and control over the bedroom searched, since the bedroom was mutually used by them for sleeping purposes. In addition, the Court emphasized that common authority does not depend on whether the person giving consent has a property interest in the property searched, although it may be a factor in determining the validity of consent. The primary rationale is that, by sharing his or her privacy with another person, the defendant assumes the risk that that person will voluntarily consent to a search.

Apparent Authority

In 1990, the case of *Illinois v. Rodriguez*[127] established the doctrine of "apparent authority," relieving the officer from being penalized for perfectly reasonable conduct. In *Rodriguez,* a woman told police that she had been beaten in a particular apartment by the defendant. The woman also told the police that the defendant was now asleep in the apartment, and she offered to let the police into the apartment with her key, so that they could arrest him. In addition, the woman referred to the defendant's apartment as "our" apartment and said that she had clothing and furniture in the apartment. With her consent, the police entered the defendant's apartment and observed contraband in plain view, which was seized. It later turned out that, although the woman once lived in the apartment, she had not been living there for a number of weeks preceding the incident.

MYTH ▶   ◀ FACT

MYTH	FACT
If an officer goes undercover and obtains consent to search, then the consent is not voluntarily given.	If a person giving consent is unaware that he or she is giving such consent to an officer, the consent is still voluntary, since no coercion is present. The consenting person assumes the risk that the individual with whom he or she is dealing is actually a friend who will not betray his or her trust, rather than an undercover government agent.

The Supreme Court held that the search was reasonable. The Court emphasized that the Fourth Amendment prohibits unreasonable searches and seizures. Therefore, what is required of police officers when they make factual determinations "is not that they always be correct, but that they always be reasonable." By stressing the importance of the "reasonableness" requirement, the Court laid the foundation for the **apparent authority doctrine**. Under this doctrine, a consent search will be deemed reasonable if the facts available to the officer at the moment of entry would cause a reasonable person to believe that the consenting party had common authority for most purposes over the premises or property.

Scope of Consent: Plain View

If consent is voluntarily given to search a premises for a particular object and during the search another item is observed in plain view, that item is admissible evidence if it was found within the scope of the consent given. For example, if a person should give consent for an officer to search a house for television sets and in making the search the officer should find other stolen electrical appliances in plain view, these appliances would normally be admissible in evidence, as their discovery would be within the scope of the consent. However, if in the same search a stolen gun were located in a small dresser drawer, the gun would probably be excluded because it was not in plain view. Searching the small dresser may be considered by the court as going beyond the scope of the consent. It would be a stretch of the imagination to expect to find a television in a small dresser drawer.

Exigent Circumstances Searches and Seizures

Another exception to the warrant requirement is an **exigent circumstances search and seizure**. By definition, an exigency is a situation that requires immediate action—it will not be deemed unreasonable for an officer to search without a warrant under exigent circumstances. Unlike a consent search, however, an officer must have probable cause to search under this exception to the warrant requirement. A variety of situations may constitute exigent circumstances, and the more important ones will be discussed in further detail in this section.

Four exigencies were specifically recognized by the United States Supreme Court in the case of *Minnesota v. Olson*:[128]

1. hot pursuit of a fleeing felon;
2. imminent destruction of evidence;
3. the need to prevent a suspect's escape; and
4. the risk of harm to the police or to others.

Hot pursuit is limited to a situation in which a suspect is followed from the point of the offense to the destination in a continuous transaction. For example, after a robbery of a cab company office, taxi drivers followed the perpetrator from the office to a residence. One driver notified the company's dispatcher, who relayed the information to the police who were en route to the scene of the robbery. Within minutes, the police arrived at the residence and their warrantless entry into it was declared lawful.[129]

APPARENT AUTHORITY DOCTRINE
The principle by which a third-party consent search will be deemed reasonable if the facts available to the officer at the moment of entry would cause a reasonable person to believe that the consenting party had common authority for most purposes over the premises or property.

EXIGENT CIRCUMSTANCES SEARCH AND SEIZURE
Another of the well-delineated exceptions to the warrant requirement, permitting a police officer to enter premises when there is a situation that requires immediate action. The Supreme Court has recognized four such circumstances: (1) hot pursuit of a fleeing felon; (2) imminent destruction of evidence; (3) the need to prevent a suspect's escape; and (4) the risk of harm to the police or to others.

As discussed in the "Blood Samples and Driving Under the Influence" subsection of this chapter, imminent destruction of evidence may be an exigency justifying a warrantless search. In the *Schmerber* case, discussed in the just-mentioned subsection, the police had probable cause to believe that the defendant had an elevated blood-alcohol level, which would dissipate if the officers were required to take the time to obtain a warrant. Therefore, the warrantless intrusion into the defendant's body was a reasonable search because it would have been impractical for the officers to obtain a search warrant. And, as held in *Missouri v. McNeely*,[130] the finding of exigency must be made in each individual case based on a totality of the circumstances. Not all DUI cases can be presumed to present such an exigency. The exigency of imminent destruction of evidence may also justify the entry into and search of a dwelling if the police have probable cause to believe that criminal evidence is within the dwelling and will be destroyed if immediate action is not taken. To justify such an entry, the officer must be able to articulate facts that would lead a person of reasonable caution to believe that the imminent destruction of evidence is threatened.

APPLICATION CASE

In *Vale v. Louisiana*,[131] officers failed to articulate such facts as would justify an exigent circumstance entry in a home to prevent destruction of evidence. In *Vale,* the officers possessed two warrants for the defendant's arrest. While the officers were outside the defendant's residence, they observed the defendant sell narcotics on the street corner to another person in a car parked on the street. The officers promptly stopped the car and arrested both the driver and the defendant, Vale. The officers then entered the defendant's residence and discovered narcotics in a bedroom. The United States Supreme Court found the search unlawful, as no exigency existed to justify the search. The Court noted that the officers had no reason to believe there was anyone else in the defendant's residence who could gain control of and destroy the narcotics. The Court held that an arrest on the street, standing alone, cannot provide its own exigent circumstances so as to justify a warrantless search of the arrestee's house.

Another exigency that has been recognized by the Supreme Court is the need to prevent a suspect's escape. An officer may enter a home or other dwelling and search for a suspected felon who the officer has probable cause to believe is presently within the home and will escape if immediate action is not taken.

APPLICATION CASE

In *Illinois v. McArthur*,[132] Mrs. McArthur tipped off two police officers about her husband's marijuana stash under the couch. One officer locked the door to the home while the other went to obtain a search warrant. The remaining officer refused to allow Mr. McArthur to enter the home without accompanying him. Two hours later, the other officer returned with a warrant and both searched the home. The officers found a marijuana pipe and a small amount of marijuana. Mr. McArthur moved to suppress the evidence on the ground that the pipe and the marijuana were fruits of the poisonous tree, namely, the unlawful restraint of him and of his house during the two-hour period while the warrant was being obtained. The Supreme Court found that the officers' conduct was reasonable under the exigent circumstances exception in light of the circumstances, which was a reasonable belief that Mr. McArthur would destroy the evidence before the police could obtain the warrant. The Court intimated that search or a seizure is reasonable as long as law enforcement imposes a limited and tailored restraint to secure law enforcement needs while protecting an individual's privacy.

Finally, an exigency justifying the search of a person or a home is the risk of harm to the police or to others, either inside or outside the dwelling. Again, the officer must have probable cause to believe that a risk of harm exists, such as a situation in which a bullet is fired through the floor of an apartment, injuring a person in the apartment below. Police entry into the apartment without a warrant to search for the shooter, other victims, and weapons is justified as an exigency.[133]

Scope of Exigent Circumstances Search

The scope of a search conducted under exigent circumstances will be defined by the emergency or exigency that justifies the search. A discussion of the *Warden v. Hayden*[134] case will illustrate the parameters of an exigent circumstances search. In *Warden,* the officers had probable cause to believe that a suspect who was involved in an armed robbery had entered a particular dwelling (it turned out to be his mother's home) moments earlier. The officers immediately went to the dwelling in question and were allowed to enter without protest by a woman living in the home (who turned out to be the suspect's mother). A number of officers spread out through the whole house, including the basement, in order to locate the defendant. The defendant was found and arrested in his own room, where he was faking sleep. Simultaneously, other officers discovered and seized items related to the armed robbery. Particularly, a shotgun and pistol were discovered in a bathroom toilet, which was opened because of the noise of running water. Clothing fitting the description of that worn by the robber was found in a basement washing machine by an officer, and various other items were found under the defendant's bed mattress and in a bedroom drawer. The Supreme Court found the full-scale search of the house reasonable because "exigencies of the situation made the [search] imperative."[135] Essentially, the officers were in hot pursuit of an armed and dangerous felon and "only a thorough search of the house for persons and weapons could have ensured that [the defendant] was the only man present and that the police had control of all weapons which could be used against them or to effect escape."[136]

The case of *Welsh v. Wisconsin*[137] is illustrative of the limits upon the exigent circumstances exception to the warrant requirement. Welsh was driving erratically and ran off the road. By the time the police arrived at the scene where his car had run off the road, Welsh had departed on foot. After checking the vehicle's registration, the police found Welsh's address and went to his home. The officers entered his home and found him in bed. They arrested him and took him to get a blood-alcohol test. The Supreme Court found that the entry into the home was not justified by exigent circumstances and therefore Welsh's conviction was overturned. Under Wisconsin law, first offense driving under the influence (DUI) was, at the time, classified as a noncriminal, civil forfeiture offense. Hence, the Court rejected the state's claim of exigency due to dissipating evidence of DUI as a basis for the warrantless entry into the home.

Plain View Doctrine

PLAIN VIEW DOCTRINE
The last of the well-delineated exceptions to the warrant requirement, providing that an officer may seize an object without a warrant if (1) the officer observes the object from a lawful vantage point; (2) the officer has a right of physical access to the object from the lawful vantage point; and (3) the nature of the object is immediately apparent as an article subject to seizure (i.e., that it is contraband or a fruit, instrumentality, or evidence of a crime).

As another exception to the warrant requirement, the plain view doctrine is intertwined with all of the other methods of conducting a reasonable search. Under the **plain view doctrine**, an officer may seize an object without a warrant if

1. the officer observes the object from a lawful vantage point;
2. the officer has a right of physical access to the object from the lawful vantage point; and
3. the nature of the object is immediately apparent as an article subject to seizure (i.e., contraband or a fruit, instrumentality, or evidence of a crime).

The first requirement, that the officer observe the object from a lawful vantage point, means that the officer cannot violate the Fourth Amendment in arriving at that vantage point. Four methods exist by which an officer may arrive at the vantage point lawfully:

1. The officer may observe the object during a search pursuant to a search warrant. For example, the officer may be executing a search warrant for narcotics in the defendant's garage when the officer discovers illegal AK-47 rifles.
2. The object may be viewed by the officer while the officer executes an arrest warrant in the arrestee's home.
3. The officer may discover the object while conducting a search justified under an exception to the warrant requirement, for example. The object may be viewed by an officer during a lawful consent search or a search justified by exigent circumstances.
4. The object may come into view during police activity that does not constitute a search or seizure, such as entering the house to take a report for a missing child.

The second requirement for the plain view exception is that the officer must have a right of physical access to the object. In essence, the officer must be able to reach out and grab the object. For example, assume an officer walking down the street observes through an open window a marijuana plant on a living room table. The officer may be at a lawful vantage point on the street, and the observation alone does not constitute a search, but the officer does not have a right of physical access to the dwelling containing the plant. The observation would constitute probable cause for a search warrant but would not justify a warrantless seizure of the plant.

Finally, the third requirement dictates the object's incriminating nature must be immediately apparent to the officer who views it. This requirement is satisfied if the officer has probable cause to believe that the object is contraband or a fruit, instrumentality, or evidence of a crime. In the previous example, the officer must have sufficient experience and knowledge to immediately recognize the plant as being marijuana.

FYI

The plain view doctrine is not limited to observations made with the sense of sight. The Supreme Court has also established a plain feel doctrine. Under the plain feel doctrine, an officer may seize an object without a warrant from the person of the defendant while conducting a lawful stop and frisk (stop and frisk will be discussed in detail in the following section). For a plain feel seizure to be upheld, the officer conducting the patdown must immediately recognize the object as contraband or a fruit, instrumentality, or evidence of a crime. The officer may not manipulate the object, e.g., by squeezing, in order to determine its incriminating nature. In addition to the plain feel doctrine, it could quite easily be argued that there should be a plain smell doctrine. Many officers are trained in detecting the smell of drugs, such as marijuana. Should an officer smell an odor that is immediately recognizable as a narcotic, and the officer is at a lawful vantage point with a right of physical access to the narcotic, then a warrantless seizure of the narcotics would be reasonable.

APPLICATION CASE

In *Bond v. United States*,[138] a Border Patrol agent boarded a bus in Texas to check the immigration status of its passengers. Satisfied that all of the passengers were lawfully in the United States, the agent walked down the aisle of the bus and squeezed the luggage in the overhead compartments, feeling a brick-like object in Bond's bag. Bond admitted to the agent that the bag was his and agreed to allow the agent to open it. The agent opened the bag and found a brick of methamphetamine. Bond was charged with offenses relating to the possession of the drugs and moved to suppress the evidence obtained by the agent, claiming the agent conducted an illegal search. The trial and appellate courts rejected Bond's argument, but the Supreme Court of the United States disagreed and reversed his convictions. In short, the Court found that the agent's manipulation of the bag, which led to his further interaction with both the bag and Bond, which ultimately led to the drugs, was a search. It gave the agent sufficient information to constitute a search. Bond had an expectation of privacy in his bag and a reasonable expectation that his bag might be handled by other passengers. The agent's squeeze exceeded "the casual contact [Bond] would have expected from other passengers" when he felt the bag in an exploratory manner, a manner that was more intrusive than a reasonable person would expect. A probing physical manipulation is a search and presumed unreasonable without a warrant.

In *Arizona v. Hicks*,[139] a bullet was fired through the floor of the defendant's apartment into the apartment below. The officers entered the defendant's apartment under exigent circumstances to search for the shooter, other victims, and weapons. While inside, an officer observed expensive stereo equipment that seemed out of place in the defendant's run-down apartment. The officer moved and turned over the record player to observe and record the serial number for the purpose of determining whether the player was stolen. The officer checked with his headquarters and was advised that the stereo was, in fact, stolen. He then seized the equipment.

The United States Supreme Court invalidated the search on the ground that the officer lacked probable cause to believe that the stereo equipment was stolen when he first observed it. Moving the turntable to view the serial number constituted another search, which required additional justification.

SEARCH AND SEIZURE ON LESS THAN PROBABLE CAUSE: STOP AND FRISK AND REASONABLE SUSPICION IN OTHER CIRCUMSTANCES

Prior to 1967–1968, the only ways a search and seizure would be found valid under the Fourth Amendment were if the officer acted with probable cause and a warrant or with probable cause and an exception to the warrant requirement. These traditional principles of probable cause, the warrant requirement, and a few, well-delineated exceptions were also applicable to the states through the Fourteenth Amendment.

In 1968, the Supreme Court decided the seminal case of *Terry v. Ohio*.[140] The Court adopted a new search and seizure standard when it found a law officer's search and seizure to be justified on less than probable cause and without a warrant. It is significant that, six months before *Terry*, in a noncriminal setting, the Court suggested that the determination of "reasonableness" of searches and seizures involves "balancing the need to search against the invasion which the search entails."[141]

In the *Terry* case, an officer with more than 30 years' experience became highly suspicious, but lacked probable cause, after observing three men who appeared to be casing a store for a robbery. The officer approached the suspects, asked for their names, and, receiving an incomprehensible reply, patted down the outside of the defendant's clothing. As a result of the patdown, the officer felt a gun in a pocket of the defendant's overcoat, which the officer then pulled out. He then arrested the defendant. The defendant was prosecuted and convicted for carrying a concealed weapon.

The United States Supreme Court upheld the defendant's conviction despite the fact that the officer lacked probable cause to make an arrest when he first stopped and frisked the defendant. In determining the reasonableness of the officer's conduct, the Court balanced the government interests in effective crime prevention and officer safety against the governmental intrusion on the individual's security. The Court found that the governmental interests outweighed the individual's interests, primarily for the reason that the intrusion on the individual's privacy was less than that of a full-scale search and seizure. Consequently, the justification to conduct less than a full-scale search and seizure, i.e., stop and frisk, need not rise to the level of probable cause. The Court set some guidelines by which an officer may conduct a stop and frisk by stating:[142]

> We merely hold today that where a police officer observes unusual conduct which leads him reasonably to conclude [what has come to be known as "reasonable suspicion"] in light of his experience that criminal activity may be afoot and that the persons with whom he is dealing may be armed and presently dangerous, where in the course of investigating this behavior he identifies himself as a policeman and makes reasonable inquiries, and where nothing in the initial stages of the encounter serves to dispel his reasonable fear for his own or others' safety, he is entitled for the protection of himself and others in the area to conduct a carefully limited search of the outer clothing of such persons in an attempt to discover weapons which might be used to assault him.

Terry was the first criminal case in which this new "balancing" test was applied. The result was authorization of a search and seizure on less than probable cause. In this case, the officer's conduct was the stop and frisk of a suspect whom the officer suspected was about to commit a crime. The circumstances of this contact, if governed by the traditional pre-existing law, would not have permitted any intervention by the officer. In *Terry,* the Court found that the officer's conduct was indeed a seizure and search of the person. However, the Court also found the officer's conduct was not as intrusive as a full-scale arrest or full-scale search.

In order to investigate suspicious behavior, an officer is justified in a wide variety of situations, with less than probable cause and without a warrant, to detain the suspect temporarily to make reasonable inquiry to confirm or dispel the suspicion. Moreover, if the officer has a suspicion that the suspect might be armed and dangerous, the officer may conduct a patdown search of the suspect to ascertain whether the suspect has a weapon that could harm the officer or others. The officer, in order to act in these ways, needs only **reasonable suspicion**. Reasonable suspicion, being a lesser standard than probable cause, does not require as much evidence of criminal wrongdoing as probable cause—nor is it necessary that the officer's information be as reliable as that required for probable cause.

Although the *Terry* case involved a combined stop and frisk, later decisions of the Supreme Court have extended the principle to stops of suspects on less than probable cause in the absence of an officer's belief that the person is armed and dangerous. Thus, an officer may temporarily detain, or **stop**, a suspect if the officer possesses reasonable suspicion, but not probable cause, that a particular individual is about to commit, is committing, or has committed a crime. During this temporary detention, the officer may question the suspect in order to confirm or dispel that suspicion. It is important to note that, unlike probable cause, reasonable suspicion does not require that the officer know with particularity the type of crime committed—particularity is only required with respect to the identity of the individual.

If the officer has a reasonable suspicion that the suspect is armed and dangerous, then the officer may conduct a limited patdown search of the person's

REASONABLE SUSPICION
That level of suspicion, less than probable cause, that permits an officer to detain a suspect temporarily to make reasonable inquiry to confirm or dispel the suspicion.

STOP
A temporary detention, not amounting to a full-blown arrest, requiring only reasonable suspicion that a particular individual is about to commit, is committing, or has committed a crime.

FRISK
A limited patdown search of the outer garments of a person to determine whether he or she possesses a weapon with which to cause injury to an officer or others.

outer clothing—a **frisk**—in an attempt to discover weapons. In those situations when an officer reasonably suspects that a particular person is engaged in a crime and is armed and dangerous, the officer may detain the person as well as conduct a patdown search of the person. The officer's power to stop and frisk a suspect is not unlimited. One of the serious issues is just how long a suspect can be detained without probable cause and have the action still be considered within the scope of reasonable police conduct. Another question is how far, if at all, an officer may go beyond a patdown of the outer clothing of a suspect. The main issue to be considered, then, is determining the scope of police action on less than probable cause under the balancing test announced in *Terry*.

The Permissible Scope of Stops

An officer may stop an individual based on a reasonable suspicion that the person is engaged in some criminal activity or is armed and dangerous. The detention cannot rise to the level of an arrest, since probable cause is required for that action. Detention, justified on the basis of reasonable suspicion, constitutes a seizure, but, because it is less intrusive than an arrest, the level of required justification is lower than the probable cause that is necessary for an arrest.

In determining whether an investigative detention based on reasonable suspicion rises to the level of a *de facto* arrest (an arrest in fact), a number of factors must be considered:

1. the length of the detention, i.e., whether the detention lasted longer than was necessary to clarify the circumstances for which the person was stopped;
2. whether the person was forcibly removed from home or another place that he or she was entitled to be; and
3. whether the officer pursued the investigation in a reasonable and diligent manner, i.e., utilized a method of investigation that was likely to confirm or dispel the officer's suspicions quickly.

What Is Reasonable Suspicion?

The short definition of reasonable suspicion is more than an inarticulable hunch and less than probable cause. As the Supreme Court held in *Terry,* reasonable suspicion exists when a law enforcement officer has a reasonable, articulable suspicion that criminal activity is afoot. Factors such as location and a suspect's behavior are used to determine reasonable suspicion. In *Illinois v. Wardlow,*[143] Wardlow fled upon seeing a caravan of police vehicles patrolling an area known for heavy drug trafficking. Two officers saw Wardlow in flight, gave chase, and caught up with him. The officers frisked Wardlow for weapons and found a handgun. Wardlow was convicted of unlawful use of a weapon by a felon. He moved to suppress the gun, claiming that the officer did not have reasonable suspicion sufficient to justify an investigative stop under the *Terry* doctrine. The trial court denied the motion, but the Illinois appellate and supreme courts reversed, and the state took the case to the United States Supreme Court. The Supreme Court held that the officers did have a reasonable suspicion that criminal activity was afoot. The Court credited the totality of the circumstances, including Wardlow's headlong flight upon seeing the officers and the fact that the surrounding area was known for heavy narcotics trafficking, as creating reasonable suspicion.

Law enforcement professionals may assess the totality of the circumstances and rely on their training and experience to determine whether reasonable suspicion exists. A case that contributes greatly to the understanding of this is *United States v. Arvizu*.[144] There, a Border Patrol agent investigating sensor activity reported in an area known for drug smuggling observed a van known to the officer as the type of vehicle used for smuggling. The van was traveling on a route commonly used by drug smugglers to circumvent a Border Patrol checkpoint. The agent pulled off the road to observe the van and, as the van approached, the agent observed the driver appearing stiff and seeming to avoid looking at the agent. In this remote area, the agent thought it odd that the driver did not wave at him, as was the custom. There were three children in the backseat, and the agent noticed that two of the children's knees were unusually high, as if their feet were propped up by something on the floor. The agent then followed the van; all three children put up their hands and waved at him in an abnormal manner, acting as though they were being instructed. The agent radioed for a registration check, learning the vehicle was registered to a residence four blocks north of the border in an area notorious for alien and drug smuggling. Finally, when the agent observed the driver signal a turn, change his mind, and then suddenly turn at the last turnoff that would allow the van to avoid the checkpoint, the agent made a vehicle stop. He asked the driver if he could search the car. The driver consented, and the agent found nearly 138 pounds of marijuana under the passengers' feet and in the back of the van.

Arvizu was charged with federal drug crimes for possession of the marijuana and moved to suppress the evidence. He was convicted, and the case went to the Supreme Court of the United States. The Court found that the Border Patrol agent acted lawfully when he stopped the van because he had reasonable suspicion that criminal activity was afoot. In its decision, the Supreme Court explained that officers may "draw on their own experience and specialized training to make inferences and deductions" and apply them to the totality of the circumstances to determine whether reasonable suspicion exists.

Anonymous tips can create problems for law enforcement. On one hand, law enforcement agents obtain information about possible criminal activity from an anonymous source and they want to investigate the tip. On the other hand, anonymous tips are sometimes unreliable and investigation may intrude on an individual's privacy. Earlier in this chapter, discussion of the case of *Illinois v. Gates*[145] demonstrated that an anonymous tip can be the basis of a finding of probable cause. But anonymous tips can also be the basis for law enforcement action based on a reasonable suspicion. In light of the balancing under *Terry* principles, the Fourth Amendment authorizes law enforcement to stop and frisk when an anonymous tip is reliable enough to raise a reasonable suspicion that criminal activity is afoot.

For example, in the case of *Alabama v. White*,[146] an officer in the Montgomery, Alabama, Police Department received a call from an anonymous person stating that the defendant, mentioned by name, would be leaving a particular address at a particular time and would enter a particularly described automobile and drive to Dobey's Motel, carrying a brown attaché case with an ounce of cocaine in it. The officer and his partner went to the location, saw the described car, and observed a woman, with nothing in her hands, entered the car and drove along the most direct route to Dobey's Motel. The officers stopped the defendant just short of the motel and told her they suspected her of carrying cocaine and asked permission to search the car. In the trunk they found a locked brown attaché case. They asked and received permission to open it and found marijuana. The officers arrested White. During processing at the station, the officers found three milligrams of cocaine in her purse.

White was charged with possession of both drugs. She moved to suppress the drugs at her trial, claiming the officers lacked reasonable suspicion to stop her. The trial court denied her motion, but the appellate court reversed her conviction and the state supreme court agreed. The state took the case to the United States Supreme Court, which reversed the decision of the state courts and upheld the reasonableness of the police officers' conduct in stopping White. The Court found that, when the officers stopped her, under the totality of the circumstances, they had sufficiently corroborated the anonymous tip to furnish reasonable suspicion that she was engaged in criminal activity. Though the Court thought this was a close case, the Court upheld the officers' actions, stating, "When significant aspects of the caller's predictions were verified, there was reason to believe not only that the caller was honest but also that he was well informed, at least well enough to justify the stop."

On the other end of the spectrum, in connection with anonymous tipsters and reasonable suspicion, is the case of *Florida v. J.L.*[147] There, police received an anonymous tip that a young black male was carrying a gun. The tipster said the young black male would be standing at a particular bus stop and he would be wearing a plaid shirt. When the officers arrived at the bus stop, they found J.L., a young black male wearing a plaid shirt. They did not see J.L. carrying the firearm or making any threatening movements. The officers approached J.L. and frisked him. They found a gun in his pocket. J.L. was charged and convicted of state firearms offenses. He moved to suppress the gun, and the state courts suppressed the gun as the fruit of an unlawful search, undertaken without reasonable suspicion. The state took the case to the United States Supreme Court, which held that the officers did not have reasonable suspicion to stop and frisk J.L. According to the Court, the officers did not have reasonable suspicion based on the anonymous tip alone. An anonymous tip is reliable when it provides predictive information so the police can test the tipster's knowledge or credibility. In this case, the tipster's information only predicted J.L.'s location and attire. Anyone seeing him standing on the street could have provided that information. Hence, the information did not describe inside information of criminal activity afoot.

APPLICATION CASE

In *Hiibel v. Sixth Judicial District Court of Nevada, Humbolt County*,[148] a deputy sheriff responded to a call reporting an assault of a young woman in a truck by a man on a particular road. The deputy went to the scene and approached a truck in which a young woman was seated and the defendant was standing alongside the truck. The officer asked the man to identify himself, but he would not. The officer repeated this request 11 times, but Hiibel, refused. Even when the officer told Hiibel that he could be arrested if he refused to identify himself, Hiibel refused. The officer arrested Hiibel, and he was convicted of violating a specific Nevada statute that requires an individual subjected to a *Terry* stop to identify himself. The case made its way to the United States Supreme Court, which upheld the conviction, stating, "The Court is now of the view that *Terry* principles permit a state to require a suspect to disclose his name in the course of a *Terry* stop."

The Duration of the Detention

The duration of the detention can be too long to be justified on grounds of reasonable suspicion. In one case, the Supreme Court found that the detention of an air traveler's luggage for 90 minutes was itself "sufficient to render the seizure unreasonable."[149] In another case, the Court concluded that a 16-hour detention of a suspected drug smuggler, who was believed to have swallowed narcotics-filled balloons, was "not unreasonably long."[150] In yet another case, the Court found that a detention of a few minutes at the station house for fingerprinting was unreasonable.[151]

In each of these cases, the time alone was arguably not determinative. In the luggage detention case, the Court also found that the officers did not pursue the investigation diligently. The length of the detention was occasioned by the need to transport the luggage from one airport to another to subject it to a dog sniff test. The Court found that the officers had more than ample time to take the dog to the airport, since they were awaiting the suspect's arrival. In the drug smuggler's case, the Court stated that the defendant brought on the length of the detention herself, through her "heroic" efforts to avoid defecating for that extended period of time. And, in the fingerprinting case, the Court found that the forcible transportation of the suspect from his home for the brief fingerprinting detention was itself a *de facto* arrest.

APPLICATION CASES

In *Michigan v. Summers*,[152] the Supreme Court of the United States held that, when executing a search warrant, an occupant of the home may be detained for the duration of the search. The Court stated that, although the restraint on the liberty of the detained occupant was significant, it was less intrusive than the search itself.

However, in *Bailey v. United States*,[153] the Court held that a detention of the defendant at a place beyond the immediate vicinity of his apartment while it was being searched was not permissible under *Summers* as a detention incident to the execution of a search warrant.

Forcible Removal of the Suspect to the Station House

As in the fingerprinting detention case previously discussed, the Court has found that the forcible removal of a suspect from his or her home or another place where the suspect is entitled to be constitutes a *de facto* arrest. Remember that in such cases there is no probable cause, but merely reasonable suspicion, for the detention. Under such circumstances, the exercise of dominion and control over a suspect in forcibly removing that suspect to the police station is far greater an intrusion than an on-the-scene detention for investigation, commonly referred to as an investigative detention.

In *Hayes v. Florida,*[154] the Supreme Court held that the forcible taking of a suspect to a police station for fingerprinting will be considered an arrest, requiring probable cause. Notwithstanding, the Supreme Court in that case indicated that officers may conduct fingerprinting in the field, if several conditions are met. These conditions include a reasonable suspicion that the suspect has committed a crime, a reasonable basis to believe that fingerprinting will establish or negate the suspect's connection with that crime, and that the procedure be carried out as quickly as possible.

Reasonable Diligence in Investigation

The final factor that will determine the reasonableness of a less-than-probable-cause detention is the diligence with which the investigating officer acts to confirm or dispel the suspicion that caused the stop in the first place. The officer need not use the least intrusive means of investigating. If, in hindsight, a less intrusive means could be said to have been available, the question will be whether the officer acted reasonably in failing to recognize and pursue those means. In the final analysis, the test will be whether the officer "pursued his investigation in a diligent and reasonable manner."[155]

A brief discussion of an important Supreme Court decision in this area will help illustrate this point. In *United States v. Sharpe,*[156] a DEA agent patrolling a road in North Carolina spotted a pickup truck and car driving in tandem. The agent thought the truck was heavily loaded and looked somewhat suspicious, so he followed the two vehicles and, after about 20 miles, called for help from the highway patrol to make an investigatory stop. When the agent and the highway patrol officer tried to stop the vehicles, the truck pulled out, sped away, and was chased and stopped down the highway by the officer. The DEA agent stopped the car, radioed for more help from the local police, and did not reach the detained pickup truck for about ten minutes. When the agent got to the truck, he smelled marijuana through the rear window of the pickup. He also learned that there was, in fact, a connection between the driver of the pickup and the driver of the car, the defendant. By the time the DEA agent returned to the car and arrested the defendant, some 30 to 40 minutes had elapsed since he first stopped the car. The Supreme Court found the detention reasonable, based only on reasonable suspicion. The Court noted that the agent's investigation was diligent and reasonable, even if he might have acted more speedily, for example, by having the patrolman investigate the pickup truck.

Extension of Frisks to Vehicles and Homes

The scope of a search based on reasonable suspicion is also limited because, if the action becomes a full-scale search, probable cause will be required. The patting down of a person an officer has reasonable suspicion to believe is armed is limited to the person's outer clothing in an attempt to discover weapons. Under this rule, it would be impermissible for the officer to thrust a hand into a person's pocket. If an officer sees or feels something during a frisk that may reasonably be a gun or other weapon, then the officer may search further than the outer clothing. A frisk may not be required when the suspect, who is believed to be armed and dangerous, makes sudden movements as if reaching for a weapon. In such circumstances, the officer is justified in reaching into the place where the officer believes the weapon to be without first frisking the suspect. If the patdown or frisk of the suspect dispels the officer's suspicion that the suspect is carrying a weapon, then the search must cease. If, on the other hand, the officer feels an object during the frisk that the officer has reason to believe is a weapon, then the officer may seize the object and continue further with the frisk. Any soft object, however bulky, will not likely justify further investigation.

In the case of *Minnesota v. Dickerson,*[157] an officer removed an object from the pocket of a person during a patdown search that turned out to be a small plastic bag containing crack cocaine. The Supreme Court found the search and seizure unlawful but said that an officer may seize an object if the officer can detect by feel during a patdown search that the object is contraband. In *Dickerson,* however, the officer never thought that the lump he felt in the pocket was a weapon but also did not immediately recognize it as cocaine. He determined the lump to be cocaine only after he "squeezed, slid, and otherwise manipulated the pocket's contents." The Court held that the officer's actions did not qualify under the **plain feel doctrine**, which was discussed earlier in this chapter. By so stating, the Court created the doctrine.

A police officer may also search the passenger compartment of an automobile on reasonable suspicion. Such a search is allowed for the purpose of protecting the police officer from weapons in the automobile that might be used against the officer. The search, or "frisk," of an automobile's passenger compartment is limited to those areas and any containers in which a weapon may be placed or hidden. The officer must possess reasonable suspicion that the person is dangerous and may gain immediate control of a weapon. The frisk of a car is limited to those areas where a weapon might be, unlike a SILA search of an automobile that allows the officer to search anywhere in the passenger compartment, regardless of whether the area searched may contain a weapon or destructible evidence.

PLAIN FEEL DOCTRINE The principle, extending the plain view doctrine to the sense of touch, that allows an officer to seize an object during a lawful patdown search, if the object's incriminating nature is immediately apparent, meaning that the officer has probable cause to believe the object is contraband or fruits, instrumentalities, or evidence of a crime.

APPLICATION CASE

In *Ybarra v. Illinois,*[158] the officers entered a small tavern with a warrant authorizing the search of the tavern and a bartender for heroin and other items. There were a number of patrons in the bar when the officers entered. The officers patted down all of the patrons, including the defendant. As a result of the patdown of the defendant, an officer discovered drugs in his possession, hidden in a cigarette package. However, the officers had no suspicion that the defendant was armed and dangerous, nor did the warrant extend to him or any other patron of the tavern. The Court held that the patdown search of the accused, without any suspicion of his being armed and dangerous, was illegal.

©Paul S. Howell/Getty Images

Fourth Amendment rights to privacy are reduced in a public school setting, allowing for search and seizure based upon reasonable suspicion of illegal activity.

A frisk of a house may also be permitted on less than probable cause. When officers arrest a person in a home or other premises and there is a reasonable suspicion that individuals who pose a danger to officers or others are concealed in the house, the officers may make a protective sweep of the building. This power to conduct a protective sweep is different from the automatic extension of the SILA area of immediate control. Keep in mind that the *Buie*[159] case, discussed in the SILA section of this chapter, extended the allowable search area into closets and other spaces immediately adjoining the place of arrest. That extension was automatic, not even requiring reasonable suspicion. The *Buie* case also authorized the protective sweep of other areas of the premises to search for dangerous persons, but only if there is reasonable suspicion that such persons might be present.

Another area where the Supreme Court has allowed a search on reasonable suspicion involves schoolchildren in public schools. In *New Jersey v. T.L.O.*,[160] a school official had searched a high school student's purse, looking for cigarettes as evidence to corroborate a teacher's report that the student had been smoking in a lavatory, which was against school rules. He found the cigarettes and noticed some rolling papers, which led to further searches of the purse, during which the official found marijuana and evidence that the student was selling the drugs. The Court upheld this warrantless search, declaring that searches of schoolchildren by school authorities may be conducted without a warrant, based on a reasonable suspicion of a violation of school rules or laws. Balancing the citizen's Fourth Amendment interests against the state's interests in this manner is consistent with the reduced expectation of privacy in public schools. The state's interest is in maintaining order and discipline in schools. The citizen's interest is in the right to be secure in his or her "person, houses, papers, and effects."

SUSPICIONLESS STOPS AND SEARCHES: THE SPECIAL NEEDS EXCEPTION TO THE PROBABLE CAUSE AND WARRANT REQUIREMENTS

There are a number of arenas where societal needs create a government interest that argues for suspicionless stops and searches of individuals. Here we are not concerned with situations such as entry into airport boarding areas, where all passengers are subject to routine stops and searches. In recent years, the Supreme Court has approved stops and searches of persons in certain situations where there is absolutely no suspicion of any particular person acting unlawfully. In these situations, the Court has found a governmental interest separate from usual law enforcement needs; the government has demonstrated special needs. A few categories that carry criminal penalties that the Court has approved are sobriety checkpoints,[161] fixed inland border checkpoints (to search for illegal aliens),[162] and probation officers' searches of probationers' homes.[163]

In the case of *Maryland v. King*,[164] the Supreme Court extended the suspicionless search doctrine to the state taking a DNA sample from a suspect arrested for "a serious offense" without grounds for believing that the results would be used in a criminal prosecution. In a 5-4 decision, the Court found sufficient government interest in using such information to further the needs of the criminal justice system, while the defendant's privacy interests did not outweigh the state's. The defendant's DNA sample was used to compare with DNA samples from cold cases, leading to his identification as the likely perpetrator of a rape committed six years before. The evidence was admitted against King at trial, and he was convicted. The decision in *King* also has implications for the search incident to arrest and inventory exceptions to the warrant and probable cause requirements of the Fourth Amendment.

APPLICATION CASE

In *United States v. Knights*,[165] Knights signed a probation order in which he agreed to submit himself, his property, and his home to searches at any time with or without a warrant, and even in the absence of probable cause. The police conducted a warrantless search of Knights' apartment based on reasonable suspicion. The court upheld the search, reasoning that the conditions of probation diminished Knights' reasonable expectation of privacy.

In addition, the Court has approved drug testing in a few areas where no criminal penalties were involved: for example, certain railway employees after railway accidents,[166] drug testing of Customs Service employees engaged in certain activities,[167] and drug testing of all high school and junior high school athletes in a school district.[168]

APPLICATION CASE

In *Board of Education v. Earls*,[169] the court upheld a school policy that required all middle and high school students who wished to participate in any "competitive" extracurricular activities—including choir, band, sports, and the academic team—to submit to a drug test. The court concluded that the drug testing policy was reasonable, even though the schools in question did not have a major drug problem, as the invasion of students' privacy caused by the drug testing was not significant.

These situations are exceptions, however, to the general rule that search or seizure must be accompanied by either individualized probable cause or reasonable suspicion. In three other cases, the Supreme Court demonstrated that there are limits to government claims for special needs that suspend the requirement of individualized suspicion. First, in *Chandler v. Miller,*[170] the Court held that Georgia's requirement that certain candidates for state office pass a mandatory drug test did not fit within the category of constitutionally permissible suspicionless searches. A significant aspect of the Court's reasoning was that the state did not show any specific suspicion that there was drug use by state officials. In short, the state did not demonstrate any special needs.

Similarly, in *Ferguson v. City of Charleston,*[171] the Court declared invalid a city's scheme that identified and tested, without consent, any maternity patient in the public hospital suspected of drug use, where the use jeopardized the health of the unborn child. Under the plan, if the results of a urine test were positive, the police would be notified and the mother would be prosecuted. The Court found that the claimed special need in this plan was one not divorced from the state's general interest in law enforcement. Hence, the Court found the plan to be unreasonable and unconstitutional.

Finally, in *City of Indianapolis v. Edmond,*[172] the Supreme Court reviewed a city's drug interdiction checkpoint plan. Under the plan, the police set up roadblock checkpoints on six occasions over a four-month period, mostly during the day. Under the written plan, a predetermined number of vehicles were stopped for two to three minutes each. At least one officer approached each car and told each driver the purpose of the stop—to check for drugs—and asked each driver to produce a license and registration. While the officer looked for signs of impairment and conducted an open-view examination of the vehicle from outside, a narcotics-detection dog walked around the outside of the vehicle, sniffing for contraband. The program had a 9 percent yield of arrests, more than half of which were for drug-related crimes. The Court struck down the city's plan as unconstitutional, distinguishing the border-stop and sobriety checkpoint cases. According to the Court, those cases involved checkpoints "designed primarily to serve purposes closely related to the problems of policing the border or the necessity of ensuring roadway safety," whereas, in this case, the primary purpose of the city's roadblock was to "detect evidence of ordinary criminal wrongdoing." In short, the city failed to demonstrate special needs justifying suspicionless stops of motorists.

OBJECTING TO THE INTRODUCTION OF EVIDENCE CLAIMED TO BE ILLEGALLY SEIZED

In order to claim that evidence has been illegally seized, an accused in a criminal case must have the right to make such a claim and must file a written request in court at the earliest opportunity. The right to make the claim has traditionally been called **standing**, and the written request is called a **motion to suppress**.

Standing

Traditionally, the right to contest an illegal search and seizure—and, for that matter, any claimed constitutional or law violation—has been known as standing. Analytically, however, standing is nothing more than the possession of a claim of a personal,

STANDING
The right to contest an illegal search and seizure, or any claimed constitutional or law violation; actually, it is nothing more than the possession of a claim of a personal, reasonable expectation of privacy in the thing seized or the place searched.

MOTION TO SUPPRESS
The written request to a court, made by a defendant in a criminal case, objecting to illegally obtained evidence.

reasonable expectation of privacy in the thing seized or the place searched. Earlier in this chapter, *Katz v. United States* and its doctrine of the expectation of privacy were discussed. The requirement of standing is nothing more than the law's demand that one who claims a Fourth Amendment violation must demonstrate a personal expectation of the privacy that was violated. If the defendant has no personal and reasonable expectation of privacy in the place searched or the things seized, there is no basis on which that person can make a Fourth Amendment complaint, and the motion to suppress the evidence will be dismissed.

Two United States Supreme Court decisions will be helpful in illustrating who may have standing. In *Rakas v. Illinois,*[173] officers stopped an automobile matching the description of a car used in a robbery that took place shortly before the stop. The officers ordered the occupants out of the car and then searched the passenger compartment. The police found rifle shells in a glove box and a sawed-off shotgun under a passenger seat. The defendant, a passenger in the car, attempted to exclude the shells and the rifle from evidence. The United States Supreme Court held that the defendant could not contest the search and seizure because he lacked a reasonable expectation of privacy in the car. According to the Court, Fourth Amendment rights are personal in nature, and therefore only the person whose rights are violated can challenge the search. Under the Court's reasoning, the owner of the car could contest the search because he possessed a reasonable expectation of privacy. The defendant, as a passenger in the car, lacked any personal expectation of privacy in the car.

Two years after *Rakas,* the Supreme Court decided the case of *Rawlings v. Kentucky.*[174] In *Rawlings,* the defendant placed a variety of controlled substances into the purse of an acquaintance in an attempt to avoid discovery by the police. When the police ordered the acquaintance to empty her purse, revealing the narcotics, the defendant admitted that the narcotics were his. The Court held that the defendant lacked a reasonable expectation of privacy in the purse. In reaching this conclusion, the Court reaffirmed that in *Rakas* it had abandoned a separate inquiry into "standing" in favor of an inquiry that focused on the substance of a defendant's legitimate expectation of privacy in the area searched.

A person may gain an expectation of privacy in another person's property, because the concept of expectation of privacy does not rest on some kind of property interest. For instance, a person may gain a reasonable expectation of privacy in another's car. If, on a regular basis, the owner of a car allows the defendant to use and exercise control over the car, then the defendant may gain a reasonable expectation of privacy in the car. The same holds true if the property in question is a dwelling. In fact, if the property searched is a dwelling as opposed to a vehicle, then it is much easier to establish an expectation of privacy, since, as the Supreme Court has pointed out, a person has a lesser expectation of privacy in a vehicle. Thus, in *Minnesota v. Olson,*[175] the Court held that an overnight guest in another's home gains a reasonable expectation of privacy in that home for Fourth Amendment purposes.

APPLICATION CASE

In *Minnesota v. Carter,*[176] a police officer peeked through a gap in the blinds on a window of an apartment and observed Carter bagging cocaine at the kitchen table with two other people. Carter and his companion from Chicago,

Johns, did not live in the apartment; they were in the apartment for the sole purpose of bagging cocaine. Based upon the view into the apartment, the police obtained evidence of cocaine-related crimes and arrested and charged Carter, Johns, and the lessee of the apartment with those crimes. At trial, Carter and Johns moved to suppress all the evidence, claiming it was fruit of an unlawful search. The trial court denied the motion, and the case ultimately went to the United States Supreme Court. The Court affirmed the trial court's ruling on the motion to suppress, finding Carter and Johns did not have an expectation of privacy in the apartment and hence could not claim the police officer's peek into the window was an illegal search. The commercial nature of Carter and Johns' visit, the relatively short time Carter and Johns were at the apartment, and the lack of connection between Carter and Johns and the resident led the Court to conclude that Carter and Johns did not have a legitimate expectation of privacy while in the apartment bagging the cocaine.

Motion to Suppress Evidence

If a defendant believes that evidence has been illegally obtained, an objection to its use by the prosecution must be made in court at the earliest opportunity. The written objection, called a motion to suppress, usually must be filed within a set time after the defendant's arraignment.

The motion to suppress evidence will set forth the reasons the defendant thinks that the evidence was illegally obtained. The objection to a search warrant might attack the search warrant itself, the scope of the search, or the seizure of some item not listed in the warrant. For example, in the case of a search incident to an arrest, the objection may be that there was insufficient probable cause to make the arrest; if the arrest was illegal, then the search and seizure of the evidence was unlawful. Or the defendant may claim that the SILA extended beyond the area under his or her immediate control, which would make the search, and therefore the seizure of evidence, unlawful. Figure 9–3 shows the motion to suppress from the O.J. Simpson trial.

A hearing is usually held on the motion to suppress evidence prior to the trial. At that hearing, the defendant will attempt to develop through testimony the reasons the evidence should be excluded. The prosecution will offer a rebuttal and present the reasons to prove that the evidence was legally obtained. If the magistrate or judge denies the motion to suppress before or at the preliminary hearing, the motion can be renewed at trial. If the magistrate or judge agrees with the defendant, the evidence will be excluded, but if the judge decides that the evidence was legally obtained, it will be admitted against the accused at the trial. The admission of evidence over the defendant's objection is grounds for appeal. If the appellate court thinks the evidence was illegally obtained and should have been excluded, the conviction, in most instances, will be reversed.

The People of the State of California, Plaintiff

v.

Orenthal James Simpson, Defendant

NOTICE OF MOTION AND MOTION TO SUPPRESS AND RETURN EVIDENCE,
TO QUASH AND TRAVERSE SEARCH WARRANT;
DOCKET-NUMBER: BA097211
Municipal Court, Los Angeles Judicial District, Los Angeles County.
Division 35

Filed: June 29, 1994

TO THE ABOVE COURT AND TO THE DISTRICT ATTORNEY OF LOS ANGELES COUNTY
AND/OR HIS REPRESENTATIVE, AND ALL INTERESTED PARTIES:

NOTICE IS HEREBY GIVEN that the Defendant, ORENTHAL JAMES SIMPSON, by and through
counsel, hereby moves for an order suppressing and returning all evidence described below and any fruits
thereof on the ground that it was obtained by a search without a warrant that was unreasonable, and that
a subsequent search with Search Warrant No. 94-0093, attached hereto as Exhibit A, was unreasonable
because the property obtained is not that described in the warrant, there was not probable cause for the
issuance of the warrant, the method of execution of the warrant violated federal and state constitutional
standards, and there were other violations of federal and state constitutional standards. Defendants will
also move to quash and traverse the aforementioned search warrant based on material misrepresentations
and omissions contained therein.

This motion will be heard on Thursday, June 30, 1994, at 8:30 A.M., or as soon thereafter as the matter
can be heard in Division 35 of the above court, located at 210 West Temple Street, Los Angeles,
California 90012, at the time of the Preliminary Hearing set for the case. This motion will rely on the
attached memorandum of points and authorities, the declaration of Gerald F. Uelmen, the files of this
case, and evidence to be presented at the hearing.

The evidence to be suppressed and returned consists of all tangible and intangible evidence obtained as a
result of any illegal act including, but not limited to the unlawful entry into the curtilage of defendant's
residence at 360 North Rockingham Avenue, West Los Angeles, California by police on June 13, 1994,
the unlawful securing of said premises, the warrantless observation and search of said premises, the
warrantless search of a 1994 Ford Bronco, California license 3CWZ788, as well as evidence obtained in
the execution of an unlawful search warrant to search said premises, and any fruits of any of the
aforementioned illegal acts. This motion specifically includes, but is not limited to each of the items
disclosed to the defendant and enumerated one through thirty-four in the Property Reports attached
hereto as Exhibit B, dated June 14, 1994, with the exception of item number seventeen.

Respectfully Submitted,

LAW OFFICES OF ROBERT L. SHAPIRO
By: ROBERT L. SHAPIRO
By: GERALD F. UELMEN
By: SARA L. CAPLAN
Attorneys for Defendant
ORENTHAL JAMES SIMPSON

DATED: June 28, 1994

FIGURE 9–3 Sample motion to suppress.

REVIEW AND APPLICATION

SUMMARY

(1) The primary purpose of the exclusionary rule is to prevent the introduction of illegally obtained evidence in trial.

(2) The two-pronged test for determining whether a search occurred under the Fourth Amendment examines whether (1) the person alleging that a search occurred has exhibited an actual, subjective expectation of privacy in the place searched; and (2) the person's expectation is one that society is prepared to recognize as reasonable or legitimate. If both conditions are present, then there is a search.

(3) The proper procedure and requirements for obtaining a search warrant are for the officer to fill out a warrant application (an affidavit) containing an adequate statement of probable cause and stating specifically the items to be found and seized.

(4) Probable cause means a fair probability that a crime has been committed, that a person possesses seizable property, or that seizable property or a person subject to arrest is located in a particular place. Probable cause may be established by facts and circumstances that would lead a person in the officer's position reasonably to believe the facts to be true. The facts may be perceived by the officer personally or reported by a known or unknown informant. If the facts are reported by an informant, the officer must have information as to the informant's basis of knowledge and reliability, or the information must be communicated under circumstances that lend credibility to the informant's information. Finally, the officer may investigate an informant's tip that is insufficient to provide probable cause, thereby gaining sufficient information to equal probable cause when combined with the tip.

(5) A search incident to a lawful arrest can be made only when an officer has executed a lawful arrest. Such a search is limited to the person of the arrestee; the area within the arrestee's immediate control; any area immediately adjoining the place of arrest from which an attack could be immediately launched, if the arrest takes place in a home or other structure; and the interior of the passenger compartment of a car and any containers, open or closed, therein if the arrest takes place while the arrestee is in a car or recently emerged from a car.

(6) The three ways that a vehicle may be searched without a warrant are (1) incident to a lawful arrest of a passenger; (2) according to the inventory exception; and (3) under the vehicle exception, when there is probable cause to believe that the vehicle contains seizable objects.

(7) The two requirements for a valid consent are that the consent must be voluntarily given and that the person giving the consent has authority, or at least apparent authority, over the property.

(8) Validity of a third-party's consent depends on whether the third party and the defendant have common authority, or apparent authority, for most purposes over the premises or property.

(9) Four circumstances have been recognized as exigent: (1) hot pursuit of a fleeing felon; (2) imminent destruction of evidence; (3) the need to prevent a suspect's escape; and (4) the risk of harm to the police or to others.

(10) The requirements of the plain view doctrine are that (1) the officer observes the object from a lawful vantage point; (2) the officer has a right of physical access to the object from the lawful vantage point; and (3) the nature of the object is immediately apparent as an article subject to seizure (i.e., that it is contraband or a fruit, instrumentality, or evidence of a crime).

(11) In order for a law enforcement officer to stop and frisk a suspect, the officer must have a reasonable suspicion that a particular person is engaged in a crime and is armed and dangerous.

(12) The standing requirement is that, before a defendant may claim a constitutional violation, he or she must demonstrate a personal, reasonable expectation of privacy in the place searched or the things seized.

KEY TERMS

exclusionary rule   268
fruit of the poisonous tree doctrine   269
independent source doctrine   269
attenuation doctrine   270
inevitable discovery doctrine   271
silver platter doctrine   271
deterrence rationale   272
good faith exception   273
impeachment exception   275
false friend doctrine   278
open fields doctrine   278
curtilage   278
seizure of property   284
seizure of a person   284
search warrant   286
fruit of a crime   287

instrumentality of a crime   287
evidence of a crime   287
contraband   287
probable cause   287
neutral magistrate   287
probable cause to search   289
probable cause to arrest   290
totality of the circumstances for probable cause   292
fair probability   293
knock and announce, or knock and notice   298
staleness doctrine   300
anticipatory warrant   301
return of the search warrant   301

search incident to a lawful arrest (SILA)   302
protective sweep   305
vehicle exception   309
inventory search   311
consent search   312
consent   312
totality of the circumstances for consent   313
common authority   315
apparent authority doctrine   317
exigent circumstances search and seizure   317
plain view doctrine   320
reasonable suspicion   323
stop   323
frisk   324
plain feel doctrine   329
standing   332
motion to suppress   332

QUESTIONS FOR REVIEW

1. What is the primary purpose of the exclusionary rule?
2. What are the conditions examined in the two-pronged test for determining, under the Fourth Amendment, whether there is a search?

3. How does an officer obtain a valid search warrant?

4. How can an officer establish probable cause?

5. What are the limitations on a search incident to lawful custodial arrest?

6. What are the three ways in which a vehicle may be searched without a warrant?

7. What are the two requirements for a valid consent?

8. What is the additional requirement for a valid consent if a third party is giving consent?

9. What circumstances have been recognized as exigent, allowing an officer to search with a warrant?

10. What elements must be satisfied before an officer may seize an object under the plain view doctrine?

11. What justification does an officer need to conduct a stop and frisk?

12. What is the standing requirement for a defendant's assertion of a constitutional violation by law enforcement officers?

WORKPLACE APPLICATIONS

1. In addition to the examples given in the chapter, list five specific examples of fruits, instrumentalities, contraband, and evidence that you could specify in a search warrant. Are there any examples that could fit into two or more categories?

2. You have received confidential, reliable information from an informant you have successfully used six times in the past. The past information has led to fifteen arrests and the seizure of two guns and several pounds of cocaine. The current information is that a large shipment of marijuana will be arriving at 789 Southwestern Avenue at 4 o'clock this afternoon in a white Cadillac. You have staked out the location, have run a check of the license plates of all vehicles seen at the location, and have ascertained the names of the owner and occupants. Write an affidavit requesting search and arrest warrants. Be sure to include all contraband, evidence, fruits, and instrumentalities that you expect to find and locations you wish to search.

3. At roll call, the lieutenant hands you and five other officers a search warrant and tells you to execute it. The place to be searched is in a trailer park, and the items to be seized are stolen cars and parts. It seems odd to you that the four cars listed on the warrant could be in a trailer park lot, but none of the other officers think anything is wrong with the warrant. After searching the trailer and lot, you do not find the items listed in the warrant, but you discover contraband in plain view. However, you discover that the name of the street was misspelled on the warrant and you have searched the wrong location. Did you conduct a legal search? Why or why not?

4. You receive an anonymous tip that there is marijuana growing in the backyard of a certain address. You go to the location to investigate and discover a six-foot wooden fence surrounding the curtilage of the house. Is it a search if you look through a knothole in the fence? If you get a ladder and look over the fence? If you get a 6'5"officer to peer over the fence? If you open the gate door a crack and just look into the yard?

5. Officers suspect that an 18-year-old male is responsible for thousands of dollars of personal property damage through the creation of gang-related graffiti all over town. Officers go to his house and, after talking with his mother, determine that the suspect is not home, that he does not have a lock on his bedroom door, and that his mother goes into his room twice a week, once to collect his laundry and again to put it away. The mother consents to a search of her son's room for spray paint cans. Is the consent valid?

ETHICAL DILEMMA

1. A search warrant that your lieutenant handed you to execute at a crack house is invalid because of a misstatement about an informant, but you are the only one who recognizes the error. You know that a reasonable officer, such as your lieutenant and your partner, would believe the warrant to be valid, and therefore the warrant will have no problem being admitted in court. The department anticipates a record-breaking seizure of cocaine and numerous arrests. Should you execute the warrant?

ENDNOTES

1. Miranda v. Arizona, 384 U.S. 436 (1966).

2. 232 U.S. 383 (1914).

3. 367 U.S. 643 (1961).

4. People v. Defore, 150 N.E. 585, 587 (1926) (Justice Cardozo, criticizing the exclusionary rule of the *Weeks* case).

5. 251 U.S. 385 (1920).

6. 371 U.S. 471 (1963).

7. ___ U.S., ___, 136 S.Ct. 2056 (2016).

8. 547 U.S. 586 (2006).

9. 467 U.S. 431 (1984).

10. *Id.* at 444.

11. 364 U.S. 206 (1960).

12. Mapp v. Ohio, 367 U.S. 643, 655 (1961).

13. 468 U.S. 897 (1984).

14. *Id.* at 926.

15. Joshua Dressler, Understanding Criminal Procedure § 20.06 [B][1], at p. 360 n.136 (7th ed. 2017).

16. *See* Illinois v. Krull, 480 U.S. 340 (1987), where the United States Supreme Court held the good faith exception applicable to an unlawful search and seizure carried out in objectively reasonable reliance upon a state statute later declared unconstitutional.

17. Joshua Dressler, Understanding Criminal Procedure § 21.09 [A], at p. 409 (3d ed. 2000).

18. *See* Arizona v. Evans, 514 U.S. 1 (1995).

19. Herring v. United States, 555 U.S. 135 (2009).

20. 564 U.S. 229 (2011).

21. *Id.* at 143–44.

22. 480 U.S. 79 (1987).

23. 540 U.S. 551 (2004).

24. 389 U.S. 347 (1967).

25. *Id.* at 351–52 (emphasis added).

26. 508 U.S. 366 (1993).

27. 385 U.S. 293 (1967).

28. 401 U.S. 745 (1971).

29. ___ U.S. ___, 2018WL3073916 (2018)

30. 265 U.S. 57 (1924).

31. 466 U.S. 170 (1984).

32. ___ U.S, ___, 2018 WL 2402551 (2018)

33. 442 U.S. 735 (1979).

34. 425 U.S. 435 (1976)

35. 460 U.S. 276 (1983).

36. 468 U.S. 705 (1984).

37. 533 U.S. 27 (2001).

38. 565 U.S. 400 (2012).

39. The description of Jones v. United States is derived from Thomkovicz & White, Criminal Procedure: Constitutional Constraints Upon Investigation and Proof 33–35 (8th ed. 2017).

40. 133 S.Ct. 1409 (2013).

41. ___ U.S. ___, 135 S. Ct. 1368 (2015)

42. State v. Grady, ___ S.E.2d ___, 2018 WL 2206344 (Ct. App. N.C. 2018).

43. 476 U.S. 207 (1986).

44. 488 U.S. 445 (1989).

45. 466 U.S. 109 (1984).

46. 462 U.S. 696 (1983).

47. 543 U.S. 405 (2005).

48. *Id.* at 409-10.

49. 568 U.S. 237 (2013).

50. ___ U.S. ___, 135 S.Ct. 1609 (2015)

51. *Id.* at 1612.

52. 569 U.S. 1 (2013).

53. 486 U.S. 109 (1988).

54. United States v. Jacobsen, 466 U.S. 109, 113 (1984).

55. United States v. Mendenhall, 446 U.S. 544, 553-54 (1980).

56. 501 U.S. 429 (1991).

57. *Id.* at 436.

58. 499 U.S. 621, 626 (1991).

59. 536 U.S. 194 (2002).

60. Coolidge v. New Hampshire, 403 U.S. 443, 467 (1971).

61. James J. Tomkovicz & Welsh S. White, Criminal Procedure: Constitutional Constraints upon Investigation and Proof 66 (8th ed. 2017) citing and quoting United States v. Garza-Hernandez, 623 F.2d 496 (7th Cir. 1980) (quoting Brinegar v. United States, 338 U.S. 160, 174-76 (1949) (emphasis added by Tomkovicz and White).

62. Illinois v. Gates, 462 U.S. 213, 238 (1983).

63. *Id.* at 235.

64. 540 U.S. 366 (2003).

65. 358 U.S. 307 (1959).

66. 423 U.S. 411 (1976).

67. 532 U.S. 318 (2001).

68. 462 U.S. 213 (1983).

69. 378 U.S. 108 (1964).

70. 393 U.S. 410 (1969).

71. Gates, 462 U.S. at 238.

72. *Gates*, 462 U.S. at 245.

73. ___ U.S. ___, 135 S.Ct. 530 (2014)

74. 568 U.S. 237 (2013).

75. 480 U.S. 79 (1987).

76. 496 U.S. 128 (1990).

77. Gooding v. United States, 416 U.S. 430 (1974).

78. Wayne Lafave, 2 Search & Seizure § 4.7(b) (5th ed. 2017).

79. *Id.*

80. 526 U.S. 603 (1999).

81. *Id.* at 614.

82. 514 U.S. 927 (1995).

83. *Id.* at 930.

84. 520 U.S. 385 (1997).

85. 547 U.S. 586 (2006).

86. 523 U.S. 65 (1998).

87. 547 U.S. 90 (2006).

88. 438 U.S. 154 (1978).

89. 395 U.S. 752 (1969).

90. 414 U.S. 218 (1973).

91. 525 U.S. 113 (1998).

92. Chimel v. California, 395 U.S. 752, 763 (1969).

93. *Id.* at 763.

94. Maryland v. Buie, 494 U.S. 325, 334 (1990).

95. 415 U.S. 800 (1980).

96. *Id.* at 803.

97. 494 U.S. 325 (1990).

98. *Id.* at 327.

99. *Id.* at 334.

100. *See* New York v. Belton, 453 U.S. 454 (1981).

101. Arizona v. Gant, 556 U.S. 332 (2009).

102. 453 U.S. 454 (1981).

103. 541 U.S. 615 (2004).

104. Arizona v. Gant, 556 U.S. 332 (2009).

105. Riley v. California, ___ U.S. ___, 134 S.Ct. 2473 (2014)

106. 384 U.S. 757 (1966).

107. 569 U.S. 141 (2013)

108. Id. at 144.

109. ___ U.S. ___, 136 S.Ct. 2160 (2016)

110. Carroll v. United States, 267 U.S. 132, 153-54 (1925).

111. Cardwell v. Lewis, 417 U.S. 583 (1974).

112. Cady v. Dombroski, 413 U.S. 433, 441 (1973).

113. ___ U.S, ___, 2018 WL 2402551 (2018)

114. 526 U.S. 599 (1999).

115. Texas v. White, 423 U.S. 67, 68 (1975).

116. Chambers v. Maroney, 399 U.S. 42 (1973).

117. 471 U.S. 386 (1985).

118. 526 U.S. 295, 302 (1999).

119. 528 U.S. 11 (1999).

120. 412 U.S. 218 (1973).

121. 519 U.S. 33 (1996).

122. 536 U.S. 194 (2002).

123. 501 U.S. 429 (1991).

124. United States v. Matlock, 415 U.S. 164, 172 n.7 (1974).

125. 547 U.S. 103 (2006).

126. United States v. Matlock, 415 U.S. 164, 172 n.7 (1974).

127. 497 U.S. 177 (1990).

128. 495 U.S. 91, 100 (1990).

129. Warden v. Hayden, 387 U.S. 294 (1967).

130. 569 U.S. 141 (2013)

131. 399 U.S. 30 (1970).

132. 531 U.S. 326 (2001).

133. *See* Arizona v. Hicks, 480 U.S. 321 (1987).

134. 387 U.S. 294 (1967).

135. *Id.* at 298.

136. *Id.* at 299.

137. 466 U.S. 740 (1984).

138. 529 U.S. 334 (2000).

139. 480 U.S. 321 (1987).

140. 392 U.S. 1 (1968).

141. Camara v. Municipal Court, 387 U.S. 253, 536-37 (1967).

142. 392 U.S. at 30.

143. 528 U.S. 119 (2000).

144. 534 U.S. 266 (2002).

145. 462 U.S. 213 (1983).

146. 496 U.S. 325 (1990).

147. 529 U.S. 266 (2000).

148. 542 U.S. 177 (2004).

149. United States v. Place, 462 U.S. 696, 710 (1983).

150. United States v. Montoya de Hernandez, 473 U.S. 551, 532 (1985).

151. Hayes v. Florida, 470 U.S. 811 (1985).

152. 452 U.S. 692 (1981).

153. 568 U.S, 186 (2013)

154. 470 U.S. 811 (1985).

155. United States v. Sharpe, 470 U.S. 675, 687 (1985).

156. *Id.*

157. 508 U.S. 366 (1993).

158. 444 U.S. 85 (1979).

159. Maryland v. Buie, 494 U.S. 325 (1990).

160. 469 U.S. 325 (1985).

161. Michigan Dept. of State Police v. Sitz, 496 U.S. 444 (1990).

162. United States v. Martinez-Fuerte, 429 U.S. 543 (1976).

163. Griffen v. Wisconsin, 483 U.S. 868 (1987).

164. 534 U.S. 112 (2001).

165. Skinner v. Railway Labor Executives' Assn, 489 U.S. 602 (1989).

166. National Treasury Employees Union v. Von Raab, 489 U.S. 656 (1989).

167. Vernonia School District 47J v. Acton, 515 U.S. 646 (1995).

168. 536 U.S. 822 (2002).

169. 520 U.S. 305 (1999).

170. 520 U.S. 305 (1997).

171. 532 U.S. 67 (2001).

172. 531 U.S. 32 (2001).

173. 439 U.S. 128 (1978).

174. 448 U.S. 98 (1980).

175. 495 U.S. 91 (1990).

176. 525 U.S. 83 (1998).

Design Element: ©Ingram Publishing

10 EXCLUSIONARY RULE— IDENTIFICATION PROCEDURES

CHAPTER OUTLINE

CHAPTER OBJECTIVES

This chapter discusses the exclusionary rule as it relates to lineups and other identification procedures. After reading this chapter you will be able to:

▶ Name three types of identification procedures.

▶ Explain when an accused is entitled to counsel at an identification procedure.

▶ Explain when an accused is not entitled to counsel at an identification procedure.

▶ Identify the constitutional grounds for an accused's claim of misidentification before trial and at trial.

▶ Explain the test for allowing an in-court identification by a witness whose pretrial identification was tainted.

▶ State the test for excluding evidence of a pretrial identification on grounds of suggestiveness.

▶ List the five factors set forth in the *Biggers* case.

▶ Summarize the law applicable to identifications when there is a claim that a pretrial identification procedure was suggestive.

▶ Name several situations that the law enforcement officer should avoid with respect to the makeup of a lineup or photographic array.

▶ State the purpose of the *Biggers* five factors analysis.

IDENTIFICATION PROCEDURES AND THE EXCLUSIONARY RULE

The exclusionary rule makes relevant evidence inadmissible at trial if a defendant's Fourth Amendment rights (the rights against unreasonable searches and seizures) have been violated. Both pretrial and in-court identifications may be inadmissible against defendants, if a defendant's Fourth, Fifth, Sixth, or Fourteenth Amendment rights were violated during the investigative identification procedure. If a search or seizure takes place before an identification procedure, and the search or seizure is found by a court to have violated the Fourth Amendment, the subsequent identification of the accused could be excluded from evidence as fruit of the poisonous tree. However, the identification may be excluded from evidence on grounds other than those related to the search and seizure, for example, grounds relating to right to counsel and due process. Therefore, the law enforcement professional must be familiar with and meet certain standards with respect to the procedures used to identify suspects.

"The vagaries of eyewitness identification are well-known; the annals of criminal law are rife with instances of mistaken identification."[1] With these words, the United States Supreme Court announced a rule requiring counsel to be present at post-indictment lineup procedures conducted for the purpose of identifying suspects as perpetrators. During 1967, in a trilogy of cases (*Wade, Stovall,* and *Gilbert*),[2] the Court explored the issues relating to identification evidence. The essence of the Court's conclusions was that misidentification due to a variety of causes was a serious problem in eyewitness testimony. Improper or suggestive pretrial procedures regarding the identification of individuals can lead to misidentification. Misidentification at trial then deprives an accused of a fair trial. Therefore, in this trilogy of cases, and others that have followed, the Court established basic guidelines to prevent or reduce the likelihood of such errors.

The presence of counsel at pretrial identifications is not always possible. However, according to the Supreme Court, the Constitution mandates that an attorney must be present at post-indictment lineups. If an attorney is not present, then any mention of the lineup is prohibited at trial. Regardless of whether or not an attorney is present, the procedure must not be unfairly suggestive. If the procedure is unfairly suggestive, the subsequent in-court identification by the witness may also be subject to the exclusionary rule, unless it can be shown that the in-court identification resulted from an independent source—i.e., was not affected by the suggestive procedure.

There are three basic types of identification procedures: lineups, show-ups, and photographic arrays. A **lineup** is the presentation to a victim or witness of a line of persons who all look similar to see if one can be identified as the perpetrator of the crime. A **show-up** is the one-on-one presentation of a suspect to a victim or witness for identification purposes. A **photographic array** is a presentation to a witness of a number of photographs for identification of the perpetrator.

IDENTIFICATION PROCEDURES AND THE RIGHT TO COUNSEL

The Sixth Amendment to the Constitution states, in part, "In all criminal prosecutions, the accused shall . . . have the assistance of counsel for his defense." The United States Supreme Court has held that the right to counsel at trial is a fundamental

LINEUP
The presentation to a victim or witness of a line of persons who all look similar to see if one can be identified as the perpetrator of the crime.

SHOW-UP
The one-on-one presentation of a suspect to a victim or witness for identification purposes.

PHOTOGRAPHIC ARRAY
The presentation to a witness of a number of photographs for the identification of the perpetrator.

right. This right applies to the states through the Fourteenth Amendment Due Process Clause whenever a defendant's trial may result in incarceration.[3] Additionally, since events may occur before trial that affect an accused's trial rights, the right to counsel may attach long before the trial itself. It is therefore necessary to determine at what stage in the pretrial process, and under what circumstances, counsel must be present when the police attempt to have a witness or victim identify a suspect.

The Critical Stage Test for the Right to Counsel

As early as 1932, the United States Supreme Court observed that "the period from arraignment to trial was 'perhaps the most critical period of the proceedings . . .' during which the accused 'requires the guiding hand of counsel . . . if the guarantee is not to prove an empty right.'"[4] The Court has also held that an accused, after indictment, is entitled to counsel during questioning by an undercover informant.[5] *Miranda* extended the right to counsel to suspects being held for custodial interrogation.[6] Therefore, it is not surprising that, in 1967, the Court held that a post-indictment lineup conducted for identification purposes is a critical stage of a criminal prosecution at which counsel is required to be present.[7]

A **critical stage** begins at the initiation of an adversarial judicial proceeding, whether by way of formal charge, preliminary hearing, indictment, information, or arraignment. Any pretrial event requiring the presence of counsel can be a critical stage, analogous to a trial, where the accused may be overpowered by his or her professional adversary. The test of a critical stage is whether at "the trial itself . . . no substitute for counsel" can be provided to a defendant in the event that "a pretrial confrontation is conducted in the absence of counsel."[8] An accused is guaranteed that he or she need not stand alone against the state at any stage of the prosecution, formal or informal, in court or out of court, where counsel's absence might detract from the accused's right to a fair trial.[9]

In *United States v. Wade,*[10] several weeks after Wade's indictment for robbery, an FBI agent arranged to place Wade in a lineup, without notice to Wade's lawyer. Wade and the others in the lineup were made to wear strips of tape on their faces, as the witness said the robber had done. They also repeated aloud the words the robbers had uttered. Two bank employees identified Wade as one of the robbers at the pretrial lineup and again at trial.

Wade moved to strike the courtroom identifications because he was denied his Sixth Amendment right to counsel at the pretrial lineup. The United States Supreme Court agreed, stating that "a major factor contributing to the high incidence of miscarriage of justice from mistaken identification has been the degree of suggestion inherent in the manner in which the prosecution presents the defendant to witnesses for pretrial identification."[11] The Court recognized the grave potential for prejudice improperly influencing the witness at the pretrial lineup. Since it may be impossible to reconstruct the pretrial lineup at trial, the presence of defense counsel at the lineup can guard against prejudicial practices, provide a means of documenting what occurred, and assure a meaningful confrontation at trial. The Court therefore held that the post-indictment lineup is a critical stage of the prosecution at which the accused is as much entitled to the aid of counsel as at the trial itself.[12] The *Wade* decision extended the exclusionary rule to post-indictment pretrial lineups in which a defendant has been denied his or her Sixth Amendment

CRITICAL STAGE
The initiation of an adversarial judicial proceeding, whether by way of formal charge, preliminary hearing, indictment, information, or arraignment.

right to counsel. The Court held, however, that Wade was not entitled to automatic reversal of his conviction "without first giving the Government the opportunity to establish by clear and convincing evidence that the in-court identifications were based upon observations of the suspect other than the lineup identification."[13] Therefore, the case was sent back to the trial court in order to give the government the chance to prove that the in-court identification was not tainted.

When Counsel Need Not Be Present

If a defendant has not been formally charged with a criminal offense, he or she is not entitled to the assistance of counsel at an identification proceeding. When a suspect who has not been indicted or otherwise formally charged is placed in a lineup, counsel need not be present.

One of the reasons counsel must be present at a post-indictment lineup is the possibility that the accused will be misled by lack of familiarity with the law or will be overpowered by a professional adversary. When a photograph of the lineup or a photographic array is shown to a witness, however, the accused is not present and cannot be misled or overpowered. Identifications made prior to the initiation of adversarial judicial proceedings are scrutinized under the Fifth and Fourteenth Amendments. The proscription is against procedures that are unnecessarily suggestive and conducive to irreparable mistaken identification.

APPLICATION CASE

In *Kirby v. Illinois*,[14] the victim of a robbery was taken to the police station, where two defendants were seated at a table. Upon entering the station, the victim immediately identified the defendants as the robbers. Neither defendant asked for legal assistance, nor had either one been advised of the right to have an attorney present.

In upholding the identification over a claim of denial of the right to counsel, the United States Supreme Court declined to "impose a per se exclusionary rule upon testimony concerning an identification that took place long before the commencement of any prosecution whatever."[15] The Court reasoned that a person's Sixth Amendment right to counsel attaches only at or after the time the adversarial judicial proceedings have been initiated. The Court also stated that adversarial judicial proceedings commence by way of formal charge, preliminary hearing, indictment, information, or arraignment, for it is only then that the government commits itself to prosecute and only then that adverse positions of government and defendant solidify.

Although defendants are not entitled to the assistance of counsel before they are formally charged, "a defendant may rebut this presumption [that absence of counsel causes no harm] by demonstrating that despite the absence of formal adversary judicial proceedings, the government had crossed the constitutionally significant divide from fact-finder to adversary."[16] This may occur when there is an unnecessary delay in formally charging an accused in order to conduct a lineup. A lineup identification under such circumstances could be found to be unlawful.

IDENTIFICATION PROCEDURES AND DUE PROCESS

Even if there is no violation of the Sixth Amendment's right to counsel, an identification may still be excluded if it is unnecessarily suggestive or in some other way conducive to irreparable mistaken identification. At the core of the issues relating to misidentification are the Due Process Clauses of the Fifth and Fourteenth Amendments. These clauses preserve the right to a fair trial. If a witness has been subjected to suggestive inducement to identify the defendant, then the possibility of misidentification is increased. In such a circumstance, the pretrial identification may be tainted. Moreover, the in-court identification, flowing from the pretrial identification, may also be objectionable. Allowing either or both identifications to come before the jury when the witness has been subject to suggestive inducement could deny the defendant a fair trial.

Effect of Illegal Pretrial Identification on In-Court Identification

It is possible for an out-of-court identification to be illegal while the identification made at trial is found admissible. On the other hand, if the in-court identification is so influenced by the illegal out-of-court identification as to be a product of it, then the in-court identification will not be admissible, either. The test is whether or not the in-court identification is sufficiently free of the taint from the out-of-court identification to be trustworthy. Moreover, any case involving a legally questionable pretrial identification inevitably involves the question of whether or not the in-court identification should be admitted. For example, even the case of *United States v. Wade,* which dealt with the right to counsel at a post-indictment lineup, involved questions about the effects of that lineup upon a witness's ability to identify a suspect later, after the lineup.

The law enforcement professional must understand this two-staged aspect of pretrial identification procedures. When a witness testifies at trial and identification of the accused is involved, the witness is permitted to testify to the fact that the defendant, seated in the courtroom, was the perpetrator. In addition, the witness is permitted to testify to the fact that the perpetrator was picked out during the identification procedure before trial.

Following is a sample transcript of a witness's trial testimony involving identification of the accused. In this case, the witness identified the accused at a pretrial lineup where defense counsel was present and the procedure was not suggestive.

Prosecutor: As you sit here today, looking around the courtroom, do you see anyone who you can identify as the person who pointed a gun at you on February 23 and told you, "Your money or your life?"

Witness: Yes, yes I do.

Prosecutor: Would you please point that person out, state where he or she is sitting, and what he or she is wearing.

Witness: It is the man sitting at counsel table next to the defense lawyer; he is dressed in a blue shirt with a red tie.

Prosecutor: Your honor, may the record reflect the fact that the witness has identified the defendant.

Judge: Yes, the record will so reflect.

Prosecutor: Turning your attention to the midmorning of February 25, do you recall attending a lineup at the police station?

Witness: Yes, I do.

Prosecutor: At that lineup, did you identify anyone as the person who robbed you two days before?

Witness: Yes I did.

Prosecutor: And who was that person?

Witness: The same person I just identified in this courtroom.

The case of *Gilbert v. California*[17] dealt with the effect of an illegal lineup on testimony at trial, where the illegality was the denial of counsel. Gilbert was indicted in a robbery-murder case. A lineup was conducted 16 days later without notice to his court-appointed lawyer. Gilbert was identified by three eyewitnesses to the crime, by the manager of the building he lived in, and by eight other witnesses to other robberies that Gilbert allegedly had committed. All of these witnesses not only identified Gilbert at trial but also testified that they had identified him at the pretrial lineup. The three eyewitnesses and building manager testified at the guilt phase of the trial. The eight other witnesses testified at the penalty phase of the trial. Gilbert was found guilty and sentenced to death.

The Supreme Court held that the lineup was unconstitutional under *Wade,* because the lineup was held after indictment and without the presence of Gilbert's counsel. In addition, the Court held that the witnesses' testimony, which had identified Gilbert at the lineup, was subject to the exclusionary rule because "[t]hat testimony is the direct result of the illegal lineup come at by exploitation of (the primary) illegality."[18] The denial of the right to counsel made the identification proceeding illegal, and no testimonial reference to it at trial should have been permitted.

However, with respect to the in-court identifications, the Court reached a different conclusion. A witness's ability to identify a person might result from the illegal lineup, or it might be based on an independent source unaffected by the illegal identification procedure. There was no evidence taken at the trial concerning the impact of the pretrial identifications upon the witnesses' in-court identifications. Therefore, the Court held that the case was to go back (remanded) to the trial court for an evidentiary hearing to find out how the lineup affected the witnesses at trial. Thus, an in-court identification will be admitted only when the prosecution can show that the witness's identification was not influenced by a tainted pretrial identification. Moreover, the prosecution must make that showing by clear and convincing evidence, not just by a preponderance of the evidence.

Only Unnecessarily Suggestive Pretrial Identifications Are Illegal

It is possible for an out-of-court identification to be suggestive yet not be illegal. The Supreme Court has considered cases in which practical considerations led police officers to try to gain identifications under circumstances that were suggestive.

As a result of these cases, it may be said that there is no *per se* exclusionary rule. The question is whether, under the **totality of the circumstances**, the identification procedure was unnecessarily suggestive.

The case of *Stovall v. Denno*[19] dealt with the issues of suggestiveness in identification procedures apart from the right to counsel. In *Stovall*, five police officers took the defendant to the hospital, where one of the victims of a robbery and stabbing was being treated for serious injuries inflicted by her attacker. Stovall was handcuffed to a police officer, was placed in front of the victim, and, at the direction of the police, repeated a few words for a voice identification by the victim. He was the only black man in the room, and his counsel was not notified of the show-up. The victim testified at trial concerning her hospital room show-up identification and made an in-court identification. The Court rejected the right to counsel claim but turned to the suggestiveness of the procedure for analysis.

The Court held that a pre- or post-indictment identification procedure that is unnecessarily suggestive and conducive to irreparable mistaken identification violates the due process rights of an accused. To determine when an identification procedure is unnecessarily suggestive, the Court stated that "a claimed violation of due process of law in the conduct of a confrontation depends on the totality of the circumstances surrounding it."[20] In *Stovall,* showing the defendant to the victim in the immediate hospital confrontation was imperative. Therefore, the Court held that, although the show-up was unnecessarily suggestive, the circumstances—the fact that the victim was the only person who could exonerate Stovall—made the show-up necessary. Overall, the Court concluded, the show-up did not create a likelihood of misidentification.

In *Neil v. Biggers,*[21] the victim was called to the police station to view a defendant seven months after being raped. Because the police could not readily find any other people fitting the defendant's unusual physical characteristics, they held a show-up (two officers walked the accused past the victim), at which the victim identified the defendant as the rapist. The defendant claimed that the show-up was unreasonably suggestive. The Court rejected the defendant's claim, rejected again any *per se* exclusionary rule for suggestive identification cases, and found that, under a five-factor test, the identification of Biggers was reliable. Those five factors are[22]

1. the opportunity of the witness to view the criminal at the time of the crime;
2. the witness's degree of attention;
3. the accuracy of the witness's prior description of the criminal;
4. the level of certainty demonstrated by the witness at the confrontation; and
5. the length of time between the crime and the confrontation.

During the attack, the victim spent up to half an hour with the assailant. She saw him under adequate artificial light in her house and under a full moon outdoors. At least twice, she faced him directly and intimately. Her initial description to the police was more than thorough and included the assailant's approximate age, height, weight, complexion, skin texture, build, and voice. Furthermore, she had "no doubt" that the suspect was the person who had raped her.[23]

The principle that not all suggestive identification procedures will lead to application of the exclusionary rule also applies to photographic identifications. In the first case in which the Supreme Court of the United States considered a suggestive eyewitness identification stemming from the presentation of photographs to witnesses, *Simmons v. United States*,[24] the Court pointed out the dangers associated with suggestive presentation of photographs to a witness. The danger of misidentification is greatly increased if the police display to the witness only the picture of a single individual who resembles the person that the victim saw. Misidentification is also greatly increased if the police show the witness pictures of several persons among which the photograph of a single individual recurs or in some way is emphasized. The chance of misidentification is also heightened if police indicate to the witness that they have other evidence that one of the persons pictured committed the crime. Regardless of how such initial misidentification comes about, the witness is more apt to retain in his or her memory the image of the photograph rather than of the person actually seen, reducing the trustworthiness of subsequent lineups or courtroom identifications.

In *Simmons*, the FBI obtained six photographs from the sister of a suspected bank robber in which the defendant appeared among a group of people. The FBI showed the photographs to five witnesses, who identified Simmons as one of two men who had robbed the bank. At trial, the five witnesses made in-court identifications of Simmons as one of the robbers. No mention was made of the pretrial photographic identifications. Relying on the Court's lineup cases of the year before, Simmons claimed that the pretrial photographic identifications so influenced the witnesses that their in-court identifications were tainted and that he was thereby denied due process.

The Supreme Court rejected the defendant's arguments. After listing the potential problems involved in photographic misidentification, the Court noted that photographic identification procedures are widely and effectively used in law enforcement. Moreover, effective cross-examination at trial can lessen the effects of possible misidentification. Therefore, the Court refused to prohibit the use of such procedures by law enforcement. Rather, the Court held that the totality of the circumstances test applicable to lineups should also be applied to photographic identification procedures, on a case-by-case basis. In *Simmons* itself, the Court found that it was not unnecessary for the FBI to resort to photographic identification and that there was, in the circumstances of the case, little chance that the procedure utilized led to misidentification of Simmons. The Court affirmed his conviction.

Even though the Supreme Court pointed out these misidentification dangers, the Court nonetheless applied to photographic identifications the same totality of the circumstances test it had applied to lineups. Moreover, the Court in *Simmons*, as well as in the subsequent case of *Manson v. Brathwaite*,[25] considering those circumstances, concluded that the photographic identifications in both cases did not violate the accused's due process rights. The Court found this to be so even though, in both cases, the photographic identification procedures were suggestive.

In *Manson v. Brathwaite*,[26] an undercover police officer purchased heroin through an open doorway while standing within two feet of the seller for two to three minutes. After the buy, the undercover officer described the seller to other officers as "a colored man, approximately five feet eleven inches tall, dark complexion, black hair, short Afro style, and having high cheekbones, and of heavy build."[27] One of the officers, recognizing the description of the individual, obtained a photo of him and left it in the undercover officer's office. While alone, the undercover officer viewed the photo for the first time and identified the person in it as the seller. The identification led to the arrest, trial, and conviction of the defendant. At the trial, the undercover officer testified about the photographic identification, the photograph was admitted into evidence, and the officer made an in-court identification of the accused.

The Supreme Court of the United States reviewed the case for a violation of Brathwaite's due process rights. The Court noted that the identification procedure in this case was suggestive (because only one photograph was used) and unnecessary (because there was no emergency or exigent circumstance). The Court rejected a *per se* rule approach to cases involving unnecessarily suggestive photo identifications. Rather, the Court applied the totality of the circumstances test measured by a requirement that the identification possess certain features of reliability. According to the Court, "reliability is the linchpin in determining the admissibility of identification testimony . . . and the factors to be considered are those set out in *Biggers*."[28] Those factors include the opportunity of the witness to view the criminal at the time of the crime, the witness's degree of attention, the accuracy of his or her prior description of the criminal, the level of certainty demonstrated at the confrontation, and the time between the crime and the confrontation.[29] Against these factors, the Court said, is to be weighed the corrupting effect of the suggestive identification itself. Applying these principles to the case before it, the Court found that the identification procedure did not violate due process, and the Court affirmed the defendant's conviction.

The law applicable to pretrial identification procedures can be summarized rather simply. When a defendant raises a question about the suggestiveness of a pretrial identification procedure, the trial court must first determine if the identification procedure was unnecessary and suggestive. If not, the court should admit the pretrial and in-court identifications by the witness. However, if the trial court finds the procedure to be unnecessary and suggestive, the court must then determine whether, under the totality of the circumstances, the suggestiveness of the procedure would give rise to a very substantial likelihood of irreparable misidentification on the one hand, or whether the identification possessed features of reliability. The reliability features utilized are those five enumerated in the *Biggers* case. Against these factors is to be weighed the corrupting effect of the suggestive identification itself. If, after applying the *Biggers* factors, the court finds the identification procedure reliable, the court should admit that identification, regardless of its suggestiveness.

The problems associated with misidentification stemming from an unnecessarily suggestive pretrial identification procedure can be illustrated by consideration of what a juror might think while observing an in-court identification of an accused

FYI

Federal Jury Practice and Instructions Criminal § 14.10 Eyewitness; Identification of the Defendant

One of the [most important] issues in this case is the identification of Defendant _____ as the person who committed the crime[s] charged in [Count[s] _____ of] the indictment. The government, as you know, has the burden of proving every issue, including identity, beyond a reasonable doubt. Although it is not essential that the witness testifying about the identification [himself] [herself] be free from all doubt as to the accuracy or correctness of the identification, the jury must be satisfied beyond a reasonable doubt that Defendant _____ is the same person who committed the crime[s] charged. If you are not convinced beyond a reasonable doubt that Defendant _____ was the person who committed the crime[s] charged in [Count[s] _____ of] the indictment, you must find Defendant _____ not guilty.

Identification testimony is, in essence, the expression of an opinion or a belief by the witness. The value of the identification depends upon the opportunity that the witness had to observe the person who committed the crime at the time of the offense and the opportunity to make a reliable identification at a later time.

In judging the identification testimony of any witness you should consider at least the following questions:

(1) Are you convinced that the witness had the ability and an adequate opportunity to observe the person who committed the crime charged?

Whether the witness had an adequate opportunity to observe the person committing the offense at the time of the offense will be affected by many things, including the length of the observation, the distance between the witness and the person observed, the lighting conditions, and whether the witness knew the person from some prior experience.

(2) Are you convinced that the identification by the witness after the offense was committed was the product of [his] [her] own recollection?

In making this determination you may take into account both the strength of the later identification and the circumstances under which the later identification was made.

If the identification by the witness was influenced by circumstances under which the identification was made, you should examine that identification with great care. You may wish to consider the length of time that had elapsed between the commission of the crime and the later opportunity of the witness to observe the defendant.

You may consider that an identification made by pointing out a defendant from a group of similar individuals is generally more reliable than an identification which results from a presentation of the defendant alone to the witness.

(3) Has the witness failed to identify the defendant on a prior opportunity or has the witness identified someone else as the person who committed the offense charged? You should examine and consider the credibility of any witness making an identification in the same manner as you would any other witness.

The burden of proving the identity of Defendant _____ as the person who committed the crime[s] charged in [Count[s] _____ of] the indictment rests totally with the government. The government must prove the identity of the defendant as the person who committed the crime[s] charged beyond a reasonable doubt. If, after examining all of the evidence, you have a reasonable doubt as to whether the defendant was the individual who committed the crime[s] charged, you should find Defendant _____ not guilty.

by a witness. When the witness is asked if he or she sees in the courtroom the perpetrator of the act on trial, a juror is likely to wonder whether the witness has seen the perpetrator between the time of the event and the beginning of the trial. The defendant is usually seated at the lawyer's table in the courtroom. Anyone observing that scene will recognize who is on trial and from that alone could identify the accused. Moreover, most people have watched television shows or films that depict the identification procedures widely in use by law enforcement. Thus, any juror is likely to wonder which, if any, of those procedures were used in the case on trial.

For these reasons alone, the facts surrounding all identification encounters between suspects and witnesses should be presented to the jury for its consideration of the validity of the pretrial identifications and their effect upon in-court identifications. The same considerations also illustrate the fact that the judge will first decide whether any pretrial identifications have been unduly suggestive. Finally, these considerations demand that the law enforcement professional take the appropriate steps to avoid unnecessary and suggestive identifications and to document the facts surrounding those encounters.

The unreliability of eyewitness testimony has been a topic of concern in the courts as well as in society generally in the United States. One of the effects of this concern is law discussed in this chapter: the exclusionary rule applied to improperly obtained eyewitness identifications. However, as to such testimony generally, the law also gives the jury specific instructions on how to look at the evidence. In the accompanying boxes are two of those instructions currently in use, the first in federal courts and the second in California courts.

TYPES OF SUGGESTIVE IDENTIFICATION PROCEDURES

Size of the Lineup or Array

A law enforcement officer presenting a single person or photograph—a show-up—is one of the most suggestive identification procedures.

FYI

Judicial Council of California Criminal Jury Instructions (2018) 315 Eyewitness Identification

You have heard eyewitness testimony identifying the defendant. As with any other witness, you must decide whether an eyewitness gave truthful and accurate testimony. In evaluating identification testimony, consider the following questions:

▶ Did the witness know or have contact with the defendant before the event?
▶ How well could the witness see the perpetrator?
▶ What were the circumstances affecting the witness's ability to observe, such as lighting, weather conditions, obstructions, distance, [and] duration of observation [, and <insert any other relevant circumstances>]?
▶ How closely was the witness paying attention?
▶ Was the witness under stress when he or she made the observation?
▶ Did the witness give a description and how does that description compare to the defendant?
▶ How much time passed between the event and the time when the witness identified the defendant?
▶ Was the witness asked to pick the perpetrator out of a group?
▶ Did the witness ever fail to identify the defendant?
▶ Did the witness ever change his or her mind about the identification?
▶ How certain was the witness when he or she made an identification?
▶ Are the witness and the defendant of different races?
▶ [Was the witness able to identify other participants in the crime?]
▶ [Was the witness able to identify the defendant in a photographic or physical lineup?]
▶ [<insert other relevant factors raised by the evidence>.]
▶ Were there any other circumstances affecting the witness's ability to make an accurate identification?

The People have the burden of proving beyond a reasonable doubt that it was the defendant who committed the crime. If the People have not met this burden, you must find the defendant not guilty.

Repeated encounters between the witness and the suspect or the repeated presentation of images of the same suspect in a single photographic array is also highly suggestive. Therefore, the officer should take care to avoid such practices.

On the other hand, as the cases discussed earlier in this chapter indicate, even though the use of a single photograph or show-up is highly suggestive, a court will nonetheless justify its use in certain **emergency or exigent circumstances**. For example, if the witness is injured and it is not clear he or she will live, courts have held that such a procedure is justified.[30]

Collaboration Between Witnesses

Collaboration between witnesses increases the rate of misidentification, making it a highly suggestive identification procedure. Officers should keep witnesses apart while they view both photographic spreads and lineups. For example, in one case,[31] a police officer passed a car matching the description of the getaway car involved in an earlier bank robbery. The officer briefly viewed the driver. The officer and a bank teller then examined two sets of photographs together. The officer saw the teller choose the photograph of the defendant. Although the court found that there was sufficient reliability in this and other identifications, the court stated a strong preference for separating the witnesses during the identification procedure.

Police Instructions or Statements to Witnesses

There are substantial risks involved in officers giving instructions to witnesses who are about to engage in an identification procedure. So, the officer should take special care. Officers should not tell a witness that the photo array or the lineup includes a defendant already in custody, since the witness may then be more likely to choose the person who most closely resembles the person they observed, rather than selecting no one at all. Officers should avoid providing information or making statements that cause a witness to focus on a particular suspect, as such actions are also highly suggestive. In one case,[32] an FBI agent showed a witness a photo array that she narrowed down to two photographs, finally choosing one. The agent then told her that she had chosen incorrectly and the other photograph was the suspect believed to have committed the robbery. The court held that this was sufficient to create a very substantial likelihood of irreparable misidentification and reversed the defendant's conviction. Although statements to witnesses by the police are not condoned, if the officer makes a neutral inquiry into the witness's choice, without focusing his or her attention on a specific defendant, the statement or question is then not viewed as suggestive but merely as investigatory.

Therefore, the rule on police statements and inquiries is that, when the police pose a neutral question or are following proper police practices to determine the strength of an identification, the procedure is not unnecessarily suggestive. However, if the police make statements that focus the witness's attention on a single person or picture, or if the police threaten the witness if he or she does not cooperate, such actions are considered highly suggestive procedures that might cause a court reviewing the identification to conclude that the identification was the result of unnecessary suggestiveness.

During lineups, show-ups, and photographic arrays, officers should record all instructions given to and conversations with the witnesses. Such recordings will help rebut any allegations from the defense that the identification process was unnecessarily suggestive.

Composition of the Lineup or Photo Array

Regardless of the size and manner of the identification procedure, it may be unnecessarily suggestive based on the composition, or content, of the lineup or photo array. Situations relating to composition that the officer should avoid include placing the accused with others of a different race in the lineup or array, asking the accused to dress in a particular way, and presenting others in the lineup or array who are so dissimilar in appearance to the defendant that he or she stands out. If the composition of the lineup or array focuses the attention of the witness on a particular suspect, it is likely to be viewed as suggestive, and the trial court will have to decide the effect under the totality of the circumstances test.

Different Appearance of the Accused

The most important thing in creating a lineup or photo array is that the lineup or array includes persons matching the defendant's general physical description. As the courts have put it,

> [P]olice stations are not theatrical casting offices; a reasonable effort to harmonize the lineup is normally all that is required.[33] . . . The test is whether the picture of the accused, [or the defendant himself in a lineup], matching descriptions given by the witness, so stood out from all the other photographs as to suggest to an identifying witness that that person was more likely to be the culprit.[34] . . . The individuals in the photographic display and lineup [should be] of the same race, possess similar physical features, and be alike in size, age, and dress.[35]

Other Suggestive Procedures Pertaining Solely to Photo Arrays

Different Type or Quality of Photos

A test used to determine if the type or quality of the photo is suggestive is whether the difference in photos tends to draw attention to a particular defendant's photograph. The quality of the photos needs to be similar enough that a witness's attention will not be drawn to one photo because it stands out for some reason. This issue usually appears when both black-and-white and color photographs are used in the same array. Similarly, if the appearance of the photo (old versus new, faded versus not faded) is substantially different, the identification is suggestive.

Photographic arrays are also known as "six-packs" because most officers use six photographs in their array. When using a six-pack, the officer should have the witness circle the photograph of the suspect identified and put the date and his or her initials next to the circle. This enables the witness to identify the photograph card positively in court if there is a substantial lapse of time before the trial begins and the witness forgets what the defendant looks like.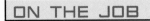

To aid in suspect identification, computerized photographic arrays can be quickly assembled. The technician keys in the physical characteristics reported by the victims or witnesses that he or she wants displayed in each of several panels of composite photographs. The system then assembles and inserts the photograph of the suspect into the photographic array.

©RICHARD NOWITZ/Science Source

The use of both black-and-white and color photographs in the same array is generally discouraged. In one case,[36] the witness was shown a small group of photos, only two of which (the accused and another suspect) were fresh and in color. The officer then asked the witness if those were the two "fellows." The court found that the dramatic difference between the color shots and the black-and-white mug shots, combined with the officer's implication that the witness was expected to choose two of the photos, was highly suggestive. In another case,[37] a witness was shown one color photograph with eleven black-and-white mug shots. The court found the procedure inherently suggestive and stated, "This color photograph of the [accused] stood out like the proverbial 'sore thumb.'"[38]

ON THE JOB

Officers often show witnesses several arrays, only one of which has the defendant in it. The officer should keep the array that the witness chose, as well as record what other arrays were shown to the witness (photocopying the six-packs is a good idea). This will aid the officer and prosecutor in court in the event the defense alleges that unnecessarily suggestive arrays were presented to the witness.

Also, remember that, if all of the photographs in the array look too much alike, the array will be subject to the criticism that the right suspect could not be picked out. On the other hand, if any one of the photographs in the array is different in some obvious way, the array will be subject to the criticism that it was suggestive.

Contents on and Around the Photographs

Not only do the type and quality of photos provide a constitutional basis to challenge a photo array, but superfluous markings on photographs may also give rise to such a challenge. Matters such as captions stating where the person depicted was arrested, the use of photo arrays in which the accused's photo contains a height measurement chart, and the surroundings in which a suspect is depicted generally (e.g., in a hospital room) have all been the bases for defendants' attacks upon photo identifications. While few of these attacks have been successful, the wise course for any officer is to present photographs as nearly similar in all respects as possible.

Alteration and Disguise of the Photographs

Although the digital alteration of all photographs in an array may be permissible, if only one picture is altered, a subsequent identification may be held to be suggestive on that ground.[39] If an officer requires a suspect to wear a disguise for his or her photo, the identification will not be viewed as suggestive if others in the array are also required to wear the same disguise.

DETERMINING THE RELIABILITY OF A SUGGESTIVE IDENTIFICATION: THE FIVE FACTORS OF THE *BIGGERS* CASE

In the *Biggers*[40] case, the United States Supreme Court set forth five factors for determining the reliability of a suggestive identification. Put another way, the question is whether, even though the pretrial identification procedure may have been unnecessary and suggestive, the identification is clothed with **indicia of reliability**. If the identification is reliable, even though the pretrial identification procedure was suggestive, the identification is admissible. These factors allow the trial court to determine if the witness had an independent basis, other than the suggestive procedure, for his or her identification. If the trial court finds that there was an independent basis for the witness's in-court identification, the identification will be allowed.

INDICIA OF RELIABILITY
Those facts indicating an identification is reliable—particularly, the five factors of the *Biggers* case.

The five factors set out in *Biggers* that must be examined are

1. the witness's opportunity to view the criminal at the time of the crime;
2. the witness's degree of attention;
3. the accuracy of the witness's prior description of the criminal;
4. the level of certainty demonstrated by the witness at the confrontation; and
5. the length of time between the crime and the confrontation.

In applying these factors, the courts have found that witnesses' identifications are more reliable

1. the longer the witness's opportunity to view the offender;
2. the greater the attention the witness gives the offender at the time of the offense;
3. the more detailed the initial description from the witness;
4. the greater the certainty demonstrated by the witness; and
5. the shorter the length of time between the crime and the lineup.

Witness's Opportunity to View the Criminal at the Time of the Crime

The test of reliability based on the witness's opportunity to view the criminal at the time of the crime is not dependent upon duration of time alone. Rather, opportunity relates to other factors. For example, in one case,[41] the witness testified that he had seen the defendant ten or fifteen times over a year-and-a-half period, from close range, in adequate light, and for a few minutes at a time. Each time the witness met the defendant, the witness was wearing his glasses and observed the defendant during daylight hours. These incidents supplied the witness with an independent basis to recognize the defendant, and therefore the trial court allowed the witness's in-court identification of the accused, even though the witness had also identified the defendant in an unnecessarily suggestive photographic array.

In another case,[42] a witness to a robbery picked out the accused in a lineup that was unnecessarily suggestive. However, the witness, during the robbery, saw the assailant's face for more than a minute, at a distance of only two to three feet—ample time to view him adequately. The witness also made a positive identification of the defendant while viewing a videotape only five days after the robbery. Based on the witness's time to view the defendant and her certainty, the trial court admitted the identification as reliable under the totality of the circumstances.

Other circumstances in which reliable independent identifications have been allowed include when the witnesses' observations of a suspect lasted anywhere from 14 seconds to 30 minutes. The test used to determine if the opportunity to view the defendant was adequate is whether the observations were from close range and with fairly good lighting.[43] The general rule is that, if the witness had a good opportunity to view the defendant, then even if the pretrial identification was suggestive, it will be admissible because the viewing opportunity provided an independent basis for the identification.

However, the law enforcement officer should still strive to avoid the use of a suggestive pretrial identification procedure. Courts will still look to the other *Biggers* factors, and, if under the totality of the circumstances the in-court identification does not appear to be reliable, it could be found inadmissible.

Witness's Degree of Attention

The second *Biggers* factor is whether the degree of attention the witness paid to the suspect during the event was sufficient that one could say that the witness's ability to identify the accused in court was based on the independent identification and not upon an unnecessarily suggestive identification procedure before trial. Several examples of cases will help illustrate the point.

In one case,[44] the witness was too busy fighting with one man to see the other, the defendant. In another case,[45] five teenage boys were unexpectedly confronted by two men, one of whom was holding a rifle. The man aimed the gun in the air and fired it. The boys continued walking, and one man shot and killed one of the boys and wounded another. The defendant was taken to the police station later that day to be viewed by the boys. The police asked the boys, "This is him, isn't it?"—to which the boys replied affirmatively. The court held that, since a show-up is presumptively more suggestive than a lineup, as well as totally unnecessary, the court had to decide whether, under the totality of the circumstances, the identification was reliable. The court held that the boys' degree of attention to the defendants fell well short of the level necessary to find their identification reliable. While the boys were able to describe the automobile used by the men and the rifle used by the shooter, they had only a minute to view the entire crime scene, including the defendants. The time the boys spent looking at things other than the defendants detracted from their ability to identify the defendants reliably. The court stated, "[W]hen one is identifying magnesium wheels, one is not looking at someone's face."[46] Therefore, the boys' degree of attention was not adequate to find the identification reliable.

The court must also consider whether an ordinary citizen, suddenly confronted by an armed robber, would be carefully observing the person in order to ensure an accurate description later on or simply staring at the muzzle of the gun. On the other hand, if the witness has been trained to have special observational skills, such as a police officer, the degree of attention required is far lower than that for an ordinary witness. This is based upon the belief that police officers pay a higher degree of attention to details than a lay witness because of the special training they receive in observational techniques. For example, in *Manson v. Brathwaite,* the officer bought two glycine bags of heroin through a door that was open only a few inches. The court held that, since Trooper Glover was a specially trained and experienced officer, he could be expected to pay scrupulous attention to detail.[47] The court recognized that Trooper Glover, because of his background, knew that he would subsequently have to find and arrest the vendor, as well as have his observations subjected to close scrutiny and examination at trial. Thus, Trooper Glover paid extra attention to all the details, especially the defendant's appearance.

Accuracy of the Description

There is no set rule for determining how accurate an initial description of the defendant must be in order to find the identification reliable on an independent basis. The courts tend to look at whether or not the witness was able to approximate the defendant's age, build, height, weight, skin color, and clothing, as well as any other physical characteristics. For example, in the case in which the five boys were stopped by the men with a rifle, the court held that they had rarely seen a case in which a defendant had been more poorly described. The only description one boy could give was that his attacker wore a white T-shirt and that he had shaggy hair. "Not one of the witnesses gave the assailant's age, build, height, weight, skin color, other clothing or other indicia of appearance."[48] The boys gave only broadly generalized descriptions that could have matched a number of people.

Manson v. Brathwaite again provides an excellent contrast. There, the witnessing undercover officer gave a detailed description to another officer shortly after completing his transaction with the defendant. "It included the vendor's race, his height, his build, the color and style of his hair, and the high cheekbone facial feature. It also included clothing the vendor wore."[49] Hence, even though the witness viewed the single photograph of the defendant two days later in a suggestive procedure, the Court held that, coupled with other indicia of reliability, the accuracy of the officer's initial description helped prove the reliability of his identification.

The standard of reliability for the initial description given by the witness falls somewhere between the two illustrative cases. Moreover, the standard is not fixed. Therefore, the witness's initial description of the suspect should be as detailed as possible. If a witness is not sure about a certain characteristic of the criminal, he or she should not guess. Instead, the officer taking the statement should record every thought expressed by the witness related to the perpetrator's description. Then, if the initial description is not completely accurate, there will be an exact record of what the witness said. Coupled with other factors of reliability, the court may find that the witness's identification is reliable based on the accuracy of the initial description, even though he or she viewed a suggestive lineup, show-up, or array.

Level of Certainty Demonstrated by the Witness at the Confrontation

Two issues surround the certainty of a witness: First is the degree of certainty required to support the admissibility of an identification, and second is the point at which the witness became certain. For example, in one case,[50] the witness saw her assailant for a period of three to four seconds from a distance of forty-five feet. When the witness said she was 95 percent sure of both her identification in a lineup before the trial and her in-court identification, the court believed her. The alleged suggestiveness occurred after the pretrial lineup and consisted of an officer telling the witness that the perpetrators were in custody. Because of the court's reliance on the high level of certainty before the suggestiveness occurred, this case demonstrates that the certainty of the witness must be used in conjunction with the other factors of reliability to find that the identification was reliable under the totality of the circumstances.

Courts have also found identifications reliable when the witness has shown a much lower level of certainty. In one case,[51] Wozniak, a witness to a bank robbery, had three to four minutes to observe the robber. She gave the police a description of the robber's race, height, weight, clothing, complexion, hair, facial hair, and tone of voice. Two days later she viewed the surveillance photographs and pointed out the robber. However, in a later, nonsuggestive photo array, she could only say that a photo of the defendant, who was depicted without the facial hair he had at the time of the robbery, "looked like" the perpetrator, although she was sure that none of the other five persons in the photo spread was the robber. The defendant was arrested on an unrelated charge and photographed with his beard, and the FBI case agent brought the photo to Wozniak's attention. Upon seeing this photo, she was positive that it was the man who had committed the robbery. The court held that, although the manner in which Wozniak's attention was directed to the photo was suggestive, there was sufficient independent indicia of reliability to admit the identification. The court ruled that, in addition to other factors, the entire set of circumstances present, including her "looks-like" identification from the six-person photo spread, provided an ample independent basis for her identification of the defendant.

Although the certainty of the witness is very important in determining the reliability of the identification of a defendant, if that certainty is not shown at the initial confrontation, a trial court is not likely to credit the identification as reliable. As the *Simmons* court recognized, "regardless of how the initial misidentification comes about, the witness thereafter is apt to retain in his memory the image of the [suggestive] photograph [or lineup] rather than of the person actually seen, reducing the trustworthiness of subsequent lineup or courtroom identification."[52]

Length of Time Between the Crime and the Confrontation

The shorter the time interval between the crime and the identification, the more reliable it is. Nonetheless, a long interval alone is usually not enough to invalidate an otherwise seemingly reliable identification.

Starting in *Biggers* itself, the United States Supreme Court held that a lapse of seven months between the rape and the confrontation was a seriously negative factor.[53] The Court has upheld this standard in a number of subsequent cases. In one case,[54] the Court held that the eight months between a robbery and the in-court confrontation was the factor most negatively affecting reliability. In another case,[55] the court held that a nine-month delay did not weigh in favor of admissibility. Although these time delays posed a problem with respect to finding the identification reliable, in all three of these cases, the courts found that under the totality of the circumstances the identifications were reliable.

Thus, a delay of more than seven months between the crime and the identification procedure is likely to be considered a negative reliability factor under the totality of the circumstances. However, where the other factors tend to demonstrate the reliability of the identification, the courts have not held the identification inadmissible due to the time delay. Therefore, the best way to ensure that time will not be a negative factor is to set up a nonsuggestive confrontation between a witness and a suspect as soon as possible.

In October 1999, the U.S. Department of Justice released a report ("Eyewitness Evidence: A Guide for Law Enforcement") that suggested ways in which eyewitness identification can become more reliable.[56] Some of the suggestions relating to lineups are that the procedure should contain a minimum of five fillers (non-suspects) who generally fit the witness's description of the perpetrator. The suspect and the fillers should all share the same unique features, e.g., scars and tattoos. The officer is cautioned to avoid using fillers who so closely resemble the suspect that a person familiar with the suspect might find it difficult to distinguish the suspect from the fillers. The suspect should be in different positions in each lineup, both across cases and with multiple witnesses in the same case, and the officer should position the suspect randomly in the lineup. If a new suspect is shown, the officer should avoid reusing fillers in lineups shown to the same witness.

The Department of Justice guide contains instructions to be given to the witness prior to viewing a lineup to ensure that the witness understands that the purpose of the identification procedure is to exculpate the innocent as well as to identify the actual perpetrator. The officer should instruct the witness that the person who committed the crime may or may not be in the set of photographs, or in the lineup. Further, the officer should assure the witness that, regardless of whether an identification is made, the police will continue to investigate the incident.

In place of the six-pack procedure, the guide suggests that individual photographs be placed in random order and viewed one at a time and that the witness be told to take as much time as needed in making a decision about each photo before moving to the next one. The guide suggests that, if an identification is made, the officer should avoid reporting to the witness any information regarding the individual selected prior to obtaining the witness's statement of certainty. The guide also says that, when presenting a simultaneous live lineup, the investigator should instruct everyone at the lineup not to suggest in any way the position or identity of the suspect in the lineup, for that will influence the witness's selection. Finally, the guide reiterates instructions usually given to law enforcement officers, such as they should avoid saying anything to the witness that may influence the witness's selection and the information that should be included in reports.

In 2014, the National Academy of Science published a report on its findings related to eyewitness identification.[57] The report made three sets of recommended best practices, the first set relating to law enforcement procedures. Those best practices are

1. Train All Law Enforcement Officers in Eyewitness Identification
2. Implement Double-Blind Lineup and Photo Array Procedures
3. Develop and Use Standardized Witness Instructions
4. Document Witness Confidence Judgments
5. Videotape the Witness Identification Process

Then, in January 2017, Deputy Attorney General Sally Q. Yates issued a memorandum to Department of Justice law enforcement and prosecutors relating to photo array identifications. Attached to the memorandum was a report of experts within the Department setting forth recommended procedures.[58] This memo and report noted, among other things, an evolving preference for a sequential (one photo at a time) rather than a simultaneous (multi-photo at one time) presentation procedure.

REVIEW AND APPLICATION

SUMMARY

(1) The three basic types of identification procedures are lineup, show-up, and photographic array.
(2) An accused is entitled to counsel at a post-indictment lineup that is conducted for identification purposes—a critical stage of a criminal proceeding.
(3) A defendant who has not been formally charged with a criminal offense is not entitled to counsel at an identification proceeding.
(4) The constitutional grounds for an accused's claim of misidentification before and at trial are the Due Process Clauses of the Fifth and Fourteenth Amendments.
(5) When a pretrial identification procedure has been deemed unnecessarily suggestive, the witness's in-court identification may be allowed if the prosecution can show by clear and convincing evidence that the witness's identification is independent of the tainted pretrial identification procedure.
(6) The test for excluding evidence of a pretrial identification on grounds of suggestiveness is whether, under the totality of the circumstances, the identification procedure was unnecessarily suggestive.
(7) The five *Biggers* factors for determining whether a suggestive pretrial identification procedure creates such a likelihood of misidentification as to violate due process are (1) the witness's opportunity to view the criminal at the time of the crime; (2) the witness's degree of attention; (3) the accuracy of the witness's prior description of the criminal; (4) the level of certainty demonstrated by the witness at the confrontation; and (5) the length of time between the crime and the confrontation.

(8) A summary of the law applicable to identifications is as follows: When a defendant raises a question about the suggestiveness of a pretrial identification procedure, the trial court must first determine if the identification procedure was unnecessary and suggestive. If it was not, the court should admit the pretrial and in-court identifications by the witness. However, if the trial court finds the procedure to be unnecessary and suggestive, the court must then determine whether, under the totality of the circumstances, the suggestiveness of the procedure would give rise to a very substantial likelihood of irreparable misidentification or whether the identification possessed features of reliability. The reliability features utilized are the five enumerated in the *Biggers* case.

(9) Some situations that the law enforcement officer should avoid with respect to the composition of a lineup or photographic array include placing the accused with others of a different gender in the lineup or array, asking the accused to dress in a particular way, and presenting others in the lineup or array who are so dissimilar in appearance to the defendant that the defendant stands out.

(10) The purpose of the *Biggers* five-factors analysis is to determine whether a witness's in-court identification is independent of a suggestive pretrial identification procedure—i.e., whether the in-court identification is reliable.

KEY TERMS

lineup 344	critical stage 345	emergency or exigent
show-up 344	totality of the	circumstances 354
photographic	circumstances	indicia of
array 344	(identification) 349	reliability 357

QUESTIONS FOR REVIEW

1. What are the three basic types of identification procedures?
2. When is an accused entitled to counsel at an identification procedure?
3. When is an accused not entitled to counsel in connection with an identification procedure?
4. What are the constitutional grounds for an accused's claim of misidentification before trial and at trial?
5. What is the test for allowing an in-court identification by a witness whose pretrial identification was tainted by an unnecessarily suggestive pretrial identification procedure?
6. What is the test for excluding evidence of a pretrial identification on grounds of suggestiveness?
7. What are the five factors set forth in the *Biggers* case to determine whether a suggestive pretrial identification procedure creates such a likelihood of misidentification as to violate due process?
8. What is the law applicable to identifications when there is a claim that a pretrial identification procedure was suggestive?

9. What are several situations that the law enforcement officer should avoid with respect to the composition of a lineup or photographic array?

10. What is the purpose of the *Biggers* five-factors analysis?

THINKING CRITICALLY ABOUT EVIDENCE

1. List several factors that can be used to make a show-up, lineup, and photographic array so unnecessarily suggestive as to invoke the exclusionary rule.

2. Having the defense counsel present at a post-indictment lineup can sometimes make the procedure difficult. If a lineup occurs before the defendant is formally charged, then the lineup can take place without an attorney. Do you think it would be proper for a law enforcement officer to delay filing a complaint intentionally against an accused solely for the purpose of having a lineup without the presence of the defense counsel?

WORKPLACE APPLICATIONS

1. You have a witness to an armed robbery. The witness is shot and is in the hospital in critical condition but is conscious and able to answer questions. Write a step-by-step plan on how you would conduct a show-up, lineup, and photographic array with this witness to establish identification.

2. A robbery occurred at noon on Thursday, and the eyewitness described the robber as a tall, young, white male with dark hair, wearing a red shirt and blue jeans and carrying a gun. During a show-up at 1 o'clock Saturday morning, the police take the witness to the defendant, who is several miles from the crime scene. The suspect is sitting in the back of a police car; when the witness arrives, the suspect is taken out of the car. The police shine their vehicle spot light on the suspect, and the witness can see that the suspect is in handcuffs. The suspect is a 20-year-old, 5'10" white male with brown hair, but he is wearing a white T-shirt and blue sweatpants. There is a gun sitting on the hood of the police car. Is the show-up so unnecessarily suggestive as to warrant the application of the exclusionary rule?

3. You are preparing photographic arrays for a witness to view in a case in which you have photographs of two suspects. Can you place the suspects' photos together on a single array, or do you have to place them on separate cards? For one defendant, the only picture you have of her is a booking photograph. Do all the other photographs have to be booking photographs? How many photographs do you have to use on a card to avoid unnecessary suggestiveness?

ETHICAL DILEMMA

1. Earlier in the week, you conducted a photographic array, or six-pack, with the only eyewitness to a double homicide. The witness correctly picked out the defendant and circled his photograph as you instructed, but you forgot to tell the witness to initial and date the six-pack card. Two weeks later, you realize that all you have is the six-pack, with a circle around the defendant, and no way of authenticating the card in court as the same card the witness looked at earlier. Do you call the witness back to the station and have him place his initials on the card next to the circle?

ENDNOTES

1. United States v. Wade, 388 U.S. 218 (1967) (footnote omitted).

2. United States v. Wade, 388 U.S. 218 (1967); Gilbert v. California, 388 U.S. 263 (1967); Stovall v. Denno, 388 U.S. 293 (1967).

3. Scott v. Illinois, 440 U.S. 367 (1979), interpreting Argersinger v. Hamlin, 407 U.S. 25 (1972), and Gideon v. Wainwright, 372 U.S. 335 (1963).

4. United States v. Wade, 388 U.S. 218, 225 (1967), quoting Powell v. Alabama, 287 U.S. 45, 57 & 69 (1932).

5. Massiah v. United States, 377 U.S. 201 (1964).

6. 384 U.S. 436 (1966).

7. United States v. Wade, 388 U.S. 218 (1967).

8. United States v. Ash, 413 U.S. 300, 316 (1973).

9. Wade, 388 U.S. at 226.

10. 388 U.S. 218 (1967).

11. *Id.* at 228.

12. *Id.* at 236–37.

13. *Id.* at 240.

14. 406 U.S. 682 (1972).

15. *Id.* at 690.

16. United States v. Larkin, 978 F.2d 964, 969 (7th Cir. 1992).

17. 388 U.S. 263 (1967).

18. *Id.* at 272–73, quoting Wong Sun v. United States, 371 U.S. 471, 488 (1963).

19. 388 U.S. 293 (1967).

20. *Id.*

21. 409 U.S. 188 (1972).

22. *Id.* at 199–200.

23. *Id.* at 200.

24. 390 U.S. 377 (1968).

25. 432 U.S. 98 (1977).

26. *Id.*

27. *Id.* at 100.

28. *Id.* at 114.

29. *Id.*

30. *See, e.g.,* Herrera v. Collins, 904 F.2d 944 (5th Cir. 1990).

31. United States v. Bagley, 772 F.2d 482, 493 (9th Cir. 1985), *cert. denied,* 475 U.S. 1023 (1986).

32. United States v. Russell, 532 F.2d 1063 (6th Cir. 1976).

33. United States v. Lewis, 547 F.2d 1030, 1035 (8th Cir. 1976), *cert. denied,* 429 U.S. 1111 (1977).

34. United States v. Jakobetz, 955 F.2d 786, 803 (2d Cir. 1992).

35. Salam v. Lockhart, 874 F.2d 525, 528 (8th Cir. 1989), *cert. denied,* 493 U.S. 898, 1989.

36. Styers v. Smith, 659 F.2d 293 (2nd Cir. 1981).

37. Passman v. Blackburn, 652 F.2d 559 (5th Cir. 1981), *cert. denied,* 455 U.S. 1022 (1982).

38. *Id.* at 570.

39. United States v. Dunbar, 767 F.2d 72, 73 (3d Cir. 1985).

40. Neil v. Biggers, 409 U.S. 188 (1972).

41. United States v. Damsky, 740 F.2d 134, 140 (2d. Cir.), *cert. denied,* 469 U.S. 918 (1984).

42. United States v. Donahue, 948 F.2d 438 (8th Cir. 1991), *cert. denied,* 503 U.S. 976 (1992).

43. *Id. See also* Herrera v. Collins, 904 F.2d 944, 948 (5th Cir.) (witness saw defendant in headlights for about fourteen seconds at fifteen feet), *cert. denied,* 498 U.S. 925 (1990); United States v. Goodman, 797 F.2d 468 (7th Cir. 1986) (witness saw defendant for fifteen to twenty seconds under good lighting at close range); United States v. Serna, 799 F.2d 842, 852 (2nd Cir. 1986) (defendant within two to three feet of witness for thirty minutes), *cert. denied,* 481 U.S. 1013 (1987).

44. Mata v. Sumner, 696 F.2d 1244, 1251–52 (9th Cir.), *vacated on other grounds,* 464 U.S. 957 (1983).

45. Valdez v. Schmer, 724 F.2d 249 (1st Cir. 1984).

46. *Id.* at 251.

47. Manson v. Brathwaite, 432 U.S. 98, 115 (1977).

48. Valdez, 724 F.2d at 252 (1st Cir. 1984).

49. 432 U.S. 98, at 115.

50. United States v. Jarrad, 754 F.2d 1451, 1455 (9th Cir.), *cert. denied,* 474 U.S. 830 (1985).

51. United States v. Monsour, 893 F.2d 126, 128 (6th Cir. 1990).

52. Simmons, 390 U.S. at 383–84.

53. Biggers, 409 U.S. 188, 201 (1972).

54. United States v. Rundell, 858 F.2d 425 (8th Cir. 1988).

55. United States v. Marchand, 564 F.2d 983, 996 (2nd Cir. 1977), *cert. denied,* 434 U.S. 1015. (1978).

56. The guide can be found on the Web at https://perma.cc/7QX9-43GW. In 2003, the National Institute of Justice republished the guide and added a multimedia training package. The package contains a slide presentation, audio and video clips of interviews and lineups, and exercises designed to enhance learning and make training sessions more interactive and visually interesting for law enforcement students. The 2003 guide can be found on the Web at https://www.ncjrs.gov/nij/eyewitness/188678.pdf.

57. See NAS, *Identifying the Culprit: Assessing Eyewitness Identification,* https://www.innocenceproject.org/wp-content/uploads/2016/02/NAS-Report-ID.pdf (last visited 6/1/2018).

58. The memorandum and report are available at https://www.justice.gov/file/923201/download (last visited 6/1/2018).

11 CIRCUMSTANTIAL EVIDENCE

CHAPTER OUTLINE

CHAPTER OBJECTIVES

This chapter focuses on another broad area of criminal evidence—circumstantial evidence. After reading this chapter you will be able to:

▶ Distinguish between direct and circumstantial evidence.

▶ State when and how the trial judge determines the relevancy of circumstantial evidence.

▶ Explain why the law generally prohibits evidence of the defendant's character.

▶ Name the principal noncharacter uses of "other crimes" evidence.

▶ Explain how motive and intent differ.

▶ Describe how the prosecution might use "other crimes" evidence.

▶ State how the prosecution may use another act of the defendant to refute a claim of mistake.

▶ Explain what *modus operandi* means in the context of the "other acts" evidence rule.

▶ Give several examples of circumstantial evidence that may be admitted to prove the accused's consciousness of guilt.

▶ Explain when the prosecution might prove the defendant's bad character.

▶ Explain when a victim's character is at issue.

▶ Describe the laws shielding victims of sex offenses and why lawmakers have enacted them.

▶ Identify how a witness's character may be attacked.

▶ Describe the test used to evaluate the admissibility of a defendant's prior uncharged felony convictions.

DIRECT EVIDENCE VERSUS CIRCUMSTANTIAL EVIDENCE

A common misconception is that circumstantial evidence is inferior evidence, but this is not so. As the federal jury instruction defining direct and circumstantial evidence states, "The law makes no distinction between the weight or value to be given to either direct or circumstantial evidence. Nor is a greater degree of certainty required of circumstantial evidence than of direct evidence."[1] This is the rule in a majority of jurisdictions. In a minority of states (California and 12 other states—see Figure 11-1), the law treats circumstantial evidence differently. In those states, the courts tell jury members that they may not find the defendant guilty based on circumstantial evidence unless the proved circumstances are (1) consistent with the theory that the defendant is guilty of the crime *and* (2) cannot be reconciled with any other rational conclusion. This instruction recognizes what is known as the "reasonable alternative hypothesis" instruction, which often benefits the accused. For example, assume a male defendant's fingerprints are found at the scene of a burglary and the police, upon investigating him, discover in his apartment a credit card in the name of the burglary victim. In such a case, the evidence is purely circumstantial, and the defendant would be entitled to the just-described jury instruction in those jurisdictions that distinguish between direct and circumstantial evidence. In *Holland v. United States,*[2] the Supreme Court of the United States said that, since there was no difference between direct and circumstantial evidence, trial courts need not give a cautionary instruction on circumstantial evidence like that used in California to satisfy the accused's right to a fair trial. A proper instruction on reasonable doubt is sufficient. Figure 11-1 shows those states that require a cautionary instruction like California's in regard to circumstantial evidence.

FIGURE 11–1 States that give circumstantial reasonable doubt instruction.

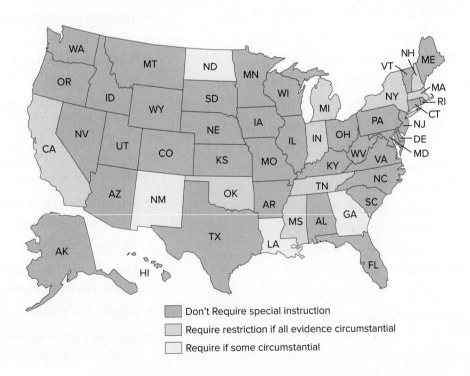

- Don't Require special instruction
- Require restriction if all evidence circumstantial
- Require if some circumstantial

Most courts, including those in jurisdictions that make *no* distinction between direct and circumstantial evidence, do continue to define the two categories of evidence for the jury. The distinction between direct and circumstantial evidence is often difficult to recognize. But because of the Supreme Court's decision in the *Holland* case, there is no constitutional basis for the reasonable alternative hypothesis instruction. Consequently, only the noted minority of state jurisdictions recognize the right of a defendant to such an instruction.

Direct Evidence Defined

Direct evidence is the testimony of a person who asserts or claims to have actual knowledge of a fact, such as an eyewitness. In a criminal trial, an example of direct evidence is the facts presented by a witness who saw the accused actually commit the crime. The jury decides whether to believe the witness's testimony; if they believe the witness, then they accept the facts the witness stated. The jury does not have to draw any inferences from the evidence presented to reach a conclusion about the defendant's guilt or innocence with direct evidence. For example, if, in a murder case, a witness saw the accused shoot the victim, the witness's testimony is direct evidence of the shooting and, if believed, is sufficient to convince the jury of the accused's guilt. It is important to note that, in this example, the observations of the witness are direct evidence only of the shooting and are not direct evidence of the cause of death, as the discussion of circumstantial evidence that follows will make clear.

DIRECT EVIDENCE
Testimony of a person who asserts or claims to have actual knowledge of a fact, such as an eyewitness.

FYI

Direct evidence is the product of a person's sensory perception. A person who states, "I heard three shots," is an "ear witness." A person who testifies, "It smelled like smoke," is a "nose witness." A person who testifies, "I felt his wrist and got no pulse," is a "touch witness." And, of course, a person who says, "I saw the man enter the bank with a gun," is an "eye witness."

Circumstantial Evidence Defined

Circumstantial evidence is an indirect approach to proving the facts in dispute. Federal law defines it as "proof of a chain of facts and circumstances indicating the existence of a fact."[3] Sometimes circumstantial evidence is called "indirect evidence" because certain facts may be inferred to have taken place when other facts are proved to have happened. The law defines circumstantial evidence as evidence that tends to establish the facts in dispute by proving the existence of another set of facts from which an inference or a presumption can be drawn. One or more inferences can arise from a series of proved facts. Returning to the hypothetical murder case, if no one saw the accused shoot the victim, the prosecution would have to prove the accused's guilt by proving the existence of other facts and circumstances from which the judge or jury infers beyond a reasonable doubt that the defendant committed the crime.

For example, consider a situation in which a witness overheard a heated argument between the accused and the victim, then heard a shot, and after that saw the accused, holding a gun, run from the room in which the victim was found dead. From these facts, an inference could be drawn that the accused was guilty of the homicide. It may appear at first glance that these facts are direct evidence,

CIRCUMSTANTIAL EVIDENCE
Evidence that tends to establish the facts in dispute by proving the existence of another set of facts from which an inference or a presumption can be drawn.

The following example was given by a Federal District Court judge to a jury to explain the difference between direct and circumstantial evidence.

Suppose that, before going to bed one cold winter night, you look out the window and see snow falling. You may conclude by direct evidence, your having seen the snow fall, that the snow banks the next morning resulted from a snowfall the night before. However, if you go to bed after looking out the window and see the dry pavement in your driveway but wake up the next morning and see banks of snow there, you may conclude by inference only, that is, by circumstantial evidence and reasoning, that it snowed the night before. In either event, you are just as certain that snow fell in the night.

as, in each instance, the witness heard or saw something. The testimony is direct evidence about what the witness heard and saw. However, it is only circumstantial evidence about the fact in issue, whether the accused shot the victim, because the witness cannot testify that he or she saw the accused shoot the victim. The witness's testimony only presents a set of circumstances from which the jury could, and likely would, infer that the defendant shot the victim and therefore was guilty.

In the case in which the witness actually saw the defendant shoot the victim, most of the observations of the defendant's actions would be direct evidence: The witness saw that the defendant had a gun in his hand, pointed it at the victim, and pulled the trigger; there was a loud noise and the victim fell to the floor, dead. Since the witness could not possibly see the bullet leave the gun and enter the victim's body, the jury could only conclude that the shot resulted in death based on the inferences from the observed circumstances.

Circumstantial evidence may also be presented by the accused in an effort to prove innocence. For example, in our hypothetical murder case, the defendant might attempt to claim self-defense. He or she might use evidence to show that the victim had a reputation for violence and, to show that the deceased was the initial attacker, might claim that the victim was carrying a knife.

Why Use Circumstantial Evidence?

Some people are skeptical of circumstantial evidence because they do not understand what it is or its significance in the prosecution of cases. Most crimes are committed without eyewitnesses, particularly homicide and burglary, so the only means of proving guilt is through the introduction of circumstantial evidence. Circumstantial evidence can be as convincing as direct evidence in proving guilt and often may be even more reliable. Law enforcement professionals must guard against being too skeptical when it comes to circumstantial evidence. It is often easy to overlook or disregard seemingly unimportant and unrelated facts that, when taken as a whole, create a high probability of conviction. Most of the scientific evidence presented by forensic experts is nothing more than circumstantial evidence, yet its reliability can be very satisfactory and convincing. A latent fingerprint discovered on a burglarized safe or on a gun identified as a murder weapon is the strongest kind of proof that the accused touched those objects. Figure 11-2 shows the latent fingerprint patterns.

On the other hand, witnesses to crimes may have difficulty remembering details, such as the time that events occurred or an accurate description of people or objects they saw. In fact, many courts instruct juries to look carefully at eyewitness identification testimony because it is so often inaccurate. Those courts tell the jury to take into account all the factors that weigh upon mistaken

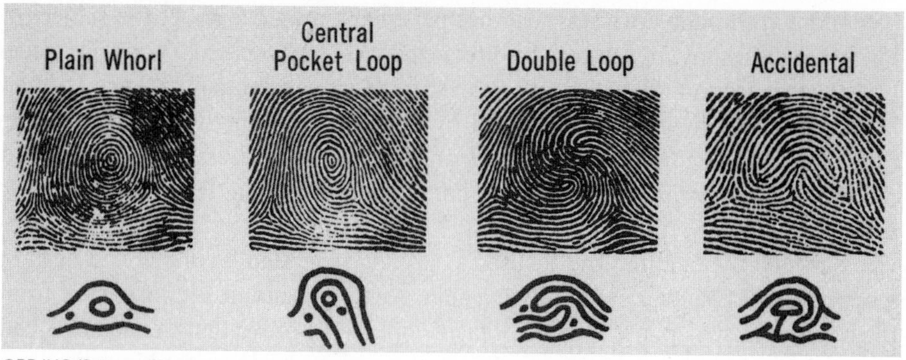

FIGURE 11–2 Basic fingerprint patterns.

Plain Whorl | Central Pocket Loop | Double Loop | Accidental

©PR INC./Science Source

eyewitness identifications, such as the opportunity for the witness to observe, the stress the witness was under at the time of the events, any cross-racial or ethnic differences between the witness and the accused, and whether there was previous contact between them. See the California jury instruction regarding eyewitness identification set forth in Chapter 10, page 353, for an example of such a cautionary instruction.

ON THE JOB

In order to document the accuracy and propriety of an eyewitness's identification of a suspect, the law enforcement officer must make a complete and accurate record of all actions and statements surrounding the witness's identification. For example, if the officer seeks to have the witness select a photograph of a suspect, a photographic array should be arranged in which the prime suspect's photograph is presented along with other photographs of similar-looking suspects. Even more important, however, is that an oral or video record should be made of everything. The array should be photocopied and all instructions recorded. It is important to remember that this identification is not meant to stand alone but is a piece of the total investigation by the officer.

The law recognizes the validity of circumstantial evidence because human experience teaches that, when a given set of circumstances repeatedly causes a result, the same result is likely to recur each time those same circumstances recur. In other words, the inferences the fact-finder draws from the evidence presented will be consistent with human experience and common sense. Thus, human experience and common sense have shown that, when a person overhears a heated argument between two people, hears a shot, sees an individual running from the room with a gun in his or her hand, and finds a deceased victim in the room, then the individual seen fleeing is likely the killer.

Relevance of Circumstantial Evidence

Whether direct or circumstantial evidence is to be introduced, the rules of admissibility are the same. First, the evidence must meet the requirement of **relevance**. In the words of FRE 401, the evidence must have "any tendency to make a fact more or less probable than it would be without the evidence." Second, the evidence must

RELEVANCE
A showing that an item of evidence has any tendency to prove or disprove a pertinent fact.

be presented through a witness who has personal knowledge about the subject of his or her testimony. In the case of direct evidence, one can usually readily recognize the connection. However, the relevance of circumstantial evidence is often hidden and may have to be explained by the attorney trying to introduce it before the judge will admit the evidence. For example, the appearance of an accused person's clothing immediately after the crime has been committed may not initially seem relevant. Nevertheless, if the charge against the accused is murder or aggravated assault, the fact that the accused's clothing suggested he or she had been in a struggle could be material in proving guilt. Another example is a love letter from the accused to the spouse of the deceased, offered to prove that the accused had the motive to kill his lover's husband—in order to have his lover for himself.

MOTION *IN LIMINE*
A motion to exclude or admit evidence, often made before trial and usually heard out of the presence of the jury.

BALANCING TEST
The requirement that relevant evidence be excluded if its "probative value is substantially outweighed by a danger of one or more of the following: unfair prejudice, confusing the issues, misleading the jury, undue delay, waste of time, or needlessly presenting cumulative evidence."

If either side tries to keep testimony or tangible evidence out of court, that party will object to the evidence. He or she may make the objection at trial when the opponent first tries to introduce the evidence, or in a motion, sometimes made pretrial. A motion to exclude or admit evidence is a **motion *in limine***. After the attorneys make written and/or oral arguments, the judge then rules on the admissibility of the evidence. Sometimes a judge has a witness testify before making a ruling on the evidence's admissibility. Keep in mind, as discussed in Chapter 3, that, just because evidence may be relevant, it may still be inadmissible if the judge determines it might be unfairly prejudicial, or if it would be confusing or a waste of time. FRE 403 has a **balancing test** that requires the judge to exclude relevant evidence if its "probative value is substantially outweighed by a danger of one or more of the following: unfair prejudice, confusing the issues, misleading the jury, undue delay, waste of time, or needlessly presenting cumulative evidence." The fact that a witness was addicted to drugs or alcohol at one time in his or her life but was not claimed to have been under the influence at the time of the events involved in the trial is an example of a relevant fact that a judge would probably exclude under the balancing test.

The relevance of circumstantial evidence is based primarily on logic, reasonableness, good sense, and good judgment. If circumstantial evidence tends to explain in a reasonable manner what happened and aids in proving the truth of issues in dispute, it is considered relevant.

A lawyer may offer a single fact in evidence that seems irrelevant. However, other facts, proven later, may make the first fact relevant to the issues in dispute. For example, evidence that an accused is an expert shot with a rifle may not have any particular significance, even in a homicide case, but, if it is proved that the homicide victim was killed with a rifle shot from a great distance, the fact that the accused was able to commit such an act could create an inference of guilt. On the other hand, if it was proved that the accused was completely unfamiliar with firearms, that fact would support an inference that he or she could not have been the shooter.

ON THE JOB

A law enforcement professional who is testifying when defense counsel objects might think it would be helpful to the prosecution if he or she were to blurt out the information that the prosecution is seeking. Such behavior is inappropriate and unprofessional. If the judge decides the jury should not have heard the information, the judge might have to declare a mistrial. In that case, the attempt to help the prosecution could cause the unnecessary expense of a retrial or even prevent the case from being tried at all. The witness should pause and wait for the judge's ruling on the objection before making any response.

Different Functions of Circumstantial Evidence

Circumstantial evidence is used in many ways in criminal prosecutions. In many cases, the entire evidence against the accused consists only of circumstantial evidence because no eyewitnesses exist to present direct evidence. For example, if an accused is on trial for burglary, all of the evidence presented by the prosecution might be nothing more than a series of events from which the jury could draw an inference of guilt. The first evidence might be from the officer who had arrested the accused during the night near the store that had been burglarized and who had found the accused in possession of articles known to have been taken during the burglary of the store. This testimony does not directly place the accused in the store or put the accused in the position of actually having burglarized the store. However, these events, or facts, create a strong suspicion of the accused's guilt. Additional testimony shows that latent fingerprints developed in the store were identified as those of the accused. With this additional bit of evidence, the case against the accused becomes stronger. Finally, a criminalist lab technician testifies to finding a small piece of glass in the pant cuff of the accused that fit in place with those taken from a broken window of the burglarized store. None of these facts, individually or collectively, directly prove that the accused is the burglar, yet, as a whole, they are as strong in establishing guilt beyond a reasonable doubt as if a witness had testified, "Yes, I saw the accused break into the store and put the jewelry in his pocket and leave."

In fact, the jury may consider this series of circumstances to be more convincing than the direct evidence of a witness who testified to seeing the accused burglarize the store. The jury may believe the witness unreliable or mistaken, but a strong inference of guilt can be drawn from the circumstantial evidence. Thus, the mere fact that the only evidence available is circumstantial does not mean that it cannot establish a strong case against the accused and, in fact, lead to a jury verdict of guilty beyond a reasonable doubt.

In a case in which a witness testified, "Yes, I saw the accused break into the store, put the jewelry in his pocket, and leave," circumstantial evidence of latent fingerprints developed inside the store and glass fragments in the pant cuff of the accused would be used to corroborate the direct evidence presented by the witness.

One of the most frequent uses of circumstantial evidence is to connect the accused with the crime, that is, to identify the accused as the one who committed the act. To establish identity, the prosecution may introduce evidence that the accused has committed other crimes with the same *modus operandi* or that he or she had the ability and means with which to commit the crime in question. The accused's previous attacks on the victim are circumstantial evidence that may be introduced to overcome an allegation that a homicide was committed in self-defense or by accident, or to prove premeditation. A defendant, to establish innocence, may also present circumstantial evidence. Some of the more prominent uses of circumstantial evidence in criminal cases are discussed in the following sections.

ADMISSIBILITY OF OTHER CRIMES, ACTS, OR WRONGS

Most people are likely to agree that a person who has previously committed other acts of misconduct or crimes is more likely to be guilty of a crime, when accused, than a person who has not previously committed a crime. Therefore, revealing to the jury the other acts of misconduct and crimes committed by a defendant in a criminal trial can create a strong suspicion of guilt. However, early in the development of the common law in England, the courts recognized that evidence of uncharged misconduct has a tremendous potential to prejudice the jury, leading it to conclude that the accused is a person of bad character. The jury might then convict the accused based on that opinion without considering the evidence of the specific crime charged. For this reason, the common law developed a rule that, normally, evidence of past acts of misconduct and crimes by the defendant, which were not a part of the charge for which he or she was presently being tried, could not be introduced during the trial.

FRE 404(a) typifies the modern **character evidence rule** generally prohibiting the use of character evidence: "Evidence of a person's character or character trait is not admissible to prove that on a particular occasion the person acted in accordance with the character or trait." The mere fact that the accused has committed other acts of misconduct or crimes does not necessarily mean the accused is guilty of the new charge. It has been held that in each case a defendant is entitled to go to trial with a clean slate and is to be tried on the facts of the case at hand and not on a past record. The evidence of other crimes introduced against the defendant may so prejudice the jury that the defendant will not receive a fair trial. The jury may be inclined to assume automatically that a defendant is guilty of the crime with which he or she is presently charged because of the uncharged acts. In short, evidence of character is often irrelevant and, even when relevant, is likely to be more prejudicial than probative.

There are times, however, when **evidence of other crimes, acts, or wrongs** committed by the accused may be introduced during a criminal trial if they are pertinent to certain trial issues other than the accused's bad character and if the judge believes the evidence is particularly necessary to assist the jury in arriving at the truth. Other crimes or misconduct of the accused can be strong circumstantial evidence of guilt when offered on such issues as, in the language of FRE 404(b), "motive, opportunity, intent, preparation, plan, knowledge, identity, or absence of mistake, or lack of accident."

This rule lists specific categories of noncharacter use of other misconduct evidence, but the categories are not exclusive or exhaustive. This evidence, sometimes called "*prior* bad acts" evidence, need not have occurred prior to the charged crime. The other misconduct may have been committed prior to, at the same time as, or after the act for which the person is charged. It just must be relevant to one of the categories of noncharacter use. Sometimes this evidence is referred to as "*similar* acts" evidence. However, the other bad acts do not always

CHARACTER
EVIDENCE RULE
The rule that states evidence of a trait of character to prove a person's conduct in conformity with that trait is inadmissible, with a few exceptions.

EVIDENCE OF OTHER CRIMES, ACTS, OR WRONGS
Evidence of bad acts used not to prove a trait of character but to prove something else, such as motive, opportunity, intent, preparation, plan, knowledge, identity, absence of mistake, or lack of accident.

MYTH ▶	◀ FACT
Uncharged misconduct evidence is admissible against an accused only if the uncharged act is similar or substantially similar to the charged act.	Uncharged misconduct evidence is admissible if it is relevant, whether similar to the charged act or not.

have to be similar, as long as they are relevant. For example, consider a defendant on trial for car theft. Evidence shows that he stole the car to use as a getaway vehicle after setting fire to his failing business in order to collect insurance. Evidence of the uncharged arson would be admissible to show motive for the car theft even though it is entirely dissimilar to the charged act. Finally, evidence of other crimes may fit into more than one category of noncharacter use. In the car theft example, the defendant's acts of arson and theft are also part of a common plan or design; the plan was to steal the car to carry out the arson.

Other Crimes to Prove Motive or Intent

Other acts of misconduct or crimes frequently become the reason or motive for repeating the same act or crime, or they may be an indication that the accused intended a particular act. Although people often use the terms "intent" and "motive" interchangeably, legally they are different. Motive can be defined as "that which leads or tempts the mind to indulge in a criminal act," and it is something that may be resorted to as a legitimate help in arriving at the ultimate act in question. * * * "[4]

A **motive** is that which moves a person to act or explains the reason a person acted. For example, evidence that a homicide victim witnessed the accused commit a bank robbery would be admissible evidence of a motive for the homicide. The motive in this case is the desire of the accused to silence the victim, so that he or she could not testify against the accused. Although the law does not require evidence of motive in any case, motive is always relevant because the accused's conduct, identity, or intent may be inferred from the motive.

For another example of how motive can be inferred from a set of circumstances, consider the case of a convict who escapes from prison, steals a car, robs a convenience store, and then speeds away down a highway. A patrol officer spots the speeding vehicle and pulls it over for a traffic violation. As the officer approaches the stopped vehicle, the convict leans over, pulls a gun from between the seats, and shoots the officer. At the trial for the killing of the patrol officer, the prosecution could use as evidence the uncharged crimes of escape, auto theft, and robbery to establish the motive of the killing. The uncharged misconduct evidence would clearly be admissible to prove that the motive for the shooting was the desire not to be identified and caught during the getaway.

Intent, on the other hand, is a state of mind; it expresses mental action that is usually coupled with an outward physical act to cause a particular result. Therefore, a crime may be divided into two component parts: the mental state, or *mens rea,* and the physical action, or *actus reus.* Intent is a necessary element of most crimes, even though only a general intent to take the physical action is required. Being a state of mind, intent is not easily proved and can only be proved by circumstantial evidence. Since we cannot look into the mind of an accused, the jury must infer intent from the evidence of what the accused said and did.

An example of the introduction of other bad acts to prove *mens rea* occurred in *Huddleston v. United States,*[5] in which the defendant was charged with one count of selling stolen goods shipped across state lines and one count of possessing stolen property. The defendant was arrested and charged after selling Memorex videocassette tapes stolen from a shipment. The government charged that the defendant possessed and sold the tapes, knowing that they were stolen. The defendant admitted

MOTIVE
That which moves a person to act or explains the reason a person acted.

INTENT
A state of mind; it expresses mental action that is usually coupled with an outward physical act to cause a particular result.

possessing and selling the tapes but denied knowing they were stolen. The facts of the case are as follows: (a) More than 32,000 blank Memorex videocassette tapes were stolen from the Overnight Express yard in South Holland, Illinois. (b) Two days later, the defendant contacted the manager of a store in Ypsilanti, Michigan, seeking her assistance in selling a large number of blank Memorex videotapes. After the defendant assured the manager that the tapes were not stolen, she agreed to help sell the tapes. (c) They sold 5,000 tapes and delivered them to various purchasers.

At trial, two instances of previous uncharged misconduct were introduced to prove that the defendant was aware that the tapes were stolen. First, the owner of a record store testified that the defendant had offered to sell him new 120 black-and-white televisions for $28 apiece. In the second instance, an undercover FBI agent, posing as a buyer for an appliance store, testified that the defendant offered to sell him a large quantity of Amana appliances. The defendant testified that a person named Leroy Wesby had provided all the videotapes, the televisions, and the appliances and that Wesby had told him that all of the merchandise was legitimately obtained. The United States Supreme Court held that, if the jury could reasonably conclude that the televisions and appliances were stolen, then this evidence could be used to prove that the defendant knew that the videotapes were also stolen because all three items had come from the same source. Thus, the previous acts of uncharged misconduct were admissible to help prove that the defendant had the required intent to possess and sell stolen goods.

Another common example in which misconduct evidence is used to prove intent is in drug cases. Most drug cases involve a charge of possession of illegal substances or possession with intent to sell. As in the *Huddleston* case, when a person accused of possessing drugs claims that he or she did not know the substance possessed was a drug or that it was illegal to possess the substance, evidence of prior criminal possession of drugs can be used to rebut the defendant's claim.

Other Crimes to Prove Plan (or Design)

Evidence of the commission of acts similar to the alleged crime may be admissible to show plan or design. Prior acts that are evidence of a common plan or design are not used to prove the intent or the mental element of a crime, but rather to prove that the defendant engaged in the conduct for which he or she is charged. An example is the California case *People v. Ewoldt.*[6] The defendant was charged with four counts of committing lewd acts upon a child and one count of annoying or molesting a child. The victim was the defendant's stepdaughter, Jennifer. At trial, the prosecution tried to introduce evidence that the defendant had committed prior uncharged lewd acts upon Jennifer, as well as evidence that the defendant had committed prior uncharged lewd acts upon the victim's older sister, Natalie. The California Supreme Court held that both instances of uncharged misconduct by the defendant were admissible. The court explained that, "[t]o establish the existence of a common design or plan, the common features must indicate the existence of a plan rather than a series of similar spontaneous acts, but the plan thus revealed need not be distinctive or unusual." The court found common features between the molestation of both girls. Both of the victims were the defendant's stepdaughters, were living with the defendant, and were similar in age when the acts occurred.

One of the most bizarre cases in which a common plan or design became an issue was *People v. Lisenba,*[7] in which the defendant was charged with the murder of his wife. Prior acts of misconduct relating to the murder of a former wife were admitted to prove that the charged murder was part of a common plan or scheme. The defendant had married his second wife and immediately thereafter took out an insurance policy on her life, with a double-indemnity clause for accidental death. A short time later, the defendant conspired with a friend to help him kill his wife and make the death appear as an accident in order to collect on the double-indemnity clause of the insurance policy. The defendant first decided to poison his wife by obtaining two rattlesnakes. With the help of his friend, the defendant tied his wife to the kitchen table and placed her feet in the box of rattlesnakes. The defendant and his friend then left the house. Upon their return, the defendant found that the venom had not had any serious effect on his wife. He then decided to drown her in the bathtub and then place the body in a backyard fishpond in a manner to make it appear that she had "accidentally" fallen into the pond. After placing the wife's body face down in the pond, the defendant then went out to dinner with another friend and his wife. When he returned home, the defendant made a pretense of searching for his wife. After searching the yard, the defendant stated that his wife had apparently fallen into the fishpond and drowned. An autopsy was performed, and the drowning was confirmed. An investigation at that time failed to reveal the circumstances of his wife's death.

The defendant meanwhile tried to collect on the insurance policy, but the insurance company refused payment on the ground that the accidental death was suspicious. This suspicion was based on the fact that, three years previously, the defendant had married a woman in Colorado and had immediately taken out an insurance policy on her life with a double-indemnity clause. Thereafter, while on an automobile ride, the defendant and his first wife were in an accident. The first wife did not die in the auto accident, but drowned in the bathtub under suspicious circumstances. The prosecution brought out the facts of this alleged accidental death during the trial for the murder of his second wife as uncharged misconduct evidence. The evidence of the prior acts of misconduct by the defendant concerning his first wife, including the existence of the double-indemnity clause insurance policy, her attempted murder, the subsequent cover-up to make it look like an accident, and the mysterious drowning, was admitted in the trial for murder of his second wife in order to prove a common scheme or plan to kill his wives for the insurance money.

Other Crimes to Prove Lack of Mistake or Accident: The Doctrine of Chances

There are some instances when the circumstances of the case or the defendant's claim requires the prosecution to disprove the possibility that no criminal conduct has taken place or that the crime occurred as the result of an accident or a mistake. For example, in a child abuse case, the parents might claim that the child received his or her injuries by accidentally falling down the stairs; thus, there was no criminal act committed upon the child. In a case like this, the prosecution could introduce uncharged misconduct evidence to prove a crime had occurred rather than an accident—i.e., the *actus reus* of a crime. The prosecution might introduce several documented previous instances in which the child suffered serious unexplained injuries in an attempt to prove that the injuries now at issue were not the result of an accident. This use of such evidence has been called the **doctrine of chances** and may be explained as an attempt to convince the jury that the charged crime is not an isolated event due to chance. According to one commentator, "The doctrine of chances rests on the objective improbability of coincidences."[8] If the same situation happens time and time again, then these "accidents" can no longer be considered coincidental.

An early example demonstrating the use of the doctrine of chances is the English case often referred to as the "Brides of the Bath," *R. v. Smith*.[9] The defendant was on trial for the drowning death of his first "wife," who was found dead in a bathtub shortly after the "marriage" and after she signed an agreement transferring her property to the accused upon her death. The defendant contended that the wife had died of an epileptic seizure and that her drowning was simply an accident. However, the prosecution introduced evidence that two subsequent "wives" had died in their baths under similar suspicious circumstances shortly after their "weddings" and after signing their property over to the accused. Thus, all three "wives" were found dead in exactly the same manner while the defendant was alone with them in their homes. At the time of all three of these "marriages," the defendant was actually married to another woman, who remained alive through it all. The defendant was convicted for the murder of his first "wife" and, on appeal, the British court held that the evidence of the subsequent two drownings was admissible to refute the possibility of coincidence. The court said that the uncharged acts went to prove that the charged drowning was a crime rather than an accident and allowed the conviction to stand. The simple reasoning behind the ruling of admissibility was that either Smith was the unluckiest man alive or he had drowned his first "wife."

APPLICATION CASE

A more recent example of the doctrine of chances use of other misconduct evidence is *Estelle v. Mcguire*,[10] in which the defendant was charged with the murder of his infant daughter. The defendant claimed that the daughter had fallen off the couch and subsequently died of the injuries she sustained. However, the prosecution introduced evidence that the child had 17 contusions on her chest, 29 contusions on her abdominal area, a split liver, a split pancreas, a lacerated large intestine, and damage to her heart and one of her lungs. There was also evidence of rectal tearing and a partially healed rib fracture, both of which were the result of previous injuries. The prosecution claimed that the child suffered from battered child syndrome, which tended to prove that the child had not suffered the injuries accidentally and that the final infliction of injury that took her life did not result from her falling off the couch.

The use of other misconduct evidence to refute the possibility of accident or mistake may also occur when the defendant, charged with some particular criminal activity, denies it occurred and claims innocence. For example, assume a man is accused of sexual molestation of one child and he admits that he was in the child's company but denies any sexual contact. The prosecution could introduce evidence that the accused molested another child on a different occasion to refute the defendant's claim of innocent association. In such a case, the evidence also could be said to be admissible because the evidence of the uncharged event tends to corroborate the evidence of the crime charged.

Other Crimes or Misconduct to Prove Identity

During a criminal case, not only must the fact that a crime has been committed be proven, but also it must be established that the defendant was the one who committed the act, unless he or she admits committing the act and claims some justification or legal excuse, such as self-defense. Proving that the defendant is the one who committed the crime for which he or she is on trial is not always easily accomplished, particularly if the defendant alleges mistaken identity or claims an alibi defense. Prior crimes known to have been committed by the defendant may sometimes be introduced into evidence in an effort to prove that the defendant committed the crime for which he or she is on trial. Motive, existence of a plan or pattern of conduct that implies a plan, absence of accident, and opportunity are theories often used to prove the identity of a perpetrator. Identity is particularly provable by evidence that the accused committed another, similar crime.

However, mere evidence that there are similarities between a prior crime committed by the accused and the charged crime at issue is often not enough to prove identity. This is so because many crimes of the same nature committed by different individuals may have marks of similarity. For example, burglary by entry through a ground floor window is a common method and, hence, evidence of such will usually be inadmissible. Most courts have gone so far as to hold that, to be admissible, evidence suggesting similarities in the manners in which the prior crimes and the currently charged crime were committed must be so unusual and distinctive as to be like a signature. A distinctive pattern of committing crimes is referred to as the ***modus operandi*** of the perpetrator. For example, a bank robber who always wears a Donald Trump mask and gray overalls is distinguished by these characteristics, which are part of his *modus operandi.*

MODUS OPERANDI
A distinctive pattern of committing crimes.

MEANS OR CAPABILITY TO COMMIT A CRIME

Circumstantial evidence is often introduced to prove that the accused had the means with which to commit a particular crime or that he or she could commit it. Examples include an employee who had the keys to a locked drawer from which valuables were stolen and an employee with a computer password to confidential files when secrets contained within the computer were stolen. Perhaps the most illustrative example is in the trial of Scott Peterson. There, the prosecution maintained that Peterson had both the means and the capability to murder his wife, Laci, and their unborn son, Conner. The first piece of circumstantial evidence was the fact that Peterson lied about his affair with Amber Frey—he did not tell the police about it, and he even lied about that on national television. Even the fact of his affair was a piece of evidence that could be used by the jury to infer a motive to kill his wife. Second was the evidence that Peterson told Frey some weeks before Laci's disappearance that he had "lost" his wife. Finally, perhaps, was Peterson's alibi—that he had gone fishing the day of Laci's disappearance—placing him in the area of San Francisco Bay, where Laci's and Conner's bodies washed up almost four months later. Each of these pieces of evidence in the totality of the circumstances would be sufficient to prove that Peterson had both the means and the capability of committing the double homicide. In fact, Peterson was convicted on this evidence.

CONSCIOUSNESS OF GUILT

Although individuals may react differently from time to time, people generally follow a standard pattern of behavior. Frequently, a person who has committed a crime will deviate from his or her usual pattern of conduct. When this occurs, proof of uncustomary acts, statements, or appearance may be introduced to show **consciousness of guilt**. It has been held that any act from which the inference of consciousness of guilt can be drawn is admissible.

CONSCIOUSNESS OF GUILT
Evidence of an accused's uncustomary acts, statements, or appearance from which guilt may be inferred.

APPLICATION CASE

In a famous trial for murder, Daniel Webster headed the prosecution of John Francis Knapp, who was charged with the murder of Joseph White. Webster claimed that Knapp had aided and abetted a man named Crowninshield, who actually struck the fatal blows. It was therefore crucial to the prosecution to show Crowninshield's guilt—although Crowninshield himself had committed suicide before the trial. In his closing argument, Daniel Webster argued to the jury that the suicide was a confession of guilt: "Meantime the guilty soul—cannot keep its own secret. It is false to itself; or rather it feels an irresistible impulse of conscience to be true to itself. It labors under its guilty possession, and knows not what to do with it. . . . It must be confessed, it will be confessed; there is no refuge from confession but suicide, and suicide is confession."[11]

Evidence of guilt can be manifested in several forms of observable behavior. If an accused person were seen fleeing from the scene of a crime, the prosecution could introduce this fact in evidence as part of the proof of guilt because the usual tendency for a person who has committed a crime is to flee from the scene. The fact that the defendant was in a highly emotional state immediately after a murder that he has been accused of committing may be introduced to show consciousness of guilt. The fact that the accused attempted to evade arrest and to escape can also be introduced. Probably the most famous example of this type of evidence is the low-speed chase of O.J. Simpson in his white Ford Bronco in connection with his first criminal trial. Other acts that may serve as evidence of consiousness of guilt include those in which the accused denies his or her identity to the police or starts using a fictitious name immediately after a crime has been committed. The failure to appear for trial, an attempt to conceal evidence, the refusal to participate in a lineup, the refusal to furnish handwriting examples, and an attempt to bribe witnesses are all circumstances that would indicate that the accused is guilty of a crime.

CHARACTER OF THE DEFENDANT

If the defendant in a criminal trial has a reputation of bad character, this reputation may be some indication of guilt because one usually acts in accordance with one's reputation. The reputation of the defendant may therefore be pertinent to the issue. Nevertheless, the universal rule, exemplified by FRE 404(a), generally prohibits the proof of character at trial. Therefore, the prosecution is not permitted to introduce evidence that the defendant is a person of bad character in order to prove guilt. Two reasons have been advanced for this prohibition. First, there is no presumption that the defendant in a criminal trial is a person of good character and much trial time is saved by not requiring the prosecution to show the bad character of the accused. Second, and probably of greater importance, if evidence is presented that the defendant has a reputation for being bad, such evidence may subject him or her to undue prejudice. There is always a danger that the jury may convict the defendant on reputation rather than on the facts of the case.

FYI

In 1995, an amendment to the FRE, adding Rules 413, 414, and 415, went into effect. These rules effectively established an exception to the rule that prohibits evidence of a trait of character to be used to prove that an accused conducted himself or herself in accordance with that trait of character and thereby likely committed the crime charged. The rules allow evidence of "similar crimes" to be admitted in sexual assault and child molestation cases. In other words, evidence of sexual misconduct or child molestation committed by a person accused of similar sexual misconduct or child molestation *is* admissible to prove that such a person has a propensity to commit such acts. Congress adopted these rules to aid law enforcement and the courts in convicting sexual offenders. These rules permit evidence of specific bad acts, but *not* evidence in the form of reputation and opinion.

However, under the universal rule, the defendant may present evidence of good character in an attempt to prove innocence [see FRE 404(a)(2)(A)]. The law permits the accused to try to show that he or she is not the kind of person who would commit the crime of which he or she has been accused. Of course, this **defendant's good character rule** requires that the evidence of good character must have some bearing upon the crime charged; that is, it must show traits in opposition to the type of crime that the defendant is accused of having committed. For example, if the defendant were charged with robbery, evidence that the defendant has a reputation for being honest would be admissible, as it would be in opposition to the charge. If, however, the defendant were charged with child molestation, a reputation for being an honest person would not be relevant and would therefore not be admissible. A defendant charged with aggravated assault might show evidence that he or she has a reputation for being a quiet and peaceful person in an attempt to prove that the assault was done in self-defense.

DEFENDANT'S GOOD CHARACTER RULE
The rule of evidence that permits an accused to introduce evidence of good character in an attempt to prove his or her innocence.

Proving the Defendant's Good Character

A defendant shows his or her good character through witnesses, referred to as "character witnesses," who are in a position to know the defendant or the defendant's reputation. Under the modern rule, typified by FRE 405(a), a character witness may testify only in the form of opinion or reputation. Character, opinion, and reputation are not the same. Generally speaking, character is a description of a person's attributes, traits, or abilities. Opinion as to character is the witness's personal judgment based on direct observation and personal knowledge of an accused's specific traits of character. Someone who knows the accused long enough and well enough to form an opinion may give opinion evidence. The longer the witness has known the accused, the more weight the opinion carries.

Reputation is the consensus of what other people in the community say about the accused's character. To prove the reputation of a person, a witness must be in a position to know what others say about that person. The character witness must know what others say about the defendant in a specific community, such as where the defendant resides, works, or socializes. It must be the general reputation reflected among a certain class of persons. For example, a gambler may have a good reputation among his associates for being honest because he pays all of his gambling debts, and he may even have the reputation of being a generous person within the same crowd. However, in the community in which he resides, he may have a bad reputation because he is considered an unsavory person. For any weight to be given to the testimony of a character witness, the witness should have recent knowledge of the defendant's reputation; that is, the knowledge should be as of, or about, the time that the crime was committed. If the knowledge of the accused's reputation is too remote in time, it may be of little consequence to the jury.

Prosecution's Proof of Defendant's Bad Character

Once the defendant has attempted to prove good character, the prosecution may present evidence to show that the defendant is of bad character. The defendant's introduction of that evidence places character in issue, and the prosecution is permitted to meet this issue by **impeachment**, refuting the defendant's contention of being good by proving the defendant is of bad character. This may be accomplished by impeaching the defendant's character witness or by the prosecution calling its own witnesses to attest to the defendant's bad character.

Impeachment of a defendant's character witness by the prosecution may follow any one of the traditional impeachment methods. In addition, however, the prosecution may try to devalue the character witness's testimony by asking the witness about specific acts of misconduct in which the defendant has engaged. Remember that the defendant's character witness may not testify to specific good deeds to prove good character on direct examination. Nonetheless, the prosecution is permitted to test the character witness's knowledge of the defendant or his or her reputation by asking whether the witness has heard of specific acts of misconduct by the defendant on cross-examination. All that the courts require of the prosecution is a good faith basis in fact that the accused has committed the misdeed.

IMPEACHMENT
The process by which the credibility of a witness is attacked.

That is, if the prosecution is in possession of information that the defendant has committed acts of misconduct, or if the prosecution knows statements have been made that the defendant committed acts of misconduct, then the inquiry of the witness may be made. The prosecution may not just make up a rumor in an effort to test the character witness. In fact, when the prosecution asks questions about acts of misconduct by the defendant, the trial judge may require proof that there is a good faith basis for the question and require the prosecution to identify the source of the information along with evidence of the source's reliability. This inquiry by the trial judge is not made in the presence of the jury.

Some people believe that permitting the prosecution to indulge in a wholesale background inquiry about the prior misconduct of a defendant is highly prejudicial in all instances and should not be allowed. On the other hand, it must be remembered that the defendant does not have to place his or her character in issue by attempting to prove good character, particularly if the defendant knows, better than anyone else, that the good character does not exist. The defendant should be aware that the prosecution cannot show bad character or prior acts of misconduct until the defendant opens the issue. Therefore, the defendant raises the issue at his or her own risk. It is only fair that the prosecution should be entitled to overcome a defendant's false allegation that he or she is of good character. It is considered in the best interests of justice to permit some inquiry to be made of the defendant's true character. Besides being asked whether the witness has ever known or heard of acts of misconduct or prior crimes, the witness may be asked whether he or she knew or heard of the defendant's prior convictions. The prosecution, however, may not independently introduce proof of those prior convictions.

When the defendant elects to put character in issue, character witnesses will testify and may be cross-examined. In all likelihood, the jury will hear testimony of both good character and bad character. It then becomes a matter of whose witnesses, or which testimony, the jury believes.

Amount of Proof to Show Good or Bad Character

No set number of witnesses is needed to prove either good or bad character. Much is dependent upon the weight given to the testimony of the character witnesses. In any event, the trial judge will allow a reasonable number of witnesses on both sides, so that the jury may make some determination. The judge will normally limit the number of witnesses after a certain point; otherwise, the presentation of character witnesses could go on indefinitely.

Proof of Prior Sexual Misconduct

In 1995, the Federal Rules of Evidence were amended to address the admissibility of evidence of a defendant's prior sexual assault or child molestation crimes in cases involving sexual assault or child molestation. Rules 413, 414, and 415 create exceptions to the general rule that evidence of past crimes may not be used "to prove a person's character in order to show that on a particular occasion the person acted in accordance with the character" [FRE 404(b)(1)]. FRE 413 specifically allows the prosecution in sexual assault cases to introduce evidence regarding other uncharged sexual misconduct by the accused. Evidence of sexual assault would therefore be automatically admissible in the prosecution's case-in-chief. Similarly, FRE 414 permits the introduction of uncharged incidents of child molestation in a case in which the accused is charged with an offense of child molestation. Such incidents may include any prior acts of molestation against the victim, as well as prior incidents involving other children. Rule 415 makes such evidence also admissible in civil damages cases brought by the victims of either sexual assault or child molestation.

APPLICATION CASE

In *United States v. McHorse*,[13] McHorse was convicted of four counts of aggravated sexual assault upon three victims, all of whom were under 12 years of age at the time of the crimes. At trial, testimony relating to similar acts was admitted under both FRE 404 and FRE 414. First, the defendant called his son, Justin, to testify on his behalf that he knew his father "couldn't" do anything bad to anybody, "would not do anything like that," and "was a great father and provided a very good home." Based on this testimony, the court ruled the son had testified as a character witness for the defendant, thus opening the door under FRE 404(a) to rebuttal by specific instances of conduct. The government was entitled to demonstrate that Justin was not fully informed as to his father's character by inquiring into Justin's knowledge of two discrete specific instances of conduct allegedly involving the defendant's daughter and half-sister. The prosecutor then asked the son if he was "aware of the fact that your own sister . . . [h]as said that he sexually abused her from the time that she was a small child" and if he was "aware of the fact that [the defendant's half-sister] has said that your father sexually abused her from the time that she was a small child to the time she was 18." Justin replied he was not aware of the daughter's allegations but was aware of the half-sister's allegations. In addition, under FRE 414, the court permitted testimony regarding the defendant's alleged conduct toward Jane Does D and E, which closely resembled that conduct upon which the trial was based.

This set of rules operates as a series of exceptions to the general rule prohibiting evidence of a trait of character to prove conduct by an accused in conformity with that trait. Congress enacted the new rules in response to the increasing public outcry against sexual offenders who continue to commit the same crimes.

These rules are particularly helpful to rebut a claim of consent. In fact, "[w]ithout question, Rules 412, 413, and 414, applied in a single case, make it easier for the government to prosecute sex offense cases."[14]

APPLICATION CASE

In *United States v. Withorn*[15] the trial court admitted R.M.'s testimony that Withorn sexually assaulted her. The incident R.M. described was substantially similar to the current victim's experience with Withorn. The victims were approximately the same age at the time of the rapes, and both assaults involved force and occurred after Withorn had isolated the victims from others. Both victims also testified that immediately after the incident Withorn threatened to harm them if they told anyone what had occurred, and in each case Withorn's defense was that the victim had consented to the sexual activity. Because of these parallels, the appellate court held that R.M.'s testimony was probative evidence showing Withorn's propensity toward the type of behavior alleged to have been committed against the victim.

CHARACTER OF VICTIMS

Homicide Victim

When one person kills another, the character of the deceased victim is generally unimportant. The crime of homicide still stands, whether the deceased victim was of good or bad character. In these circumstances, the law does not require that the prosecution present any evidence concerning the character of the deceased. However, when the character of a victim does become an issue at trial, the traditional rule, as stated in FRE 404(a)(2)(B) and (C), allows for the introduction of a pertinent trait of character of the alleged victim of the crime offered by an accused, or by the prosecution to rebut the same, or evidence of a character trait of peacefulness of the alleged victim offered by the prosecution in a homicide case to rebut evidence that the alleged victim was the first aggressor.

The character of the victim usually becomes an issue in homicide and assault cases. For example, in a homicide case, the defendant may admit to killing the victim but claim that the homicide was the result of self-defense. The defendant might try to prove that the victim was violent and aggressive, both in fact and in reputation. The defense could call character witnesses to prove the aggressive nature of the victim through both opinion and reputation testimony.

When the defendant introduces this kind of evidence, the prosecution may also present witnesses to prove the opposite, that the victim was reputed to be meek and mild. Rule 404(a)(2)(B)(ii) provides that, when an accused attacks the character of an alleged *victim* under 404(a)(2)(B), the door is opened to attack the same character trait of the *accused.* For example, if the defense offers evidence of the alleged victim's violent disposition, the prosecution can admit evidence of the defendant's violent disposition.

Self-defense may be based on one of two theories: fear and first aggressor. If the defendant claims that she killed in self-defense based on fear, then she must also show that she personally *knew* of that aggressive character. In making that showing, the defendant is allowed to introduce all evidence showing the basis of her fear of the victim, including specific instances of aggressive conduct by the victim. Such specific instances evidence is not admissible to prove that the victim acted in conformity with an aggressive character trait, but rather to prove that the defendant justifiably *feared* the victim. To support the defendant's claim of fear, the defendant must actually have known of the matters claimed to justify the fear.

On the other hand, if the defendant claims that the victim was the first aggressor, then she may offer evidence of the victim's character for aggressiveness to prove aggressive *action*. The defendant need not have had knowledge of the victim's aggressiveness beforehand. The proof of the character trait, however, is limited to reputation and opinion evidence; the defendant cannot introduce evidence of specific instances of conduct.

When the defendant tries to prove that he or she acted in self-defense and introduces evidence that the deceased was known as a person of violent character in general, the defendant must also show that the defendant had knowledge of the victim's violent character. Knowledge of the violent character of the victim is necessary if the defendant is going to allege that he or she thought his or her life was endangered. The evidence that the defendant can use includes reputation, opinion, and specific instances of aggressive conduct by the victim. Any evidence about the victim's aggressive character known to the defendant is relevant to support the defendant's claim that he or she feared the victim. This evidence, strictly speaking, is not offered to prove the victim's character in the sense that the victim acted in conformity with the character trait of aggressiveness on the occasion in question. Rather, the evidence is only offered to show the defendant *believed* the victim was likely to be an aggressor.

If, however, the defendant's self-defense claim is that the victim was the first aggressor, then under FRE 404(a)(2)(B) the defendant may introduce evidence of the bad character of the deceased even though he or she had no knowledge of it in an effort to prove that the deceased was the aggressor and, therefore, the defendant acted in self-defense. Since the victim's character trait is not itself an element of the defense, however, the defendant is limited to proof in the form of reputation or opinion evidence. FRE 405 defines the forms of evidence that may be used to prove character, when character is provable, and limits the use of specific instances of conduct evidence to those cases in which "character or a trait of character is an essential element of a charge, claim, or defense. . . ." Although being the first aggressor is an element of the defense of self-defense based on this theory, the *character trait* of aggressiveness is not itself an element of the defense. An example of elemental use of character evidence is a case involving the defense of entrapment, in which the defendant claims he or she was not "predisposed" to commit the crime. In such a case, the defendant's character, in the sense of being criminally predisposed, could be proved by specific instances of criminal conduct.

SELF-DEFENSE
The justifiable use of force to protect oneself from a real or threatened attack. Generally, a person is justified in using a reasonable amount of force in self-defense if he or she believes that the danger of bodily harm is imminent and that force is necessary to avoid this danger.

Victim in Sex Offense Cases

Discussion of the issues involved in sex offense prosecutions poses difficult problems for many people, as do the prosecutions themselves. When engaging in a study or discussion of these problems, it is necessary to maintain a serious attitude and to be sensitive to the feelings of those who may have suffered similar attacks.

Historically, courts have allowed the defendant in rape and sexual assault cases to introduce evidence of the victim's prior sexual history in an attempt to raise a doubt about her consent or to discredit her story. FRE 404(a)(2) permitted the defense to put the victim on trial. The trial courts permitted defense counsel to cross-examine the victim about her sex life, call witnesses to testify about the victim's sexual activity, or introduce evidence that she had a reputation of being promiscuous or unchaste. This evidence was used to prove that the victim voluntarily submitted to the defendant's sexual advances or, because she was not chaste, should not be believed. The introduction of this type of evidence both embarrassed and demoralized rape victims, leading many victims to refrain from reporting forcible rapes. In recent years, these attacks by the defense upon the victims of sexual assault have been sharply curtailed by the courts.

In response to this growing trend, many states have enacted "rape shield laws," such as FRE 412, to prevent such injustices. **Rape shield laws** provide that, although evidence of the sexual conduct of the victim arguably has some minimal probative value, such evidence is nonetheless inadmissible because of its substantial prejudicial effect upon the victim and society's interest in law enforcement. Under Rule 412, evidence that the victim engaged in other sexual behavior or proof of the victim's sexual predisposition is inadmissible. This provision applies to both criminal and civil cases. However, three exceptions to this rule exist:

1. Evidence of other sexual acts by the victim is admissible to prove that a person other than the accused was the source of the semen, injury, or other physical evidence.

2. Evidence of other sexual acts between the victim and the accused may be used to prove either that the victim consented to the sexual conduct in question or that the accused honestly, but mistakenly, believed the victim did consent.

3. Evidence may be presented if its exclusion would violate the constitutional rights of the defendant. At stake in this exception is the defendant's Fifth and Sixth Amendment rights to a full defense and fair trial.

RAPE SHIELD LAWS
Laws that prohibit a person accused of a sexual offense from introducing evidence of the sexual background or behavior of the victim.

FYI

Many rape victims are reluctant to report their attacks. Most fear not being believed by the police, as well as the possibility of public exposure. Many are afraid that they will somehow be blamed for the attack. Several Hollywood movies, such as *The Accused* and *Thelma and Louise,* have addressed this issue exceptionally well by putting the viewer in the position of the victim.

In 2004, the sexual assault case against Kobe Bryant for the alleged rape of a 19-year-old woman in his hotel room was dismissed. Kobe admitted he had sex with the woman, but he claimed it had been consensual. Almost one year after the charges were filed, the case was dismissed because the woman refused to testify. Her decision not to testify came after the public release of a transcript of a closed hearing that ultimately led to the trial judge's ruling that certain evidence could be admitted at trial under Colorado's rape shield law.

The closed-door hearing involved testimony from a defense DNA expert that the accuser had another man's semen on her thigh and inside her vagina, indicating that she had had sex with someone other than Bryant between the time of the alleged sexual assault and her medical examination. It was noted that a physical exam of Bryant after the incident produced no indication of a second man's DNA, leading the expert to say that she believed that the accuser had had sex with the other man, referred to in court records as "Mr. X," in the hours after she was with Bryant. This theory called into question whether the woman had lied during her testimony in an earlier hearing. She said that she had had sex only once in the days surrounding the Bryant incident and that the other man had worn a condom.

Prosecutors had expected the existence of "Mr. X" to be kept secret—and kept out of open court—under Colorado's rape shield laws. But a court reporter inadvertently e-mailed transcripts of the DNA expert's testimony to reporters in late June, and the news coverage of the hearing was widespread. The crowning blow, experts said, came July 23, when the court decided to admit the "Mr. X" evidence, as well as the accuser's sexual history with two key witnesses. This evidence was not barred by the rape shield law, according to the judge, because under Colorado's counterpart to FRE 412(1)—Colo. Rev. Stat. § 18-3-407—it was admissible to prove that a person other than the accused was the source of the semen, injury, or other physical evidence.

Two examples may help clarify the third exception in the previous list. First is the case of *State v. Cassidy*.[16] This was essentially an acquaintance rape case in which the accused and the victim had a previous occasional sexual relationship and met in a bar one evening. The victim accompanied the accused home, agreed to have sex, and, according to her, was brutally sexually assaulted when she changed her mind. The defendant's story was that the two were having consensual sexual intercourse when suddenly the victim became hysterical, screaming about her husband who was killed in Vietnam. She said she "shouldn't be doing this" and that she wanted to die and wanted to be with her husband. According to the defendant, he managed to get the victim to leave. The trial court permitted evidence of the prior sexual conduct between the defendant and the complainant but refused to admit evidence of a sexual encounter between the victim and another man, who testified in the absence of the jury as part of the defendant's offer of proof. This testimony was to the effect that she and he had gone to her home together about a year before the night in question. They had had sexual relations, during which she began "going crazy" and screaming about her husband who was killed in Vietnam, after which the victim quieted down and went to sleep. This evidence was held inadmissible under Connecticut's rape shield law largely because the victim had not made a rape claim against the other man.

In contrast is the case of *Olden v. Kentucky*.[17] In that rape case, the African American defendant wanted to introduce evidence that the victim, who was Caucasian, was living with another African American man when she went for a ride with the defendant and had consensual sex. The defendant believed that the victim fabricated the sexual assault charge to save her relationship with the other man. The Supreme Court of Kentucky held that the trial court should not have excluded the evidence under Kentucky's rape shield law but that the evidence was still properly held inadmissible at trial because of "prejudice" related to the mixed races of the participants. In addition, the trial court held that the Kentucky rape shield law required exclusion of the evidence. The Supreme Court of the United States overturned the conviction, stating that denial of the defendant's right to introduce the evidence of the victim's relationship with the other man deprived the defendant of his Sixth Amendment rights to confrontation.

These cases illustrate just some of the varying circumstances that might arise under the third exception to the rape shield law. The circumstances under which the defense may claim the need to introduce evidence of a sex crime victim's conduct in the name of the constitutional rights of the defendant are as varied as the ingenuity of counsel. The courts are likely to keep in mind, however, that the rape shield laws were designed to balance the fair trial rights of the defense against the interests of society in the effective prosecution of sexual offenses, along with the important rights of the victims of such crimes.

State of Mind of Homicide Victim When Defendant Claims Self-Defense or Accident

When the defendant has been charged with homicide and the defense contends that the killing was an accident or was in self-defense, the prosecution may present evidence that reflects the state of mind of the deceased. Statements made by the victim indicating fear of the defendant may be introduced. For example, if a husband is charged with the homicide of his wife, statements of the wife to others that she was afraid of her husband or statements concerning threats made by him to kill her are held to be admissible. Very often, neighbors and close family friends are good sources of such information. These statements, although retold by a third party, would not be considered inadmissible hearsay because they are offered to prove the state of mind or emotional feelings of the victim prior to death. The victim's state of mind is relevant because it is offered to overcome the allegation that the killing was by accident or in self-defense. Thus, if the victim was in fear of harm by the accused, then this evidence is relevant to prove that the accused was the one responsible for the murder. Likewise, as previously mentioned, a defendant may also present statements showing that the victim made death threats against the defendant. The defendant may offer these statements to substantiate his or her contention of acting in self-defense.

MYTH ▶	◀ FACT
Statements by a homicide victim that he or she feared the accused are readily admissible to prove the guilt of the accused.	Statements by a homicide victim indicating fear of the accused are not generally admissible to prove the guilt of the defendant. It is only when the defendant claims self-defense or accident that the victim's fear of the accused becomes relevant.

CHARACTER OF WITNESS

The final area in which character evidence may be introduced is in attacking or supporting the credibility of a witness. Universally, evidence relating to a witness's untruthfulness may be used to attack that witness, either by cross-examination as to bad acts bearing upon untruthfulness or by introduction of evidence of conviction of a serious crime or a crime involving dishonesty. Such evidence is relevant because a jury will take a witness's testimony seriously only if the jury believes that the witness is telling the truth on the stand. It should be noted that evidence of truthful character is admissible only as rebuttal evidence once the character of the witness has been attacked. The side opposing the witness must attack the truthfulness of a witness, either through opinion or reputation evidence, before rebuttal evidence of the witness's truthfulness can be introduced. Not every witness's character will be attacked. Usually, only the character of witnesses who testify to pertinent information regarding the guilt or innocence of the accused will be called into question, such as co-conspirators, informants, and alibi witnesses.

Along with opinion and reputation evidence, specific instances of conduct relating directly to the witness's truthfulness or felony convictions may be asked about on cross-examination. Specific instances of conduct that relate to the witness's honesty, such as previous instances of perjury or false statements, are always proper subjects for inquiry. Also, any previous serious criminal convictions, defined as crimes that are punishable by death or imprisonment in excess of one year, may also be introduced, but their admissibility is subject to the trial court's balancing probative value against potential for unfair prejudice. As mentioned previously, under FRE 403, for example, the trial judge must determine that the probative value of the conviction is substantially outweighed by its potential for unfair prejudice to rule the evidence inadmissible.

If the witness has not suffered a conviction for a serious crime or one involving dishonesty, then the cross-examining lawyer must accept any response that the witness gives to an inquiry of whether he or she committed prior bad acts bearing upon untruthfulness. If the witness denies that such conduct ever occurred, the questioner may not go on to prove that the conduct in question did, in fact, occur. Any party may attack the credibility of a witness, including the party who has called the witness. Usually, the defense will attack an informant for the prosecution for untruthfulness or try to get the informant to contradict previous out-of-court statements during his or her in-court testimony.

The Accused as Witness

Although constitutionally the accused does not have to take the stand in his or her own defense, often he or she chooses to do so. In that event, the accused is considered a witness and his or her character for truthfulness also becomes an issue. The prosecution may then open inquiry into the defendant's character for untruthfulness and may call character witnesses to attest to the defendant's lack of truthfulness. The prosecution may also introduce specific instances of conduct in an attempt to discredit the defendant's honesty, but this type of evidence is usually severely limited. Under FRE 609, for example, an accused's previous conviction, which carries a punishment of death or imprisonment in excess of one year, may be admitted but is subject to a special balancing test weighted in favor of exclusion of the evidence. This special balancing test requires that the trial judge must find that evidentiary value of the previous conviction is greater than the prejudicial effect to the accused before it can be admitted. In other words, if the evidence is even slightly more prejudicial than probative, then the judge must find it inadmissible. Thus, in a homicide trial, a previous conviction for murder may not be admissible, as it would be highly prejudicial to the current charge. Nevertheless, a previous conviction for embezzlement would not have the same prejudicial effect and therefore would likely be admitted. Previous convictions that involve dishonesty or false statements do not have to be balanced and are automatically admissible under FRE 609(a)(2). The rule also provides a time limit on the convictions that may be introduced. Any conviction that is more than ten years old is generally not admissible.

REVIEW AND APPLICATION

SUMMARY

(1) Direct evidence is the testimony of a person who asserts or claims to have actual knowledge of a fact, such as an eyewitness. Circumstantial evidence is evidence that tends to establish the facts in dispute by proving another set of facts from which an inference or a presumption can be drawn.

(2) The judge decides the relevance of circumstantial evidence either when someone objects to its admission at trial or upon a motion *in limine* made at any time. To meet the requirement of relevance, the evidence must have "any tendency to make the existence of any fact that is of consequence to the determination of the action more probable or less probable than it would be without the evidence."

(3) The law generally prohibits evidence of the defendant's character because it is often irrelevant and, even when relevant, is likely to be more prejudicial than probative.

(4) The principal noncharacter uses of other crimes, acts, or wrongs are to prove motive, opportunity, intent, preparation, plan, knowledge, identity, and absence of mistake or accident.

(5) A motive is that which moves a person to act or explains the reason a person acted. Intent, on the other hand, is a state of mind; it expresses mental action that is usually coupled with an outward physical act to cause a particular result.

(6) Similar uncharged acts of the accused may be introduced to show that the defendant performed the charged acts as part of a common design or plan, where the common features indicate the existence of a plan rather than a series of similar, spontaneous acts. When such evidence is used, it is for the purpose of showing that the accused did the charged act.

(7) The prosecution may use other misconduct evidence to disprove the possibility that no criminal conduct has taken place or that the crime occurred as the result of a mistake or an accident. It may also use such evidence when the defendant, charged with some particular criminal activity, denies it occurred and claims innocence. For example, assume a man is accused of sexual molestation of one child and he admits that he was in the child's company but denies any sexual contact. The prosecution could introduce evidence that the accused molested another child on a different occasion to refute the defendant's claim of innocent association.

(8) *Modus operandi* is a distinctive pattern of committing crimes that, in the context of the other acts evidence rule, can be used to prove identity.

(9) Some examples of circumstantial evidence of consciousness of guilt are fleeing from the scene of a crime, being in a highly emotional state after a murder, using a fictitious name with the police, refusing a sobriety test, and refusing to appear in a lineup.

(10) The prosecution may introduce evidence of the defendant's bad character under two circumstances: (1) When the defendant has "put character in issue" by introducing evidence of good character, the prosecution can rebut that evidence with evidence of bad character; and (2) when the defendant is charged with sexual assault or child molestation, then the prosecution can introduce evidence of past sex offenses or child molestation offenses, under FRE 413 or 414, to prove the defendant has a propensity to commit such acts.

(11) A victim's character usually becomes an issue in murder and assault cases when the defendant claims self-defense based on either a fear of attack by the victim or a claim that the victim was the first aggressor.

(12) Rape shield laws generally prohibit the accused in sexual assault or rape cases from introducing evidence of the victim's character for sexual behavior. These laws were enacted to promote the reporting and prosecution of such cases by protecting the victims of these crimes from being put on trial themselves.

(13) A party may attack an opposing witness's character by (1) introducing evidence of a conviction of a crime punishable by death or imprisonment in excess of one year; (2) introducing evidence of previous instances of perjury or false statements; and (3) inquiring, on cross-examination, whether the witness engaged in conduct bearing upon untruthfulness, but the questioner must accept the witness's answer and cannot introduce rebuttal evidence.

(14) The special balancing test requires that the trial judge determine that the probative value of the evidence of a previous conviction outweighs the prejudicial effect to the accused before it can be admitted. In other words, if the evidence is even slightly more prejudicial than probative, then the judge must keep it out.

KEY TERMS

direct evidence 369
circumstantial
    evidence 369
relevance 371
motion *in limine* 372
balancing test 372
character evidence
    rule 374

evidence of other
    crimes, acts, or
    wrongs 374
motive 375
intent 375
doctrine of
    chances 378
modus operandi 379

consciousness of
    guilt 380
defendant's good
    character rule 381
impeachment 382
self-defense 386
rape shield
    laws 387

QUESTIONS FOR REVIEW

1. What is the difference between direct and circumstantial evidence?
2. When and how does the trial judge determine the relevance of circumstantial evidence?
3. Why does the law generally prohibit evidence of the defendant's character?
4. What are the principal noncharacter uses of "other crimes" evidence?
5. What is the difference between motive and intent?
6. How might the prosecution use "other crimes" evidence to prove a defendant had a design or plan?
7. How might the prosecution use another act of the defendant to refute a claim of mistake or accident?
8. What does the term *modus operandi* mean in the context of the "other acts" evidence rule?
9. Under what circumstances may the prosecution prove the defendant's bad character if the defendant has not taken the stand?
10. What are the laws shielding victims of sex offenses?
11. What are the ways opposing counsel might attack a witness's character?
12. Describe the special balancing test used in evaluating the admissibility of prior uncharged felony convictions of a defendant who takes the stand.

THINKING CRITICALLY ABOUT EVIDENCE

1. A defendant is charged with the crime of pickpocketing. The victim testifies that the defendant approached him on the street and said that his wife had just given birth to a baby boy. The defendant then put his arm around the victim and offered him a cigar. After the defendant left, the victim noticed that his wallet was missing from his back pocket. The prosecution wishes to call several other witnesses to testify that the defendant had approached them also with the same story and that their wallets had also been stolen. Should the judge allow the prosecution to call these witnesses? Explain why or why not.

2. In the trial of O.J. Simpson, Judge Lance Ito allowed the prosecution to introduce evidence of Mr. Simpson's misconduct involving some acts of domestic violence. For example, some five years before she died, Mr. Simpson attacked and hit his then-wife Nicole Brown Simpson. Under what doctrine was this act of uncharged misconduct permitted to be introduced into evidence? Was Judge Ito's ruling correct?

WORKPLACE APPLICATION

1. An officer is investigating a sexual assault (rape) case. The officer learns that the victim of the assault is a prostitute. How does this fact influence the officer's investigation and presentation of the case to the prosecutor? How do you think defense counsel will attempt to discredit the victim during trial?

ETHICAL DILEMMA

1. The investigating officer is testifying at a burglary trial. The prosecutor asks what first drew the officer's attention to the accused as a suspect in the case. The officer's suspicion was based on information from informants who identified the accused in connection with another burglary in the same neighborhood two weeks before. The officer arrested the suspect based upon this information and before the accused's fingerprints were found at the scene of the crime. How should the officer answer the prosecutor's question?

ENDNOTES

1. 1A Fed. Jury Prac. & Instr. § 12.04 (6th ed. 2018).

2. Holland v. United States, 348 U.S. 121 (1954).

3. 1A Fed. Jury Prac. & Instr. § 12.04 (6th ed. 2018).

4. Johnson v. State, 872 P.2d 93, 96–97 (Wyo. 1994), quoting Thompson v. United States, 144 F. 14, 18 (1st Cir.1906),

5. 485 U.S. 681 (1988).

6. 7 Cal. 4th 380 (1994).

7. 14 Cal. 2d 403 (1939).

8. Edward J. Imwinkelried, *The Dispute over the Doctrine of Chances,* 7 Crim. Just. 16, 18 (1992 Fall).

9. 11 Crim. App. 229 (1915).

10. 502 U.S. 62 (1991).

11. Commonwealth v. Knapp, Sup. Jud. Ct. of Mass., 1830, VII Am. St. Tr. 395, 516, as cited and quoted in Roger C. Park & Richard D. Friedman, Evidence, Cases and Materials 221–22 (12th ed. 2013).

12. Michaelson v. United States, 335 U.S. 469, n. 16 citing People v. Lauadero, 85 N.E. 132 (N.Y. 1908) (1948).

13. 179 F.3d 889 (10th Cir.), *cert. denied* 528 U.S. 944 (1999).

14. United States v. Withorn, 204 F.3d 790 (8th Cir. 2000).

15. *Id.*

16. 3 Conn. App. 374, 489 A.2d 386, *cert. denied* 196 Conn. 803, 492 A.2d 1239 (1985).

17. 488 U.S. 227 (1988).

Design Element: ©Ingram Publishing

12 | DOCUMENTARY EVIDENCE AND THE RIGHT OF DISCOVERY

CHAPTER OUTLINE

CHAPTER OBJECTIVES

This chapter explores the rules of evidence relating to documents as evidence and the right of discovery of evidence before the trial begins (pretrial). After reading this chapter you will be able to:

▶ Name the two classifications of documents and each of their categories.

▶ List the six situations in which secondary evidence of the contents of a writing may be introduced.

▶ Explain the three foundational elements that must be shown before secondary evidence is admitted.

▶ State when a defendant is not required to comply with a subpoena *duces tecum* and produce a document in his or her possession.

▶ Name the three types of discovery the defendant can obtain from the prosecution under FRCrP 16 and which type is granted reciprocal discovery.

▶ Describe what statements are covered by the Jencks Act.

▶ Identify the range of matters that may be subject to discovery by the defendant in a criminal case.

▶ List the defenses that the accused may be required to disclose to the prosecution prior to trial.

DOCUMENTS AS A KIND OF EVIDENCE

Documents—writings, recordings, and photographs—are another kind of evidence by which facts are presented during a judicial proceeding. The FRE, Rule 1001(a), defines a "writing" as "letters, words, numbers, or their equivalent, set down in any form." Rule 1001(b) defines "recording" as "letters, words, numbers, or their equivalent recorded in any manner." And Rule 1001(c) defines "photograph" as "a photographic image or its equivalent stored in any form." Documents may be classified as (1) public or (2) private. Public documents may be further categorized as (1) laws; (2) judicial records; (3) other official documents, such as records or driver's licenses, marriage applications, and birth certificates; and (4) public records of private writings, such as records of deeds and mortgages. Private documents are the private writings or recordings of individuals, such as letters, memoranda, answering machine messages, e-mail messages, text messages, suicide notes, and wills.

Although private documents generally play a more significant role in the trial of civil matters, there are times when they become an important part of a criminal case. For example, the submission into evidence of an extortion note may be necessary to prove a charge of extortion; a suicide note or a threatening letter may be a part of the proof in a homicide case; or the "date book" of a prostitute may be presented in a prostitution trial. These articles also fall into the category of real evidence, as well as the documents category.

The use of documentary evidence implicates two fundamental aspects of the rules of evidence: authentication and the best evidence rule. Authentication is a foundational requirement that authorship or genuineness be established. The best evidence rule requires that, when one seeks to prove the contents of a writing, recording, or photograph, the original must be presented, unless there is good reason the original cannot be provided.

AUTHENTICATION

AUTHENTICATION
A prerequisite to the introduction of evidence of a document that requires the party introducing the document to show that the document is what it is claimed to be.

Authentication is a prerequisite to the introduction in evidence of a document—or, for that matter, many types of evidence. The rule of authentication requires that the party introducing the document show that the document is what the party claims it to be. For instance, if the prosecution is trying to introduce an extortion note against the defendant in support of an extortion charge, the prosecution must first show that the note was made by or at the direction of the defendant. More specifically, the prosecution must introduce evidence sufficient to support a jury finding that the note is indeed attributable to the defendant. This can be done in several ways, for example, through the testimony of a witness with appropriate knowledge, the testimony in the form of nonexpert opinion on handwriting, a comparison of handwriting by the jury or an expert, or a showing of distinctive characteristics in the note.

The common law once required that a witness with knowledge of the document attest to the fact that the document was genuine, and that it was what its proponent claimed it to be. The modern rule, for example, FRE 901(b), expressly allows an unlimited number of ways to authenticate a piece of evidence. The Chief United States Magistrate Judge for the District Court of Maryland, in a 2007 decision in *Lorraine v. Markel American Insurance Company*,[1] noted that electronically stored information is admissible in evidence subject to the same authentication requirements as any other evidence. For that matter, such evidence is subject to all the rules of evidence. And, though the *Lorraine* case was a civil case, its holding is equally applicable in a criminal trial.

In addition to authentication, the party introducing the document must show the relevance of the document to the issues of the case. After this has been done, the document will be offered into evidence. Meeting the requirements of authentication and relevance is known as **laying the foundation** for the introduction of the writing, recording, or photograph into evidence. If the judge agrees that the evidence of the document's genuineness is enough to convince the jury and that the document is connected with the issues of the case and is what it is claimed to be, the judge will admit it into evidence, and the document will then speak for itself.

BEST EVIDENCE RULE

In proving the terms of a writing, the original writing must be produced, unless the document is shown to be unavailable for some reason other than the bad faith act of the party seeking to introduce the document. This provision is known as the **best evidence rule**. The rule says that, if information is to be offered during a trial concerning what is contained in a writing, the best evidence, or best proof, of the contents of the writing is the writing itself. The original writing must, therefore, be introduced and must be proven to be genuine. Today this rule is not as important as it once was, for FRE 1003 allows a duplicate to be admitted to the same extent as the original, unless there is a question as to its authenticity or if it would be unfair to do so. A **duplicate** has been described as a copy "produced by methods possessing an accuracy which virtually eliminates the possibility of error."[2] Photocopies, or copies made by any mechanical means, are acceptable. Copies produced manually, either handwritten or typed, are not considered duplicates. The genuineness of a document or writing is proven through the process of authentication described previously.

The best evidence rule was adopted many years ago and, although the reasons were good at the time, they are not as compelling today due to modern technology. The first reason was that the rule came into being at a time when the only way in which copies of a document could be made was to copy the wording and symbols by hand. It was common knowledge that copying by hand created a great likelihood of mistakes and inaccuracies. Moreover, hand copying opened the door to possible fraud and deceit. Another reason for preferring the original document was the danger of misinterpretation and the possibility of omitting important portions of the contents during the testimony because of faulty memory. With

LAYING THE FOUNDATION
Meeting the requirements of authentication and relevance in order to introduce a writing, recording, or photograph into evidence.

BEST EVIDENCE RULE
The rule that requires that, in proving the terms of a writing the original writing must be produced, unless the document is shown to be unavailable for some reason other than the bad faith act of the party seeking to introduce the document.

DUPLICATE
A copy produced by methods possessing an accuracy that virtually eliminates the possibility of error.

FYI

The way the best evidence rule operates can be somewhat confusing. The rule only applies when one seeks to prove the contents of a writing, recording, or photograph. Therefore, the way a lawyer asks a question about a writing or the way a witness answers may determine whether or not the rule applies. For example, assume that the questioning lawyer is trying to prove that the testifying officer wrote a report about the investigation. If the questioning lawyer asks the witness, "What did the report say?" that question seeks to prove the content of the writing (the report) by its form and would violate the best evidence rule and would be objected to, and the answer would be ruled inadmissible. However, if the lawyer asked instead, "What did you do after you investigated?" that question avoids the best evidence rule entirely. Similarly, if the witness responded, "I wrote a report in which I stated . . . ," that would violate the best evidence rule. But if the officer merely answered, "I wrote a report," that would avoid the best evidence rule entirely.

MYTH ▶	◀ FACT
The best evidence rule requires that the best evidence available to prove a point be offered during a trial or other proceeding.	The best evidence rule applies only to writings, recordings, and photographs. It is a rule that requires that the original of the writing, recording, or photograph be presented, unless there is some valid reason for tendering secondary evidence. Otherwise, there is no "better evidence" rule such as stated in this myth. There is no legal requirement that the best available evidence to prove a specific point be introduced. In some limited circumstances, if a party had the ability to produce evidence and failed to do so, the jury can be instructed by the judge that they may infer that the evidence would have been unfavorable to the party that withheld it.

the advent of copiers, faxes, smartphones, digital scanners, and other devices, strict adherence to the best evidence rule is no longer necessary.

The best evidence rule is very easy to satisfy. First, most modern "copies" of a writing constitute a "duplicate." Photocopies, faxes, and computer-generated "copies" of writings qualify as duplicates. A duplicate of a recording is any counterpart produced from the same matrix as the original by means of mechanical or electronic recording. Under the modern best evidence rule, a duplicate is admissible as though it were an original. The negative and any print constitute the original of a photograph. Therefore, most means of producing copies today will result in a "copy" that satisfies the best evidence rule. Finally, if the lawyer asks his or her questions in the proper form, the witness will not be called upon to testify in such a way as to violate the best evidence rule.

Primary Versus Secondary Evidence

PRIMARY EVIDENCE
An original document.

When an original document is produced in court, it is known as the **primary evidence** in relation to its own contents. When the original is introduced, that constitutes compliance with the best evidence rule. Where it is either impossible or impractical to produce the original document in court, a party may prove the contents of the document by way of an exception to the best evidence rule. The FRE allow a party to prove the contents of a document by other evidence, such as by any other form of the writing—even oral testimony. When other evidence is substituted for the original document, the substitute is known as **secondary evidence**.

SECONDARY EVIDENCE
Evidence substituted for the original document.

The most common form of secondary evidence is testimony from a witness. Anytime a witness testifies in such a way as to state in court the contents of a writing, recording, or photograph, that testimony constitutes secondary evidence. Whether or not that testimony will violate the best evidence rule depends upon whether or not one of the exceptions to the requirement of the original has been shown to exist.

The following are the most frequently encountered situations in which secondary evidence of the contents of a writing may be introduced. These exceptions occur when the original writing, recording, or photograph

1. has been lost or destroyed;
2. is unobtainable by any available judicial process or procedure;
3. is in the possession of an adverse party and, after a notice to produce it, the adverse party fails to do so;
4. is in the custody of a public officer;
5. relates to a collateral matter; or
6. is voluminous and cannot be examined without a great loss of time, making a summary of the writing's contents sufficient.

Whenever secondary evidence is offered in lieu of the original document, the necessary foundation must be laid before the secondary evidence is admitted. Three things must be shown:

1. that there has been a writing in existence;
2. that the secondary evidence is a genuine copy of the original or accurately relates the contents of the original; and
3. the reason, or justification, that the secondary evidence is being offered instead of the original.

Lost or Destroyed Writings, Recordings, or Photographs

When a party alleges that the original document cannot be produced because it was lost, there must be a showing that the party seeking to prove its contents diligently searched for the document. The extensiveness of the search necessary will vary depending upon the kind of document involved and its importance to the case. The party must show, at the least, that contact was made with the last person known to have had the document or with the persons most likely to know its whereabouts, and that the last place where the document was known to be was searched without result.

The document may be unobtainable because it is out of the state or otherwise beyond the reach of the court. The party seeking to prove the contents of such a document must first show that the document could not be obtained through the use of a subpoena or some other judicial process. Once the party establishes that such efforts have been made, he or she may then prove the contents of the document by secondary evidence.

A document that is unobtainable from a third person's possession is essentially lost. Thus, when the party seeking to prove the contents of the writing can prove that the original document is in the hands of a third party, who for some reason refuses to cooperate and release the document, even in the face of a subpoena, secondary evidence may then be admitted in the same manner as if the original were lost.

When a party claims that a writing has been destroyed, that party must also show that the destruction was unintentional. If the writing was destroyed intentionally, the party must show that the intentional destruction was not in bad faith or with fraudulent intent. Otherwise, the introduction of secondary evidence will be denied.

Document in Possession of Adverse Party

When an original document is in the hands of a defendant in a criminal trial, notice must be given to the defendant to produce the original before secondary evidence may be introduced in its place. There is no particular form necessary for this notice. It may be merely an oral request to produce the document, but a reasonable time must be allowed for the holder to comply. As a practical matter, though, formal notice, known as **notice to produce**, should be given. If the document is essential at trial, a **subpoena** *duces tecum* should be served on the defendant rather than a notice to produce. The Fifth Amendment privilege against self-incrimination allows the defendant to withhold a document lawfully, if such document would incriminate the defendant. The privilege against self-incrimination does not prevent secondary evidence from being admitted to prove the contents of the writing or document.

Collateral Matter

Secondary evidence of the contents of a document may be utilized when such a document is not closely related to a controlling issue at trial. Hence, if the contents of a document are only incidentally related to the issues at trial, the original need not be produced. In such cases, the document is said to relate to a **collateral matter**. For instance, the charge of grand theft requires that the property stolen be above a specific dollar amount. Assuming the grand theft charge involves a stolen diamond, a witness would likely be allowed to testify that the diamond was purchased from a licensed pawn broker without production of the broker's license, despite the fact that the license is "best evidence." If, on the other hand, a genuine dispute exists as to the contents of the document, the judge will not likely consider the document as relating to a collateral matter.

Document in Custody of Public Officer

In most instances, original public records can be produced in court. However, the possibility of loss or destruction is too great; therefore, it is impracticable to do so in most cases. Thus, the modern rule—for example, FRE 1005—expressly exempts public records from the requirements of the best evidence rule. In addition to the threat of loss or destruction, the production of public records causes inconvenience to the public as a whole, as well as to the people in charge of such documents. Consequently, secondary evidence in the form of a copy of an original is admissible to prove the contents of the record. Authentication of the copy does not require additional evidence, as long as the copy is accompanied by a statement from the person, official, or clerk having custody of the record certifying that the document is a true copy of the original. Often, a certified copy of a public record also has an official seal. This is known as a **certified copy** of the original document.

Sometimes in criminal cases, the prosecution must prove that the accused was convicted of a crime in another state or in another court proceeding. In such cases, the record of conviction must be certified by the clerk of the court, attesting that the document is a true copy of the original. The presiding judge of that jurisdiction must also certify that the clerk correctly certified the form.

NOTICE TO PRODUCE
A formal, written notice issued by one party to another requiring the production of a document.

SUBPOENA
DUCES TECUM
A subpoena, or order to appear in court, commanding a person to bring specified documents or objects with him or her.

COLLATERAL MATTER
A matter only incidentally related to the issues at trial. When the contents of a document relate to such a matter, the original document need not be produced in court.

CERTIFIED COPY
A copy of a document to which is attached a statement by the person, official, or clerk having custody of the record certifying that the document is a true copy of the original.

This kind of copy is sometimes referred to as an **exemplified copy** of the original.[3] Verification by both the clerk and the judge is necessary because the record is most important to the issues of the case, and therefore someone in addition to the officer having custody of the record should attest to the accuracy of the copy.

Original Documents Too Voluminous to Examine

Sometimes at trial, it is necessary to use information from the records of a business or other entity to shed light on the issues of the case. Although this situation occurs more frequently in civil trials, criminal trials may also involve such records. The FRE specifically provide that a summary, chart, or calculation of voluminous records may be presented in the place of the records themselves. The records, though, must be made available for examination and/or copying by the other party at a reasonable time and place. This exception to the best evidence rule, known as the **voluminous records rule**, is simply a way of expediting the judicial process.

What Is an Original Document?

In cases in which there is only one original document and that document is produced in court, the best evidence rule has been satisfied and no problem arises. It is therefore necessary to determine what constitutes an **original document**. The FRE define an original document as the document itself, "or any counterpart intended to have the same effect by the person who executed or issued it." Additionally, "[f]or electronically stored information, 'original' means any printout—or other output readable by sight—if it accurately reflects the information." With respect to photographs, the original is the negative or any print made from the negative. It should be emphasized again that, although an original document is the best evidence, a duplicate of the original is admissible to the same extent as the original.

Inscribed Chattel

An **inscribed chattel** is an object with words and/or images written, painted, or engraved on it. For instance, the name or insignia of a business is often painted on the side of a truck, or the name or identification number of a law enforcement officer is engraved on his or her badge. In these situations, if the best evidence rule were strictly followed, the property (e.g., the badge and the truck) would have to be produced in court as the "originals." Fortunately, the best evidence rule may not strictly apply to inscribed chattels. A judge has considerable discretion in allowing the introduction of secondary evidence to prove the terms of an inscription on a chattel. In determining whether or not to apply the best evidence rule to inscribed chattels, the judge will look at factors "such as the need for precise information as to the exact inscription, the ease or difficulty of production, and simplicity or complexity of the inscription."[4] If the judge determines that it is not necessary to produce the chattel, then ordinarily a witness who observed the inscription on the chattel will be allowed to testify as to the inscription, and the object need not be produced in court.

EXEMPLIFIED COPY
A copy of a record of conviction that has been certified by the clerk of the court, as well as by the presiding judge of the particular jurisdiction, stating that the clerk correctly certified the form.

VOLUMINOUS RECORDS RULE
An exception to the best evidence rule that permits a summary, chart, or calculation of voluminous records to be presented in the place of the records themselves.

ORIGINAL DOCUMENT
The document itself, "or any counterpart intended to have the same effect by the person who executed or issued it." Additionally, "[f]or electronically stored information, 'original' means any printout—or other output readable by sight—if it accurately reflects the information." With respect to photographs, the original is the negative or any print made from the negative.

INSCRIBED CHATTEL
An object with words and/or images written, painted, or engraved on it, such as a police officer's badge. Generally, such objects are not subject to the best evidence rule.

In *United States v. Duffy,*[5] the defendant was convicted of interstate transportation of a motor vehicle. He was accused of stealing a car from a dealership at which he was employed in Florida and driving it to California, where it was found. Duffy claimed that he did not take the car but had hitchhiked from Florida to California, where he was found. Among the evidence against Duffy at trial was a shirt found in a suitcase in the trunk of the car. The shirt had a laundry mark reading "D-U-F," according to the testimony of the police officer who found it. The defense objected to this testimony, insisting that the shirt itself had to be brought to court to prove the contents of the inscription. Both the trial court and the United States Court of Appeals for the Fifth Circuit disagreed, concluding that the object was a chattel not subject to the best evidence rule.

THE RIGHT OF DISCOVERY IN CRIMINAL CASES

DISCOVERY
The right afforded to the adversary in a trial to examine, inspect, and copy the evidence in the hands of the other side.

EXCULPATORY EVIDENCE
Evidence favorable to the defense.

The right of **discovery** is a right afforded to the adversary in a trial to examine, inspect, and copy the evidence in the hands of the other side. Until the mid-twentieth century, there were no formal provisions for discovery in criminal cases. Both the prosecutor and the defense counsel were limited to discovery of the other's case by what they could learn from their own factual investigations, pretrial proceedings, and informal exchange of information, if any. A constitutional obligation required the prosecutor to reveal evidence favorable to the defense (**exculpatory evidence**), but this was a narrow exception to the prevailing status of no discovery in criminal cases generally. A major impediment to discovery in criminal cases has been the view that fairness requires discovery to be reciprocal. Because of the defendant's Fifth Amendment self-incrimination and attorney-client privileges in criminal cases, such reciprocity is impossible. To a large extent, these impediments to discovery still exist in principle. However, a number of events—the 1946 enactment of Rule 16 of the Federal Rules of Criminal Procedure (FRCrP); the establishment of defense discovery rights by California case law in the 1950s;[6] the proposals for discovery suggested in an American Bar Association study first published in 1968 and approved in 1970;[7] the adoption of the ABA's proposals in a number of states, including Florida, Illinois, and New Jersey, between 1968 and 1970;[8] and the adoption of similar provisions in other states—have led to a substantial increase in discovery in criminal cases by both the prosecution and the defense. In fact, it is fair to say that, although there is only limited discovery in criminal cases in federal courts, the majority of states allow broad discovery in criminal cases.

FRCrP 16 provides for discovery in criminal cases to achieve a number of goals, including providing the defendant with sufficient information to plead and prepare for trial, avoiding surprises to both sides, promoting judicial economy, and speeding up the trial process. The rule permits, upon request, the defendant to discover from the prosecution

1. any written statements or transcriptions or recordings of oral statements made by the defendant possessed by the prosecution;
2. the defendant's prior criminal record; and
3. documents, photographs, tangible objects, results of physical and mental examinations, and test reports possessed by the prosecution that the prosecution intends to use as evidence or that the court deems material to the defendant's trial preparation. If any of the materials specified in this item are granted to the defendant, the prosecution is granted reciprocal discovery.

Because of the "one-way street" limitation, discovery historically has been relatively rare in criminal cases, with three major exceptions:

1. the right of the defendant to discover the identity of a confidential informant when vital to the defense, and at the time of trial in any event, in many cases;
2. the obligation of the prosecution to disclose evidence favorable to the defense—*Brady* **material**, named after the Supreme Court decision in *Brady v. Maryland;*[9] and
3. the defendant's right to discover written or recorded statements of witnesses, required to be turned over in accordance with the Jencks Act[10] in federal court and under similar state statutes.

In the absence of a statute or court rule, the trial court has complete discretion in granting or denying a defendant's discovery requests. The defendant will often have the burden of showing that the discovery request is necessary and material to the defense, is in the interest of a fair trial, and is not merely a "fishing expedition."

In *Brady v. Maryland,*[11] the United States Supreme Court announced for the first time a general prosecutorial duty to disclose exculpatory evidence to the defendant before trial, i.e., any evidence that would tend to exonerate the defendant. Brady and a man named Boblit were tried separately for murder, convicted, and sentenced to death. Brady admitted his participation in the crime but claimed that Boblit had done the actual killing. Prior to the trial, Brady's counsel asked the prosecution to allow him to examine Boblit's out-of-court statements. Several of those statements were shown to him, but one in which Boblit admitted the actual killing was withheld and did not come to Brady's notice until after Brady had been tried, convicted, and sentenced and after his conviction had been affirmed on appeal.

The Supreme Court held that the prosecution's suppression of evidence favorable to an accused upon request violates due process where the evidence is material either to guilt or to punishment, irrespective of good faith or bad faith on the part of the prosecution. In so concluding, the Court stated:[12]

> Society wins not only when the guilty are convicted but when criminal trials are fair; our system of the administration of justice suffers when any accused is treated unfairly. An inscription on the walls of the Department of Justice states the proposition candidly for the federal domain: "The United States wins its point whenever justice is done its citizens in the courts."

BRADY MATERIAL
Information favorable to the defense, in the possession of the prosecution, material to the defendant's case that must be disclosed to the defense. The term is derived from the case of *Brady v. Maryland*.

If a police officer has or knows of facts and evidence that would tend to exonerate the defendant, the officer should inform the prosecutor. Otherwise, subsequent revelation of this information may result in a mistrial, a new trial on appeal, or reversal of the conviction in a subsequent *habeas corpus* proceeding.

In cases subsequent to *Brady,* the Court has stated that "a failure by the government to disclose material exculpatory information in its possession [is] a constitutional violation only when a reasonable probability exists that, absent the failure to disclose, the result of the trial (conviction) would have been different."[13]

APPLICATION CASE

The case of *Banks v. Dretke*[14] is illustrative of the consequences of the prosecution's failure to comply with *Brady* requirements. Banks was convicted of capital murder and sentenced to death in a Texas court. The prosecution's case included testimony, in both the guilt and penalty phases, of two witnesses, Cook and Farr. Prior to trial, the prosecution offered the defense counsel full discovery without the necessity of a motion; however, the prosecution did not disclose that Cook had been extensively coached in his testimony and Farr had been a paid informant who had instigated Banks' procuring a gun after the killing, a fact that Farr testified to at the penalty phase to prove that Banks had a continuing violent disposition. That fact could have played a substantial role in the ultimate death penalty determination. In addition, the prosecution did not reveal the fact that both of these witnesses gave false testimony. All of this information ultimately came to light in the federal *habeas corpus* proceedings instituted by Banks to overturn his conviction and the sentence of death.

The case ultimately went to the United States Supreme Court. The Court found that the failure of the prosecutor to disclose that Farr was a paid informant and that Cook was coached by Deputy Huff had violated the *Brady* standards. According to the Court's *Brady* rules, in order for a defendant to succeed on a *Brady* claim,

1. the evidence at issue must be favorable to the accused because it is exculpatory or impeaching;
2. the defendant must show that the state suppressed the evidence at issue; and
3. the defendant must show that prejudice ensued.

With respect to the first requirement, the Court found that Farr's paid informant status plainly qualified as evidence advantageous to Banks, as did Cook's extensive coaching. As for the second requirement, the Court found that the conduct of the prosecution in withholding the information and allowing false testimony amounted to deliberate suppression of such information. Finally, the Court observed that prejudice, for *Brady* purposes, means "material" in the sense that "the favorable evidence could reasonably be taken to put the whole case in such a different light as to undermine confidence in the verdict."

The Court found this third requirement satisfied on the view that, if the jury had known that Farr was a paid informant and Cook was coached, they may not have given any weight to their testimony, especially Farr's uncorroborated testimony that Banks was violent and would commit other violent acts. As a result, the Court affirmed the appellate court's decision to set aside the death penalty.

DISCOVERY THROUGH PRELIMINARY HEARING

Generally, the defendant must make a discovery request prior to trial. However, in many jurisdictions, even before the accused might have the opportunity to consider such a request, the prosecution may be required to present evidence at a preliminary hearing. A **preliminary hearing** is a stage in the criminal prosecution that is held for the purpose of determining whether probable cause exists to believe the accused has committed a particular offense. It is impossible to hold a preliminary hearing without the prosecution revealing a portion of its case. At the preliminary hearing, the prosecution must present evidence sufficient to convince the magistrate that there is probable cause to believe the accused committed a particular crime in order for the accused to be bound over for trial. Probable cause is a low standard and, in most instances, the prosecution will satisfy this standard. (Probable cause was discussed in Chapter 8.)

PRELIMINARY HEARING
The stage in the criminal prosecution that is held for the purpose of determining whether probable cause exists to believe the accused has committed a particular offense.

Thus, even before the modern advent of discovery in criminal cases, the defendant had discovery to some extent through the preliminary hearing. Then (and now, to some extent), the prosecuting attorney was faced with a dilemma with respect to the defendant's discovery through the preliminary hearing. The prosecutor must present a reasonable amount of evidence in support of probable cause. On the other hand, the prosecutor does not want to reveal every aspect of the case to the defense because the defense could then plan a response and perhaps even fabricate one. To the extent that the defendant is entitled to learn of the evidence by the right of discovery, the prosecution is at an even greater disadvantage, as it cannot withhold part of its case at the preliminary hearing.

There are some advantages to the prosecution in presenting as much evidence as possible at the preliminary hearing. Witnesses may be more willing to cooperate and testify more truthfully immediately after the crime has been committed than months later, when the trial may take place. The events are fresher in the witnesses' minds at the time of the preliminary hearing than at the trial, which might be months later. Once the witnesses have testified under oath at the preliminary hearing, their testimony is set and may even be used in the event of recalcitrance, absence, sickness, or death. On the other hand, the prosecutor may wish to present a very strong case at the preliminary hearing to encourage the defense to enter into plea negotiations. If the defendant and defense counsel see that the prosecution's case is too strong to justify risking a trial, the incentive to plead guilty will be substantial. Nonetheless, in many cases in which the likelihood of trial is high, most prosecutors will present as little of the case as necessary to establish probable cause. The principal reason for this is the desire to prevent the defense from discovering too much of the case through the preliminary hearing.

Although a preliminary hearing affords the accused an opportunity to discover evidence in the hands of the prosecution, a preliminary hearing is not guaranteed in jurisdictions that prosecute by way of indictment rather than information. Some jurisdictions and the federal court system may not hold a defendant over for trial unless a grand jury has indicted the defendant. Accordingly, if the defendant is indicted by a grand jury before there is a preliminary hearing, the preliminary hearing is superceded by the grand jury's determination or is not held at all. The defendant is at a great disadvantage with respect to the discovery afforded by a preliminary hearing in an indictment jurisdiction, since he or she is not allowed to be present during the grand jury proceedings and only the prosecutor is allowed to present evidence to the grand jurors.

GROWTH OF THE RIGHT OF DISCOVERY

Although historically the accused had a limited right of discovery through the preliminary hearing, the argument persisted that this was not sufficient to enable the defense to prepare a case properly. Eventually, this argument prevailed and the right of discovery was developed and adopted, in varying degrees, in all jurisdictions. As stated earlier in this chapter, one of the first statutes granting the right of discovery to an accused was that adopted by the federal government in 1946, Rule 16 of the FRCrP, which currently provides in pertinent part:[15]

> Upon a defendant's request, the government must disclose to the defendant, and make available for inspection, copying, or photographing, all of the following:
>   (i) any relevant written or recorded statement by the defendant if:
>   ▶ the statement is within the government's possession, custody, or control; and
>   ▶ the attorney for the government knows—or through due diligence could know—that the statement exists;
>   (ii) the portion of any written record containing the substance of any relevant oral statement made before or after arrest if the defendant made the statement in response to interrogation by a person the defendant knew was a government agent; and
>   (iii) the defendant's recorded testimony before a grand jury relating to the charged offense.

Rule 16 was followed 11 years later by the United States Supreme Court decision in the *Jencks* case.[16] The *Jencks* case was followed within a few months by the Jencks Act, adopted by Congress to lessen the effect of the *Jencks* decision. The **Jencks Act** deals only with the right of the defendant to discover statements made by a government witness. The act covers only statements written by the witness or transcribed at the same time the statement was made and either signed or adopted by the witness. Moreover, if there is such a statement, by the terms of the Jencks Act, the defendant is not entitled to discovery of it "until said witness has testified on direct examination in the trial of the case."[17] Thus, the effect of the act is to deprive the defendant of pretrial discovery of recorded or adopted witnesses' statements, since they are discoverable only after the witness has testified on direct examination at trial. Following the *Jencks*

JENCKS ACT
A federal statute that deals only with the right of the defendant to discover statements made by a government witness. The statute is named after the case of *Jencks v. United States*.

case, a number of states adopted some right of discovery by the defendant, through either court decisions or statutes.

Jencks, a labor union official, was convicted of violating a federal law by filing an alleged false affidavit in which he denied that he had ever been a member of the Communist Party. During his trial, two witnesses working in connection with the FBI testified that they had observed Jencks engaging in Communist Party activities. Upon cross-examination, these witnesses admitted that they had made reports to the FBI about the actions of Jencks. The defense attorney made a motion to the court requesting that these reports be produced, so that he could inspect them. The motion was denied by the trial judge on the grounds that there was no showing that there was any inconsistency between the reports made to the FBI and the testimony of the witnesses.

After Jencks was convicted, the case was appealed to the United States Supreme Court on the grounds that Jencks was denied due process because of the government's failure to produce the requested reports. The Supreme Court reversed the conviction and stated that the refusal of the trial court to order the production of the reports was in error. The Court held that a defendant in a criminal trial is entitled to inspect all reports in the hands of the government that touch on witnesses' testimony.

The broad wording of the majority opinion in the *Jencks* case seemed to grant an unlimited right to the defendant in a criminal case to examine government reports. Criticism of the decision resulted, based on national security concerns. In fact, in his dissenting opinion in the *Jencks* case, Justice Clark stated: "Unless the Congress changes the rule announced by the Court today, those intelligence agencies of our Government engaged in law enforcement may as well close up shop, for the Court has opened their files to the criminal and thus afforded him a Roman holiday for rummaging through confidential information as well as vital national secrets."[18] A few months later, Congress passed the Jencks Act, 18 U.S.C. § 3500, which tempered the effects of the *Jencks* decision.

PRETRIAL DISCOVERY

As discovery first developed in criminal cases, it was confined to discovery at the time of trial. Now, however, those jurisdictions that have considered the issue have extended the right to allow discovery pretrial. Jurisdictions differ as to when the right may be exercised. Some jurisdictions permit discovery within a certain number of days after arraignment or filing of charges.[19] Other jurisdictions allow the defendant to make a discovery request before arraignment[20] or a preliminary hearing.[21] At the other extreme, there are jurisdictions that do not permit defense discovery until after the preliminary hearing.[22]

The defense invariably will argue that discovery should commence as soon as possible and before the preliminary hearing. This argument is based upon the fact that defense counsel has the right to cross-examine prosecution witnesses during the preliminary hearing and therefore would like to inspect the statements and other evidence in order to be better prepared. Rule 16 of the FRCrP makes no mention of the time when discovery may be requested, which implies that it may be as soon as possible and prior to the filing of an indictment or information. This rule has served as a model for some states.

Matters That May Be Examined

Jurisdictions vary as to what evidence may be examined by the defendant. A defendant may have the right to examine such items of evidence as a grand jury transcript, a list of prosecution witnesses, copies of written statements made by the defendant or others, tapes or memoranda of oral statements, certain types of official or business documents, scientific or technical reports, weapons and other physical evidence, fingerprints, and photographs. Some jurisdictions permit the defendant, or the defendant's attorney, to inspect almost every piece of evidence in the hands of the prosecution or the law enforcement agency involved. Included in the right of discovery are

1. statements of the accused, including the right to hear or copy any recordings made of conversations with the accused;
2. statements of prospective prosecution witnesses;
3. names and addresses of prospective witnesses;
4. names and addresses of certain informants, particularly when probable cause for the arrest may stem from such informant, or if the informant was a participant in the crime or a witness thereto;
5. notes and documents made by witnesses, including the peace officer, used to refresh their memory prior to testifying;
6. notebooks used by the officer during the course of investigating the case;
7. photographs of the defendant shown to the victim of a crime for identification purposes;
8. scientific reports, such as crime-laboratory reports;
9. photographs pertaining to the crime; and
10. real evidence collected during the investigation.

Defendant's Right to Information About Prospective Witnesses

Defense access to names, addresses, and other information regarding witnesses and prospective witnesses has been one of the focal points in the debate over the right of discovery in criminal cases. This is not surprising, since the release of such information may lead to witness intimidation. There is no provision in federal law for the defense's access to witness information before trial. However, the trend in the states is just the opposite. Interestingly, in this country and in England, there long existed the practice of endorsing (listing) the names of witnesses for the prosecution upon the indictment or information. At least 19 states have enforced statutes requiring endorsement as a discovery tool since before 1900, and an additional 4 states had enforced such statutes by 1939.[23] As of August 2018, 29 states require the prosecutor to provide witness lists to the defense before trial. In addition, 19 states require that the indictment or information be endorsed with the names of witnesses, or that the identity of the grand jury witnesses be provided to the defense. Figure 12–1 shows those states that require witness disclosure by the prosecution to the defense.

States	Disclose Trial Witness	Disclose Grand Jury Witness	States	Disclose Trial Witness	Disclose Grand Jury Witness
Alabama	No	No	Montana	Yes	Yes
Alaska	Yes	No	Nebraska	Yes	No
Arizona	Yes		Nevada	Yes	Yes
Arkansas	Yes	No	New Hampshire	Yes	No
California	Yes	Yes	New Jersey	Yes	
Colorado	Yes	Yes	New Mexico	Yes	No
Connecticut	No	No	New York	Yes	Yes
Delaware	No	No	North Carolina	Yes	No
DC	No	No	North Dakota	Yes	Yes
Florida	Yes	Yes	Ohio	Yes	No
Georgia	Yes		Oklahoma	Yes	Yes
Hawaii	Yes	No	Oregon	Yes	No
Idaho			Pennsylvania	Yes	Yes
Illinois	Yes	No	Rhode Island	Yes	Yes
Indiana			South Carolina	No	No
Iowa	Yes	No	South Dakota	No	No
Kansas	Yes	Yes	Tennessee	Yes	Yes
Kentucky	No	Yes	Texas	Yes	Yes
Louisiana	No	No	Utah	Yes	
Maine	Yes		Vermont	Yes	Yes
Maryland	Yes		Virginia	No	
Massachusetts	Yes	Yes	Washington	Yes	No
Michigan	Yes	Yes	West Virginia	Yes	No
Minnesota	Yes	Yes	Wisconsin	Yes	No
Mississippi	Yes	No	Wyoming	No	No
Missouri	Yes	Yes			

FIGURE 12–1 States that require witness disclosure by prosecution to defense.

Defendant's Right to Identity of Informers

The debate over the defendant's right to discovery is nowhere more heated than in the area of the identity of informers. As was pointed out in Chapter 3, the right of discovery afforded the defendant has not abolished the privilege of the law enforcement officer to retain the confidentiality of the informer's identity. However, the privilege has been severely restricted. The courts hold that the disclosure of an informer's identity is required if it appears from the evidence that the informer is a material witness on the issue of the defendant's guilt or innocence. Failure to disclose the identity would deny the defendant the right to a fair trial, leading to the dismissal of the charges against the defendant. The guidelines as to whether an informer is a material witness are not clearly established. The courts have ruled that, if an informer participated in the crime or was an eyewitness to the crime, the informer is a material witness. The burden is on the defendant to prove the informer's status as a material witness. This burden is discharged when the defendant demonstrates a reasonable possibility that the informer whose identity is sought could give evidence on the issue of the guilt or innocence of the defendant.

Procedure for Pretrial Discovery by Defendant

Generally, an informal request made by the defense attorney to the prosecuting attorney to inspect the prosecution's evidence is sufficient to obtain permission to do so. This informal request, depending upon the jurisdiction, may be made orally or in writing.[24] In some jurisdictions, though, the defense must make a formal request for discovery by filing either a motion or a notice of intent to participate in discovery.[25] The defense may not participate in discovery if the judge determines that it is simply a "fishing expedition" by the defense in an effort to see what evidence the prosecution holds in the hopes of benefitting the defense's case. Normally, however, the defense attorney simply has to state that the inspection of the prosecution's evidence is deemed necessary for the preparation of the defense. In most instances, the right of discovery is then placed into operation and the judge issues an order for pretrial discovery.

When the defense requests pretrial discovery, either formally or informally, the prosecuting attorney generally prefers to be consulted before any disclosure for examination is made. In this way, the prosecuting attorney can better control what must be released for examination.

PROSECUTION'S RIGHT OF DISCOVERY

The most significant impediments to prosecution discovery rights are defendants' self-incrimination rights and the attorney-client privilege. Compelling the accused to produce evidence is, to some degree, compelling the accused to be a witness against himself or herself. Nonetheless, there has been substantial movement in the direction of allowing prosecution discovery of the defense case, within certain limits. Generally speaking, the prosecution may be given reciprocal discovery. Since 1966, Rule 16 of the FRCrP has provided for some reciprocal discovery. For example, Rule 16(b)(1)(A) provides the following:

> If a defendant requests disclosure under Rule 16(a)(1)(E) and the government complies, then the defendant must permit the government, upon request, to inspect and to copy or photograph books, papers, documents, data, photographs, tangible objects, buildings or places, or copies or portions of any of these items if:
>   (i) the item is within the defendant's possession, custody, or control; and
>   (ii) the defendant intends to use the item in the defendant's case-in-chief at trial.

Such reciprocal discovery was upheld by the United States Supreme Court in 1975.[26] Sections (a)(2) and (b)(2) of Rule 16 limit the right of discovery by both the defendant and the prosecution—protecting both self-incrimination rights and attorney-client privileges. Moreover, the prosecution may demand notice of the defendant's intention to offer a defense of alibi (FRCrP 12.1) or insanity (FRCrP 12.2).

At the state level, as broader rights of discovery have been granted to the defendant, the rights of the prosecution to discover aspects of the defendant's case have also been broadened. The defendant may be required to disclose to the prosecution various defenses, such as alibi, self-defense, insanity, and entrapment. In 1970, the United States Supreme Court upheld Florida's rule granting prosecution discovery of an alibi defense.[27] When the defendant must disclose defenses, he or she must also furnish the prosecution with names of prospective witnesses, as well as other information that may be requested by the prosecution.

DEFENDANT'S RIGHT TO ORIGINAL INVESTIGATIVE NOTES AND RECORDINGS

Once an officer writes a report, he or she may destroy the original notes upon which the report was based. The departmental policy may even mandate such destruction of notes. Generally, this is not a problem, since the majority of courts considering the matter have held that the defendant is not entitled to discovery of the officer's original investigative notes. However, in some instances, courts have ruled otherwise.

In the 1976 case of *United States v. Harris,*[28] the United States Court of Appeals for the Ninth Circuit held that the FBI must preserve the original notes taken by agents during interviews with prospective government witnesses or an accused. The court stated that the preservation of such evidence was necessary in order to permit the federal courts to play their proper role in deciding what evidence must be produced pursuant to the Jencks Act or other applicable law. Further, the court rejected the contention that the good faith destruction of rough notes in accordance with normal FBI policy was justifiable. Thus, the court found that notes taken by FBI agents in interviews with prospective government witnesses or the accused—as were involved in the *Harris* case itself—constitute potentially discoverable materials.

Since the time of the *Harris* decision, the Supreme Court of the United States has not addressed the issue, and there is a split of authority in the federal circuits. There is also a difference of views among the states. Defendants' claims that their rights were violated by the destruction of notes generally claim that the state's refusal to produce the notes deprived a defendant of liberty without due process of law in violation of the Fourteenth Amendment to the United States Constitution. *Brady v. Maryland*[29] requires the state to disclose to a defendant exculpatory material in the prosecutor's possession. Thus, a defendant may claim that the state's failure to produce an officer's original notes was a *Brady* violation. In addition, defendants often raise the issue that a specific state discovery statute was violated because the officer's notes relating to statements made by the defendant were not produced. Such claims are generally evaluated under the standards of

Jurisdiction	Permits Generally	Case by case review for due process or other const violation or does not permit	Undecided
Alabama		Waldrop v. State, 859 So.2d 1138 (2000) (one instance, cautions might be brady violation	
Alaska	Emery v. State, 2002 WL 1842987 (2002)		
Arizona	**State v. Axley**, 646 P.2d 268, Ariz., 1982. (MG)		
Arkansas			Not decided-no case/statues
California	People v. Von Villas (1992) 10 Cal.App. 4th 201, 248; People v. Garcia (1986) 183 Cal.App.3d 335, 348-350; 81 Ops. Cal. Atty. Gen. 397, 1998 WL 911746 (Cal.A.G.)		
Colorado		People v. Morgan, 681 P.2d 970 (1984); People v. Erickson 883 P.2d 511, Colo.App.,1994. OK if not constitutionally material	
Connecticut		State v. Vessichio, 500 A.2d 1311 Conn.,1985., State v. Zayas, 489 A.2d 380, Conn. App.,1985 (HAVE Jenks act like discovery state, in this Case OK, but "cannot condone"	
Delaware			Not decided MG
DC		U. S. v. Jackson, 450 A.2d 419 D.C.,1982. (Not permit MG)	
Florida			Not decided MG
Georgia	Mitchell v. State, 529 S.E.2d 169 Ga.App.,2000. (Permits, MG)		
Hawaii		State v. Maluia, 539 P.2d 1200. Hawaii 1975. case by case, have statute like jenks act, but notes incorporated are usually not statements under Jenks	
Idaho			Not decided-no case/statutes MG
Illinois	People v Wilson, 626 N.E.2d 1282 (1993) (MG TOO)		

FIGURE 12–2 States that permit destruction of police officer's notes if incorporated into a report

Indiana		Pmt- Albrecht v. State, 737 N.E. 2d 719 (2000), case by case, bad only if in bad faith or deprive of right	
Iowa	State v. Bowers, 661 N.W. 2d 536, 543 (2003)		
Kansas		Doesn't permit-St. v. Eubanks,577 P.2d 1208 (1978) MG Added State v. Walters, 655 P.2d 947, Kan. App.,1982	
Kentucky			Not decided-no cases/ statues (mg)
Louisiana			Not decided-no cases/ statues (mg)
Maine			Not decided-no cases/ statues (mg)
Maryland			Not decided-no cases/ statues (mg)
Massachusetts	Pmt-Com. v. Coll, 34 Mass. App. Ct 79 (1993) Could not find this case** Com. v. Pina 430 Mass. 66 (1999)		
Michigan		Pmt-People v. Synder, 2001 WL 672873, Mich. App.; People v. Cervante 1998 WL 1990401, Mich. App People v. Petrella 336 N.W.2d 761 Mich.App.,1983. Apr (added by MG, unsure)	
Minnesota	State v. Wilson, 535 N.W. 2d 597 (1995) (MG)		
Mississippi			Not decided (MG)
Missouri	Pmt- St. v. Burke, 809 S.W. 2d 391 (1990); State v. Buss, 768 S.W.2d 197 (Mo.App. E.D. 1989). (MG Added)		

FIGURE 12–2 (*Continued*)

State			
Montana	Pmt- St. v. Wright, 17 P.3d 982 (2000) (MG)		
Nebraska		NMG: State v. Davlin, 639 N.W.2d 631 (2002) St.v Parsons, 412 N.W. 2d 480(1987) (case by case)	
Nevada		Haynes v. State, 739 P.2d 497, Nev.,1987. One instance; reverse if establish prejudice (MG)	
New Hampshire	St. v Coolidge, 260 A.2d 547 (1969) (MG) Coolidge v. New Hampshire, 403 U.S. 443, 91 S. Ct. 2022, 29 L. Ed. 2d 564 (1971) is the most recent case		
New Jersey	Pmt- St. v. Dreher, 302 N.J. Super. 408 (1997) (MG agree)		
New Mexico			Not decided (MG)
New York		People v. Butler, 596 N.Y.S.2d 276, N.Y.A.D. 4 Dept.,1993. (MG not permit) Pmt- People v. Jarvis, 249 A.D.2d 417 (1998) – one case, ok if no prejudice	
North Carolina		State v. Nance, 579 S.E.2d 456 (N.C.App.,2003.) one instance, not matter unless show destroy in bad faith and would have been exculpatory	
North Dakota			Not decided (MG)
Ohio	State v. Drake 1993 WL 437602 Not Reported in N.E.2d Ohio App. 8 Dist.,1993.		
Oklahoma			Not decided (MG)
Oregon	State v. Armstrong, 692 P.2d 699 (Or.App.1984) mg		
Pennsylvania	Pmt- Com. v. McElroy, 665 A.2d 813, 819 (1995)		
Rhode Island		State v. Garcia, 643 A.2d 180 R.I.,1994. (state fire investigator, violate due process or discovery rule	Not decided
South Carolina			Not decided (MG)

FIGURE 12-2 (*Continued*)

South Dakota		Not decided (MG)
Tennessee		Not decided (MG)
Texas		Not decided (MG)
Utah		Not decided (MG)
Vermont	Pmt- St. v. Gibney, 825 A.2d 32 (2003)	
Virginia		Not decided (MG)
Washington		Not decided (MG)
West Virginia		Not decided(MG)
Wisconsin	Pmt- St. v. Noble, 246 Wis. 2d 533 (2001) (MG AGREE)	
Wyoming		Not decided (MG)

FIGURE 12–2 (Continued)

Arizona v. Youngblood,[30] where the United States Supreme Court held that the failure of police to preserve potentially useful evidence was not a denial of due process of law absent the defendant's showing of bad faith on the part of the police. The Court also indicated its unwillingness to read the fundamental fairness requirement of the Due Process Clause as imposing on police an undifferentiated and absolute duty to retain and preserve all material that might be of conceivable evidentiary significance in a particular prosecution. Thus, when claims of constitutional violations are raised as a result of the destruction of notes, the state courts, which decide such matters on a case-by-case basis, will determine if the evidence was exculpatory (*Brady*) or if the material has evidentiary significance in the action (*Youngblood*).

Thus, the law enforcement professional should exercise caution when deciding whether or not to destroy original notes, especially when those notes record a defendant's or witness's statements. The same is true of recordings of interviews after the recording has been transcribed. The problem arises most frequently when the defendant claims that the officer's report or interview transcript is inaccurate. Significantly, even in jurisdictions where the destruction of interview notes or recordings has been criticized, the courts have not held the principle applicable to original notes relating to other matters, such as notes dealing with surveillances. See Figure 12–2 for a summary of the law in each jurisdiction relating to destruction of officers' notes.

SUMMARY

(1) Documents may be classified as (1) public or (2) private. Public documents may be further categorized as (1) laws; (2) judicial records; (3) other official documents, such as records or driver's licenses, marriage applications, and birth certificates; and (4) public records of private writings, such as records of deeds and mortgages. Private documents are the private writings or recordings of individuals, such as letters, memoranda, answering machine messages, suicide notes, and wills.

(2) The situations in which secondary evidence of the contents of a writing may be introduced is when the original writing (1) has been lost or destroyed; (2) is unobtainable by any available judicial process or procedure; (3) is in the possession of an adverse party and, after a notice to produce it, the adverse party fails to do so; (4) is in the custody of a public officer; (5) relates to a collateral matter; and (6) is voluminous and cannot be examined without a great loss of time, and a summary of the writing's contents will suffice.

(3) The three foundational elements that must be shown before secondary evidence is admitted are (1) that there has been a writing in existence; (2) that the secondary evidence is a genuine copy of the original or accurately relates the contents of the original; and (3) the reason or justification that the secondary evidence is being offered instead of the original.

(4) The Fifth Amendment privilege against self-incrimination allows the defendant lawfully to refuse to comply with a subpoena *duces tecum* and withhold a document, if such document would incriminate the defendant.

(5) Under FRCrP 16, the defendant can discover from the prosecution (1) any written statements, recordings, or transcriptions of oral statements made by the defendant possessed by the prosecution; (2) the defendant's prior criminal record; and (3) documents, photographs, tangible objects, results of physical and mental examinations, and test reports possessed by the prosecution that the prosecution intends to use as evidence or that the court deems material to the defendant's trial preparation. If any of the materials specified in item 3 are granted to the defendant, the prosecution is granted reciprocal discovery.

(6) The Jencks Act covers only statements from a government witness written by that witness or transcribed at the same time the statement was made and either signed or adopted by the witness.

(7) The matters that may be subject to discovery by the defendant include such items of evidence as a grand jury transcript, a list of prosecution witnesses, copies of written statements made by the defendant or others, tapes or memoranda of oral statements, certain types of official or business documents, scientific or technical reports, weapons and other

physical evidence, fingerprints, and photographs. Some jurisdictions permit the defendant, or the defendant's attorney, to inspect almost every piece of evidence in the hands of the prosecution or the law enforcement agency involved.

(8) The defendant may be required to disclose to the prosecution various defenses, such as alibi, self-defense, insanity, and entrapment.

KEY TERMS

authentication 398	subpoena *duces*	discovery 404
laying the	*tecum* 402	exculpatory
foundation 399	collateral matter 402	evidence 404
best evidence rule 399	certified copy 402	*Brady* material 405
duplicate 399	exemplified copy 403	preliminary
primary evidence 400	voluminous records	hearing 407
secondary	rule 403	Jencks Act 408
evidence 400	original document 403	
notice to produce 402	inscribed chattel 403	

QUESTIONS FOR REVIEW

1. What are the two classifications of documents and each of their categories?
2. What are the five situations in which secondary evidence of the contents of a writing may be introduced?
3. What are the three foundational elements that must be shown before secondary evidence is admitted?
4. When is a defendant not required to comply with a subpoena *duces tecum* and produce a document in his or her possession?
5. What are the three types of discovery the defendant can obtain from the prosecution under FRCrP 16 and which type is granted reciprocal discovery?
6. What statements are covered by the Jencks Act?
7. What range of matters may be subject to discovery by the defendant in a criminal case?
8. What defenses may the accused be required to disclose to the prosecution prior to trial?

THINKING CRITICALLY ABOUT EVIDENCE

1. An officer arrests the defendant for possession of a stolen vehicle. At the preliminary hearing, the arresting officer assists the prosecutor. As potential witnesses, the prosecution has the owner of the vehicle who reported it stolen, a witness who saw the defendant near the car before it was stolen, the assisting officer, and the officer's partner who participated in the arrest. Keeping in mind the purpose of the preliminary hearing, whom should the prosecutor put on the witness stand and why?

WORKPLACE APPLICATIONS

1. An officer serves a search warrant at an illegal gambling establishment and finds photocopies of a pay/owe sheet; photographs of patrons gambling; and a computer containing files of hundreds of pages of bank account transactions, phone numbers, and correspondence. Keeping the best evidence rule and primary and secondary evidence in mind, write an explanation of how each item could be admitted into evidence.

2. The prosecutor tells several officers involved in a drug bust to give her "all notes and reports" of the incident that they possess. One of the officers interviewed a witness and recorded it but did not take any notes or include anything the witness said in a report, as the witness offered no useful information. Is the officer required to turn the recording over to the prosecutor, so that she can give it to the defense? Explain.

ETHICAL DILEMMA

1. An officer retires and moves to a state far from the area where he worked. Back in his home city, a defendant in a spousal abuse case is requesting discovery from the prosecution. The retired officer's partner knows that the retired officer kept a notebook that had notes from every call that resulted in an arrest, including the arrest of this defendant. The working partner believes the notes are not significant to the case. Telling the prosecutor about the notes means that the retired officer will have to search them out and produce them. Should the working partner tell the prosecutor about the notebook's existence?

ENDNOTES

1. 241 F.R.D. 534 (D. Md. 2007).

2. Fed. R. Evid. 1001(4), advisory committee note (original note), the Rule is now 1001(e).

3. *See, e.g.,* State v. Williams, 797 S.W.2d 734 (Mo. Ct. App. 1990).

4. Lawson v. State, 803 N.E.2d 237 (Int. App. 2004), citing Charles T. McCormick, Evidence § 234 (4th ed. 1992).

5. 454 F.2d 809 (5th Cir. 1972).

6. People v. Riser, 305 P.2d 1 (Cal.1956) (production of prosecution witness statements during trial). *See also* People v. Lopez, 384 P.2d 16 (Cal.1963) (pretrial discovery of government witness identity).

7. American Bar Ass'n, Project on Criminal Justice Standards, Standards Relating to Discovery and Procedure Before Trial (Approved Draft, 1970).

8. C. Clennon, *Pre-Trial Discovery of Witness Lists: A Modest Proposal to Improve the Administration of Criminal Justice in the Superior Court of the District of Columbia,* 38 Cath. U.L. Rev. 641, 651–52 nn.57–59 (1989).

9. 373 U.S. 83 (1963).

10. 18 U.S.C. § 3500.

11. 373 U.S. 83 (1963).

12. *Id.* at 87.

13. C. Clennon, *Pre-Trial Discovery of Witness Lists: A Modest Proposal to Improve the Administration of Criminal Justice in the Superior Court of the District of Columbia,* 38 Cath. U.L. Rev. 641, 656 (1989), citing United States v. Bagley, 473 U.S. 667, 682 (1985) (quoting Strickland v. Washington, 466 U.S. 668, 694 (1984)).

14. 540 U.S. 668 (2004).

15. Fed. R. Crim. P. 16 (a)(1)(B).

16. Jencks v. United States, 353 U.S. 657 (1957).

17. 18 U.S.C. § 3500 (a).

18. 353 U.S. at 681–82.

19. *See, e.g.,* Fla. Crim. P. Rule 3. 220 (2004). R.I. Super. Ct. R. Crim. P. Rule 16(g)(1) (2004). Tenn. Davidson County Logal Rule; Rhode Island Superior Ct. Rules of Crim. Pro.; Fla. R. Crim. P.

20. N.J. R. Crim. Rule 3:13–3 (2001).

21. Minn. R. Crim. P. Rule 9.01 (2004).

22. Illinois R. Crim. P. Rule 32.26 (2004).

Design Element: ©Ingram Publishing

23. C. Clennon, *Pre-Trial Discovery of Witness Lists: A Modest Proposal to Improve the Administration of Criminal Justice in the Superior Court of the District of Columbia,* 38 Cath. U.L. Rev. 641, 657–58 nn.96–98 (1989).

24. *E.g.,* R.I. Super. R. Crim. P. 16; N.J. Court Rules, R. 3:13–3.

25. *E.g.,* Fla. R. Crim. P. 3.220; Va. Sup. Ct. R 3A:11.

26. United States v. Nobles, 422 U.S. 225 (1975).

27. Williams v. Florida, 399 U.S. 78 (1970).

28. 543 F.2d 1247 (9th Cir. 1976).

29. 373 U.S. 83 (1963).

30. 488 U.S. 51 (1988).

13 PHYSICAL EVIDENCE

CHAPTER OUTLINE

CHAPTER OBJECTIVES

This chapter examines the law of evidence as it relates to the collection of physical evidence. After reading this chapter you will be able to:

▶ Name the five examples of how authentication can be accomplished.

▶ Identify the four general categories of physical evidence.

▶ List the order and persons in a typical chain of custody.

▶ State the three methods an officer can use to identify positively the object in court as the one that the officer found at the crime scene.

▶ Identify the information that should be placed on a typical tag.

▶ Describe how items of evidence should be packaged for long-term storage in an evidence locker.

▶ Explain the balancing test of FRE 403 for admitting gruesome objects into evidence.

WHAT IS PHYSICAL EVIDENCE?

PHYSICAL EVIDENCE
Material objects in
a criminal trial, for
example, a gun, a knife,
bloodstained clothing,
a latent fingerprint, or a
photograph.

REAL EVIDENCE
In terms of physical
evidence, the object itself.

**DEMONSTRATIVE
EVIDENCE**
Evidence used solely
to illustrate a witness's
testimony. A representation
of the object to be entered
into evidence: a copy, an
imitation, a model, or a
reproduction.

RELEVANT EVIDENCE
Evidence that "has any
tendency to make a fact
more or less probable
than it would be without
the evidence; and . . . the
fact is of consequence in
determining the action."

AUTHENTICATION
The presentation of proof
to show that an object is
what its proponent claims
it to be.

**LAYING THE
FOUNDATION**
The identification process
to show that an object is
authentic.

As previous chapters have shown, there are numerous kinds of evidence. One kind of evidence is **physical evidence**, or material objects. In a criminal trial, physical evidence may be a gun, a knife, bloodstained clothing, a latent fingerprint, or a photograph. Two forms of physical evidence are "demonstrative" and "real evidence." **Real evidence** is the object itself. **Demonstrative evidence** is a representation of the real thing: a copy, an imitation, a model, or a reproduction. For example, the gun used in a shooting is real evidence, while another gun of the same manufacture and model is demonstrative evidence. Another example of demonstrative evidence is a diagram of the scene of a crime, drawn in the courtroom by an investigating officer to help illustrate his testimony describing the scene. The distinction, however, is usually just academic, as the terms "physical evidence," "real evidence," and "demonstrative evidence" are used interchangeably.

Once physical evidence has been identified by a witness, authenticated, and introduced into evidence as an exhibit, the physical evidence speaks for itself. The jury does not have to rely upon the testimony of a witness to explain what was found and to provide a description. The jurors can usually hold, feel, inspect, and examine the object and see for themselves the information that it contains.

Physical Evidence Must Be Relevant

For physical evidence to be admissible, it must have some connection to the facts of the case; it must be relevant to the issues of the trial, and it must assist in proving the facts in dispute. FRE 401 defines **relevant evidence** as evidence that "has any tendency to make a fact more or less probable than it would be without the evidence; and . . . the fact is of consequence in determining the action." If an object is a part of the transaction of the crime and assists in explaining and unfolding the story of the case, the object will be relevant and may be introduced into evidence and shown to the jury.

Generally, only relevant evidence is admissible; irrelevant evidence is inadmissible. However, FRE 403 states that even relevant evidence can be excluded if it is unduly prejudicial, confuses the issues, misleads the jury, or is a waste of the court's time. Essentially, the trial court balances the worth of the evidence to prove or disprove some fact against its potential for unfair impact on the jury. The court can exclude the evidence if its prejudicial or distracting effect substantially outweighs its probative value.

Laying Foundation for Physical Evidence

Before any physical object may be admitted in evidence and shown to the jury, enough proof must be presented to satisfy FRE 901 requirements that the object is what its proponent claims it to be. This **authentication**, or identification, process is called **laying the foundation** for the object. This can be accomplished in a number of ways, for example, through the following:

1. testimony of a witness who has firsthand knowledge;
2. a nonexpert who was familiar with a person's handwriting and did not gain the knowledge of the handwriting for the purpose of the litigation, such as a spouse or roommate;

3. allowing the jury or an expert to compare the object to an example and decide its authenticity;

4. distinctive characteristics and surrounding circumstances, such as sending a bill to an address and receiving payment from the bill; or

5. voice identification that can be learned firsthand or through a mechanical or electronic transmission, such as a television or digital answering device.

Some evidence is self-authenticating and does not require authentication to be admitted into court. For example, FRE 902 lists certified copies of public records, domestic public documents under seal, foreign public documents, and official publications, such as books, pamphlets, newspapers, and periodicals, as self-authenticating evidence. Although these documents are self-authenticating, a witness may be called to produce them at trial.

The burden of authentication of physical evidence in a criminal trial most often falls upon the law enforcement professional because he or she normally discovers the object while investigating the crime and knows how the object connects the accused to the crime. The officer may be aware of the object's connection to the case because it was removed from the accused at the time of the arrest or taken from the crime scene. Other witnesses besides the officer may have to assist in the authentication of the object, as one officer may not have knowledge of all the connecting facts. For example, if the accused were charged with robbing a man of his wallet and money, and an officer arrested the accused and removed a wallet from his possession, the officer would be able to connect the wallet to the accused. However, the victim of the robbery would have to identify the wallet as the one taken in the robbery in order to connect it with the crime.

Introducing Physical Evidence

Using the example of the robbery case, the prosecutor needs to prove that the wallet is connected with the facts of the case in order to have it admitted into evidence. The victim could testify that there was a wallet, and the arresting officer could relate the facts about the arrest and the discovery of the wallet in the possession of the accused, all without the prosecutor introducing the wallet into evidence. However, as evidence, the wallet speaks for itself. It shows the jury that the object is relevant and authentic. The evidence also emphasizes the facts of the case and substantiates the oral testimony of the witnesses. The trial judge will send the physical evidence to the jury room for examination during the deliberation to assist the jury in remembering the facts as they were presented during the trial.

There is no rule requiring the prosecutor to call witnesses in any particular sequence. Good lawyers, however, try to present witnesses in a logical order. In the wallet robbery example, the prosecutor might first call the victim of the robbery to the stand to establish the fact that the robbery took place. The victim could also testify to elements of the crime, such as the taking of the wallet through means of force or fear. The following steps are usually taken in order to get the wallet, or any other object, introduced into evidence. The prosecutor will mark the wallet in numeric order for identification purposes, such as "People's Exhibit Number 1, for Identification." Normally, the prosecutor's exhibits are marked with numbers, while the defense's exhibits are marked with letters.

Next, the prosecutor will lay the foundation for the witness to identify the wallet by giving it to the witness and asking if the witness recognizes it as being the same wallet that was taken during the robbery. The prosecutor will then offer the wallet to the judge as evidence and request that the judge accept it into evidence. At this time, the opposing counsel may raise any legal objections to the introduction of the wallet, and the prosecutor will respond. Ultimately, the judge will rule on the objections and either sustain or overrule them and receive the wallet into evidence. Once the evidence is admitted, it can be considered by the jury.

In theory, the jury must disregard an object until it is admitted into evidence. However, this is not easily accomplished because the authentication of the object usually takes place in the presence of the jury. If the object is not admitted, it is almost impossible for jurors to erase the memory of the object from their minds. Once the object has been introduced, the jurors may consider it with respect to the differing viewpoints in the case and give the evidence the weight they think it deserves. They may examine and inspect it at the time it is introduced, and the attorneys may refer to it during their closing arguments.

Attacking Physical Evidence

Due to the great impact physical evidence has on a jury, a defense attorney will often do everything possible to prevent an object from being introduced as evidence. The defense attorney might argue that the object is unduly prejudicial to the defendant, as with gruesome photographs, or that the person collecting the object was prejudiced toward the defendant and planted the evidence. The attorney can try to show that the object is not relevant and has not been positively connected to the case. Or the defense might try to prove that the officer cannot positively identify the object as the same object that was recovered at the crime scene. The defense attorney might try to prove that the object was tampered with, collected by an incompetent investigator, or contaminated in such a way that the object can no longer prove the fact intended. Often, when the defense counsel's objections are successful, it is due to improper handling of the investigation of the crime, which includes the collection, identification, and preservation of the object. Before discussing the investigation of a crime, it is important to identify some of the sources of physical evidence, as well as some of the kinds of objects that may be considered as a part of a crime, or transaction, and thereby be relevant to the issues of a case.

SOURCES OF PHYSICAL EVIDENCE

The law enforcement officer, or investigator, or criminalist can find physical evidence in many places. Physical evidence can be used to determine what crime has been committed, to lead to other evidence, to enable the officer to reconstruct the crime, and to assist in convicting the perpetrator. The most logical and lucrative place to find physical evidence is at the crime scene. The perpetrator's person, vehicle, home, place of business, and base of operations are prime sources of evidence. Even a search of the areas surrounding these places, or along a getaway route, could turn up discarded evidence.

Kinds of Physical Evidence

It is impossible to list all the kinds of physical evidence that may be considered to be a part of the transaction of a crime, because there can be as many kinds as there are objects in existence. However, kinds of physical evidence, as a matter of convenience, may be classified under four general categories: fruits of a crime, instrumentalities used in committing the crime, contraband, and evidence. The **fruit of a crime** is property that is seizable by a police officer, such as stolen or embezzled property. An **instrumentality of a crime** is property that is seizable by a police officer that was used as the means of committing a crime, such as a gun. **Contraband** is any item that is illegal for a person to possess, such as an illegally sawed-off shotgun or an illegal drug, such as crack cocaine. **Evidence of a crime** is any object that demonstrates that a crime has been committed. Any object discovered during an investigation that falls within one of these categories should be admitted in evidence with little difficulty, since it is connected with the crime and relevant. The only problem that may arise is the proper authentication of the object. It is in this matter that collection, identification, and preservation play a paramount role.

Chain of Custody

When the prosecutor seeks to introduce an object into evidence, the burden is on the government to prove that the object in court is the same item that was collected by the officer out on the street and that it is in the same condition, or substantially the same condition, as when it was collected. The prosecutor needs to obtain testimony that traces who has had control of the object and where the object has been since it was collected. The persons involved in the possession of the object usually include the collecting officer, the transport officer (who takes it to the crime laboratory for analysis or directly to the police evidence locker for booking), crime lab personnel, the custodian of the records of the evidence locker, and the officer who takes the object to court. Many departments simplify the process by requiring that the collecting officer transport the object to the crime laboratory or book it into evidence. The same officer then retrieves the object and takes it to court. The object will usually have a chronological log attached to it that must be filled out by everyone who handles the object, including laboratory technicians, booking officers, investigators, and prosecutors.

> **FYI**
>
> It may be impossible to show that evidence is in *exactly* the same condition as when it was discovered. Sometimes, as with drugs that have been subjected to testing, the evidence might be diminished or otherwise altered in some manner. Therefore, the party offering the evidence is permitted to show that it is in "substantially" the same condition as when it was found.

Securing the Crime Scene and Collecting Physical Evidence

The fact-finding activities that take place at the scene of a crime immediately after the crime has been reported to or discovered by police officers are all part of what is called the preliminary investigation. In most cases, many of these initial

FRUIT OF A CRIME
Property that is seizable by a police officer, such as stolen or embezzled property.

INSTRUMENTALITY OF A CRIME
Property that is seizable by a police officer that was used as the means of committing a crime, such as a gun.

CONTRABAND
An object or material that is illegal for a person to possess, such as an illegally sawed-off shotgun or an illegal drug, such as crack cocaine.

EVIDENCE OF A CRIME
Any object that demonstrates that a crime has been committed.

activities are undertaken by uniformed patrol officers from the police agency responding to the call for assistance.

One of the first things a new officer learns is the necessity of protecting the integrity of a crime scene. Upon arrival at a crime scene, the officer should quickly determine if anyone is injured or needs medical treatment and, if so, summon the necessary health professionals. Next, the officer should survey the crime scene, quickly determine whom to interview, and move nonessential individuals out of the area. As soon as possible, the crime scene area should be cordoned off or otherwise closed to nonessential individuals. This will keep contamination of the crime scene to a minimum. The reality at many crime scenes is that some contamination of the scene is unavoidable, especially in cases where a crowd gathers before the officer arrives, or when multiple people are injured. The officer must exercise good judgment to protect as much of the scene as possible. Improper protection of a crime scene may result in evidence becoming contaminated or even destroyed and may lead to the exclusion of key objects in a trial or affect the worth of the evidence in the eyes of the jury.

Each type of physical evidence, whether an intact object, pieces of an object, blood, glass, liquids, or gasses, must be collected, marked or tagged, packaged, transported, and stored properly to be later admitted into evidence in court. It is beyond the scope of this text to discuss in detail the specific methods for securing and processing the crime scene and any evidence found there. Those techniques are taught in other police science courses, such as crime scene investigation and criminal investigation courses. This chapter deals with the general principles that law enforcement professionals must follow to preserve the integrity of any evidence for use at trial.

In small police departments, the officer may be the one who takes photographs and acts as the primary investigative agent. The local police chief will call for a forensic or other type of investigative specialist only if he or she feels the circumstances warrant their involvement. In most urban departments, a photographer or videographer and a criminalist or forensic specialist will be part of any major crime scene investigation. In either case, the next phase of the investigation will be a detailed search of the scene and any associated places and persons to collect and analyze whatever evidence can be found. At this stage, a number of different activities are conducted, including the lifting of latent fingerprints, the taking of blood samples, the plotting of bullet trajectories, the notation of gun powder patterns, the analysis of wound patterns, and the gathering of materials upon which trace evidence may have been deposited.

In many instances, investigators and criminalists will process key pieces of evidence taken by them directly from the crime scene. In other cases, the patrol officer will be responsible for collecting and processing all crime scene evidence. Regardless of who collects the evidence, the individual removing the item from the scene of the crime must be able to present satisfactory proof at the time of trial that the object has a connection to the case and to the specific crime for which the accused is being tried. Thus, for example, the item will be marked in some distinctive way, with initials and date, so that the person collecting it can point to how he or she knows this is the item collected. At trial, the officer must be able to identify positively the object as the one that he or she found at the scene. The officer must also be able to establish that the object has not been tampered with or altered in any way that might disqualify it as evidence. Tainted evidence, even if admitted in court, may lose all or some of its evidentiary value.

CONNECTING OBJECTS WITH ISSUES AT TRIAL: CHAIN OF CUSTODY, OR POSSESSION

Objects that constitute fruits, instrumentalities, or evidence of the crime or are contraband may be introduced in evidence and exhibited to the jury if it is proven that such objects offered as evidence relate to the crime charged. To do this, someone must be in a position to testify that the object was connected with the crime or found at the scene. The officer who investigated the case may or may not be able to do this, depending upon certain circumstances, because the officer can testify only to his or her own actions and observations. The officer can describe the crime scene only as it was upon his or her arrival. Seldom is the officer the first one at a crime scene. Thus, proof that a particular object was a part of the scene may depend on the testimony of some other witness. It is vital that the officer obtain the names, addresses, and phone numbers of those present. The officer must also ascertain whether the scene is in its original state or whether anything has been removed, tampered with, or handled. The person who originally discovered the crime scene can be a very important link in the chain of proof showing that a particular object has a connection with the crime.

The typical record of **chain of custody,** or possession, includes the person who initially observed the object, the possession of the object by the officer, transportation to the laboratory, possession by laboratory technicians, retrieval by another officer and transportation to police storage facilities, and the final transport to court. If there is a break in the chain of custody, the claim of proof that the item is in the same condition as when it was found at the crime scene may be compromised, and the item may no longer be admissible in evidence. A log is usually attached to the item, and each person who handles the item must record his or her name, department, and date of handling to help ensure that the chain of custody is kept intact.

CHAIN OF CUSTODY
The maintenance of custody and control over an object to such a degree that the custodian can prove the object is in the same condition as when custody was obtained.

Maintaining the chain of custody is particularly important when the object is one that is not unique or when questions could be raised about changes in the condition of the object, unique or not. Chain of custody must be carefully maintained for common, fungible objects (things that are not immediately identifiable when mixed with like items), such as "a plastic bag containing one ounce of a white, powdery substance."

On the other hand, an officer who finds a particular weapon at the scene of a homicide may secure the weapon by tagging it and sealing it in a plastic evidence bag. This will make the particular gun identifiable, even though thousands of guns of the same make and model were manufactured. If the defendant were to claim that someone altered the condition of the gun from the time it was collected by the officer to the time it was delivered in court, then proof of an uninterrupted chain of custody could be critical for the admission of the gun into evidence.

In order to ensure admissibility at trial, three procedures may be used to identify an object positively:

1. The officer may keep the object in his or her complete and exclusive custody and control from the time it was found until it is presented in court.
2. The officer may maintain a complete and accurate record of the chain of custody.
3. The officer may tag or mark the object in some distinctive manner.

Identification by Custody and Control

One of the most effective means by which the officer can identify an object to be introduced in evidence is for the officer to keep the object in his or her personal possession, or **exclusive control**, from the time the officer picks it up at the crime scene until he or she produces it in court. Realistically, this is impractical for a number of reasons. First, it is virtually impossible for an officer to maintain control of many objects. There simply are not enough storage facilities available. Second, and probably most important, the object may require examination or analysis by experts. Finally, exclusive control is also impractical because of the right of discovery by the defendant. This right gives the defendant the privilege of reviewing the physical evidence that may be introduced during trial. Consequently, the officer may lose, or at least be required to share, control of objects during this review by the defendant or his or her counsel.

Although there may be instances when the officer is not required to release physical evidence to anyone else, some consideration should be given to what is entailed in complete custody and control of objects. Obviously, complete custody and control does not mean that the officer must carry the object at all times, but it does mean that, from the time the officer picks it up at the crime scene until it is produced in court, the object must be continually under his or her exclusive control. In other words, after picking up the object at the scene of the crime, the officer must transport it to the station or to another place where the officer will store it, and it must be kept where no one else has the opportunity to handle the object outside the officer's presence. This necessitates a locker, or cabinet, to which only the officer has access. Complete custody and control further implies that, if the object is to be viewed or examined by another, the officer must be present. This is a burdensome system of identification.

The following is a sample transcript of an officer identifying an object by means of exclusive custody and control:

Prosecutor: Officer Smith, did you find any items at the crime scene?

Officer Smith: Yes, I found a one-page, typed letter lying by the body.

Prosecutor: What did you do with the letter?

Officer Smith: After the videographer and photographer both finished recording the location of the object, and the criminalist failed to find any latent prints on the letter, I personally transported it to the crime lab to have the type print analyzed.

Prosecutor: Whom did you leave the letter with at the crime lab?

Officer Smith: Well, I didn't really leave it with anyone. I personally took it to an analyst named John Roe and stood by for an hour while he analyzed the letter.

Prosecutor: Did the letter ever leave your sight?

Officer Smith: No, Mr. Roe let me watch the entire analysis process, which is quite interesting, and then I took the letter back, sealed it in a manila envelope, and took it home.

Prosecutor: What do you mean by "you took it home"?

Officer Smith: Well, it was the end of my shift, and my lieutenant said that the guy who was arrested for the crime would have his preliminary hearing in a few days, so he said I could hold on to the letter until then, provided that I didn't lose exclusive control of the letter. So, I took it home, locked it in my wall safe hidden behind a picture in my living room, and set my burglar alarm anytime I left the house.

Prosecutor: Does anyone else have access to the wall safe in your home?

Officer Smith: No, I live alone, and I have never given the safe combination to anyone else.

Prosecutor: Did you ever take it out of the safe before today?

Officer Smith: Yes, I took it out at your request yesterday and took it to the defense counsel's office to show it to him.

Prosecutor: Did you let it out of your sight at that time?

Officer Smith: No, I was with the letter at all times.

Prosecutor: Where did you take the letter next?

Officer Smith: Back home to my safe, where it remained until I brought it to court today.

Prosecutor: Officer Smith, can you identify this object marked People's Exhibit 1 for identification?

Officer Smith: Yes, it is the same letter that I found at the crime scene.

Identification by Proof of Chain of Custody

Some objects found at the crime scene by an officer, by their very nature, must pass through the hands of others besides the officer under circumstances in which the officer cannot maintain custody and control. This is particularly true when an object must be examined by an expert in a crime laboratory for an extended period of time. For example, a criminalist who extracts DNA samples from a bloodstain collected at a crime scene may require a number of days of possession of the stain before sending the samples off to another crime lab for comparison and analysis. In such a circumstance, the officer loses complete custody and control of the object. When this takes place, the officer must know to whom the object was released and the purpose for which it was released. In other words, the officer must maintain a record of the chain of possession.

Proof of **chain of custody,** or possession, specifically means the knowledge, or accounting, of each person who has come into possession of a physical object found at a crime scene, from the time it was discovered until it is presented in court. Such an accounting allows the jury to be sure that the object is what it purports to be and has not been altered or tampered with. This accounting is important for two basic reasons: first, to establish that the object presented in court is the one that was found at the scene and is thus a part of the transaction and, second, to establish that the object examined and analyzed by the expert was the one found in connection with the crime and that it was not altered or tampered with between being found and being analyzed. If this proof is not available, the object, as well as the expert's analysis, may be excluded from evidence.

As an example of how the doctrine of chain of possession works and how it can be most important to the prosecution of a case, assume that an officer, Officer A, discovers a knife on a suspect in a murder case. On this knife is a stain that is believed to be blood. Officer A wants the stain examined by a laboratory expert to determine whether the stain is blood, whether it is of human origin, and the blood type.

Officer A gives the knife to Officer B to take to the police station, where it is to be sent to the crime laboratory. On arrival at the station, Officer B finds that Officer C is going to the crime laboratory with some other physical evidence, so Officer B sends the knife with Officer C. Officer C takes the knife to the laboratory and turns it over to Clerk D. Clerk D gives the knife to Expert E, who makes a scientific examination of the stains on the knife. Expert E concludes from examination that the brownish stains are blood and are of human origin. He also finds that the blood is of the AB grouping, which is a rare type and is the same type as that of the murder victim. The knife and the analysis of the expert become very important to the prosecution of the suspect. In the meantime, Officer A asks Officer F, who is going to the laboratory, to pick up the knife and return it to the station. Officer F picks up the knife, returns it to the station, and places the knife in the evidence room until the time of the trial.

On the day of the trial, Officer A gets the knife from the evidence room and takes it to court. There may be something distinctive about this knife that enables Officer A to identify it positively as the one he took from the suspect, even though it has been out of his possession. But how can Officer A positively testify in a convincing manner that the stains that were on the knife when it was taken from the suspect are the same ones examined by the expert? Officer A cannot do so because the knife has gone through several hands. It cannot be proven that someone did not use the knife for some purpose between the time it was found and the time it was examined, or that the blood examined was the blood that was on the knife originally. Since this proof is not available, the knife, as well as the analysis, would be excluded from evidence. However, if all the persons who came in contact with the knife are known, are available to testify concerning their part in the transaction, and can establish that the knife had not been tampered with, the knife and the analysis would be admitted in evidence.

FYI

In the example of Officer A and the bloodstained knife, it would have been a much better procedure for Officer A to have maintained possession of the knife until he was able to take it to the crime laboratory personally and turn it over directly to the blood-analysis expert. This procedure could have eliminated three potential witnesses—Officer B, who took the knife to the station; Officer C, who transported the knife to the crime laboratory; and Clerk D, who accepted the knife from Officer C. Ideally, Officer A would also have retrieved the knife directly from the crime laboratory after the analysis.

Although an accurate and complete record is maintained of the chain of custody of physical evidence, the objects should go through as few hands as possible. This is because, the fewer the number of persons who come in contact with the physical evidence, the less the chance that it will be tampered with, altered, or lost entirely. Probably even more important, each person who comes in contact with the physical evidence may have to be called as a witness to establish the fact that the evidence analyzed was, in fact, found in connection with the crime at issue. The necessity of using a long line of witnesses to prove a relatively small segment of the case can be time-consuming, as well as tedious for the jury. Jury members could well lose interest in the case, and the value of the physical evidence would be lost entirely. Also, when a number of witnesses are required to prove a point, the unavailability of one witness in the chain may be enough to exclude the object from being introduced into evidence.

For purposes of chain of custody, an object may be treated differently once it has been subjected to analysis. Before analysis, proof must be presented that no tampering, contamination, or substitution took place between the time the object was found and the time it was subjected to the analysis. After the analysis, all that is necessary is that the officer who found the object be able to recognize it at the time it is produced in court. However, there are many objects that do not lend themselves to ready recognition, so the chain of custody, even after an analysis, should not be overlooked.

MARKING OBJECTS FOR IDENTIFICATION

The identification of physical evidence by means of complete custody is not always practical, and identification by maintaining a record of the chain of custody sometimes breaks down because of a missing piece of information or an inaccuracy. Therefore, the officer may wish to make an object more recognizable at the time of trial as the one he or she found in connection with a particular crime. As the prosecution can introduce only relevant objects into evidence against a defendant, the identification of an object in court is extremely important. If the officer is not positive that an object is the same one he or she found, then the object has no relevance to the case and cannot be used against the defendant. Many cases are won by the government because the jury finds the physical objects offered as evidence convincing beyond a reasonable doubt, not because the testimony of an officer, an expert, or a witness is especially compelling. The jurors are convinced because the physical evidence speaks plainly for itself, and they believe the physical evidence to be more reliable than mere human perception and memory.

ON THE JOB

The following example helps emphasize the importance of marking an object that is to be used as physical evidence.

Assume that the only physical evidence found at a murder scene was human tissue and blood found under the victim's nails, presumably obtained from scratching her killer. An officer collected the sample in a vial but failed to mark it in any identifying manner. The sample went to the crime laboratory and was analyzed. However, because there were two unmarked samples that arrived that day, no one at the lab knew which sample belonged to which case. When the defendant's case went to trial a year later, even though one of the samples had the defendant's DNA and blood type, the officer could not state in court that the sample was the same one that he had collected at the crime scene. Therefore, the evidence was not admitted and the prosecution was forced to drop all charges for lack of evidence. Although this is an extreme case, the moral of the story is the same for all similar situations: If you cannot identify the object as being the same object that you found at the crime scene, you cannot use that object as evidence, and you will be forced to use other evidence, if any exists, to convict the defendant.

It is generally most efficient and desirable for the officer who discovered the object to mark it in such a manner that he or she will recognize it at a later date. The mark should be made at the time the object is removed from its original position and should be distinctive, so that the officer will recognize it as the one he or she placed on the object. The officer's initials and the date of the marking will usually be sufficient to enable the officer to identify the object at a later time.

An object should be marked at the time it is found, whether the officer plans to maintain complete custody and control of the object or maintain an accurate record of the chain of possession. Then, in the event of an unexpected release of the object to another, or a gap in the record of chain of possession, the officer will still be able to recognize the object and connect it with the specific crime and scene. Even if an object is not to be examined scientifically or released to anyone else, the officer should mark it so that, when the officer is on the witness stand, there will be no doubt in his or her mind that it is the original object. Because the officer will have no doubt about the identification, the officer's testimony will likely eradicate any doubt on the part of the jury that the object produced in court is the one the officer found at the scene of the crime.

In most instances, there is a considerable lapse of time between the discovery of physical evidence and its production in court. The officer may believe at the time of discovery that he or she will readily recognize the evidence in the future. This is not always possible, and there may be an allegation by the defense on the possibility of a substitution in connection with the object in question. Therefore, the officer must be in a position to testify, without any doubt, that the object produced in court is the same one found in connection with the transaction at hand.

As acceptable and convincing as marking a piece of evidence for identification is, it is not without its complications. First of all, marking physical evidence can be a time-consuming procedure, and the many other responsibilities at a crime scene frequently do not allow the time necessary to do the job thoroughly. Also, many objects found at a crime scene are not easy to mark, such as objects with hard surfaces, soil specimens, hairs, and fibers. These objects may have to be transported to the station, where proper tools for marking are available. Finally, some objects should not be marked directly, such as bullet fragments, because any marking could ruin the surface and destroy striation markings on the fragment. Irrespective of such problems, the importance of marking physical evidence cannot be overemphasized.

If the officer finds it impossible to mark an object properly at the crime scene, the object (hairs, fibers, or other trace evidence) should be placed in a paper or plastic bag, or other container, and marked for identification. The item might have a tag attached to it with an identifying notation on the tag, or a tag can be placed in or attached to the protective packaging.

It is not possible to outline the exact ways in which the various objects found at a crime scene should be marked, but, because of the unique problems that are presented in marking certain objects, a few guidelines will be set forth. Anytime an officer or a criminalist is marking an object, he or she must be extremely careful to make the marking so as not to interfere with any scientific examination that may be performed in connection with the object. Also, the law enforcement professional must exert every effort not to obliterate any latent prints that may be on the object.

Nothing in the rules of evidence requires that a marking for identification purposes be extensive. The mark should consist of the marker's initials or some other unique mark that will enable the officer to recognize it at a later time. A simple "X" mark should be avoided. The data that usually accompany the identification of an object, such as where, when, and by whom found, may be written on a tag that is attached to the object.

Even though an object is marked for identification, a record of the chain of custody is still very important. This is particularly true when physical evidence must be examined by an expert. Again, it must be proven that the evidence was in the same condition when examined as when it was found at the crime scene.

Besides the distinctive identifying mark made on the object by the officer or other law enforcement professional removing it from the crime scene, additional information should accompany the object from the time of its discovery until it is presented in court. It is not only impractical but also inadvisable to maintain these data on the article itself. The data are best recorded on a tag, sticker, or slip of paper attached to the article or to the container in which it is kept.

Although there will be notes or other official records that will provide information on the physical evidence, the law enforcement professional should also include an evidence tag with the article itself to provide for easy identification and retrieval from the evidence locker. The tag also enables the quick refreshing of memory concerning the article at the time of the trial and assists in maintaining a more accurate and complete record of the chain of possession.

There is no set format for recording the information on the tag or for the contents of the tag. Typically, the tag should contain (1) the case number; (2) the name of the defendant; (3) the name of the victim; (4) the name of the law enforcement professional who found the object; (5) the date, time, and place where the object was found; (6) a brief description of the article (this is important in case the tag becomes detached from the object and because some objects cannot be recognized from appearance alone); (7) the signature of the person finding the object; (8) the person to whom the object was released and the reason for the release; (9) the date and time of release; and (10) the ultimate disposition of the object—what will be done with the object if it is not used as evidence.

In many instances, the tag can be attached to the object by a string or wire. For example, the string or wire can be attached to the handlebars of a bicycle, the buttons or zipper on a piece of clothing, or a weapon. Stickers can be placed on large items, such as televisions, stereos, or video recorders, as well as on small items, such as vials of blood, urine samples, or plastic bags containing drugs. Tags on slips of paper can be placed in envelopes with documents, such as checks, insurance or proof of ownership records, or sales receipts.

When the physical evidence is returned to the collecting officer from another person (perhaps an expert) to whom the collecting officer released it, the collecting officer should examine the physical evidence to make certain that it is the proper evidence. The collecting officer should make a record of the return date, verify the identifying marks, and note any change in the appearance of the evidence. This is particularly necessary when the physical evidence has been examined by a laboratory expert because the laboratory expert may have removed a portion of the physical evidence or changed its appearance in some way. By examining the evidence upon its return, the officer will not be caught by surprise on the witness stand and will be prepared to explain any changes that have occurred in the evidence.

STORAGE OF PHYSICAL EVIDENCE

With a little experience, the average law enforcement professional will become proficient in collecting, marking for identification, and tagging physical evidence. However, much of the value that could be derived from the evidence is often lost because of deficient storage procedures. Many law enforcement agencies have little storage space or inadequate facilities, and proper storage of physical evidence is difficult. As a result, the property control officer may have to place objects found at crime scenes on top of lockers and file cabinets or in a large closet along with hundreds of similar items. When the time for trial comes, the property control officer finds it difficult to testify convincingly that he or she had complete custody and control of the object, that an accurate record of the chain of possession exists, or that there was no tampering with the evidence. Any of these circumstances may cause the object to be excluded from evidence.

A well-run law enforcement agency takes extra care to ensure the proper storage of physical evidence, especially since defense counsel are focusing their attacks more and more on the foundations for physical evidence. Today, more than ever, officers and prosecutors have to rely on scientific investigations and the presentation of physical evidence to prove the defendant's guilt. Therefore, no chances should be taken on physical evidence being lost or excluded because of improper storage. Each department should have a separate room, or rooms, set aside for the storage of physical evidence. The evidence storage room door should have a combination lock or special key that only the property control officer and his or her supervisor have the means to open. Additionally, the evidence locker should be organized by item type. For example, refrigerators should hold perishable items, such as blood and urine; separate cabinets or lockers should be used for clothing, narcotics, weapons, tools, explosives or ammunition, and electronic items, such as stereos, smartphones, digital recorders, laptop computers, tablets, and other digital devices. Large items, such as bicycles, should be placed in a corner, or outside with vehicles in a secure, enclosed area that is protected by camera surveillance to ensure the safety of the evidence.

The property control officer maintains a log of all items that are placed in the evidence storage area and their location, as well as all people who enter and the items retrieved. This maintains the chain of custody and control of the evidence inside the locker and, in many states, allows the department to know when a lost or unclaimed item in police possession has gone unclaimed for the statutory time period, allowing it to be auctioned off.

Objects should be stored in a manner in which they can retain their original shape and appearance as much as possible. When objects are to be stored for a considerable period of time, it is advisable to place them in cartons or paper or plastic bags in order to prevent dirt, dust, and the elements from affecting their appearance. The cartons or bags should be sealed and marked with the proper identifying data on the outside of each package, from which the contents may be easily determined. Such storage will prevent unauthorized handling, as well as aid in keeping objects from being soiled or losing their appearance. There have been times when articles were excluded from evidence because of marked alterations in their appearance. If the physical evidence is going to create confusion instead of clarifying a fact in the case, it will be excluded.

Because of the shortage of personnel and the routine nature of many investigations, it is not practical to assign two officers to investigate all crimes. But it is advisable in major cases to have two officers, crime scene investigators, criminalists, or other law enforcement professionals present when the physical evidence is collected and marked for identification. Either person could then testify concerning the object and its connection with the case and thereby refute any allegations of planting evidence. Otherwise, if only one officer has knowledge of the physical evidence and if that officer should become unavailable, the evidence would most likely be found inadmissible and its value lost to the prosecution of the case.

DELIVERING PHYSICAL EVIDENCE

Many police departments require the officers to deliver physical evidence personally to the crime laboratory for scientific investigations. However, in some areas, the only practical way of transmitting physical evidence to a crime laboratory for scientific examination is by mail or other delivery service. Even in large cities, such delivery methods are commonly used. To maintain the chain of possession of the evidence, the officer who collects the object should wrap it, seal the container, and properly initial it. Included on the outside of the package should be a cover letter describing the object to be examined and the desired examination, thus eliminating any unnecessary handling of the item. After the object has been wrapped, sealed, and initialed by the officer, the whole package, including the cover letter, should be wrapped with an outer wrapping suitable for shipping and properly addressed to the crime laboratory with the notation that the package contains evidence. The package should be sent by a method that requires a recipient's signature.

Explosives and narcotics should never be shipped without meeting the federal shipping guidelines. A separate letter or phone call to the crime laboratory should be made, advising that a package is in transit; this letter should also describe the object being transmitted and the desired examination. The crime laboratory can then be on alert for the package, and the number of persons handling the package can be limited.

PREPARATION OF PHYSICAL EVIDENCE FOR USE IN COURT

Much of the impact of physical evidence can be lost if the manner in which it is exhibited is not well planned. Many people are reluctant to touch evidence items, such as a bloodied object or a weapon, and, consequently, the jurors pass up the opportunity to examine the objects fully as they are introduced in court. Some thought should be given to placing the various objects in suitable containers with transparent tops or sides. This way, the jurors can freely pass the object from one to another with little apprehension about holding or inspecting the object. Weapons should be placed in a box or mounted on a board, and, though a fatal bullet may appear perfectly clean, there are those who prefer not to touch something that has brought about the death of a human being. The projectile should be laid on cotton and placed in a small plastic box for the jurors' examination. A plaster of paris cast of a shoe track that has dirt and debris still on it, and the shoe that is alleged to have made the track, should be placed in a container for better inspection by the jury.

With the use of a little ingenuity and planning, physical evidence can be most effectively displayed to the jury and its use as evidence greatly enhanced. Physical evidence emphasizes and substantiates an officer's testimony. In all jurisdictions, jurors take the physical evidence with them while deliberating to enable them to recall the testimony of the investigating officer better and to have it at hand for consideration.

GRUESOME OBJECTS

Often, the physical evidence collected at the scene of a crime, particularly in murder cases, is gruesome or repulsive. Consequently, the courts seek to avoid unduly prejudicing the jury against the defendant, and most judges conduct the balancing test of FRE 403 to avoid unnecessarily exhibiting gory objects that may "inflame the jury and excite their emotions."[1] FRE 403 states that relevant evidence may be excluded "if its probative value is substantially outweighed by a danger of one or more of the following: unfair prejudice, confusing the issues, misleading the jury, undue delay, wasting time, or needlessly presenting cumulative evidence." The court weighs the importance of the gruesome object to the prosecution against the effect the evidence will have on the jury. The evidence will be admitted unless the prejudice against the defendant is substantially greater than the value of the evidence to the jury in determining the outcome of the case. Therefore, the mere fact that some object may excite the jurors or cause them to recoil is not enough to exclude it from evidence.

Photographs of the Crime Scene or Corpses

In *State v. Thompson,*[2] the court stated:[3]

> Photographs of homicide victims are admissible at trial even if they are "gory, gruesome, horrible or revolting so long as they are used by a witness to illustrate his testimony and so long as an excessive number of photographs are not used solely to arouse the passions of the jury."

The principle stated in the *Thompson* case helps assure that prosecutors will be able to admit any gruesome evidence necessary to prove their case and that victims of the most gruesome murders will still be able to obtain justice.[4]

Gruesome photographs have been admitted to show the crime scene, including the physical layout of the murder location and the area where significant objects, such as the body, spent cartridges, bullet holes, and blood spatter, were found. These types of photographs can often help clarify testimony. Gruesome photographs of the body and/or the autopsy have been admitted to show the location of wounds as well as the extent of the injuries. For example, in a California case, a videotape of the victim was properly admitted into evidence. "The videotape was relevant in depicting the position of the victim's body in the tub—gagged, a pillow case secured over the head, and arms and legs bound behind the back—supporting the prosecution's theory that the defendant, contrary to the defense presented at the trial, had acted with malice and the intent to kill, and that the killing was deliberate and premeditated. The videotape also corroborated Officer Perkins's testimony describing the crime scene."[5]

In all jurisdictions, a gruesome photograph will be excluded if its probative value is substantially outweighed by its potential for unfair prejudice. The purpose of this rule is to prevent a conviction based solely on the violence and depravity of the crime because the jury has viewed graphic and gruesome photos of the victim's body or crime scene. Of all the jurisdictions, Utah law imposes a greater burden on the prosecution before a gruesome photograph can be admitted into evidence: "[T]he introduction of potentially prejudicial photographs of a corpse is generally inappropriate if the only relevant evidence they convey can be put before the jury readily and accurately by other means not accompanied by the potential prejudice."[6] In 2016, that court rejected the prior case law and fell in line with the almost universal view that the principles of Rule 403, the Utah version of which is identical to the FRE, govern.[7]

Videos of the Crime Scene or Corpses

Under FRE 1001(2), the term "photographs" includes still photographs, as well as video recordings and motion pictures. A properly authenticated video is generally admissible, within the discretion of the trial court, if it is relevant to the issues in the case. Under the same principles stated in the *Thompson* case, the question before the court is whether the video's probative value is substantially outweighed by its possible prejudicial effect. Crime scene videos are generally admissible if relevant to show motive, intent, method, malice, premeditation, or the atrociousness of the crime, even though photographs of the scene have also been admitted. As with photographs, however, the admissibility of crime scene videos challenged because of their alleged gruesome or inflammatory nature must generally be determined on a case-by-case basis by weighing their probative value against the danger of unfair prejudice. Hence, on a case-by-case basis, all jurisdictions allow videos into evidence even though they are claimed to be too gruesome, unless the potential for unfair prejudice substantially outweighs the probative value.[8]

PHYSICAL OBJECTS NOT PRODUCED IN COURT

There is no requirement that all physical evidence in a case must be produced or introduced into evidence. There is only the requirement that the defendant be afforded a fair trial. The prosecuting attorney has the final decision in determining which evidence will be presented, if at all, and how it will be presented. The prosecutor has several options in presenting information to the jury, even if a particular physical object is too large to bring into the courtroom or presents logistical problems, such as a courthouse ban on explosives or highly toxic chemicals.

Photographs, video recordings, constructed models, and witness testimony are traditional methods of introducing these objects. The proliferation of state-of-the-art computer technology has allowed physical objects to "come to life" before the eyes of the jury. In many jurisdictions, absent witnesses can be examined over closed circuit television in the courtroom.[9] Photographs from the crime scene can be projected upon a screen, and large-screen projection units can display video taken from the crime scene, in addition to displaying computer-generated graphics, such as flow charts, spreadsheets, and computer-aided sketches of the crime scene. Computer-generated animations can also be used to re-create the crime or accident scene.

These methods of presenting evidence of objects can require a substantial amount of time to prepare. The prosecutor, therefore, needs to determine which method of presenting the evidence will be most effective with the jury, and then allot the necessary time.

Courtroom demonstrations and experiments may also be used to depict facts or events. Such a demonstration is admissible as long as it is relevant, presents a reasonably accurate representation of the facts or events depicted, and aids the jury in understanding the matter depicted or the subject of the experiment. Demonstrations and experiments can be very effective, but they also can be very risky. Unless the demonstration or experiment has been well rehearsed, it can backfire. A famous example of a questionable demonstration is the prosecution's demand that O.J. Simpson try on a bloody glove in the presence of the jury in the first criminal trial against Simpson. Simpson made a convincing display of the difficulty of fitting his hand into the glove. His counsel, Johnny Cochran, later quipped, "If it doesn't fit, you must acquit." And the jury did just that.

VIEWING OF THE CRIME SCENE BY THE JURY

Photographs and videos of crime scenes are frequently displayed to jurors to enable them to understand and follow the testimony of the witnesses better. However, there are times when the jury goes to the scene of a crime to view the physical aspects of the location. This is usually done when it is anticipated that there will be a great deal of testimony regarding the crime scene and the judge believes the jurors will have a better understanding of the issues involved if they have viewed the scene. The trial judge has the discretion of allowing the jury to view the crime scene,[10] taking into consideration the time the viewing will take and the value of the viewing. If the jury will gain little more information through the viewing than can be accomplished through a series of photographs or videos, or if the scene has been materially altered and would mislead the jury, the judge will likely deny the viewing. In some states, the viewing is conducted under the supervision of a person appointed by the court to ensure there is no communication with the jury on any subject connected with the trial.[11] It is difficult, if not impossible, for a jury to erase a crime scene completely from their minds and, due to the harm that may be done and misconduct that may take place, a trial judge may be reluctant to permit a jury to view a crime scene.

The trial judge has control of how the viewing will be handled; he or she can answer questions posed by the jurors and asked of the attorneys.[12] Also, it is not required that the defendant be present at the viewing,[13] although, if comments are going to be made to the jury, such as pointing to certain features of the scene, the defendant's attorney must be present and the comments must be recorded.[14] If the defendant is present, though, the judge can order the defendant handcuffed or shackled.[15]

REVIEW AND APPLICATION

SUMMARY

(1) Authentication can be accomplished through (1) testimony of a witness who has firsthand knowledge; (2) a nonexpert who was familiar with a person's handwriting and did not gain the knowledge of the handwriting for the purpose of the litigation, such as a spouse or roommate;

(3) allowing the jury or an expert to compare the object to an example and decide its authentication; (4) distinctive characteristics and surrounding circumstances, such as sending a bill to an address and receiving payment from the bill; or (5) voice identification that can be learned firsthand or through a mechanical or electronic transmission, such as a television or an answering machine.

(2) The four general categories of physical evidence are fruits of a crime, instrumentalities of a crime, contraband, and evidence of a crime.

(3) The typical record of chain of custody, or possession, includes the person who initially observed the object, the possession of the object by the officer, transportation to the laboratory, possession by the laboratory technician, retrieval by another officer and transportation to police storage facilities, and final transport to court.

(4) An officer can do the following to identify an object positively in court as the one that the officer found at the crime scene:

    (a) The officer may keep the object in his or her complete and exclusive custody and control from the time it was found until it is presented in court.

    (b) The officer may maintain a complete and accurate record of the chain of custody.

    (c) The officer may mark the object in some distinctive manner, making it readily recognizable later.

(5) Typically, the tag should contain (1) the case number; (2) the name of the defendant; (3) the name of the victim; (4) the name of the person who found the object; (5) the date, time, and place where the object was found; (6) a brief description of the article (this is important in case the tag becomes detached from the object and because some objects cannot be recognized from appearance alone); (7) the signature of the law enforcement professional finding the object; (8) the person to whom the object was released and the reason for the release; (9) the date and time of the release; and (10) the ultimate disposition of the object—what will be done with the object if it is not used as evidence.

(6) It is advisable to place items of evidence in cartons or paper or plastic bags in order to prevent dirt, dust, and the elements from affecting their appearance. The cartons or bags should be sealed and marked with the proper identifying data on the outside of each package, from which the contents may be easily determined.

(7) FRE 403 states, "Although relevant, evidence may be excluded if its probative value is substantially outweighed by the danger of unfair prejudice, confusion of the issues, or misleading the jury, or by considerations of undue delay, waste of time, or needless presentation of cumulative evidence." The court weighs the importance of the gruesome object to the prosecution against the effect the evidence will have on the jury. The evidence will be admitted unless the prejudice against the defendant is substantially greater than the value of the evidence to the jury in determining the outcome of the case. Therefore, the mere fact that some object may excite the jurors or cause them to recoil is not enough to exclude it from evidence.

KEY TERMS

QUESTIONS FOR REVIEW

1. What are five examples of how authentication can be accomplished?
2. What are the four general categories of physical evidence?
3. What are the order and persons in a typical chain of custody?
4. What are the three methods an officer can use to positively identify an object in court as the one that the officer found at the crime scene?
5. What information should be placed in a typical tag?
6. How should items of evidence be packaged for long-term storage in an evidence locker?
7. What is the balancing test of FRE 403 for admitting gruesome objects into evidence?

THINKING CRITICALLY ABOUT EVIDENCE

1. Consider the crimes of rape, embezzlement, and car jacking. For each crime, make a list of (a) several sources of physical evidence and (b) examples of the four kinds of physical evidence that you would look for while investigating those crimes.

WORKPLACE APPLICATION

1. An officer responds to a "man down" call and discovers that the victim, lying in the middle of the road, was shot in a drive-by shooting. A crowd had gathered around the body, but it disperses upon the officer's arrival. Cars are still driving down the street. The officer, with the help of several other officers, cordons off the area, interviews witnesses, and searches for evidence. The officers discover that the vehicle containing the shooters grazed a parked car and knocked off its side mirror. The mirror frame is found lying in the road. Additionally, several shell casings are found, one run over by a car and two others undamaged, in the street. What type of information might be gained from these pieces of evidence? How will the officer ensure that the mirror frame and the casings can be authenticated when the officer is called to testify in court?

ETHICAL DILEMMA

1. An officer recovers a balloon full of tar heroin from a suspect during a drug bust. The officer books the item into evidence, forgetting to write his initials on the balloon. Two days later, the officer retrieves the balloon from the

evidence locker to take to the defendant's preliminary hearing and notices his mistake. The chain of custody log is complete and there are no breaches, but the officer knows it will be easier to prove the heroin's authenticity at the preliminary hearing, and ultimately at the trial, if his initials are on the balloon. No one else is aware that the officer forgot to initial the balloon. Should the officer initial the evidence? Explain your answer.

ENDNOTES

1. *See, e.g.,* United States v. Waloke, 962 F.2d 824, 829 (8th Cir. 1992).

2. State v. Thompson, 402 S.E.2d 386, 394 (N.C. 1991), quoting State v. Murphy, 365 S.E.2d 615, 617 (N.C. 1988).

3. *Id.* at 394. *See* generally M.C. Dransfield, Annotation, *Admissibility of Photograph of Corpse in Prosecution for Homicide or Civil Action for Causing Death,* 73 A.L.R. 2d 769 (1960 & Supp. 2018) (a collection of cases, the majority of which admit gruesome photographs of victims' corpses).

4. *See* 2 Handbook of Fed. Evid. § 401:7, text accompanying n.27 (8th ed. 2018).

5. People v. Sims, 853 P.2d 992, 1020 (Cal. 1993).

6. State v. Lefferty, 749 P.2d 1239, 1257 (Utah 1988), citing State v. Garcia, 663 P.2d 60, 64 (Utah 1983).

7. Met v. State, 388 P.3d 447, 469 (Utah 2016).

8. Danny R. Veilleux, *Admissibility in Homicide Prosecution of Allegedly Gruesome or Inflammatory Visual Recording of Crime Scene,* 37 A.L.R. 5th 515 (1996 & 2018 Supp.).

9. Annotation, *Closed-Circuit Television Witness Examination,* 61 A.L.R. 4th 1155 (1988 & Supp. 2004).

10. *See* People v. O'Brien, 61 Cal. App.3d 766, 780 (1976); State v. Cintron, 665 A.2d 95 (Conn. App. 1995); Harper v. State, 337 S.E.2d 117 (Ga. App. 1987).

11. *See, e.g.,* Cal. Penal Code § 1119, Fl. St. at § 918.05.

12. *See* People v. Mayfield, 928 P.2d 485 (Cal. 1997).

13. *See* Snyder v. Massachusetts, 291 U.S. 97 (1934) (defendant's due process rights are not violated if he or she is absent during the jury's viewing of the crime scene); Amazon v. State, 487 So. 2d 8, 10 (Fla. 1986); Valdez v. United States, 244 U.S. 432 (1917) (defendant's Sixth Amendment right to confrontation is not violated if he or she is absent during the jury's viewing of the crime scene if such rights were voluntarily waived).

14. *See, e.g.,* Arnold v. S. Carolina, 467 U.S. 1265 (1984).

15. *See* Woodards v. Cardwell, 30 F.2d 978, 982 (6th Cir. 1970), *cert. denied,* 401 U.S. 911 (1971); State v. Landrum, 559 N.E.2d 710, 724 (Oh. 1990); People v. Hardy 825 P.2d 781, 836 (Cal. 1992).

Design Element: ©Ingram Publishing

14 PHOTOGRAPHIC, RECORDED, AND COMPUTER-GENERATED EVIDENCE

CHAPTER OUTLINE

CHAPTER OBJECTIVES

This chapter examines the rules of evidence as they relate to visual and audio presentations in the courtroom. After reading this chapter you will be able to:

▶ Define the kinds of evidence included in the terms "writings" and "recordings" in the FRE.

▶ State the circumstances in which video and audio evidence may be used in court.

▶ Decide when to use a hard copy or a projected image in presenting evidence.

▶ List the various uses of photographic and recorded evidence.

▶ State the first rule of admissibility of photographic and recorded evidence.

▶ Determine when a gruesome photograph or video recording is likely to be admitted.

▶ State the second rule of admissibility of photographic and recorded evidence.

▶ Identify those witnesses who can authenticate a photograph or recording.

▶ List the three methods of authentication of photographs and recordings.

▶ List the data to be included on the crime scene identification card.

▶ State when a posed or reconstructed scene is acceptable.

▶ Identify the methods of presenting photographic or recorded evidence.

PHOTOGRAPHS, RECORDINGS, AND THE LIKE AS EVIDENCE

Early in the twentieth century, courts were often unwilling to accept photographs as evidence. Today, however, photographs are accepted as physical evidence as readily as a gun used in a murder or a knife used in an assault. Moreover, modern technology has generated a variety of forms of evidence that depict or record both sounds and images and that are readily admitted as evidence on the same basis as photographs. Included in this category are scanned copies, photocopies, motion picture films, video and audio recordings, X-rays, computer-generated images projected on a screen or printed onto paper, and all manner of digitally produced media.

Photographs, films, video recordings, and digital recordings of the scene of a crime or accident are indispensable as a means of preserving such evidence in the event of deterioration or alteration of the scene. The prosecution in a criminal case routinely introduces at trial still photographs or videos of the crime scene. Similarly, recorded audio and video preserve actions or spoken words and are especially effective in contradicting claims made by parties and witnesses at trial. For example, in the first O.J. Simpson criminal trial, the prosecution used Simpson's fitness video to contradict his claim that he suffered from a debilitating arthritic condition.

The FRE have defined photographic and recorded evidence in nonexclusive language in order to allow the most scientifically advanced forms of evidence. Additionally, since tangible evidence can be substantive (real) evidence or demonstrative evidence, photographic and recorded evidence falls within both categories. Thus, such evidence can be used to aid the jury in understanding the circumstances and can be used by the jury to decide a question of fact in a case.

FRE 1001 defines **writings and recordings** as "letters, words, or numbers, or their equivalent, set down in any form [for writings] . . . [or] recorded in any manner [for recordings]." **Photographs** "means a photographic image or its equivalent stored in any form."

To introduce a photograph or recording in evidence, certain legal steps must be followed: for example, showing relevance, laying the foundation, and satisfying the best evidence rule. Because of these requirements, and because of the importance of audio and visual aids in the trial of a case, especially a criminal case, this entire chapter is devoted to this subject. Describing the techniques of photography, videography, and computer-generated imaging is beyond the scope of this text. The discussion, therefore, will be confined to the rules of evidence as they apply to the introduction of audiovisual evidence offered as substantive evidence or to aid the jury in understanding the case.

Prints Versus Projected Images

Prints and projected images are readily admissible when used to illustrate testimony. Furthermore, photographs, slides, films, videos, and projected computer-generated images rarely cause difficulty when being qualified for use at trial, or, as it is called, authenticated and identified. In other words, laying the foundation for such evidence is generally easy to accomplish. Visual aids will be admitted when they enable the judge or jury to better understand the evidence

WRITINGS AND RECORDINGS
Letters, words, or numbers, or their equivalent, set down in any form for writings or recorded in any manner for recordings.

PHOTOGRAPHS
Photographic images or their equivalent stored in any form.

presented during trial. Photographs, as well as videos and computer output, may be used as either substantive evidence or demonstrative evidence. If the visual aid is used by the jury in deciding facts, such as the number and location of wounds, then the visual aid is used as **substantive evidence**. On the other hand, if the visual aid is used solely to illustrate testimony given by a witness, then the visual aid is demonstrative evidence only. This distinction is important because if photographs, slides, videos, films, and computer output are classified as demonstrative, they will be admitted with a minimum of foundation, and even if not totally accurate in every detail. As long as the pictorial image will assist the jury in understanding the testimony of a witness or will illuminate an idea, the judge has discretion to allow the jury to see the demonstrative aid.

Many courts distinguish between photographs used as "pictorial testimony" and photographs admitted on the "silent witness" theory. When a photograph is used as **pictorial testimony**, that is, used to illustrate a witness's testimony, a sponsoring witness must testify that it is a fair and accurate representation of the subject matter, based on that witness's personal observation. However, photographs or videos, taken by an automatic camera with no operator present may be introduced to document the events recorded under the **silent witness** theory. When a photograph or video is offered as a silent witness, for example, an image from a video camera at an automated teller showing someone tampering with the teller, the video is admissible as evidence of the events without a sponsoring witness, since, in fact, there is none. A witness must simply testify as to how the equipment works and that the video was removed from the equipment and is from the date and time in question.

The advantages and disadvantages of using projected images rather than hard copies should be considered before deciding on which version to use at trial. It is often necessary for counsel and the judge to discuss an exhibit before it can be shown to the jury. Each side is entitled to view all visual aids offered in evidence by the opposition before the visuals may be admitted. In a sidebar discussion with both attorneys, the judge decides whether there is some reason to keep the evidence from the jury. If the judge decides not to admit the exhibit, the jury will never hear the discussion or see the visuals. If the exhibit is a projected image or is otherwise displayed in full view in the courtroom, the jury must be excused or some other procedure followed so that the images are not shown in the jury's presence. Such problems can be avoided by having small prints made of the projected images that are going to be used, thereby preventing jury exposure during the discussion on admitting the exhibits. The advantage of using projected images rather than prints is that the large images on the screen can be viewed by the entire jury at once, whereas prints must be viewed individually by jurors. Generally, the preferable course is to have both projectable images and prints made, thus avoiding some of the difficulties that may arise when such evidence is used.

Videos

With the growth of video technology, officers have increasingly used video in all aspects of law enforcement, and courts have readily admitted such evidence at trial. Since video evidence falls under the heading of photographs, all rules that apply to

SUBSTANTIVE
EVIDENCE
Evidence used to decide the existence or nonexistence of a fact.

PICTORIAL
TESTIMONY
Photographic evidence used to illustrate a witness's testimony.

SILENT WITNESS
A photograph, film, or video that has been taken by an automatic camera with no operator present and introduced to document an event.

photographs also apply to videos. Courts uniformly agree that the question of the admissibility of video evidence is a matter of discretion for the trial court.

Photocopy, X-Ray, and Computer-Generated Output

Though these images may require slightly more effort to authenticate, forms of "high-tech" evidence, including computer-generated output, X-rays, and photocopies, are also held to the same standards of admissibility as videos and photographs. Computer-generated reproductions, summaries, and models of complex undertakings have gained acceptance in the courts, provided that the evidence is relevant, is not hearsay, and is supported by a proper foundation. Computer simulations also can be used in re-creating a crime or an accident scene. Such simulations can attract and fix the attention of the jury and may be more effective than a mundane lecture by a witness.

X-ray plates or negatives may be displayed to the jury, although interpreting an X-ray usually requires testimony by an expert. On the other hand, a copy created by a photographic or other reproduction method, such as xerography (commonly referred to as a Xerox copy), is admissible to the same extent as an original. Thus, a properly authenticated, relevant Xerox or photocopy of a document, photograph, or diagram will be readily admitted into evidence.

A wide variety of forms of demonstrative evidence and visual aids exist, and the number of variations continues to increase as computer and electronic technology continues to advance. However, the traditional photograph continues to be used frequently, most likely because photographs are still simpler to produce than images created using other high-tech methods. And with the advent of smartphones with built-in cameras of rather high quality, photos taken by such means abound.

Photographic, recorded, and computer-generated evidence has an extremely wide variety of uses. Such evidence can be used

1. to show the scene of any incident, including the crime scene;
2. to demonstrate a theory as to how events occurred or might have occurred;
3. to record the behavior of a party or witness;
4. to document surveillance of an individual;
5. to record police lineups, identification procedures, and the act of identification itself;
6. to record activities of those being investigated for driving under the influence, including the administration of field sobriety tests;
7. to record interviews of suspects, victims, or witnesses;
8. to record depositions or to preserve testimony;

FYI

The best evidence rule requires that, to prove the content of a writing, recording, or photograph, the original is usually required. However, an "original" of a photograph includes the negative or any print made from the negative, according to FRE 1001(d). Moreover, FRE 1003 states that, in most cases, a "duplicate is admissible to the same extent as an original." A duplicate, as defined in FRE 1001(e), is a "counterpart produced by a mechanical, photographic, chemical, electronic, or other equivalent process or technique that accurately reproduces the original."

In other words, mechanically or electronically reproduced copies of writings, photographs, videos, motion pictures, audiotapes, and computer images are all admissible to the same extent as the original form of such materials.

©South_agency/E+/Getty Images

Photographs of murder scenes often assist the jury in arriving at a decision in a case.

9. to record criminal confessions; and
10. to record or generate crime re-enactments and accident re-creations.

Clearly, this list is not exclusive. The potential uses of such evidence can be of extraordinary help to the officer in seeing that his or her work does not simply end with the arrest but culminates in a conviction.

The Rise of Technology

By the end of the 1980s, the technological revolution had reached the point at which computers, VCRs, Xerox, and photocopy machines had become commonplace in the office and in the home. Now, DVD players, MP3 players (such as iPods, iPhones, and Androids), digital recorders, laptop computers, smartphones that take pictures, and multipurpose PDAs that function as a computer, phone, and camera are all readily available. This technology is so pervasive that labeling it high-tech almost seems inappropriate. As the United States Supreme Court said in its smartphone case of *Riley v. California*,[1] ". . . modern cell phones . . . are now such a pervasive and insistent part of daily life that the proverbial visitor from Mars might conclude they were an important feature of human anatomy." Indeed, as early as 1980, the rules governing civil trials were changed to accommodate the extensive use of videotaping of deposition testimony. As computer technology advanced during the 1980s, so did acceptance of computer output as evidence in the courtroom. The computer as a method for displaying evidence has become commonplace in the courtroom, with one of its most useful aspects being the ability to create graphics easily. With the advent of computers in court, charts, diagrams, and maps can be created quickly, cheaply, and more accurately then ever before. Also, mass storage drives and disks in computers, not to mention plug-in thumb or flash drives, have the capacity to store photographic-quality images, full sets of documents in digital format, and both video and audio digital presentations. These materials can be organized utilizing sophisticated software programs for presentation in the courtroom, where they may be projected or printed on paper or manipulated in a variety of ways to enhance the effect on the judge and jury.

As long as a complete foundation is laid for the introduction of such high-tech evidence, it will usually be found admissible. First, the evidence must be relevant. In deciding whether the photograph, video, or other items of evidence are relevant and admissible, the judge must balance the relevance of the evidence against any potential the evidence might have to unfairly prejudice the jury. Second, the evidence must be authenticated in order to establish its source and accuracy. Finally, the evidence must not violate the hearsay or some other exclusionary rule. The requirements of relevance and authentication, both of which may be called **foundation**, will be discussed in the following paragraphs as they relate to photographic, recorded, and computer-generated evidence.

No law enforcement professional should minimize the value of photographs or video recordings. The comments to the FRE state that photographs, charts, and diagrams may be used even if a fact is not disputed. Therefore, if one has the choice of whether to take many photographs rather than just a few, or to shoot more video rather than less, one should always err on the side of producing too much evidence.

FIRST RULE OF ADMISSIBILITY— FOUNDATION FOR RELEVANCE

Photographic or recorded evidence, to be admissible, must have some nexus, or connection, with the facts of the case. In other words, the evidence must be relevant. Showing relevance is the first step in laying a foundation for the admission of any item of evidence. As stated in preceding chapters, the rule of **relevance** requires only that the evidence have any tendency to make the existence of any fact of consequence more or less probable than it would be without the evidence. The operative language is "any tendency." The evidence need only help make the fact *somewhat* more or less probable. Further, since in most states the fact to which the evidence is directed need not be in dispute, illustrative evidence is universally offered and admitted. This is so even if the fact illustrated or amplified is proven by other evidence, even eyewitness testimony. Such illustrative evidence may be admitted either to serve as background, to aid the jury in understanding the facts illustrated or represented, or to depict actual objects, persons, relationships, or events. The principle that a picture is worth a thousand words usually prevails over attempts to keep these forms of evidence from the jury.

The next step in the foundational inquiry is the **balancing test**, sometimes referred to as **legal relevancy**. Even if the photograph or video is relevant, the judge may decide it should not be admitted into evidence if its probative value is substantially outweighed by the danger of unfair prejudice, confusion of the issues, or the chance of misleading the jury. The judge might refuse to admit the evidence based merely on the fact that he or she thinks it would take up valuable time. Or the judge might feel that the evidence could confuse the jury and find it inadmissible for that reason. If demonstrative, such evidence must be carefully presented, so that it enlightens the jury without overwhelming them or inflaming their passions. When the video, photograph, or computer animation is used to prove the existence of an object or

FOUNDATION
The requirements of relevance and authentication, which must be met for admission of an item of evidence.

RELEVANCE
A showing that an item of evidence has any tendency to make the existence of any fact of consequence more or less probable than it would be without the evidence.

BALANCING TEST, OR LEGAL RELEVANCY
The requirement that relevant evidence not be admitted if its probative value is substantially outweighed by the danger of unfair prejudice, confusion of the issues, or misleading the jury.

a scenario, rather than as background information or as a visual aid, the potential for unfair prejudice is even greater. For example, if a jury is to use the photograph or video to determine a factual issue, such as the likelihood that a particular knife caused the wounds that killed the victim, the relevance of the photo or video is very great, but so is the potential for the jury to have an emotional reaction. This does not mean the judge should keep the photo or video from the jury. However, the judge must decide whether, in that case, the jury can be expected to decide the fact fairly if they look at the photo or video.

A further distinction in the context of balancing for unfair prejudice is that of color photographs versus black-and-white photographs. Since a color photograph is intrinsically more vivid than a black-and-white photograph, it may tip the balance against admissibility. The gruesome nature of the crime may become more pronounced through the color photograph, inflaming the jurors and preventing them from rationally considering all the evidence. Thus, black-and-white photographs may save the evidence from exclusion in certain situations if used instead of colored photographs, slides, or videos.

Gruesome Photographs and Videos

An example in the context of the balancing test is a photograph of a murder victim or of a person who has been subjected to aggravated assault. The mere fact that a photograph may be unpleasant or gruesome to look upon does not make it too prejudicial so as to be inadmissible. By its very nature, the more gruesome the crime, the more gruesome the photographs that will be admitted. (See the discussion of gruesome images in Chapter 13.)

For instance, the photograph may be so relevant that the danger of unfair prejudice is outweighed by its probative value and hence is admissible. Relevant photographs, despite their gruesomeness and potential for prejudice, "generally will be admitted when they tend to prove such things as the existence of a crime, the cause of death, the number and location of the wounds, the manner in which they were inflicted, the amount of force used, the willfulness of the act in question, a person's identity, or to corroborate evidence concerning an unusual cause of death."[2] Further, the photograph may be the only piece of evidence; therefore, necessity would compel its introduction. All of these considerations are within

ON THE JOB

When making a visual record of a grisly scene, one should keep in mind the importance of minimizing the gruesomeness while not tampering with the scene. For example, if a color photo is so gruesome as not to be admissible, try converting the photo to black-and-white. Also, consider shooting the scene in both black-and-white and color to begin with. With today's digital image cameras and processing software, converting color to black-and-white is quite simple.

ON THE JOB

A mortal wound may be depicted in a photograph to aid the jury in determining the cause of death or whether a particular object was the cause of death. In such a case, the officer taking the photograph should take a close-up of the wound so as to reduce the gruesome impact by framing out the remainder of the corpse. Then, even if the photograph is in color, the judge is more likely to conclude that the probative value outweighs the potential for unfair prejudice.

the trial judge's discretion. If the photograph is so repugnant and its potential for inflaming the jury substantially outweighs its probative value, then the judge will rule to exclude it from evidence. The law enforcement professional must be aware of these considerations when investigating a crime scene. Overreliance on this type of evidence can easily lead to the loss of a case, should the judge rule the crime scene photographs inadmissible.

Nude Photographs

The mere fact that a photograph reflects a part of a human body that would not ordinarily be exposed to public view does not render it inadmissible. Be aware, though, that, depending on the qualities of the subject matter photographed, the prejudicial effect or the potential for confusing the issues within the trial may preclude the admission of the photograph. For example, the picture of a nude, mutilated body may overwhelm the jury's emotional stability while having such little tendency to make a fact of consequence, such as intent, more or less probable that the judge would undoubtedly exclude the photograph.

Some cautionary notes should be kept in mind when photographing nude persons. If a homicide is discovered and the victim is nude, the scene must be recorded just as it is. No effort should be made to cover any portion of the body before the scene is properly photographed or videoed from all angles. To preserve the dignity of the deceased or to prevent embarrassment to relatives, it may be advisable to cover exposed sex organs. Such photographs may be taken; however, photographs must also be taken of the crime scene just as it is discovered. These initial, unaltered photographs are quite important, as they may answer questions that arise during the trial. Also, the chance of destroying other physical evidence or tainting evidence generally while attempting to cover the body is always present, necessitating the taking of photographs as the scene is discovered.

If, on the other hand, the victim of a battery is alive and there are injuries on private portions of the body, certain precautions should be considered before photographing such a person in the nude. Seldom, if ever, is a victim of an attack permitted to display wounds on private portions of the body in the courtroom. If these wounds are to be viewed by the court and jury, it must be through photographs. Again, if the photographs are relevant to show the extent and location of injuries received and are not unduly prejudicial, they are admissible even though they are taken of a person in the nude. However, those images that are not pertinent to the case may be excluded for reasons of wasted time, cumulative evidence, and undue delay. Thus, it is best that the private areas of the body be covered.

In 1993, in the first case in which rock superstar Michael Jackson was under investigation for child molestation, one of the alleged victims indicated that Jackson had a unique mark on his penis. Investigators from the Santa Barbara County, California, Sheriff's Department and the Los Angeles Police Department obtained a warrant to search his body to determine whether the description of Jackson provided by his alleged victim was accurate. Jackson later described the search: "They served a search warrant on me which allowed them to view and photograph my body, including my penis, my buttocks, my lower torso, thighs and any other area that they wanted. . . . It was the most humiliating ordeal of my life, one that no person should ever have to suffer."[4] Jackson subsequently chose to settle the case out-of-court, and the photographs were never made public.

Obviously, the gender of the victim should determine the gender of the officer taking the photos. If the photograph is of an exposed body of a deceased person, then the gender of the photographer will be of less concern. In all other cases, if possible, the gender of the photographer should be the same as that of the person being photographed.

SECOND RULE OF ADMISSIBILITY— FOUNDATION FOR AUTHENTICATION

The primary purpose of the introduction into evidence of a photograph or recording is to give a clearer understanding of what happened in a particular case and to assist the jurors in arriving at the truth. Thus, according to the second rule of admissibility, the photograph or recording must be a true and accurate representation of the matter depicted. This is the requirement of the foundation of authentication or identification, which must be satisfied for the evidence to be admissible.

Accuracy Is Required

To achieve accuracy, a crime scene should be photographed or videoed as soon as possible after its discovery and before there have been any alterations to the scene. To avoid later confusion, the officer must keep an accurate record of all photographs, film, or video shot at the scene. If objects have been removed, positions changed, or other items added, the photograph or video will not be an accurate account of the scene and, being inaccurate, may be excluded. Although some change in the crime scene may not automatically lead to inadmissibility, if the change is such that the explanation of the change is more confusing than clarifying to the jury, the judge may refuse to admit such evidence showing the scene. This dilemma can be avoided through effective authentication—showing that, even though there are some differences, the item is still essentially an accurate depiction of the scene in all important respects. Authentication is not as complex as the term might lead one to believe. However, unless there are injured persons or animals at a crime scene that require immediate removal, no change should be made at the scene until it can be properly recorded by photograph or video.

Proof of Accuracy

There is no presumption that a photograph or recording is a true and accurate depiction of the scene contained within it. There must be a witness who can testify that the scene depicted or the sounds reproduced are true and accurate. All that is required is testimony from a witness that a photograph, a recording, an illustration, or computer output is what the person offering it claims it to be. Thus, authentication is simply an initial requirement that the photograph or video is a fair and accurate representation of the thing it endeavors to explain. That does not mean it must be perfect; it means that the audio or visual aid must not be confusing or misleading, even if it is not identical in every detail. Courts were once reluctant to accept in evidence any film or video that had been spliced, but they are now more receptive to admitting film or video in which irrelevant portions have been edited out.

Photographer Not Necessary to Verify Accuracy

ATTESTING WITNESS
A person who can authenticate or verify the accuracy of the evidence.

The **attesting witness**, that is, the person who can authenticate or verify the accuracy of the evidence, may be anyone familiar with the scene or the matter depicted. The witness does not have to be the photographer who took the picture or the operator of the equipment that recorded the event. The attesting witness need not have been present when the photograph was taken. The only thing necessary is that the witness must be familiar with the scene depicted in the photograph and be in a position to testify that it is an accurate representation of that which the evidence purports to depict.

Although anyone familiar with a crime scene may verify the accuracy of a photograph depicting the scene, the most logical person to verify its accuracy is the person who took it. Although generally it is not important how a photograph was taken, there are times when related questions arise. Some judges have permitted questions about how a photograph was taken, the conditions under which the picture was made, and the operation of the equipment that the photographer used. Such questioning is usually allowed under the contention that it is necessary to establish the accuracy, or lack thereof, of the photograph. When such questions are permitted, the photographer may be the only one who can supply the answers.

MYTH ►	◄ FACT
Only the person who took a photograph, shot a video, or recorded a conversation can authenticate the photograph, video, or audio recording.	Anyone who can testify with knowledge as to the accuracy of the contents of a photograph, a video, or an audio recording is qualified to authenticate such evidence.

ON THE JOB

The professional who shoots the photographs or videos at a crime scene should record the following in personal notes and in the police report:

1. the equipment and procedures used;
2. the rationale for each choice and procedure; and
3. the conditions at the time the photograph or video was shot.

It may be months, or even years, before testimony regarding the evidence is required, and recollecting details after so long may be difficult.

Generally, however, the method and equipment used in taking the photograph are of little or no consequence. There is no legal requirement that any particular type of camera be used. It matters little whether the photograph was taken with an inexpensive, disposable camera or an elaborate, professional model on film or on disk. The main requirement is that the photograph should be an accurate representation. In general, better cameras provide more detailed photographs, but distortions can occur regardless of the equipment used.

Videos and computer-generated output also require testimony to demonstrate reliability and accuracy; usually, anyone who can attest to the fact that the depiction is fair and accurate will suffice. If a computer-generated reconstruction is used, testimony to qualify the hardware and software used may be necessary, as would be testimony to demonstrate the reliability of the data used. Such complex authentication often requires expert testimony. Evidence that is simply demonstrative, however, may only require a witness who can testify that the evidence is fair and accurate and will either aid a witness in giving testimony or aid the jury in understanding testimony.

Photographer Need Not Be an Expert

There is no legal requirement that the photographer or videographer have any particular amount of experience in photography or filmmaking for the evidence to be admissible. An expert photographer or videographer is more likely to get a better product under adverse conditions than an inexperienced one, but the important thing is the accuracy of the photograph or video and not the experience of the person who operated the equipment. Remember, it is the veracity of the witness testifying to the accuracy of the photograph or video that is of greatest importance. Sometimes, however, depending on the circumstances, additional proof that the operator was experienced and the camera or video equipment was in good working order might be required by the trial judge. Such evidence may also be persuasive to the jury.

If, however, the evidence is computer-generated output or an X-ray, the operator will usually be an expert or someone with special knowledge of the equipment being used. Since such equipment is inherently complex, the operator will usually be someone with special training and will have to be qualified before being allowed to authenticate such high-tech data or computer-generated evidence.

A nonexpert witness who has taken a photograph or made a video should not attempt to provide a technical explanation of the photographic or videographic process. Technically, the witness need only testify that the scene is accurately depicted. Even qualified witnesses need not answer technical questions concerning shutter speeds, refractions, and other esoteric subjects, unless they are being qualified as an expert witness. If such a line of questioning is objected to, the judge will usually direct that it be discontinued. Normally, the judge will admit or reject photo or video evidence for reasons other than the experience and qualifications of the operator.

Even experienced photographers will usually avoid being qualified as a photographic or videographic expert. This is not often necessary for the photographs or videos to be introduced into evidence. The more technical and complex the testimony becomes, the more likely the judge or jury will discount it. Also, the professional may be placed in an embarrassing position, should the photographs be ultimately rejected. This does not mean that the prosecuting attorney may not show that the professional has considerable experience in photography or video making when attempting to impress the jury with the weight of the evidence; however, there is a vast difference between proving ability in photography and filmmaking and qualifying a witness as an expert.

Frequently, a law enforcement professional will verify the accuracy of a photograph or video by stating that he or she knows that it is an accurate reproduction of the crime scene because he or she took the picture. Or the professional may testify that he or she was present when the picture was taken and that the photograph fairly and

MYTH ▶   ◀ FACT

MYTH	FACT
Because of the ease with which digital images can be manipulated, a digital image or recording must be proven, by some special witness, not to have been altered. The actual photographer or recorder must testify and say that he or she produced the image or recording without tampering with it.	Anyone can lay the foundation to admit an image or a recording merely by testifying that it is what it is claimed to be and fairly and accurately represents the scene or records the images or sounds. Even though alteration is possible, it is up to the jury to decide, if the claim is made, whether the witness attesting to accuracy should be believed. It might, in some cases, enhance credibility for chain of custody evidence to be introduced, but it is not required by the law.

accurately depicts the scene. However, at times, the person who took the photograph will be unable to attest honestly that the photograph or recording is accurate, simply because the person does not remember taking the photograph. To avoid this situation, the law enforcement professional must ensure that he or she can identify the photograph or recording later. This may be done in one of three ways. First, the photographer may maintain complete possession of the photograph or recording until it is produced in court. Second, the photographer may maintain a chain of custody, or possession, of the photograph or recording. Third, the photographer may place some identifiable object within the scene depicted.

Foundation by Chain of Custody, or Possession

Aside from a witness testifying to its accuracy, another method of authenticating a photograph or recording is to present evidence showing that the photograph or recording has been in the constant custody, or possession, of one or more persons and that the evidence is in the same condition as it was originally. This showing of **chain of custody** was discussed in Chapter 13. This method for laying the necessary foundation is especially helpful when the photograph cannot be easily identified or when the potential for interference with the evidence is present. When the photograph, video, or X-ray can be easily identified, then testimony by a witness as to its accuracy is normally sufficient. Most photographs and videos today are produced digitally on some form of media that can be logged in for maintenance. In such case, the disk, flash card, or other memory media may be held for chain of custody purposes.

FYI

Laying a foundation to identify an object as the thing it is claimed to be rarely poses any problems. If the object is unique or is made unique, then most identification difficulties will be bypassed. For this reason, when a law enforcement professional marks an object, including photographs, with his or her initials, the date, or another distinctive characteristic, the object is no longer fungible with other, similar objects and can be readily identified both in-court and out-of-court. If the item is different enough, then no continual possession or chain of custody may be required to lay the foundation for identification.

Foundation by Distinctive Characteristic

Perhaps the most practical means of identifying a video or photograph as the one the professional took is to place an object with a **distinctive characteristic** within the crime scene before shooting the photograph or video. Placing an object in the scene may seem contrary to the admonition about taking a photograph of a crime scene before any changes are made to the scene. If, however, the recognizable object is intelligently selected and carefully placed within the camera range, no difficulty should be encountered in having the photograph admitted in evidence. The object placed in the scene should be clearly placed there for identification purposes and not be something that may be confused with a part of the crime scene. The object itself will create a distinctive characteristic within the crime scene, thereby identifying the video or photograph as the one the officer shot.

In placing an object in the crime scene for identification purposes, four matters must be considered: (1) What should be used? (2) Where should it be placed? (3) What identification data should be included? (4) Should measurement devices be placed at the scene?

What Should Be Used for Identification Purposes

It is very helpful, when preparing to photograph or video record a scene, to place in the frame an **identification card** to indicate details of what is shown. It should be obvious to the viewer that such an object is for identification purposes only and is not a part of the crime scene itself. When the photograph or video is taken close to the scene or article (for example, a footprint), a small, 3-by-5-inch card with proper notations on it may suffice as an object for identification purposes. A business card giving the law enforcement professional's name and department placed in the close-up scene would also be acceptable.

Where the Object Should Be Placed

The identification card should be strategically placed in the scene photographed or recorded. The photographer should be particularly careful when the scene must be searched for evidence because any intrusion into the scene for purposes of placing the identification card or other object may result in evidence being tainted or destroyed. It is not necessary that the identifiable object be placed in the center of the picture. The preferred practice is to place the identification card or object within camera range in either the lower right- or left-hand corner. Even if the card or object is slightly out of focus, it will not affect the identification of the photograph or video. Also, the card or other identifiable object should be carefully placed within the scene to avoid a possible allegation that it is hiding some detail of the crime scene. Such a problem can be avoided by first photographing or recording the scene at a distance and incrementally moving forward in order to show greater detail, advancing the identification card into the scene as additional photographs are taken. Under no circumstances should identification information be added digitally after the photographs have been taken. No matter how innocent, a response to the question "Did you add any information to the photograph after you left the scene?" could result in the photograph being inadmissible or could shed doubt on the accuracy of what was depicted.

What Data Should Be Included on the Identification Card

The identification data written on the card placed in the crime scene should be kept to a minimum. Actually, all that is necessary is enough information to identify the card or object as the one the professional placed in the scene. Keeping in mind the original purpose of this card, to facilitate identification of the photograph or video, all that is necessary is the officer's handwritten initials on the card or object. The professional may also include the date, the time, and the case number, if known, on the card or object. Any additional information may lead to problems for the professional at the time of trial.

If the exact time cannot readily be determined, it is proper to record the approximate time. Accuracy in recording data is the guiding rule, but an approximation is allowable if an exact reading is impossible. Usually, the time of day has little or no value as far as a video or photograph is concerned. Testimony to an approximate time is normally more than satisfactory. Many cameras have a time stamp automatically imprinted on the film or recording at the option of the user. In such a case, the photographer or videographer should be certain that the timer is set properly; if it is not, the time should not be imprinted. Inaccurate time stamping can cause substantial difficulties at trial, especially if a clock within camera range or other evidence in the case shows a different time. For example, in the first O.J. Simpson criminal trial, the videotape of Simpson's bedroom, failing to depict a pair of socks the prosecution claimed were present in the bedroom at that time, had a time stamp, which the camera operator testified was incorrect. This raised a question of whether the socks, which contained blood, were planted. This discrepancy led to great difficulties in substantiating the prosecution's case and allowed the defense to buttress its argument that the evidence was tampered with or otherwise tainted.

Including any statement on the card or object about the kind of crime involved could prove disastrous, since the actual charge for which the defendant is tried may not be the one initially indicated. For example, consider a situation in which the word "suicide" has been included on the data card, but the death is later determined to be a homicide. Photographs or video marked with the word "suicide" would then have to be offered as evidence in the trial of the defendant for murder. Such a mistake does not render the evidence inadmissible, but it does create a needlessly embarrassing situation for an officer and could result in confusion at trial. Another example of this type of blunder is a set of crime scene photos with the notation "robbery-rape" written on the identification card within the photographs, but the accused is later tried only for robbery. Because any reference to an uncharged rape could inflame the minds of the jury, the photographs might be excluded from evidence.

Numbering on the photographs taken at the crime scene, placed there either by criminalists or by the officers taking the photographs, can also lead to unnecessary problems. Should all the photographs not be produced in court, the defense attorney will be able to make an issue of the seemingly missing evidence. As a practical matter, there is no legal rule requiring that all physical evidence or all witnesses who have some knowledge of the case be produced during a trial. In most instances, a photographer will take more photographs than are necessary, attempting to ensure that the scene is photographed from all angles or to ensure that the equipment has not malfunctioned. Such circumstances can, of course, be easily explained. Also, should the issue arise, the additional photographs could be produced, placing an even greater emphasis on the subject at issue. However, to avoid the placement of numbers in the photographs, the sequence of photos made can be recorded in the photographer's field notes. Also, contact sheets and prints of the negative strips can help record and document the photographer's progress through the crime scene.

Placement of Measurement Devices in the Scene

The size of an object, a hole, or an opening depicted in a photograph may be of particular significance. The most practical way to show size is to place a ruler or other standard measuring device near the object or opening photographed. Some departments have adopted a gummed tape upon which a standard measure in inches is printed. This device is particularly advantageous when small objects are to be photographed. In placing the measuring device beside any object, the device should be positioned such that there is some space between the object and the measuring device. This helps overcome any allegation that something was being hidden. Such a space need be only slight.

Also, there should be no advertising matter or other written data on the measuring device except for identification data, such as the officer's or criminalist's initials and the name of the department.

POSED PHOTOGRAPHS
AND VIDEO RECORDINGS

A crime scene should be captured by photograph or video as soon as possible after discovery and before any changes are made in it. However, there are times when a photograph or video cannot be taken before alterations are made in a crime scene or before objects are moved. When circumstances dictate, an effort can be made to reconstruct the scene as closely as possible to its original state. This is referred to as a "posed," or "artificially reconstructed," crime scene. For example, if a dead body has been removed, someone might assume the position of the body in the photograph. Similarly, if a gun has been moved at the crime scene, it can be replaced in its original position, as nearly as possible, for the photograph.

There is no rule stating that such a reconstructed video or photograph is inadmissible. Such evidence is, however, generally regarded with disfavor in light of a strong perception that posed pictures may mislead the jury. Questions may arise during the trial over the exact position of the victim's body or the exact location of the gun. When people, automobiles, and other objects are placed to conform to witnesses' descriptions of the original crime or collision, difficulties often result. Posed, or artificially reconstructed, scenes may be admitted when the positions of persons and objects are undisputed. However, if a posed photograph or reconstructed video portrays only the version of the facts supported by the testimony of the proponent's witness, then it will generally be inadmissible. The problem in such a situation is the tendency of the photograph or video to emphasize unduly only one side's testimony. This could result in the jury taking one party's reconstruction as the fact of what really occurred. Even worse, the jury might consider such conduct an attempt to tamper with evidence, holding it against the presenting party's case.

Nevertheless, there are times when only relative positions or locations of objects in a crime scene are of importance and a reconstructed scene filmed or recorded for this purpose, if properly explained, would be admissible. Someone who saw the original crime scene must still testify to the accuracy of the reconstructed scene. If a posed photograph or video is taken, and if the original object or an exact duplicate cannot be used, something entirely dissimilar can be used instead. This often helps avoid confusion on the part of the jury. For example, if there was a gun in the actual crime scene, and another gun of a different make or caliber is placed in the staged scene, the jury may have difficulty in distinguishing between the gun used in the crime and the one captured on film. If, however, a stick or other marker is used, the jury can quickly determine that it is the position of the object, not the object itself, that is important.

METHODS OF PRESENTATION IN THE COURTROOM

Photographic Prints as Evidence

Photographic prints, whether black-and-white or color, need not be of any particular size as a matter of law. However, the law enforcement professional should be aware that the jury must be able to examine the evidence easily; therefore, a large blowup of the photograph may be most useful. The generally accepted size is an 8-by-10-inch enlargement. This size print has certain advantages. It is large enough to bring out sufficient detail, it is easy for the jurors to handle, and it fits conveniently into the court file. Even more effective are overhead projections, using transparencies, video projection, or computer-assisted projection, onto a screen large enough for everyone in the courtroom to see. Such images may also be delivered to a monitor placed before the witness, jury, judge, and lawyers. Many courtrooms have equipment allowing such delivery of images. Presentation of images by projection is the preferred method, and most courtrooms will accommodate bringing in portable equipment if the courtroom does not have permanently placed equipment.

Demonstrative Diagrams, Charts, and Boards

If a print is to be used by a witness during testimony to point out or explain certain facts, such as fingerprint comparisons or blood trace evidence, the print should be enlarged to a size that can be readily seen by the jury as they are seated in the jury box. Perhaps the most practical method of doing this is to have the prints blown up to an appropriate size and attached to a large board, i.e., a demonstrative board. This will allow easy handling of the prints so as to place them in the optimal position for viewing by the jury. Explanatory notes may be attached, so that the jury can quickly decipher what each print is and what it relates to. The prosecutors in the nanny trial in which Louise Woodward was charged with homicide in the death of the baby she was attending made use of such demonstrative boards, which were used to depict trauma to the baby. In addition, blown-up images and demonstrative boards or computer-generated slide show presentations can be extremely practical when the jury must evaluate a comparison, such as that between a latent fingerprint and a known exemplar. Even in the case of fingerprint comparison, such a visual aid is effective, as the jury can see for themselves the similarities between a latent print and that of the accused. Although the jury may be completely unfamiliar with fingerprints, they are still able to appreciate the depicted similarities.

ON THE JOB

Not all trials can be supported by the resources used in high-profile cases. Nonetheless, the use of diagrams and other visual aids is critical to the effective presentation of the facts to the jury. Therefore, all law enforcement professionals should endeavor to create diagrams depicting the events from the inception of any investigation or report. A witness who can produce a diagram usable at trial is especially appreciated. A witness who can draw an effective, large-scale diagram should use that method, but the possibility of using overhead projectors to blow up images, or computers to generate images, should be considered as well.

Projected Images

Projected images are extremely helpful to present graphics and written words on a large screen. Transparencies are most commonly used with "overheads." Transparencies are see-through sheets with imprinted text or images, which are simply placed on the overhead projector and then projected onto a screen. A unique quality of transparencies is that the operator can write on the transparency or point to specific aspects of the transparency from the overhead projector.

In addition, images may be projected overhead from a variety of sources other than transparencies. Video cameras may be linked directly to a projector to transmit an image onto a screen in the courtroom. A computer may be used to transmit images from a video source or an image contained on a flash drive, CD, DVD, or hard drive. Furthermore, computer-generated animations can be projected onto overhead screens or onto a video screen in the jury box. Any of these projection methods achieve the same result. They give the jury a sense of the image depicted in the scene.

The televised trial of O.J. Simpson in 1994–1995 introduced the world to the "courtroom of the year 2000." In that case, Judge Lance Ito and attorneys Marsha Clark and Johnny Cochran repeatedly asked something called **ELMO** to carry out various tasks. They were referring to a sophisticated, integrated, computer-controlled projection system, which included a visual presenter made by ELMO Manufacturing, a company located in Chatsworth, California. The ELMO visual presenter is a top-lit video camera mounted on a pole, pointing down, that looks much like a photographic enlarger. It transmits the image it receives onto a monitor. "ELMO" is an acronym that stands for "Electronic Light Magnetic Optical." ELMO was only one of the many components of the advanced systems used in the Simpson trial. The courtroom equipment in Los Angeles County consisted of both hardware and software: two video disk systems (one for the prosecution and one for the defense); Microsoft's PowerPoint presentation software program; two Invizn presentation systems (a proprietary computer-based document presentation system, one each for prosecution and defense); one ELMO visual presenter; one videocassette recorder; one Sony Video Printer (a special printer that prints telestrated video to special paper); one Point Maker Telestrator; computer-controlled integration of all these inputs (using Interactive Presentation Solutions software); two 20" Sony monitors on the floor for four of the jurors; one 84" parabolic screen; one Marquee 8000 data projector; and monitors for Judge Ito, the witness, and the attorneys. All of the computer-generated signals, both video and data, were strung through a switcher that controlled the projector and monitors for the jury (one output) and monitors for the judge, witness, and counsel (another output). The output seen by the jury was also transmitted to the media and was controlled with a kill switch by Judge Ito. The controller system was put in place and operated by Trial Presentation Technologies of Culver City, California, at an estimated cost of about $500,000, which was donated to Los Angeles County by the company. The estimated cost of all equipment use and services by the court, prosecution, and defense was $1.5 million.[5]

Since the Simpson trial, the use of simpler devices, known as visual presenters or document cameras, has become common, if not widespread. A document camera is a device that resembles an overhead transparency projector. However, the document camera can project any object placed on its surface and can connect to other devices, such as computers. Whereas the ELMO and all its peripheral

ELMO
A computer-controlled projection system, including a visual presenter, for use in the courtroom. ELMO is actually the name of the company that created the system; the acronym stands for "Electronic Light Magnetic Optical."

equipment used in the Simpson trial were extremely costly, a document camera and video projector are comparatively inexpensive. Today's visual presenters, including ones marketed under the ELMO name, are very small devices that can be purchased for about $400 and fit easily on a desk.

Many courtrooms are outfitted with smart podia that link to computers, document cameras, video projectors, and video players, all within the control of counsel and the judge. This equipment can be utilized by integration into sophisticated programs enabling the lawyers to present evidence in a multimedia format. Even if a courtroom is not so outfitted, when a case is important enough, portable equipment can be brought into the courtroom to achieve the same result.

CONSIDERATION OF OTHER MATTERS

How Many Photographs Should Be Taken

The amount of video captured or the number of photographs taken for evidentiary purposes has no fixed number, nor are there any criteria for what should be captured on film. The video or photographs of a crime scene should thoroughly and accurately record all the information available. Undoubtedly, the more serious the crime committed, the more the crime scene should be recorded or photographed.

The documentation of crime scenes and crime scene investigations by video or digital recording has become a matter of routine for many police departments. In high-profile cases, the media may be present and recording much of the crime scene activity. Thus, it is prudent for the officer to make as accurate a record as possible of law enforcement activities to preserve the integrity of the scene and the evidence contained therein.

In a homicide case, it may be a good idea to include a scene of the general area where the homicide took place. If the homicide was committed in a residence, a photograph or video of the street in front of the house is often used advantageously during the trial. The exterior of the house itself should be filmed, as well as an overall shot taken of the room in which the homicide actually took place. A video and photograph should be taken of the body, showing the exact position in which it was found and its location in the room, and close-up shots should be taken of the body depicting the wounds. Further shots should be taken of all other pertinent objects that may have a connection with the crime, including possible entrances and exits.

In a traffic accident case, at least one picture should be taken in the direction in which each vehicle was traveling. A video or photograph should be taken showing the visibility of the drivers as they approached the point of impact. Close-up shots should be taken of the damage to the vehicles and of skid marks, if any. Skid marks may be recorded better from the direction opposite from which each vehicle was traveling. This is because skid marks are usually more pronounced nearer the point of impact and can be more clearly followed going against the line of tread.

Preparing Photographs, Videos, and Computer Output for Trial Use

Before going to court, the law enforcement professional who is going to testify should review the photographs, videos, recordings, and computer-generated evidence that the prosecution plans to introduce. The professional should make

©Guy Cali/Getty Images

A document camera, which can project any object placed on its surface, is a very versatile multimedia projection device in the courtroom.

certain all the evidence needed is available and that photographs have been properly printed, videos and other recordings properly edited, and computer output accurately portrayed.

It is permissible for the officer who will be asked to introduce photographs or a video in evidence to initial the tape cassette or disk or the back of the prints before their introduction. In fact, this initialing is advisable unless there is some identification within the video or photograph itself that will enable the officer to recognize the photographs or video readily on the stand. In the case of prints, no marks should be placed on the face of the photograph before it is shown to a witness on the stand. If it becomes necessary to point out something on the photograph by marking it, this should be done from the stand while testifying. "Retouching," or altering, a negative or a print renders the evidence inadmissible. This does not apply to editing irrelevant portions, done only at the direction of the prosecuting attorney. This does not imply that portions of a negative may not be cropped when an enlargement is made to bring out details. There is no legal requirement that every print must include the entire negative. However, it is recommended that one print of the entire negative be prepared, should there be an allegation of excluding or hiding evidence or of changing the appearance of a scene.

Photographic, Video, Software, and Equipment to Be Used

The kind of camera, lenses, video recording media, software, or equipment used is relatively unimportant in most law enforcement uses. In the case of computer-generated output, however, the accuracy of name-brand equipment and commercially available software may be verified more readily than little-known equipment and software. In fact, judicial notice may be taken of its accuracy. With respect to videos and photographs, the main objective is to get as good a representation of the thing photographed or recorded as possible. This can best be accomplished by standardizing the camera, video recorder, or memory media used. Through standardization, officers become familiar and proficient with the equipment.

X-RAY PHOTOGRAPHS

X-ray photographs fall within the definition of photographs under the FRE, but they require more in the way of introduction than do ordinary photographs. X-ray photographs involve a technical field and depict that which is not visible to the eye. These photographs must be introduced through an expert witness, usually the person who took the photographs. The competency of the witness, as well as the accuracy of the machine, will have to be established. Also, the procedure for taking the photographs may have to be explained. Usually, the X-ray photographs will have to be interpreted by another expert witness who is capable of reading them.

SUMMARY

(1) The FRE defines the terms "writings" and "recordings" as letters, words, or numbers, or their equivalent, set down in any form for writings or recorded in any manner for recordings.

(2) Video or audio evidence may be used by the jury in deciding facts as substantive evidence. Or such evidence may be used solely to illustrate testimony given by a witness as demonstrative evidence.

(3) If there is any question about an image's admissibility into evidence, the judge must decide that question before the jury can see the image. In such a case, a hard copy of the image is useful to present to the judge. Also, a hard copy is good to present to the jury for their individual viewing and to take into the jury room for deliberations. The advantage of using projected images is that the large images on the screen can be viewed by the entire jury at once.

(4) Here is a partial list of the uses of photographic and recorded evidence: (1) to show the scene of any incident, including the crime scene; (2) to demonstrate a theory as to how events occurred or might have occurred; (3) to record the behavior of a party or witness; (4) to document surveillance of an individual; (5) to record police lineups, identification procedures, and the act of identification itself; (6) to record the activities of those being investigated for driving under the influence, including the administration of field sobriety tests; (7) to record interviews of suspects, witnesses, or victims; (8) to record depositions or to preserve testimony; (9) to record criminal confessions; and (10) to record or generate crime re-enactments and accident re-creations.

(5) The first rule of admissibility of photographic and recorded evidence is that the evidence must be relevant.

(6) Relevant photographs or videos, despite their gruesomeness and potential for prejudice, will usually be admitted when they tend to prove such things as the existence of a crime, the cause of death, the number and location of the wounds, the manner in which they were inflicted, the amount of force used, the willfulness of the act in question, or a person's identity or to corroborate evidence concerning an unusual cause of death. When it is necessary to prove the manner of death or extent of injury in an assault case, even photographs or videos of nude bodies may be admissible over objection.

(7) According to the second rule of admissibility, the photograph or recording must be a true and accurate representation of the matter depicted.

(8) To authenticate a photograph or recording, the witness must be able to testify that the scene depicted or the sounds reproduced are true and accurate.

(9) The three methods of authentication other than by attesting witnesses are (1) maintaining complete possession of the photograph or recording until it is produced in court; (2) maintaining a chain of custody of the photograph or recording; and (3) placing an object with a distinctive characteristic in the scene depicted.

(10) The data that should be included on the identification card should be limited to that which is minimally necessary for authentication and identification, such as the officer's initials, the date, and perhaps the time.

(11) Although posed, or reconstructed, scenes are inadvisable, they may be acceptable when photographs or video cannot be shot before the crime scene is altered or objects are moved. The scene must be reconstructed as closely as possible to its original state.

(12) The methods of presentation include photographic prints; demonstrative diagrams, charts, and boards; overhead projectors and transparencies; and other projection devices in a high-tech courtroom.

KEY TERMS

QUESTIONS FOR REVIEW

1. What types of evidence are included in the terms "writings" and "recordings" in the FRE?
2. Under what circumstances may video and audio evidence be used in court?
3. What factors should be considered when deciding whether to use a hard copy or a projected image in presenting evidence?
4. What are the various uses of photographic and recorded evidence?
5. What is the first rule of admissibility of photographic and recorded evidence?
6. When is a photograph or video likely to be admitted even if it depicts a gruesome scene or a nude person?
7. What is the second rule of admissibility of photographic and recorded evidence?
8. Who can be called as a witness to authenticate a photograph or recording?
9. What are the three methods of authentication of photographs and recordings other than by an attesting witness?
10. What data should be included in the identification card placed at a crime scene for photographing?
11. When is a posed, or reconstructed, scene acceptable?
12. What are the various methods of presentation of photographic or recorded evidence in court?

THINKING CRITICALLY ABOUT EVIDENCE

1. A defendant is on trial for murder. The victim was stabbed to death with a serrated knife. A serrated knife, which the prosecution claims is the murder weapon, was found in the possession of the accused and has been admitted into evidence. The prosecutor wants to introduce a color blow-up of a photograph of the part of the victim's body bearing the wound, taken at the morgue during the autopsy, so that the jury can see that the wound was caused by the claimed murder weapon. The prosecutor also wishes to project the image of the photograph on a large screen in the front of the open courtroom. What do you think the judge will allow into evidence? Will the prosecutor be able to use the photograph, the projected image, or both?

2. In the case of a particularly heinous and gruesome crime, the prosecution may feel that the jury should see all the photos related to the crime to impress upon them the viciousness of the crime. Explain how this strategy could backfire for the prosecution.

WORKPLACE APPLICATIONS

1. You are the investigating officer in an armed robbery case. The victim has just attended a lineup, where she picked a suspect from a group of six individuals. You took a photograph of the persons standing in the lineup just at the moment the victim made the identification. Write a brief report of the event and describe what you would do to ensure that the photograph could be used in court to prove the identification and the authentication process.

2. You are the investigating officer at the scene of a homicide. The victim is lying naked on a bed, with a rope around her neck, apparently having died of strangulation. You are charged with photographing the scene. Make a list of photographs you need to take and how you will identify them later in court.

ENDNOTES

1. ___ U.S. ___, ___,134 S.Ct. 2473, 2484 (2014).

2. 2 Handbook of Fed. Evid. § 401:7, text accompanying n.27 (8th ed. 2018).

3. People v. O.J. Simpson, 1995 WL 350931, p. 15–16 (Cal. Super. Trans., June 6, 1995).

4. Los Angeles Times, December 23, 1993, p. 1, 1993 WL. 2239535.

5. The source of this information regarding the equipment and software used in the O.J. Simpson trial was Adam Matthew Ormond, Partner, Trial Presentation Technologies.

15 | HOW TO TESTIFY EFFECTIVELY

CHAPTER OUTLINE

The Law Enforcement Professional's Role

Problems of the New Professional: Notification to Appear

What to Do Before the Trial

What to Wear in Court

Where to Appear and What to Do

Conduct Before and During the Court Session

Conferring with the Prosecuting Attorney

Being Called to the Stand

On the Witness Stand

Voice and Grammar

Profanity and Vulgarity

Jargon

References to the Accused

Answering Questions on the Stand

When the Witness Forgets Testimony

Cross-Examination

After Testifying

Review Case After Verdict

Review and Application

CHAPTER OBJECTIVES

This chapter considers matters relating to the officer's appearance in court to testify. After reading this chapter you will be able to:

▶ Name the different methods used to notify a law enforcement professional to appear in court.

▶ Describe the appropriate clothing for law enforcement professionals to wear to court.

▶ Identify those people to whom the law enforcement professional should not speak during recesses.

▶ Explain what a law enforcement professional should do while testifying with respect to objections.

▶ State what a law enforcement professional should do when he or she does not remember the answer to a question asked.

▶ Explain what a law enforcement professional should do when asked an argumentative question on cross-examination that the defense attorney insists should be answered yes or no.

THE LAW ENFORCEMENT PROFESSIONAL'S ROLE

The law enforcement professional plays a key role in the successful prosecution of a criminal defendant. During the investigation of a crime, officers interview witnesses, preserve the crime scene, and collect physical evidence, all of which are essential in proving a defendant guilty beyond a reasonable doubt at trial. In some jurisdictions, criminalists or crime scene investigators perform some of these functions. Sometimes these investigators would like to avoid appearing in court and testifying–usually with good reason. They are called to court on their days off, required to cancel or cut their vacations short, or have to give up their precious hours of sleep to be in court. Also, many officers and other law enforcement professionals, like most witnesses, are apprehensive about appearing in court. Nonetheless, these witnesses must overcome all of these difficulties and do their best when this all-important final phase of the criminal process is at hand.

Most witnesses are nervous about testifying. Testifying in court is a new and strange experience for most people. Even people with the most outgoing personalities may feel conspicuous and uncomfortable on the witness stand. There is the potential of being embarrassed by cross-examination questions, contradicted by other witnesses, or unable to remember important details. Just the fact that the attention of the entire courtroom is focused upon the witness is enough to intimidate most people. The law enforcement professional is not immune from these worries, and a new officer may be especially apprehensive about his or her first few appearances as a witness. Even the most experienced witness may feel some tension when called to testify if a case has an unusual fact pattern or is difficult to prove, or if the defendant is very sympathetic. What the witness says on the stand and how it is said may make the difference between a conviction and an acquittal.

However, most fears can be eliminated by observing a few rules on how to testify effectively and convincingly. It is impossible to list everything a law enforcement professional should know to become a good witness or to explain every situation that may arise during the trial proceedings, but one very simple rule, the most important one, will eradicate most of a witness's worries. Testify truthfully. Even if an officer has failed to follow department procedures fully, being truthful is still the best course. Failure to own up to mistakes can lead to being tripped up on cross-examination and cause even more damage. The professional who tells the truth will not have to be concerned about being tripped up on cross-examination, being contradicted, or not having his or her testimony corroborated by other witnesses. The witness's role is to tell whatever he or she knows about the facts, and an officer who testifies truthfully, fully, and fairly about what he or she observed should have nothing to fear and should be comfortable in any courtroom setting.

PROBLEMS OF THE NEW PROFESSIONAL: NOTIFICATION TO APPEAR

A new law enforcement professional needs to know many basic, but important, details about testifying in court. For example, a novice officer may have several questions about being called to testify: What do I wear? Where do I appear?

What do I do when I get there? What do I take with me? These questions will be addressed in this chapter.

As pointed out in Chapter 5, prospective witnesses are usually notified that they are to appear in court by having a **subpoena** served on them. The subpoena tells them where and when to appear in court. There are several ways a law enforcement professional may receive notification to appear in court to testify. He or she may receive a subpoena, the same as any other witness. The subpoena will have the date, the time, the courtroom that the witness should appear in, and whether the witness is on-call or should make a personal appearance. Being **on-call** means that the person is not needed to appear personally in court unless called by the prosecutor. The witness should remain close to the courthouse, so that he or she can be there quickly if the prosecutor calls. When on-call, the witness should provide the prosecutor or court clerk with a phone, cell phone, or pager number where the officer can be reached when needed.

The defendant's name and case name should appear on the subpoena, allowing the professional to begin preparing for the case. The officer may be served directly with the subpoena or, if the department is large enough, through a subpoena control department. The subpoena control department accepts subpoenas for all the department's officers. The watch commander or supervisor and the officer are notified of the service. The supervisors can then rearrange the schedule to accommodate the officer's time in court.

The law enforcement professional may not receive a subpoena at all but may merely receive a call from the prosecutor, advising that he or she is needed as a witness in a particular case. Many prosecutors believe that the formality of having a subpoena issued for a law enforcement professional is unnecessary. The usual advantage of serving a prospective witness with a subpoena is that the subpoena is a court order demanding the presence of the person in court as a witness. This is not necessary with a law enforcement professional, as he or she will appear without being compelled. On the other hand, in heavily populated areas, prosecuting attorneys may find it convenient to have subpoenas issued for all witnesses, including law enforcement professionals. The prosecutors thus eliminate individual calls to the people involved and are less likely to overlook a necessary witness.

SUBPOENA
A court order demanding the presence of the person in court as a witness.

ON-CALL
A direction in a subpoena that states that the officer is not needed to appear personally in court unless called by the prosecutor. Such a direction requires that the officer remain nearby and readily available for a court appearance.

ON THE JOB

One of the best preparations for a new law enforcement professional who has never before testified is to attend a number of trials and observe others testifying. After just a few witnesses have been observed, what constitutes "good" testimony and "bad" testimony should become apparent.

WHAT TO DO BEFORE THE TRIAL

Upon receipt of notice to appear as a witness, one should do a number of things before the court date. While the prosecutor's office is preparing for trial, the law enforcement professional must give all the facts of the case to the prosecutor, even facts revealing weaknesses or problems in the case. All facts surrounding the execution of a search warrant, arrest, collection and analysis of evidence, and interrogation of the defendant should also be discussed with the prosecutor. It is dangerous to ignore portions of the case in the hope that the case can be successfully prosecuted without these facts coming out.

Next, the prospective witness should completely refamiliarize himself or herself with the facts of the case prior to trial. Usually, a considerable period of time elapses between the investigation and the related trial. The individual has usually investigated numerous other cases in the interim and will find it impossible to remember all the details that must be related during testimony unless the case file is reviewed. The officer should ascertain from the prosecutor just what he or she is expected to testify about. A new officer should discuss the case with his or her partner or superior officers, who will be able to give advice on how to present the facts and physical evidence effectively. If the officer, criminalist, or other law enforcement professional is going to testify about the collection of evidence or the analysis of physical evidence, the witness should be familiar with the test conducted as well as the specific results. At a minimum, an officer or a criminalist who may be qualified as an expert to conduct certain tests, such as blood analysis, fingerprint comparison, DNA testing, fiber content analysis, or soil testing, should review with his or her supervisor the types of questions that can be expected to elicit why the witness is qualified to run the tests and interpret the results.

If the professional is responsible for the introduction of physical evidence, he or she should check the evidence locker to make certain the evidence is available and should prepare it for proper presentation. Necessary arrangements should be made, so that the law enforcement professional is available on the trial date; nothing, including vacations, should interfere with being in court on the date and at the time scheduled. The officer may need to change shifts and make certain his or her superiors are notified of the subpoena, so that the officer's normal assignments are covered during the court time.

WHAT TO WEAR IN COURT

The moment a witness enters the courtroom, whether he or she is a law enforcement professional or not, the jury begins to make its appraisal of the person. Overall appearance—particularly the manner of dress—makes the first impression, and the first impression may be a lasting one that overshadows even the witness's testimony. The law enforcement professional should not handicap his or her testimony by wearing inappropriate attire to court.

The general rule is to wear to court what one wears to work. If the officer wears a uniform to work, then that is what he or she should wear to court. If the officer is a detective or other professional or in some other unit that does not require that uniforms be worn, then business attire is appropriate for court. Professionals who go to court on their days off may also choose to wear a suit instead of their uniform because they are going to court in their personal vehicles. Many prosecutors suggest that law enforcement professionals appear in court in civilian clothing rather than in uniform. Their suggestion is based on the reasoning that jurors tend to associate the officer in uniform with any traffic citations they might have received. To some jurors, the uniform and badge may represent an authority that they resent and could affect the weight given to an officer's testimony. The new officer should ask the prosecutor if he or she has a preference as to what the officer should wear; however, there is nothing improper about an officer wearing a uniform to testify. An officer should refrain from wearing a nightstick or baton in the courtroom and should remove a uniform hat or motorcycle helmet prior to entering the courtroom.

Many times, the law enforcement professional will not have a pretrial interview with the prosecutor. This is particularly true of misdemeanor trials and other minor offenses. The officer should take the initiative to seek out the prosecuting attorney and try to meet before testifying to discuss the case. This is especially true when there is some problem the attorney may not know about.

If one is going to appear in court wearing civilian clothing, both male and female witnesses should wear conservative business attire. Men should wear a white or solid-color dress shirt and a modest tie with a matching jacket. Women should wear a business suit or a conservative blouse and dress slacks or a skirt. Long hair should be pulled back neatly from the face, and the witness should avoid any flashy jewelry, such as dangling earrings or large necklaces. The witness should also avoid looking too casual. Sports clothing, jeans, shorts, open-collared shirts, and athletic shoes are inappropriate.

Whether in uniform or civilian clothing, the law enforcement professional should wear well-shined shoes and clothing that is clean and pressed. Pockets should not bulge with pencils, notebooks, and other items that may distract from testimony. A witness is not allowed to refer to personal notes on the stand unless an attorney approaches with notes from which to read. Therefore, witnesses should not take notes with them to the witness stand. If a witness in court appears casual, unkempt, or careless, the jury may assume the person's work to be of the same caliber and give little weight to his or her testimony.

WHERE TO APPEAR AND WHAT TO DO

When a witness receives a notice to appear in court, he or she is usually advised exactly where and when to appear. If the witness is to appear on the first day of the trial, he or she must go to the designated courtroom and wait for further instructions. If the trial of the case is continued, the judge will advise the witnesses that they are excused but are to return on a certain date. Generally, this is the only notice that witnesses will receive for the new appearance date. If the prosecuting attorney has told the witness that he or she does not have to appear until sometime after the trial has started, the witness should be in court at the appointed time and should notify the prosecutor of his or her presence. This can be done by advising the prosecutor when court is not in session or through the bailiff or court clerk after the court session has commenced.

In most instances, witnesses are excluded from the courtroom during a trial. This is to prevent one witness from hearing another witness's testimony and is known as the **rule on witnesses**, or the witness sequestration rule. Before going into the courtroom, the law enforcement professional should determine whether the witnesses have been excluded in order to comply with the judge's exclusion order. If the witnesses have been excluded and the officer goes into the courtroom and sits down, the officer may be severely reprimanded by the judge. Worse, the law enforcement professional's presence, unless discovered immediately, may be cause for a mistrial. The officer may be asked to wait in a room with other witnesses, in an officer's waiting room, or in the hallway outside the courtroom. It is important

RULE ON WITNESSES
The rule, often invoked by a trial judge, that witnesses be excluded from the courtroom during trial, so that one witness cannot hear the testimony of another.

An exception to the rule that sequesters witnesses is that a person whose presence is shown by a party to be essential to the presentation of its case may remain in the courtroom. In many instances, a law enforcement professional in charge of an investigation, especially in a complex case, may be permitted to stay in the courtroom and even sit at the counsel table to assist the prosecution. Under those circumstances, if the assisting officer is also a witness, the fact that the officer was present throughout the testimony of other witnesses is likely to be noted by opposing counsel. It is imperative for an officer in this situation to maintain a high degree of professionalism throughout his or her time in the courtroom.

that the witness not discuss the nature of his or her testimony with other witnesses.

It is mandatory that the witness be at the required place at the required time. There is no excuse for being late or missing a court appearance, regardless of how many continuances have been granted or may be anticipated. However, if for some reason a witness is going to be late, he or she should telephone the prosecutor or the court clerk, explain the reason for the delay, and give an estimated time of arrival. This enables the prosecutor to rearrange the order of the witnesses, if possible, and allows the judge to plan the court's calendar accordingly. A witness's inability to follow simple instructions, such as showing up on time or calling when he or she is going to be late, can only have a negative impact— on the person's reputation, the judge's temperament, and the weight the jury awards to the person's testimony.

CONDUCT BEFORE AND DURING THE COURT SESSION

If the witnesses are not excluded from the courtroom, the law enforcement professional may gain important insights into how, or how not, to testify effectively by paying close attention to the trial as it progresses. One should observe the prosecutor's direct examination, the demeanor of the judge, and the defense attorney's cross-examination. As a spectator, the officer will be able to judge, along with the jury, which witnesses are most persuasive. The officer can also choose those qualities he or she wishes to emulate while on the stand. However, the more likely scenario is that the witnesses will be excluded from the courtroom, in which case the officer should remain in the immediate area in order to be ready to testify when needed.

Before court is in session and during recess periods, many people congregate near the courtroom, waiting for court to convene. Some of these individuals are prospective jurors, and, inasmuch as jurors frequently formulate opinions of witnesses before they ever take the witness stand, prospective witnesses should be discreet and circumspect about their language, conversation, and conduct even before entering the courtroom. An officer in uniform should be aware that

Usually, the judge excludes the witnesses from the courtroom during the trial. This ensures that the witnesses will not be influenced by one another's testimony. Therefore, it is unlikely that the new law enforcement professional will get to see any of the trial before testifying for the first time. It is a good idea to visit a courtroom and watch part of a trial before appearing as a witness for the first time. Preferably, the visit should be to the courtroom in which one will appear, but watching any trial in progress would prove helpful.

he or she can be easily identified as an officer. An ill-advised remark about the case, a political figure, or an ethnic group or loud or boisterous conduct by an officer may prejudice a juror, so that anything the officer says on the stand will be disregarded.

If witnesses are not excluded from the courtroom, officers should avoid carrying on conversations or passing notes and papers among themselves while the trial is in progress. The witness should avoid displaying emotion in the courtroom. It is only natural for the officer who has investigated the case thoroughly to be convinced of the defendant's guilt, but the officer must not convey that belief to the jury and should assume a completely neutral position. The officer must not give the impression to the jury of being prejudiced against the defendant or trying to "railroad" the defendant into jail. The officer must be careful while the prosecuting or defense attorneys are speaking to avoid facial expressions that will convey the officer's feelings to the jury. Any indication of bias should be avoided, as some jurors, by their nature, are wary of law enforcement officers. Jurors' feelings may be aggravated by seemingly insignificant actions, such as the officer rolling his or her eyes, which only builds an unfavorable impression and lessens the effect of the officer's testimony. The officer should at all times show the greatest dignity, poise, and decorum possible.

Unfortunately, some officers have found that certain actions in which they have engaged during trial recesses have worked to their disadvantage. The officer should not engage in conversations with the defense attorney or defense witnesses during recesses, no matter how innocent or pleasant the encounter may appear. An officer can always be recalled to the witness stand to repeat some ill-timed remark made to a defense attorney or a defense witness during a recess period.

The officer should also avoid contact with the defendant or defense witnesses, both before and during the trial. Although the officer should appear impartial during the trial, jurors may not understand a seeming bond of friendship between an officer and the defendant after they have heard the officer relate some unflattering facts about the defendant's conduct. Any openly hostile remarks to the defendant would also show a lack of impartiality.

There should also be no communication between an officer and any member of the jury. This may be difficult if the officer is acquainted with one of the jurors socially; however, any conversation between an officer and a jury member is grounds for a mistrial. Remember that a mistrial may result in the defendant's going free, as a subsequent prosecution may be barred by double jeopardy. All of the foregoing suggestions apply equally to law enforcement personnel called upon to testify in court.

Conferring with the Prosecuting Attorney

Any conference with the prosecuting attorney concerning one's testimony should take place prior to the trial date. The prospective witness will have an opportunity to talk with the prosecutor during pretrial conferences and before the preliminary hearing. At the trial, the prosecutor must deal with many witnesses, many of whom have never testified before. Additionally, the law enforcement professional should bring his or her own copies of reports so as not to inconvenience the prosecutor by having to borrow the latter's reports.

Being Called to the Stand

THE WELL
That area in the courtroom, between the judge's bench and counsel tables, that is off-limits without the judge's permission.

When called as a witness, walk toward the witness stand, which is next to the judge on the side closest to the jury. Never walk in front of the judge, between the judge's bench and the attorneys' tables. This area is called **the well** and is considered off-limits. The well should be entered only upon the judge's direction.

Procedures differ among courts as to the exact place where the oath is administered. In some courts, it is administered to the standing witness outside the witness box. In other courts, the witness is permitted to enter the witness box and then is asked to stand to take the oath. Be sure to determine in advance the position where the oath is given.

After the oath has been given, reply with the words "I do" in a sincere, firm voice, loud enough for the jury to hear. Once a witness has been given the oath, it is usually not necessary for it to be given a second time, should the witness be called back to the stand during the same trial.

ON THE WITNESS STAND

Once seated in the witness stand, avoid slouching or slumping in the seat, chewing gum, or having something else in your mouth while testifying. Avoid fidgety behavior, such as playing with a pen or pencil, continually clearing your throat, scratching or rubbing your nose, or pulling your earlobes. Common sense dictates that you will want to appear as professional, natural, and personable as possible before the jury. Avoid robot-like mannerisms that signal to the jury inexperience, discomfort, or something to hide.

Voice and Grammar

While testifying, speak into the microphone, if there is one, using a normal conversational tone and level. As the attorneys are asking questions, look at each questioning attorney but then direct the answer to the jury. This enables eye contact with the jury, thus giving the jury, not the judge or attorneys, the facts of the case. Avoiding eye contact with the jury may be interpreted as an attempt to hide something from the jurors.

Avoid sentence fillers, such as "uh," "well," "you know," or "like," when testifying. When used in excess, these words can be annoying to the jury and can signal uncertainty about an answer, even if that is not the case. Improper grammar should also be avoided because it can also irritate the jurors and suggest ignorance, lack of training, or lack of experience in testifying. Using careless speech, such as the words "have went," "have came," "have took," "ain't," or "irregardless," can only make an unfavorable impression on jurors, leading them to believe that you are as careless with your work as with the words you choose.

As a witness, the law enforcement professional must remember that he or she is speaking "on the record." In other words, a court reporter is taking down everything that is spoken in the

The area in the courtroom in front of the judge's bench, between the bench and counsel tables, is known as the well. Traditionally, the area is at least one sword's length from the judge's bench and is off-limits to all persons appearing in the courtroom. This tradition, which originally offered protection to the judge, is still customary today. No one should enter the well without asking the judge for permission to do so. Officers, in particular, should avoid walking into the well en route to and from the witness stand.

courtroom. Therefore, the witness must be sure to speak in a tone and manner that will enable the reporter to hear the testimony. Moreover, the witness must be sure not to speak at the same time that anyone else is speaking. Finally, the witness must be sure to communicate in words, not gestures or hand movements.

Profanity and Vulgarity

Law enforcement professionals are in constant contact with the criminal world, where profanity and vulgarity are part of normal speech. Although officers may use the same vocabulary as the criminal in daily conversations, these profane or vulgar terms must be avoided while testifying, unless the witness is repeating the exact language used in a conversation. When the witness must quote exact language for the jury to hear, the witness should tell the jury that he or she is, in fact, quoting exactly the words used. Also, a word or phrase may not seem to be vulgar to the average juror but may be viewed as profane by a particular listener. For example, the term "your mother" is used by some street gangs as the ultimate "four-letter" fighting word. In this case, the witness will need to explain the profanity of this phrase to the jurors, so that they can give it the proper evidentiary value.

Jargon

Persons in all walks of life, including law enforcement professionals, use a form of occupational jargon that, in most instances, is meaningless to those outside the occupation. Initials, numbers, and code section numbers are used when speaking of certain violations—such as "51-50," the California Health and Welfare Code and Institutions § 5150 for a person who is mentally unstable. This jargon, as well as the language of criminals that has been adopted into an officer's vocabulary, should be avoided or else thoroughly explained when testifying; otherwise, the jury will lose the meaning of the officer's testimony.

For example, officers frequently refer to marijuana as "bud," an armed robbery as a "2-11," and a police helicopter as a "whirly-bird." In one state, the vehicle code section making drunken driving a violation was section 502. Officers referred to this violation as a "five-o-deuce," and this term became so much a part of the language of one officer that he used it while testifying. The defense attorney challenged his remark concerning the alleged violation. The officer became so confused that he could not recall the correct code section and ended up looking terribly incompetent. In short, the law enforcement witness should avoid all jargon that could ultimately confuse the jury or the witness.

References to the Accused

A law enforcement witness will undoubtedly have to refer to the accused, usually when identifying the defendant and testifying as to his or her conduct. The witness's voice should avoid any inflection that shows prejudice toward the defendant. When identifying the defendant for the first time, the witness should look to the defense table, where the defendant is sitting, identify the defendant, and describe what he or she is wearing. The witness should avoid pointing at the defendant because it is accusatory and because the court reporter cannot reflect gestures, such as pointing, on the record. For example, the witness can identify the defendant by saying, "The person that I arrested that night is in the courtroom today and is the female wearing a county jail blue jumpsuit at the defense counsel's table."

Although the witness may refer to the accused as "the defendant," some defense attorneys will object, arguing that the accused should be referred to by name. If everyone else involved in the trial is referred to by name, it can be argued that referring to the accused as the defendant is demeaning. Therefore, the officer may wish to call the defendant by name to avoid any appearance of intentionally demeaning the accused.

Answering Questions on the Stand

The first few questions asked of the law enforcement witness by the prosecuting attorney will be background questions, such as occupation, years on the force, unit of assignment (such as patrol or narcotics), and specialized training in a certain area, such as drug detection. Although the witness may find it tedious to recite such basic information or a lengthy training history, this information is required for the trial record. Equally important, the jury will be hearing this information for the first time, and it will be the jury's first opportunity to view the law enforcement witness. The jury will use this early portion of the testimony to formulate its opinion about the officer.

The following example presents a typical background line of questioning of a law enforcement officer by a prosecutor.

> **Prosecutor:** Please state your name and spell it for the record.
> **Officer:** My name is Jane Roe. J-a-n-e R-o-e.
> **Prosecutor:** Ms. Roe, you are employed by the New York City Police, aren't you?
> **Officer:** Yes.
> **Prosecutor:** Please state your rank and duty assignment on the date of May 27, 2018.
> **Officer:** I was, and am, a lieutenant assigned to the homicide division of the 24th precinct; actually, I am supervisor of the homicide division.
> **Prosecutor:** Lieutenant Roe, how long have you been a police officer?

Officer: Nineteen years.

Prosecutor: What training and experience have you had in determining the trajectory path of a bullet?

Officer: I have a bachelor's degree from SUNY Buffalo in criminal justice and a master's degree in forensic science. I attended a one-week training course in 2010 on weapons and their firing patterns and an eight-hour class on determining the origin of a fired bullet, and I have been a member of numerous forensics societies for approximately fifteen years. For the past five years, I have taught new detectives how to determine the trajectory, the angle, and the origin of a bullet and have taught new police cadets the basic bullet trajectory science, so that they can begin investigations before the detectives arrive. I have investigated the trajectory of a bullet in approximately 300 to 400 cases.

Prosecutor: Have you ever testified as an expert in determining the trajectory of a bullet?

Officer: Yes, I have testified as an expert approximately 40 to 50 times in the Supreme Court.

As the prosecuting attorney begins the interrogation of the officer concerning the facts of the case, the defense attorney will undoubtedly make objections to some of the questions asked. When an objection is made, the judge may **sustain the objection**, which means that the question may not be answered, or **overrule the objection**, which authorizes the witness to answer the question. Before answering any questions, whether it is during direct examination or cross-examination, the witness should allow sufficient time for an objection to be made. It is actually to the advantage of the witness to wait a second or two before replying, taking an opportunity to think about the question and to form an intelligent answer. However, it is not necessary for the officer to look at the defense attorney after each question is asked by the prosecution to see whether an objection is forthcoming. If an objection is made to a question asked, the witness *must* wait for the judge to rule upon the objection. Judges find it highly irritating to have to strike, or eliminate from the record, the witness's testimony continually because he or she did not wait for the judge to make a ruling on the objection. If the objection is overruled and the witness does not recall the question or does not understand the question, the witness should ask to have the question repeated. The witness should never guess what was asked.

As the direct examination progresses, frequently the witness tends to relax and settle down because the prosecutor is an ally and the questioning is going well. Once cross-examination begins, however, the witness frequently sits erect and pushes forward to the edge of the chair, as if to meet the enemy. To avoid such a sudden change of demeanor, the witness should not look too relaxed during direct examination and should avoid changing his or her expression and body language once cross-examination begins. The witness should maintain the same conversational tone during cross-examination, avoid becoming emotional or sarcastic, and not make wisecracks or argue with the defense attorney.

SUSTAIN THE OBJECTION
A ruling by the judge that prohibits the witness from answering the question posed.

OVERRULE THE OBJECTION
A ruling by the judge that permits the witness to answer the question posed.

ON THE JOB

As often as possible, a police officer on the witness stand should limit his or her responses to "yes," "no," and "I don't know," especially on cross-examination. The officer should never volunteer information not required to answer the questions truthfully.

Some defense attorneys are overzealous in their effort to represent the defendant and become very aggressive and antagonistic during the cross-examination. Although it may be difficult for the officer to maintain his or her composure, the defense attorney usually acts this way for one reason—to get the witness to lose his or her temper. The defense attorney may take advantage of the witness losing his or her temper on the stand by alleging that the witness also lost his or her temper with the defendant and that the confession or consent to search was obtained because the defendant was fearful. The jury is more likely to believe the defense's allegations if they have witnessed an angry outburst on the stand. Conversely, if the witness can remain calm during an aggressive personal attack by the defense attorney, the jury will undoubtedly respect and believe the witness, and the defense attorney's tactics will actually work to the advantage of the law enforcement officer.

When asked a question, whether on direct or cross-examination, the witness should answer the question as concisely, accurately, and clearly as possible and should not volunteer information. By volunteering information, the witness may unnecessarily open up an area for cross-examination, or he or she may bring out matters that the prosecutor planned to emphasize at a later point in the trial with a different witness. Frequently during cross-examination, the defense attorney will continue to look at the officer after the officer has completed the answer. Officers sometimes think that the attorney is waiting for more information and will add to their testimony, usually with information that is outside the scope of the defense attorney's question and could lead to additional cross-examination. Although all questions should be answered as completely as possible, the witness should stop when this is done and wait for the next question, ignoring any pause by the defense attorney.

During the direct examination, the witness who may know or think that the prosecutor has overlooked an important fact may mention it to the prosecutor at the first opportunity. It may be necessary to wait until a recess, but the witness should not volunteer it on the stand, as the prosecutor may have intentionally excluded that testimony. After completing testimony, if the officer sincerely believes that there was a very important point overlooked, he or she may quietly mention it to the prosecutor after leaving the stand. If the prosecutor thinks that the omitted testimony is important enough, he or she may recall the witness to the stand. However, if the prosecutor chooses to disregard the point, the officer should not argue. It is the prosecuting attorney's, not the officer's, responsibility to guide the prosecution of the defendant.

Officers should not mention the criminal record or prior conviction of a defendant unless specifically asked. The defendant's other acts of misconduct, crimes, and criminal record may be revealed only under very limited circumstances, and referring to such matters during the officer's testimony may result in a mistrial.

FYI

The general structure of cross-examination allows the defense attorney to question the witness only on subject areas that were raised or suggested during direct examination. This limitation is based on the rule that cross-examination is limited to the scope of the subject matter of direct examination. This rule prevents "fishing expeditions" by the defense and allows for cross-examination only on issues that the prosecution chooses to present against the defendant. By volunteering information, the witness can open up areas not intended by the prosecution and for which the prosecution is not prepared.

When the Witness Forgets Testimony

Although the law enforcement professional should become as familiar as possible with the facts of the case, he or she is not expected to be able to recall certain minute details, such as serial numbers, measurements, and license numbers. Even major facts may slip from the mind of any witness. The witness should not feel embarrassed if he or she cannot recall every detail of the case, as the investigation may have taken place several years earlier and the witness will have worked on a number of other cases since then. If unable to remember, the witness should simply state, "I do not recall at this time, but I did write that information in my report. If I am able to review my report, which I made when the facts were still fresh in my memory, I'm sure it will refresh my memory." Once the witness has reviewed the report, he or she must be able to say truthfully that his or her memory is refreshed. Then, when the witness answers the question, his or her testimony is completely truthful.

Any document that a witness uses to refresh his or her memory while on the stand may be examined by the defense attorney. If the witness uses a pocket notebook for this purpose, the defense attorney may peruse the entire notebook. For this reason, the officer should put all information that he or she believes will be needed for trial in the report or utilize a loose-leaf notebook, so that the pages pertaining to the case at hand may be removed and taken to the stand. In jurisdictions where the defense is permitted to examine anything the officer uses before trial to refresh his or her memory about the facts of the case, the defense may also examine the entire notebook unless those pages pertaining to the case can be removed and furnished to the defense.

Cross-Examination

Defense attorneys differ in their approach to witnesses upon cross-examination. Some attorneys assume a friendly attitude toward the witness. The defense attorney may be very complimentary to an officer. Each question may be posed in a manner that gives the impression that it is a privilege to be permitted to make such an inquiry of the witness. Such an approach may lull the witness into a state of false security, causing the officer to become overconfident and, as a result, possibly make careless remarks when answering the questions on cross-examination.

Other attorneys endeavor to browbeat witnesses or assume an extremely adversarial attitude toward them, particularly when the witnesses being cross-examined are police officers. The defense attorney may make insinuating remarks in an effort to devalue the witness's testimony, and the witness may be taxed to the extreme to maintain composure. A witness who cannot remain composed may react emotionally and do or say things that are detrimental to the prosecution of the case. This is usually what the defense attorney is hoping for. A law enforcement witness should never become engaged in a verbal altercation with a defense attorney.

Various kinds of questions are asked of a law enforcement witness by the defense attorney. Frequently, questions are asked that demand a yes or no answer. Some questions cannot be answered intelligently with a simple yes or no, for example, "Have you stopped beating suspects in handcuffs?" Such a question implies that the witness has beaten suspects in custody in the past and that the only fact now involved is whether he or she continues to do so or has stopped. If the officer has never beaten a suspect in custody, either a yes or a no would be incorrect and not a truthful statement. This is an excellent example of an argumentative question that is objectionable. However, if the prosecutor fails to object to such a question or to some other that the witness cannot answer intelligently with a yes or no, the witness should inform the judge, "This question cannot be answered by a yes or no response." If the judge insists on an answer, there is no choice but to answer with a yes or no, depending upon which is the most correct. The witness will have the opportunity to explain the answer fully during re-direct examination.

A question from the defense attorney that may confuse a new officer is "Have you discussed this case with anyone?" Many people think that it is improper to discuss the facts of a case with anyone else. Any witness, law enforcement professional or not, who has not discussed the case with the prosecutor is not properly prepared to testify intelligently. The facts should also be discussed by all of the officers who were involved in the case to make sure each knows what to testify about and what real evidence to present. The fact that the case has been discussed with others before the trial does not mean that a story has been fabricated or that the testimony is going to be falsely related. The witness should readily admit discussing the case with superiors and the prosecutor but should explain that he or she was not told what to say, except to relate the facts truthfully and accurately.

Many times, a defense attorney will ask an obviously absurd question, for example, "You didn't see the shooting, did you?" Such a question may be designed to elicit an equally absurd or curt response. Such questions should be answered with the same courtesy and seriousness as all others. A question may be asked in an ambiguous or misleading manner, such as "Do you want the jury to believe . . . " or "Is it your testimony that. . . ." If a question is asked in a misleading or ambiguous way, the witness should ask that the question be clarified. Sometimes questions are asked in rapid sequence, with the hope that the officer will reply equally rapidly, possibly resulting in inaccuracies. The witness should not yield to the pressure of giving a quick answer. If the witness needs time to regain composure, did not hear the question, or did not understand the question, he or she may request that the question be repeated. If the witness does not know the answer to a question, he or she should have no hesitancy in stating, "I do not know." Neither should the witness be reluctant about answering a question that may seem favorable to the defendant. The witness will gain more respect and favor with the jury by telling his or her entire story in an impartial and impersonal manner than if the witness appears biased against the defendant.

One mistake often made during cross-examination is to try to determine the motive behind a question asked by the defense attorney. In doing so, the witness may gear the answer to what he or she believes is the motive and thus fail to give a direct and concise answer to the question. The witness may even include material that is not pertinent or give an entirely irrelevant answer as a result of thinking about an alleged motive rather than the question asked. Anytime a witness tries to outthink the attorney instead of adhering to the truth with short, concise answers, the witness can end up in serious trouble and cause difficult problems for the prosecution.

Occasionally, the law enforcement professional may find that his or her service record will become the subject of cross-examination. It is a good idea to keep track of the number and types of cases in which you have been involved, as well as the number of cases in which you have testified. Also, you should be ready to identify training classes and college courses you have taken and any awards you have received. Having this information ready can only help you on the stand.

AFTER TESTIFYING

After completing both direct and cross-examination testimony, the law enforcement professional appearing as a witness should make certain that he or she is permanently excused before exiting the courthouse. Many times, the prosecutor or defense attorney recalls witnesses for further testimony, so the witness will need to ascertain whether he or she will be called again to testify before leaving.

REVIEW CASE AFTER VERDICT

Having testified in the best manner possible, a law enforcement professional should not take an acquittal personally. A professional who failed to testify properly should endeavor to determine his or her mistakes, correct them, and assist others in not making the same mistakes. Whether an acquittal is granted or a conviction obtained, the professional should review the case to determine mistakes made in the testimony, the collection and preservation of the evidence, and the interviews with witnesses. The professional should examine all facets of the case in an effort to improve investigation and courtroom techniques continually. This will enable the person to grow as a witness, as an investigator, and as a professional officer.

REVIEW AND APPLICATION

SUMMARY

(1) The law enforcement professional may receive a subpoena, much like any other witness. He or she may be served directly with the subpoena or, if the department is large enough, through a subpoena control department. He or she may not receive a subpoena at all but may merely receive a call from the prosecutor, advising that he or she is needed as a witness in a particular case.

(2) The general rule for a law enforcement professional is to wear to court what he or she wears to work. If the officer wears a uniform to work, then that is what he or she should wear to court. A professional who does not wear a uniform should wear business attire to court. Those who go to court on their days off may also choose to wear a suit instead of their uniform, as they are going to court in their personal vehicles.

(3) A witness should not speak to jurors, defense counsel, defense witnesses, and the defendant during court recess.

(4) After each question posed on direct and cross-examination, the witness should pause for a second to see if there are any objections. If there is an objection, the witness should not answer the question until the judge has ruled. If the judge sustains the objection, the witness may not answer the question. If the judge overrules the objection, the witness may then answer the question.

(5) A law enforcement professional who cannot remember the answer to a question asked should state that he or she does not remember. If there is anything that the witness believes will refresh his or her recollection, such as a written report, he or she should so state. If, and only if, the witness's memory is refreshed, he or she may truthfully respond to the question.

(6) When asked an argumentative question on cross-examination to which the defense attorney insists upon a yes or no answer, the witness should wait for the prosecutor to object. If there is no objection, the witness should inform the judge that he or she cannot answer the question intelligently with a yes or a no. If the judge insists that the witness answer the question, he or she should answer as best he or she can and try to explain fully on re-direct examination.

KEY TERMS

subpoena 471	the well 476	overrule the
on-call 471	sustain the	objection 479
rule on witnesses 473	objection 479	

QUESTIONS FOR REVIEW

1. What are the methods used to notify a witness to appear in court?
2. What is appropriate clothing for law enforcement professionals to wear to court?
3. Identify the persons that the law enforcement witness should not speak to during recesses.
4. Explain what a law enforcement witness should do while testifying with respect to objections.
5. State what a law enforcement witness should do when he or she does not remember the answer to a question asked.
6. Explain what a law enforcement witness should do when asked an argumentative question on cross-examination that the defense attorney insists should be answered yes or no.

Design Element: ©Ingram Publishing

GLOSSARY

accident investigator The person who investigates the causes and results of vehicle accidents.

acoustical spectrography The branch of science that consists of composing the voice or sound into harmonic components and obtaining a visual pattern of the sound—a spectrogram.

admission Any statement, verbal or otherwise, made by a party that can be used in evidence against him or her.

adoptive opposing party's statement (admission) A "statement" that occurs when a party, though not making the statement himself or herself, adopts a statement made by another, usually by silence in the face of an accusation.

adverse witness A witness aligned with the opposing side.

affidavit A written statement, sworn under oath, in which the officer states the facts within his or her personal knowledge that support the criminal complaint.

affirmative defense A reason under the law that allows a defendant to claim to be exonerated, one that the defendant must affirmatively claim and prove.

anticipatory warrant A warrant issued with a provision that it be executed upon the occurrence of a triggering condition.

apparent authority doctrine The principle by which a third-party consent search will be deemed reasonable if the facts available to the officer at the moment of entry would cause a reasonable person to believe that the consenting party had common authority for most purposes over the premises or property.

arraignment and plea The defendant's appearance in court after the filing of a formal charge, at which the defendant enters a formal plea to the charges, and at which issues about right to counsel and bail are decided by the judge.

attenuation doctrine The exception to the fruit of the poisonous tree doctrine in which the connection between the unlawful conduct of the police and the discovery of the challenged evidence is so unrelated as to dissipate the taint.

attesting witness A person who can authenticate or verify the accuracy of the evidence.

attorney One who is authorized to practice law in a given state or nation.

authentication The presentation of proof to show that an object is what its proponent claims it to be.

bail A deposit of cash, other property, or a bond guaranteeing that the accused will appear in court.

balancing test, or legal relevancy The requirement that relevant evidence not be admitted if its probative value is substantially outweighed by the danger of unfair prejudice, confusion of the issues, or misleading the jury.

best evidence rule The rule that requires that, in proving the terms of a document, the original writing must be produced, unless the document is shown to be unavailable for some reason other than the bad faith act of the party seeking to introduce the document.

bias A witness's interest in the case or its outcome.

bond A written promise to pay the bail sum, posted by a financially responsible person, usually a professional bondsman.

booking A formal processing of the arrested person by the police that involves recording the arrest, fingerprinting, photographing, and inventorying all the personal items taken from the suspect.

***Brady* material** Information favorable to the defense, in the possession of the prosecution, material to the defendant's case that must be disclosed to the defense.

burden of proof The law's requirement that a particular party introduce evidence in a lawsuit and persuade the fact-finder that the evidence is believable.

business or public records The hearsay exceptions that permit certain written reports or records that record acts, events, conditions, opinions, or diagnoses to be admitted into evidence without requiring the person with knowledge of the facts contained in the records to be called as a witness.

case-in-chief That portion of the trial that comprises the main evidence, for either the prosecution or the defense.

certified copy A copy of a document to which is attached a statement by the person, official, or clerk having custody of the record certifying that the document is a true copy of the original.

chain of custody A method of authentication in which evidence is presented showing that the photograph or recording has been in the constant possession of one or more persons and that the evidence is in the same condition as it was originally.

challenges for cause The motion that a prospective juror should be excluded because he or she is incapable of being impartial.

character evidence rule The rule that states evidence of a trait of character to prove a person's conduct in conformity with that trait is inadmissible, with a few exceptions.

character witness A person who has sufficient personal knowledge of another individual to be in a position to render an opinion or testify to the reputation of the character of the person in question.

circumstantial evidence Evidence that tends to establish the facts in dispute by proving the existence of another set of facts from which an inference or a presumption can be drawn.

clergy Priests, ministers, religious practitioners, or similar functionaries who have been ordained by a religious denomination or organization.

client One who goes to an attorney seeking professional services or advice.

collateral matter A matter only incidentally related to the issues at trial. When the contents of a document relate to such a matter, the original document need not be produced in court.

common authority Mutual use of the property searched by persons generally having joint access to or control over the property for most purposes.

communicant One who seeks out the clergy in a religious capacity for the purpose of securing spiritual advice.

conclusion The ultimate inference drawn from a fact observed; a synonym for "opinion."

conclusive presumption A presumption that the law demands or directs be made from a set of facts and that cannot be refuted by evidence.

confession A conscious acknowledgment of guilt by an accused.

Confrontation Clause The provision of the Sixth Amendment to the Constitution of the United States that guarantees the defendant in a criminal case the right "to be confronted with the witnesses against him."

consciousness of guilt Evidence of an accused's uncustomary acts, statements, or appearance from which guilt may be inferred.

consent A voluntary agreement by a citizen to an officer, allowing the officer to search the citizen's property, given without coercion and with authority over the place or thing to be searched.

consent search Another of the well-delineated exceptions to the warrant requirement, as well as an exception to the probable cause requirement.

contempt The power of a court to punish persons for failure to obey court orders or coerce them into obeying court orders.

contraband An object or material that is illegal for anyone to possess.

contradiction by cross-examination Impeachment by asking the witness about facts that are directly in opposition to those testified to by the witness on direct examination.

contradiction generally The form of impeachment that asserts the opposite of a statement or specifically denies a statement.

contradictory evidence Evidence used to prove a fact contrary to what has been asserted by a party or witness.

corpus delicti Required proof, other than a confession, that a crime has been committed.

corroborative evidence Evidence that is supportive of other evidence already given, tending to strengthen or confirm the prior evidence introduced.

credibility The quality in a witness that renders the witness's evidence worthy of belief.

crimes experts Persons, often law enforcement officers, who are experts in the methodology and paraphernalia involved in committing specific crimes.

criminal complaint A document that charges the defendant with a specific crime, usually signed by a law enforcement officer or prosecutor.

criminalist A specialist in the application of science to crime and the law.

critical stage The initiation of an adversarial judicial proceeding, whether by way of formal charge, preliminary hearing, indictment, information, or arraignment.

cross-examination The rigorous examination of a witness by opposing counsel in which the questioner seeks to detract from the witness's credibility, often by using leading questions.

cumulative evidence Evidence that repeats earlier testimonial or tangible evidence.

curtilage The land immediately surrounding a home and associated with it, where one has a reasonable expectation of privacy.

custodial interrogations Interrogations conducted with the suspect *in custody*. Such interrogations can occur only after the suspect has been read, and waived, his or her *Miranda* rights.

custody Custody results when a police officer restrains a person in a manner consistent with a formal arrest, regardless of the situation or intent of the officer.

dangerous patient exception An exception to psychotherapist-patient privilege, existing in most states, which provides that, if the psychotherapist has reasonable cause to believe that the patient is in such mental or emotional condition as to be dangerous to himself or herself, or to another person or another's property, the disclosure of the communications is necessary to prevent the threatened danger.

Daubert-Kumho **test** The new test for admissibility of expert testimony, requiring the trial judge to determine that the subject of an expert's testimony has achieved the stature of "scientific knowledge" based on five factors: (1) testing of the theory or technique; (2) peer review and publication of the theory or technique; (3) the particular scientific technique's known or potential rate of error; (4) the existence and maintenance of standards controlling the technique's operation; and (5) the theory or technique's "general acceptance."

declarant A person who makes a statement.

declaration against interest An exception to the hearsay rule for a statement made by a person who is not a party to the case and who is unavailable as a witness. To qualify as a declaration against interest, the person's statement must have been contrary to the person's interests at the time it was made.

defendant's good character rule The rule of evidence that permits an accused to introduce evidence of good character in an attempt to prove his or her innocence.

deliberate elicitation When the law enforcement officer acts with the purpose of eliciting an incriminating response from a suspect after counsel has been obtained or the adversarial proceeding has begun.

demonstrative evidence Evidence used solely to illustrate a witness's testimony. A representation of the object to be entered into evidence: a copy, an imitation, a model, or a reproduction.

deposition A written declaration, under oath, made upon notice to the adverse party, during which the adversary is present and cross-examines.

deterrence rationale The rationale for the exclusionary rule that rests upon the view that, to deter police officers from disregarding the Constitution, it is necessary to exclude from evidence at trial the evidentiary fruits of illegal police conduct.

direct evidence Testimony of a person who asserts or claims to have actual knowledge of a fact, such as an eyewitness.

direct examination The questioning of a witness by the side who calls that witness.

discovery The right afforded to the adversary in a trial to examine, inspect, and copy the evidence in the hands of the other side.

distinctive characteristic A method of authentication whereby a unique object is placed in the scene of a photograph or recording for purposes of identification.

DNA experts Persons educated in genetics, biology, chemistry, or other sciences who work with and present DNA evidence.

doctrine of chances The use of evidence of other, similar occurrences to show that the charged crime is not an isolated event due to chance.

doctrine of completeness The rule that provides that if a party seeks to admit part of a document, the opposing party may "require the introduction at that time of any other part or any other writing or recorded statement which ought in fairness to be considered contemporaneously with it."

document examiner An expert in the analysis of documents who identifies documents, paper, handwriting, and the like.

duplicate A copy produced by methods possessing an accuracy that virtually eliminates the possibility of error.

dying declaration An exception to the hearsay rule that provides that a statement made by an unavailable declarant may be admitted into evidence in a prosecution for a homicide or, in a civil case, a statement that the declarant, while believing the declarant's death to be imminent, made about its cause or circumstance.

ELMO A computer-controlled projection system, including a visual presenter, for use in the courtroom. ELMO is actually the name of the company that created the system; the acronym stands for "Electronic Light Magnetic Optical."

emergency or exigent circumstances Those circumstances that will justify a suggestive presentation of a suspect to a witness, such as when the witness is in danger of dying.

evidence Information that people base decisions on. In a legal sense, evidence is the information presented in court during a trial that enables the judge and jury to decide a particular case.

evidence locker A place, usually in a police station, where evidence gathered by law enforcement officers is deposited and kept safe from tampering pending its use in court.

evidence of a crime Any object that demonstrates that a crime has been committed.

evidence of other crimes, acts, or wrongs Evidence of bad acts used not to prove a trait of character but to prove something else, such as motive, opportunity, intent, preparation, plan, knowledge, identity, absence of mistake, or lack of accident.

evidentiary objections Legal arguments raised by opposing counsel during trial to prevent a witness from testifying or other evidence from being admitted.

excited utterance A statement relating to a startling event or condition, made while the declarant was under the stress of excitement that it caused.

exclusionary rule The rule that provides that illegally obtained evidence will be excluded from use in a criminal trial.

exclusive control Personal possession of an object of evidence from the time the officer picks it up at the crime scene until it is produced in court.

exculpatory evidence Any evidence that tends to prove the innocence of an accused.

exemplified copy A copy of a record of conviction that has been certified by the clerk of the court, as well as by the presiding judge of the particular jurisdiction, stating that the clerk correctly certified the form.

exigent circumstances search and seizure Another of the well-delineated exceptions to the warrant requirement permitting a police officer to enter premises in a situation requiring immediate action. The Supreme Court has recognized four such circumstances: (1) hot pursuit of a fleeing felon; (2) imminent destruction of evidence; (3) need to prevent a suspect's escape; and (4) risk of harm to the police or to others.

expert on mental illness An expert on the mental condition of persons, usually a psychologist or psychiatrist.

expert witness A person skilled in some art, trade, science, or profession. An expert must have knowledge, skill, experience, training, or education that is beyond that of the average person.

fair probability The test for the amount of belief of suspicion required for a determination of probable cause.

false friend doctrine The doctrine, in defining one's reasonable expectation of privacy, that what a person willingly reveals to another, on the assumption that the other is a friend, is thereby revealed to the world if the so-called friend turns out to be no friend at all.

Federal Rules of Evidence (FRE) The most common codification of evidence law—the rules that apply in all federal courts throughout the United States and in the 43 states that have relied upon them as a model in adopting their own evidence codes.

fingerprint expert An expert in the identification of fingerprints by comparing unknown and known samples of fingerprints.

footprint expert An expert in the identification of unknown footprints and walking patterns.

former testimony The exception to the hearsay rule that allows into evidence testimony given by a now unavailable witness at a prior proceeding.

foundation The requirements of relevance and authentication, which must be met for admission of an item of evidence.

frisk A limited patdown search of the outer garments of a person to determine whether he or she possesses a weapon with which to cause injury to an officer or others.

fruit of a crime Property that is seizable by a police officer, such as stolen or embezzled property.

fruit of the poisonous tree doctrine The principle that any evidence derived from a violation of a defendant's constitutional rights is inadmissible.

Frye test The former test for admissibility of expert testimony. Required that the testimony be based on scientific methodology "generally accepted as reliable in the relevant scientific community."

good faith exception This exception to the exclusionary rule allows the admission of evidence even if there is some technical defect in the warrant, as long as the executing officer has an objectively reasonable belief that the warrant is valid.

grand jury A panel of persons chosen through strict court procedures to review criminal investigations and, in some instances, to conduct criminal investigations. Grand juries decide whether to charge crimes, in the form of an indictment, in the cases presented to them or investigated by them.

habeas corpus A form of legal action that seeks to free a prisoner from unlawful confinement.

hearing in camera A judge's consideration, privately, in chambers, of the validity of a claim; here, specifically, a claim that a privilege does or does not exist.

hearsay A statement that the declarant does not make while testifying at the current trial or hearing and a party offers in evidence to prove the truth of the matter asserted in the statement.

holder of a privilege That person who benefits from the privilege and who has the power to waive it.

hung jury A jury that cannot reach a verdict.

hypothetical questions Questions based on facts, data, or opinions that have some relation to the matter at issue and upon which the expert witness is asked to render an opinion.

identification card A card or paper containing identification data placed at a crime scene before photographing or recording for purposes of enabling easy authentication.

impeachment A process or a result that diminishes or destroys the believability of a witness's testimony.

impeachment exception An exception to the exclusionary rule that applies to *Miranda* or the Fourth Amendment, which allows statements taken in violation of *Miranda* or the Fourth Amendment to be used at trial to impeach the testimony of the accused.

implied, or adoptive, opposing party's admission Silence in the face of an accusation when a reasonable person would respond.

incompetency The inability to act as a witness. Today, there are few grounds for incompetency, and in federal courts and all states except Arkansas (where atheists are not competent), all persons are competent to be a witness.

inconsistent statements Statements inconsistent with the present testimony. Such statements are logically relevant to impeach a witness because one who speaks inconsistently is less likely to be accurate or truthful.

independent source doctrine One of three exceptions to the fruit of the poisonous tree doctrine. This exception holds that, if the same information or knowledge is also gained through a source independent of the illegality and this fact can be shown by the prosecution, the information can be admissible through this source but not through the illegal search.

indicia of reliability Those facts indicating an identification is reliable—particularly, the five factors of the *Biggers* case.

indictment A formal written accusation by a grand jury charging a specified person with the commission of a specified crime, usually a felony.

inevitable discovery doctrine An exception to the fruit of the poisonous tree doctrine that states that the challenged evidence is admissible if the prosecution can show that the evidence would have been inevitably discovered, even in the absence of the police illegality.

inference A conclusion drawn from an observation or a series of observations.

information A formal written accusation submitted to the court by the prosecutor, alleging that a specified person has committed a specified crime.

inscribed chattel An object with words and/or images written, painted, or engraved on it.

instrumentality of a crime Property that is seizable by a police officer that was used as the means of committing a crime, such as a gun.

intent A state of mind; it expresses mental action that is usually coupled with an outward physical act to cause a particular result.

interrogation Express questioning or its functional equivalent, that is, any words or actions on the part of the police (other than those normally attendant to arrest and custody) that the police should know are reasonably likely to elicit an incriminating response from the suspect.

inventory search Another of the well-delineated exceptions to the warrant requirement that permits a police officer to inventory the property of a vehicle or person for the protection of the property and the police.

jails The facilities used to maintain custody of persons arrested pending prosecution and to maintain custody of those sentenced to short periods of confinement, usually less than one year.

Jencks Act A federal statute that deals only with the right of the defendant to discover statements made by a government witness. The statute is named after the case of *Jencks v. United States.*

judgment of acquittal A judicial decision on whether the prosecution has satisfied its burden during the presentation of its case-in-chief.

judicial notice The acceptance of a fact by a judge without formal proof, in the form of testimony or tangible evidence, being presented. A substitute for evidence.

jurisdiction The power or authority of the court to act with respect to any case before it.

jury deliberation The review of evidence by the jury in an attempt to reach a verdict.

jury nullification The power of a jury in a criminal case to acquit a defendant for any reason or no reason at all.

knock and announce, or knock and notice The constitutional requirement that, before an officer may execute a search warrant by forcibly entering the premises, the officer must knock and announce his or her presence and purpose for entering.

law of evidence The rules that govern what a jury can hear and see during the trial of a case.

lay opinion testimony In an American courtroom, testimony by nonexpert witnesses in the form of opinion; must be based on rational inference from the facts observed and necessary for a clear understanding of the witnesses' testimony.

lay witness A person who has some personal knowledge about the facts of the case and who has been called upon to relate this information in court.

laying the foundation The identification process to show that an object is authentic.

leading question A question that suggests to the witness the answer sought by the questioner.

lineup The presentation to a victim or witness of a line of persons who all look similar to see if one can be identified as the perpetrator of the crime.

mandatory presumption The form of presumption that *requires* the jury to find the presumed fact from the existence of the basic fact.

marital communications privilege The rule that any communication between spouses during the marriage is privileged.

Massachusetts procedure An alternative procedure by which a court decides whether a confession is voluntary. If the judge decides that the confession is voluntary, the judge instructs the jury as to the definition of voluntariness and tells the jury to consider the confession as evidence only if it finds that the confession was voluntary.

material evidence Evidence that pertains to a fact of consequence to the case on trial.

medical examiner or coroner The government medical expert called to give opinion testimony as to the cause of death in a homicide.

Miranda **warnings** The warnings required by the case of *Miranda v. Arizona* to be given to a suspect in custody before interrogation by a police officer can be valid.

modus operandi A distinctive pattern of committing crimes.

motion *in limine* A motion to exclude or admit evidence, often made before trial and usually heard out of the presence of the jury.

motion to suppress The written request to a court made by a defendant in a criminal case objecting to illegally obtained evidence.

motive That which moves a person to act or explains the reason a person acted.

narrative The form of interrogation in which the witness relates what happened in his or her own words, without interruption.

neutral magistrate A person who acts as magistrate (or judge) who can issue a warrant upon application of a law enforcement officer. Such person cannot be associated with law enforcement or the prosecution.

news reporter A publisher, an editor, a reporter, or other person connected with or employed by a newspaper, magazine, or other periodical publication or by a radio or television station.

notice to produce A formal, written notice issued by one party to another requiring the production of a document.

on-call A direction in a subpoena that states that the officer is not needed to appear personally in court unless called by the prosecutor. It requires that the officer be readily available.

open fields doctrine The doctrine, in determining one's reasonable expectation of privacy, which states that people do not have a legitimate expectation of privacy in open fields, even if law enforcement officers trespass upon private property in order to observe the open fields.

opening statement A summary of how the prosecution expects its evidence to show the defendant guilty beyond a reasonable doubt or how the defense attorney expects to raise a reasonable doubt.

operative legal fact A statement that creates or destroys a legal relationship, right, power, or duty.

opposing party's statement (admission) Any statement, verbal or otherwise, made by a party that can be used in evidence against him or her.

original document The document itself, "or any counterpart intended to have the same effect by the person who executed or issued it." Additionally, "[f]or electronically stored information, 'original' means any printout—or other output readable by sight—if it accurately reflects the information." With respect to photographs, the original is the negative or any print made from the negative.

orthodox procedure The prevalent procedure by which a court decides whether a confession is voluntary. In this procedure, the trial judge decides whether the confession is voluntary, in which case the confession is introduced into evidence and the judge instructs the jury to consider the confession along with all the other evidence presented.

overrule the objection A ruling by the judge that permits the witness to answer the question posed.

parole service An agency of the state correctional system that is similar to the probation department but supervises those released on parole from the penitentiary.

paroled When a person who has been convicted of a felony and sentenced to a term in prison is released under supervision into the community prior to the expiration of the full sentence.

past recollection recorded A record of a fact, known by a witness at one time but not presently remembered, that will qualify as evidence.

patient Any person who consults a psychotherapist or physician for the purpose of the diagnosis or the treatment of a mental or emotional condition.

peremptory challenge The motion that excludes a prospective juror from the jury panel without specific reason or justification.

perjury Knowingly making a false statement about a matter material to a case or swearing or affirming to the truth of a previously made statement that one knows to be untrue. May be a misdemeanor or felony.

persuasion burden The element of the burden of proof that requires a party to persuade the trier of fact on the issue at trial.

photographic array The presentation to a witness of a number of photographs for the identification of the perpetrator.

photographs Photographic images or their equivalent stored in any form.

physical evidence Material objects in a criminal trial, for example, a gun, a knife, bloodstained clothing, a latent fingerprint, or a photograph.

pictorial testimony Photographic evidence used to illustrate a witness's testimony.

plain feel doctrine The principle, extending the plain view doctrine to the sense of touch, that allows an officer to seize an object during a lawful patdown search, if the object's incriminating nature is immediately apparent, meaning that the officer has probable cause to believe the object is contraband or fruits, instrumentalities, or evidence of a crime.

plain view doctrine The last of the well-delineated exceptions to the warrant requirement providing that an officer may seize an object without a warrant if (1) the officer observes the object from a lawful vantage point; (2) the officer has a right of physical access to the object from the lawful vantage point; and (3) the nature of the object is immediately apparent as an article subject to seizure.

polygraph experts Persons expert in the workings, use, and results of tests using polygraphs.

preliminary hearing A court proceeding in which a judge decides whether there is enough evidence that an accused person committed a crime to hold that person for trial.

present sense impression A statement describing or explaining an event or a condition, made while or immediately after the declarant perceived it.

presumption A substitute for evidence whereby the fact-finder is allowed to conclude that a certain fact exists because some other fact is found to exist.

pretrial discovery A reciprocal exchange of information between the prosecuting and defending attorneys, before trial, either as ordered by the court in a particular case or required by statute or rule.

prima facie **case** The amount of proof the prosecution must present in its case-in-chief—evidence sufficient to establish that a crime was committed and that the defendant probably did it.

prima facie **criminal** A case in which the prosecution has established that a crime has been committed and that the accused probably committed it.

prima facie **criminal evidence** A case in which the prosecution has established that a crime has been committed and that the accused probably committed it.

prima facie **evidence** Evidence that, standing alone, unexplained or uncontradicted, is sufficient to establish a given fact or group of facts constituting a party's claim or defense.

primary evidence An original document.

prior consistent statement A statement made previously that is consistent with the present testimony of the witness. It is admissible only to rebut an express or implied charge that the declarant recently fabricated it or acted from a recent improper influence or motive in so testifying.

prior inconsistent statement A witness's previously made statement that contradicts the witness's current in-court testimony.

prisons Penal institutions maintained by the state or federal government consisting of state penitentiaries, reformatories, and juvenile training facilities.

privilege against self-incrimination The constitutionally based right that permits a witness to refuse to answer any question if the answer would tend to show that the witness is guilty of a crime and would subject the witness to the danger of prosecution and conviction.

privileged communications Exchanges of confidential information between persons who are in a privileged relationship.

probable cause: Although the Fourth Amendment provides that no warrant shall be issued except upon probable cause, it does not spell out what probable cause is. The definition of probable cause has been developed primarily through court decisions and interpretation.

probable cause to arrest When the facts and circumstances within the officer's knowledge, and of which he or she has reasonably trustworthy information, are sufficient to warrant a person of reasonable caution to believe, by a fair probability, that a particular individual has committed, or is committing, a particular offense.

probable cause to search When the facts and circumstances within an officer's knowledge, and of which he or she has reasonably trustworthy information, are sufficient in themselves to warrant a person of reasonable caution in the belief that *an item subject to seizure will be found in the place to be searched.*

probation The most frequent sentence imposed on first-time offenders, whereby the offender is released back into the community and required to obey the rules and conditions set out in writing by the probation officer after approval by the judge.

probation department An agency that investigates defendants prior to sentencing, provides a pre-sentence probation report to the court, and supervises persons placed on probation after conviction.

production burden The element of the burden of proof that requires a party to produce evidence at trial on a particular issue.

prompt arraignment rule The rule requiring an arrested person to be brought before a committing magistrate without unnecessary delay. Such a delay can cause statements made by the arrested person to be found inadmissible. Also known as the *McNabb-Mallory* rule.

proposed privilege rules Those privilege rules drafted but not adopted as the Federal Rules of Evidence.

protective sweep A quick and limited search of a premises, incident to an arrest and conducted to protect the safety of police officers or others. It is narrowly confined to a cursory visual inspection of those places in which a person might be hiding.

psychotherapist A person who has been authorized to practice medicine and devotes a substantial portion of his or her time to the practice of psychiatry or a person who is recognized by the laws of the particular jurisdiction as a certified psychologist.

public safety exception An exception to the requirement of *Miranda* warnings when police officers ask questions reasonably prompted by a concern for the public safety.

qualifying to be a witness To qualify to be a witness, a person must possess witness capacity: have personal knowledge of facts relevant to the case, be able to understand the obligation to tell the truth, and take the oath or affirm that he or she will testify truthfully.

rape shield laws Laws that prohibit a person accused of a sexual offense from introducing evidence of the sexual background or behavior of the victim.

real evidence In terms of physical evidence, the object itself.

reasonable doubt The standard of proof in a criminal case. A doubt based upon reason: that which would make a reasonable person hesitate to act in connection with important affairs of life.

reasonable suspicion That level of suspicion, less than probable cause, which permits an officer to detain a suspect temporarily to make reasonable inquiry to confirm or dispel the suspicion.

rebuttable presumption A presumption that allows for the opposing party's introduction of contradictory evidence to rebut the presumption's conclusion.

recognizance A promise to appear in court.

re-cross-examination Further questioning, after redirect examination, for clarification purposes.

redirect examination Further questioning, after cross-examination, for the limited purpose of rebutting or clarifying information brought out during cross-examination.

refreshing recollection The process or fact of reviving a witness's memory by a variety of means.

relevance A showing that an item of evidence has any tendency to make the existence of any fact of consequence more or less probable than it would be without the evidence.

relevant evidence Evidence that "has any tendency to make a fact more or less probable than it would be without the evidence; and . . . the fact is of consequence in determining the action."

res gestae Literally, "the thing done." The term is used most commonly to refer to the spontaneous utterance exceptions to the hearsay rule but could be meant to encompass any number of other exceptions. Therefore, it is ambiguous and its use should be avoided.

return of the search warrant A separate document attached to a warrant, that gives a list of the property seized in connection with the search and must be returned to the court after the search and seizure has been completed.

routine booking question exception An exception to the requirement of *Miranda* warnings that allows questions to be asked to secure the biographical data necessary to complete booking or pretrial services.

rule on witnesses The rule, often invoked by a trial judge, that witnesses be excluded from the courtroom during trial, so that one witness cannot hear the testimony of another.

rulings on objections The judge's decision on evidentiary objections: overruled, the witness may testify; sustained, the witness must not answer the question.

search incident to a lawful arrest (SILA) One of the well-delineated exceptions to the warrant requirement that permits an officer, without a warrant and further probable cause, to search the person of and certain areas around an arrestee incident to a lawful arrest.

search warrant A written order issued upon probable cause by a neutral and detached magistrate, in the name of the people, to a peace officer directing the officer to search a particular person or place and to seize specifically described property and bring it before the magistrate.

secondary evidence Evidence substituted for the original document.

seizure of a person A seizure of the person occurs when, (1) by means of physical force or show of authority, the person's freedom of movement is restrained and only if, (2) in view of all of the circumstances surrounding the incident, a reasonable person would not have believed he or she was free to leave.

seizure of property A seizure that occurs when there is some meaningful interference with an individual's possessory interests in that property.

self-authentication The principle that authenticity of a document may be determined on its face, without resort to outside evidence.

self-defense The justifiable use of force to protect oneself from a real or threatened attack. Generally, a person is justified in using a reasonable amount of force in self-defense if he or she believes that the danger of bodily harm is imminent and that force is necessary to avoid this danger.

sequestered jury A jury removed from any outside influence.

show-up The one-on-one presentation of a suspect to a victim or witness for identification purposes.

silent witness A photograph, film, or video that has been taken by an automatic camera with no operator present and introduced to document an event.

silver platter doctrine The doctrine that allowed state officers who obtained evidence illegally to hand it over to federal officers for prosecution in federal court.

spousal incapacity privilege The marital privilege that gives a spouse called to testify against his or her spouse the privilege to refuse to testify.

staleness doctrine The principle that, once a warrant is issued, it may not be held indefinitely by the officer before the search is made.

standing The right to contest an illegal search and seizure, or any claimed constitutional or law violation.

state of mind The exception to the hearsay rule that allows into evidence a declarant's assertion of his or her then-existing state of mind to prove that the person actually had such a state of mind.

state of mind of the declarant A statement offered to show the state of mind of the person who uttered the statement, not of the person who heard the statement.

state of mind of the hearer A statement that creates or affects the state of mind of another who hears the statement.

statements for purposes of medical diagnosis or treatment The exception to the hearsay rule that allows into evidence statements that are made for—and are reasonably pertinent to—medical diagnosis or treatment; and describe medical history; past or present symptoms or sensations; their inception; or their general cause.

statements of prior identification Statements made out of court identifying a person made after the declarant has seen that person.

stipulation Facts upon which the trial parties and their attorneys agree that may be presented during the trial without formal proof being required.

stop A temporary detention, not amounting to a full-blown arrest, requiring only reasonable suspicion that a particular individual is about to commit, is committing, or has committed a crime.

subpoena A court order demanding the presence of the person in court as a witness.

subpoena *duces tecum* A subpoena, or order to appear in court, commanding a person to bring specified documents or objects with him or her.

substantive evidence Evidence used to decide the existence or nonexistence of a fact.

sustain the objection A ruling by the judge that prohibits the witness from answering the question posed.

the well That area in the courtroom, between the judge's bench and counsel tables, that is off-limits without the judge's permission.

totality of the circumstances The test for voluntariness of a confession.

totality of the circumstances (identification) The test for suggestiveness that, in contrast to the *per se* rule, takes into account all surrounding circumstances to determine whether the exclusionary rule applies.

totality of the circumstances for consent The test for consent that takes into account all of the circumstances surrounding the giving of consent to determine whether a person has voluntarily consented.

totality of the circumstances for probable cause The test for probable cause, which is a fluid concept based on nontechnical, common-sense considerations.

"traces of the mind" theory The theory that allows into evidence statements that prove the declarant has knowledge that he or she could have gained only by actually having perceived some unusual event, circumstances, or surroundings.

true presumption A presumption that requires that, when the jury finds the basic fact to exist, it must find the presumed fact to exist in the absence of evidence to the contrary being introduced.

unresponsive answer A witness's answer that does not address the subject matter of the question or goes beyond the scope of the question asked and relates to some other matter.

vehicle exception Another of the well-delineated exceptions to the warrant requirement by which an officer may search the interior of a vehicle if he or she has probable cause to believe that it contains contraband or fruits, instrumentalities, or evidence of a crime.

venire The pool of prospective jurors from which the jury panel is selected.

venue The neighborhood, place, or county in which an act is declared to have been done or, in fact, happened, thus defining the particular county or geographical area in which a court with jurisdiction may hear and determine a case.

vicarious opposing party's statement (admission) A statement not actually made by the party but by an individual acting on behalf of a party as either a person expressly authorized to speak on behalf of the party, an employee, or a co-conspirator.

voiceprint expert An expert in voice identification, using the science of acoustical spectrography.

voir dire The process of questioning a panel of pro-spective jurors to select the final panel; roughly it means "to speak the truth."

voir dire of a proposed expert witness The questioning process by which an expert witness is qualified.

voluminous records rule An exception to the best evidence rule that permits a summary, chart, or calculation of voluminous records to be presented in the place of the records themselves.

witness capacity The elements of witness capacity are the ability to perceive, remember, and narrate in an understandable manner, as well as sincerity.

witness immunity Rules allowing witnesses to be spared from prosecution if the witnesses furnish facts that might otherwise incriminate themselves.

witness stand The seat taken by a witness to testify at trial.

witness *voir dire* The process of hearing, usually conducted out of the presence of the jury, by which a judge decides the qualification of a witness to testify.

writings and recordings Letters, words, or numbers, or their equivalent, set down in any form for writings or recorded in any manner for recordings.

CASE INDEX

SUBJECT INDEX

forensic scientist, 141. *See also* criminalist

former testimony exception, 211–212

foundation, 450

Fourteenth Amendment's Due Process Clause, 36

Fourth Amendment. *See* search and seizure

Franks test, 302

FRCrP 16, 404–405, 408, 412

FRE, 7–8, 184–185

free and voluntary rule, 231

Freedom of Information Act (FOIA), 104–105

freedom of the press, 106

Frey, Amber, 379

frisk, 324

fruit of a crime, 287, 427

fruit of the poisonous tree doctrine, 248–250, 269

Frye test, 133

Fuhrman, Mark, 125, 166

further questioning (subsequent examinations), 48

G

garbage, 283, 284

genetic fingerprint, 137

geographical facts, 64–65

Geragos, Mark, 40

Goldman, Ronald, 390, 452

"good cop, bad cop," 236

good faith exception, 272–273

Gordon, Larry Darnell, 120

gory objects, 438

GPS tracking device, 281–282

grammar and voice, 41, 476–477

grand jury, 7, 21–22

grisly scene, 451

groundless objections, 46

gruesome objects, 438–439

gruesome photos and videos, 451–452

H

habeas corpus, 17

handwriting, authentication of, 130–131, 140

Health Insurance Portability and Accountability Act of 1996 (HIPAA), 98

hearing *in camera,* 89

hearsay (objection), 47

hearsay, defined, 180

hearsay rule, 180–218
  admissions, 194–195
  business and public records, 212–217
  categories of exemptions, 192
  Confrontation Clause, 182–183
  declaration against interest, 199–200
  dying declaration, 195–199
  former testimony, 211–212
  medical diagnosis or treatment, 209–210
  myth *vs.* fact, 181, 185, 187, 189, 193, 194, 196, 211
  not offered for truth of matter asserted, 188–192
  offered for truth of matter asserted, 186
  overview (flowchart), 188
  overview (table), 223–224
  past recollection recorded, 218
  pedigree or family history, 217–218
  principles and examples, 223–224
  prior statements by witnesses, 192–194
  rationale for the rule, 182–184
  spontaneous utterances, 200–205
  state of mind, 205–211
  statement, defined, 184–185

high-tech evidence, 449–450

HIPAA, 98

historical overview
  confession, 230–231
  jury size, 31
  rules of evidence, 7–8
  trial by jury, 6–7

Hoffa, Jimmy, 277

holder of a privilege, 88

Homeland Security, 13

homicide victim, 385–386, 389

hostile remarks, 166

hot pursuit, 317

hung jury, 51

"hurry up and wait," 117

husband and wife relationship
  communication overheard by third party, 92–93
  crime or fraud exception, 92
  information gained before marriage, 91–92
  marital communications privilege, 90–91
  spousal incapacity privilege, 89–90

hypnosis, 66, 67

hypothetical question, 138

I

ICE, 13

identification by custody and control, 430–431

identification by proof of chain of custody, 431–433

identification card, 458

identification procedures, 344–362
  Bigger's five-factor analysis, 357–362
  collaboration between witnesses, 354
  Department of Justice guide, 361
  different appearances of accused, 355
  exclusionary rule and, 344
  photo arrays, 355–357
  police instructions or statements to witness, 354–355
  right to counsel, 344–347
  sample jury instructions, 347–348
  size of lineup or array, 353–354
  types, 344
  unnecessarily suggestive pretrial identification, 348–353

identity, 129

identity of informer privilege, 103–105

ignorance of the law, 73

"immediate control" of arrestee, 303

imminent destruction of evidence, 317, 318

probation department, 18
production burden, 70
profanity and vulgarity, 477
projected images, 446–447, 462–463
prompt arraignment rule, 232
proof beyond a reasonable doubt, 29, 36–37
proof by a preponderance of the evidence, 29, 37, 69
proposed privilege rules, 87, 88
Prosecuting Attorney, 13
prosecuting attorney, 13. *See also* prosecutor
"prosecution rests its case," 49
prosecution's case-in-chief, 41–43
prosecution's rebuttal, 49–50
prosecutor, 13–14
    responsibilities before trial begins, 36
    right to discovery, 412–413
    trial, at (*See* trial process (jury trial))
protective sweep, 305
PSI, 9
psychiatrist, 142
psychological pressure (confession), 235–236
psychologist, 142
psychotherapist, defined, 100
psychotherapist-patient privilege, 99–100
public documents, 398
public records, 212–213, 214, 402–403
public safety exception, 245–246
public statutes, 64

Q

qualifying to be a witness, 81
questioned document comparisons, 140

R

Raleigh, Walter, 181, 182
rape shield laws, 60, 387–388
Rashomon (film), 28
Rashomon syndrome, 28
re-cross-examination, 48
real evidence, 424. *See also* physical evidence

real-life examples. *See* O. J. Simpson trial
reasonable alternative hypothesis instruction, 368
reasonable diligence in investigation, 328
reasonable doubt, 28, 29, 36–37
reasonable expectation of privacy, 277
reasonable suspicion, 37, 323, 324–326
rebuttable presumption, 70, 72
rebuttal evidence, 49–50
recognizance, 20
reconstructed crime scene, 460
recorded recollection, 146–147
recording, 398
recording interviews/encounters, 202, 231, 371
redirect examination, 48
refreshing recollection, 145–149
rehabilitation of impeached witness, 168–169
rejoinder, 50
release on own recognizance, 20
relevance, 371, 450
relevant evidence, 58–60, 424
religious advisor, 102
religious beliefs and opinions, 168
reputation, 381, 382
reputation evidence, 162, 218
res gestae, 201
return of the search warrant, 301
right to counsel
    attorney-client privilege, 94
    confession, 250–254
    giving physical evidence, 309
    identification procedures, 344–347
right to fair trial, 71
routine booking question exception, 246
rule on witnesses, 120, 473
rules of evidence, 5–6
rulings on objections, 46

S

sanity
    lay opinion testimony, 130
    presumption, 71–72
scientific knowledge, 133

scientific/medical facts, 65–67
search and seizure
    aerial surveillance, 282
    apparent authority, 316–317
    blood samples, 308
    confession, 254
    consent search, 312–317
    curtilage, 278
    defendant's claim of constitutional violation, 332–335
    driving under the influence, 308
    exigent circumstances search, 317–320
    false friend doctrine, 277–278
    frisk, 324
    "immediate control" of arrestee, 303
    inventory search, 311–312
    methods of satisfying reasonability requirement, 285–286
    motion to suppress, 334–335
    myth *vs.* fact, 316
    open fields doctrine, 278
    plain feel doctrine, 329
    plain view doctrine, 320–322
    protective sweep, 305
    reasonable expectation of privacy, 277
    reasonable suspicion, 323, 324–326
    refusal to give samples, 309
    scope, 275
    search/seizure are two separate acts, 275
    search warrant (*See* search warrant)
    seizure of a person, 284
    seizure of property, 284
    SILA exception, 302–309
    standing requirement, 332–333
    stop, 323
    stop and frisk, 322–330
    suspicionless search, 330–332
    technologically enhanced searches, 279–282
    Terry doctrine, 324–325
    vehicle exception, 309–311
search incident to a lawful arrest (SILA), 286, 302–309

search warrant, 286–302
anonymous source, 291–292
anticipatory warrant, 301
confidential informant, 291–292
defendant's attack on the warrant, 302
defined, 286
fair probability, 289, 293
Franks test, 302
grounds for issuing warrant, 287
knock and notice, 298–300
nighttime service of warrant, 295–296
number of officers involved in search, 300
particularity of description of property, 294
probable cause, 289–290, 334
procedure for obtaining warrant, 287–294
return of the search warrant, 301
sample warrant, 288
staleness doctrine, 300–301
time limit on execution of warrant, 300
time limit on length of search, 300–301
use of force in execution of warrant, 298–300
who may serve a warrant, 296–298
secondary evidence, 400–401
Secret Service, 13
segregation of witnesses, 120
seizure of a person, 284
seizure of property, 284
selection of jury, 32–33
self-authentication, 214
self-defense, 60–61, 386, 389
self-impeachment, 168. *See also* impeachment
self-incriminating question, 126
self-incrimination, 170–173
claiming the privilege against, 170–171
defendant's compulsion to take witness stand, 173
defendant's obligation to physical acts/evidence, 173
general rule, 170
refusal to give samples, 309

testimonial compulsion, 173
waiving the privilege, 171–172
witness's immunity against prosecution, 172–173
self-representation, 39
self-serving statement, 230
sentencing, 9, 12, 51–52
sequestered jury, 51
sexual assault/child molestation cases, 381, 384–385, 386–389
show-up, 344
SILA exception, 302–309
silence
admission, 230
defendant, 173
silent witness, 447
silver platter doctrine, 271
"similar acts" evidence, 374–375
Simpson, Nicole Brown, 452
Simpson, O. J. *See* O. J. Simpson trial
six-pack, 355
Sixth Amendment right to counsel. *See* right to counsel
skid-mark expert, 141
sobriety, 129
source of information, search warrant, 290–292
spectrum of levels of proof, 37
speed expert, 141
speed of vehicles, 128
spontaneous utterances, 200–205
availability of declarant, 205
excited utterance, 201–202
foundation and rationale for exceptions, 202–203
present sense impression, 201
time element, 203–204
utterance must relate to event just preceding it, 204
spousal incapacity privilege, 89–90
staleness doctrine, 300–301
standards of proof, 37
standing, 332–333
Starr, Kenneth, 93
state court system, 16–17
state evidence codes, 8
state of mind exception, 205–211
availability of declarant, 208
foundation and rationale for exception, 207

inferring declarant's subsequent conduct, 207–208
medical diagnosis or treatment, 209–210
state of mind declaration, defined, 206–207
statements of causation, 210–211
state of mind of the declarant, 190
state of mind of the hearer, 189–190
statement of cause or condition or pain, 210–211
statements for purposes of medical diagnosis or treatment, 209–210
statements of prior identification, 193–194
State's Attorney, 13
Stewart, Larry, 167
Stewart, Martha, 167
stipulations, 74
Stoll, John, 83
stop, 323
stop and frisk, 322–330
storage of physical evidence, 435–437
"stricken from the record," 46
subpoena, 117–119, 471
subpoena control department, 471
subpoena *duces tecum,* 117, 402
substantive evidence, 447
suggestive pretrial identification, 348–353
superior court, 17
surrebuttal evidence, 50
suspicionless search, 330–332.
See also search and seizure
sustain the objection, 479

T

tainted evidence, 428
technological revolution, 449–450
technologically enhanced searches, 279–282
Terry doctrine, 324–325
testifying. *See* testimony of law enforcement officers
"testimonial compulsion," 173
testimonial statements, 215, 217

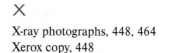